TURKISH ART
AND ARCHITECTURE

Istanbul, Mausoleum of Hürrem Sultan, 1558, tile panels from interior (see pages 228 and 276)

TURKISH ART AND ARCHITECTURE

Oktay Aslanapa

PRAEGER PUBLISHERS
New York · Washington

BOOKS THAT MATTER

Published in the United States of America in 1971
by Praeger Publishers, Inc., 111 Fourth Avenue,
New York, N.Y. 10003

Library of Congress Catalog Card Number: 72-144222

Printed in Great Britain

To
My wife Günseli

Contents

CONTENTS

Maps

Photographs

COLOUR PLATES

The colour plates of monuments or objects in Turkey are from transparencies provided by Halûk Doğanbey.

MONOCHROME PLATES

PHOTOGRAPHS

PHOTOGRAPHS

PHOTOGRAPHS

Plans

Buildings outside Turkey

Buildings in Turkey

PLANS

PLANS

RESTORATION

Designs and Carpet Patterns

DESIGNS

Buildings outside Turkey

Buildings in Turkey

CARPET PATTERNS

Carpet 1

Grateful acknowledgement is made to the following for the black and white photographs

Eski Eserler ve Müzeler Genel Md.: 1, 20, 21, 39, 53, 73, 102, 139, 248; Ersin-Günay Alok: 2, 36, 51; Turizm Tanıtma Bak.: 3, 22, 28, 43, 44, 56, 59, 63, 75, 83, 88, 89, 91, 92, 93, 98, 105, 114, 125, 128, 132, 135, 138, 161, 175, 178, 184, 190, 192, 193, 203; Rahmi Ünal: 6, 10, 14, 33, 38, 57, 60, 62, 64, 68, 69, 70, 71, 74, 76, 94, 95, 99, 103, 110, 112, 115, 202; Halûk Karamağaralı: 7, 8, 11, 12, 13, 16, 46, 61, 65, 79, 80, 81, 209; Oluş Arık: 15, 23, 24, 47, 72, 100, 104, 108; Istanbul Alman Arkeoloji-Enstitüsü: 17, 30, 37, 48, 78, 126, 159, 169, 181, 183, 199, 204; Ayda Arel: 129; Orta Doğu Teknik Üniversitesi: 141; Adil Arkan: 143, 150, 151, 152, 157, 160, 162, 165, 166, 167, 168, 170, 172, 173, 174, 176, 177, 179, 180, 182, 185, 186, 187, 188, 191, 216, 217, 242; Halûk Doğanbey: 149, 154, 158, 198, 201, 236; Turgut Belda: 196; Topkapı Sarayı Müzesi: 223, 224; Victoria and Albert Museum, London: 206, 218, 229; Staatliche Museen, Berlin: 210; Boston Museum of Fine Arts: 219, 220; Philadelphia Museum of Art, A. J. Wyatt: 225, 226; Seattle Museum of Art: 227.

Preface

The excavations and researches carried out in recent years in Anatolia, as well as in Iran, Afghanistan and Turkestan, have shed a completely new light on Turkish art. The preparation of a book such as this has necessitated bringing together the results of all this work, as published in hundreds of books and articles in every language. Our principal objective has been to examine, from various points of view, the links connecting monuments of art and architecture created in widely separated areas, and to reveal by means of plans and diagrams the unity and continuity of Turkish art.

The place of Turkish art within Islamic Art as a whole has long been a subject of controversy. In those regions in which Islamic Art developed it was founded on an already established basis of pre-Islamic civilisation, the most important of these being the Late Antique and Christian cultures of Syria, and the Sasanian arts of Iraq and Iran. The Arabic, Persian and Turkish elements added to these formed the basis of the development of Islamic Art. The majority of the states in the Islamic world were founded by the Turks and for nearly one thousand years, from the 9th century onwards the Turks, apart from some minor instances, remained the dominant element in the Islamic world. Consequently, it is obvious that the development of Turkish art will have been influenced by a number of different arts deriving from various countries. The tomb of Ismā'īl the Samanid at Bukhara dating from the first half of the 10th century played an important role, as a monument of revolutionary design derived from the Sasanian fire-temples, in the development of Karakhanid and Seljuk tomb design, and to this was added the influence of the external appearance of Buddhist stupas. The plan of the Ghaznevid palaces, itself derived from the Sasanids, shows the influence of 'Abbāsid palace architecture. Other architectural forms such as the iwan, the squinch and the dome are also forms derived from the Sasanids. But in spite of this, in all monuments of Turkish art, in whatever geographical region they may be, one is immediately struck by a characteristic style which clearly distinguishes them from any other artistic productions.

In recent works dealing with the art of Islam, such as K. Otto-Dorn's volume *Die Kunst des Islam* published in 1964, and Ernst Grube's volume *The World of Islam* published in 1966, more than half the book is in each case devoted to Turkish art. In the work by Derek Hill and Oleg Grabar published in 1964 and 1967 entitled *Islamic Architecture and Its Decoration A.D.*

800–1500, about half the book is given up to Turkish art. Thus in works dealing with Islamic Art which are based on researches carried out in recent years Turkish art occupies an increasingly important place.

The attractive works produced in architecture and the other arts in the Safavid period from the 16th century onwards reflect most vividly the marked difference of style between Iranian and Turkish works of art. Although forms deriving from the Seljuks are to be found in Īl-Khānid art and even in Safavid architecture we find the real continuation of Great Seljuk art in all its various aspects not in Iran but in Anatolia. This is a powerful indication of the strength of continuity and development in Turkish art. As for the art produced by the Ottomans this might well be described as a new and original exploitation, on a world scale, in lands that had witnessed the fusion of the world's richest cultures, of all the various styles of Turkish art that had preceded it.

Treatment of such a subject as Turkish art with the tremendous temporal and geographical sweep which this covers demands that it should be broken up into sections. It seems more natural to consider it in terms of dynasties since, with the constant invasions of the Middle Ages and the vast movements of populations this implies, geographical areas rarely have the requisite homogeneity to provide a firm basis for classification. On occasions the dynastic and the geographical criteria come into conflict and, inevitably, displacement of some sort is required. But it has seemed less confusing to deal with, for example, the 9th century Ṭūlūnids of Egypt out of sequence and in association with the Syrian Zengids because the architectural tradition they founded is more to be related to the Middle East than to Central Asia. It must also be remembered that classification in terms of dynasties is not just another way of giving dates; the Karakhanids, for example, survive well after the appearance of the Great Seljuks on the scene, but it has seemed more accurate to continue to speak of Karakhanid rather than Seljuk architecture in some cases because these earlier schools depended upon an older tradition and not upon the innovations of the Seljuks. Dating is not always secure but the works discussed in this volume have been dated as far as the present state of our knowledge permits. Some of the principal Turkish dynasties have been shown on pp. 346–354 as a general guide to chronology.

I wish to express my heartfelt thanks to Assistant Professor Dr. Şerare Yetkin for constant help in the preparation of this book, to Assistant Tülây Reyhanli for her care in sorting and typing the manuscripts, to Professor Ibrahim Kafesoğlu and Professor Faruk Sümer for their help in historical matters, to Professor Bahadır Alkım for his help in various fields, to Professor Semavi Eyice, Assistant Dr. Sadi Dilaver, Assistant Dr. Yıldız Demiriz and Library Assistant Nil Aykon for their help in preparing and typing the bibliography, to Assistant Professor Dr. Nurhan Atasoy, Dr. Güner Inal and James Mellart for help of various kinds, to my student Ara Altun for her careful drawing of the plans, to Mahmud Cüda for drawing the maps, and to Bingül Erisir and Gönül Güreşsever for the designs. For the photographs I must express my particular thanks to the Ministry of Tourism and Edvin Rizi, Assistant Professor Dr. Halûk Karamağaralı, the German Archaeological Institute of Istanbul, the Directorate-General of Antiquities and Museums, Zeren Akalay and Filiz Öğütmen of the Library of the Topkapı

Saray Museum, Kemal Çığ, Director of the Topkapı Saray Museum, and Can Kerametli, Director of the Museum of Turkish and Islamic Art, and his assistants, and I also wish to thank Mr. Adair Mill for undertaking the difficult task of translating this book into English. Last but not least, I would like to thank my publisher's specialist reader, and Mr. Alan Pringle and his secretary Miss E. Z. Gordon and the staff of Faber and Faber for their constant collaboration and help in making the book ready for the press.

OKTAY ASLANAPA

Note on Transliteration

Although Turkish, Arabic and Persian for the greater part of the Islamic period have used the same alphabet the sounds which these three languages produce are almost all different. The result is that a system of transcription or transliteration which is adequate to one will distort the sound or the orthography of the others. In the present book where the overwhelming consideration would appear to be ease of reference, there is no attempt to be doctrinaire. Any system will lead to inconsistencies or incongruities and it cannot be pretended that the following principles are entirely devoid of them. However, it is hoped that these inevitable deficiencies are to some extent counterbalanced by their greater accessibility to the non-specialist:

(1) Turkish, Persian or Arabic words or place-names which have a common English form are used in this form—caliph, sultan, emir, vizir, mosque, kiosk, except when they are part of a proper name. Thus 'the kiosk of Qılıch Arslan' at Konya, but 'the Çinili Köşk' (the tiled pavilion) at Istanbul.

(2) Arabic or Turkish words relating to institutions which do not have a common English equivalent will be incorporated into the text. Thus, 'masjid' (Ar.), a minor place for prayer, but 'medrese', 'türbe', 'kümbed' (all Turkish). In the latter cases, which are all Turkish forms of Arabic or Persian words, these have been used because there is arguably a difference between the Arabic or Persian institutions and their Anatolian equivalents. The one qualification is that Turkish possessive suffixes have been dropped, thus the Topkapı Saray, not Sarayı, the Mama Khātūn Türbe, not Türbesi, since this would only confuse readers who do not read Turkish.

(3) Place-names

Since the most important point about place-names is that they should easily be looked up in an atlas the following considerations have prevailed:

(i) Sites or towns in the Soviet Union are transliterated strictly from the Russian: thus Uzgend (not Özkent), Nakhichevan, not Nakhjawān etc.

(ii) Modern Turkish place-names within Turkey are spelt as they would appear on a Turkish atlas. Thus Harput (not Khart'pert'), Çankırı, Şebinkarahisar. The Turkish alphabet is similar to the English except for the letters c (j), ç (ch), ş (sh), ğ (gh) and ı (a deeper form of English i), and for ö and ü which are pronounced as they would be in German.

(iii) Other place-names, in Persia, Syria or Afghanistan etc., are spelt as they would appear on local maps except where there is a well-known English equivalent (thus, 'Damascus', not 'Dimishq'). In just a few cases in the Balkans, where place-names have often changed radically in the past twenty years, the older name has been used as being more likely to be familiar to an English-speaking public.

(4) Personal names and titles

Unfortunately, any system, however detailed, breaks down when faced with combinations of Arabic, Persian or Turkish in a name. As far as possible, up to the end of the Seljuk period Arabic names have been transliterated strictly according to the system used by the *Encyclopaedia of Islam* (with the substitution of q for ḳ), though where Persian or Turkish also occur an attempt has been made not to distort either component. Thus Saʿd al-Dīn *Köpek*, the vizir of ʿAlā al-Dīn Kayqubād, not *Kubak*, as the Arabic would demand. In some of these cases it is not at all clear which is the correct form e.g. Kalūk or Kölük, Sukman or Sökmen. In particularly dubious cases the alternative has been indicated in brackets, but the choice of one or the other must not be assumed to indicate an irrevocable commitment to any linguistic, etymological or historical hypothesis.

In the Ottoman period to transliterate all Arabic names strictly would create absurd situations where names now familiar to us would appear totally strange. Modern Turkish has for the most part been preferred here, sometimes with the use of the macron or diacritical marks where, as in the case of book-titles, this might make for ease of reference. A few examples follow:

	the Caliph al-Muʿtaṣim the Qāghān (Khāqān) Bilge Khān Mu'mine Khātūn 'Izz al-Dīn Kaykā'ūs	all Seljuk or pre-Seljuk
but	Rüstem Pasha Mehmed the Conqueror Osman, Ahmed, Ömer	Ottoman
and	Nüzhet al-Akhbār der Sefer-i Sigetvar, the history of the Hungarian campaign of Süleyman the Magnificent	

In these latter cases, in contrast to the verbatim transcription of Turkish place-names, for ease of reference, a phonetic transliteration of modern Turkish has been used.

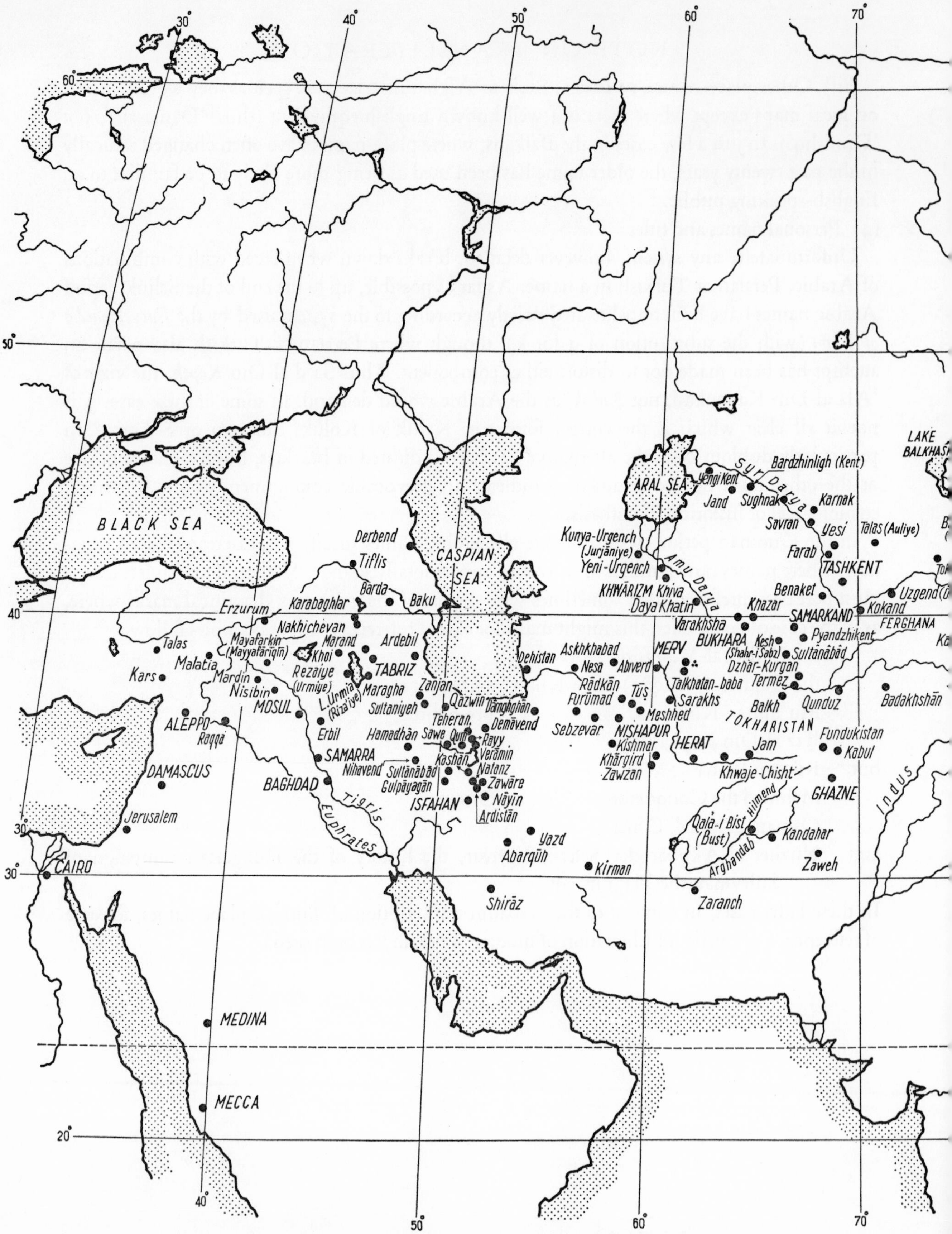

MAP I The Turks in World History, and their Capitals

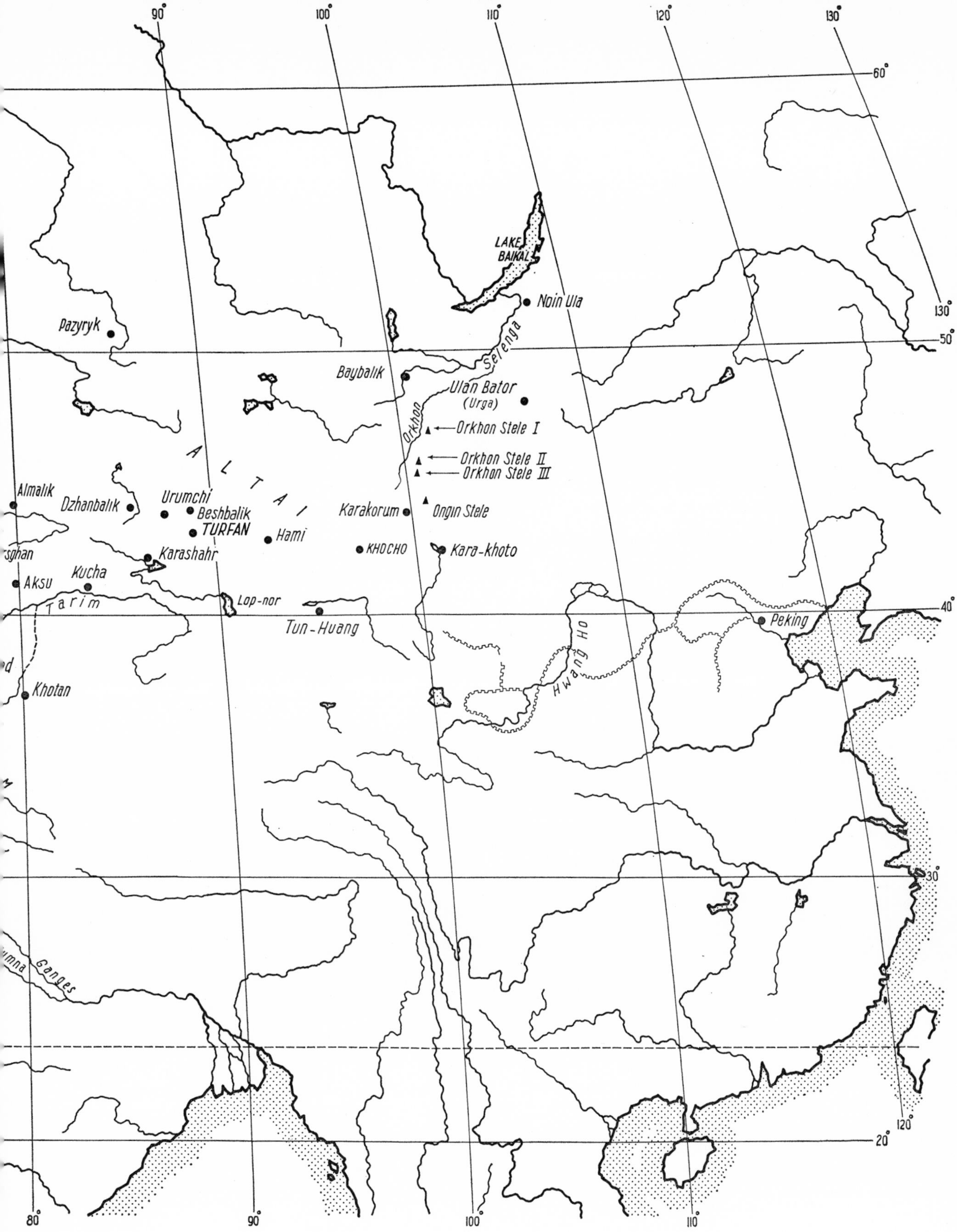
LAKE BAIKAL
Noin Ula
Pazyryk
Serenga
Baybalık
Ulan Bator
(Urga)
Orkhon
Orkhon Stele I
Orkhon Stele II
Orkhon Stele III
ALTAI
Almalık
Dzhanbalık
Urumchi
Beshbalik
TURFAN
Hami
Karakorum
Ongın Stele
KHOCHO
Kara-khoto
Karashahr
Kucha
Aksu
Tarim
Lop-nor
Tun-Huang
Hwang Ho
Peking
Khotan
Ganges

1

THE PRE-ISLAMIC TURKS AND THEIR ARTS

In order to achieve a thorough understanding of Turkish art in Anatolia it is necessary to dwell at least in outline on the arts produced by the Turks, or in countries under Turkish rule, prior to the Turkish settlement of Anatolia. Some eighty different Turkish states have been established in the course of history, from Emirates to Empires. Amongst the various elements, such as a common mother-tongue, common customs and traditions, that bound these various states together in spite of various political and religious differences, we must also count artistic activity. The Turks always brought their own culture and their own arts to the territories they conquered and settled in, and so changed the whole face of the country by stamping their own seal upon it. One cannot help noticing the unity and continuity of Turkish art of various different periods in territories stretching from Mongolia and Eastern Turkestan to Algiers and Budapest, and from the Crimea to Egypt.

As it is very difficult to obtain original photographs of the Pre-Anatolian periods that we shall be treating as an introduction or preparation for the study of Turkish art in Anatolia, we shall be able to demonstrate the links between them only by means of plans and diagrams. At the same time a certain amount of historical information will help towards a clearer understanding of the works of art themselves.

It has been suggested, as the result of various historical investigations, that the original homeland of the Turks before they set out on their migrations consisted of the area between the Altai and Ural Mountains and the steppes to the north and the north-east of the Caspian Sea. In the migrations that began before the Christian era the Turks branched out in various directions. The Asiatic Huns known in Chinese annals by the name Hiung-Nu and first seen in northern China in the 1st millennium B.C. are generally regarded as the first Turks to play a part in history. After a treaty with the Huns in 308 B.C. the Chinese began the Great Wall of China as a protection against the Turks, and completed it 90 years later in 214 B.C. In the middle of the 1st century A.D. the Empire of the Huns split into two. One branch consisted of the Huns that appeared in Europe in the 4th century A.D. and, under the leadership of Attila (434–453), overran much of Europe almost as far as the English Channel.

Another branch of the Huns migrated into Khurasan and established a great state towards the middle of the 5th century. These mingled with the Hephthalites, and, as the White Huns, established an empire that stretched from the Caucasus to Northern India. The rule of the White Huns collapsed in 564 when their territories were divided between the Gök Turks and the Sasanids.

As for the Huns who remained in China they were able to preserve their rule here and there until the middle of the 4th century.

At the end of the 3rd century the Turks known by the Chinese as T'o-ba and by the Gök Turks as Tabghach established an empire in South Mongolia and North China, and after capturing the Chinese imperial capital of Lo'Yang they conquered in 430 the territories of Shensi and Kansu. According to Chinese written sources these Tabghach were a branch of the Asiatic Huns. In 495, under the influence of Buddhism, the Tabghach language was forbidden and Turkish words removed from all official documents. The Turkish state subsequently became wholly Chinese in character.

The first people to use the word 'Turk' as the official name of a state and a community were the Gök Turks who settled on the Ötügen plateau to the west of the river Orkhon in the middle of the 6th century and who in a very short time set up a great empire stretching from Manchuria to the Black Sea. They called themselves either Turks or Turuks. In one of the inscriptions the word Gök (Kök) Türk is used referring to the sky (gök) or the sky god. Chinese sources make it quite plain that the Gök Turks were descended from the Asiatic Huns. This Gök Turk Empire, which enjoyed its most brilliant period during the reign of Mukan Qāghān (553–572), played a very important part in the Turkicisation of Central Asia. In 630 the empire, which from the time of its establishment in 552 by Bumin Qāghān and his brother Istemi Yabghu had been divided into a Western and an Eastern administrative district, came under Chinese suzerainty, but in 682, as a result of political struggles waged by Ilterish Qāghān (mentioned in Chinese sources under the name Qutlugh) and the great statesman Tonyukuk the administrative centre of the eastern Gök Turk state regained control of Ötügen. During the reign of Qapaghan Qāghān (692–716) the Turks of Central Asia were united into a single state. Bilge Qāghān, who succeeded Qapaghan, and his brother Kültegin are the best-known rulers of the Gök Turk state. The name 'Turk' is first found in the writings of a Byzantine author Aghathias (died 582) in connection with the Gök Turks, in the Arabic sources in the poetry of Nabiga al-Zubyānī, one of the poets of the Pre-Islamic period, who died around 600, and in Russian in the annals of the 11th and 12th centuries. Byzantine sources (Menandros) state that a letter sent by Istemi Yabghu to the Emperor Justinian in 568 was written in Turkish. An inscription dated 692 was erected in the name of Ilterish Qāghān beside the Ongin river to the south of the River Orkhon.

The oldest written documents in Turkish history are the Orkhon Inscriptions of the Gök Turks. These are carved from right to left and top to bottom on slabs of stone 3.75 metres high and 1.5–1.3 metres wide. There are three of these stones, the first being erected in 727 for Bilge

Tonyukuk, the second in 731 for Kültegin and the third in 735 for Bilge Qāghān. They are written in the oldest known form of Turkish script but in an advanced form of the Turkish language that can be read even today without too much difficulty. Prototypes of these inscriptions are found in the Yenisei region dating from the 6th and 7th centuries. Tonyukuk composed his own inscription, and the other two were composed by Prince Yolugh Tekin, a descendant of the Gök Turk Qāghāns, who thus occupies an important place in old Turkish literature.

The runic script of the White Huns resembled that of the Gök Turks. We learn from Priskos, however, that the Western Huns had styles of writing peculiar to themselves.

It was from the Gök Turks that the Turks as a whole derived their name, and it was the history of the Gök Turks that laid the foundations for later Turkish history. The Gök Turk state had comprised all the tribes of Turkish descent apart from the two small communities of the Yakuts in the Far East and the Oghurs (Bulgars) in the west. When the empire of the Gök Turks collapsed the various Turkish tribes that migrated in every direction kept their Turkish name, the Turkish language, and Turkish culture alive wherever they went. The movement of the Turks was subsequently always towards the west, but in Turkestan, Transoxania, India, Iran, Anatolia, Syria and the Balkans they retained their Turkish consciousness as a heritage of the Gök Turk empire. The Gök Turks, who had established an empire stretching from Manchuria and Mongolia to the shores of the Black Sea and the frontiers of the Sasanid and Byzantine Empires, held an important place in later Turkish history and in their own time established relations with other states. The daughter of Istemi Yabghu married the Sasanian Shahanshah Anushirwan and became an Empress in the Sasanian palace.

The Uighurs

The Uighurs, who are first mentioned in the Orkhon inscriptions in connection with their rebellion against Gök Turk suzerainty in the year 717 and who had long been known in Chinese sources as descendants of the Asiatic Huns, lived on the eastern shore of the River Selenga in dependence to the Gök Turks. In 745 they overthrew the Gök Turks and established an Uighur state. The founder of this state was Qutlugh Bilge Qāghān and its capital Qarabalgasun. In 747 he was succeeded by his son Moyunchur (Mo-yen Chur) who in an inscription he himself had written and erected near the Shine-Usu Lake in North Mongolia related the founding and expansion of the Uighur state and his own and his father's victories.

During the reign of his son Bögü (Alp Qutlugh Bilge Qāghān) Manichaeism was accepted by the Qāghān as the State religion, and a number of temples were built.

The inscription written in the Gök Turk alphabet of the Uighurs and erected in Qarabalgasun by the Uighur Qāghān Alp Bilge (808–821) relates how Manichaeism spread amongst the Uighurs during the reign of Bögü Han. Of the three languages in which the Qarabalgasun inscription is written that in Gök Turk is so worn as to be scarcely legible, whilst of the sections translated into Soghdian and Chinese only the Chinese can be clearly deciphered. The warlike spirit of the Uighurs, however, was softened and blunted by the vegetarian diet enforced by the Manichaean religion and in 840 they were defeated by the Kirghiz, their Qāghān was killed, and their capital Qarabalgasun captured. After this a large part of the Uighurs withdrew to the Tarim region and settled in the vicinity of the Tanri Mts., Turfan and Besh Balig. Other Uighur cities were Kucha, Kashgar, and Hami (Urumchi). In 947 the capital appears to have been Khocho (the present-day Kara Khocho in East Turkestan), and the summer capital Besh Balig. The later Uighur rulers were known as Iduk-Kut, and their capital Khocho became known as the city of Iduk-Kut (Idikut shehri).

Buddhism became widespread in the Uighur state of East Turkestan after 870, even beginning to outstrip Manichaeism, whilst at the same time we find Nestorian Christianity and, though at first only to a very small extent, Islam. Buddhist religious literature had a brilliant development in the Uighur language. Until the beginning of the 10th century the Uighurs had employed the Gök Turk alphabet, but after that they wrote in their own Uighur script, which is thus the second oldest Turkish alphabet.

The Chinese ambassador Wang-yen-to, who visited the Uighur Qāghān Arslan Khān at Turfan in 981, gives a detailed description of the brilliance of Uighur civilisation and of his reception at the Court. According to the latest researches the art of printing in movable type was discovered by the Uighurs in the 9th or 10th century. Sacks of these letters made of hard wood were recovered during excavations. The older Chinese art of printing employed a block system. It is generally agreed that the Uighurs played an important part in the spread of the printing-press towards the West. Like the Gök Turks the Uighurs used the twelve animal calendar. The Uighur state continued to exist in East Turkestan up to the beginning of the 13th century when, in 1209, it became a dependency of Chingiz Khan. After this the Uighur dynasty continued under the old name of Iduk-Kut until the beginning of the Ming dynasty (1368), when the Iduk-Kut ceased to exist.

Even after the political domination of the Uighurs (who were always referred to in Islamic sources as the Dokuz Oghuz) had collapsed, their culture and civilisation still continued to exert an influence for many years. The Uighur script was very highly developed, and came to be employed by all the Turkish tribes. The Mongols adopted both the Uighur alphabet and their own brand of Buddhism, and for many years they employed Uighur as the official language. Güyük Khān, who died in 1248, wrote to the Pope in Uighur. The same script was used in the Īl-Khānid period in Persia, and the Uighur script was later used for the laws of Timur and the edicts of the Golden Horde. Uighur continued to be employed on coins and in official inter-state correspondence up to the end of the 15th century. Mime, ballet, vocal and orchestral music, and a primitive form of theatre were to be found amongst the Uighurs, and were regarded by the Chinese as very original and attractive. The art of story-telling was also very advanced. From the dramatic point of view the Uighur versions of the stories were far superior to the Chinese.

The Pre-Islamic Art of the Turks

In the tombs excavated by the Russian archaeologist Rudenko in the district of Pazyryk in the foothills of the Altai Mountains in Siberia a number of artefacts were found, together with

I Konya, Sirçalı Medrese, 1242, iwan (see page 132)

human and animal bodies preserved in ice. No agreement has been reached as to the exact dating of these remains but it is very probable that they date from the 3rd or 2nd century B.C. That each of the ten horses sacrificed here bears a different crest indicates that they were presented by ten different tribes, and the cutting of the ears, tails and manes is a sign of mourning that was later widespread among the Turks. The caftans, felt socks and boots found there are typical attire of the nomadic Turks. The tombs found at Pazyryk and those at Katanda and Shiba may be said to be the oldest princely burials in the Altai Mountains to display the culture of the Great Hun Empire. The decorations on the horse trappings, small tables, household vessels, and wooden objects such as pestles all belong to the common culture of the Hunnic age. The rugs found in the Pazyryk burials display Achaemenid influence, though the rows of reindeer figures one behind the other are foreign to both the Achaemenids and to Iran in general, whilst mirrors and other objects are clearly influenced by Chinese art. It is possible moreover to see an original Hunnic style in decorations made by applying thin coloured pieces of leather to felt. Examples on a saddle cloth depicting an eagle attacking a mountain goat, a gryphon and other animal combats are in a style very reminiscent of the textile work found at Noin-Ula.

Of the 212 tombs that have been excavated in the Noin-Ula region near where the River Selenga debouches into Lake Baykal, numbers 1, 6, 12, 23 and 25 have been ascribed to Hun princes. Here too, objects resembling those in the Pazyryk burials as well as articles from China and Persia were found frozen in the ice. One of the appliqué textiles of thin coloured leather on felt depicts a gryphon with the head of a long-eared eagle attacking a stag from behind whilst embroideries on wool portray Hun warriors on swift horses, and two heads with moustaches display great power of portraiture.

There is a striking resemblance between the objects found in the Pazyryk and Noin-Ula burials, and the designs composed of thin coloured leather on felt.

The culture of the Hunnic state comprises five hundred years of common culture and tradition from the end of the 3rd century B.C. to the end of the 3rd century A.D.

Artistic activity amongst Tabghach took on a more definite form. Cave temples decorated with pictures and rich sculpture at Tunhuang on the Eastern edge of the Gobi Desert were founded under their rule. Although there is a great deal of Chinese influence in Tabghach art the decoration based on textile patterns to be found in the mural paintings shows an obvious connection with the art of the Huns and other nomads. Any descendants of the Khan in the Tabghach court could marry one of the princesses after having acquired the art of carving statues of Buddha. They had a very strong affection for Buddhist art. Clay figurines found in tombs of noble ladies of the Tabghach court show very delicate taste and workmanship and indicate an advanced art of sculpture.

An increasing amount of research has been devoted to the art of the Gök Turks in recent years. In the course of surveys and excavations carried out by the Archaeological Institute of Czechoslovakia under the direction of Lumir Jisl in the summer of 1958 in the Orkhon valley the still extant sections of the mausoleum of the great Turkish hero Kültegin were unearthed, together with a number of statues. The tomb had been previously rifled and utterly devastated, and the statues reduced to fragments, most of which were lost. Originally these statues had depicted Kültegin and his wife seated side by side. Of these only the marble head of the statue of Kültegin, the body of his wife which had split into two pieces, and fragments of the nose, mouth and chin sections of her head have been recovered. When regarded full face the head of Kültegin is seen to possess very expressive features created by means of soft modelling. One is struck by the relief device of an eagle with outspread wings on the front of his crown. This device was already known and admired by the Huns, and the eagle with ears and horns was a great symbol of strength. Figures of a pair of rams guarding the tomb, and a headless tortoise carrying an inscribed stone, and *balbals*—statues portraying enemies overcome by the heroes—were also recovered. Chinese sources affirm that there was an altar in the tomb, that the statue of Kültegin was made of stone and that his battles were depicted on all four walls, whilst the chronicles of the T'ang dynasty mention that six artists were sent there to decorate it.

Chinese artists may indeed have worked on the marble statues but one ought to point out that the *balbals* are typical of Gök Turk sculpture and display a certain feeling for the art of portraiture. Most of the innumerable *balbals* left by the Gök Turks have disappeared, but it is clear that they painted their statues as well as their inscriptions. Inscriptions have been found painted in red and black. A *balbal* found in recent years and now in the national museum of Ulan Bator has eyes, nose, moustaches, mouth and ears defined in brown and yellow.

The attire depicted in the Gök Turk sculptures conforms to the type of dress worn until recent times by the Turks of Central Asia. The fragments of embossed belts are noteworthy. A dagger was slung at the back of these, and small bags hanging from the belts took the place of pockets. As very little research has been carried out on Gök Turk art it is difficult to form a clear idea concerning it, but the arts must have been as developed as the language and literature though as a result of tomb robbery and destruction little of their work now remains.

Art was highly developed amongst the Uighur Turks and more of their works have come down to us. Their architecture resembles Buddhist and Manichaean religious art in combining Indian and Persian forms. Manichaean temples are in the form of fire-temples with domes on squinches. Domed tombs have also been found in the vicinity of Khocho. The dome may have come from Persia, but, as the concept of burial did not exist in the Zoroastrian religion, the conception of a *tomb* did not yet exist. The first tombs therefore were the domed funerary monuments built by the Uighurs at Khocho. In another domed structure in the vicinity of Komul, which would appear to be a tomb, the squinches in the corners are replaced for the first time by large triangles, a feature that is not to be found in Persia. Later, however, in Seljuk and Ottoman architecture, these triangles are a very important feature of dome construction.

The dominant features of the domestic architecture of the Uighurs are quite distinct from those of China. An art of Buddhist sculpture had developed amongst the Uighurs under Indian, Greek and Chinese influence, but at the same time the Uighurs produced a new, realistic and quite original type of sculpture derived from the *balbals* of the Gök Turks.

A clay statue, 47 cm. in height, of a kneeling figure carrying a load on its shoulder, found at Kızıl, is typical of Uighur art of the 8th and 9th centuries. The complexion is shown as fair, and the hair and head-dress black. Two animal statues taken in plaster from moulds found at

Sorchuk are of even greater interest. In one of these, a highly stylised horse's head 27 cm. in height, the mane and forelocks are so accentuated as to give the impression of a demon. A second figure, 38 cm. in height, portraying an elephant's head, is grotesque in appearance and even more stylised than the first. It is obviously the work of someone who had never seen an elephant. There are elephants' heads resembling this in the mural paintings at Kucha. The heads of animals that were found in plenty in that region, such as horses, camels and goats, were portrayed, however, with quite astonishing realism.

The Uighurs were the real representatives of old Turkish art, and a considerable number of works have come down from them. In Eastern Turkestan, the old homeland of the Uighurs, there are thousands of rock-cut temples. Their walls and ceilings were decorated with frescos, most of which were removed by the Germans who explored and excavated Turfan and taken to the Ethnographical Museum in Berlin. Most of these were destroyed in the last war. The subjects of the frescos are essentially Buddhist in character. Buddhist and Manichaean wall paintings and miniatures dating from the 8th and 9th centuries found in the ruins of the old Uighur cities are the oldest specimens of Turkish painting yet known. In these, priests, donors and musicians are grouped symmetrically in rows and portrayed in bright colours, azure and crimson.

In the frescos are to be seen individuals who had commissioned their own portraits, various groups of people, Indian and Chinese priests, Tokharians and Persians. Thus the art of lending an individual, personal quality to the representation of the human face, in other words the art of portraiture, arose some time after 750 in the mural paintings of the Uighur Turks. Until that time faces were, like bodies, drawn in accordance with certain stereotyped patterns, and the results distinguished one from the other by means of names inscribed below. As Professor Von Gabain very aptly pointed out, by directing their attention to peoples different from themselves and dividing them up into different physical types the Uighurs came to see themselves more clearly. Eventually they developed the art of portraiture to such an extent that an individual likeness can be observed even in pictures of priests arranged in rows, despite their identical posture and attire.

The Gök Turks played an important part in the birth of the art of portraiture. The ancient Turks preserved the memory of their heroes for eternity by inscribing their names, title and age on stones known as Bengü or Mengü. Therefore it was essential that each hero's Bengü should be determined in such a way that it was impossible for it to be changed later. The influence of this conception on the Uighurs must later have given rise to the art of portraiture. Besides distinguishing and dating the various physical types and creating an art of portraiture the Uighurs introduced another innovation to painting in their likenesses of the Gods, and in both of these spheres they exerted a certain influence on Chinese painting.

Although the Qāghān and the nobles had accepted Manichaeism the Uighur people remained faithful to Buddhism. There were also a small number of Nestorian Christians. The most important monument of Uighur Buddhist painting is a temple at Bezeklik in the vicinity of Murtuk. In the Bezeklik frescos Uighur princes are portrayed with great realism. At Sorchuk the frescos depicting men and women donors all display skill in individual portraiture.

Uighur miniatures, in the pages remaining from Manichaeist books, depict both religious and profane scenes. Besides these there were discovered large illuminated pages and banners, which were kept in Manichaean temples and employed in their religious rites. This Uighur art of miniature painting later became a basic source for the development of the Islamic miniature.

From the 8th and 9th centuries onwards the arts of portraiture and miniature painting which had developed amongst the Uighurs steadily progressed, and later, in the 13th century, this brilliant inheritance of the artistic Turks was carried to the West and to the Islamic world by the Mongols and the new empire they founded.

Although in addition to these there was a considerable amount of artistic activity from the 4th century onwards in other Turkish states established in various regions from Asia to Europe before their conversion to Islam—by peoples such as the Avars, Turgishes, Karluk, Kirghiz, Pechenegs, Uses (the Oghuzes who migrated to Europe), the Kipchaks and the Cumans, the Hungarians, the Bulgarians (the Volga and Danube Bulgars) and the Khazars—nevertheless, since they have few artistic relations with Turkish art of Anatolia, we have not dwelt upon them.

The Turks in Islam

The Turks (Atrāk) first appeared in the Islamic world when a small number of Turks from Ferghana, Tashkent and Transoxiana began to be enrolled in the ranks of the imperial bodyguard and the security forces of the ʿAbbāsid caliphs in the second half of the 8th century. In the 9th century their numbers increased rapidly, and by the time of the Caliph al Muʿtaṣim the Imperial bodyguard was composed entirely of Turks. Once the Turks and the Turkish bodyguard were settled in the new centre of Sāmarrā founded by al-Muʿtaṣim on the banks of the Tigris north of Baghdad in 838 the influence of Turkish art began to be apparent. The bevelled style employed in the plaster decoration in houses and palaces, a form of decoration made by the use of wooden moulds on wet plaster, is an innovation introduced into Islamic art by the Turks. This style appears in Central Asian metalwork before Sāmarrā and in Turkish architectural decoration after Sāmarrā.

The foundation of the two Turkish states of the Ṭūlūnids and the Ikshīdids in Egypt between the second half of the 9th century and the second half of the 10th century provided a firm foundation for the development of Islamic art.

On the voluntary conversion of the Turks to Islam, however, a great and completely original artistic movement accompanied the foundation of Muslim Turkish states in Asia, and it was by the Karakhanids, the first of these, that the first solid foundations of Turkish Islamic art were laid. (Map I.)

2

KARAKHANID ART

The first Islamic Turkish state to be founded in Asia was that of the Karakhanids. Before their conversion to Islam they had been known variously as the Turkestan Uighur Khans, the Ilig Khans, the Āl-i Afrasiyāb, etc. This state was founded by the Karluk Turks, who were joined by the Chighil and Yaghma Turks. When the Uighur Principate to which the Yabghu of the Karluks owed allegiance was dispersed by the Kirghiz in 840, he looked upon himself as a Turkish prince and took the title of Karakhan. The home territory of the Karakhanids lay between Kashgar and the Semirech'ye. Their rule lasted from the middle of the 9th century to the beginning of the 13th century (842–1212).

Towards 920 Satuk Boghra Khan accepted Islam as the official religion and adopted the name ʿAbd al-Karīm. After that date the Turks were converted to Islam in ever increasing numbers. Satuk Boghra Khan was killed in 959 in a battle against the ruler of the Eastern Karakhanids, the Great Khan Arslan Khan, at Balasagun, and was buried at Artuch, to the north of Kashgar. He was succeeded as ruler of the Eastern Karakhanids by his son Baytash Musa, who defeated the Great Qāghān Arslan Khan circa 960 and thus ensured the conversion of all the Karakhanids to Islam. In 999 the Karakhanids captured Bukhara and so put an end to the state of the Samanids. From this period there are still extant several valuable works of Turkish language and literature, such as the Kudatgu (or Kutadgu) Bilig written by Yusuf Khaṣṣ Ḥājib in verse in Uighur script at Kashgar in 1069 and dedicated to Boghra Khan, and the three-volume Dīwān Lughat al-Turk written by Maḥmūd of Kashgar in 1074, which is a work of the greatest importance from the point of view of the history of Turkish culture. Although Maḥmūd of Kashgar's work is properly Karakhanid it was written in Baghdad under the Great Seljuks.

The Turkish philosopher Muḥammad Farabī (died 950), who was born in the Turkish town of Qarachuk (later Farab) on the eastern bank of the Oxus, was the first to develop Islamic philosophy on the foundation of ancient Greek thought, and commented upon and interpreted the works of Aristotle. He wrote as many as 160 works on scientific and philosophic subjects. Another great Turkish scholar was Al-Birūnī of Khwārizm (died 1048), one of the greatest mathematicians of his time, who wrote more than 110 works on various branches of science including geometry, algebra, mathematics and geography.

Mosques

In the earliest buildings of the 10th century we see adobe structures gradually replaced by brick. In the Small Deggaron Mosque of the 11th century in the town of Khazar about 40 km. from Bukhara we find a blend of adobe and brick. The dome, which is 6.5 metres in diameter and rests on four pointed vaults supported on low round piers 30 cm. in diameter, shows a small-scale, centralised type of plan, with small domes averaging 3.6 metres in diameter in each of the corners (Plan Ia). The walls are of adobe, whereas the piers and arches supporting the central dome are of brick. The columns it contains have been altered from their original form. The interior of the mosque produces a most powerful impression with the simplicity of its brick patterning, the lightness of its arches and the mature harmony of its plan and architecture.

This early Karakhanid structure is very interesting when we consider the large-scale mosques constructed on a centralised plan with four half-domes that were to be produced in Ottoman architecture of the 16th century. The 10th and 12th centuries formed a period of brilliant development in Karakhanid brick architecture. The Talkhatan Baba Mosque about 30 km. from the old city of Merv and dating from the end of the 11th or the beginning of the 12th century, is constructed wholly of brick and is quite extraordinary in appearance from the point of view of both plan and architecture. The mosque is rectangular in shape and measures 18 × 10 metres. It is a single-domed structure which has been extended on each side by means of small cross vaults (Plan Ib). The façades are articulated by niches. The rich architectural decoration formed by the various patterning of the bricks in these foreshadows the later Karakhanid structures. The mosque opens outwards through a triple arch, a wide central arch flanked by two narrower ones, and the brick decoration to be seen on the façades is repeated in the brick pointed arched niche of the mihrab. The Talkhatan Baba Mosque is noteworthy as being the first step towards a type of plan scheme with a single dome extended on each side that was to be employed by the architect Sinan in the Ottoman period in the 16th century. Most of the Karakhanid mosques have survived to our own times after undergoing various repairs, additions and alterations.

The Maghāk-i ʿAṭṭārī Mosque, in Bukhara, stands on the site of an old Karakhanid mosque that had been built in the 11th century. Although traces of four columns from the original building are plainly visible it is impossible to reconstruct the original plan. Possibly this too was a centralised type of plan scheme. Although the original form has been destroyed the monumental south porch with its slightly pointed arches surviving from the original Karakhanid structure is remarkable for its highly developed architectural decoration in which foliate and geometrical motifs are formed into one harmonious whole by the use of epigraphic motifs. The first composition of patterns on a ground of small, burnished bricks, carved

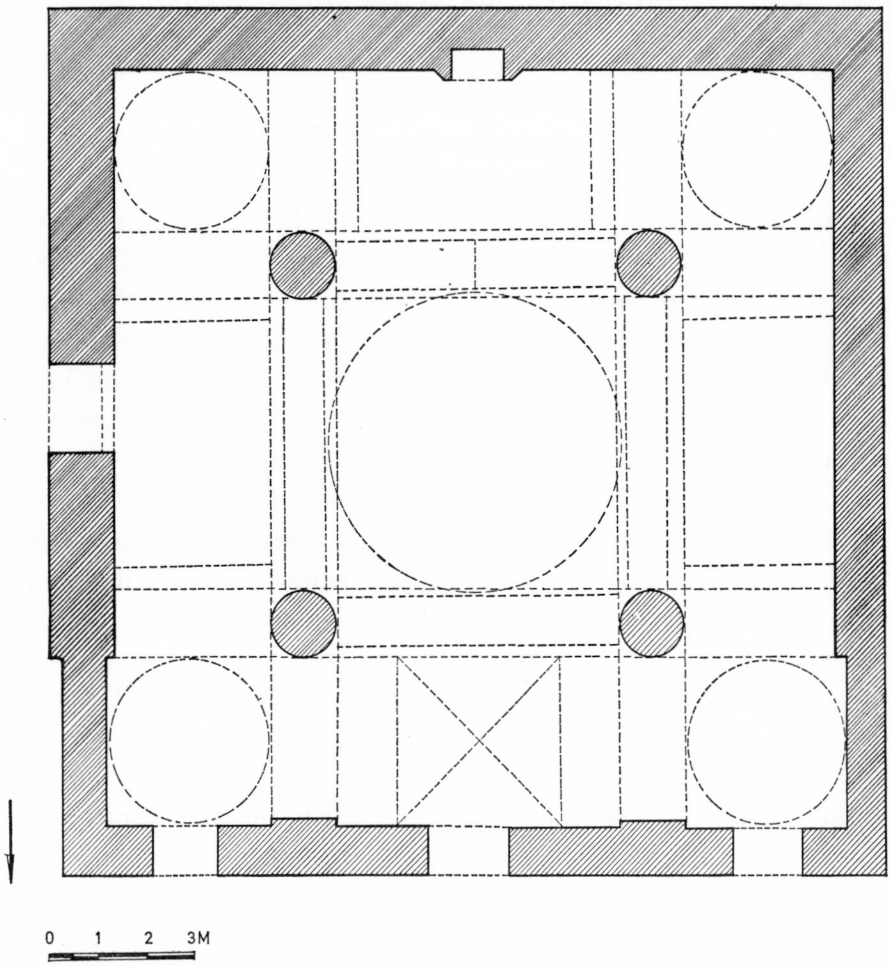

Plan Ia. Khazar, Mosque

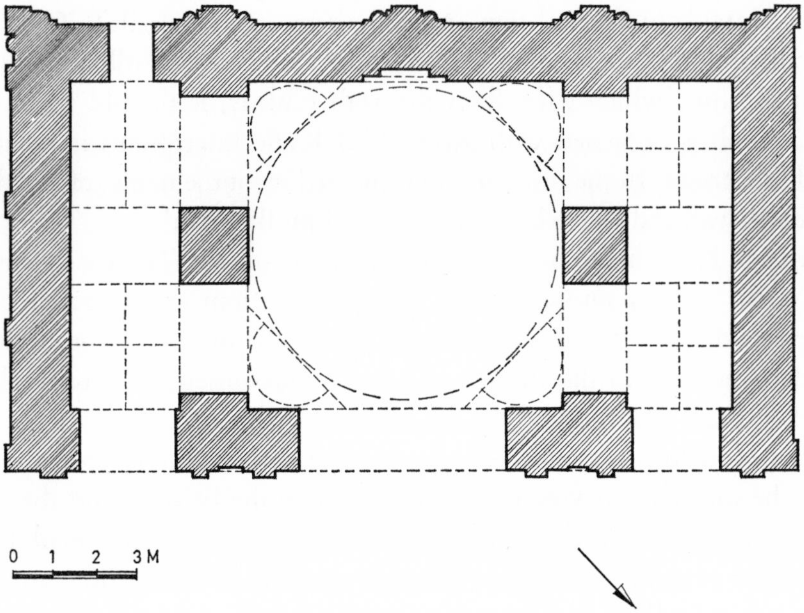

Plan Ib. Talkhatan Baba, Mosque

terracotta and stucco modelling is executed with very great technical skill. A fourfold braid pattern resulting from the intersection of octagonal figures, to be seen in the lowest panel of the geometrical decorations forming a border on each side of the porch niche, played a most important role in Karakhanid architectural decoration and was to be employed, but always with a new tone and spirit, in various types of art from the Ghaznevids and Great Seljuks right up to the Anatolian Seljuks and even the Ottomans. The general composition of the porch niche was continued in Anatolian Seljuk architecture and also in Timurid architecture. The present plan of the Maghāk-i ʿAṭṭārī Mosque, with its three-aisled plan on six columns, is ascribed to the 12th century, when Karakhanid architecture was at its highest peak of development. It is of great importance as a prototype of the three-aisled mosques of Anatolia.

Most of the monuments of Bukhara were built by Muḥammad bin Sulaymān Arslan Khān (1087–1130). One of these—the Masjid-i Jumʿa (Friday Mosque)—dates from the beginning of the 12th century, but the present Kalyan Mosque dates from the time of the Shaybanid ruler Uzbek Khan (1514). Of the original mosque only the minaret remains, and of that only 47 metres of the original height. In the ceramic inscription on its body we find the name Arslan Khan, and the date 521/1127. The minaret is in the form of a thick cylinder tapering towards the top, and is decorated by thirteen bands of geometrical reliefs. The Kalyan minaret dominates the whole city and has come to stand as the symbol of Bukhara. It has been claimed that the parapet surrounded by pointed arches and supported by spiral brackets is original. A prototype of this minaret is to be seen in another Karakhanid minaret constructed at Uzgend in the 11th century. The base of this latter is 9.4 metres in diameter and its height 17 metres. It is built of thick bricks and is surrounded by alternate wide and narrow courses of geometrical designs. The style and decoration of the Kalyan minaret are much inferior. It may well have been constructed by a Karakhanid craftsman from Uzgend in imitation of the original.

In 516/1119–20 Arslan Khān converted an old hunting park on the outskirts of Bukhara dating from the Karakhanid period into an open-air mosque (muṣalla). This consisted only of a mihrab wall, and the congregation prayed under the trees. The qibla wall (west wall) of the Namāzgāh Mosque, which dates from the 16th century, is the old mihrab wall of the muṣalla. The mihrab is decorated with geometrical Kufic inscriptions in small, burnished, yellow and reddish bricks. In the inscription on the pediment the names of Allah and the first four caliphs are repeated, and on the borders the text 'al-mulk li'llāh'.

Of the other large Karakhanid mosque at Dzhar Kurgan near Termez (Tirmidh) only the brick minaret dated 1108–9 survives. This minaret rises from an octagonal base, the shaft being decorated with sixteen semicylindrical flutes with an inscription from the Koran forming a wide band around the summit. There are also inscriptions on each facet of the base. The fourfold braid motifs round the door formed by intersecting of the octagons are also to be found here. Monotony is avoided by the alternate horizontal and vertical zigzag placing of the bricks. The minaret was very much higher before the balcony and the upper portion collapsed in an earthquake. As the architect's name is given as Muḥammad al-Sarakhsī we may assume that he came from Sarakhs. The architectural device of decorating the shaft of the minaret by semicylindrical flutes was continued for centuries in Turkish architecture in

II Istanbul, Çinili Köşk, 1473, exterior, main entrance (see page 247)

both mausolea and minarets, and was developed in a number of different variations. The nearest examples to the fluted minaret are the Radkan tomb dating from the 13th century, the fluted minaret at Antalya, and the Çifte Minare Medrese at Erzurum. A similar architectural principle—with certain modifications and with more slender proportions—can be seen continued in the minaret of Sultan Mas'ūd III at Ghazne constructed at almost exactly the same time as the Dzhar Kurgan minaret, the Quṭb Minar minaret constructed by Quṭb al-Dīn Aybek in Delhi in 1206, and in several minarets built by the Anatolian Seljuks and even by the Ottomans. The Burana minaret at Balasagun in Eastern Turkestan indicates the presence of another Karakhanid mosque of the 11th century.

The Vabkent minaret to the north of Bukhara dating from 1196 is an almost identical replica of the Kalyan minaret and introduces nothing new.

According to Narshakhī's history of Bukhara, 'As most of the minarets of the Samanids were constructed of wood they caught fire very easily. The Karakhanids, on the other hand, built monumental minarets in brick.' Consequently the oldest minarets still extant in Turkestan belong to the Karakhanid period.

Tombs

The Arab Ata tomb at Tim in the vicinity of the Zarafshan valley dated to 367/978 is the oldest example of Karakhanid funerary architecture still standing. It is a single-domed structure on four walls (6 × 6 metres) in which the concept of a defined façade is powerfully asserted. It differs from the Samanid tomb in Bukhara dating from the first half of the 10th century in its heightened tripartite squinches and in the fact that the porch concealing the monumental dome lends the small building the appearance of being much larger and higher than it really is. The rich geometrical brick decoration of the Arab Ata tomb, to be seen on the upper part of the façade of the large pointed arched porch articulated by a row of three niches, its inscription band—a large portion of which has been destroyed—and its mature architecture, all foreshadow the later brilliant development of Karakhanid tomb construction.

The early 12th-century tombs of Ayshe Bibi and Baladzhi Khātūn (near the Dzhambul station on the Turkestan–Siberia railway) at Talas in what is now Kazakhstan show the rapid developments that took place in Karakhanid tomb architecture. The tomb of Ayshe Bibi measures 7 × 7 metres. Its dome has collapsed, but it is remarkable for its deep, narrow porch niche on thick, decorated corner pilasters, and for its strange engaged pilasters at the two corners, wide at the top and bottom and slender in the middle. All the façades and the two minarets are decorated with 64 different designs in high relief and faced with terracotta in square, cross and star patterns. So rich and splendid a tomb must have been built for Ayshe Bibi, the daughter of a sultan and the wife of a khan. She was in fact the daughter of the Great Seljuk Sultan Alp Arslan and became the wife of the Karakhanid ruler Shams al-Mulūk Naṣr bin Ibrāhīm (1068–1082). This ruler is known to have been responsible for a number of architectural monuments in his dominions. It is natural that he should have built a tomb worthy of his wife Ayshe.

The tomb of Baladzhi Khātūn is of the same dimensions but is much simpler in appearance. Inside it has a squinched dome with eight grooves, whilst the exterior is surmounted by a cone in the form of a pyramid with 16 facets. A long, narrow niche is cut into the façade on each side of the portal, and there is no decoration except for a straggling *naskhī* inscription in terracotta along the upper edge. Baladzhi Khātūn may well have been a relation of Ayshe Bibi.

The most lively example of Karakhanid tomb architecture may be seen in that part of Uzgend that stretches to the east of the Ferghana valley, in what is now Kirghizstan. Here are to be found a group of three tombs arranged in a row, of the oldest and largest of which only a squinch of the central dome and a portion of the porch are still standing. The tomb is dated 403 (1012) and is of Nāṣir bin ʿAlī, the great ruler of the Karakhanids, who adopted the title Arslan Ilig Khan. This building was originally 8.5 sq. metres in size and consisted of a squinched dome set on four walls. When Von Viller saw it in 1924–5 the front wall had been restored. A section with five round arches surrounded by rounded mouldings under the single surviving squinch is decorated with stylised lotus and palmettes in stucco reminiscent of the bevelled style of 9th-century Sāmarrā.

The star patterns and fourfold braid motifs produced by the intersection of the semi-octagons executed in brick on the wide border still surviving from the portal, are very important as the first example of a geometric pattern that, after undergoing various modifications, was later to become a traditional motif in Turkish art (Design Ia). It is possible to follow the development of this decorative motif throughout all subsequent periods of Turkish art, both in architecture and in the other arts. Another form of the pattern produced in Karakhanid art by the intersection of octagons is to be seen in the brick decorations on the porch of the Maghāk-i ʿAṭṭārī mosque at Bukhara and on the narrow course in the middle of the Uzgend minaret. In the tomb of Nāṣir bin ʿAlī we see, in addition to the usual geometrical patterns, the first appearance of stylised foliate motifs.

A second tomb, which stands to the north and is the best preserved of the three, was, according to the inscription above the arch of the portal niche, built by Jalāl al-Dīn Ḥusayn in 547/1152. That he came of Turkish stock is shown by his Turkish name 'Alp Qılıch Tängä Bilge Türk Tughrul Qāghān'. He died in the year 1156. This Karakhanid tomb, consisting of a dome with squinches set on four walls, is, for its façade and external appearance, which are epoch-making, one of the most important works in the history of Turkish architecture. A pointed arched niche is surrounded by a wide geometrical border and the corners at both sides are softened by means of round piers. The *rūmī* (foliate scroll or arabesque) motif is to be seen for the first time in the *naskhī* inscription on the arch of the porch niche. The finely detailed decoration composed of veined *rūmī*, lotuses and palmettes in the inscription above the portal completely covers the façade, which is divided into three shallow niches with pointed arches. Most of these have crumbled away in recent years. Large 8-sided stars in terracotta on the interior face of the arch of the porch niche are connected to each other by four arms, and the spaces between them are filled with tendrils, palmettes and *rūmī* decoration. One is struck by the richness of an art of decoration, developed within such great simplicity. There is a magnificent inscription surrounding the pointed arch of the porch niche, and at the very point of the

Design Ia. Uzgend, Tomb of Nāṣir bin ʿAlī, 1012–13, detail of raised brick design on porch

arch there is an inset in turquoise faience. On either side of this inset there is a blank circular medallion which must have been at one time inset with tiles.

According to the inscription on the third tomb, which stands at the southern end of the oldest tomb, it was built in 582/1187 and completed in ten months. Here too the central portion of the inscription on the arch of the porch niche in which the name was written has disappeared. Although vertical lines are predominant in this tomb, its main architectural lines seem to be modelled upon the tomb of Jalāl al-Dīn Ḥusayn, which had been built some 35 years before. The form of the façade had thus become traditional, and played an important part both in the architecture of the Anatolian Seljuks and, with the first tomb structure of the Shāh-i Zinde Cemetery at Samarkand, in Timurid architecture.

In this tomb the architectural details have been arranged in the form of decorations, and follow each other from the exterior to the interior. Rich lozenge patterns on the round, brick corner piers, an inscribed arch supported on pilasters in a deep porch niche, inscription borders in plaited Kufic lettering and other geometrical decorations, together with *naskhī* border inscriptions embellished with tendrils, *rūmī* arabesques and palmettes in relief, indicate how great an advance had taken place in so short a time. The side façade is articulated by three niches with pointed arches and is an exact replica of the main façade of the tomb of Baladzhi Khātūn.

In spite of the richness of its decoration the mausoleum is monumentally weak compared with the other two tombs. From its date it would appear to belong to Jalāl al-Dīn Ḥusayn's grandson, Muḥammad bin Naṣr. The latter's Turkish name was Tughrul Qāghān, and he reigned in Ferghana with his capital at Uzgend. As coins bearing his name were minted in 1182 his tomb must have been built several years later.

The tomb of Sheikh Faḍl at Sefid Bulend near the old capital of Kassan to the north of Ferghana is one of the most important specimens of Karakhanid architecture. The exterior of this three-storey building, which is 14 metres high and is constructed entirely of brick, is a fusion of tomb and shrine. The squinch section is in the form of an octagonal storey supported by four walls around a cubiform inner space, and the structure terminates in a shallow cone rising in three steps. In contrast to the simple external appearance of this plain brick building, the interior displays wealth of decoration. The walls of the domed central area show a remarkably sound understanding of architectural decoration rarely to be found elsewhere.

The stucco decoration begins at the base of the walls in rows of trefoil arches. After this there is a row of large ornate roundels surrounded by Kufic inscriptions and framed by alternate curved and angular mouldings. The upper section of the walls terminates in an inscription frieze in raised Kufic of mature style. The squinches are surrounded by pointed arches with rounded mouldings, and another Kufic inscription from the Koran encircles the building just above this. It would appear that the interior of the dome was also covered with carved stucco.

The tomb of Sheikh Faḍl has no dating inscription but its architectural style suggests the middle of the 12th century, between the tombs of Nāṣir bin 'Alī and Jalāl al-Dīn Ḥusayn at Uzgend.

Although in addition to these there are fifteen or twenty Karakhanid tombs known we have touched upon only the most typical, in order to give a general idea of their characteristics.

Caravansarais

The oldest caravansarais in the history of Turkish architecture are those of the Karakhanids, and these were known as Ribāṭs. The plan and architecture of the Karakhanid caravansarais were later imitated in the caravansarais constructed by the Great Seljuks and the Anatolian Seljuks.

Shams al-Mulūk Naṣr bin Ibrāhīm, the Karakhanid Sultan who married the daughter of Alp Arslan, built two caravansarais—one of them on the Bukhara–Samarkand road, and the other on the Samarkand–Khodzhend road. The more important of the two is the Ribāṭ-i Malik (on the Bukhara–Samarkand road) built in 471/1078–9. Judging from the traces of its walls it must have been a square construction 86 × 86 metres. Identical vaulted rooms and chambers were deployed in two storeys around the central courtyard. The building was constructed entirely of adobe faced with brick. Only the south wall and porch are still standing.

This wall is buttressed at the corners by towers and is articulated by large semicircular brick piers crowned by a series of pointed arches set in successive receding planes. The type of façade architecture here applied to a caravansarai is typical of the Merv district. It can be seen in several castles in the area and throws light on the history of a number of ruins of the type in Merv, Khiva and Termez. The pointed arched porch (known in Turkestan by the Persian word Pīshṭāq) that rises up exactly in the centre of the façade, is remarkable in that although it belongs to the second half of the 11th century it already displays the traditional mature form of the Turkish porch. The porch is of monumental proportions (12 × 15 metres). The walls are 12 metres high. Its arch is defined by an inscription from the Koran in Kufic lettering, whilst a wide rectangular border decorated with large star and cross patterns in raised brick, and limited by a moulding of double knotted *tori* at each end, surrounds the arch. This type of porch, which first appears with the Karakhanids, forms a basic element in the architecture of the Great Seljuk, Anatolian Seljuk and Timurid periods.

On the upper section of the walls is a Persian inscription in brick, but both the beginning and end of this, which was in Kufic, have disappeared. Bartold read the date of this building and the name of the ruler who built it in a gloss in a manuscript of the Kitāb-i Mullah Zāde, and thus threw light on the missing portions of the inscription. It has been suggested that the cylindrical 15.5 metres high tower at the left-hand corner of the front façade was a minaret. It is encircled by a wide inscription band just below the parapet. The façade, with the porch in the centre, the cylindrical towers at each corner, the large piers in the side walls and the long niches terminating in pointed arched tympani adorned with geometrical patterns, all of which can be seen in an engraving made in 1841, is an example of a monumental and unforgettable type of façade architecture.

Other Karakhanid caravansarais are of various plans and types, and clearly exerted an influence on the Turkish caravansarais erected in later periods.

The Dakhistan Caravansarai (Turkmenistan) is a very ruined structure of the 11th century that resembles in its square plan (37 × 37 metres), its side and corner towers and its central arcaded courtyard, both the Ribāṭ-i Zaʿfarān on the Nishapur–Sebzevar road, which is thought to have been built by Malikshāh in the 11th century, and the Ribāṭ-i Anushīrwān at Ekhvan east of Simnan. But instead of the four iwans seen in the Ribāṭ-i Zaʿfarān and Ribāṭ-i Anushīrwān there is only one iwan, in the entrance of the Dakhistan Caravansarai, so that it may well be older than the others.

The Akchakale Caravansarai on the Merv–Amul road, almost all of which is now buried in the Kara Kum desert, is the finest of the others. The building is a mixture of adobe and brick, and in its plan and external appearance it is a prototype of the Ribāṭ-i Sharaf, built by the Great Seljuks on the Nishapur–Merv road in 1114–5. It is composed of two 4-iwan arcaded courtyards one behind the other. The plan of the Akchakale Caravansarai forms a harmonious whole, and would appear to belong to the end of the 11th century. (Plan 11a.)

The Daya Khātūn Caravansarai on the old road leading from Amul to Khwārizm, on the banks of the Oxus (Amu Darya) has a square plan scheme with four iwans and towers of two types, one solid and the other hollow, at the corners and sides. The two rooms in the

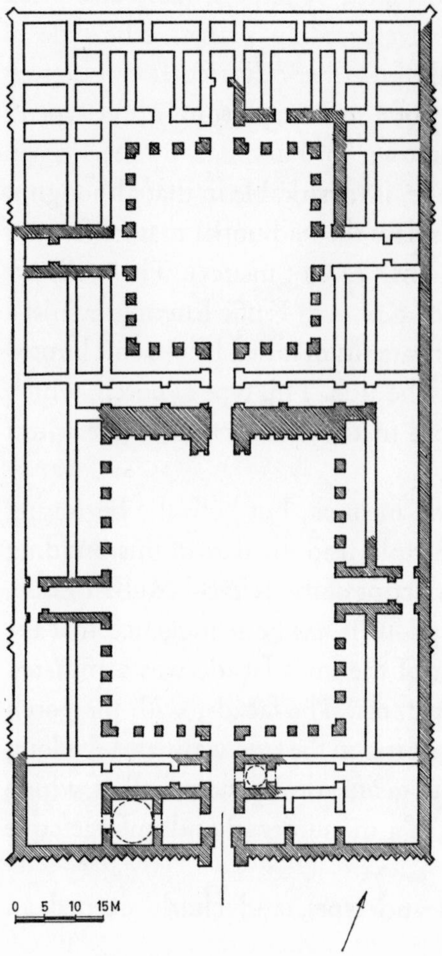

Plan IIa. Akchakale, Caravansarai

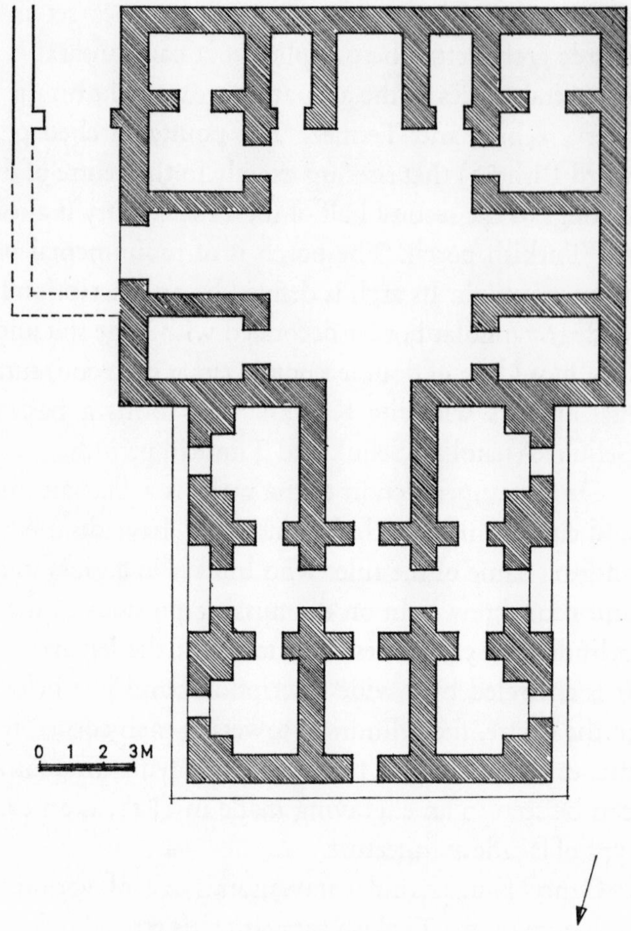

Plan IIb. Kurtlutepe Shehir (Bashan), Caravansarai

north-west corner and behind the west iwan are identical in plan with the rooms in the Ribāṭ-i Sharaf. The very sound brick architecture and unusual brick bonding remind one of the Talkhatan Baba Mosque. It is thus possible to place the Daya Khātūn Caravansarai at the end of the 11th century.

The caravansarai in the ruins of Kurtlutepe Shehir (Bashan) differs in plan from the others and appears as a small-scale replica of the Seljuk caravansarais of Anatolia. The open courtyard in front and the covered hall behind present the plan scheme of the great Anatolian Sultan Hans. (Plan IIb.) This caravansarai probably dates from the end of the 11th or the beginning of the 12th century.

The Karakhanid caravansarais are important monuments of Turkish architecture, which later exerted an obvious influence on the plan and architecture not only of caravansarais but also of medreses and mosques.

3

GHAZNEVID ART

The Turkish state founded in 977 by Sebük Tekin with its capital at Ghazne came to be known as the Ghaznevid state. Tekin was succeeded in 998 by his son Sultan Maḥmūd, who, after seventeen campaigns, conquered the whole of northern India and converted the country to Islam under a Turkish administration. Sultan Maḥmūd also added the provinces of Khwārizm and Khurāsān to his empire, but in 1040 his son Mas'ūd I was defeated by the Seljuks and lost all his dominions outside India and Afghanistan. From this date until 1191 the Ghaznevid state remained a dependency of the Seljuks.

Originally a small town of little importance, Ghazne had become, under Ghaznevid rule, one of the greatest centres of culture in Asia. Sultan Maḥmūd founded medreses and libraries, and gathered scholars together in his palace. The poet Firdawsī completed his Shāh Nāme at his court and dedicated the work to him, whilst Farrūḥī declared him to have been the head of the Shāhanshāhs (that is, the greatest of all rulers) in 1038. Turks had settled here before the Ghaznevids, a point of cardinal historic importance from the point of view of the influence exerted by Ghaznevid Turkish art on both Great Seljuk art and the Turkish art of India.

Mosques

According to written sources ('Utbī), the magnificent 'Arūs al-Falak (Bride of Heaven) Mosque built by Sultan Maḥmūd at Ghazne was covered by a roof supported on wooden pillars brought from India, and contained decoration of dazzling richness in which red, gold and lapis lazuli were used. There is no doubt that other mosques were also built in Ghazne.

The problem of the towers at Ghazne, which has for long given rise to various unfounded theories, has at last been solved. Photographs taken from a distance show them standing in a large ruin resembling a mosque, and prove that they must have been minarets. If excavations were made this mosque could be unearthed. One of the minarets was, according to its inscription, built by Sultan Mas'ūd III. The upper portion of the minaret, a circular shaft, was in the form of a slightly tapering cylinder whilst the lower portion which is still extant is of brick and flanged in the form of an 8-pointed star, the whole resting on a low stone base. The minaret was originally 48 metres in height, but the cylindrical upper portion was destroyed in an earthquake. There is a spiral staircase within it. Brick decoration consisting of various foliate motifs and geometrical designs, together with very rich Kufic inscriptions, was begun at the top of the structure, but the lower sections were left unfinished. It would appear that the decoration remained incomplete on the death of Sultan Mas'ūd in 1115.

Up to 1953 the second minaret had been ascribed to Sultan Maḥmūd and was thought to be older than the first. After researches carried out by J. Sourdel-Thomine, however, it was seen from the inscription to belong to Bahram Shāh (1117–1149). This is, in fact, a simplified copy of the minaret of Mas'ūd III. Geometrical patterns predominate in the decoration.

Of all the Ghaznevid mosques the most important from the architectural point of view is the Great Mosque at Lashkari Bazar, the possible plan of which was suggested as a result of excavations carried out by the French archaeologist D. Schlumberger in 1951. The mosque appeared to have been a large, plain, two-aisled structure built against the walls surrounding an esplanade to the south of the great Ghaznevid summer palace near the ruins of Bust in South Afghanistan, and forming a rectangle 86 × 10.5 metres in size. Four rectangular brick piers in front of the mihrab no doubt supported a dome. The columns on each side of this central dome supported the north and south wings of the aisles. It appears that there were two rows of columns in front of the esplanade wall. Because of the hot climate the mosque was open on to the courtyard and on two sides. It is not clear how the aisles on each side of the dome in front of the mihrab were roofed. Two rows of small domes has been suggested but this does not give a satisfying plan. It is more likely that a flat roof or vaulting was employed. (Vaulting is seen later in the Artukid mosques in Anatolia, which have a plan similar to this one.) (Plan Ic.) The plan of the mosque and the quality and bonding of the bricks suggest that it was built in the first half of the 11th century during the reign of Sultan Maḥmūd (998–1030), and Schlumberger is also of this opinion.

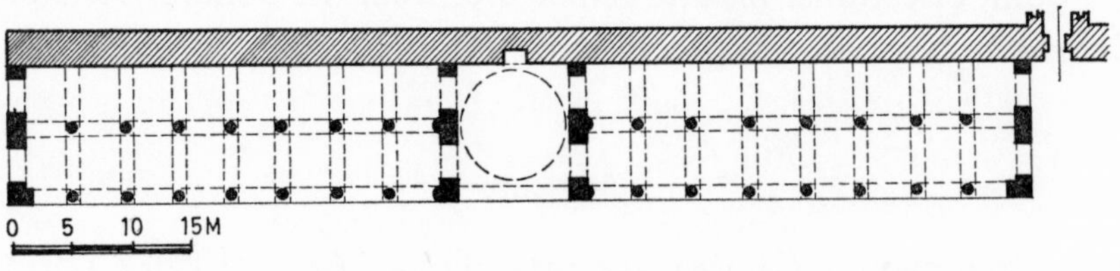

Plan Ic. Lashkari Bazar, Great Mosque

The mosque was destroyed at a later date, and the decorated columns that were lost during repairs were replaced by thick piers, the dome was reduced in size and a new mihrab was placed in front of the old one. After having been used for some time in this state the mosque was again destroyed. The first destruction and restoration were carried out in the time of the Ghurids. Its complete and final destruction was the work of the Mongols.

The Great Mosque at Lashkari Bazar is very important from the point of view of architectural development. The dome spanning the width of two aisles in front of the mihrab occurs here before it is to be found in the first Great Seljuk mosques in Persia. The type of mosque plan involving a dome over the mihrab was developed in various mosques built by the Great Seljuks in Iran, and exerted a wide and continuous influence, being carried by the Artukids to Anatolia, and thence by the Turkish Mamluks as far as Cairo, where it is so be seen in the Mosque of Baybars.

It is generally agreed too that an arch at Bust is the entrance iwan of a Ghaznevid mosque of the 12th century. Its form has been ruined as the result of a very unskilful restoration.

Tombs

The tombs of the Ghaznevids are, from the architectural point of view, very undistinguished compared with those of the Karakhanids. The richly decorated sandalwood doors of the tomb of Sultan Maḥmūd at Rawḍa 2 kilometres to the east of Ghazne are now in the Agra fort. Only the tomb of Arslan Jadhīb at Sengbest shows a highly developed architecture. We learn from the author of the Tarīkh-i Yamīnī that Arslan Jadhīb (997–1028), the Ghaznevid governor of Tūṣ, built a ribāṭ (or convent) in Sengbest, his birth-place, and was buried in the same town.

This tomb is of brick, and is in the form of a square 12.5 × 12.5 metres, roofed by a dome on squinches. The walls and the dome are decorated by zigzag and stepped patterning as well as by painted decoration. On the upper part of the wall there is a broad inscription half a metre high composed of white Kufic script on a polychrome ground of fine scrolls. Under the dome there is a second, narrower Kufic inscription in cut brick.

Beside the tomb there is a tapering cylindrical minaret 22 metres in height, the upper section of which has collapsed. The tomb was erected by Arslan Jadhīb while he was governor of Tūṣ and he was buried here on his death in 1028.

Although a number of medreses are known to have been built in the Ghaznevid period nothing of any of these remains. The word 'medrese' occurs in inscriptions found in the Pīr-i Falizvan cemetery at Ghazne during recent Italian excavations. The Tarīkh-i Yamīnī mentions medreses of the time of Maḥmūd of Ghazne, but it is quite impossible to form any idea of the medrese architecture of that time from these references.

Palaces

The historian Bayhāqī tells us that Sultan Mas'ūd I (1030–1041) possessed great skill as an architect and that he himself drew up the plans of his palace, the actual building of which he completed in four years with the help of an architect named 'Abd al-Malik (1036). The palace complex of Lashkari Bazar near the citadel of Bust was unearthed for the first time by Schlumberger in 1948. This was formerly known as Lashkargāh (the Barracks).

The Great Palace to the south is the largest and most important of the three buildings on the bank of the River Hilmend. It stands on a bend of the river, which it faces on two fronts. It has a marvellous appearance in both site and outlook. The Great Mosque, as we have seen, is situated against the southern wall of the Great Palace. It dates from the beginning of the 11th century and is the oldest palace remaining from the reign of Sultan Maḥmūd. Before it there is an esplanade, from which a wide avenue led to an outer gate. Here there is a two-storeyed façade articulated by niches with highly ornate terracotta and stucco decoration. There is also carved, polychrome stucco decoration, a fragment of which is now in the Kabul Museum.

The palace measures 164 metres from north to south, 92 metres from east to west, and, together with the outer courtyard, has a total length of $\frac{1}{2}$ km. (Plan IIIa.) The greater part of the building is constructed of adobe on brick foundations, but the more important parts are made entirely of brick. A deeply recessed door in the centre of the façade leads into a cruciform chamber which in turn opens into the 4-iwan courtyard of the palace (63 × 45 metres). Thus the 4-iwan courtyard plan we have already seen in Karakhanid caravansarais reappears in a more highly developed form in Ghaznevid architecture. The harem apartments are situated in the corners concealed from the main courtyard, and contain within them small 4-iwan courtyards. The north iwan 10.5 metres in height is higher and wider than the others and leads into the throne room. Although there are several points of resemblance between this palace and the Jawsāq Palace at Sāmarrā in Iraq the 4-iwan courtyard is an innovation derived from Karakhanid architecture. In the Parthian Palace at Ashur there is a primitive type of irregular 4-iwan courtyard, but the iwans were not defined. We can see cruciform chambers in Sasanian and ʿAbbāsid architecture, but in the Great Palace of Lashkari Bazar these architectural forms have been arranged to form a successful and harmonious whole.

One of the most remarkable innovations is to be seen in the decorative work of the throne room. The upper section of the walls is covered with highly embossed and deeply carved decorations in terracotta consisting of palmettes and *rūmī* (foliate arabesque) motifs in geometrical panels in the centre with Kufic inscription borders. Some of these are now in the Kabul Museum. On the lower portion of the walls there are polychrome mural paintings in tempera depicting forty-four soldiers arranged in file. There were originally seventy of these, and the heads of those remaining have unfortunately been obliterated and only the bodies remain. Their attire consists of magnificent brightly coloured caftans embroidered in various designs, soft boots, and trousers descending as far as the top of the boots, a type of dress which is typical of the Turks of Central Asia. The birds of prey to be seen amongst the soldiers indicate the presence of falconers. Of a weapon resting on their shoulders only the shaft is left. A fragment of fresco on an ornamental pilaster among the ruins depicts a man's head with the round face and almond-shaped eyes traditionally associated with the Turks. The soldiers' caftans are tied at the waist by a belt, and from this were suspended straps on which bags and various necessary articles were hung. There are ṭirāz bands (woven inscription bands in the name and titles of the ruler they served) on their arms. This type of attire, which is found in Uighur frescos, can also be seen in paintings at Sāmarrā in which Turks are portrayed.

There is a very striking resemblance between Uighur frescos of the 8th and 9th centuries and those at Lashkari Bazar. Information concerning the identity of the soldiers in these frescos is

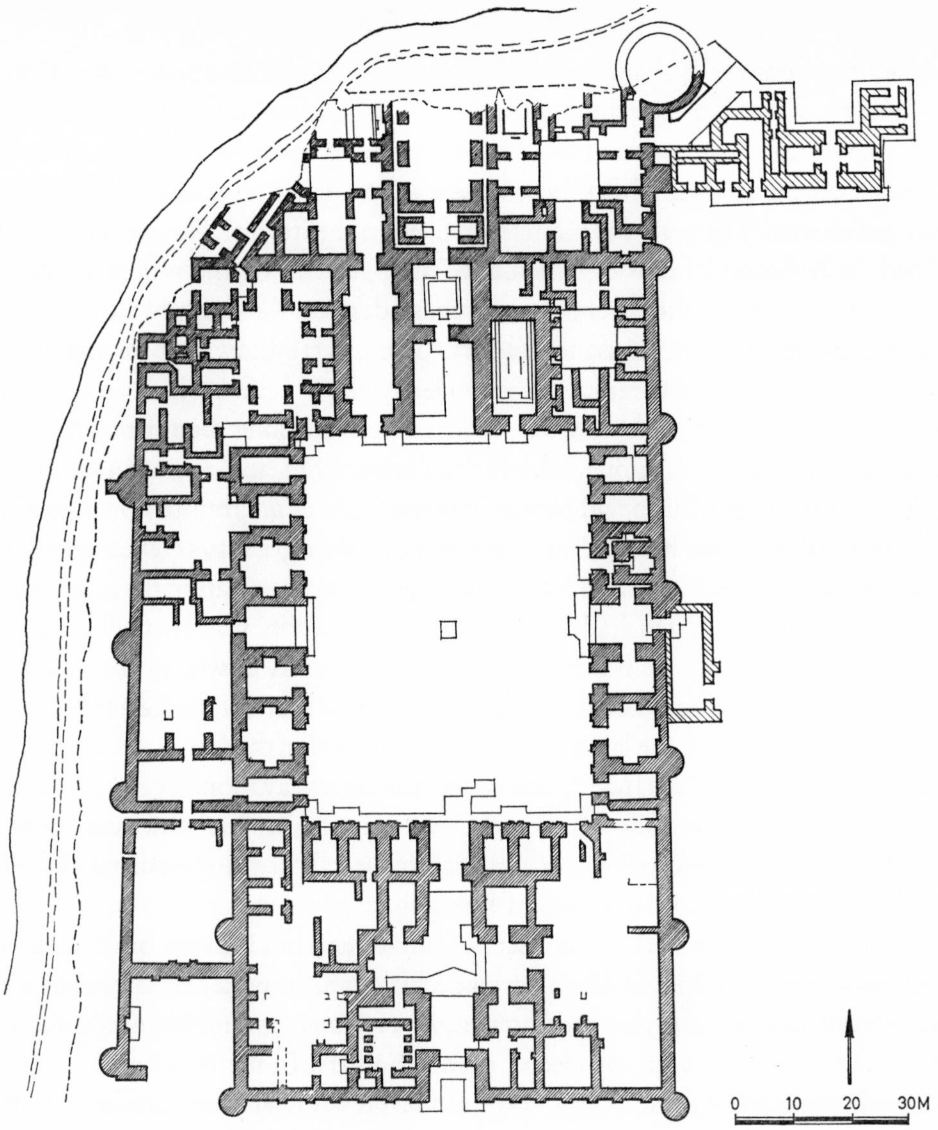

Plan IIIa. Lashkari Bazar, Palace, general plan

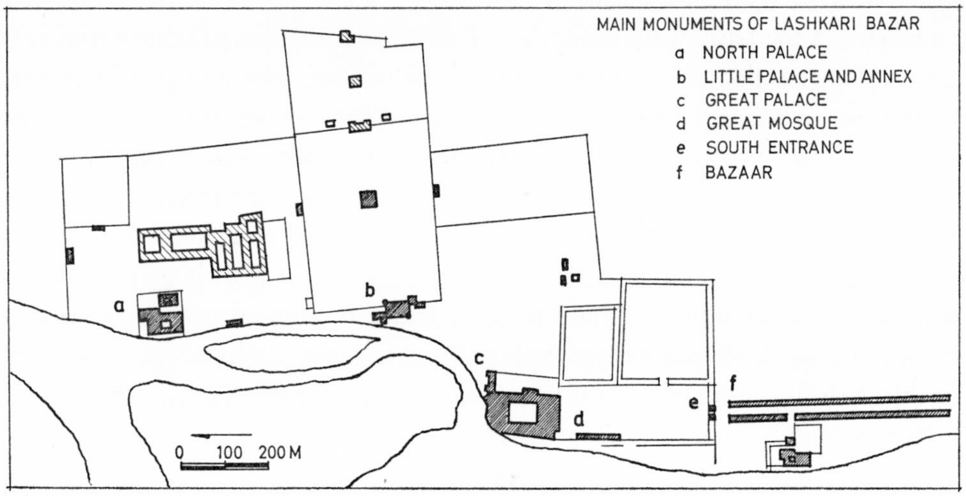

given in these lines from the Ṭabaqāt-i Nāṣirī of Juzjānī. 'The Ghaznevid Sultan Maḥmūd had an imperial bodyguard of four thousand soldiers. On ceremonial occasions two thousand soldiers were drawn up on each side of the throne. Those on the right wore fur caps with four aigrettes and carried gilt maces, whilst those on the left wore fur caps with two aigrettes and carried silver gilt maces.' These are the soldiers depicted in the frescos. The weapons resting on their shoulders are maces, the heads of which have disappeared, together with the heads of the soldiers. Bayhāqī, describing the reception of ambassadors on the death of Sultan Maḥmūd, mentions a bodyguard of four thousand soldiers. These were drawn up facing the throne according to rank. The different ranks are very clearly shown, being indicated by different styles of caftan and by jewelled, gold or silver belts. There was a long ornamental canal behind the throne room with three pools, one behind the throne room and another two on the east and west sides. None of the Ghaznevid frescos have survived *in situ*, but two in a good state of preservation were taken to the Kabul Museum. In Schlumberger's 1951 excavations a small mosque with stucco decoration and a mihrab was found in the west part of the area to the south of the section in which the frescos had been discovered, and this was brought to the Kabul Museum in 1964. The Palace and Great Mosque were burned down by the Ghurid ruler 'Alā al-Dīn Jihānsūz, and later restored in a very primitive fashion by the Ghurids themselves. The small mosque is ascribed to the late 12th century, at the end of the Ghurid period.

The palace of Sultan Mas'ūd III was uncovered during excavations begun at Ghazne by the Italians under the direction of Bombaci and Scerrato in the summer and autumn of 1957–1958 and continued up to recent years. On a mihrab niche can be read the name of the Sultan and the date—the second day of the month of Ramadhan in the year 505 (3 March 1112). A *naskhī* inscription gives the name of the architect as Muḥammad bin Ḥusayn bin Mubārak.

This Ghaznevid palace, which is of very great architectural importance, is constructed on a 4-iwan courtyard plan. The courtyard measures 50.6 × 31.9 metres, and the south iwan, which includes the throne room, is wider and deeper than the others. In the north-west corner of the courtyard a small rectangular mosque was constructed, probably at some later date, with piers arranged in two rows of four, and a stepped mihrab. (Plan IIIb.) The walls surrounding the courtyard are of brick, and in the upper sections the niches and iwan façades are framed by highly ornate yellow, red and blue painted geometrical designs and inscriptions in terracotta and stucco relief. At the base of the walls, 44 of the carved marble panels 70 cm. in height which originally surrounded the courtyard still remain *in situ*. These originally consisted of 510 panels covering 250 metres. On the upper section there is an inscription entirely in Persian in floriated Kufic. This is the second Persian inscription to be found in Turkish architecture, the first being in the Ribāṭ-i Malik. Originally 250 metres long, it remains unparalleled in length. From the traces remaining it would appear that the lettering and decorations were painted azure on a bright crimson ground. The lower edges of the marble panels were decorated with a narrow band of arabesques and tendrils, whilst the central parts—which were just over half a metre wide—were ornamented with palmettes, lotuses and more arabesques in low relief—filling the trefoil arches typical of Ghaznevid art. Trefoil arches are also to be seen in the stucco revetments of Sāmarrā. On these marble panels there can also be seen figures of

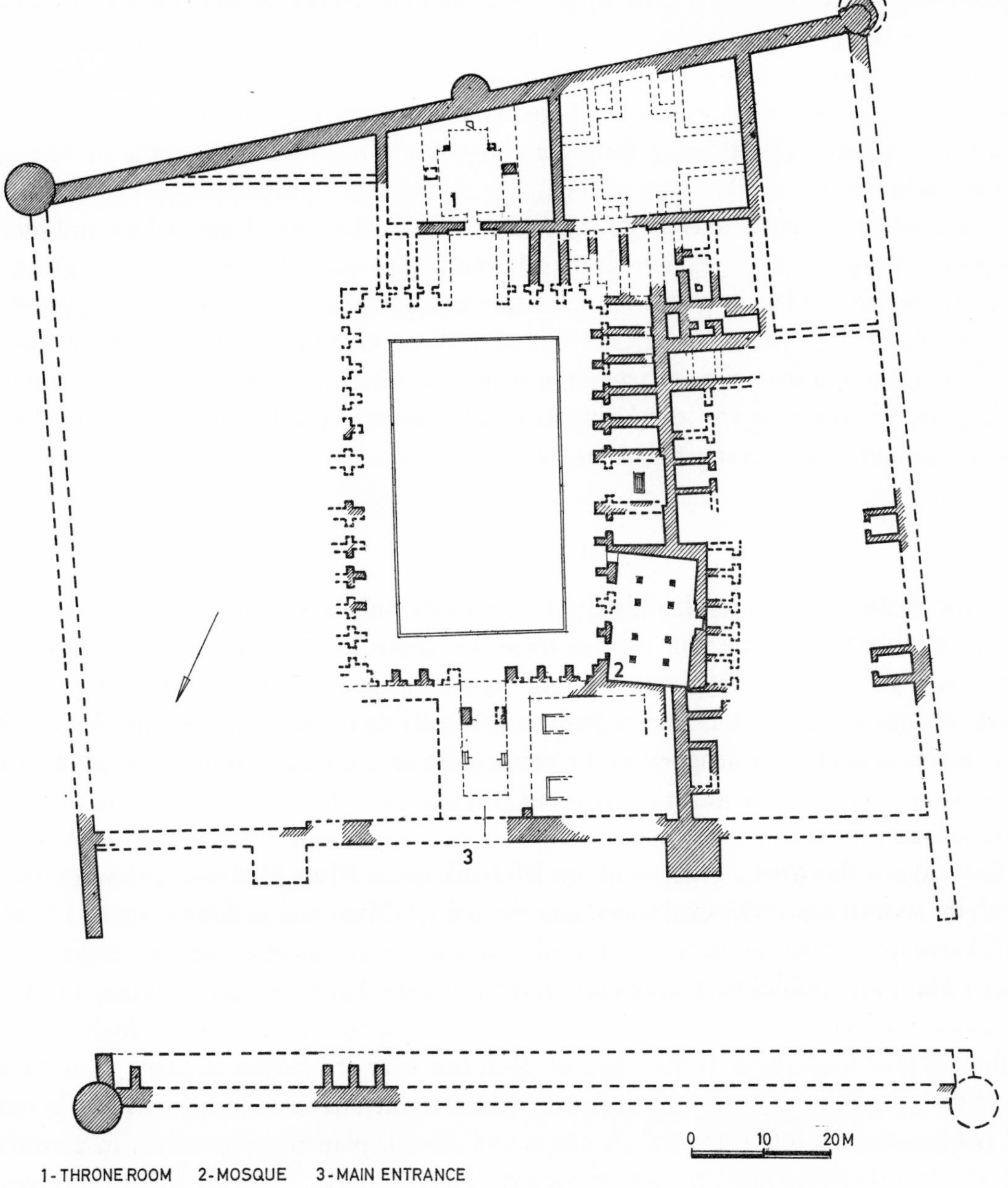

Plan IIIb. Ghazne, palace of Masʿūd III

animal and birds set amidst scrolls. The palace at Ghazne was situated in the seat of government and built entirely of brick; and with its marble panels, marble pavements and the polychrome decorations on its façade it must have been far more splendid and spectacular than the palace of Lashkari Bazar.

In the last year of his reign Sultan Masʿūd III built a mosque with the spoils that he brought back with him from his Indian campaign. The minaret of this mosque is still standing and bears an inscription containing his name. The palace also forms the centre of a large complex of buildings comprising a covered market, a market-place, a mosque and a minaret. Excavations may yet shed some light on the plan of this complex. During the excavations tiles have been found decorated with birds of prey, rosettes and flowers in relief under a green, yellow or brown monochrome glaze, dating from the end of the Ghaznevid period, the middle of the 12th century.

On the death of Sultan Masʿūd his son Arslan Shāh abandoned this palace and took up residence in his own palace, known as the Dawlatkhāne, where he was crowned. The palace at Ghazne was burned to the ground in 1150 after having been looted and destroyed for a whole week by ʿAlā al-Dīn Jihānsūz the Ghurid and his mountain tribesmen. Bahram Shāh, however, later succeeded for a time in regaining control at Ghazne, which was then occupied by the Seljuks, the Ghurids and the Khwārizmshāhs in turn, until it was finally razed to the ground by the armies of Chingiz Khān in 1221.

Caravansarais

After the ribāṭs of the Karakhanids the Ghaznevids built a number of monumental constructions of the same name, but most of these have been lost with the passage of time. The ribāṭ beside the tomb at Sengbest was built as a caravansarai. Besides this the Ghaznevid Sultan Maḥmūd built a caravansarai known as the Ribāṭ-i Shāhī on the Tūṣ–Sarakhs road about five parasangs from Sengbest in the year 410/1019–20. Ḥamdullāh Mustawfī Qazwīnī, in his geographical work entitled Nuzhat al-Qulūb written in 740/1340, when describing the great caravan routes, mentions the Ribāṭ-i Māhī as being about 6 parasangs from Sengbest. A. Godard saw this from a distance on the left bank of the River Meshhed and on comparing it with the written sources he established that the Ribāṭ-i Māhī was in fact the Ribāṭ-i Shāhī of the Ghaznevids. In recent years Derek Hill and Clevenger measured and photographed the Ribāṭ-i Māhī and published a brief account of it (in the *Illustrated London News*, 13 August 1966, and in *Islamic Architecture and its Decoration*, London, 1967). The Ribāṭ-i Māhī is situated on the Sarakhs road about 50 km. east of Meshhed near the Soviet frontier. It is roughly square (70.68 × 71.92 metres) with a 4-iwan central courtyard surrounded by rows of rooms, and is buttressed by round towers. A conjectural sketch plan may be drawn in accordance with the measurements and photographs given (Plan IIc.). The Ribāṭ-i Māhī continues the Karakhanid architectural tradition in such features as the 4-iwan courtyard plan and the brick ornamentation, but the most remarkable originality of this building is the union of iwan and dome, which is here found realised in Ghaznevid architecture as early as the first quarter of the 11th century (1019–20) long before experiments of the Great Seljuks in this direction. The inner and side walls of the iwan vaults are decorated with palmette and *rūmī* arabesque insets in geometrical panels. These geometrical decorations are a different form of the designs on the Uzgend tomb, with a fourfold braid pattern produced by the intersection of octagons having each alternate side broken (Design Ib). An inscription band of large, floriated Kufic in cut brick encircling the iwans is in the Ghaznevid style and resembles the inscription in the tomb

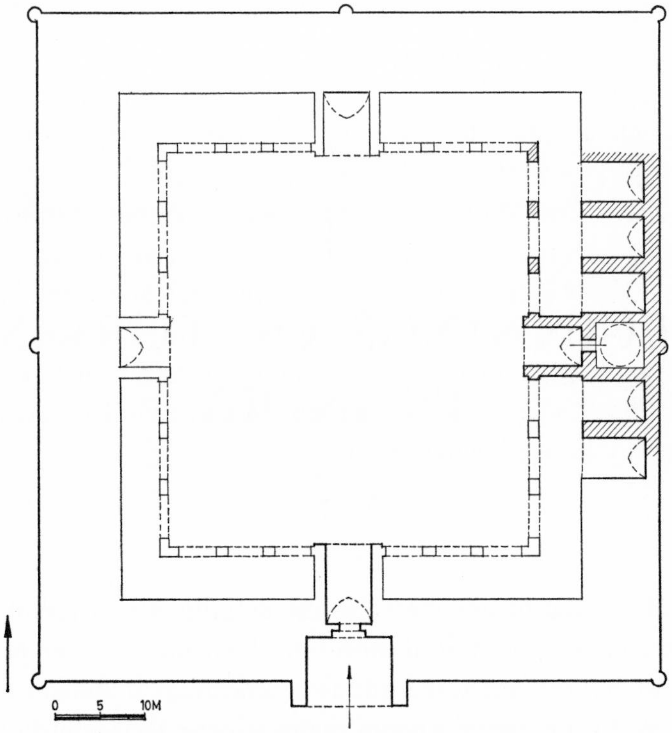

Plan IIc. Sarakhs road, Ribāṭ-i Māhī

of Arslan Jadhīb at Sengbest. The mihrab dome in the Great Mosque at Lashkari Bazar, by occupying a definite position in the inner space, prepares the way for the later Seljuk mosques of Iran, whilst the Ribāṭ-i Māhī both prepared the way for the combination of iwan and dome to be found in Seljuk mosques, and, as a prototype of the Seljuk caravansarais, provides a link between Karakhanid and Seljuk architecture.

Design Ib. Ribāṭ (*or* Rubāṭ)-i Māhī, section of decoration on entrance porch

4

THE BEGINNINGS OF TURKISH ART IN INDIA

Although the 'Umayyad armies entered the Indus Valley as early as the beginning of the 8th century, Islam was not firmly established in India until the Ghaznevid period. The Ghaznevid Sultan Maḥmūd opened the way for Turkish art by his conquest of the Punjab. In 1193 Quṭb al-Dīn Aybek, the founder of the dynasty of the Delhi sultans in the first part of the 13th century, employed the columns around the ruins of a Jaiṇ temple to build the mosque of Quwwat al-Islām and in 1230 Iltutmish doubled its size. Later it became entirely Seljuk in appearance as a result of the addition of inscriptions and a façade consisting of three pointed arches, of which the central one was higher and wider than the other two.

Quṭb al-Dīn Aybek built the Quṭb Minar minaret beside this mosque in 1219. Constructed of red sandstone and 73 metres in height, this is the highest minaret in the world. It is composed of a very thick shaft narrowing towards the top, with five storeys and four balconies. It is surrounded by bold fluted projections, those on the lower portion being alternately round and angled, those on the first storey round, those on the second storey angled. The shaft is also embellished by the addition of inscriptions and decorative bands. The diameter of the minaret is 15 metres at the base and 2 metres at the summit. Each of the five storeys is narrower and shorter than the one below. A later Delhi Sultan 'Alā al-Dīn Ḥalji (1296–1316) began to build a similar style of minaret twice the size of the Quṭb Minar but was unable to complete it. The completed lower portion of this colossal minaret gives some idea of the projected measurements. The Quṭb Minar, together with the Karakhanid Dzhar Kurgan minaret, may be looked upon as a more magnificent sequel, in which brick has been replaced by stone, to the minaret of Sultan Mas'ūd III at Ghazne. Its two upper storeys collapsed and were repaired in marble in the second half of the 14th century. This minaret stands as a symbol both of the Delhi Sultans who produced the first original examples of Turkish art in India, and of the city of Delhi. The Delhi dynasty came to an end in 1555. But from the middle of the 16th century North and Central India passed under the rule of the Chaghatay-Moghul emperors.

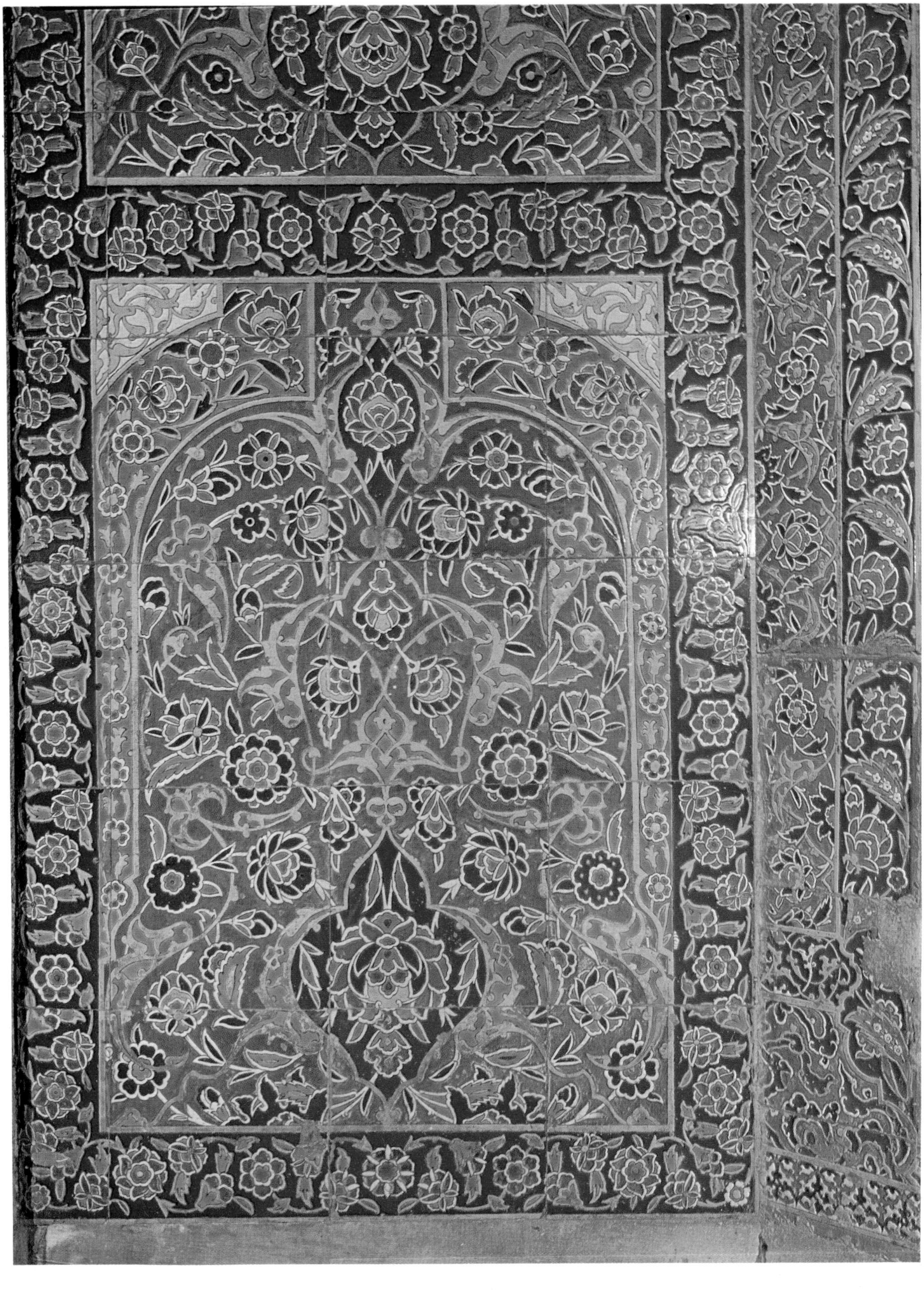

III Istanbul, Mausoleum of Shehzade, 1543, tile panel from inner walls (see page 276)

5

THE ART OF THE GREAT SELJUKS

The state founded in Khurasan by Duqāq's son Seljuk and his grandson, who belonged to the Qiniq tribe of the Oghuz Turks (the Oghuzes took the name of 'Turcoman' on accepting Islam) who had at one time formed the backbone of the Gök Turks, very quickly expanded into an empire during the reigns of the three sultans, Tughrul Bek, Alp Arslan and Malikshāh. Sultan Tughrul Bek established his capital in the city of Rayy in the year 1040. After the death of Sultan Sanjar in 1157 the Seljuks of Iraq assumed the dominant role in Iran, and this continued until the death of Sultan Tughrul in 1193. The Seljuks of Kirman came to an end in 1211 and the place of the dynasty was taken by the Khwārizmshāhs. The Seljuks of Syria lost their supremacy after 1117. In Azerbaidzhan, however, the rule of the Seljuk Atabeks continued until the Mongol invasion.

Mosques

Before the Karakhanid and Ghaznevid mosques became known to scholars the history of Turkish mosque architecture began with the Great Seljuks in Iran, and this gave rise to a number of quite insoluble problems and a large number of continually changing hypotheses. Surveys and excavations undertaken in recent years now show, however, that the type of mosque plan with dome over the mihrab and unity of space had already been tackled in Karakhanid and Ghaznevid architecture. The Seljuks in Iran utilised and developed the advances already made by earlier Turkish architecture and so created a monumental, large-scale type of mosque architecture. After that time, the mosque plan with mihrab dome and 4-iwan courtyard prevailed throughout Iran and the whole of the Middle East. The researches of Godard have for the first time produced an overall view of Seljuk architecture in Iran.

The earliest surviving Seljuk mosque is the Masjid-i Jum'a (Friday Mosque) at Isfahan, the most important parts of which were re-built in the reign of Malikshāh (1072–1092). According to the inscriptions the large mihrab dome and the small domed chamber to the north, outside the courtyard, directly opposite this, were built during the reign of Malikshāh, whilst the 4-iwan courtyard and surrounding arcades were constructed later in the Seljuk period. The mosque was subsequently enlarged by a long series of additions and modifications testified to by some thirty inscriptions, and has been repaired several times during the 19th and 20th centuries.

In 1080, Niẓām al-Mulk built in Malikshāh's name a large dome chamber over the mihrab in the south precincts of the original ʿAbbāsid courtyard mosque built largely of adobe and dating back as far as the Caliph al-Manṣūr. In the original structure there were very probably aisles with wooden roofs on each side of this mihrab dome, though when the four iwans were added this plan was changed. The central domed area measures 15 metres square and opens out into the mosque on three sides through nine arches (Plan 1d). The group of eight thick,

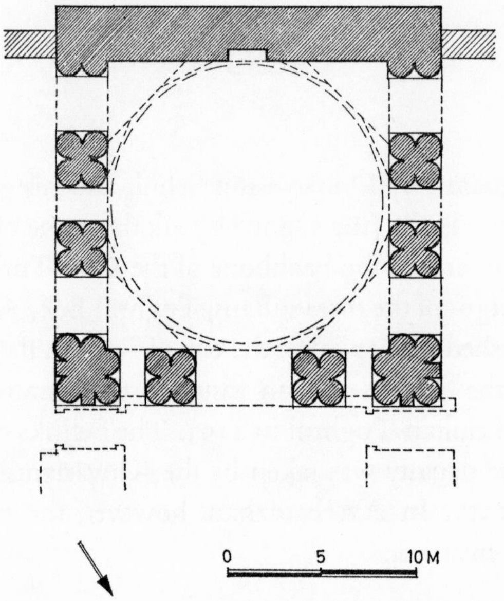

Plan Id. Isfahan, Great Mosque, dome of Malikshāh

heavy, plaster-coated piers on which the dome rests gives a striking contrast with the rich architectural forms of the dome and the squinch zone. As there is a marked difference both within and without between the dome and the substructure it has been suggested that the dome may have been built on thick piers remaining from the original building. The exterior is dominated by the slightly pointed structure of the brick dome.

The second dome, known as the Gunbadh-i Khākī, 11 metres in diameter and 22 metres in height, was built in 481/1088 for the Karakhanid princess Terken Khātūn, the daughter of the Karakhanid Sultan Naṣr bin Ibrāhīm Tamghach Khān (1053–1068) and the wife of Malikshāh. It was built by the Seljuk vizir, Tāj al-Mulk, the rival of Niẓām al-Mulk, who took the latter's place when he died. The dome rises directly from the roof. The structure has no façade opening on to the exterior and is entered by a small door leading into a dark corridor. Nevertheless, taken as a whole, this structure is one of the most mature and successful works of Great Seljuk architecture from both the technical and the aesthetic point of view. The arches and the corners of the piers supporting the dome are softened by rounded engaged pilasters which continue into a torus moulding round the arch. As Pope very aptly pointed out, the unity of the upper and lower structures reminds one of Gothic. The development has its origin in Karakhanid dome architecture. This building, one of the finest examples of Seljuk architecture, was built about eight years after the dome of Malikshāh, and was meant as a quiet retreat worthy of a Karakhanid princess and the wife of a sultan, where she might rest and pray on her visits to the mosque. There is no mihrab, but the arch on the south side is on the same axis as the main mihrab. The tripartite squinches in both domes are similar in form to those already employed in 367/978 in the Karakhanid tomb of Arab Ata.

Later Seljuk mosques in Iran, with their slightly pointed brick domes on squinches, may be regarded as a series of small-scale variations on the dome of Malikshāh in Isfahan. The first of these is the Gulpayagan Mosque built by Abū Shujāʿ Muḥammad, the son of Malikshāh, in the years 1105–8. It consists of a very slightly tapering dome with stalactite squinches on a square central area measuring 10.63 × 10.63 metres. The dome rests on thick, massive brick piers joined by arches. The interior is decorated with geometrical panels reminiscent of the Gunbadh-i Khākī. The squinches are invisible from the outside. Under the Qajars in the 19th century the mosque was given a 4-iwan plan. The Seljuk Masjid-i Jumʿa at Qazwīn dating from 1113 or 1119 is a domed building with powerful plain squinches set on solid brick walls, whose simplicity is matched by its magnificence. On the walls there is a frieze composed of three-lobed arches such as we have already seen in the palace of Sultan Masʿūd at Ghazne, whilst the floriated Kufic inscription above with its bold lettering increases the monumental effect of the simple space. A *naskhī* inscription surrounding the squinch arches informs us that the mosque was built by Abū Shujāʿ Muḥammad the son of Malikshāh.

The Masjid-i Ḥaydarīye at Qazwīn was built in the same period. It is a domed building with simple squinches and stout brick walls. It opens out on three sides through wide arches and the upper sections are covered entirely by a plaited and floriated Kufic inscription. Higher up there is a narrow border of circular and star-shaped turquoise and cobalt-glazed tiles connected by drop-shaped tiles. On the other hand the gaudy, ostentatious stucco decorations around the mihrab and on the mihrab wall are not in harmony with the dignified style of the architecture.

The first building to realise in a single plan all the innovations introduced by the various Seljuk mosques in Iran is the Masjid-i Jumʿa at Zaware, which dates from 1135. A Seljuk mosque with mihrab dome, four iwans and a minaret, it is the beginning of a splendid development. Here we see the 4-iwan plan of the Karakhanid and Ghaznevid caravansarais and palaces utilised for the first time in a Seljuk mosque. The dome, 7.45 metres in diameter, has finally taken up its position as an integral part of the whole plan. (Plan Ie.) The mihrab, with its rich stucco ornament, was constructed twenty-one years later, in 1156. Parts of the Kufic inscription band encircling the upper part of the walls have crumbled away. Various geometrical designs are produced by varied arrangements of bricks in the squinch zone and within the dome itself, where they are arranged in lozenge patterns.

A number of other 4-iwan mosques were built in the same style as the Zaware Mosque, the

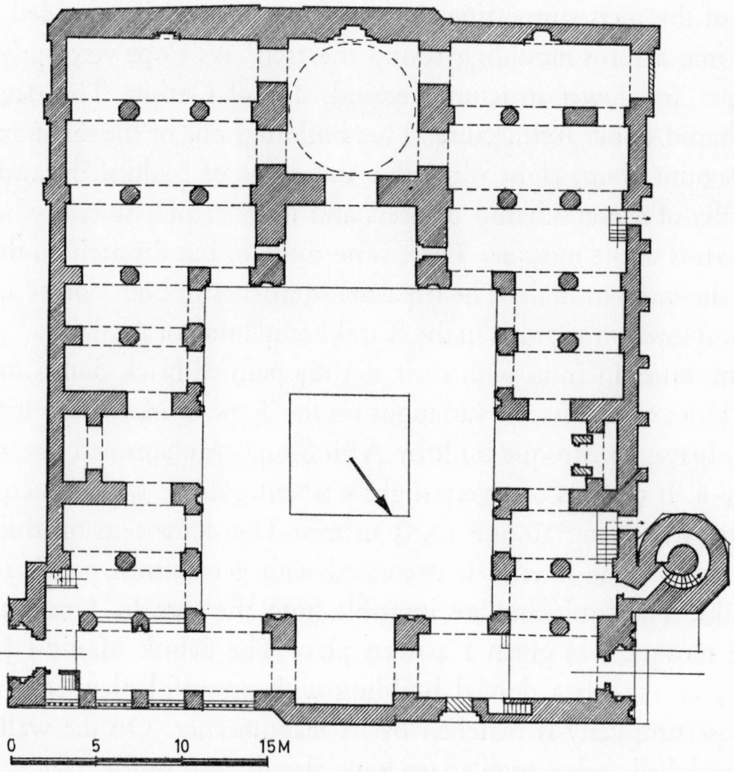

Plan Ie. Zaware, Great Mosque

plan of which aroused such great admiration, the most notable of these being the Masjid-i Jumʿa at Ardistan and at Isfahan.

The Masjid-i Jumʿa at Ardistan was built on the site of an old ʿAbbāsid mosque and is one of the most remarkable works of the Seljuks in Iran. It is a single-dome structure constructed prior to the Zaware Mosque and it is generally agreed that its dome was taken as a model for the dome of the Zaware Mosque some 15 km. away, since their dimensions are identical. The upper part of the brick walls is surrounded by an inscription in floriated *thuluth* script. Above this there is a squinch and dome system closely resembling the Gunbadh-i Khākī in the Isfahan Masjid-i Jumʿa. The patterns formed by the varied placing of the bricks, and the lozenge patterns in the dome, show a more meticulous workmanship than the Zaware Mosque. Unlike other Seljuk mosques, the inner faces of the arches between the piers supporting the dome are embellished with inscriptions and stucco ornament giving an interior richness of space that does not spoil the nobility of the architecture. In the years 553–5/1158–60 the Ardistan Mosque, although it had been built only a few years before, was made to conform to the 4-iwan plan scheme of the Mosque at Zaware.

In contrast to the rich interior dome structure, which had already reached complete maturity in Isfahan, the exterior consists of massive cubiform surfaces composed of compact brickwork utterly devoid of all ornament. The silhouette of the dome, which rests on a cubiform base and tapers slightly after passing through an octagonal transition zone, stands as a symbol of the

Seljuk dome's solidity and strength. For the first time the Seljuks created an original type of mosque architecture in Iran, and in doing this they utilised the innovations introduced by the Karakhanids and Ghaznevids. The dome became the predominant feature of the exterior. The combination of dome and iwan, which had been tackled earlier by the Ghaznevids, is to be found in its most successful form amongst the Seljuks. The history of the dome on squinches with an adjoining iwan stretches as far back as the Sasanians and the Parthians. Likewise the column, pier, arch and vault were architectural elements used in every historical period. But the Seljuks' achievement consisted in utilising all these in new forms of architecture, in creating an original architectural style by applying these elements in the form of original plans to mosques, medreses and caravansarais alike, and so expressing the national character of their art. As Godard has very aptly pointed out, not a single example of the combination of dome and iwan is to be seen in the Islamic period either in eastern or western Iran before the time of the Seljuks, so that it was the Seljuks who rediscovered the combination. It is possible that the Seljuks took this conception from the Ghaznevids. Again as Godard has pointed out, the Seljuk 4-iwan plan, which lends Seljuk mosques their monumental appearance and which is to be found from Iran to Central Asia, is not an ideal plan for a building in which a large congregation is to gather to worship. The mihrab is concealed by the iwans, and worshippers cannot see one another. As the main mihrab was small, mihrabs had to be constructed in various sections of the building, and two-storeyed arcades were built so that the iwans would not appear too high. The iwans and their half-domes appear incongruous when viewed from the rear. However, the Seljuks created a monumental style of architecture by combining conflicting elements, and, as a result, this type of plan, although unsuitable for a mosque from the practical point of view, has prevailed throughout Asia and the whole of Iran up to the present day.

Very little remains of the Zawzan Mosque, a large-scale building constructed by the Khwārizmshāhs in Khurāsān on the lines of the Seljuk mosques of Iran. Today only the two iwans are still standing, at an interval of 45 metres. There is no dome. The mosque differs from the Seljuk type in having only two iwans. From the traces of the arches on each side of the qibla iwan (13.5 × 27.9 metres) it would appear that the courtyard was surrounded by a single-storey arcade. Some peculiar features, such as upper galleries to each side of the iwan, a door to the left of the mihrab and the incorrect orientation of the mihrab, make it plain that the iwan was planned according to an already existing building. According to written sources (Ṭabaqāt-i Nāṣirī, Nuzhat al-Qulūb), when the province of Kirman was conquered by the Khwārizmshāhs in 1210, Qiwām al-Dīn Mu'ayyad al-Mulk (1199–1221) from Zawzan, who had been appointed governor of Zawzan by ʿAlā al-Dīn Muḥammad bin Tekesh, built a great palace in that city. The palace was situated behind the mosque. The iwan, the vault of which has now collapsed, rose to a height of 30 metres. Dark blue and turquoise medallions on the rear wall, inscriptions, and a magnificent tiled panel measuring 13 × 15 metres, are examples of the oldest and richest decoration to survive from Iran from the first part of the 13th century. The dark blue glazed Kufic inscription is very difficult to read, but the date 616/1219 mentioned in a *naskhī* inscription at the end of this points to the time of Sultan ʿAlā al-Dīn Muḥammad bin Tekesh.

The ceramic revetment of the building, which escaped untouched from the devastation wrought by the Mongols and continued the Seljuk tradition, is parallel with the first tiled Seljuk structures in Anatolia and provides important evidence from the point of view of the art of Turkish ceramic decoration.

The Masjid-i Jumʿa at Furumad in the north of Khurāsān is another 2-iwan mosque built on a similar plan but on a smaller scale and at a slightly later date. The Zengids and Seljuks built a number of 2-iwan medreses in Syria and Anatolia respectively, but the iwan type of mosque plan was not generally adopted in Western Turkish architecture.

Minarets

After the Turkish rulers had experimented with several different forms, as can be seen in the Karakhanid and Ghaznevid minarets as well as in the Quṭb Minar in Delhi, the Seljuks in Iran made widespread use of the long, slender, cylindrical minaret, which they found to conform most closely to their tastes. The Jar Minar of 515/1122 and the Sīn minaret of 1129, both near Isfahan, consist of a thick cylindrical upper portion and an octagonal lower section, but, apart from a few exceptions such as these, the type of minaret on a square or polygonal lower section completely disappears. The oldest surviving Seljuk structure is the tall, slender, graceful, cylindrical, tapering minaret dating from 450/1058 from the time of Tughrul Bek in the Masjid-i Jumʿa at Dāmghān. The side inscription band round the central portion with its raised interlacing Kufic inscriptions set in square panels of pale turquoise glaze lends this minaret special importance as the first work of Seljuk architecture employing ceramic decoration. In addition to this the body is encircled by five narrow courses of lozenges or geometrical forms produced by the varied placing of the bricks, and has a very impressive appearance. The second Seljuk minaret from the time of Tughrul Bek is the minaret of the Masjid-i Maydān at Saveh constructed in 453/1061.

Although the Masjid-i Pā Minār at Zaware is devoid of any architectural importance and the Seljuk stucco work has been covered over with Īl-Khānid plaster decorations, it possesses an elegant cylindrical minaret of the time of Alp Arslan dating from the year 461/1068. The Kufic inscription with *rūmī* on brick just beneath this is the third Seljuk inscription, after the inscriptions of the Dāmghān and Saveh minarets. Other Seljuk minarets before the end of the 11th century are the minaret of the Masjid-i Jumʿa at Kashan, dating from the year 466/1073, and the minaret of the Masjid-i Jumʿa at Barsiyan, not far from Isfahan, dating from the year 491/1097–8. Throughout the 12th century and later the Seljuks continued to develop and embellish this elegant, cylindrical type of minaret.

Funerary Architecture, Tombs and Domed Mausolea

The development of tomb architecture under the Great Seljuks is, like the development of mosque architecture, based on the works of the Karakhanids and Ghaznevids. The Gunbadh-i ʿAlī at Abarqūh to the south of Isfahan and the Chihil Dukhtarān (Forty

Maidens) tomb at Dāmghān were both built in 448/1056 in the time of Tughrul Bek. The Gunbadh-i ʿAlī is a squat octagonal structure utterly devoid of ornament terminating in a stalactite cornice and surmounted by a dome. Unlike other mausolea in Iran it is built of stone. There is a narrow Kufic inscription band immediately below the stalactite cornice. No doubt the dome was originally surmounted by an 8-sided pyramidal cone. The mausolea dating from the first half of the century at Lajim, Resget and West Radkan to the south of the Caspian are plain cylindrical brick constructions of very slight monumental significance. The Gunbadh-i ʿAlī at Abarqūh, in spite of its squat body, achieves monumental effect through its large stalactite cornice in high relief and its inscription course. The Chihil Dukhtarān tomb is a cylindrical brick structure with a conical dome. Noteworthy features of this building are the broad Kufic inscription band round the upper edge of the body and the geometrical friezes of brick above and below this. Although it resembles the earlier Pīr-i ʿAlamdār tomb also at Dāmghān and dating from 428/1027, the severe and monotonous external appearance of the Pīr-i ʿAlamdār mausoleum is here replaced by mature proportions that produce a more monumental effect.

Two mausolea recently discovered in Iran by Stronach and Young throw a great deal of light on the burial monuments of this early Seljuk period. These two magnificent tombs, situated in the region known as Kharraqān between Qazwīn and Hamadhān, stand 29 metres apart on a perfectly flat area of ground. They are octagonal structures constructed entirely of a brick, 13 metres in height and 11 metres in diameter, with double domes. At the corners of each tomb there are massive cylindrical towers of the same form and diameter. There are stairs inside both the towers of the first mausoleum and in one of the towers of the second, the towers with the staircases being wider than the others. These buttress towers are continued upwards to form the eight ribs of the outer dome. The inscriptions and the richly variegated brick ornament make these mausolea a treasury of Turkish decorative art, and this type of decoration is utilised in Anatolia in both stone architecture and ceramic decoration right up to the last periods of Ottoman art. The inscription on the first tomb to the east is composed in an unusual arrangement of Kufic on the upper part of the entrance façade and on the outer dome. According to this inscription the mausoleum was built by the architect Muḥammad bin Makkī of Zinjān in 460/1067–8, that is, in the reign of Alp Arslan and before the battle of Malazgirt (Manzikert). Each facet is decorated with a pointed arch, and among the more than twenty different patterns which occur in the geometrical brick decoration on each of these facets is to be seen the fourfold braid motif produced by the intersection of octagons, which is found in Anatolian Turkish art in architecture, faience and woodwork and as far back as the tomb of Naṣr bin ʿAlī at Uzgend dating from 1012, and which is repeated twice in the broad band of decoration under the dome. The points of the 8-pointed stars on one of the façades with pointed arches are joined to form swastikas, thus producing another decorative motif which, while occurring later in a more developed form in the faience decoration of the Anatolian Seljuks, is also to be found in the decoration of the Mustanṣiriyya Madrasa in Baghdad. (Design Id.) The interior of the dome is also octagonal. An imperceptible transition to the dome is achieved by the use of niches with pointed arches. The walls and the interior of the dome were covered with the earliest surviving examples of Seljuk painted decoration, though those in the dome have now fallen away. On the walls, designs composed of lamps suspended by chains with decorative motifs above including stars and peacocks in roundels are depicted in blue, light green, pink, brown and black. The remains of a floriated Kufic inscription on the lower edge of the dome recall the inscription in the Ghaznevid tomb of Arslan Jadhīb.

That the Seljuks should have been able to produce at so early a date such a rich, monumental structure must be viewed as a brilliant development of Karakhanid and Ghaznevid architecture based upon a conception of tomb construction the roots of which go far back into the past.

According to a five-line Kufic inscription above the door of the second mausoleum, it was built in 486/1093 by the architect Abu'l-Ma'āli bin Makkī of Zinjān for Abū Manṣūr Bek Elsi bin Tekin. This tomb was built twenty-six years later than the first, in the time of Nāṣr al-Dīn Maḥmūd, the son of Malikshāh, and the architect, to judge from his patronymic, must have been either the brother or the son of the architect of the first. The brick decorative work is of exceptional wealth and variety, and is composed of more than fifty different patterns, none of which resembles any of those in the first mausoleum. The bricks have been placed more firmly but a little coarsely. The various patterns produced by intersecting hexagons and octagons to be seen in these two mausolea form a source for later Anatolian Turkish architectural decoration. The interior has bare brick walls, the only decoration being the trefoil arches in the squinch zone and the ornament of an unfinished brick mihrab.

A third monument in a similar style is the Demavend mausoleum. This is an octagonal brick structure 9.9 metres in height and 4.85 metres in diameter with round corner piers and an 8-sided pyramidal dome. In this case each facet is divided up into three square sections covered with a variety of decorative motifs, all of which are quite different from those on the two preceding mausolea. Above the modern rectangular door there are two niches with pointed, lobed arches, and above that a panel containing four stars joined by crosses. The interior of the mausoleum is cylindrical, and the bricks on the dome are arranged in a herring-bone pattern. It has no inscription, but its style suggests a date in the third quarter of the 11th century and it takes its place with the two preceding tombs in displaying the creative power of Seljuk decorative art. These Seljuk tombs, all three of which are later than the Gunbadh-i 'Alī, are all typical in being built on an octagonal plan.

Again in recent years, D. Bivar has discovered two tombs (mazārs or shrines) built by the Great Seljuks in the area of Sar-i Pul in Afghanistan (Anbir, the centre of Juzjan). One of these, the tomb of Yaḥyā bin Zayd, a descendant of 'Alī and Fāṭima, who was known as the Imam Hurd, is a simple square adobe building with a rectangular addition in front. But inside there are very rich stucco decorations and Kufic inscriptions. The decoration of the mihrab recalls the stucco decoration of the Nayin Mosque dated circa 960 A.D. In an inscription surrounding the arch and base of the mihrab niche the name of the builder is given as Aḥmad of Tirmīdh (Termez), which implies that the architect came from the Karakhanid region. The magnificent floriated Kufic inscriptions conform to the style of Ghaznevid epigraphy. An unusual feature of the foundation inscription is the relation of how Yaḥyā bin Zayd was killed. Its style points to a date at the end of the 11th century. The wide floriated and plaited

Kufic inscription around the upper part of the walls is in a highly developed style of finer quality. The unusual squinches in the form of receding arches are worthy of note.

The second of these Seljuk shrines, known as the Imam Kalan, stands 1 km. to the west and has features similar to the first, though the inscriptions and decorative work are in a very dilapidated condition. On the arch leading into the domed area there is a worn inscription in *thuluth* lettering—the first example from the Seljuk period of this script. If the number 9 (*tisʿa*) in this inscription is accepted as 509 then the date must be 1115. The badly damaged stucco decoration on the mihrab of the shrine is similar to that on the mihrab in the Masjid-i Jumʿa at Zaware.

This development under the Seljuks reveals a much more systematic execution as seen in the mausoleum of Abu'l-Faḍl in Sarakhs at the end of the 11th century, the mausoleum of Abū Saʿīd in Mekhne, the Yarty Gumbez near Sarakhs (1098), the tomb of ʿAbd-Allāh ibn Burayd at Vekil Bazar, and the Alemberdar mausolea at Astanababa; and in the 12th century the mausoleum of Muḥammad ibn Zayd at Merv (1112).

Two of these Seljuk tombs in the south of what is now Turkmenistan are large-scale buildings with domes over 10 metres in diameter, which at the same time continue the Karakhanid tradition of brick architecture. These are the tomb of Abu'l-Faḍl at Old Sarakhs and the tomb of Abū Saʿīd at Mekhne. The first, commonly known as Sarakhs Baba, is a double-domed structure surrounded by thick brick walls divided into wide niches by pointed arches and with a projecting porch on the east façade. The outer dome has collapsed leaving the inner dome standing bare, thus destroying the harmonious proportions of the exterior. Inside, the thick walls have been relieved by cutting a rectangular niche on each side. The appearance of such a double-domed tomb at the end of the 11th century in the first Seljuk period is an innovation of very great importance. Later very great progress was to be made in the conception of the double-domed structure in Samarkand and other towns of Turkestan.

The tomb of Abū Saʿīd is a double-domed structure with thicker walls. Pointed arched niches have been cut high in the walls, and judging from its present condition, the bottom half of the walls, which are decorated with various brick patterns, was left unarticulated. The inner dome is supported on stalactite squinches, and the inner walls are divided into two rows of pointed arched niches, the niches in the lower row being wider than those in the upper. As a domed structure with façades and porches there is an obvious resemblance between the general appearance of this building and that of the Karakhanid tomb of Arab Ata.

At the beginning of the 12th century the course of Seljuk architecture continues with the tomb at Ṭūṣ traditionally supposed to be that of al-Ghazzālī, and known as the Hārūnīye. The slightly tapering inner dome remained uncovered on the collapse of the outer dome. Its external appearance achieves an unusual monumental character by means of a double tier of wall niches and the softening of the corners by means of slender colonnettes. Until quite recently the Ṭūṣ tomb was usually dated to periods as late as the 14th century, but with the discovery of the Seljuk tombs at Old Sarakhs and Mekhne it may now be assigned on stylistic grounds to the year of al-Ghazzālī's death at the beginning of the 12th century (1111).

Although this tomb has a rather elongated plan (18.6 × 25 metres) owing to the addition of an entrance iwan at the front and three small vaulted chambers at the back, as a domed structure it may be regarded as a preparation for the magnificent tomb of Sultan Sanjar in the city of Merv, where the dome is supported on a drum formed by exterior galleries.

The tomb of Sultan Sanjar, the last of the Great Seljuk rulers, dating from the year 1157, incorporates all the developments and innovations introduced in the course of Seljuk tomb architecture up to that date, and takes a place amongst the world's greatest architectural masterpieces. The architect was Muḥammad bin Atsīz of Sarakhs. The dome has a diameter of 17 metres, making it the largest dome to be constructed in that area up to that time. The later tomb of Khwāja Aḥmad Yasawī in the city of Yasī (now Turkestan) in Central Asia, dating from 1360, has a dome 18 metres in diameter, but no other dome of such proportions had previously been constructed. The tomb of Sanjar was originally a double-domed structure like the Seljuk tombs preceding it. The outer dome has now collapsed but according to Yāqūt, who visited it in the years 1217–19, its turquoise glazed bricks made it visible for miles around. The dome is supported on squinches over a central chamber 27 × 27 metres, surrounded by walls of an incredible thickness (up to 6 metres), and the interior of the dome is embellished by ribs arranged in star patterns. Even today the height of the central chamber from the ground to the top of the dome is 36 metres. The transition to the dome is prepared in the upper part of the plain brick walls by means of galleries composed alternately of one wide segmented arch and one narrow pointed arch, with piers in the corners decorated with geometrical brick patterns. From the point of view of the main external features there is a striking resemblance between the tomb of Sultan Sanjar and a number of Buddhist stupas of East Asia, the Moritim stupa and the stupas at Aksu and Subashi. A stupa is actually a solid structure but stupas having an inner space have also been constructed. Buddhism was the religion of the Turks before the acceptance of Islam and it was suggested years ago by E. Diez that the example of the Uighur stupas of the Buddhist period influenced the considerable heightening of the drum of the domes of Islamic monuments. This is obviously true. The outer gallery in the tomb of Sultan Sanjar is a step towards the heightening of the dome. A type of domed tomb having the drum heightened in the form of a tower was carried westwards with the Turks and, in the monuments of Mamluk architecture, gave a completely new appearance to medieval Cairo. The close resemblance between the group of tombs in the Shāh-i Zinde at Samarkand reflects this very vividly. Of the Shāh-i Zinde tombs the most typical and at the same time the most spectacular is the tomb of Mūsā Pasha (1337–1412), known as Qāḍīzāde-i Rūmī, the great Turkish mathematician and astronomer who came from Bursa to Samarkand. It stands out from the other tombs because of its slightly ovoid dome set on a high drum decorated with faience mosaic. Mūsā Pasha, after finishing his education in Bursa, went first to Khurāsān and thence to Samarkand, where he was appointed head of the observatory by Ulugh Bek (1394–1449) and became head professor in the medrese. His students Fatḥ Allāh Shirvānī and 'Alī Qushju came to Anatolia and taught astronomy and mathematics there. On the death of Mūsā Pasha Ulugh Bek built this tomb in his memory.

FUNERARY ARCHITECTURE, TOMBS AND DOMED MAUSOLEA

The continuously developing tradition of dome architecture in the Karakhanid, Ghaznevid and Great Seljuk periods extends as far as the tomb of Öljeytü Khudābende at Sulṭānīye, the tomb of Timur (Gūr-i Mīr) in Samarkand and the Taj Mahal near Agra in India built in the years 1630–48 by Shāh Jihān for his late wife.

Both in tomb and mosque architecture the problem of the dome and the domed mosque remained unsolved throughout the whole of Asia. It is true that experiments were made with the external appearance of various forms of dome, and that domes of immense size, such as the dome of the tomb of Muḥammad 'Ādil Shāh at Bijapur in India, were constructed, but apart from the Blue Mosque in Tabriz built by the Karakoyunlu Jihānshāh (1436–67) in the middle of the 15th century, no large-scale domed building with a plan of centralised type was constructed, and even in this case it is necessary to take into consideration the influence of the Turkish architecture developing in Anatolia. It was only with the Turks in Anatolia that the problem of the dome was tackled with complete mastery in all its various aspects and developed to its fullest possible extent.

Parallel with the development of the funerary architecture of the Great Seljuks various innovations continued to be introduced into tomb architecture throughout the 12th century.

The beginning of the octagonal tomb-tower in its simplest form is to be seen in the Gunbadh-i 'Alī at Abarqūh as far back as the time of Tughrul Bek. In the Seljuk mosques of Iran the dome is generally supported on the exterior by an octagonal base. The octagonal plan to be found in mausolea such as the Kharraqān and Demavend tombs remained the basic plan in use up to the end of the 11th century, whilst in decoration, in spite of the rich variety of designs, purely geometrical patterns prevailed.

An anonymous tomb of the twelfth century at Rayy dated 534/1139 is a cylindrical brick structure with large angled flanges. A stalactite frieze along the upper edge has been simplified, thereby losing its plastic strength. The conical roof has collapsed.

As for the Azerbaidzhan area, the Gunbadh-i Surkh (Gunbadh-i Qirmiz) at Maragha, which takes its name from the red colour of its bricks, shows a return to the square plan and domed squinches of the Karakhanid tombs. The back and side façades are each articulated by two blind niches, while the porch lunette and corner columns are embellished with faience mosaic and small square turquoise glazed bricks respectively. Judging from the octagonal base rising from the cubiform body, the top of the dome must formerly have been covered with a pyramidal roof.

The dome and conical roof of the cylindrical brick mausoleum at Maragha dating from 563/1167 have collapsed, but it is still remarkable for its turquoise glazed Kufic inscription and its brick patterning. The Gunbadh-i Kābūd (or Blue Tomb), on the other hand, which dates from 593/1196, is a spectacular building with an octagonal body, the corners of which are softened by columns, a band of Kufic inscription and a stalactite frieze above, and turquoise tiles enriching the exterior façades. Each of the eight facets is completely covered with geometrical designs and terminates above in a stalactite niche with pointed arch. Inside, the base of the dome is encircled by a *thuluth* inscription in raised lettering. Thus in Maragha, which is one of the centres of tomb architecture, in the south of Azerbaidzhan, three different types of mausoleum, the square, the cylindrical and the octagonal, were constructed.

Nakhichevan, in Northern Azerbaidzhan, is a rich centre of tomb architecture. Here one can see the products of the brilliant artistic activity under the Atabeks of Azerbaidzhan, founded in 1146. The tomb of Yūsuf bin Kuthayyir, constructed in 1162, achieves a high degree of monumentality by means of an octagonal pyramidal roof resting on an octagonal body, a broad interlacing Kufic inscription on the upper edge and geometrical patterns covering the façades. (Design Ie.) In the Kufic inscription above the portal the architect's

Design Ie. Nakhichevan, Tomb of Yūsuf bin Kuthayyir

name is given as ʿAjamī bin Abū Bakr. The tomb was built during the reign of Shams al-Dīn Yildegiz (or Ildeniz), the founder of the Atabeks of Azerbaidzhan.

But the most magnificent monument in Nakhichevan is the large brick tomb, 25 metres in height, built for Mu'mine Khātūn, the wife of Shams al-Dīn, by her son Kızıl Arslan, in 1186. The interior is cylindrical and the exterior decagonal. The pyramidal roof has collapsed. Each face is conceived as a long narrow mihrab niche with a rectangular moulding and terminates above in a Kufic inscription and stalactite cornice. The decoration, which completely covers all the faces, is enlivened with turquoise tiles. With this building the architect ʿAjamī bin Abū Bakr created his finest masterpiece. The precincts of the tomb were entered through a pointed arched porch originally flanked by twin cylindrical minarets. The monumental porch has collapsed and can be seen only in old photographs. Twin minaret porches of this type later became a popular feature of Anatolian Seljuk architecture. Beginning with the minarets at the two corners of the façade of the Karakhanid tomb of Ayshe Bibi, this tradition thus passed through Azerbaidzhan into Anatolia, where the finest examples were produced. On the other hand the Gunbadh-i ʿAlawiyyān at Hamadhān in Western Iran, which is usually assigned to the end of the 12th century, is a domed structure resting on four walls which revives the façade architecture of the Uzgend tombs. The stucco decoration we have seen in the Seljuk mosques attains here its fullest development. This stucco decoration, which achieves on the mihrab wall what amounts to a free-standing plastic appearance, foreshadows the stonework in the Great Mosque at Divriği, in Central Anatolia.

Of the buildings that perpetuate in brick the forms of ancient Turkish tents, we may mention the tomb known as the Mīl-i Radkan at East Radkan in Khurāsān (Eastern Iran). This is a cylindrical structure 22 metres in height with 36 semicylindrical flutings, surmounted in the interior by a dome, on the exterior by a conical roof. On the upper edge there is a monumental Kufic inscription in turquoise tiles 1.5 metres in width, but more than half of this has disappeared. On the body there is a striking decoration of turquoise tiles arranged in lozenge patterns. A palmette frieze under the inscription descending on to the fluting recalls fringe patterns. The close resemblance between these and other ornaments and textile patterns indicates their derivation from tent decoration. Rubruk mentions having seen this type of tent when he visited Möngke Khān at Karakorum in 1253. The tents, which were supported by wooden poles arranged in a circle and resting on round disks, were covered with coloured cloths, and had conical roofs of felt, a hole being left in the centre for ventilation and for use as a chimney. The Radkan tomb displays some of these features translated into brick; yet its date is fifty years before Rubruk's visit. The inscription is very worn and only *sitta mi'a* (600) can be read. Max van Berchem has filled the empty space with the word *ithnayn* (two), which is the most suitable suggestion and would thus give the date 602/1205–6. This fluted form of construction was found as early as the beginning of the 12th century in the Karakhanid minaret of Dzhar Kurgan dating from 1108. The upper storey, now collapsed, of the body of the Sultan Mas'ūd minaret of 1114 at Ghazne was surrounded by semicylindrical fluting. The Quṭb Minar of Quṭb al-Dīn Aybek at Delhi (1200) had a fluted body with alternately circular and angular fluting. Thus it would appear reasonable from both the historical and the architectural point of view to place the Radkan tomb at the beginning of the 13th century, which coincides with the Khwārizmshāh period. The fluted minaret constructed by 'Alā al-Dīn Kayqubād I at Antalya shows the continuation of the fluted style in Anatolia.

A second monument to reproduce tent architecture in brick is the mausoleum at Kishmar in Khurāsān. It has a cylindrical body 18 metres in height with alternately round and angular flutes rising from a twelve-sided base 4 metres high. The centres of the lozenge motifs on the flutes are hollowed out and inset with turquoise tiles. A *naskhī* inscription above the entrance is illegible but the style of the building points to the middle, or perhaps the second half of the 13th century.

Throughout the 13th century and Īl-Khānid period there was no great change in Seljuk tomb architecture, and the same types of tomb construction were continued with only minor alterations. Of the tombs in the Nakhichevan region, a richly ornamented stone mausoleum dating from the 13th century in the village of Dzhuga shows similarities with Anatolian Seljuk architecture. This tomb is a twelve-sided structure on a square base with flattened corners. The pyramidal roof has collapsed. Each of the twelve facets is ornamented, the various designs being composed of geometrical stars and interlacing ornament. There is a slight but obvious similarity with the Döner Kümbed dated 1276 at Kayseri.

A cylindrical mausoleum with twelve semicylindrical flutes and rich glazed brick and tile decorations in the village of Karabaghlar is a late, 14th-century continuation of the Radkan tomb type. The body is covered with the names of Allāh, Muḥammad and the first four caliphs in Kufic lettering in glazed brick. The fluted conical roof has collapsed. Attached to it is the second occurrence in Azerbaidzhan of the monumental type of porch with twin minarets, the first being that at Nakhichevan.

A tomb in the village of Barda, dated 1322, is remarkable for its cylindrical brick body 14 metres in height set on a low plinth of cut stone. It is completely covered with the word Allāh in decorative Kufic, while on the upper edge a few words have remained of a broad inscription band. On the porch there is ceramic decoration and an inscription mentioning the name of the architect, Aḥmad. The conical roof has collapsed. This tomb has a strong resemblance to the Ḥasan Bek mausoleum of 1348, known as the Güdük Minaret, dating from the Ertenid period, at Sivas, and the 14th-century Sırçalı Kümbed at Kayseri.

Three mausolea belonging to the period of the Khwārizmshāhs give us some idea of their funerary monuments. Of these, the tomb of Aksaray-ding in southern Khwārizm dating from the 12th century has a high square body topped by a narrow drum and a conical cap. The others are in Old Urgench. The mausoleum of Fakhr al-Dīn Rāḍī, who died in Herat in 1208, has a remarkable exterior. It is constructed entirely of brick, and consists of a 12-sided body resting on a square plinth and terminating in a pyramidal dome. The façade, articulated by three pointed niches surrounded by a rectangular moulding, is surrounded by an inscription band and faced with terracotta panels with foliate motifs. The pyramidal roof is embellished with zigzags and lozenges in turquoise glazed brick. The inner space is roofed by a dome the same height as the drum. The tomb of the Khwārizmshāh Sultan Tekesh (1172–1200) rises from a square plinth in the form of a cylindrical body adorned with niches, having a dome inside and a conical roof outside. Most of the turquoise glazed bricks covering the conical roof have fallen away.

The whole strength of the Karakhanid tombs is concentrated upon the interior with dome resting on four walls, and the façade decoration. In the Khwārizmshāh tombs however, which date from the 12th and the beginning of the 13th century and two of which are situated in the ruins now known as Kunya Urgench, more importance is given to the external appearance as a whole, and the whole strength is concentrated upon the exterior.

Medreses

The first state medreses were founded in Ghazne at the beginning of the 11th century in order to combat Shiʿism, promote Sunnism and train state officials. Although we know the names of four of these medreses of the time of the Ghaznevid Sultan Maḥmūd—the Baykhāqīye, the Saʿīdīye, and those of Abū Saʿd al-Astarābādī and Abū Isḥāq al-Isfaraynī there is no information concerning their architectural features. The word 'medrese' occurs in a funerary inscription at Pīr-i Falizvan, found during the recent Italian excavations under Bombaci. It has been suggested that a medrese adjoined the ribāṭ erected beside the tomb of the Ghaznevid governor of Tūṣ, Arslan Jadhīb, at Sengbest. In a rough sketch drawn by Niedermayer in 1913 one can perceive a rectangular courtyard with rows of rooms on each side, and either one iwan at both back and front, or one iwan at the front.

In the Great Seljuk period these educational establishments were transformed into an extensive state organisation of residential institutions in which state officials were trained. The first of these was set up in Nishapur, and was also the first to be given the name *medrese*. Nāṣir-i

Khusraw records that the Nishapur medrese was founded on the orders of the Great Seljuk Sultan Tughrul Bek, and that when he passed through Nishapur on 22nd April 1046 the construction was already quite far advanced. This type of architecture developed rapidly with the large medreses founded at Baghdad, Tūṣ, Baṣra, Isfahan, Herat and Balkh about the same time and in the years immediately following. The Baghdad medrese was completed in 1067.

In the Seljuk and Atabek periods these buildings spread throughout the Empire as far as Iraq, Syria, Egypt and Anatolia. Such a rapid development of the conception and architecture of the medrese amongst the Turks is very largely due to the rôle which the monastic life and monastic architecture had played during the Buddhist period before their conversion to Islam. E. Diez has very rightly pointed out that the origin of the medrese type of architecture should be sought in the Buddhist monastery.

Two Great Seljuk medreses of the time of Malikshāh are to be found in Khārgird and Rayy. Unfortunately nothing remains of any of the others.

The Khārgird medrese in Khurāsān (circa 1087) is a complete ruin. Nothing can be seen except the qibla iwan, the vaulting of which has collapsed. Although Godard's excavations were regarded with some scepticism by Creswell and it has been suggested that the building was in fact a mosque, they have revealed the traces of four iwans around a square courtyard. The qibla iwan, which is still standing is 7.04 metres wide and the side walls are pierced by three pointed arches. A highly embossed floriated Kufic inscription in fine quality yellow brick is the finest inscription of its kind in the whole of Iran, and is now in the Teheran museum. The inscription is 90 cm. wide and the lettering is raised to a height of 6–10 cm. from its ground. The upper half is in the form of a decoration of foliate arabesques and palmettes, whilst the stems of the letters in the lower portion are intertwined. A large part of this inscription, however, including the final section with the date, has disappeared.

The mihrab of the second 4-iwan building excavated by Godard at Rayy in 1937, with its rich stucco decoration, is not exactly aligned to Mecca. The north and south iwans are equal in size but are smaller than the east and west iwans, which is against the general rule. The confronted pheasants and other birds amongst a decoration composed of veined arabesques, palmettes and tendrils are worthy of note. Creswell suggested that the evidence pointed to a house and that there were no cells for the students, but the Kufic inscription around the mihrab is not in accord with this hypothesis.

The Great Seljuks adopted the 4-iwan plan previously developed in Karakhanid and Ghaznevid architecture and applied it to medreses and mosques, thus inventing the 4-iwan type of mosque plan.

Caravansarais

The Great Seljuks produced monumental works by utilising the type of caravansarai architecture developed by the Karakhanids and Ghaznevids.

The Caravansarai known as the Ribāṭ-i Anushīrwān at Ehvan on the Dāmghān–Simnān road is called after the Ziyarid Sharaf al-Maʿāli Anushīrwān (1029–1049), and shows certain similarities to the Karakhanid Dakhistan and Daya Khātūn caravansarais. It is built on a square plan (72 × 72 metres) with strong fortress-like walls, and is buttressed at the corners and sides with round towers. It has a 4-iwan courtyard surrounded by arcades resting on piers, behind which long rectangular-shaped rooms are arranged in symmetrical rows. In three of the corners there are chambers in the form of small domes surrounded by four iwans, which derive from Sāmarrā and the ʿAbbāsids. At the side there is a bath house. The iwans measured 17 × 5 metres, and the space behind the iwan directly opposite the entrance may originally have been domed. The entrance iwan is not situated precisely on the central axis.

The Ribāṭ-i Zaʿfarān built by Malikshāh in the same area (between Nishapur and Sebzevar) belongs to a period later than first caravansarais of the time of Tughrul Bek, and has an original plan displaying certain developments in technique. According to Herzfeld's sketch plan it is in the form of a square (75 × 75 metres), with towers at the corners and single rooms deployed symmetrically around a 4-iwan courtyard. There is a mosque to the right of the entrance. It was a mud brick structure on a high brick plinth, but the bricks have crumbled leaving the building in a very ruinous state. According to notes taken by Godard who explored this region in 1940, the Ribāṭ-i Zaʿfarān has now completely disappeared.

One of the most important of the Great Seljuk monuments is the Ribāṭ-i Sharaf that once lay between Nishapur and Merv, in a deserted region crossed by the great Khurāsān road between Meshhed and Sarakhs. Godard published the results of the extensive survey and excavations he carried out in this caravansarai, and both the stylistic peculiarities and what we know of the history of this building suggest that it was constructed in the time of Abū Shujāʿ Muḥammad, the son of Malikshāh, in 508/1114–5. It displays the strength of Seljuk architecture in its decoration, which closely resembles that of the Ribāṭ-i Māhī, and in its balanced, symmetrical plan. The main building is approximately square, and the rectangular section in front of this is composed of chambers arranged around a 4-iwan courtyard. (Plan IId.) Although the ribāṭ resembles a fortress from the outside, its interior resembles a palace in richness. The first section is plainer, but the second, main section, consisting of a domed mosque, an arcaded courtyard and private apartments forming a small 4-iwan courtyard on both sides of the magnificent Great Iwan, contains every form of comfort. The upper section of a broad Kufic inscription encircling the monumental rear iwan has fallen away. Below this there is a Kufic inscription of a single line, again in brick. The writer of the inscription is given as Abū Manṣūr Asad bin Muḥammad of Sarakhs. At the beginning of the broad inscription there is the name Abu'l-Qāsim, and at the end on the left a fragmentary date *sanat thamana* . . 8. Godard compared the building with Karakhanid works such as the Ribāṭ-i Malik, the mihrab in the Namāzgāh Mosque in Bukhara and the tombs at Uzgend, and has very aptly completed this date as 508/1114–5. With the discovery of the Ribāṭ-i Māhī nearby, a prototype appears. The interior of the iwan was later completely covered with stucco decoration, and a wide inscription in floriated *thuluth* on raised plaster encircles the whole length of the sides and back of the iwan. After the collapse of the vaulting the ribāṭ fell into a very ruinous state. In this sole remaining *thuluth* inscription we find the name of the Sultan Sanjar and the name of his wife Āl-i Afrasiyāb Qutlugh Bilge Terken bint al-Qāghān (the daughter of the Karakhanid

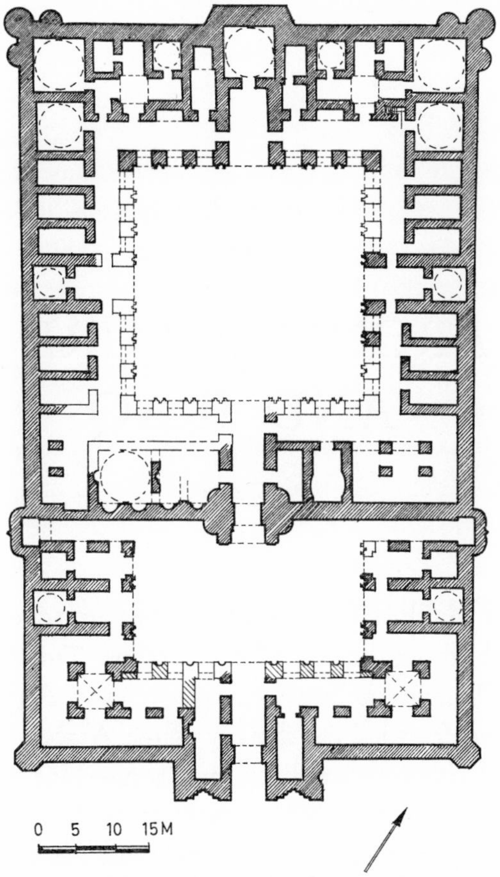

Plan IId. Nishapur–Merv road, Ribāṭ-i Sharaf

Muḥammad Arslan Khān), and the date 549/1154–5. Behind this inscription the original plainer wall decorations are still visible.

Sultan Sanjar was taken prisoner in a rising of the Oghuz tribe at the beginning of 548/1153, but he was still recognised as their sultan. He remained, together with his wife, as a prisoner in the hands of the Oghuz until the beginning of 551/1156. On the death of his wife he returned to Merv and died at the beginning of 1157 at the age of 72.

Both the Ribāṭ-i Sharaf (its original name is not known) and the Ribāṭ-i Māhī were destroyed in the Oghuz uprising. Terken Khātūn, who inherited from her father a taste for architecture, had both the ribāṭs repaired in 549 during the period of her imprisonment. The large inscription and all the alterations and decorations date from this time. The wall niches, the geometrical interlacing patterns in cut brick and the bold Kufic inscriptions reveal the original state of the building in 1114.

6

ZENGID ARCHITECTURE IN SYRIA AND IRAQ

The Great Seljuk sultan Malikshāh captured Aleppo in 1086 and appointed Aqsunqur governor. He was put to death for having rebelled against Tutush, the brother of Malikshāh and one of the Seljuks of Damascus (1086–1094). In 1127 Aqsunqur's son, 'Imād al-Dīn Zengī, became Atabek, and founded the dynasty of the Atabeks in Mosul. On his death in 1146 his territories were divided between his two sons—Nūr al-Dīn Zengī in Syria and Sayf al-Dīn Ghāzī I in Mosul and Iraq. The dynasty of the Atabeks of Damascus, founded by Tutush's slave Tughtekin in 1104, came to an end with the capture of Damascus by Nūr al-Dīn Zengī in 1154. On the death of Nāṣir al-Dīn Maḥmūd, the last of the Atabeks of Mosul, in 1233, his slave and vizir Badr al-Dīn Lu'lu' founded a dynasty that lasted until 1262.

Nūr al-Dīn Zengī's powerful personality and artistic gifts enabled him to open the way for the development of a new architectural style in Aleppo and Damascus based on Seljuk art. The Ayyubid Ṣalāḥ al-Dīn who had been brought up in his palace then founded a state of his own in Syria where he further developed this type of art, and carried it as far as Egypt. In the twenty-eight years between 1146 and 1174 Nūr al-Dīn Zengī filled the principal cities of Syria with great works of architecture, and transformed Aleppo, which he found in ruins, into one of the most flourishing cities of Syria.

No great changes were introduced in mosque architecture, which remained under the influence of the 'Umayyad mosque plan. The 'Umayyad Great Mosque in Aleppo, which had been destroyed, was restored by Nūr al-Dīn Zengī, but the square minaret in carved stone had been built earlier in the time of Malikshāh and Tutush.

The Great Mosque in Mosul may also be attributed to Nūr al-Dīn Zengī, but it has undergone many repairs and changes of form and plan. In an inscription on the old mihrab we find the name of a craftsman, Muṣṭafa al-Baghdādī, and the date 543/1148. The ornament of the octagonal piers with decorative capitals is in the same style as the mihrab, and so points to a dating of 1148. As F. Sarre has pointed out, Sayf al-Dīn Ghāzī I began the construction of the mosque and completed the mihrab, and on his death in 1170 Nūr al-Dīn Zengī came to Mosul and completed the half-finished building. From the first building there remains the brick minaret at the south-east corner of the wide rectangular courtyard. This minaret is 15 metres high, and its cylindrical body is composed of seven different ornamental bands surmounted by a helmet-shaped roof. The dome over the mihrab, the stucco decoration on the octagonal drum and the second mihrab in the courtyard all date from the time of Badr al-Dīn Lu'lu' (1233–1252). The mosque was repaired and modified by the Akkoyunlu Uzun Ḥasan (1466–1478), and by the Ottomans in 1640 and 1844, so that it comprises in itself all the different periods of Turkish architecture in Mosul.

It was Nūr al-Dīn Zengī's ambition to recapture Jerusalem from the Crusaders and he had a magnificent wooden minbar constructed to be placed in the Aqṣā Mosque. He did not, however, live long enough to realise his ambition, and it was Saladin who erected the minbar in its destined position. Until that time the minbar had been kept in the Great Mosque at Aleppo.

Nūr al-Dīn Zengī's original contribution to architecture is to be found in his medreses. According to the chronicler Ibn Shiḥna, 'Sulayman, the minister of Ilghāzī (1108–1122) of the Mardin Artukids, built the first medrese in Aleppo, known as the Zajjājiyya, in 1122. But this met with the hostility of the Shi'ites, who tore down at night what had been constructed during the day.' We have, however, no information regarding the plan of this first medrese.

The oldest medrese still standing in Syria is the medrese built for the Hanafite sect by Gümüshtekin, the governor of Bosra under the Atabeks of Damascus, in 1136. It was a rectangular structure with a square domed courtyard (6 × 6 metres). The courtyard was destroyed by the Wahhabis in the nineteenth century, and the dome collapsed. The mosque is seven metres in depth and on the qibla side opens out on to the courtyard through three arches. According to Creswell the whole structure, apart from the courtyard, was covered with a flat roof (Plan IV). It is most surprising that the first medrese in Syria should have been a domed structure quite different from those of the Great Seljuks, but in fact it was a structure similar in appearance to the Niksar and Tokat medreses of the Danishmendids in Anatolia in the 12th century. But whereas in Anatolia the domed type of medrese was to have a brilliant future, in Syria it was not continued. In Zengid medreses experiments were made with the various forms of the traditional iwan-type medrese.

The thick walled, iwan-type medreses built by Nūr al-Dīn Zengī at Aleppo, Manbij, Hama, Homs, Baalbek, Rihaba and other towns in Syria were severe, serviceable buildings in a simple architectural style. They performed the function of fortresses of Sunnism and in particular the Hanafites, defending them by means of learning and culture.

The Khan al-Tutun medrese built for the Hanafites in Aleppo in 1168 is now in ruins. Shadbakht, Nūr al-Dīn Zengī's governor in Aleppo, built the Bākhtiyya Madrasa for the Hanafites in 1193. The mosque opens into a courtyard through three arches, and possesses one of the most ornate mihrabs in Aleppo, faced with marble and porphyry, and its ornament with knotted interlacing decoration became typical of Ayyubid art in the Zengid tradition. Similar motifs were utilised in Seljuk architecture in Konya in the courtyard façade of the porch of the

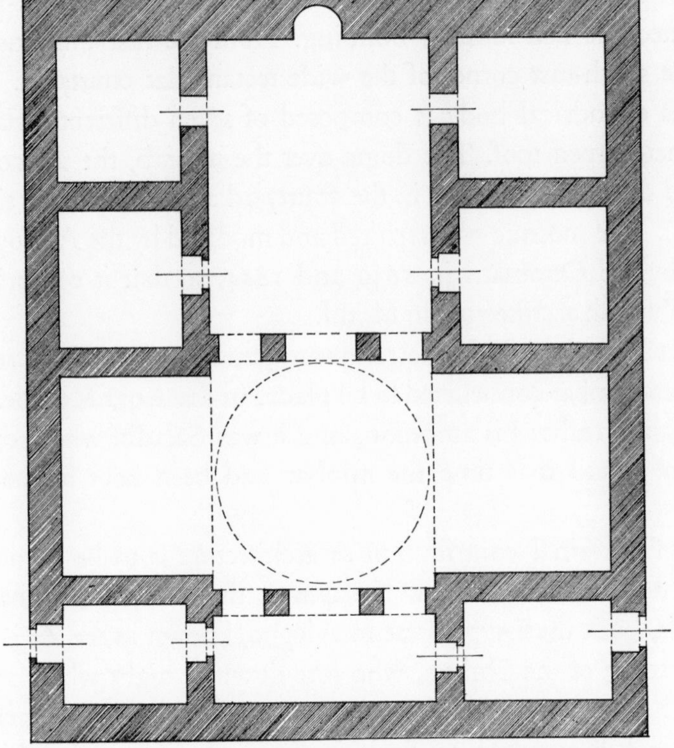

Plan IV. Bosra, Madrasa of Gümüshtekin

ʿAlā al-Dīn Mosque and in the porch decoration of the Karatay medrese, and continued to be used in Syria after the time of the Zengids in the Ayyubid period and even later.

One of the important monuments built by Nūr al-Dīn Zengī in Damascus is the Nūriyya Madrasa which was constructed for the Hanafites in 567/1172 and includes Nūr al-Dīn Zengī's tomb, a structure with a stalactite dome to the left of the entrance. At the end of the ½ metre wide inscription from the Koran in large raised *thuluth* lettering on the stone cenotaph is written 'qabr al-shahīd Nūr al-Dīn bin Zengī' ('the grave of the martyr, Nūr al-Dīn'). On the south side of a rectangular courtyard there is a typical mosque opening out through three arches, and a rectangular pool at the centre of the courtyard. The canal linking the central pool to an ornamental fountain on the rear wall of the west iwan is an architectural innovation. The idea of an iwan with an ornamental fountain was repeated in the Artukid Palace in Diyarbekir (1220) on the one hand, and in the Sultan ʿIsā medrese (1385) and the later Sultan Qāsim medrese at Mardin on the other, whilst its influence can be seen as far afield as the Maristan of Qalā'ūn in Cairo (1285). The second of Nūr al-Dīn's medreses, the ʿĀdiliyya Madrasa in Damascus on the same plan, was begun by Nūr al-Dīn and completed by the Ayyubids after his death. The courtyard is square in shape and has no fountain.

Of the Dār al-Ḥadīth (a school for teaching Muslim tradition) built by Nūr al-Dīn at Damascus only the north wing facing the street and the mosque on the south side are still standing. Another of the most important buildings constructed by him in Damascus is a

IV Edirne, Selimiye Mosque, 1574, tile panels from interior (see pages 276 and 277)

maristan (hospital). In this one finds the most mature and most balanced form of the 4-iwan courtyard plan. The architecture is modern in conception with lavatories and latrines arranged in rows around a small courtyard with a pool, to the right of the monumental vestibule. Herzfeld rightly states that apart from the repairs carried out by Qalā'ūn in the south iwan and the fountain added to the façade, the whole building is the work of Nūr al-Dīn Zengī and dates from the year 549/1154. Generous endowments ensured the continued existence of the hospital.

Nūr al-Dīn was a great ruler and patron of the arts, and saved Egypt, which had been converted to Shiism by the Fatimids and was in a state of complete chaos, through one of his lieutenants Saladin, thus preparing the ground for the Ayyubid dynasty. Saladin when Sultan continued his work and transported both medrese architecture and the Hanafite rite to Egypt. The Ayyubid dynasty lasted for seventy-nine years. The mosques and thirty-odd medreses constructed during this period were simple unpretentious buildings continuing the Zengid style without introducing any architectural innovations.

Although Saladin is far better known in Europe, for his part in the Crusades, Nūr al-Dīn Zengī was, as Herzfeld has pointed out, much the greater ruler.

The branch of the Atabeks of Mosul founded by Badr al-Dīn Lu'lu' (1233–1252) created a number of works in Mosul on the sound foundations of Zengid architecture. But in place of the dignified Zengid style based on sound materials, fine architectural proportions and geometrical decoration, a flamboyant, small-scale type of architecture employing cheap materials and drowned in tasteless decoration prevailed. Besides foliate motifs a good deal of importance was given to figural representation.

The triple-vaulted vestibule of the Qarā Saray constructed by Badr al-Dīn Lu'lu' on the site of the old Zengid palace in Mosul is still standing. The rough masonry was covered with rich stucco decoration which overlaid all the walls in several registers. Above there is an inscription 60 centimetres broad written in highly embossed *thuluth* script on a background of spiral scrolls with the ends of their convolutions terminating in birds' and animals' heads. Lately, work similar to this carved in stone in 632/1234–5 by a craftsman Zayn al-Dīn bin Abī Rashīd has been discovered in the fortifications in the gulf of Baku in Azerbaidzhan. These inscriptions with human and animal heads were recovered from the sea and replaced in their original position on the walls; some of them are now exhibited in the palace of the Shīrvān Shāhs at Baku. If their sound craftmanship is accepted as a prototype then we must ascribe the Qarā Saray to the year 632/1235. Beneath this broad inscription frieze there is a row of niches 15 centimetres in width with trilobed arches, each niche being occupied by busts in relief of figures wearing caftans, with heraldic birds with outspread wings, possibly eagles, occupying the spaces between the niches. As Sarre has pointed out, these resemble the figures in a book of Automata (Kitāb fī Maʿrifat al-Ḥiyal al-Handasiyya) written by al-Jazarī at Diyarbekir for an Artukid sultan, between 1182 and 1206.

Badr al-Dīn Lu'lu' built shrines for the two Shiite saints, Yaḥyā and ʿAwn al-Dīn. These are domed buildings with octagonal drums on high square bases, the first being surmounted by a plain, the second by a fluted pyramid.

7
ṬŪLŪNID ART IN EGYPT

Aḥmad ibn Ṭūlūn, the founder of the first Turkish state in Egypt, was a highly cultured man of good education and upbringing who opened a new and brilliant period. In a very short time he restored Egypt's prosperity and founded a new city named al-Qaṭā'i' near Fusṭāṭ. Here he built for himself a splendid palace, a polo field and a Dār al-'Imāra. The Bāb al-Ṣalāt (Gate of Supplication), one of the nine gates of the palace, was connected to the Mosque of Ibn Ṭūlūn 600 metres away by three wide streets. Ibn Ṭūlūn entered the mosque by the central street, whilst his retinue entered by the two side streets. He constructed also a hospital and an aqueduct which is still standing today. The amount of development accomplished and the number of buildings constructed in fifteen years by Aḥmad ibn Ṭūlūn are notable. The period up to his sudden death in 884 was a golden age for Egypt, and this development was continued under his son, Khumarawayh.

It is a mistake to regard the Mosque of Ibn Ṭūlūn, which took three years to build (876–879) and measures 122 metres by 140 metres, as merely a replica of the Mosque of al-Mutawakkil at Sāmarrā. Like the mosques in Sāmarrā and Ibn Ṭūlūn's own native city of Bukhara the Ibn Ṭūlūn Mosque is constructed of brick, and the inner and outer faces of the arches and the upper edge of the walls are covered with very hard white stucco ornament comprising as many as sixty different ornamental motifs. Below the wooden rafters is to be found a Kufic inscription 2 km. in length—the longest inscription in the world. According to researches carried out by Creswell the minaret, 40.5 metres high, standing outside the walls of the original mosque was built in imitation of the Malwiyya minaret in Sāmarrā and must originally have consisted of a spiral brick construction rising directly from the ground. During the repairs carried out by the Mamluk sultan Lajīn in 1296 the lower half may have been enclosed by a square limestone tower.

With its great size, the nobility of its architecture and the elegant simplicity of its plan the Mosque of Ibn Ṭūlūn still stands as the symbol of a great period that lasted for thirty-seven years, and powerfully enlivens the silhouette of Cairo.

According to Schnyder's investigation there are a number of clues suggesting that polychrome lustre pottery was manufactured in Ṭūlūnid workshops after models from Baghdad and Sāmarrā. There were centres of ceramic manufacture at Baḥnasa and ʿAshmūnayn in Upper Egypt, and there is no doubt that there was as brilliant a development in ceramics as there was in architecture and the other arts.

After the Ṭūlūnids there was a period of about thirty years during which Egypt and Syria were administered by ʿAbbāsid governors, and which has passed by without trace.

In 934 Akshid or Ikshīd, the son of Tughach, the governor of Damascus, founded a Turkish state that was to last for thirty-four years (935–969), after which time Egypt came under the sway of the Fatimids. The Ikshīdids did not create an original style of architecture except for one development. Of the buildings they constructed the Mashhad of the Sharīf Ṭabāṭaba (943) was an irregular structure of which only the outer walls are still standing. Creswell has shown, on the basis of excavations and research, that it was originally a nine-domed structure with arches resting on cruciform piers, only the bases of which have survived. This multi-domed type of plan is of some importance in the middle of the 10th century. The decorative style of the Ṭūlūnid period is seen continued on the stucco mihrabs constructed by the Ikshīdids. During the Ikshīdid period only monochrome lustre pottery was manufactured, the polychrome lustre wares of Sāmarrā not being imitated.

8

TURKISH MAMLUK ART IN EGYPT

In 1171 Saladin put an end to the Fatimid caliphate, which had endured for two hundred years after the Ikshīdids, and in 1174, on the death of Nūr al-Dīn Zengī, he founded the Ayyubid dynasty. In 1187 he and his brother al-Malik al-ʿĀdil temporarily interrupted the Latin Kingdom of Jerusalem with the capture of that city. They introduced a number of innovations into military architecture as a result of their experience in warfare, and it was by Saladin and al-Malik al-ʿĀdil that most of the citadel and the walls of Cairo were constructed. But the most important innovation from the point of view of the history of art was the introduction into Egypt by the Ayyubids of the Zengid style of medrese architecture.

The first of these medreses is the tomb of Abū Manṣūr Ismāʿīl (1216), the oldest iwan structure in Egypt, and originally, according to Creswell, a 2-iwan Shafiite medrese. Of the Kāmiliyya Madrasa dating from 622/1225, only the north iwan is still standing. The medrese of al-Malik al-Ṣāliḥ Najm al-Dīn Ayyūb (1241–2) is a twin 4-iwan medrese composed of two blocks each having two iwans, a plan which foreshadows later developments, with a central minaret and the tomb of the founder. The mihrab of the tomb is among the first examples in Egypt of Zengid coloured marble decoration. During the Ayyubid period in Egypt, which lasted for 79 years, the stone architecture of the Fatimids was largely replaced by brick, delicacy prevailed in the stucco decorations and variegated designs in the window grilles. Few works were constructed of a monumental character, the Ayyubids serving in this respect rather as a means of transition from Zengid art to Turkish Mamluk art, but the buildings constructed by the Mamluks up to the end of the 14th century still dominate the city of Cairo. Most of these buildings are in the form of complexes, and the medreses and tombs are far more striking than the mosques. The Mamluks forged lasting links with Anatolian Turkish architecture, with Great Seljuk and Zengid architecture and with the type of domed mausoleum with high drum to be found in the vicinity of Samarkand and Bukhara; they thus introduced a new architectural style while remaining faithful to Turkish architectural traditions.

Mosques

The only early Mamluk monument built as a mosque is a large, approximately square structure measuring 100 × 100 metres built by the Turkish hero Baybars in the years 1266–69, of which only a few walls are still standing. Its plan of parallel aisles is similar to that of the Mosque of Ibn Ṭūlūn, but it has a courtyard with a 4-iwan plan scheme, with an iwan cutting each of the arcades towards the porches, and perpendicular aisles in front of the mihrab dome opening out through three arches on to the courtyard. There was a square minaret over the main door, but the most important innovation in the Mosque of Baybars is the manner in which the idea of a domed area over the mihrab has been utilised. As Creswell has pointed out, this dome is a

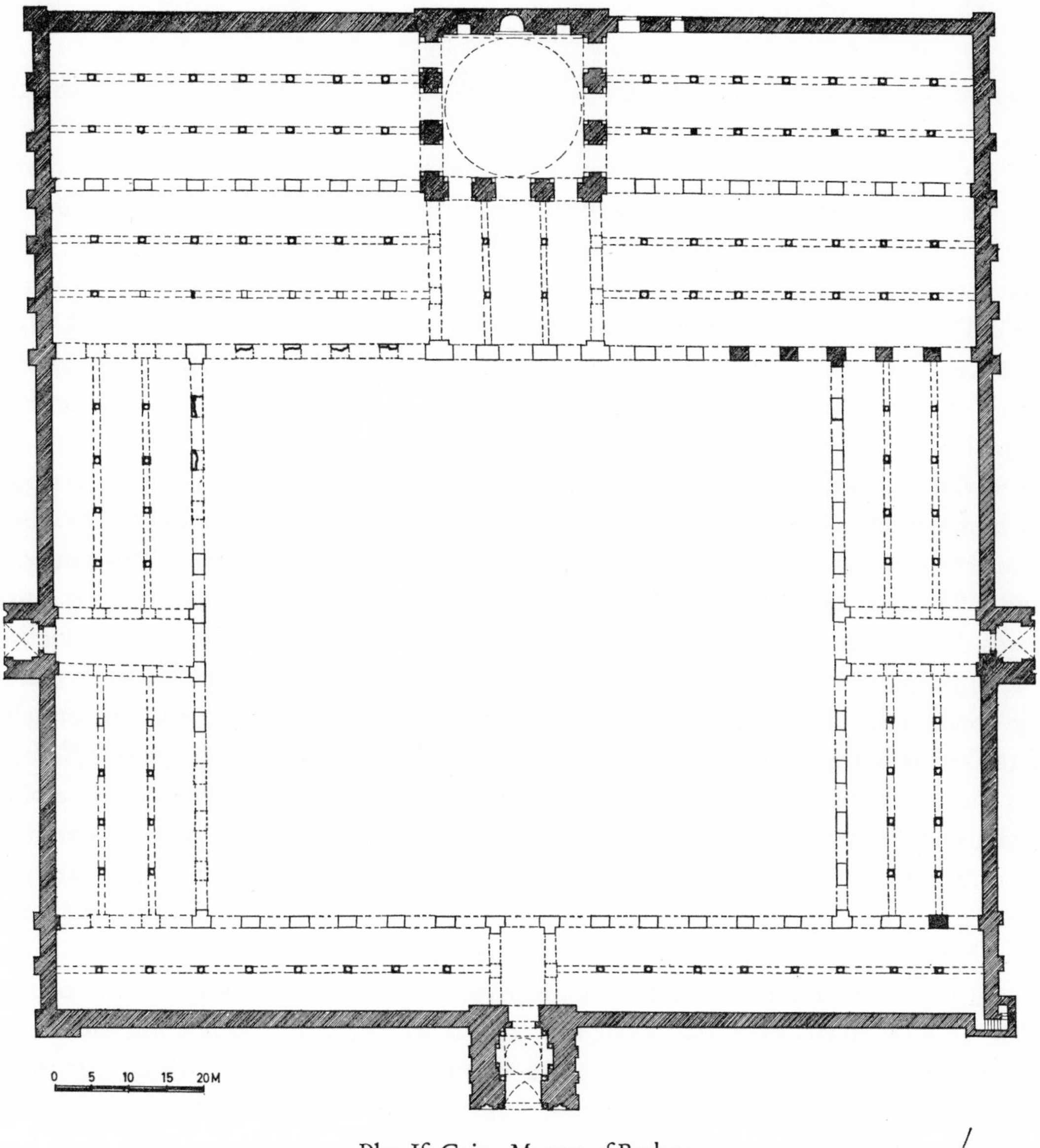

Plan If. Cairo, Mosque of Baybars

replica of the dome of Malikshāh in the Masjid-i Jum'a at Isfahan (1080) even in its diameter (15 metres). After the Zaware Mosque of 1135 the dome had become an integral part of mosque architecture, and, as can be seen in the Great Mosque in Mayyafāriqīn (Silvan) built by the Artukid sultan Najm al-Dīn Alpī in 1157, the type of mosque plan that evolved in the mosques of the Great Seljuks in Iran was finally transported to Anatolia (Plan If). Here the aisles on each side of the dome are covered with a wooden roof, as in the Mosque of Baybars in Cairo. After being employed in the Artukid Great Mosques at Mardin (1176–1186) and Dunaysir (1204) this architectural feature was carried as far as Egypt in the Mosque of Baybars. We have already seen that the mihrab dome was used as a dominant feature in mosque architecture in the Great Mosque at Lashkari Bazar as early as the beginning of the 11th century.

Medreses

A medrese with a 4-iwan courtyard, the Madrasa Ẓāhiriyya completed by Baybars in 1263 in Cairo, was demolished in 1874 during road building and only the lower half of the west corner has survived. The three richly decorated windows and the figures of panthers above the portal arch are remarkable. Old engravings inform us that here was to be found the oldest stalactite porch in Egypt, modelled on the porch of the Madrasa of Shadbakht in Aleppo. This is also indicated by the magnificent stalactite porch of the Ẓāhiriyya Madrasa in Damascus (1277). This medrese was completed after the death of Baybars by his son al-Malik al-Sa'īd Bereke Khān, who was himself buried here in 1281. The interior is ruined, but it would seem that this medrese, of which only the arch of the south iwan is still standing, was built on a 2-iwan plan.

Other early Mamluk monuments in or near Cairo are a bridge of Baybars, the canal regulator at Illahun, the tomb of the 'Abbāsid caliphs enclosed in a large courtyard (Ḥosh), whilst in Alexandria there was the Qaṣr al-'Umayd, demolished at the end of the 19th century. The bridge is 79 metres long, and just above the pointed arches on the north face there is a row of leopards or panthers in high relief. The panther formed the crest of Baybars, and one is also struck by the panther figures on the castle and bridge at Birejik in Mesopotamia. Baybars, the heroic commander of the Turkish forces that utterly routed the proud, up till then undefeated Mongol armies at the battle of 'Ayn Jālūt in 1260 and killed the Mongol general Kitbughā, was at the same time a great ruler and a great patron of the arts. In the monuments he built he created a dignified and noble architectural style, but his successors combined various different types of architectural plans in the construction of large pretentious building complexes. Unfortunately, most of the monuments of Baybars were allowed to fall into ruin and a certain number have completely disappeared.

The first characteristic plan of a large-scale Mamluk architectural complex is to be seen in the Maristan (hospital) of Sultan Qalā'ūn. The Maristan, which was completed after 11 months' work at the beginning of 1285, is a vast complex covering a whole quarter composed of a tomb, a medrese and a hospital. Some idea of its size can be given by the fact that the façade, which is articulated by pointed arched niches and pierced by three tiers of windows of various forms, is 100 metres long and has walls reaching a height of 20 metres. The square minaret and the dome of the tomb rise above the square block of the main building. The south iwan of the medrese has been transformed into a three-aisled mosque opening on to an open courtyard through a triple arch. A corridor separating the tomb from the medrese led to the maristan behind, which is now in ruins. Before Qalā'ūn became sultan he was treated in the Maristan of Nūr al-Dīn Zengī in Damascus in 1276, and it was here that he received the inspiration for his own maristan in Cairo. This hospital was built on a 4-iwan plan. The large iwans, on the south-east and north-west sides, are 13 metres in depth and had selsebils, waterways and pools behind them. In the north corner there were two other courtyards forming separate sections for male and female mental patients. Some of the marble and coloured stone mosaics of the fountains, waterways and pools can still be seen. Qalā'ūn introduced into Egypt the lavish use of this type of marble and coloured stone mosaic, to be found also on the walls and piers of his tomb and the mihrabs of both the tomb and the mosque, a type of decoration which was later to become a traditional feature of Mamluk architecture. The sebil (or public fountain) added on the north corner of the façade of the medrese by his son al-Nāṣir Muḥammad in 1326 is important as the first known example of ceramic revetment in Egypt.

The architecture, plan and façade of the Qalā'ūn complex are in a mixed style, and the building as a whole failed to achieve a balanced system of architecture. The façade recalls Romanesque or Gothic architecture, but apart from features such as horseshoe arches and double-arched windows introduced from Western Islam, the whole architecture is linked to the Seljuks and the Zengid style.

After the mosque of Baybars and the foundation of Qalā'ūn, a second period of architecture opens with the mosque-medrese of Sultan Ḥasan (1356–62), the largest monument of the Turkish Mamluks. It is an irregular rectangle 150 × 68 metres, and conforms to the classical plan in having a square courtyard 32 × 32 metres with an iwan with pointed arch on each of the four sides. The monumental façade rises to a height of 37 metres, thus reaching its utmost development. The façade architecture is the beginning of a style that was to be continued in the 'Isā Bek Mosque at Ephesus (1375) and the Sheikh Ṣāfī Mosque at Ardebil (1642–67), and is to be seen in a more restrained form in Ottoman architecture. The porch on the right corner of the façade, 20 metres high, clearly shows the influence of the Sultan Hans of the Anatolian Seljuks.

There was no great architectural development during the period of the Circassian Mamluks, which lasted from the end of the 14th century until the Ottoman conquest of Egypt by Sultan Selim I in 1517, but decoration became more ornate and more importance was given to surfaces. Strong influences from Turkestan were manifested in tomb architecture and then continued in all the domed architecture in Cairo up to the time of the Ottomans. These were domes rather resembling Mamluk helmets raised on high cylindrical drums.

Tombs of this type lent 15th-century Cairo a completely new silhouette. The close resemblance between tombs at the Shāh-i Zinde built at Samarkand during the same century and the Mamluk tombs in Cairo popularly known as the Tombs of the Caliphs reflects this most vividly.

9

TURKISH ART IN ANATOLIA

From the beginning of the 11th century onwards Turkish tribes began to enter Anatolia, and within five or ten years after the Battle of Manzikert or Malazgırt (1071), in which the Byzantine Emperor Romanus Diogenes was defeated by the Great Seljuk sultan Alp Arslan, they had conquered the whole of Anatolia. The names of twenty-four Oghuz tribes from Turkestan still remain as the names of villages in Anatolia today.

Turkish art in Anatolia drew its strength from the depths of its own history, though it was nourished from roots that stretched out into Karakhanid, Ghaznevid and Great Seljuk art. The Turks arrived in Anatolia, a province which had been dominated by the finest cultures in the world, bringing with them very powerful material and spiritual cultural values, and established their own culture so firmly that they were never to be erased. The first Anatolian Seljuk period up to the middle of the 12th century was a period of strife and confusion, with no artistic activity of any importance.

It was the Turcoman states such as the Danishmendids in Sivas, Kayseri and Malatya (1092–1178), the Artukids in Ḥiṣn Kayfā, Mardin, Harput and Diyarbekir (1098–1234), the Saltukids in Erzurum (1092–1202) and the Mengüjükids in Erzincan, Kemah, Şebinkarahisar and Divriği (1118–1252), which found occasion to create the first Turkish architectural monuments in Anatolia.

There was a brilliant, many-sided development in every sphere of Turkish art based on the firm foundations that had been laid in previous periods. In Anatolian Turkish architecture the problem of the dome, which had been tackled first by the Uighurs, the Karakhanids and the Ghaznevids and then later by the Great Seljuks, attained a magnificent monumental solution unparalleled anywhere in the world. This can be seen most vividly in Ottoman mosque architecture. (Map III.)

V Edirne, Selimiye Mosque, 1574, tile panels from door and walls of Sultan's loggia (see pages 225 and 277)

The First Mosques (Artukid, Danishmendid, Saltukid, Mengüjükid)

According to the floriated Kufic inscription, in which the name of Sultan Malikshāh and the date 484 (1091–2) are mentioned, the Great Mosque at Diyarbekir, the first of the Turkish mosques in Anatolia, was originally a Great Seljuk building (Fig. 1). Malikshāh had rebuilt the dome in the 'Umayyad mosque in Damascus, and in the mosque at Diyarbekir he seems to have repeated the original plan of the 'Umayyad mosque in a simpler style of architecture without a dome. (Plan 1.) The western façade of the courtyard, with its two tiers of arcades and the columns and mouldings from an old Roman theatre, was built by the Atabek Il-Aldi. The name of Malikshāh's son Abū Shujā' is also mentioned in an inscription dated 511/1117–18.

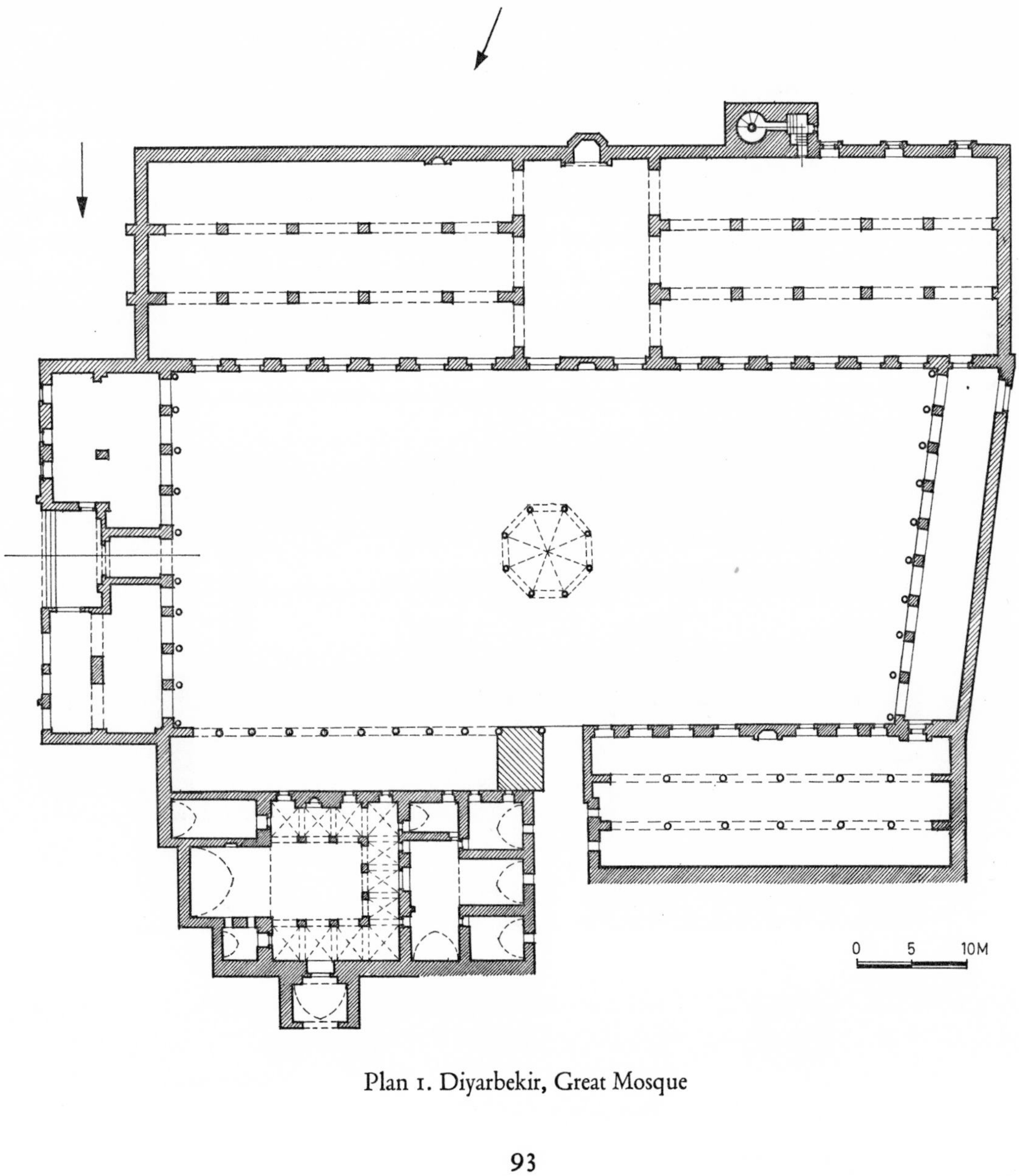

Plan 1. Diyarbekir, Great Mosque

The inscription in floriated Kufic on the arcade and the decorations on the mouldings are original (Fig. 2). This lively courtyard façade, which recalls the buildings of the 'Umayyad period, was repeated on the east side by Maḥmūd bin Il-Aldi, who had formed an independent Inalid state in 559 (1163). Here we come across the first example of the broken arch later to be used in Bursa, and the combination of Kufic inscriptions with ancient motifs is carried out with conspicuous success. In an inscription of Il-Aldi dated 550/1155–6 the name of the architect is mentioned as 'Al-bannā' Hibat Allāh Gurgānī'. The square minaret was constructed at this time.

The Great Mosque at Diyarbekir, with its arcaded courtyard in front, its domeless transept and its square minaret, had, as a whole, no influence on later Turkish architecture. The real development lies in that group of Anatolian mosques in which the mihrab dome forms an essential element of the plan. The Great Mosque at Siirt was slightly later and, according to the inscription on the base of the minaret, underwent repairs in 523/1129. The history of Siirt connects the mosque with the name Mughīth al-Dīn Maḥmūd of the Seljuks of Irak and gives the date 523, thus providing a link with the Great Seljuks. The original structure consisted of a dome on squinches resting on four brick piers two of which bear the traces of a mihrab, and has been enlarged on both the eastern and western sides by the addition of a small dome, an iwan and vaults perpendicular to this. (Plan 2.) The mihrab niches have round lobed arches set in the old brick piers, and traces of turquoise tiles and of an inscription from the Koran in floriated *thuluth* script can still be seen. The leaning minaret which has become the symbol of the town of Siirt, recalls the brick minaret of the Great Mosque at Mosul, though the thick cylindrical minaret of Siirt is much simpler and more archaic in appearance. The

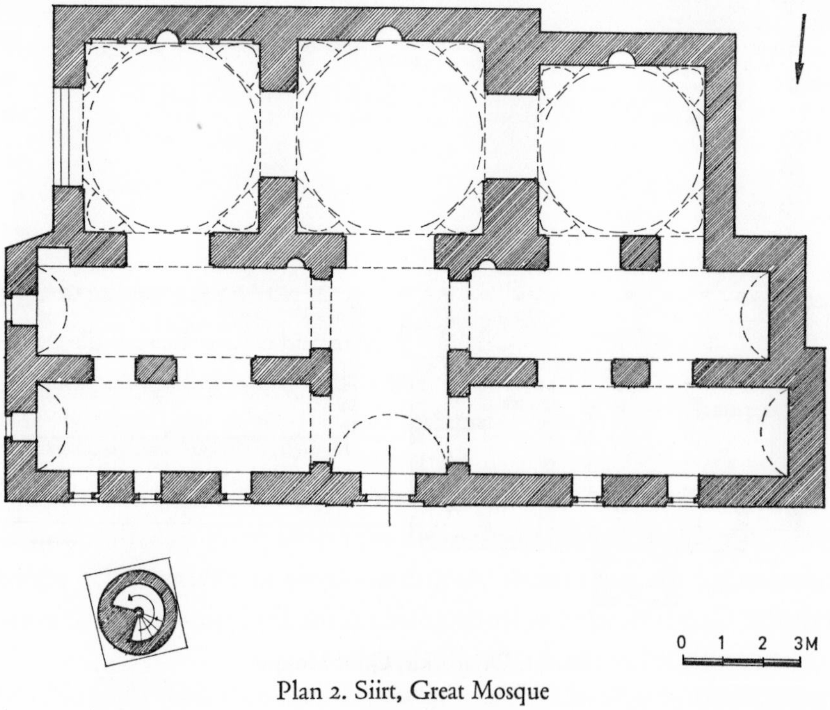

Plan 2. Siirt, Great Mosque

decorations of this latter minaret consist of the Kufic inscriptions on the high square plinth, then geometrical interlacing patterns, braid and star motifs, and turquoise glazed tiles. The plan of this mosque, which was probably completed in the 13th century, has a characteristic quality of exploration and experiment.

As for the little-known Great Mosque at Bitlis, the Kufic renovation inscription sunk in a pier on the façade beginning 'Jaddada (or Judida) binā' hadhā'l-jāmi' . . .' ('The building of the mosque was restored . . .') is dated 455/1150. It is not known to whom the name

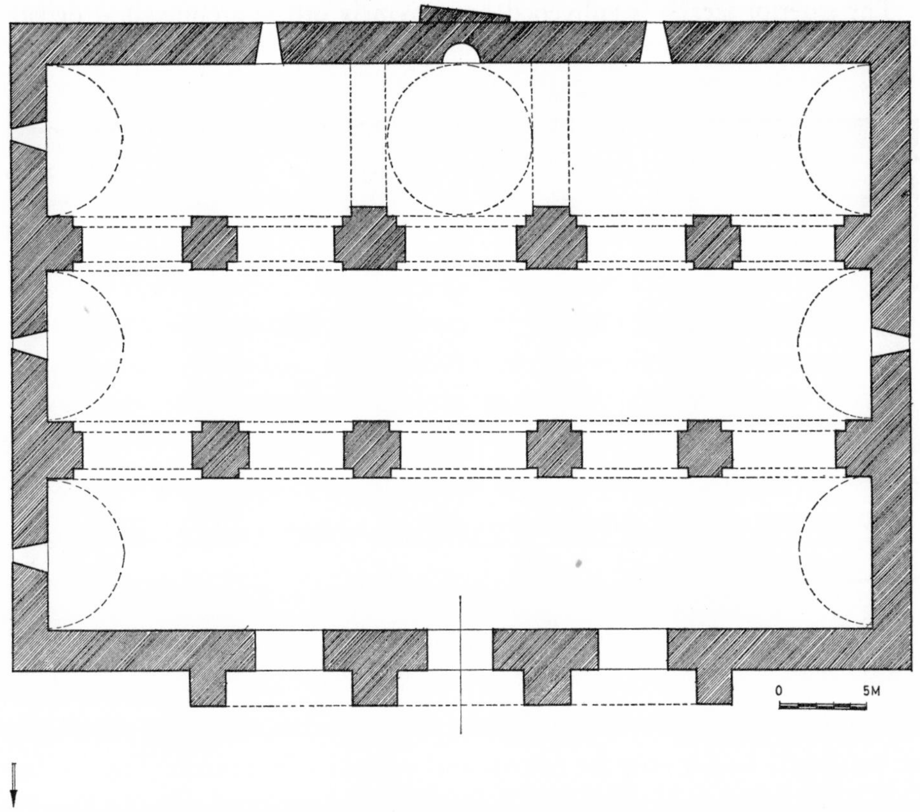

Plan 3. Bitlis, Great Mosque

Abū'l Muẓāffar Muḥammad mentioned in the inscription refers. Here a plan closely resembling those later employed in the Artukid mosques is used for the first time and in very simple form. (Plan 3.) The only remarkable feature of the exterior is the conical roof covering the mihrab dome. Like the Great Mosque at Siirt this has no courtyard. The disappearance of the courtyard in the mosques following the Great Mosque at Diyarbekir shows the importance then given to increasing the size of the actual mosque and the problem of the dome.

With the inclusion for the first time of the mihrab dome in a symmetrical plan and with its sound stonework the Great Mosque at Bitlis points to the beginning of an important development that was to be continued in the Artukid mosques.

The magnificent Artukid style of architecture begins with the Great Mosque at Mayyafāriqīn

(Silvan). The dome of Malikshāh in the Friday Mosque at Isfahan is here utilised with the same plan as a mihrab dome. It has a diameter of 13.5 metres and rests on stalactite squinches like those in the Gulpayagan Mosque completely dominating both the interior and the exterior of the whole building. By combining the mihrab dome of the Ghaznevid Great Mosque at Lashkari Bazar with Malikshāh's conception of the dome, Turkish mosque architecture in Anatolia achieved a monumental form. (Plan 4.) On the base of the dome there is an inscription of the Artukid Najm al-Dīn Alpī (1152–76). Examination of the written sources shows that the mosque was completed in its present form by Najm al-Dīn Alpī between 1152 and 1157. The exterior façade is enlivened by extremely ornate architectural decoration and

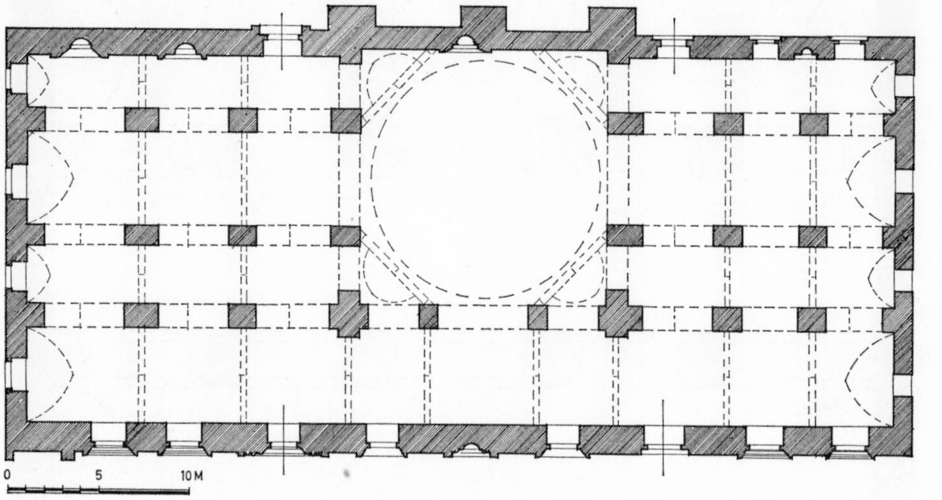

Plan 4. Silvan, Great Mosque

is covered from one end to the other by slightly pointed arches resting on squat pillars above the rows of windows. Today only the eastern and western sides remain (Fig. 3). In 1913 the mosque underwent a thorough restoration at the hands of stonemasons who were completely unfamiliar with its style, with the result that the mosque was considerably damaged by the addition of porches and columns in very bad taste.

The plan of the Great Mosque at Mardin (12th century) has the characteristic quality of Artukid architecture. The mihrab dome rests on six piers and dominates the whole of the inner space. It is fluted on the exterior, a feature that was to become traditional in Mardin after this. The inscription is dated 572/1176 and mentions the name of al-Malik al-Ghāzī Quṭb al-Dīn of Diyarbekir. The inscription on the east façade dating from 1186 is in the name of the Artukid Yawlāq Arslan. The wooden minbar was built later by the Artukid sultan Dā'ūd (1367–76). The arcaded courtyard appears again in the Great Mosque at Mardin, but of the cross-vaulted arcades only five sections on the north side are still standing.

In the Great Mosque at Harput, which was built by the Artukid Fakhr al-Dīn Qarā Arslan in the year 551/1156–7, the courtyard with a central pool has been diminished in size and

1 Diyarbekir, Great Mosque, general view

2 Diyarbekir, Great Mosque, courtyard arcades

3
Mayyafāriqīn (Silvan),
Great Mosque, exterior

4
Dunaysir (Kızıltepe),
Great Mosque, general view

5
Dunaysir (Kızıltepe),
Great Mosque, detail of mihrab

6 Divriği, Castle Mosque, porch

7 Divriği, Castle Mosque, interior

8 Divriği, Great Mosque, exterior

9 Divriği, Great Mosque, blazon at side of west porch

10 Divriği, Great Mosque, east porch

11 Divriği, Great Mosque, interior

12 Divriği, Great Mosque, mihrab

13 Divriği, Great Mosque, minbar

14 Divriği, Hospital, porch

15 Divriği, Hospital, interior

16 Divriği, Hospital, stone vault

17 Konya, Mosque of ʿAlā al-Dīn, courtyard façade. (Photographed before 1900)

18 Konya, Mosque of ʿAlā al-Dīn, interior. (Photographed before 1900)

19 Konya, Mosque of ʿAlā al-Dīn, dome, transitional section of 'Turkish triangles' and upper part of mihrab

20 Konya, Mosque of ʿAlā al-Dīn, minbar

21 Niğde, Mosque of ʿAlā al-Dīn, exterior

22 Malatya, Great Mosque, exterior of dome

23 Malatya, Great Mosque, iwan

24 Malatya, Great Mosque, detail from right-hand side of iwan with artisan's inscription in square cartouche

26 Konya, Sırçalı Masjid, mihrab decorated with ceramic mosaic

25 Konya, Sirçalı Masjid, portico

27 Beyşehir, Eshrefoghlu Mosque, doorway with faience mosaic

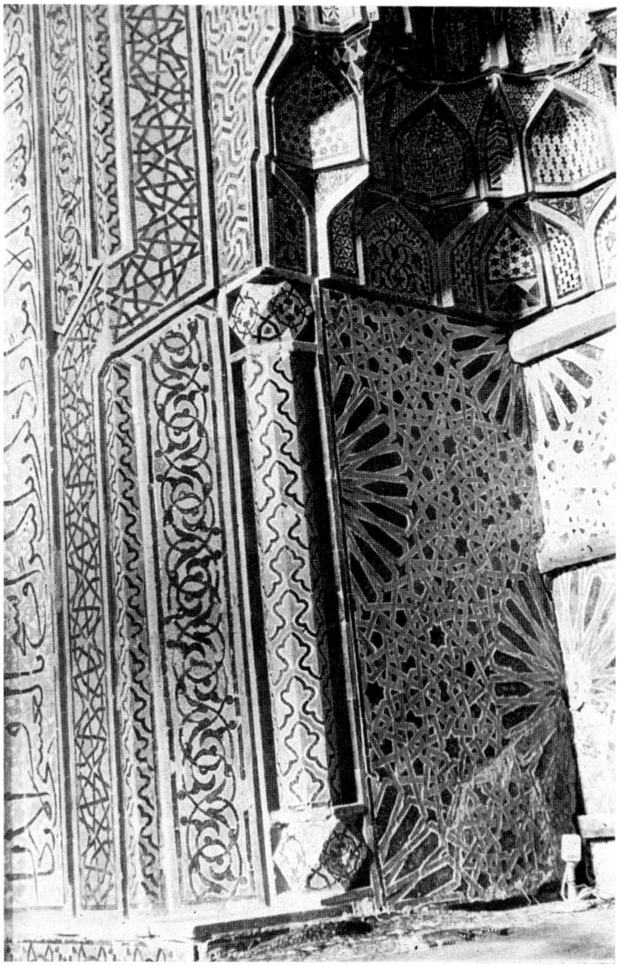

29 Beyşehir, Eshrefoghlu Mosque, detail from mihrab

28 Beyşehir, Eshrefoghlu Mosque, wooden columns

30
Konya, Mosque of Sahib Ata, porch.
(Photographed before 1900)

31 Konya, Mosque of Sahib Ata, artisan's signature on sebil niche on right-hand side of porch

32 Konya, Mosque of Sahib Ata, mihrab decorated with ceramic mosaic

33 Isparta, Atabey, Medrese of Ertokush, porch

34 Isparta, Atabey, Medrese of Ertokush, interior

35 Konya, Medrese of Karatay, exterior

36 Konya, Medrese of Karatay, interior

37 Konya, Ince Minare Medrese (Photographed before 1900)

38 Konya, Ince Minare Medrese, detail of porch

39 Konya, Ince Minare Medrese, interior of dome

40 Kirşehir, Medrese of Jājā Bek, detail of porch

41 Çay, Medrese, exterior

42 Diyarbekir, Zinciriye Medrese, courtyard

43 Diyarbekir, Mesudiye Medrese, double storeyed *riwāqs* (arcades)

44 Kayseri, Çifte Medrese, porch of hospital

placed inside the mosque, and the interior opens into this through pointed arches. (Plan 5.) The plan of the mosque, with its mihrab dome 8 metres in diameter, recalls the Friday Mosque at Zaware (1135). The body of the thick cylindrical minaret that rises up on the inner side of the north-west wall of the courtyard is decorated with unusual brick patterning and preserves the archaic form of the first structure.

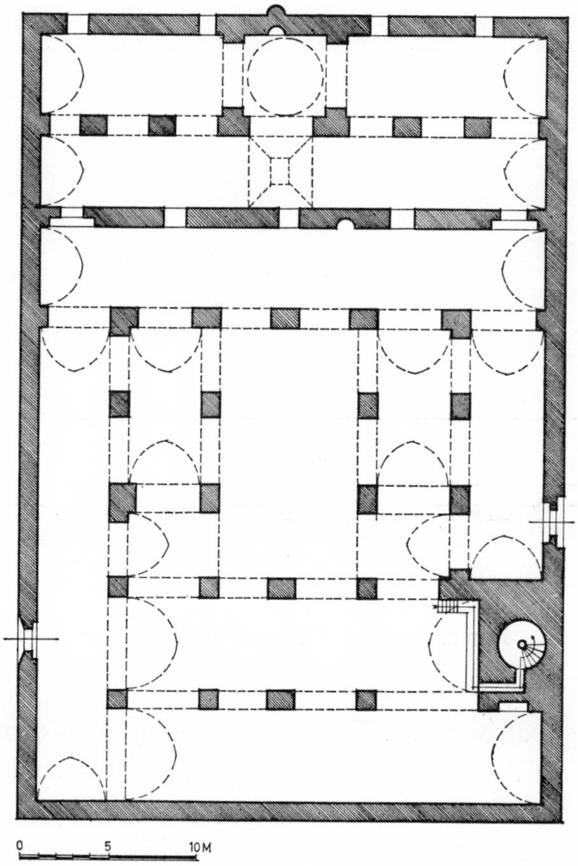

Plan 5. Harput, Great Mosque

The masterpiece of Artukid mosque architecture is the Great Mosque at Dunaysir (Kızıltepe), which is now in a very ruinous condition (Fig. 4). According to the inscription on the lobed arch of the mihrab the building was begun by Yawlāq Arslan and completed by his brother Artuk Arslan in the year 601 (1204) (Fig. 5). In external appearance and in several details there are obvious resemblances to the Great Mosque at Mayyafāriqīn. The mihrab dome has squinches each different from the other and has a diameter of 9.75 metres, 4 metres smaller than that of Mayyafāriqīn. (Plan 6.) The square minaret and the courtyard are in ruins, and only a few traces of the walls remain. The most meticulous care had been lavished on the construction of the building and its magnificent stonework, and the whole displays a wealth of architectural ornament. The cusped arches of the main door in two different colours of stone

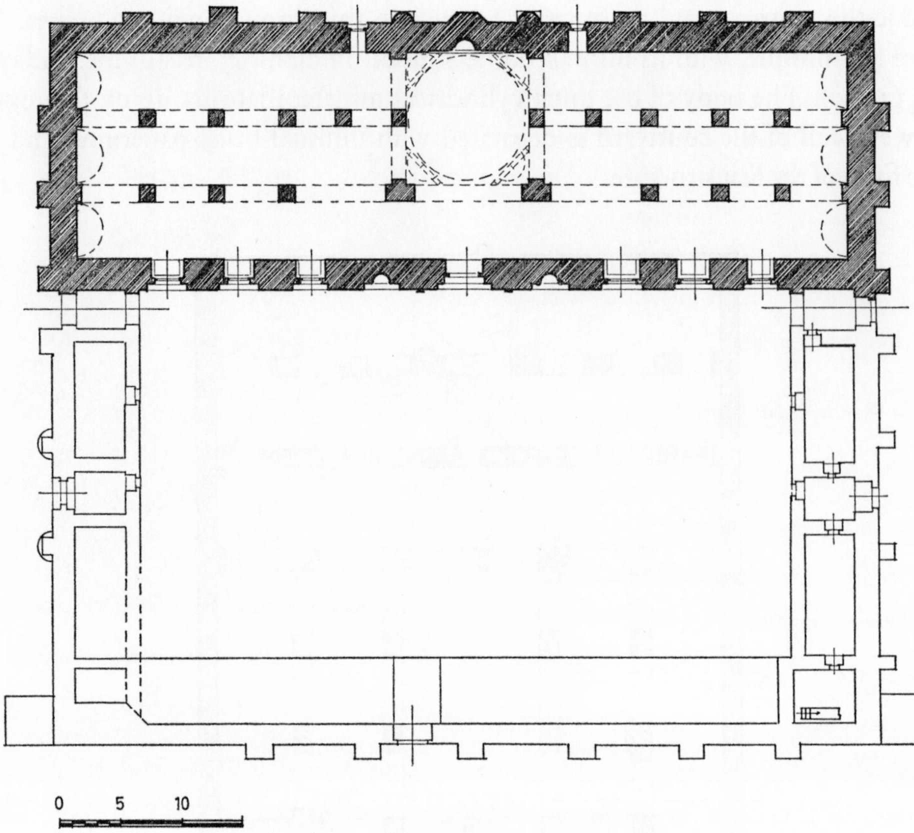

Plan 6. Kızıltepe (Dunaysir) Great Mosque

bear the imprint of Zengid architecture. Two external mihrabs on each side of the main door with different insets within the same composition recall the Great Mosque at Mayyafāriqīn. (Plate 5.) The main mihrab inside the mosque is surrounded by a lobed arch surmounted by a *naskhī* inscription, whilst a two-stepped niche terminating in a scallop shell shows the influence of Zengid architecture. In the niche itself, in addition to geometrical stars, delicate tendrils, foliate arabesques and palmettes, we find the motif of a lamp hanging on chains.

The Artukid mosques fuse Great Seljuk and Zengid influences in a powerful creative urge, and display the new style of Anatolian mosque architecture on a monumental scale. Various innovations were introduced in the second half of the twelfth century, such as the inclusion of a mihrab dome within the general plan and its dominating place in both the interior and exterior design, an arcaded courtyard, the reduction in the size of the courtyard and its inclusion as part of the interior, and cut stone masonry with its rich and varied decoration. The later periods of Anatolian Turkish architecture developed rapidly on the sound foundations laid by the Artukids.

The Great Mosque at Urfa was built on the site of an older mosque, and is in the form of a shallow rectangle with three rows of cross-vaulting on piers parallel to the qibla wall. The dome over the mihrab on squinches is a little to the east of the central axis. Because of the short, heavy piers the interior is low and depressing. The transverse-vaulted portico in front of the mosque opening out on to the courtyard through fourteen pointed arches is important in that this is the first appearance of this architectural feature in Anatolia. This mosque closely resembles the Great Mosque at Aleppo, the plan of which was given its present form by Nūr al-Dīn Zengī, and which must have been built by the Zengids in the third quarter of the 12th century. Part of the courtyard, which is very large and is surrounded by thick walls, was used as a cemetery. The octagonal minaret which stands on the north wall at a considerable distance from the mosque, may be an old bell-tower.

None of the 12th-century Danishmendid mosques have survived in their original form up to the present day. The Great Mosque at Niksar is mentioned by Evliya Çelebi under the name of the Mosque of Melik Gazi, by which name it is still known today. An old tradition places the date of its construction in the year 1145, but there is no inscription. Unlike the Artukid mosques it is a transverse-vaulted structure with five aisles lying parallel to the qibla wall. The original plan has been marred as a result of repairs, but its main features conform to the style of the 12th century. The mihrab, with its stalactite niche, is in Seljuk style, but the slightly off-centre portal is an Ottoman feature. As A. Gabriel has remarked, the Great Mosque at Niksar may serve as a souvenir of the Danishmendids, but it is of little architectural importance.

According to an inscription, the Danishmendid Great Mosque at Kayseri was built in the year 602/1205 during the reign of Kaykhusraw bin Qılıch Arslan by Muẓaffar al-Dīn Maḥmūd, son of the Emir Yaghıbasan. Nevertheless it is reasonable to suppose that this is merely a renovation inscription and that the first mosque would naturally be connected with Yaghıbasan himself in the middle of the 12th century. From the main features of the plan, which has been altered as the result of subsequent repairs, it was obviously a rather elongated structure with a mihrab dome and a small open dome in the centre, the whole being a smaller, closed version of the central courtyard of the Harput mosque. The main axis is defined by the junction of the open dome, which spans the strengthened piers and the empty space left by the intersection of the vaulting in the centre, with the mihrab dome. The whole building is dominated on the outside by the mihrab dome and the minaret rising from the middle of the west side. The thick cylindrical minaret on an octagonal plinth, the mihrab dome, the open dome and the squat pointed arches on thick, four-cornered piers are all typical of the 12th century.

Although the Kölük Mosque in Kayseri has also suffered from repairs it resembles the Great Mosque in the definition of the main axis by a dome on squinches over the mihrab and the small open dome with pendentives, as well as in its use of transverse vaulting, and it is possible that it also was founded by Yaghıbasan. (Plan 7.) An inscription mentions repairs carried out by Atsız Elti, the daughter of Maḥmūd bin Yaghıbasan, in the year 607/1210. The portal combines all the traditional elements, and displays, even at this early date, the mature composition of the later Seljuk portals.

Stone ornament was the prevailing feature in Kayseri architecture, and the magnificent mihrab of the Külük Mosque in faience mosaic possessing a delicacy of style that was to be

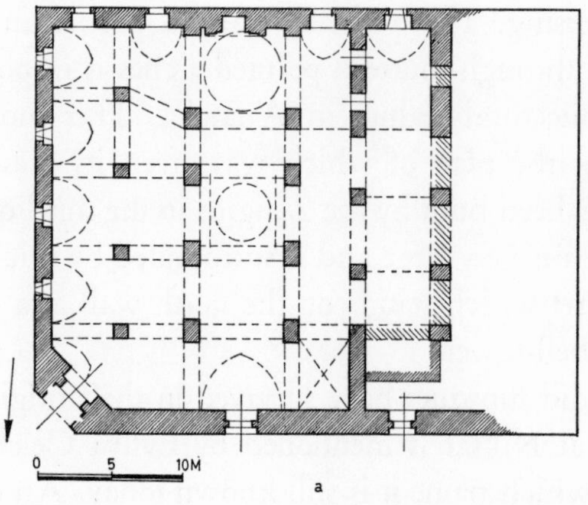

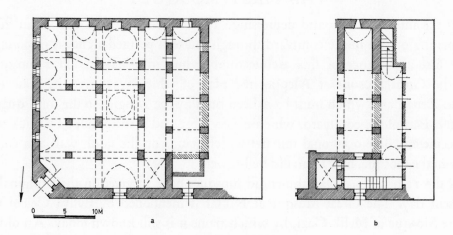

Plan 7. Kayseri, Kölük Mosque

attained only in the second half of the 13th century, remains unique. It must, therefore be later than the great faience mihrab in the ʿAlā al-Dīn Mosque in Konya. The colours, too, are richer. The corner pilasters and the meander border of an original stone mihrab are visible beneath the tile mihrab.

It is natural that the Danishmendids should have built a Great Mosque in their own capital of Sivas, and the mosque here has long been attributed to them, but during the repairs carried out in 1955 two Seljuk inscriptions were unearthed and published by Zeki Oral. According to one of them the mosque was built by Qızıl Arslan in the year 593/1197 during the reign of the ruler of Sivas, Quṭb al-Dīn Malikshāh, one of the sons of Qılıch Arslan II. A second inscription mentions the names of Kaykā'ūs bin Kaykhusraw and Yūsuf, and the date 609/1213. The beginning of the inscription is missing. A monumental impression is produced by the large area (31 × 51 metres) and the aisles perpendicular to the qibla. There is a shallow rectangular courtyard with two outer mihrabs indicating a portico and traces of the bases of its arches. (Plan 8.) The plan has preserved its old form, derived from the Danishmendids. Before the latest repairs traces of a stone mihrab with geometrical decorations composed of concentric octagons joined by two arms projecting from each of the sides were visible behind the brick mihrab. (Design 1.) The mosque is covered with a flat earthen roof, and from the outside the only remarkable feature is the minaret. This is a cylindrical structure of brick arranged in basket-work patterns and resting on an octagonal base. The minaret is encircled by a verse inscription in turquoise tiles in monumental plaited Kufic, and there is a second inscription band just below the balcony. The style and decoration of the minaret are in conformity with the date of the second inscription (1213). Compared with the Artukid mosques those of the Danishmendids introduced very little that was new.

The first known Saltukid mosque is an unusual type of masjid in the form of a domed mausoleum that dominates the Inner Citadel at Erzurum. The mihrab sunk in a half tower in the walls appears to be of disproportionate size, but is given its qibla orientation by the actual direction of the tower. (Plan 9.) Some idea of the quality of the original mihrab is

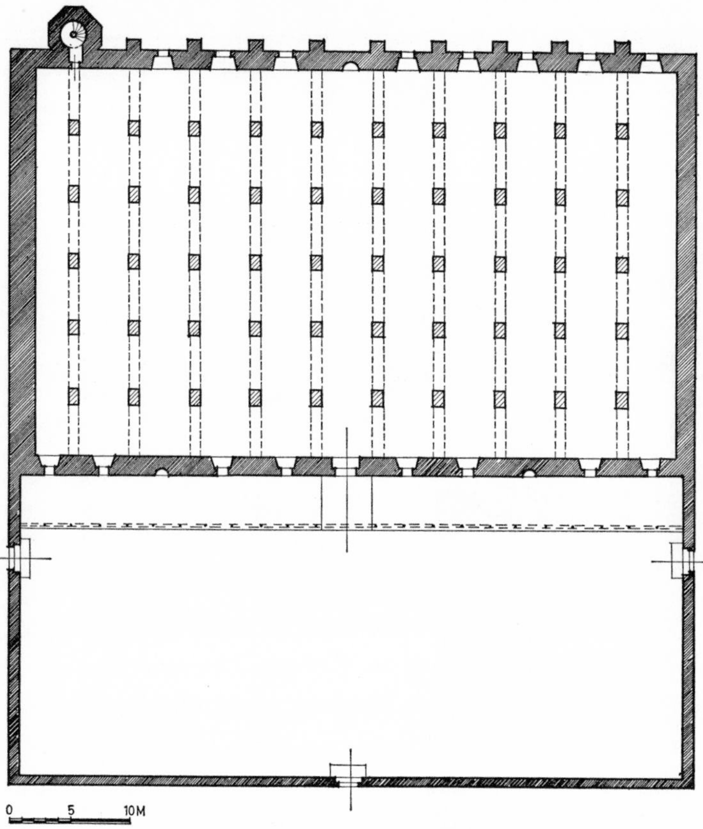

Plan 8. Sivas, Great Mosque

Design 1. Sivas, Great Mosque, stone mihrab

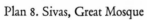

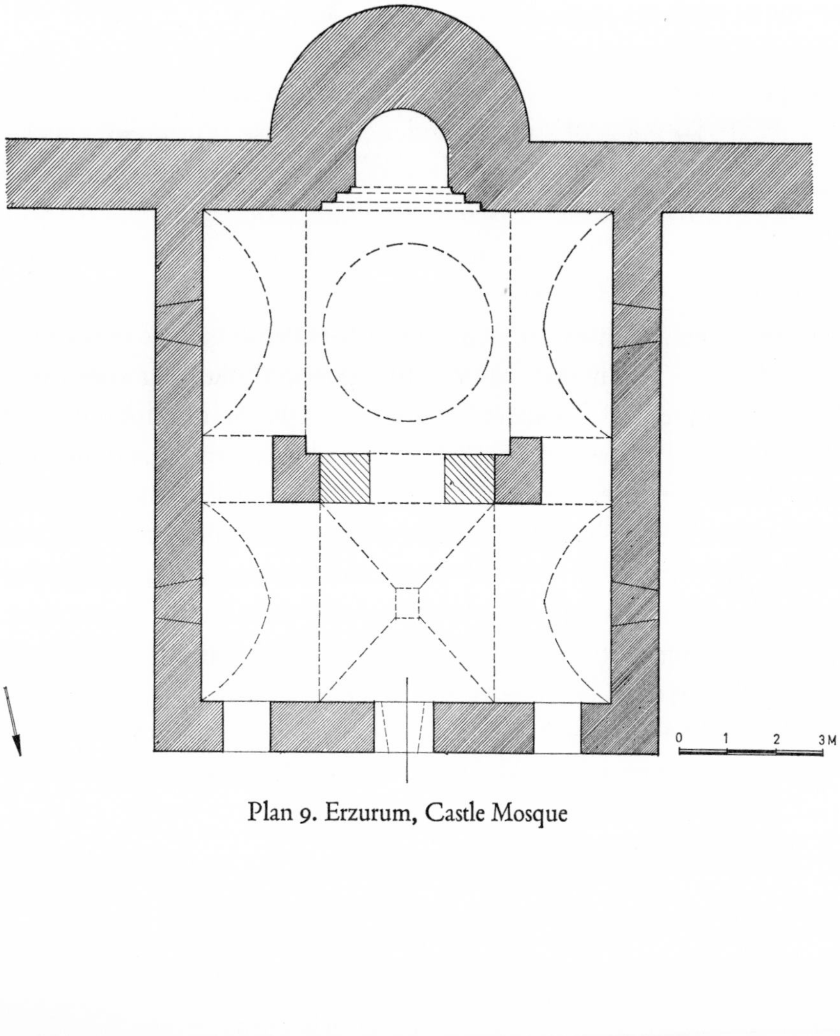

Plan 9. Erzurum, Castle Mosque

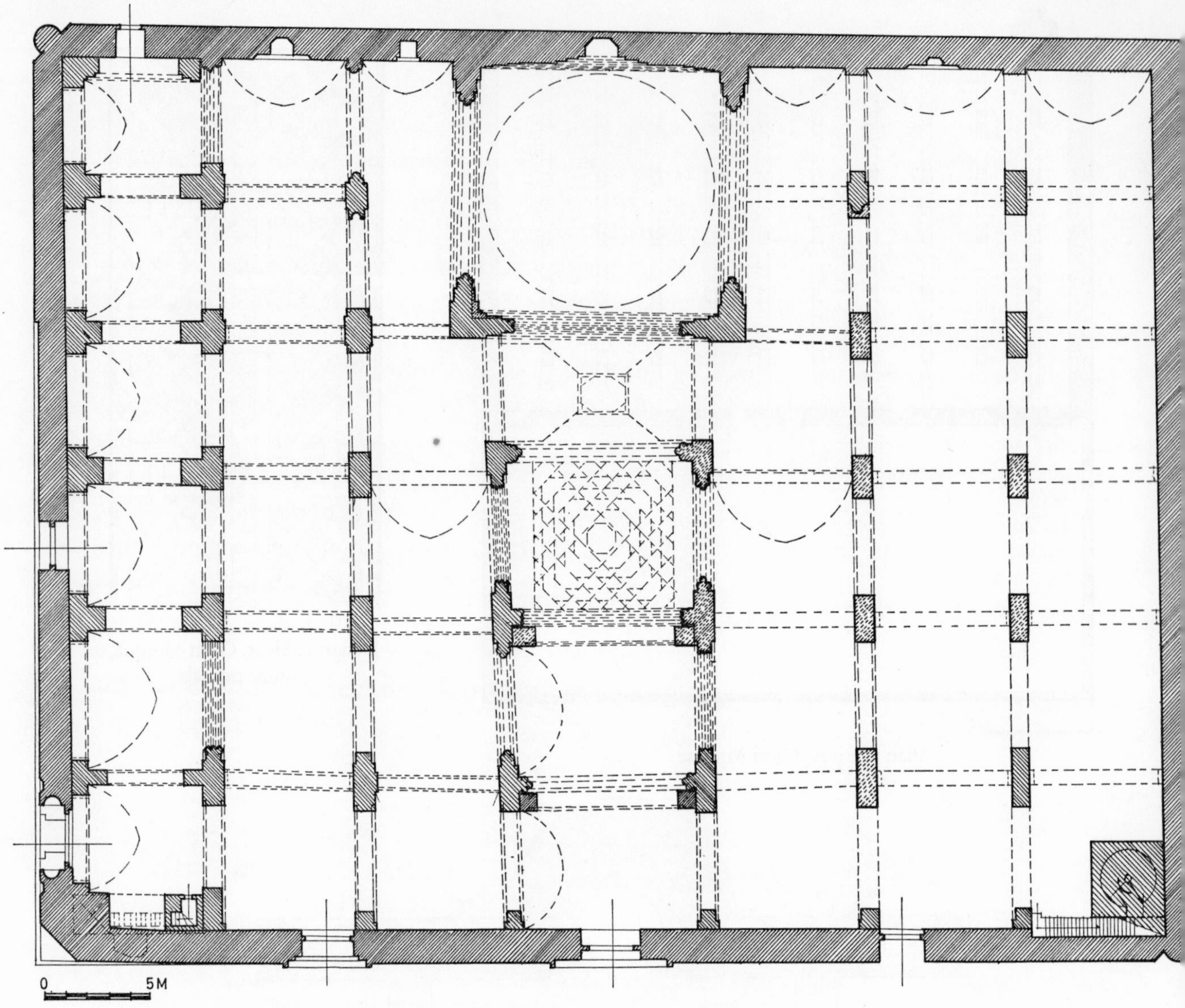

Plan 10. Erzurum, Great Mosque

given by the outer border, with its geometrical chain-patterning. The present mihrab is in the most striking bad taste. The masjid has no inscription. Quite near rises up the cylindrical brick tower known as the Tepsi Minare, which bears a Kufic inscription in carved brick on the upper edge beginning 'Inanch Beygü Alp Ṭughrul Bek', and mentions a patronymic 'bin Abū'l-Qāsim'. It has no date. As Abū'l-Qāsim was Atabek in the last quarter of the 11th century the Tepsi Minare must have been built towards the second half of the 12th century. The Kufic inscription, the brickwork and the general appearance are in agreement with a 12th century style. Although the Masjid may be attributed to the same century the similarity in external appearance between it and the Ahlat and Kayseri mausolea suggests that it took its final form in the 13th century.

The Great Mosque at Erzurum is a very simple building of cut stone without a courtyard. It has been spoilt as the result of several repairs, five of which are recorded in the inscriptions.

There is now a wooden dome in front of the mihrab in place of the large dome with pendentives that used to rest on light pointed arches with stepped mouldings and *tori.* Its designation in the oldest repair inscription, dated 1639, as the Atabek mosque points to the Saltukid period. In his *Tarihçe-i Erzurum* (History of Erzurum) Nüsret mentions having read on an old panel that the mosque had been built by Abū'l-Fatḥ Muḥammad in 575/1179. Lynch also saw this inscription. It is quite impossible that the present dome and vaulting system could have been constructed during repairs. From the point of view of the development of style it seems reasonable to suppose that in its general features it shows the continuation of a Saltukid mosque plan of the 12th century (Plan 10), with repairs made by modifying to some extent the old dome and vaulting system. The mihrab wall is obviously old. The wide rectangular border surrounding the simple stalactite mihrab niche is ornamented in high relief with braid motifs produced by intersecting octagons. These produce an unusual kind of composition by linking large octagons in groups of four. (Design 2.) Some of the old stones carved in this way were used in repair work above the inner arch of the door on the north wall. The other surviving examples of Saltukid mosques are far from providing any sound information on the general plan of the buildings of the dynasty.

The oldest building of the Mengüjükids is the little Castle Mosque at Divriği, built, according to its inscription, by Shāhanshāh in year 576/1180–1. A signature gives the name of Ḥasan bin Fīrūz of Maragha, thus showing that the architect was from Azerbaidzhan. This

Design 2. Erzurum, Great Mosque, stone mihrab

small 12th-century mosque is particularly important in that its date is definitely known and the plan has not been altered in any way. It has a long rectangular plan with central vaults perpendicular to the qibla and side aisles having four domes set on pendentives. The stepped porch niche with inscriptions and various decorations in stone and brick is very striking. (Fig. 6.) The wide border surrounding it is carved with a geometrical design composed of braided patterns produced by the intersection of elongated hexagons (Design 3). The turquoise tiles

Design 3. Divriği, Castle Mosque, decoration of porch

placed in the hexagonal spaces produced by the patterning of the bricks in the spandrels of the door arch are remarkable as being, together with those on the Siirt minaret, the first examples of tile decoration in Anatolia. The pediment (lunette) of the brick arch is also covered with star-shaped octagonal interlaces. The door-frames and the capitals of the corner pilasters have been most skilfully decorated with scrolls, foliate arabesques and palmettes as well as geometrical designs. There is a side door on the north side of the west wall made completely of stone and having very simple decoration. In the niche arch overlapping rows of hexagons are linked by double arms projecting from their sides. Besides this large hexagons formed by these arms link the smaller hexagons together (Design 4). This little mosque, in

Design 4. Divriği, Castle Mosque, decoration of side entrance

which brick and stone are still used together in the façade, and floriated Kufic, geometrical and plant motifs are once more utilised, is indeed filled with creative fervour.

In contrast to its ornate exterior, the interior architecture is simple and impressive, with a mihrab niche surmounted by a scallop-niche and capitals adorned with a palmette-lotus frieze and stylised lions' heads. The symmetrical system of roofing the different sections of the three-aisled space with equal domes and vaulting is an innovation. (Fig. 7.) The mosque has no courtyard. An inscription in the name of Sulaymān bin Shāhanshāh and the carved wooden minbar were taken to another mosque and are now lost; only a piece of the door-frame with a few interlacing ornaments and an incomplete inscription have survived.

The largest Mengüjükid building at Divriği is the Great Mosque complex containing a hospital built by Aḥmad Shāh, the grandson of Shāhanshāh, in 626/1228–9. This is full of innovations, and of a feeling of joy in creation. (Fig. 8.) An inscription on the main north porch mentions the name of ʿAlā al-Dīn Kayqubād and recognises Aḥmad Shāh as being under the suzerainty of the Seljuk Sultan. According to an inscription on the hospital, which is contiguous to the mosque on the south side, this part of the complex was built by Malika Turan Malik, the daughter of Bahram Shāh of the Erzincan and Kemah Mengüjükids, and the wife of Aḥmad Shāh. On the exterior the whole building is dominated by the folded pyramidal roof covering the mihrab dome. Sixteen of the vaults are original, the others having undergone repairs, and the slim octagonal piers supporting them have been strengthened by thick stone sheaths (Plan 11). A cistern or ice-house was dug under the central section. The

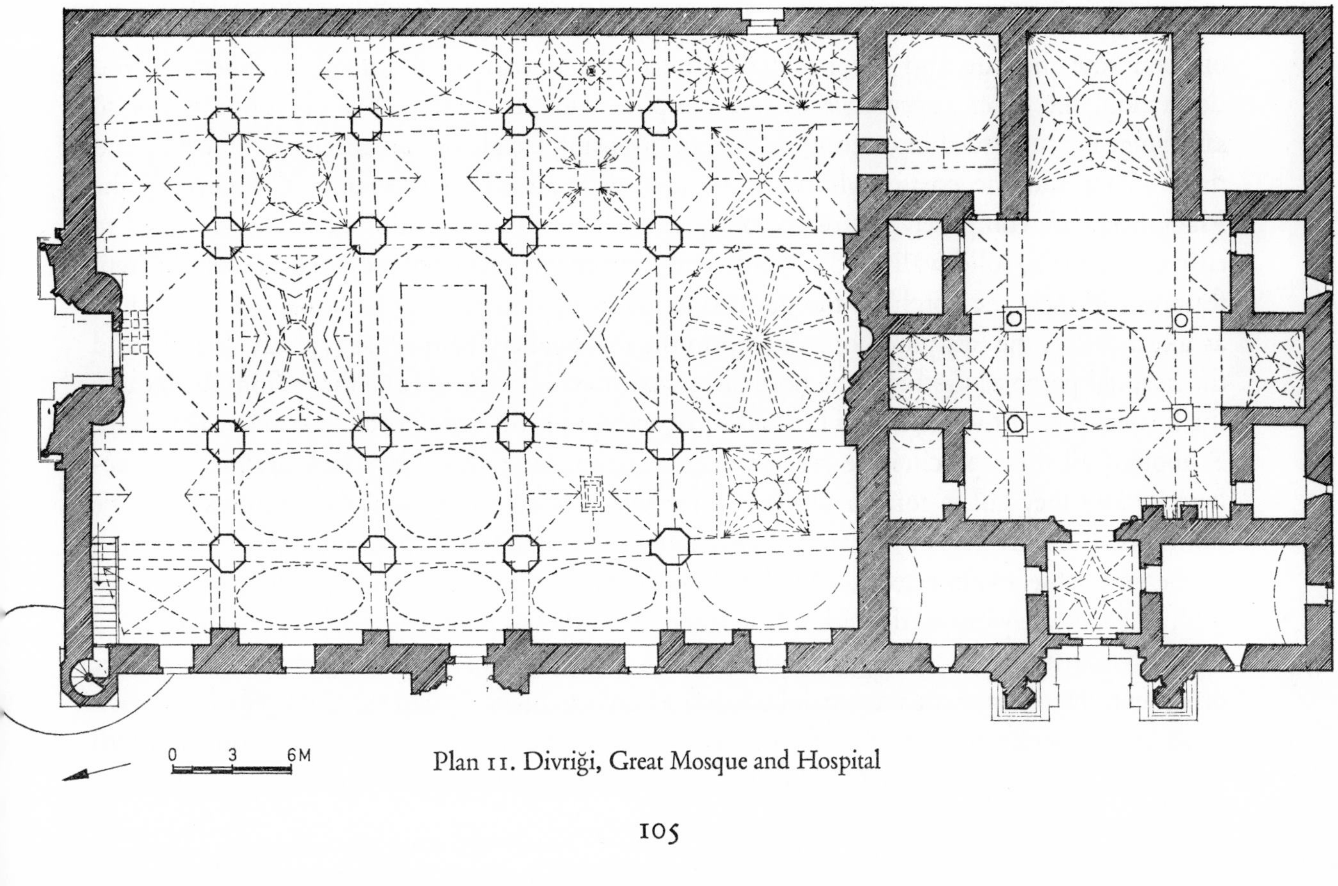

Plan 11. Divriği, Great Mosque and Hospital

central area with its stone vaulting and its sculptural ornament of bold palmettes and geometrical braided designs is rich and impressive in appearance. (Fig. 11.) The stone mihrab is very strongly defined and is set in a very large but simple niche containing rows of large baroque palmettes in high relief that seem to leap out of the wall, and surrounded by powerful mouldings. This is the only mihrab of such dimensions and of such richness of decoration to survive in Anatolia. (Fig. 12.)

The magnificent ebony minbar is the work of Aḥmad of Tiflis, and was constructed 12 years after the completion of the mosque. (Fig. 13.) The minbar is built up of rows of geometrical stars worked with delicate foliate arabesques and scrolls. Its style is much more advanced than that of the minbar of the Castle Mosque and resembles a collection of calligraphy, with as many as twenty inscriptions in relief in various types of composition. We have no information, however, about the calligrapher Muḥammad, whose first name only is mentioned in the inscription. Of the royal gallery, which was constructed of wood and had a separate door on the east side, only the floor beams remain.

The hospital is much more successful architecturally than the adjoining mosque, and is at the same time monumental in appearance and simple, peaceful and attractive in effect. (Fig. 15.) It preserves its original form and belongs architecturally to the group of domed medreses. There is an open lantern in the central section. (Fig. 16.)

A chamber in the north-east corner opening on to the mosque is a tomb. The dome may have originally been covered with a conical roof. The word 'Allāh' and designs similar to foliate arabesques can be seen on the gilt, semi-hexagonal turquoise tiles on some of the cenotaphs it contains. Although the architect Khurramshāh of Ahlat, whose name is recorded on both the mosque and the hospital, created a masterpiece of interior architecture and decoration, the outer appearance of the complex with its light yellow cut stone is not so satisfying. He succeeded in creating neither an imposing façade nor an effective silhouette; and the minaret and the coarse cylindrical buttress wall added in the reign of Süleyman the Magnificent are completely out of harmony with the rest of the building. It was intended to enliven the plain, solid walls of the façade with four magnificent porches each having different features. Of these the porch on the north side might be described as baroque, the west porch as like a textile, the east porch opening on to the royal gallery behind, as typically Seljuk, and the hospital porch as Gothic. The north and west porches protrude one metre from the façade, the hospital porch two metres; whilst all three, except for the west porch, rise above the walls. Although all these porches are masterpieces in contrasting styles they lack architectural coherence and they fail to form a unified whole with the architecture of the complex. On the north porch the surfaces of the large, powerfully plastic, exuberant, baroque-type designs, such as the very loosely connected double leaves, palmettes, lotuses and round panels, are covered with very delicately carved flowers, foliate arabesques and star patterns.

The western porch produces a quieter effect with its more delicate designs and surface ornament. The deep niche has a trilobed arch set on ornamental pilasters, and is filled with rich prismatic stalactites reminiscent of woodwork. A double-headed, stylised eagle on the north side of the wall may have been the blazon of ʿAlā al-Dīn Kayqubād, whilst a falcon standing on one leg with its head to one side on the adjacent wall may have been the blazon of Aḥmad Shāh. (Fig. 9.)

The east porch would appear to have been built in 1241, at the same time as the minbar, and is in classical Seljuk style. (Fig. 10.)

The hospital porch completely dominates the western façade with its Gothic magnificence and opens out invitingly through a wide pointed arch. The large sculptured designs in high relief are less numerous and resemble those of the north porch. (Fig. 14.) On the large circular mouldings to each side of the portal are portrayed two human heads similar to the symbolic figures to be found in other Seljuk hospitals. One of these has been partially erased. The figure with long plaited hair represents the moon, the other represents the sun. Two other human heads can be seen sunk between the mouldings on the inner left side of the entrance. It has been suggested that these are portraits of Aḥmad Shāh and his wife, Turan Malik, but this theory seems most unlikely.

The mosque, hospital and tomb form together the oldest complex foundation in Anatolia. It is full of the most surprising innovations, and shows some similarities to buildings constructed only in the second half of the century. But this brilliant architectural achievement of the Mengüjükids remained as a regional style with little further development. Its ornament is the translation into stone of the plastic style of the stucco work so highly developed by the Great Seljuks in Iran—as for example the interior of the Gunbadh-i ʿAlawiyyān at Hamadhān, the stucco mihrab in the Friday Mosque at Ardistan and the stucco mihrab in the tomb of Pīr Ḥamza Sabz Pūsh at Abarqūh. It is obvious from the innumerable tombstones to be found at Ahlat that the architect Khurramshāh's native town was one of the oldest and richest centres of stonework in Anatolia. It seems likely that he brought from there the originality and technical ingenuity of the ancient craftsmanship and drew up a work programme for the masons. Basing themselves on Great Seljuk architecture the Mengüjükids thus created for themselves an original style in the form of a truly magnificent synthesis. The same questing spirit finds expression in the Great Mosque and its complex at Divriği, where various influences are fused in a dynamic creative urge.

Seljuk Mosques in Anatolia

From the 13th century onwards Seljuk architecture gradually developed into the prevailing style of architecture in Anatolia. The plan of the ʿAlā al-Dīn Mosque in Konya was modified with the passage of time, and fails to form an organic whole. The inscriptions of Sultan Masʿūd and Qılıch Arslan II on the magnificent ebony minbar constructed for the first mosque in 550/1155 also mention the name of the master builder Mengüberti of Ahlat. (Fig. 20.) This minbar is the oldest inscribed and dated Seljuk work of art, and one would expect the mosque that contained it to possess an architecture worthy of it. But as a matter of fact the mosque is divided between two very different periods. It combines the mihrab dome and flat roofed iwan of traditional Turkish architecture with six parallel aisles on columns on the east side, and four on the west (Plan 12). Beside the domed area stands a decagonal tomb built by Qılıch Arslan

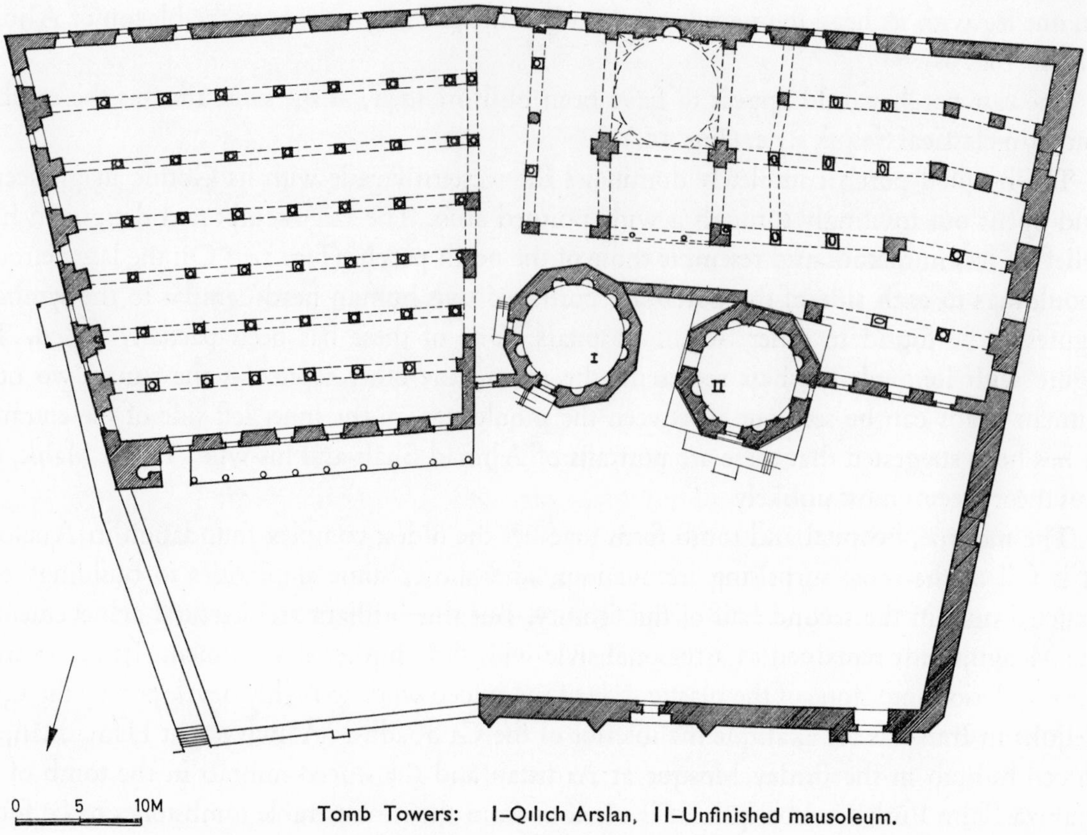

Plan 12. Konya, Mosque of ʿAlā al-Dīn

together with a half-finished octagonal mausoleum, whilst to the north lies a courtyard embracing all sections within a monumental façade. On this façade, which is covered by so many inscriptions that it resembles an exhibition of calligraphy, the names of the two master-craftsmen Muḥammad Ḥawlān al-Dimishqī and Karīm al-Dīn Erdishāh occurs, together with those of the Atabek Ayāz and two Seljuk Sultans Kaykā'ūs I and Kayqubād I. The gradual heightening from left to right of the niche arches resting on re-used columns in the upper sections is an unusual feature. (Fig. 17.) The porch is set high in the wall and dominates the whole façade with its composition of geometrical knotted interlacing patterns in bi-coloured stone and marble derived from Zengid architecture. The tympanum above the inscription is filled with star and cross motifs resembling the ancient fourfold braid motif produced by intersecting octagons. But it is doubtful if this porch, the doorway of which has been filled in with cut stone, was ever used as an entrance, since there is no passage from the courtyard façade into the mosque itself. The architect was from Damascus and brought with him Zengid ornamental features. On the mausoleum of Qılıch Arslan, in which the Seljuk sultans are buried, is mentioned the name of the architect Yūsuf bin ʿAbd al-Ghaffār of Khojand.

The most important section of the mosque from the point of view of architecture and ornament is the domed interior. In the repairs of 1891 an extremely ugly mihrab in white marble was placed right in the centre of the old mihrab, and today only the upper half of the mihrab and the triangular panels of ceramic mosaic in the transition to the dome survive. The style and technique of the geometrical and plant designs in turquoise, cobalt, and manganese-purple faience mosaic is too highly developed for the early date of the minbar, and conforms more to the date of the completion of the mosque, which, according to an inscription in the name of ʿAlā al-Dīn Kayqubād, was in 616 (1219). (Fig. 19.)

According to the theory proposed by F. Sarre in 1910 and supported by D. Lamb in 1915, the wide columned hall on the east must originally have been a courtyard. They claim that in spite of the restorations this section is more recent than the others and must have been added as an afterthought to the original plan. On the other hand we have the view put forward by C. E. Arseven in 1926—which is once more becoming generally accepted—that the multi-columned section is the original structure. (Fig. 18.) This section is in a primitive style of architecture with pointed arches and re-used columns supporting a flat roof, and may be regarded as having been included in the plan as a passage leading to the mosque and to the domed mausoleum in which the Seljuk Sultans were buried, which at the same time would provide space for a large congregation. It is reasonable to suppose that the mihrab dome should be the kernel of the first Seljuk mosque. During the repairs and additions begun by Kaykā'ūs I and completed in the reign of Kayqubād I the piered section on the west was probably built first, and the seven-aisled hall on the east later. Although ʿAlā al-Dīn Kayqubād is mentioned in the inscriptions as having merely completed the building the fact that the whole structure is known as the ʿAlā al-Dīn Mosque would seem to indicate that the tile decoration, the mihrab and the monumental façade on the north were his work. The half-finished octagonal mausoleum belongs to the same period.

Another Seljuk work dating back to the beginning of the 13th century is the mosque at Akşehir, which has been very much damaged by repairs. It has a plan similar to that of a mosque at Develi with aisles perpendicular to the qibla on piers and columns and a mihrab dome. According to the inscription on the minaret, which rises in the form of a thick cylindrical shaft on an octagonal base, it was built in the reign of Kaykā'ūs I in 610/1213. Remains of the old tile decorations can be seen in the niches on the base. The mosque is recorded in a *waqfiyya* or deed of endowment as having been enlarged and repaired by ʿAlā al-Dīn Kayqubād I. In the course of recent repairs the original mihrab was revealed beneath the plaster. This is in an early style of decoration using only geometrical designs in turquoise and manganese-purple. The words 'Allāh' and 'Allāhu akbar' ('God is great') in corrupt *thuluth* are repeated in a broad inscription band under the faience stalactites.

The mosque of ʿAlā al-Dīn Kayqubād at Niğde survives in its original plan, and combines all the features of traditional Seljuk mosque architecture in their original form. The aisles are neither parallel to the qibla wall nor exactly perpendicular to it. A compromise has been achieved. (Plan 13.) The monumental main door, which is much higher than the lateral wall, is on the east side, whilst there is a second smaller porch beside the minaret on the north-east corner. (Fig. 21.) An open lantern in the central section is a reminder of the old open

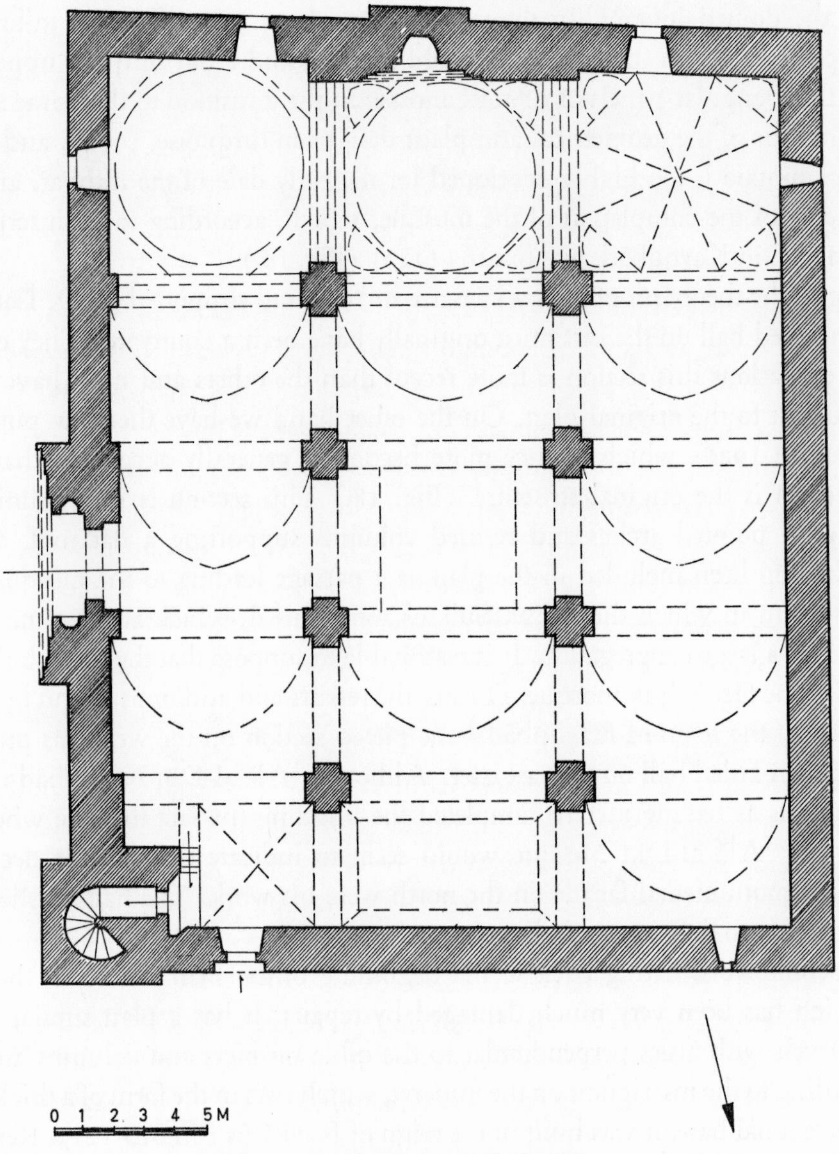

Plan 13. Niğde, Mosque of ʿAlā al-Dīn

courtyard of earlier Turkish mosques. The interior is embellished by various types of ornament in the three domes. The mihrab dome rests on stone squinches with stalactite insets. The ornament on the mihrab contains no vegetal motifs, being composed entirely of geometrical stars, entrelacs and braid designs and rosettes. The interior of the niche has been left empty. The clumsy, tasteless minbar was added later. The minaret is original as far as the balcony. The magnificent porch is almost entirely covered with ornament. In an inscription on the porch it is recorded that it was constructed by Bishāra bin ʿAbd Allāh in the year 620/1223, during the reign of Sultan ʿAlā al-Dīn Kayqubād I. (The Besharebek Masjid in Konya was built by Imrahor Zayd al-Dīn Bishārabek.) Beneath this are two human portraits in high relief with long plaits of hair hanging down each side of their faces, and between them is the builder's inscription in which the names of master Ṣidq bin Maḥmūd and his brother Ghāzī are mentioned. At the top of the arch in the central section of the mosque the architect's name is mentioned once more as the builder Ṣidq bin Maḥmūd. In sum, the 'Alā al-Dīn Mosque at Niğde represents an important development and a serious step towards combining the various traditional features of Anatolian Seljuk mosque architecture. The empty, heavy, archaic effect of the interior is softened to some extent by an open lantern and the exterior ornament.

It seems that the Great Mosque in Malatya was built by 'Alā al-Dīn Kayqubād in 1224, but that the plan and architecture were altered during modifications begun a quarter of a century later. The richest and most important brick sections, such as the dome over the mihrab, which reveals the true quality of the original structure, and the iwan and pooled courtyard adjoining it, survive from the first mosque. (Fig. 22.) It derives directly from the Great Seljuk mosques of Iran (the mosque, for example, at Zaware) both in plan and in the quality of the brickwork. (Fig. 23.) According to an inscription the architect was Ya'qūb bin Abū Bakr of Malatya. (Fig. 24.) The whole of the iwan façade is enlivened by turquoise and manganese-purple tile mosaics and inscriptions. The vaulting of the iwan, which is joined to the domed interior by means of prismatic triangles, is decorated with large geometrical forms resembling Kufic script produced by the unusual patterning of the bricks. Beneath a Koranic inscription in tile mosaic the name of the calligrapher is given, 'kataba Aḥmad bin Ya'qūb' ('Aḥmad bin Ya'qūb wrote this'). The brick dome is supported on an octagonal drum with the tripartite squinches first seen in the Karakhanid tomb of Arab Ata and continued in the Great Seljuk mosques. Inside the dome the bricks are arranged in the form of a spiral, with a 6-pointed interlacing star (seal of Solomon) in the centre, and a *naskhī* inscription round the 16-sided drum. All the sections later added to the mosque were constructed of stone and surround the original brick structure. Although the salient stone monumental western porch has undergone repairs it has preserved its architectural value. An inscription records that it was built by Shihāb al-Dīn Ilyās in 645/1247, during the reign of Kaykā'ūs II, and mentions Ustādh Khusraw as the name of another master-builder. The eastern porch is in a simpler style, and a great deal of space is given to foliate motifs in addition to geometrical interlacing patterns. An inscription records that the mosque was repaired in 672/1273–4 and again mentions Ustādh Khusraw as the master-builder. The porches and surrounding walls of the original mosque must have been of stone, but have undergone repairs and modifications. A *naskhī* inscription in the section walled off from the rest of the mosque mentions the foundation of a Qayṣariyya,[1] or hostel, and gives the titles of a Mamluk, Al-Maqarr al-Ashraf al-Sayfī al-Qushlī. At the end of the 14th century Malatya was under Mamluk suzerainty. From the style of the architecture it would appear that this addition, together with the dome behind the east porch and the porch in the south wall, was made at this time. (Plan 14.)

It has been aptly suggested that the magnificent inscription ornamented with haphazardly arranged rows of scrolls and arabesques on the wall of the Saray or Ali Bey Mosque in the new town of Malatya is the remains of the inscription from the Great Mosque of 'Alā al-Dīn

[1] Possibly the inscription reads 'hadhā'l-qayṣariyya al-mubāraka . . .', i.e. it relates to the foundation of a *qayṣariyya* or lock-up market.

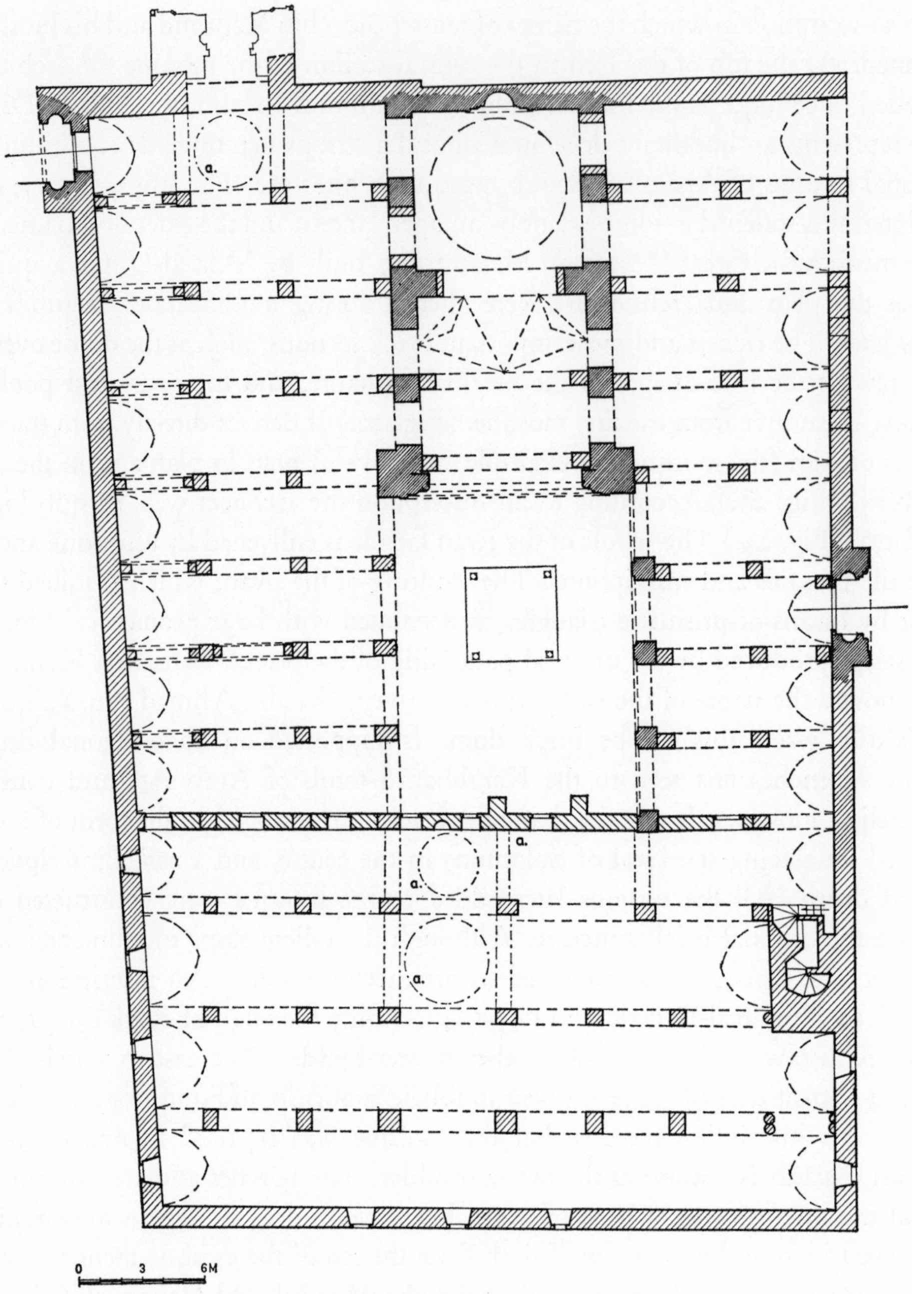

Plan 14. Malatya, Great Mosque

Kayqubād. This may well have belonged to a porch in the north façade that was later removed during the alterations carried out in the Mamluk period.

Although the Great Mosque at Malatya thus displays four different periods of architecture, it adopted, with some modifications, the plan and architecture of the Great Seljuk Mosques of Iran at a time of the most vigorous development of Seljuk architecture, and may be described as the only structure still remaining in Anatolia that provides a direct link with them.

The Khwand foundation at Kayseri is the first complex built by the Anatolian Seljuks and consists of a mosque, a medrese, a mausoleum and a hammam. It was completed by Mahperi Khātūn the wife of Kayqubād I in the year 636/1238 during the reign of her son Kaykhusraw II. It is built entirely of cut stone. The definition of the main axis by means of the mihrab dome, the iwan and the small square courtyard links it to the Great Mosque at Malatya, whilst the extension of the mihrab section towards the sides places it in the same category as the Great Mosques of Erzurum and Kayseri. The symmetry of the mosque plan

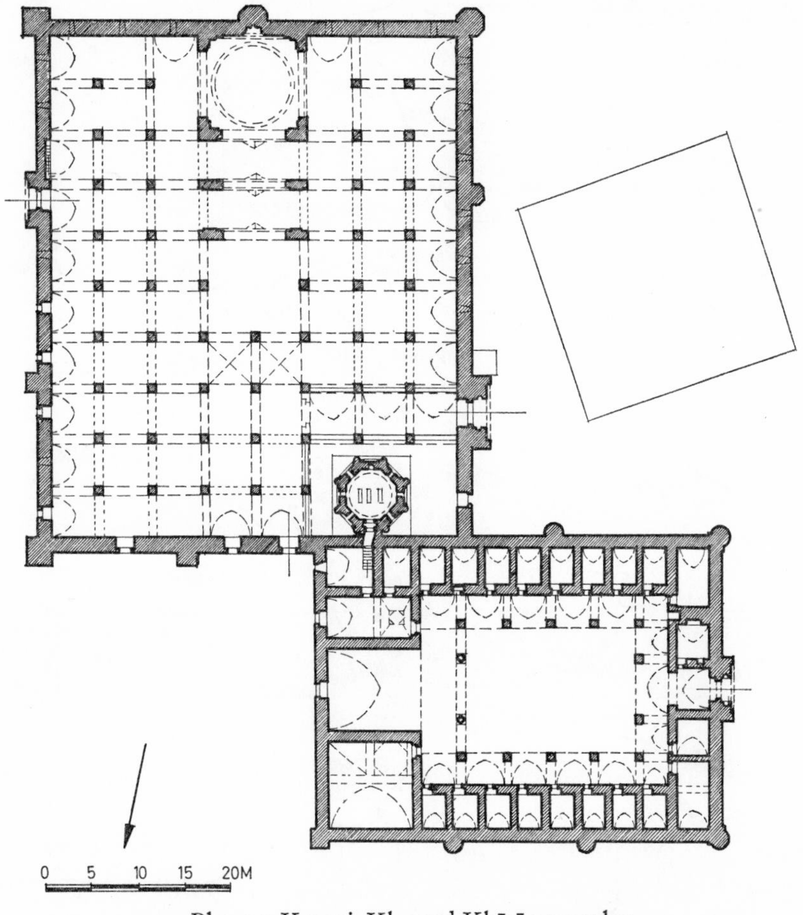

Plan 15. Kayseri, Khwand Khātūn complex

has, however, been spoilt by the addition of the octagonal domed mausoleum in the north-west corner. The medrese is joined to the mosque at the same point. (Plan 15.) The solid buttresses at the corners and sides give the mosque the appearance of a castle entered by two gates. The larger and more monumental western porch is remarkable for its geometrical decoration and its marble inscription. The eastern porch, which carries the original foundation inscription, is simpler in style. The composition of the mihrab is most unusual, and the absence of any inscriptions and, apart from the acanthus capitals, the preponderance of geometrical ornament is a surprising feature. The continual appearance of new forms in the Seljuk mihrabs testifies to the creative vigour of their art.

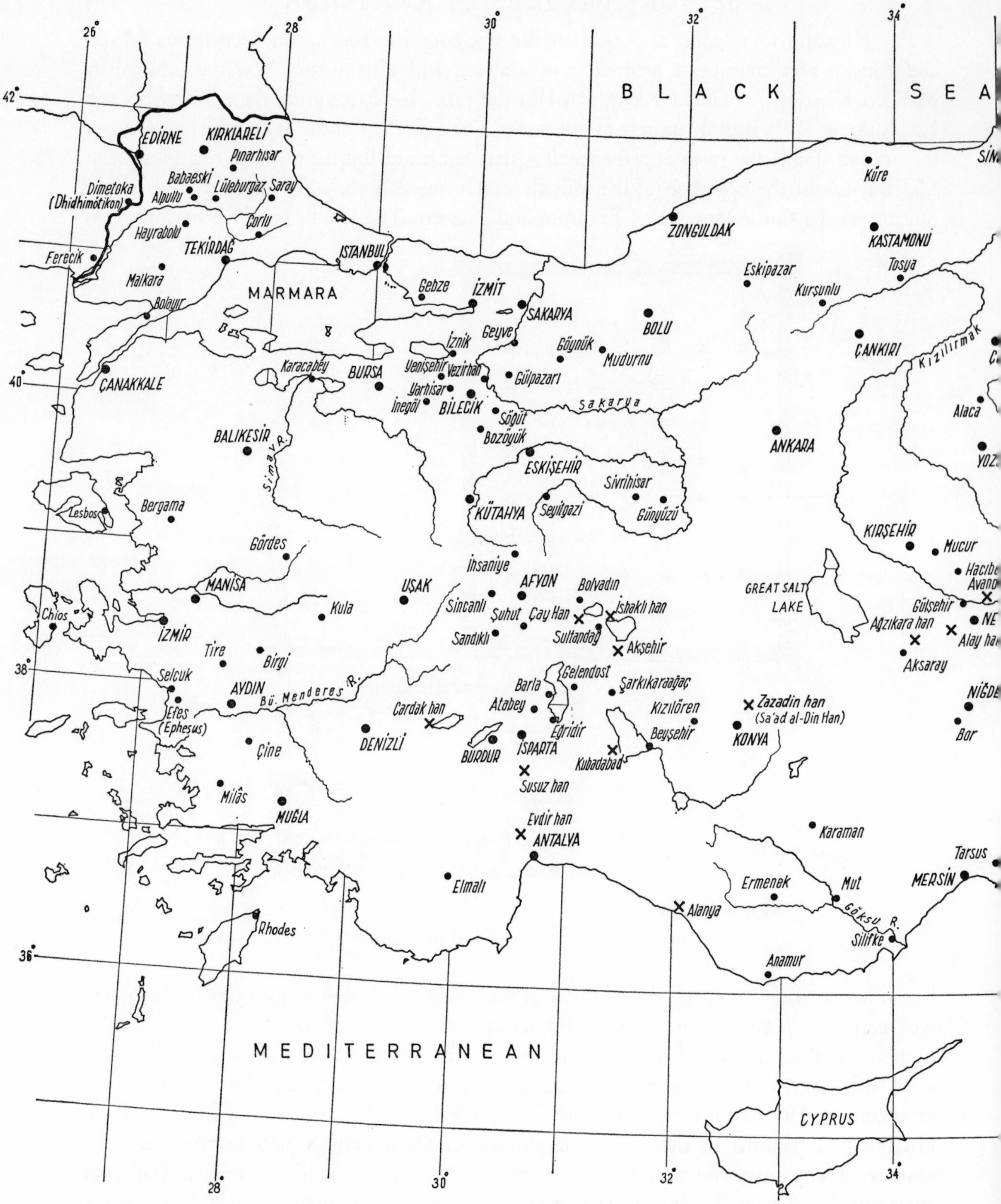

MAP II The Turkish Republic

ARTVİN
Şavşa
Ardahan
KARS
Oltu
Sarıkamış
Erevan
RİZE
TRABZON
GİRESUN
ORDU
Yeşilırmak
Niksar
GÜMÜŞANE
Çoruh R.
İspir
Bayburt
TOKAT
Pasinler
Araxes R.
Iğdır
Aşkale
Tercan
ERZURUM
ERZİNCAN
AĞRI
Doğubayazid
SİVAS
Kemah
Divriği
Patnos
Malazgirt
Erciş
Muradiye
TUNCELİ
Mazgirt
BİNGÖL
Pertek
Harput
ELAZIĞ
Murat R.
MUŞ
Ahlat
LAKE VAN
VAN
Fethiye Köyü
Pazarören
Darende
MALATYA
Elbistan
BİTLİS
Gevaş
Başkale
Silvan (Mayyafāriqīn)
DİYARBEKİR
SİİRT
Tigris
Ḥiṣn Kayfā
HAKKARİ
ADIYAMAN
MARAŞ
Ceyhan R.
Euphrates
MARDİN
Nusaybin
Kızıltepe
(Dunyasir)
GAZİANTEP
Birecik
URFA
Harran
Payas
0
100
200 Km.
38°
40°
42°
44°
36°

Another Seljuk complex is the Hacı Kılıç mosque at Kayseri, dated 647/1249, in which mosque and medrese have been fused and an arcaded courtyard is shared by both. It was built by Abū'l-Qāsim of Tūş, one of Kayqubād I's emirs, whose own tomb is at Tokat. (Plan 16.) In the mosque the mihrab dome and the central aisle are well defined. The two porches in the form of salient masses on the east façade of the mosque and medrese conform to the classical type of Seljuk porch. Inside the mosque the original architectural decoration can be seen only in the stone mihrab. There are no inscriptions. Apart from geometrical star

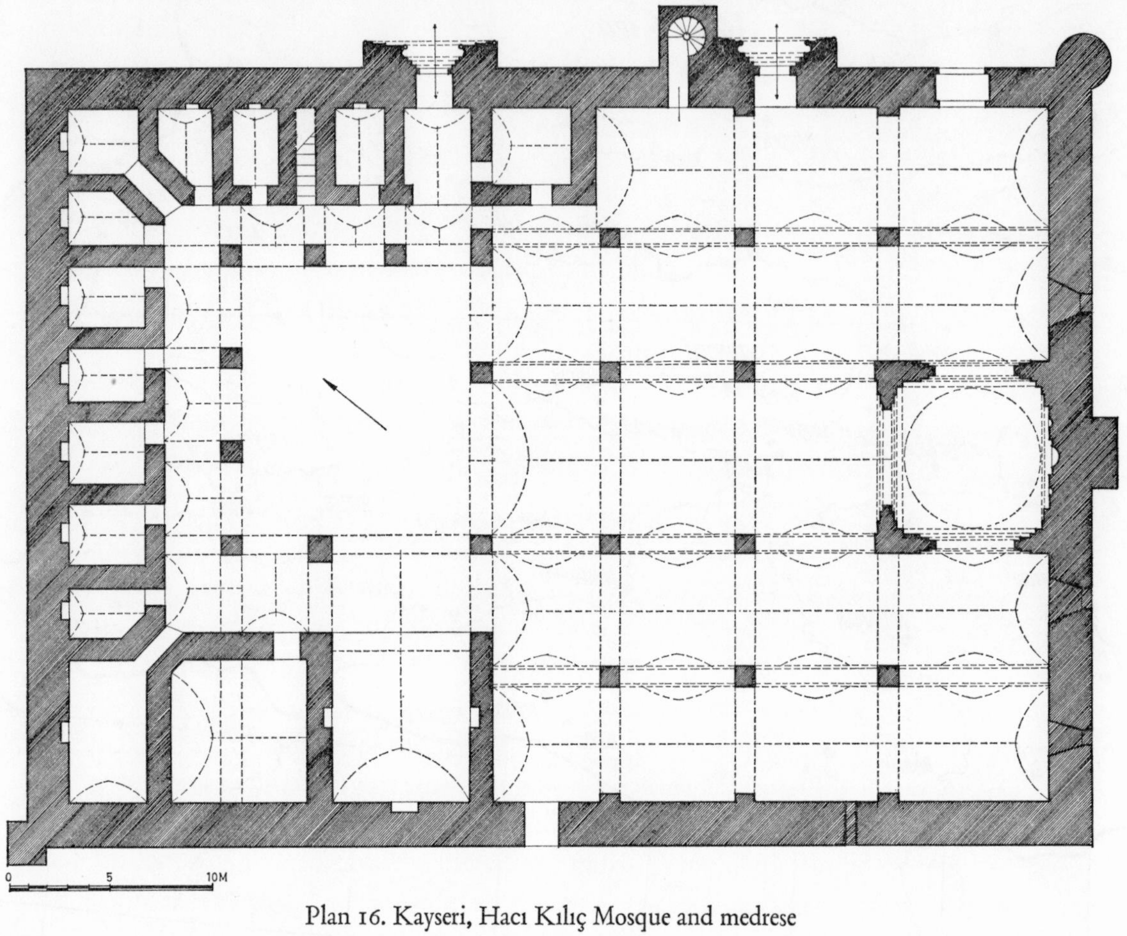

Plan 16. Kayseri, Hacı Kılıç Mosque and medrese

patterns, entrelacs and foliate arabesques, and *tori*, the geometrical knotted interlacing motifs of Zengid ornament are repeated above the pointed niche arches and in the corner fillings. These are here seen for the second time in Anatolia, their first appearance being on the courtyard façade of the ʿAlā al-Dīn Mosque at Konya; they then reappear on the porch façade of the Karatay Medrese at Konya.

The Burmalı Minare (Spiral Minaret) Mosque at Amasya was built during the reign of Kaykhusraw II by his vizir Farrūḥ and his brother the Treasurer Yūsuf in 634–44/1237–47. It is constructed entirely of cut stone and has three aisles perpendicular to the qibla. The wider central aisle in front of the mihrab is roofed by three domes, whilst the side aisles are vaulted and are less than half the width of the central one. The porch in the form of a rather deep iwan with slightly pointed arches is a little off centre. On the east side there is an octagonal mausoleum adjoining the wall, whilst on the west side there is a spiral minaret which was added at a later date. An inscription carved into the ground of one of the square green-glazed tiles surrounding the mihrab mentions the name of a master-builder from Aksaray, Muḥammad bin Maḥmūd al-Āqsarāyī. The Spiral Minaret Mosque adjoining the tomb has been deformed by various repairs, and it is impossible to see what the original plan was.

The thick hewn stone walls of the little-known Great Mosque at Bünyan, a small town in the vilayet of Kayseri, produce the effect of a castle. The mosque has three aisles resting on four piers with arches perpendicular to the qibla, and is covered with a flat wooden roof. The most important feature of the mosque is the porch, with its inscription and its ornament. It is astonishing to find in a mosque stylised figures of gryphons' and lions' heads amongst scrolls, in addition to geometrical and vegetal decoration, and ornament resembling plaited Kufic. According to the only partially legible inscription in Seljuk *thuluth* the mosque was built by the architect Kāluyān bin (?) Karabuda in the year 654/1256 on the orders of the Amīr al-Umarā'. It would thus appear that the architects Kölüg (Kölüg is an old Turkish name meaning brave) or Kalūk known from other Seljuk monuments and Kāluyān are two different architects, the patronymic of the former being 'Abdallāh, and the father of the other having some name resembling Karabuda.

According to its inscription the Great Mosque at Sinop was founded by the Pervāne Sulaymān, one of the greatest of the Seljuk vizirs, in 666/1267. With its disproportionately large courtyard surrounded by walls 12 metres in height, and its two aisles lying parallel to the qibla, it recalls the Great Mosque at Urfa. The aisle in front of the mihrab is higher and is roofed by three domes with two transverse vaults at each side, whilst the other aisle has five transverse vaults with one dome at each side. The most important feature of this mosque, which has undergone two radical restorations and modifications, is the marble mihrab. This form of mihrab, with its border decoration of elongated hexagons linking together hexagons formed by pipe mouldings, is continued later in Kastamonu during the Jandarid period.

The Gök Medrese Mosque at Amasya, which is generally agreed to have been built in 665/1266–7 by the Seljuk governor Turumtay, is a three-aisled structure roofed by means of domes and vaulting extending into its depth. The mosque has a façade of unusual composition, with a single high window on each side of an iwan-shaped porch, and cylindrical buttressing towers at the corners. It is in a serious, dignified style with the mature proportions and simple ornament of squared stone architecture. The faceted pyramidal roof on the east side has collapsed and the octagonal mausoleum is contiguous to the mosque. (Turumtay's own four-cornered tomb is opposite the façade, and is separated from it by a street.) The unusual arrangement of domes and vaulting is the result of various repairs. The mihrab dome is the same size as the others. As can be seen from its name the entrance section of this extremely long mosque was used as a medrese.

Towards the end of the 13th century, the last of the Seljuk mosques was the Great Mosque at Develi, a town in the vilayet of Kayseri. According to its inscription it was built in the year

680/1281 by Göcher Arslan and his wife Sivasti Khātūn. The pointed arched vaults of the aisle lying perpendicular to the qibla are covered with a flat earth roof, and on the exterior this is surmounted only by the mihrab dome. (Plan 17.) The main axis is strongly defined by the porch, an open lantern in the roof and the mihrab dome, and produces a T transept with the parallel aisle in front of the mihrab wall. The mihrab niche is magnificently decorated with geometrical star interlacing patterns, *naskhī* script and embossed borders of scrolls and foliate arabesque. The richness of its appearance is heightened by panels of dark-coloured porphyry and embossed medallions. This Seljuk stonework continues in a very simplified form the

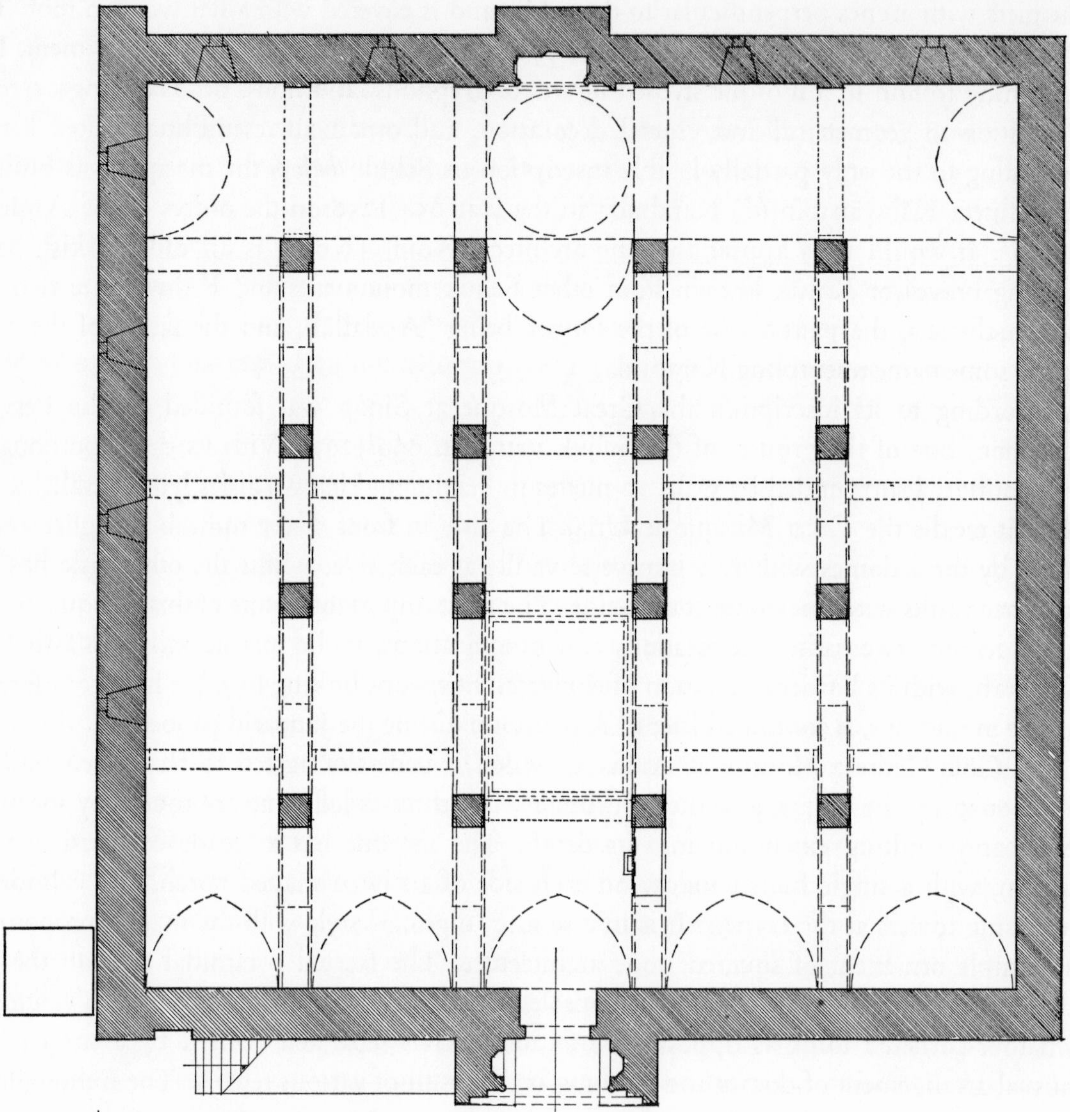

Plan 17. Develi (Kayseri), Great Mosque

stone ornament of the Zengids and Mamluks, and will be seen later from time to time in Emirate and Ottoman architecture. The Great Mosque at Develi proves that Seljuk mosque architecture preserved its strength and vitality to the very end.

Seljuk Masjids and Wooden Mosques in Anatolia

In modern Turkish the word '*mescid*' is used for small district mosques without a minbar which are not employed for Friday or Bayram prayers; the word therefore is used in a slightly different sense from that in which it is used over a wide area from Iran to Turkestan where it normally covers all places of prayer.

In Konya there are some ten of these Seljuk masjids still standing. Some are single-domed structures, though several of them have a flat roof. Most of them have either vaulted or flat-roofed vestibules, sometimes with an open portico, sometimes walled in with doors and windows. These are the prototypes of the porticos of the 14th century. Of them the single-domed Besharebek Masjid dated 613/1213, the Erdemshah Masjid of 617/1220, the small Karatay Masjid built by Karatay's brother Rumtash in 646/1248 and the Taş Masjid by the Vizir Ḥajjī Farrūḥ dating from 612/1215 have front sections in the form of vaults opening out through doors and windows. In the Sırçalı Masjid belonging to the second half of the 13th century, however, a developed form of portico opening through three arches is to be seen. (Fig. 25.)

The Taş Masjid (or Ḥajjī Farrūḥ Masjid) is the work of Ramadhān bin Kunesh of Kayseri, and is remarkable in possessing fan squinches and the first richly ornamented examples of a carved stone Seljuk porch and mihrab at a date as early as 1215. The portal niche is surrounded by a wide border worked with hexagons joined by two arms on each side, but on the level of the door the designs change to geometrical star interlacing patterns. The inner porch leading from the front section into the masjid itself was half completed on a large, monumental scale, with geometrical interlacing patterns and braiding, but as the building progressed a portico and the present portal must have been added in front. The stone mihrab is as richly decorated as the porch. The niche is surrounded by a very wide border decorated with concentric hexagons joined by arms on each side. This type of geometrical design is also to be found on the old stone mihrab of the Great Mosque at Sivas, the Sitte Melik Mausoleum at Divriği (1195) and in the portals of the undated Alay Han near Aksaray, which thus provides evidence for dating the Alay Han around 1215. Thus the Taş Masjid in Konya assumes a very important place in Anatolian mosque architecture on account of its peculiar stone ornament, its fan-shaped squinches and the vestibule (portico)—features, here displayed on a small scale, which are rarely to be met with in Seljuk mosques. (Plan 18.)

The Sırçalı Masjid is remarkable for its brick architecture, the Turkish triangles in the transition zone below the dome, unusual brick work, faience mosaic decoration in the three-arched portico and one of the finest Seljuk ceramic mihrabs. (Plan 19. Fig. 26.) Finally the Karatay Masjid on the outskirts of Konya, dated to the middle of the 13th century, shares in this development in its now characteristic use of the prismatic triangles to be seen in the dome

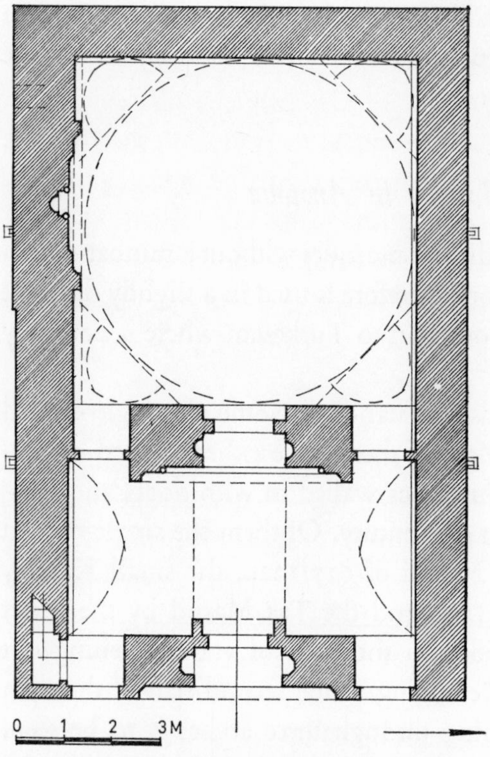

Plan 18. Konya, Taş Masjid

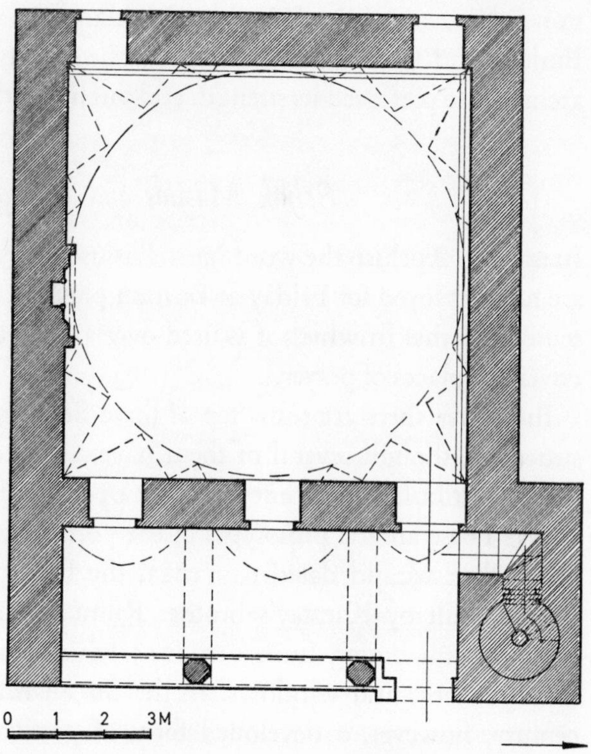

Plan 19. Konya, Sırçalı Masjid

of the ʿAlā al-Dīn Mosque and the Sırçalı Masjid and with the large portico in front now used as a dwelling.

Other Seljuk buildings outside Konya are the Güdük Minare Masjid of 624/1226 in Akşehir, the façade of which is articulated with pointed brick arches and faced with cruciform and star-shaped tiles, and the single-domed structure there with Turkish triangles known as Little Aya Sofya. The latter has faience mosaic decoration on the drum and in the interior of the dome, some of the designs being geometrical, others resembling plaited Kufic.

The Alaca Masjid of 678/1279 at Harput is remarkable for its tile mihrab and tile decorations. Its central dome with vaults at each side recalls the plan of a zāwīya (a lodging place for dervishes). Several other undated masjids might be included with these, but the masjids in the Seljuk capital of Konya form the most important group embracing within themselves the whole development of this form.

Mosques covered with flat wooden roofs supported on wooden pillars form a third group in Anatolian Seljuk mosque architecture. This type was brought to Anatolia as a continuation of the ʿArūs al-Falak (Bride of Heaven) Mosque of the Ghaznevid Sultan Maḥmūd, which we know from written sources, and the wooden-pillared Karakhanid mosques in the cities of medieval Turkestan. Richly ornamented wooden capitals in the museums of Samarkand and Tashkent, two wooden pillars, one from the Oburdan Mosque the other from the Kurut Mosque, in the museums of Tashkent and Pyandzhikent, and 24 wooden pillars from the Friday Mosque at Khiva, are all that remains of the wooden mosques of the 10th to the

12th centuries. In Anatolia some idea of structures of this type may be gleaned from the Great Mosque at Afyon Karahisar dated 671/1272, the Great Mosque at Sivrihisar dated 673/1275, the Arslanhane Mosque in Ankara dated 689/1289–90 and the Eshrefoghlu Mosque at Beyşehir dated 696/1297. The Great Mosque at Afyon was restored in 1341, and produces an effect of peace and quiet spaciousness with its forty wooden pillars with large stalactite capitals in carved wood arranged in nine aisles perpendicular to the qibla wall. The capitals and roof beams are decorated with polychrome painted decoration. The simple stone mihrab with its stalactite niche and bold Koranic inscription border and the wooden minbar dated 1272 richly decorated with geometrical interlacing patterns complete the warm atmosphere of the mosque.

An important place is occupied in this group by the Great Mosque at Sivrihisar which, according to its inscription beginning 'Al Sulṭānī' and containing the word *masjid*, was restored by the Seljuk emir Mikā'īl bin 'Abd Allāh in 673/1275 and underwent extensive repairs at the orders of the famous qāḍī Hızır Bek in 1440. This is a six-aisled structure in the form of a long, shallow rectangle with rafters running parallel to the qibla on 67 wooden columns. Four of the columns are original, and have upper sections decorated with rich relief carving, and with green and black painted decoration. The columns present a strange spectacle with various antique stone capitals side by side with plain wooden ones. The magnificent minbar in walnut with its delicately worked foliate arabesque and palmette insets in geometrical panels and its openwork baluster grilles is one of the finest Seljuk works of art. The fourfold braid pattern produced by the intersecting octagonals in the square inset grilles on the throne section is the continuation of a Turkish ornamental tradition going back to the Karakhanids and the Ghaznevids. The very plain stalactite stucco mihrab niche beside this magnificent minbar must date from the repairs carried out by the Qāḍī Hızır Bek. The symbolic figure of the archangel Michael to the left of the inscription on the east door alludes to the Emir Mikā'īl, who was the first to restore the mosque. A five-line Seljuk inscription over the outer door of the minaret which was rebuilt in 1413 mentions the date 629/1232. If this inscription, which contains merely the word *'imāra*, had belonged to the mosque it would have been placed over one of the mosque doors. There is in fact a tradition that the Great Mosque was first built as an *imaret* or rest-house and was only later converted into a mosque. However the inscription is known to have belonged to another masjid next to the mosque.

According to the inscription on its minbar the Arslanhane Mosque in Ankara was built by two members (*Akhīs*) of a corporation or guild. Here too antique capitals have been set on wooden pillars. The mihrab is a masterpiece of Seljuk art belonging to the end of the century (1290), and displays a harmonious unity of stucco decoration with turquoise and manganese-purple ceramic inlays. The minbar is the last brilliant example of Seljuk woodwork in which inscriptions are combined with foliate arabesques and palmettes among scrolls, geometrical interlacing patterns and baluster grilles in a mature composition.

The largest and most original of all the mosques with wooden columns is the Eshrefoghlu Mosque of Sulaymān Bek at Beyşehir. This has seven aisles running perpendicular to the mihrab, set on 48 wooden columns with stalactite capitals. The central aisle, which is wider and higher than the others, the mihrab dome, and the open central section, which performs the function of an ice-house or cistern, are strongly defined both internally and externally (Plan 20). The conical mausoleum of the Eshrefoghulları is contiguous to the mosque on the east side. The main door is set in the diagonal façade produced by the truncation of the eastern corner, and has an ornamental fountain on the left and a minaret on the right. The carved stone and woodwork, the painted decoration and the tile mosaics form a harmonious whole within the

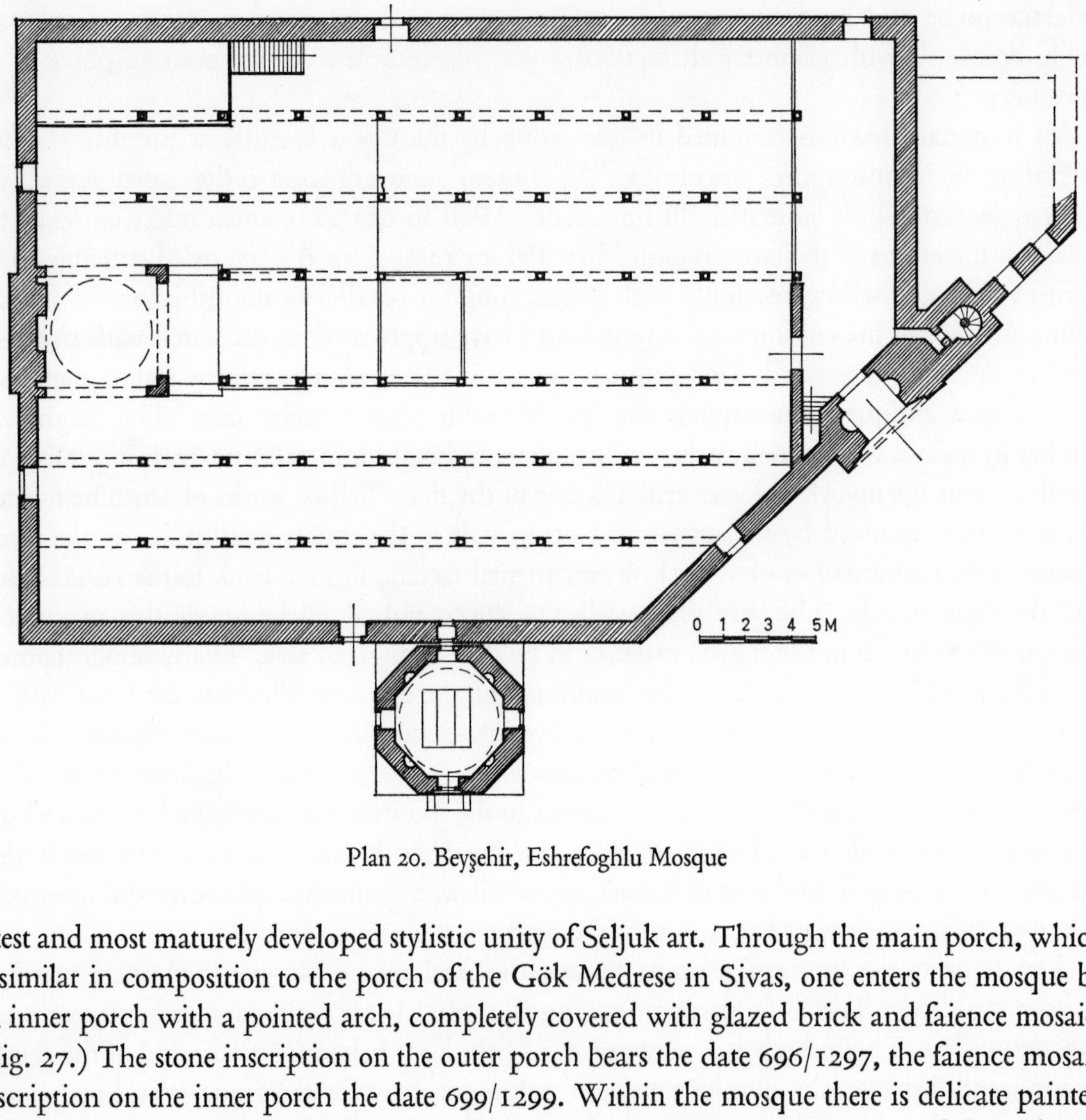

Plan 20. Beyşehir, Eshrefoghlu Mosque

latest and most maturely developed stylistic unity of Seljuk art. Through the main porch, which is similar in composition to the porch of the Gök Medrese in Sivas, one enters the mosque by an inner porch with a pointed arch, completely covered with glazed brick and faience mosaic. (Fig. 27.) The stone inscription on the outer porch bears the date 696/1297, the faience mosaic inscription on the inner porch the date 699/1299. Within the mosque there is delicate painted decoration on the rafters, on the spaces between the brackets and on some of the stalactite capitals. (Fig. 28.) The mihrab niche is more than 6 metres high and is covered with turquoise, cobalt and manganese purple faience mosaic. The composition of a star opening like the sun within the niche (Fig. 29) recalls the faience mosaic in the dome of the Karatay Medrese in Konya. The mihrab dome is faced with glazed brick and tiles, and the lozenge patterns recall the dome of the Çay Medrese, whilst the fan-shaped triangles in the transition section recall the domes in the Ince Minare Medrese and the tomb of Sahib Ata at Konya. The mihrab dome is defined on the exterior by a pyramidal dome. The walnut minbar is the work of an artisan, ʿIsā, and is worked with delicacy but in conformity with the rich, flamboyant style of the mosque.

Recent research and explorations have shown that the Sahib Ata Mosque in Konya was originally a structure supported on wooden columns and extended as far as the present façade with its twin minarets (Fig. 30). Of the interior decoration only the magnificent faience mosaic mihrab survives, the present mosque having been rebuilt at a distance of 8 metres from the porch. From the inscription on the porch we learn that it was begun by the Seljuk vizir Sahib Ata and constructed by the architect Kalūk (Kölüg) bin ʿAbd Allāh (Fig. 31). This dating makes it the oldest known wooden-columned mosque of the Anatolian Seljuks (656/1258). With the addition of a tomb and khānqāh (dervish monastery) in 682/1283 the structure took on the features of a complex. The porch of the mosque is the prototype of the twin minaret façades in Anatolia, and also presents the oldest example of the Seljuk ornamental sebil (fountain) in the form of a deep niche on the façade. The minaret on the left has collapsed, whilst the one on the right is still standing up to as far as the balcony. The ornament on the faience mosaic mihrab consists of geometrical designs and stars with delicate scrolls and foliate arabesques, with no writing whatsoever (Fig. 32). Judging from the fact that the stone and brick ornament of the monumental twin minaret façade is of as high a quality as the finest details on the faience mosaic mihrab, it would seem that this first wooden-columned Seljuk mosque must have been as magnificent as the Eshrefoghlu Mosque at Beyşehir.

The strength and creative power of Seljuk mosque architecture in Anatolia continued right up to the end in wooden-columned mosques as vigorously as in stone or brick mosques and masjids, and may be said to have produced its finest masterpiece in the Eshrefoghlu Mosque at the very end of the century.

Medreses (Danishmendid, Mengüjükid, Artukid, Seljuk)

The first medreses in Anatolia are to be found, like the mosques, in the areas under Danishmendid and Artukid domination. As many as 67 medreses have survived from between the middle of the 12th century and the end of the 15th century, of which 15 are partly standing. The Anatolian medreses may be divided into two different categories—the domed type and the iwan type—whilst both the plan and the architectural decoration show a continuous and unflagging development right up to the end. The achievement of so rich and varied an architectural creation starting from a general plan that underwent no change in its basic features shows with what dynamism Turkish art began and how sound were the foundations on which it was based. Apart from being institutions for the study of theology and Islamic law the medreses also included various institutions such as hospitals for the teaching and practice of medicine, and observatories. In other words they were not devoted entirely to religious studies.

A domed medrese plan appeared in which the courtyard is covered by a dome or by vaulting. It is noteworthy that the first medreses in Anatolia were of this type. The Gümüshtekin medrese at Bosra in Syria was the first example of this (1136) and remained as the sole example of this type in Syria without any successors. Nevertheless the domed medreses that began to appear in Anatolia 15 years later showed a continuous development, and in their conception of unified space they prepared the way for the architecture of the large Ottoman mosques.

The first domed medreses were built by the Danishmendid Emir Yaghıbasan at Tokat in 546–52/1151–7 and at Niksar in 552/1157–8. These were simple unadorned buildings of rough stone and are now in a very ruinous condition. In the first the dome on squinches is still standing; in the second, at Niksar, it has collapsed. In these two early Anatolian medreses of the 12th century the large dome rests on narrow iwans on two sides and on blind walls on the

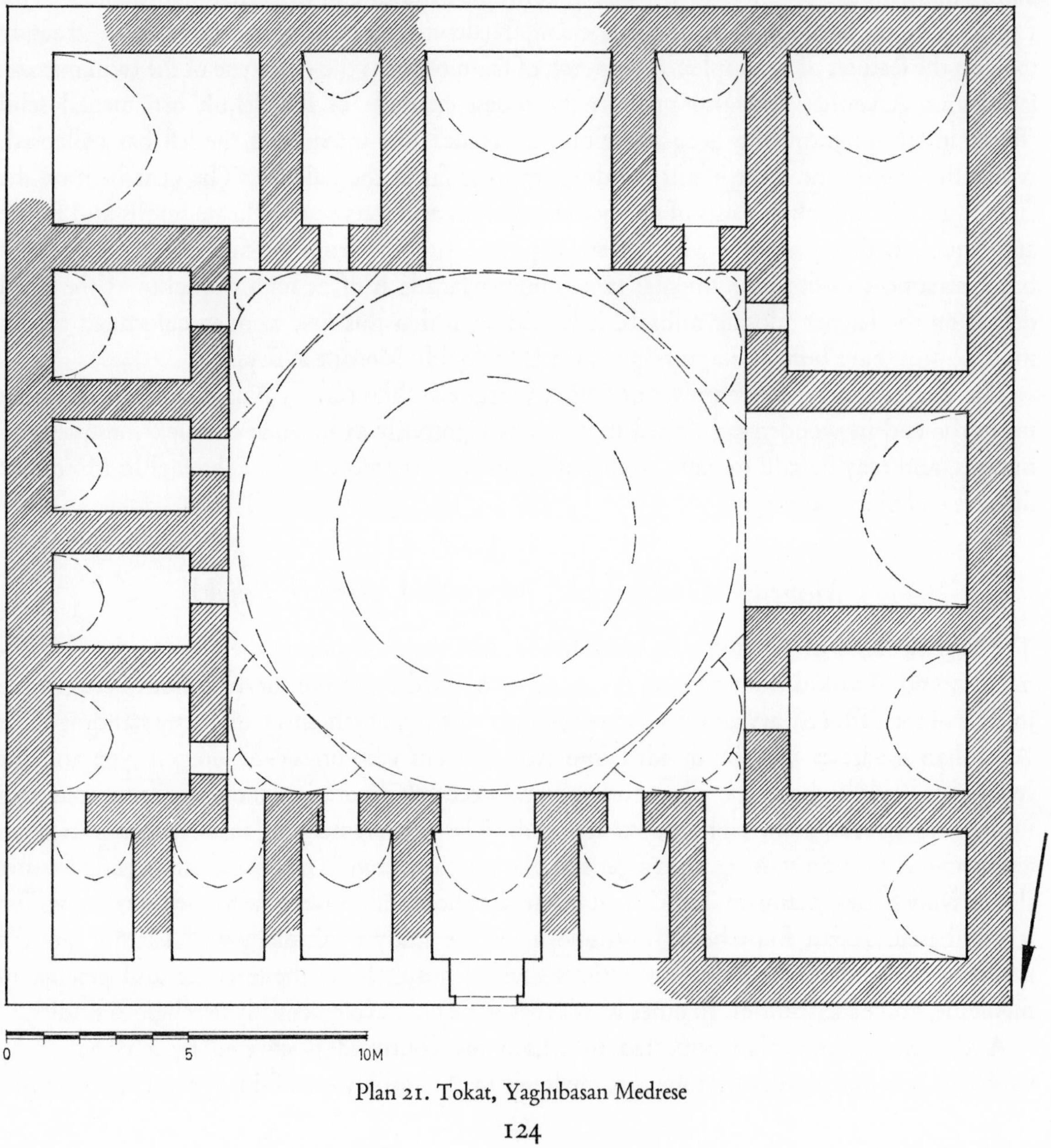

Plan 21. Tokat, Yaghıbasan Medrese

other two. The large and small vaulted chambers surrounding it are each entered by a single brick door. The opening nearly 10 metres wide in the middle of a dome on squinches 14 metres in diameter at Tokat shows that the 11 metre dome at Niksar was similar in form. Although the plan and proportions are confused, and there is a complete lack of ornament, these buildings are important as first experiments in this form. (Plan 21.) In the later two-storeyed medrese, now in ruins, built by the Seljuks at Boyalıköy near Sincanlı, a town in the vilayet of Afyon, in 607/1210, the dome rests on corner piers supported by vaulting. It has a symmetrical, balanced plan.

In the Ertokush Medrese at Atabey near Isparta dating from 621/1224 the inscription and border decoration on the porch and the sound cut stone construction show a fully developed architectural style. (Fig. 33.) The central dome rests on four pillars and is connected to the sides by vaulting. The centre of the dome is open and has a pool beneath it. There are some interesting innovations; as, for example, an octagonal mausoleum behind the great iwan, the domes on squinches on each side, and, the two other entrances, one on each side, in the form of narrow corridors, in addition to the main entrance (Plan 22). Inside the building an unusual

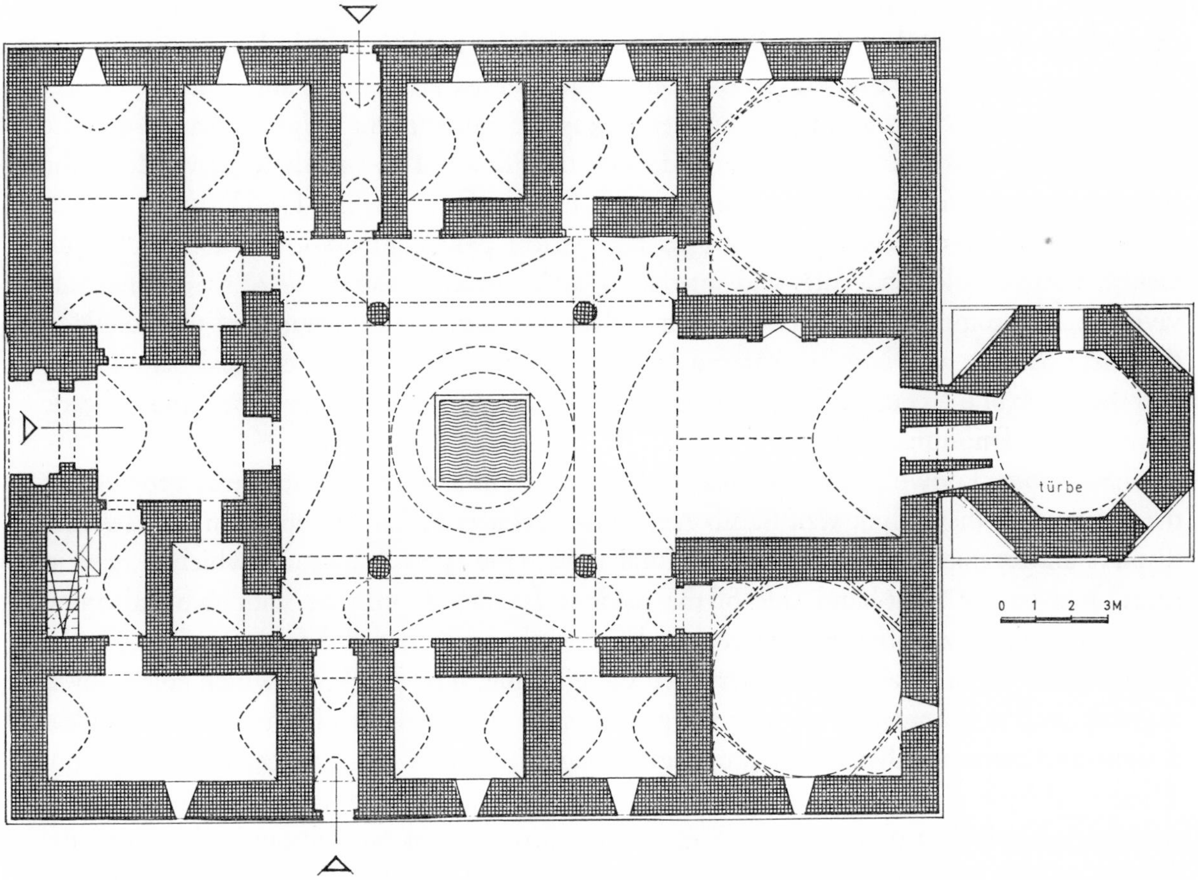

Plan 22. Isparta (Atabey), Medrese of Ertokush

effect of space has been achieved based solely on the strength of the architecture (Fig. 34.) It seems reasonable to suppose that the tomb chamber which opens into the main iwan through three arches is older and was attached to the medrese at a later date.

The Hospital of the Mengüjükid Queen, Turan Malik, at Divriği is far superior in style and quality to these first domed Seljuk medreses. It opens out through a magnificent porch of Gothic exuberance (see Fig. 14). On each side two heads with plaited hair representing the sun and the moon are in very poor condition. The hospital is in two storeys, and the richly decorated stone architecture of the three vaults covering the central section, a second dome and the vaulting in the rest of the building produce a far more spacious and imposing effect than its actual size would lead one to expect (see Figs. 15–16).

The domed chambers on each side of the great iwan first seen in the Ertokush Medrese at Atabey are to be found very frequently repeated in later Seljuk buildings. The Karatay Medrese in Konya dating from 649/1251 is the richest of all these Seljuk monumental structures (Figs. 35–36). The large central dome contains a small oculus with a pool beneath. The faience mosaic decoration covering the walls and dome increases the sense of space by its harmony with the architecture. The heightened dome has lost all sense of heaviness, and fuses completely (Fig. 36) with the great iwan to produce a special unity that prepares the way for the architecture of the later large Ottoman mosques. The bold geometrical stars in turquoise and lapis lazuli in faience mosaic on the dome resting on fan pendentives almost seem to reflect the sky. The porch bears an inscription mentioning the names of the Seljuk Sultan and of the Vizir Karatay who built the medrese, and, with the fillings of its spandrels derived from the Zengids, seen for the first time in the courtyard façade of the 'Alā al-Dīn Mosque, and its stone entrelacs in contrasting colours, its geometrical panels, raised inscriptions in Seljuk *thuluth*, finely detailed stalactites and interlacing arch motifs, presents one of the noblest surviving Seljuk compositions in carved stone. Here, the Baroque exuberance of the portals of the Great Mosque at Divriği is replaced by the sedate lines of a wholly classical Seljuk style, and the porch of the courtyard façade of the 'Alā al-Dīn Mosque has developed into a façade composition of monumental scale.

The complex known as the Ince Minare Medrese built at Konya in the years 1260–65 on the orders of another Seljuk vizir Sahib Ata by the architect Kalūk (Kölüg) bin 'Abd Allāh displays an extremely spectacular architectural unity. (Fig. 37.) A mosque, which is now in ruins, was on the right-hand side of the medrese façade. A minaret with two balconies, enlivened with glazed brick mosaic, rose up between the mosque and the medrese. In 1901 the section above the first balcony was destroyed by lightning. The porch, on which epigraphy is superbly used as a border, is set with the greatest skill and, with its high relief artichoke leaf designs and geometrical patterns, produces a magnificent and original façade composition. These exuberant plastic forms are combined with the surface ornaments that dominate the composition to form a single whole. (Fig. 38.) As Berenson has pointed out in discussing the strength of Seljuk architecture displayed by this stonework, 'it has an elegance, a distinction of design and a subtle delicacy of ornament surpassing any other known to me since French Gothic at its best.' Inside, the central space is roofed by a very much simplified form of the dome of the Karatay Medrese and forms a contrast with the richness of the exterior. The vigorous forms of brick architecture prevail. (Fig. 39.)

Although the domed medrese dated 1278 at Çay, a town in the vilayet of Afyon, shows a close relationship with its predecessors in Konya, its plan presents a more balanced and stable character. (Plan 23 and Fig. 41.) The name of the architect, Oghulbek bin Muḥammad, is mentioned in an inscription. On the porch, in addition to the inscription, there is a relief of a

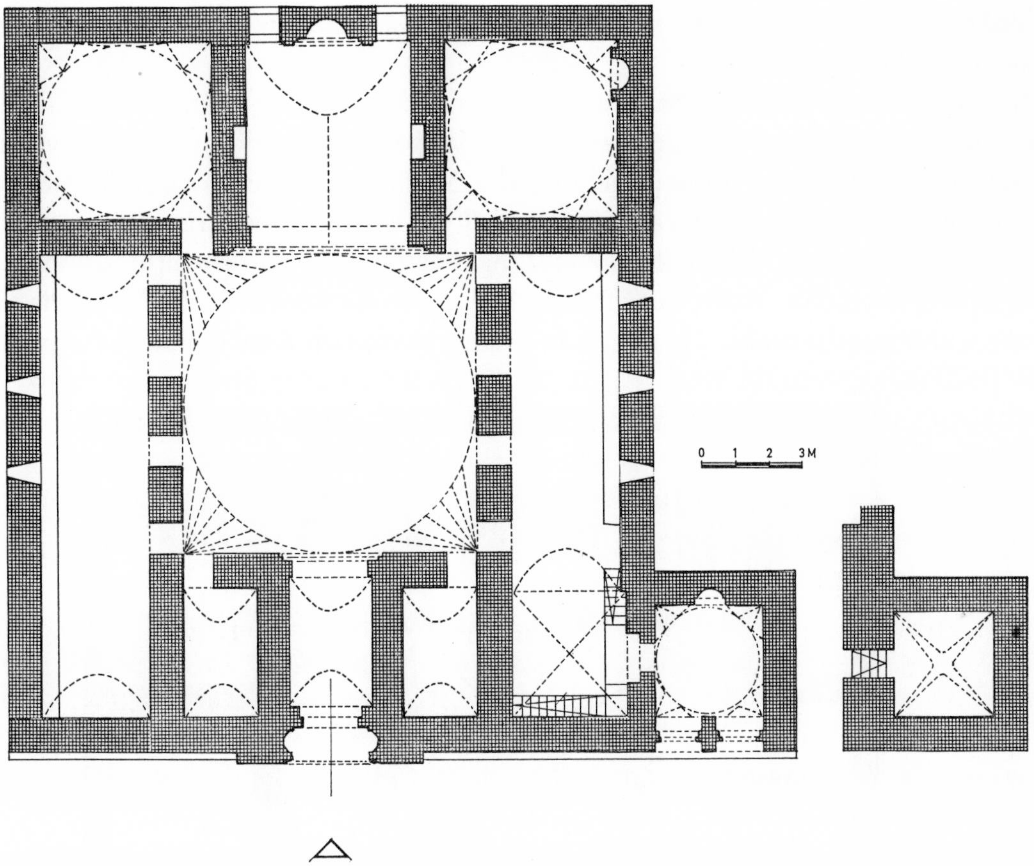

Plan 23. Çay (Afyon), Medrese

lion forming a heraldic device. The large dome is completely covered inside with faience decoration and is the richest in appearance after that of the Karatay Medrese, which it closely resembles. The dome in the upper floor of the two-storeyed guest-house added to the right of the one-storeyed medrese is also decorated with glazed brick. The mihrab of the great iwan now used as a mosque, and the façade and arch of the entrance iwan, were covered with faience mosaic, but most of that on the mihrab has fallen away.

It is generally agreed that the Caca (Jājā) Bey Medrese at Kırşehir dating from 671/1272–3 was built as an observatory and later transformed into a mosque. The façade presents an unusual appearance with its high porch in two different colours of stone in the centre, the tomb on the left and two corner towers. (Fig. 40.) The minaret has been placed at the rear. The dome is open in the centre and was used for astronomical observation. The tomb and minaret are ornamented with tiles.

Although they were few in number the domed medreses of the 13th century displayed a brilliant development. This new type of structure appeared in the middle of the 12th century, and, passing from the Danishmendids to the Seljuks, produced its finest masterpieces within a space of fifty years. The domed medrese was an invention of Anatolian Turkish architecture; on the one hand it prepared the way for Ottoman mosque architecture, while on the other it provided the basis from which the plans for *Khānqāhs, tekkes* and *zāwīyas* (all various forms of dervish monastery) were developed.

Whilst nine domed medreses have survived from the period up to the end of the 13th century, and even those are in a ruined condition, eighteen iwan medreses have survived from the same period. The first of these is the Zinciriye Medrese in Diyarbekir (1198), now used as a museum. The small courtyard is surrounded by arcades with various types of arches resting on piers. (Fig. 42.) The influence of Zengid architecture is apparent in the extremely rich stone ornamentation. Apart from the single dome in the corner on the left of the Great iwan the whole space is vaulted (Plan 24). In contrast to the rich decoration and the animated

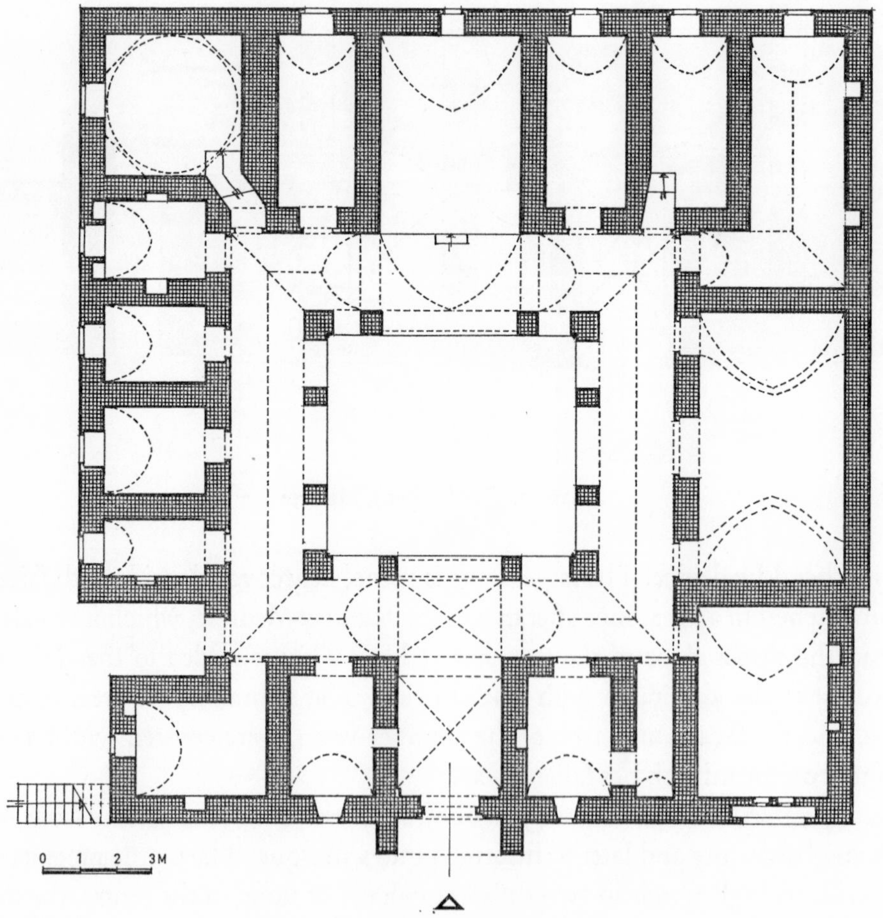

Plan 24. Diyarbekir, Zinciriye Medrese

45 Sivas, Hospital of Kaykā'ūs, general view of great iwan from courtyard

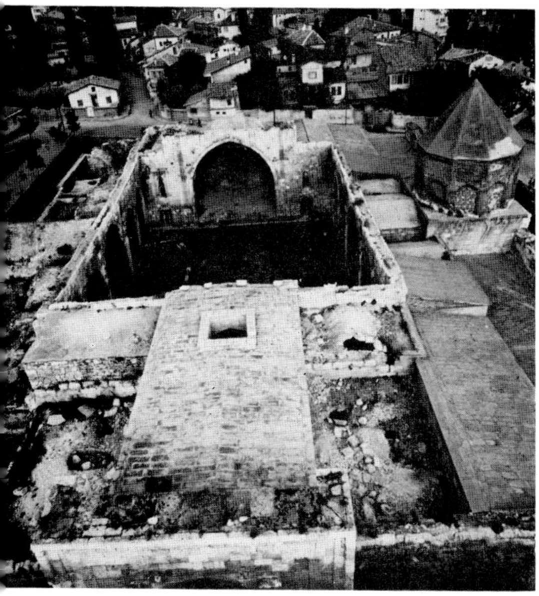

Sivas, Hospital of Kaykā'ūs, view from roof of porch

47 Sivas, Hospital of Kaykā'ūs, detail of decagonal sides of tomb

48 Konya, Sırçalı Medrese, porch. (Photographed before 1900)

49 Akşehir, Taş Medrese, minaret

50 Sivas, Gök Medrese, façade

51 Sivas, Gök Medrese, detail of left side of porch

52 Sivas, Gök Medrese, relief boss of composite animals' heads at left corner of doorway

54 Sivas, Çifte Minare Medrese, detail of porch

53 Sivas, Çifte Minare Medrese, porch

55 Sivas, Medrese of Muẓaffar Burūjirdī, porch

56 Erzurum, Çifte Minare Medrese, façade

57 Erzurum, Çifte Minare Medrese, iwans and double-storeyed *riwāqs* seen from courtyard

58 Erzurum, Çifte Minare Medrese, relief of palm tree with two-headed eagle and dragon on porch

59 Erzurum, Çifte Minare Medrese, detail of porch

60 Amasya, Halifet Ghāzī Kümbed, detail of porch

63 Erzurum, The Three Mausolea (so-called tomb of the Emir Saltuk on the left)

61 Divriği, Sitte Melik Kümbed

62 Divriği, Sitte Melik Kümbed, detail of portal

64 Konya, Mausoleum of Qılıch Arslan

65 Sivas, Mausoleum of Sultan Kaykā'ūs, rear view

66 Sivas, Mausoleum of Sultan Kaykā'ūs, detail of faience mosaic on entrance wall

69
Tercan, Mama Khātūn Kümbed,
external porch

67 Tercan, Mama Khātūn Kümbed,
view from nearby hill

68 Tercan, Mama Khātūn Kümbed,
surrounding wall

70 Tercan, Mama Khātūn Kümbed, lobed tomb

71 Afyon, Sincanlı-Boyalıköy, mausoleum

73 Kirşchir, Melik Ghāzī Kümbed

72 Kayseri, Mausoleum of Khwand Khātūn, detail

75 Kayseri, Döner Kümbed, general view

74 Amasya, Gök Medrese Cami Kümbed (tomb attached to so-called Gök Medrese Mosque)

77 Amasya, Turumtay Türbe, general view

76 Erzurum, Çifte Minare Medrese, rear view of mausoleum

78 Konya, Mausoleum of Sahib Ata, interior view with cenotaphs covered with ceramic mosaic. (Photographed before 1900)

79 Ahlat Ulu Kümbed, general view

80 Ahlat, Ulu Kümbed, detail

81 Ahlat, one of two mausolea, the Kümbed of Bughatay Aka

82 Konya, Gömech Khātūn, iwan mausoleum

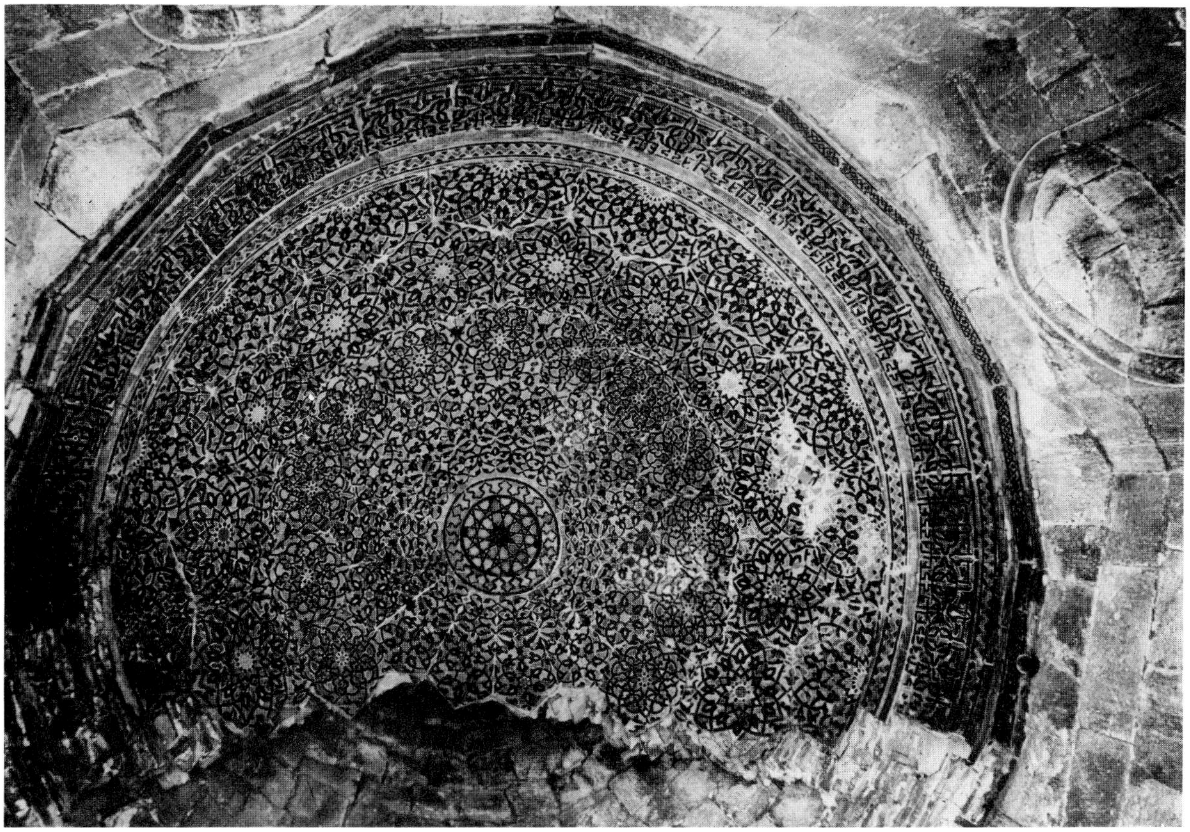

83 Beyşehir, Eshrefoghlu Mausoleum, dome with ceramic mosaic

84 Aksaray-Kayseri road, Alay Han, porch. (Photographed before 1900)

85 Antalya-Isparta road, Evdir Han, porch

86 Aksaray-Konya road, Sultan Han, outer porch. (Photographed before 1900)

87 Aksaray-Konya road, Sultan Han, side niche of outer porch

88 Aksaray-Konya road, Sultan Han, view of collapsed vaults of courtyard *riwāqs*

90 Aksaray-Konya road, Sultan Han, detail of inner porch

89 Aksaray-Konya road, Sultan Han, mosque and inner porch

design of the arches within, the exterior is dominated by an extremely simple hewn stone architecture. On the southern wall we find the name of the architect, ʿIsā Abū Dirham, and the date 595/1198.

A second Artukid structure, the two-storeyed Mesudiye (Masʿūdiyya) Medrese (1198–1223), attached to the south arcade of the Great Mosque at Diyarbekir, has a very long architectural history. (Fig. 43.) Architecturally it closely resembles the Zinciriye Medrese. It was built by the Artukid Sultan Sukman or Sökmen II for the four Sunnite sects, and was completed during the reign of Mawḍūḍ. The architect Jaʿfar bin Maḥmūd, whose name is mentioned in an inscription, came from Aleppo and shows here too the influence of Zengid stone architecture. The small courtyard has a very impressive appearance with its two-storeyed arcades with variegated arches resting on piers, and an inscription course encircling the whole between the two storeys. The arches on the upper storey are simpler. The great iwan rises through both storeys. One is struck by a spectacular mihrab opposite the entrance. Another room was built as a masjid with a second and simpler mihrab. The external appearance is very plain. The plans of these first Artukid medreses display features which link them to the later Seljuk medreses.

From the period of the Artukids of Mardin the ruins of only three iwan medreses have survived. One of these, the Khwārizm Medrese, was built in 608/1211 by Tāj al-Dīn Masʿūd, a freed slave of Artuk Arslan, near Koçhisar, a town in the vilayet of Mardin. On the east and north sides a few of the piers of the arcade surrounding the rectangular courtyard are still standing, whilst on the south side a mosque consisting of two aisles, each with three transverse vaults, opens outwards through a single iwan. The domes of the arcades have collapsed, together with the cells behind. On the west there is a common entrance protruding from the front to form a separate chamber. In so far as the courtyard here forms the junction between the mosque and the medrese this building may be regarded as a prototype of the Hacı Kılıç mosque and its medrese in Kayseri.

The Hatuniye Medrese in Mardin built by Sitt Radaviye, the wife of Najm al-Dīn Alpī and the mother of Quṭb al-Dīn (572–80/1176/7–1184/5), is very much damaged and has lost its original form. There is a small mosque on the south.

The 2-iwan Shahidiye Medrese dating from the time of Najm al-Dīn Ghāzī I (637–58/1239–60) is also greatly damaged, though there are remains of a small mosque on the south side.

The mosque on the south side of each of the three Mardin Artukid medreses may well be a sign of Zengid influence.

The first Seljuk medrese in Kayseri is the Çifte (Twin) Medrese (60 × 40 metres), a simple 4-iwan structure consisting of the Medical School founded by Ghiyāth al-Dīn Kaykhusraw I and the hospital of his sister Jawhar Nasība (602/1205). (Fig. 44.) The two buildings are joined by a corridor. We see for the first time a pyramidal domed mausoleum in the medrese section, and this may well be that of the sister. The figure of a lion on the right-hand side of the porch may well be in memory of their father Qılıch Arslan. The building is of importance as the oldest hospital building in Anatolia (Plan 25).

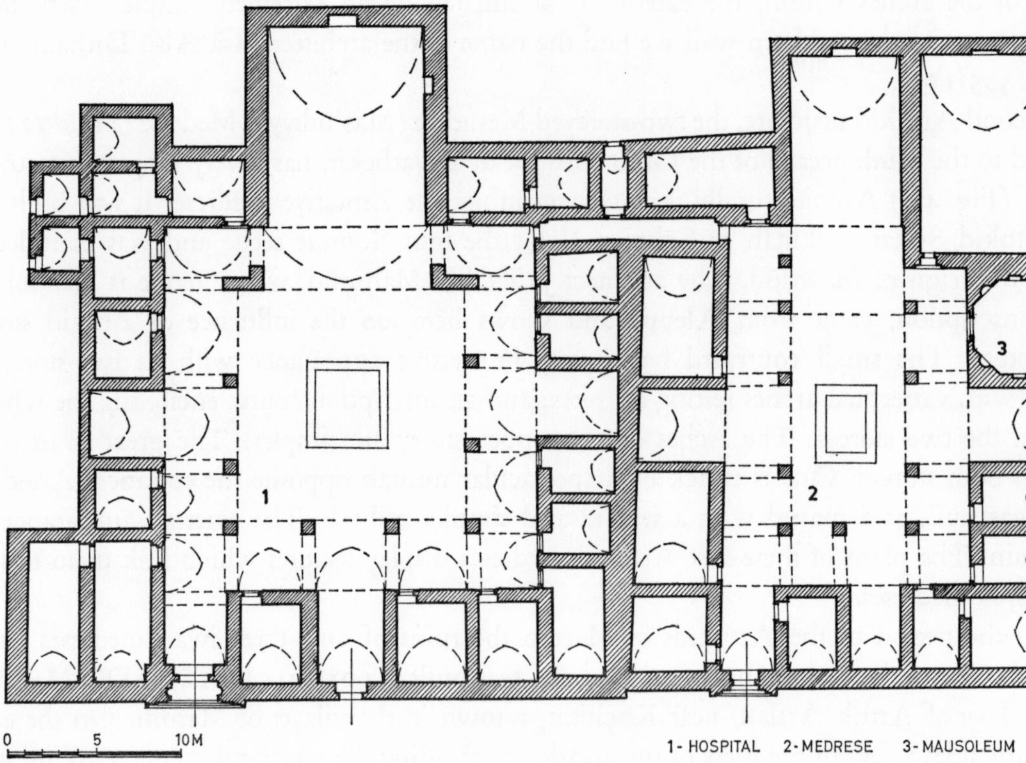

Plan 25. Kayseri, Çifte Medrese

A few years later, in 614/1217–18, Sultan 'Izz al-Dīn Kaykā'ūs I constructed the largest of the Seljuk hospitals (48 × 68 metres) in the town of Sivas. (Fig. 46.) It is a 4-iwan structure with an arcaded courtyard surrounded by dormitories and rooms with fireplaces (Plan 26). On each side of the arch of the great iwan, now in ruins, there are badly damaged male and female heads representing the sun and the moon. (Fig. 45.) Behind the iwan to the right the tall 10-sided plinth of the tomb of Kaykā'ūs reminds one of a domed mausoleum. (Fig. 47.) The hospital and tomb are highly monumental examples of mixed brick and faience mosaic technique, and their plaited Kufic lettering, entrelacs and stars in white, turquoise and cobalt are quite dazzling. The magnificent faience decoration of the craftsman, Aḥmad of Marand on the façade of the tomb recalls Great Seljuk ornament. As Marand is a town in Azerbaidzhan not far from Tabriz it is obvious that these influences arrived directly from Azerbaidzhan. It is typical that the first monumental tile decoration in Anatolia should be so closely linked to the Great Seljuks. This foreshadows the brilliant later development of Seljuk tile technique. Tiles similar to those on the cenotaph in the tomb covered the walls of the pavilion at Keykubadiye near Kayseri. An inscription on the mausoleum façade in raised white lettering on a blue ground, referring to the sensitive poet-sultan, who died of tuberculosis, reads as follows: 'My wealth was of no use to me. My Sultanate is finished. The day of my journey from this transitory world to the next was the 4th Shawwāl 617' (1219 A.D.). The main inscription of the hospital is carved on the stone of the porch. Here we can see an early form of Seljuk

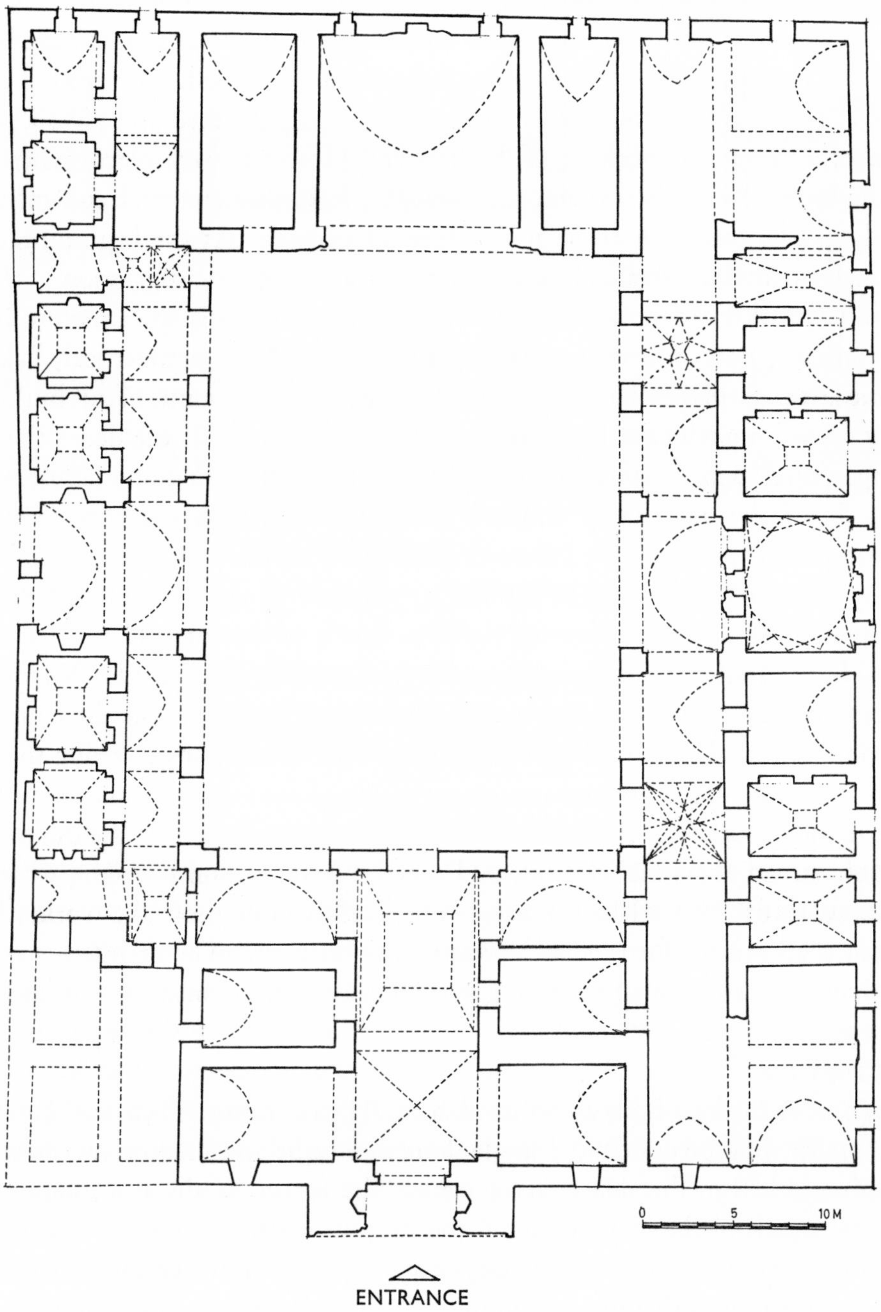

Plan 26. Sivas, Hospital of Kaykā'ūs

porch composition, with its border entrelacs and the lions' and bulls' heads symbolising the sun and the moon on either side of the arch of the stalactite niche. The braid motif produced by intersecting hexagons of the original decoration on the upper edge is an old Turkish motif (see Design Ie). These designs originate from the tombs at Kharraqān, and are also to be seen in the Mama Khātūn tomb at Tercan and in the mausoleum of the Gök Medrese in Amasya.

They appear in the mausolea of Yūsuf bin Kuthayyir and Mu'mine Khātūn at Nakhichevan before crossing over into Anatolia. Beside the hospital there would appear to have been a small medical school, now in ruins, entered through the iwan on the left. The deed of endowment of the hospital drawn up by Kaykā'ūs I in 1220 has been published and gives a great deal of information concerning the working of the hospital. Hospitals were places where the theory taught in the medical schools was put into practice. Eye, skin, internal and mental diseases were treated, and lessons were given at the patient's bedside. At the beginning of the 13th century mental patients were treated by means of music and hypnotic suggestion.

The Sırçalı (or tiled) Medrese at Konya (1242) is a monumental structure of the two-storeyed, iwan type, now in a very ruinous condition. With its symmetrical, balanced plan it is one of the first examples of the traditional Seljuk medrese. The name of this building, which is one of the most important medreses in Anatolia, derives from its tile decoration. It has an unusual appearance, with a salient porch in the centre of the cut stone façade, geometrical ornament, a foundation inscription and two small windows with stalactite decoration. The fourfold braid pattern produced by intersecting octagons on the border of the slightly pointed arch defining the porch niche marks the first appearance of this type of pattern in Konya. (Fig. 48.) In an elevated position on the right-hand side of the entrance is the tomb of Badr al-Dīn Muṣliḥ, the builder of the medrese, who was tutor to 'Alā al-Dīn Kayqubād II. A faience mihrab can be seen on the south wall of the large iwan opposite the courtyard. Most of the tiles on the mihrab and in the rich 4-coloured tile decorations covering the iwan have fallen away. There are domed classrooms on each side of the iwan, but the second storey has collapsed. On the inside of the iwan arch the architect's name is given as the builder, Muḥammad bin Muḥammad al-Bannā' al-Tūṣī. A Persian inscription[1] on the right, which has now crumbled away, read: 'What I have created is unrivalled throughout the world; I shall pass away but this shall remain for ever and preserve my memory.' The architect was connected with Tūṣ through his grandfather, and learned his craft in Konya. A building with tile decoration approaching that of the Sırçalı Medrese would have been impossible in Iran at that date. (Plate I.)

The Taş (Stone) Medrese built by Sahib Ata in Akşehir in 648/1250 was originally in the form of a complex, but today only the single domed mosque and medrese on the same façade, and the tomb attached to the side iwan, survive. The façade produces a monumental effect with its marble porch, its brick portico and the iwan of the tomb built of bi-coloured stone. The minaret rises up at the end of the façade (Fig. 49). The great iwan is in ruins, as well as part of the arcade with its four antique columns and capitals on each side. Another characteristic feature of the medrese is the brick minaret with its thick cylindrical body and two balconies, a prototype of the Ince Minare in Konya, for the tall double minarets to be seen in two of the buildings constructed by Sahib Ata remained unimitated for a considerable time, to reappear in the works of the Ottomans. The large marble iwan, now in ruins, forms a contrast with the brick arcades. The tomb, masjid and minaret of this 3-iwan medrese are decorated with faience

[1] Now in the East Berlin Pergamon Museum.

mosaics. The arcades and the cells behind are in ruins, so that the most important feature is now the original appearance of the façade.

Four other Seljuk medreses devoted to the teaching of Islamic law are in Kayseri, the Khwand Medrese, adjoining the mosque of that name and now used as a museum, the Sarāj al-Dīn Medrese of the same date (1238), the Sahibiye Medrese built by Sahib Ata in 1268 and the Hacı Kılıç Medrese of 1275, also adjoining a mosque. A characteristic feature of the Sahib Ata Medrese is the long dormitories surrounding the 4-iwan courtyard. The façade resembles that of the Khwand Medrese with its porch and corner buttresses. The Sarāj al-Dīn Medrese is simple in its architecture, with its three iwans side by side and a fourth iwan as entrance.

It is interesting to note that in Sivas three large medreses were built in the year 1271, as if in competition one with the other. There are two two-storeyed medreses with 4-iwans, the Gök and Burūjirdī Medreses, as well as the Çifte Minare Medrese, of which only the façade remains. The Gök Medrese has the most spectacular façade architecture of any of Sahib Ata's buildings, with a monumental marble portal with twin minarets, the first Seljuk *çeşme* (or public fountain) on the left of this, and corner buttresses with decoration in relief. (Fig. 50.) The porch with twin minarets is a feature deriving from his mosque in Konya, and this is the first instance of it in a medrese. (Fig. 51.) A relief boss on either side of the doorway depicting 12 different animal heads is a reminiscence of the old Turkish animal calendar. (Fig. 52.) At the tip of the wide palmette leaves under the large stars in high relief on either side of the porch, can be seen the figure of an eared eagle in the centre with birds carved among raised foliate motifs on each side. There is a domed masjid on the right-hand side of the entrance and a classroom to the left. The lower sections of the faience mosaic mihrab in the masjid have fallen away. The mixed brick and tile decoration found in the Hospital of Kaykā'ūs displays here the highest peak of Seljuk tile technique in the tiles covering the iwans. The tile decoration on the 10-faceted pyramidal outer roof of the tomb attached to the Hospital and on the rear wall of the Gök Medrese iwan continues the ornamental tradition of the brickwork of the Great Seljuk tombs at Kharraqān. With the mature plan and proportions of the arcades surrounding the pooled courtyard, the harmonious combination of bold reliefs with delicately worked stone decoration on the porch and façade, and its rich faience mosaic the Gök Medrese is the most highly developed example of Anatolian Seljuk medrese architecture. We learn from medieval written sources that it consisted of 24 rooms arranged in two storeys. The architect was Kāluyān of Konya. The name is written on the porch, on each side of the door.

The Burūjirdī Medrese has a firmly established symmetrical plan, and for the first time the inner arrangement of the rooms is reflected in the façade. (Fig. 55.) The tomb and the masjid, with their larger domes, are placed on each side of a domed vestibule. The dome of the tomb belonging to the founder of the medrese, Muẓaffar Burūjirdī, who came from Burūjird near Hamadhān, is decorated with faience mosaic. The tile decoration on the cenotaphs has fallen away. The medrese is in two storeys with 4 iwans, and the flat-roofed arcades supported by four columns on each side display a wholly classical maturity of style.

The Çifte Minare Medrese immediately opposite the Hospital of Kaykā'ūs was built by the Īl-Khānid vizir Shams al-Dīn Juwaynī. (Fig. 53.) Recent excavations have shown it to be a two-storeyed 4-iwan structure. Another chamber can be seen behind the façade projecting beyond the main building towards the left. Here the two minarets spring from the porch. (Fig. 54.) The long façade is articulated by fluted half-towers, by a niche on the right similar to the porch of the Ince Minare Medrese in Konya, and by other niches arranged in asymmetrical rows on each side. The minarets are of brick with decorative tile-work. Although Kalūk (Kölüg) bin ʿAbdallāh has been put forward as the architect of this medrese there is no indication of this in the inscriptions.

According to written sources the Gök Medrese at Tokat was built after 1270 by the Seljuk vizir the Pervāne Muʿīn al-Dīn Sulaymān. It has no inscription. The courtyard is in two storeys with 2 iwans, and the arcades are arranged in unusual fashion with slender columns on the lower storey and strong piers on the upper. Behind the arcades are rows of cells. Only a few fragments remain of the tile-work on the tomb and to the right of the iwan on the cenotaphs it contains, but some idea of the richness of the ceramic decoration is given by the faience mosaic stretching in the form of four border courses on the façade and side walls of the iwan, which was used as a mosque. It is clear that the arches of the arcade and the inner walls of the iwan were also covered with tile decoration. The medrese takes its name from the turquoise colour of the tiles in it.

The Çifte Minare or Hatuniye Medrese in Erzurum is a two-storeyed, 4-iwan structure built against the town wall, which in its high façade and interior plan combines and utilises on the largest and most magnificent scale all the various elements of Anatolian Seljuk architecture. (Fig. 56.) Some of the columns of the arcades are decorated in relief, and it resembles the Gök Medrese at Sivas in the composition of the porch with its ornament composed entirely of foliate motifs (Fig. 59) and in the *çeşme* on the left-hand side of the façade. The large-veined date palms of the Gök Medrese at Sivas are here worked with a sounder plastic understanding, and their base terminates in a dragon's head with a double-headed heraldic eagle above (Fig. 58). As only one side is built against the town wall the strengthening towers at the corners have been drawn a little inside and left without ornament. The Çifte Minare at Erzurum is not only the largest medrese in Anatolia (35 × 48 metres) (Fig. 57), but at the same time forms a completely harmonious unity in architecture, plan and ornament that recalls the Hospital at Divriği. There is a domed masjid on the right of the entrance. Although a mausoleum adjoining the south iwan and opening inwards through three arches, as in the Ertokush Medrese at Atabey, now appears in the plan as an incongruous addition, this is due to the collapse of the sections on each side of the iwan. There is no inscription and the stone ornament of the façade was left only half completed.

For a long time the medrese was attributed to ʿAlā al-Dīn Kayqubād I's daughter Khwānd Khātūn, and was assigned to 1253. More recently it has been suggested that it was built around 1290 by Padishāh Khātūn, the wife of the Īl-Khān Gaykhātū who succeeded Arghūn Khan on his death in 1291. The first of these dates may be rather early, but the second is certainly much too late. It seems very unlikely that Padishāh Khātūn would build a medrese in Erzurum immediately upon her arrival from Kirman. Moreover the conception of the single independent medrese on a monumental scale, was uncharacteristic of the Īl-Khānid period in Iran. The medrese remained from the beginning to the end, throughout its whole development, an essentially Turkish institution. Although after the Battle of Köse Dağ in 1243 Anatolia came under Īl-Khānid suzerainty the organisation of the Seljuk State remained firm until the Mamluk Sultan Baybars's Anatolian campaign of 1277. It was only after this that the oppressive rule of the Īl-Khānids began. It is reasonable to suppose that the most splendid of Seljuk medreses in Erzurum must have been built before 1277 and, as in Sivas, in a wholly Seljuk style. The highly developed, ornate composition of the porch and façade of the Gök Medrese at Sivas is to be found in a simplified form in Erzurum, and a date after 1271 would thus seem more suitable for the Erzurum medrese. As for the problem of its founder, light will no doubt be thrown on this by an examination of the written sources. Owing to the intensifying of Īl-Khānid tyranny and oppression the building was left incomplete and no foundation inscription was placed on it.

Funerary Architecture (Danishmendid, Mengüjükid, Saltukid, Seljuk)

Although the funerary architecture of Anatolia is on a very modest scale compared with Karakhanid, Ghaznevid and Great Seljuk funerary monuments, it displays a quite incredible wealth of architectural forms, together with a spirit of creative exploration and experiment that resulted in the development of various new forms of domed mausoleum and tomb. At first the domed mausolea were built either of stone or of brick, but later they began to be built only of stone. At first, too, they stood as independent buildings, but in the course of time they very often began to be included in the plans of mosques and medreses. As for their forms, although the prevailing one was the tomb with a pyramidal or conical roof set on an octagonal, decagonal, duodecagonal or cylindrical body, we also find, less frequently, tombs with lobed bodies, domed tombs on a square plan, vaulted tombs on a rectangular plan and heightened monumental tombs rising from a square base. The tomb chamber is covered by a dome beneath the exterior conical or pyramidal roofing, and underground there is a crypt known as the *mumyalık*. The brick tombs show the influence of the domed mausolea in the Maragha region of Azerbaidzhan. No funerary monuments are known belonging to the Artukid period, but several dating from 12th-century Anatolia have survived.

Six tombs remain from the Danishmendid period. The octagonal tomb at Amasya built for Halifet Ghāzī, the vizir of Melik Danishmend Ghāzī, is now in a very ruinous state. The facings of the conical spire have fallen away, but the building is remarkable for the main façade to the north, which is composed in the form of a porch, for its rich stone ornament consisting of geometrical entrelacs, high-relief mouldings, and rosettes with foliate and braided designs (Fig. 60). There is another façade to the west. Although there is an abundance of ornament, the composition is spoilt by the haphazard arrangement of the rosettes and the lack of harmony in their proportions, which distorts the symmetry of the whole. The Halifet Ghāzī Tomb suggests a period that lacked confidence in stylistic endeavour and experiment. According to tradition the tomb was built in 540/1145–6, and this date is in conformity with the style of the architectural decoration.

Another Danishmendid structure is a plain square building at Niksar known as the Melik Ghāzī Türbe and roofed by a dome supported on Turkish triangles. An inscription from the Yaghıbasan Medrese dated 552/1157 was placed on the wall above the door inside this tomb at some later date. It is no longer in position.

The Kulak Kümbed also at Niksar is an octagonal building of cut stone roofed by a dome. Inside there is no ornament of note apart from a tombstone with a Kufic inscription. It may well date from the end of the 12th century. The shafts of the letters of the inscription on the architrave under the arch of the porch are adorned with the old Turkish fourfold braid motif produced by intersecting octagons.

The Hacı Çikrik Türbe is a rectangular, vaulted structure containing three burials. Its inscription, dating from 578/1182, has been published. It is important as the first appearance of this particular type.

Whilst the preceding mausolea were built of stone, the Kırk Kızlar (Forty Maidens) tomb at Niksar is an octagonal brick structure on a stone foundation. Its pyramidal roofing has collapsed, revealing a brick dome beneath. The tomb appears originally to have had very rich brick and tile ornament, but it is now in a very dilapidated condition and would appear to have been abandoned to its fate. An inscription mentioning a certain Aḥmad bin Abū Bakr has disappeared. If the final word of this signature, which is now effaced, was in fact 'al-Marandī' it would mean that this building was the work of the same architect as the Hospital of Kaykā'ūs I at Sivas, a theory corroborated by the similarity in the style of the brick architecture. If this is the case 617/1220 would be a likely construction date.

A tomb in a village near Pazarören in the vilayet of Kayseri is a four-sided structure entirely of brick on a low plinth of cut stone displaying extremely meticulous workmanship in its brick facing, which is arranged in various geometrical patterns, such as lozenges and zigzags. The upper section is ruined, and the pyramidal roof has collapsed revealing a dome on squinches. Inside, the lower portion of the walls is plastered, but in the squinches and the dome the original brick herring-bone patterns have survived. The *mumyalık* (crypt) has an unusual plan, with transverse vaults. Its geometrical brick ornament and the long, narrow stalactite niches on each side of the façade are characteristic of an early period. Although it cannot definitely be attributed to Melik Danishmend Ghāzī, judging by its similarities to the Gunbadh-i Surkh at Maragha, the Kırk Kızlar Kümbed at Niksar and the tomb in the Hospital of Kaykā'ūs I at Sivas it would seem to date from the end of the 12th century.

As for Mengüjükid tombs, that of the Mengüjükid treasurer Qamar al-Dīn at Divriği is a plain octagonal structure of cut stone with a pyramidal roof and a porch with a lobed arch. The date of the inscription above the arch of the porch is 592/1196. Nothing now remains of the tiles or *bacini* that once filled the round cavities of various sizes below the conical roof.

The Sitte Melik mausoleum, also at Divriği, has a pyramidal roof over an octagonal body of cut stone and shows originality in the organisation of the entrance façade in the form of a porch and in the long narrow vertical niches of various sizes and with various types of ornament on the other sides. (Fig. 61.) It has undergone repairs in recent years. The old Turkish fourfold braid motif produced by intersecting octagons appears once more on the pilasters of the stalactite niches. The outer edge of the façade is surrounded by deeply hollowed grooves, whilst the inner part is surrounded by geometrical patterns, composed of concentric octagons joined by means of four arms, in the form of a wide border with two rows above (Fig. 62). This type of ornament, which we have already seen in the old stone mihrab of the Great Mosque at Sivas, continues in exactly the same form under the Seljuks in the Alay Han and in the mihrab of the Taş Masjid (founded by Hajji Farrūḥ) at Konya.

The magnificent inscription in raised *thuluth* lettering with scrolls and foliate arabesques is squeezed under the decoration above, so losing half of its effect and becoming bound up with the ornamental patterns. The last portion of the inscription, which mentions the date 592/1195, has been added underneath in a plainer and coarser *naskhī* script. The pyramidal roof is supported by finely detailed stalactite cornices and is encircled by an inscription based on the lower edge. Under the cornice is quite a wide border of geometrical entrelacs. According to the dating inscription the mausoleum was built for the Mengüjükid Emir Sulaymān bin Sayf al-Dīn Shāhanshāh. In the inscriptions his name is given with the Turkish titles of Alp Qutlugh Tughrul Tekin. On the inscription on the façade to the right only the name of the architect's father—Bahram—can be read. This tomb, which is known as the Sitte Melik Kümbed after a woman who was buried here in the 14th century, is one of the finest funerary monuments remaining from the 12th century and is of a quality and style that might be regarded as preparing the way for the Great Mosque of Divriği.

The tomb of Mengüjükid Melik Ghāzī at Kemah on the Upper Euphrates is a tall octagonal brick building, the pyramidal roof of which has been restored in wood. The sides of the octagon are set in rectangular frames which form projections at the corners in the form of piers. Underneath the roof and above the frames there are Kufic Koranic inscriptions in brick mosaic. The entrance façade is organised in the form of a porch, and the pediment of the pointed arch is ornamented with geometrical entrelacs with a single-line Kufic inscription beneath. The arch of the tympanum which rests on corner pilasters is enlivened with alternate circles and lozenges in brick mosaic. The octagonal crypt has an unusual plan with the vault rising from an octagonal pier in the centre. The interior of the tomb is cylindrical with two inscriptions in Persian and Arabic written on the walls in black ink at a later date. The Arabic inscription records the marriage of the Mengüjükid Bahramshāh to one of the daughters of Qılıch Arslan. Judging from this inscription and from the similarity of the decoration to the brick-work in the Maragha tombs and the tomb of Kaykā'ūs I at Sivas this mausoleum would appear to date from the beginning of the 13th century and thus to an early period in the development of the domed funerary monument. When ʿAlā al-Dīn Dā'ūd bin Bahramshāh, the Emir of the province of Erzincan, handed over his territories to ʿAlā al-Dīn Kayqubād I in 619/1219 he was assigned Akşehir and Ilgın, whilst Kemah passed to the Seljuks. The tomb must, therefore, have been built prior to this date.

The so-called tomb of the Emir Saltuk, the largest of the three tombs to the south of the Çifte Minare Medrese at Erzurum, and which is attributed to the Saltukids, is remarkable for the soundness of its architecture and the monumentality of its squared stone construction. (Fig. 63.) It has undergone a great deal of repair and is now covered by a low conical roof resembling a dome. The lower part of the tomb is in the form of an octagon, each side of which terminates in a triangular lunette, whilst the upper part is a tall cylinder. The exterior of this two-storeyed tomb is immediately distinguished from other Anatolian domed mausolea by features that recall late Romanesque architecture. Blind windows with round double arches supported on a central column are repeated in the centre of each side and are connected to each other by means of a string course moulding on the lower edge. Underneath this on the entrance façade there is a door with a round arch. The round-arched niches between the triangular lunettes on the upper storey contain various reliefs, including snakes, heads of hares, bats, eagles, and human heads between the horns of oxen. These are blazons or heraldic emblems from the old Turkish animal calendar.

The style of this tomb, together with certain similarities to the domed masjid in the Saltukid citadel of Erzurum, indicates a date at the end of the 12th century. It remains, however, as a single experiment without any successors in Anatolia.

As for Seljuk mausolea, that of Qılıch Arslan II adjoining the north side of the ʿAlā al-Dīn Mosque at Konya is the only one still remaining from the 12th century. This consists of a decagonal prismatic body of cut stone with a pyramidal roof. The interior is a cylindrical domed area articulated by niches. The porch, which faces the north, has now been transformed into a window and a door has been opened in the niche facing the mosque. Only a few fragments remain of a Koranic inscription in faience with the Ayyat al-Kursī (the Verse of the Throne) in raised white lettering on a lapis lazuli ground below the 10-sided pyramidal roof. An undated two-line inscription on stone under the roof on the east façade states that the mausoleum was built by Qılıch Arslan bin Masʿūd. Lower down, on the rectangular frame of the original porch arch, we find the name of the architect, Yūsuf bin ʿAbd al-Ghaffār of Khojend, a town near Nishapur, or Khojan near Samarkand. The original door, which opened out in the form of a broken arch and has now been converted into a window, is surrounded by a border of palmettes and double foliate arabesques, whilst a large square re-used carved stone block is set centrally in the upper section (Fig. 64) of the tympanum of the porch. In the tomb itself there are eight cenotaphs of various sizes. Four of these are covered with tiles with raised white lettering on a cobalt ground and some of them are also decorated with scrolls. At the head of the second cenotaph from the right is written, 'Lord, spare Qılıch Arslan bin Masʿūd, the builder of this tomb, martyr and suppliant, father of conquests.' On the first cenotaph can be seen two tiles with the names Sulaymān and Qılıch Arslan. These tiles were damaged during repairs and other tiles were inserted between them, but it is quite clear that perhaps as many as eight Seljuk sultans are buried in this modest mausoleum. As Qılıch Arslan II died in 1192 a mausoleum bearing an inscription in his name must have been constructed prior to this date. The tomb, with its plain decagonal prismatic exterior, its stone and tile ornament, its inscription and its door with a broken arch set within the slightly pointed arched porch, is one of the first experimental works of the Seljuks. (The broken arch, much used later at Bursa, was also employed in the western arcade of the Great Mosque at Diyarbekir.)

An octagonal tomb near the former, and adjoining the north wall, was left unfinished and is completed only as far as the pyramidal roof. An inscription on the courtyard façade of the mosque mentions that the mosque was built by the Atabek Ayāz on the orders of Kaykā'ūs I in 616/1219. That the tomb was left unfinished may have been due to the Sultan's death in the same year. It is of cut stone faced with marble. Within it is a duodecagonal structure articulated by niches with one window cut in the qibla wall on each side of a mihrab. The slightly pointed arch is lobed on the outer face and is surrounded by a border with geometrical entrelacs in low relief. The trefoil-shaped inscription panel of the arch was left blank. Corner pilasters with zigzag patterns, bi-coloured marble voussoirs, and various arch decorations surrounding these to be seen on the porch giving on to the courtyard façade of the mosque combine to form a highly successful porch composition. The stalactite mihrab niche is in the form of a semi-octagon containing three long niches with round arches, each surrounded by braid-work designs. This tomb is incomplete in every way, and it is clear that it must belong to the year of Kaykā'ūs I's death.

The mausoleum attached to the Çifte Medrese at Kayseri is one of the earliest Seljuk tomb structures (602/1206), and stands just behind the furthest right of the 4 iwans. It is constructed entirely of cut stone, externally being in the form of an octagon with a pyramidal spire, whilst inside it is roofed by a dome on squinches. On each side of the octagon there is a niche which is reflected on the exterior in the form of a projecting semicylinder. The upper edge is encircled by an inscription band. Although it contains no remains of any graves or cenotaphs there is no doubt that it is the tomb of Jawhar Nasība, the daughter of Qılıch Arslan and the founder of the Dār al-Shifā' (Hospital) which is now known as the Çifte Medrese.

Only one other tomb of a Seljuk sultan has survived apart from the mausoleum of Qılıch Arslan discussed above. This is the tomb in the right-hand iwan of the Dār al-Shifā' (Hospital) built by Kaykā'ūs I in Sivas in 614/1217. A tomb with a ten-sided exterior is raised over a chamber roofed with a brick dome on Turkish triangles over a square interior. The original pyramidal roofing has collapsed and has been replaced by a wooden replica. (Fig. 65.) This is the second ten-sided mausoleum we have encountered, the other being that of Qılıch Arslan at Konya. It is thus clear that only the mausolea of Seljuk sultans were ten-sided though a ten-sided tomb had been built earlier for the princess Mu'mine Khātūn at Nakhichevan. A ceramic inscription in raised white lettering on a dark blue ground under the tympanum enclosed by a large arch on the façade of the tomb informs us that the sultan died in 617/1219. The façade beneath this is pierced centrally by a door with a window on each side. This magnificent façade, which is articulated by heightened pointed arched pediments and a harmonious arrangement of narrow rectangular mouldings surrounding these, is the first monumental structure in Anatolia to display Seljuk brick and tile mosaic ornamentation and points forward to the later brilliant development of the art of faience mosaic. (Fig. 66.) The name of the master-builder Aḥmad of Marand can be read at the bottom of the right-hand tympanum in the form of two cartouches of turquoise tiles with Kufic script produced by scratching away the surrounding glaze, and it is obvious that he came from Azerbaidzhan. The façade is constructed of bright red brick of the finest quality and is decorated with turquoise, manganese-purple and white glazed bricks and tiles in the form of plaited Kufic inscriptions and mosaic patterns of geometrical stars and entrelacs. Inside the dome the simple mature brick technique, with glazed insets here and there, can be seen in all its delicacy. The cenotaph of the sultan in front of the mihrab together with the other cenotaphs the tomb contains are all covered with large tiles worked in a composition of geometrical star entrelacs, white entrelacs with black contours and insets of cobalt and turquoise.

Each of the surfaces of the ten sides of the drum rising above the roof are framed in pointed arches and worked with a mosaic of various geometrical patterns of reddish bricks on plaster. The brick decoration in the Kharraqān mausolea of the Great Seljuks are exactly repeated here in the compositions consisting of octagonal stars produced by interlinked swastikas. (Designs Id and 7.) The same type of ornament is to be found later in the faience mosaic covering the rear wall of the side iwan in the Gök Medrese in Sivas, the rear wall of the iwan of the Sırçalı and the rear wall of the iwan of the Karatay Medrese at Konya. The linking of the octagons arranged in rows in the brick ornament of the other niche by means of two arms projecting from each side is a repetition of the pattern to be found on the side door of the Castle Mosque at Divriği. The influence of the Great Seljuks can thus be traced in various forms in later Anatolian decorative arts, and the roots connecting Anatolian brick structure to the funerary architecture of Azerbaidzhan and Great Seljuk Art can be clearly seen in this tomb.

One of the most important funerary monuments of Anatolia is the tomb at Tercan known as the Mama Khātūn Kümbed. This is a structure of meticulous workmanship constructed entirely of cut stone, and of a style of architecture quite unique in Anatolia. (Fig. 67.) The actual tomb is covered by a fluted conical spire on a cylindrical body with semicylindrical flutes and is surrounded by a wide enclosing wall in the form of a circle (Plan 27). Eleven deep niches with pointed arches were opened in the inner side of this enclosure wall, and these may well have been destined for the reception of additional cenotaphs. There is an entrance to a staircase on the right of a *çeşme* in the small niche at the left of the outer porch, which itself is a little higher than the walls. The actual tomb is defined by very simple but monumental cut stone construction. The round fluting on the outside separated by grooves is reflected in the interior by long narrow semicylindrical niches with ribs between them stretching as far as the centre of the dome. The rectangular frame of the door of the mausoleum is completely devoid of any ornament save for a lotus palmette frieze. (Fig. 70.) In contrast to this the entrance façade, which includes the outer porch, forms a very harmonious composition, with rich ornament in which vegetal motifs play a very small role. (Fig. 68.) Carved stalactites, wide borders of geometrical entrelacs framing the narrow porch niche, a chain braid pattern, Kufic and *naskhī* inscriptions with slender scrolls and foliate arabesques, a plain plaited Kufic inscription surrounding the side niches of the porch, corner pilasters ornamented with geometrical patterns, all combine to produce a rare triumph of harmony of style. (Fig. 69.) Old Turkish motifs are seen repeated in the fourfold braid patterns produced by intersecting octagons on the double border surrounding the long, narrow, pointed arched niches at each side (Design 8). The brick ornament of the Kharraqān tombs and the tombs at Nakhichevan of Yūsuf bin Kuthayyir and Mu'mine Khātūn is translated into stone in the intersecting

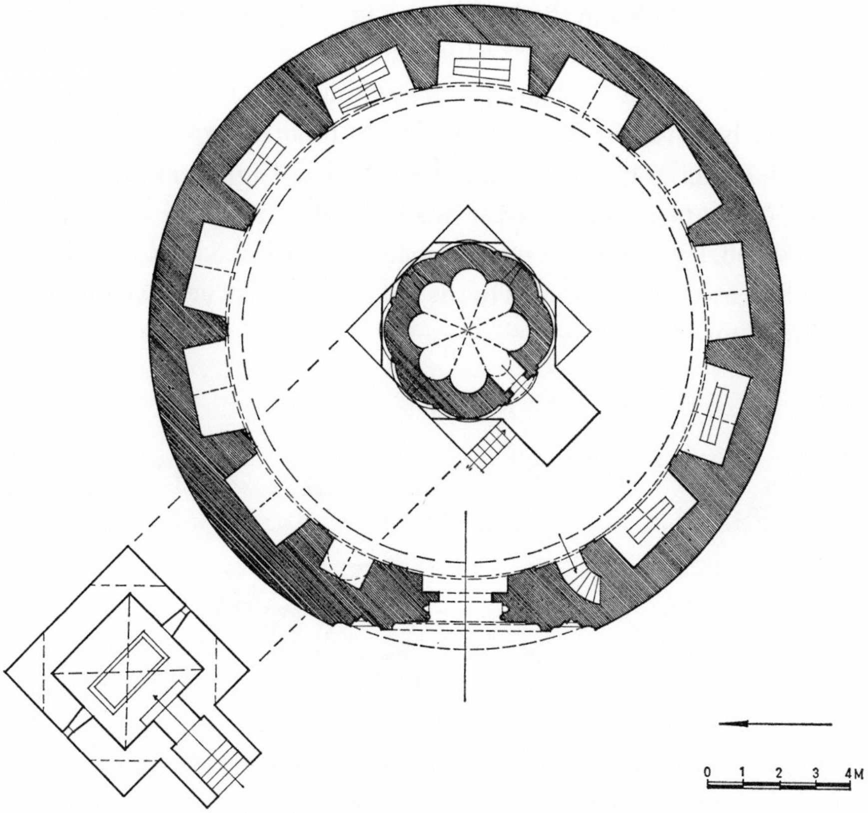

Plan 27. Tercan, Mausoleum of Mama Khātūn

Design 8. Tercan, Mausoleum of Mama Khātūn, decoration of side niche of entrance porch

hexagons to be seen in the insets in the form of pointed arches on the bottom row of the stalactites above the chain braid motif and the floriated *naskhī* inscription in the left-hand niche of the porch. The name of the architect, Abū'l-Ni'ma bin Mufaḍḍal of Ahlat, can be read in a *naskhi* inscription between the chain braid motif and the lotus, palmette and stalactite frieze on the side niches of the porch. This shows that he came from Ahlat in the province of Van, an old centre of stone masonry. The inscription is undated, and there has been a great deal of discussion about the date of the building. The style, however, points to the beginning of the 13th century. The quality of the architecture was severely damaged in the latest, very crudely executed repairs. As for the plan, in excavations carried out in recent years in Central Asia V. M. Masson has discovered a number of old funerary monuments which have been dated to the 6th–4th centuries B.C. in Transoxiana, and at Tagisken to the east of Lake Aral. The main features of the plan of the Tercan mausoleum can already be seen in these ancient tombs, which show, too, how the forms of other mausolea are linked to Central Asia. Although some scholars wish to ascribe these tombs to the Sakas, they may very well be 3rd century B.C. burial places of the Huns. (See below)

Tagisken, Mausolea (restoration)

The Kureysh Baba mausoleum at Sincanlı-Boyalıköy in the vilayet of Afyon dating from the beginning of the 13th century is a building of simple architectural design consisting of an octagonal body in cut stone of two different colours surmounted by a brick pyramidal spire. The door of the tomb is reached by staircases rising from either side of the crypt door. Each facet is articulated by a rectangular blind niche, whilst the entrance façade is organised in the form of a small porch of the same height. (Fig. 71.) The borders under the pyramidal roof and around the porch are worked with fourfold braid motifs produced by intersecting octagons. The inscription plaque is empty.

The Ertokush Mausoleum attached to the medrese at Atabey dated 621/1223 is an octagonal structure of cut stone in alternate courses of light and dark red, surmounted on the inside by a dome, and on the outside by a pyramidal brick roof. Traces of tiles can be seen on the cenotaph inside. On the exterior an unusual type of brick architecture has been applied in the use of brick filling the corners of the octagonal stone body. The mausoleum is entered through three doors at the rear of the western iwan of the medrese. There is no door from the outside. The tomb must have been built before the medrese and later attached to it. The cenotaph inside the tomb is faced with open-work turquoise tiles, and the ornamental patterns from the Ghaznevid Ribāṭ-i Māhī can be seen in the large fourfold braid patterns formed by intersecting octagons in which each alternate side is broken (see Design Ib).

The ʿAlī Tūṣī Türbe at Tokat dated 631/1234 is in the form of an octagonal tomb tower with a dome within on squinches. The pyramidal exterior roof has collapsed. The two rectangular windows with pointed arched pediments on the façade of the brick building are decorated with Kufic inscriptions in manganese-purple, turquoise and lapis lazuli faience mosaic, geometrical entrelacs and intersecting hexagons. In a two-line *naskhī* inscription on a long, narrow stone cartouche above the windows can be read the name of Abū'l-Qāsim bin ʿAlī al-Tūṣī, one of Kayqubād I's governors, and the date 631/1234. The governor, who was a native of Tūṣ, had the tomb built in his lifetime. The surfaces of the remaining walls are covered with plaster. On the outside the form of the tomb is octagonal, whilst on the inside the square chamber is roofed by a dome on squinches. The pyramidal roof has collapsed.

The tomb of Mahperi Khwand Khātūn, the wife of ʿAlā al-Dīn Kayqubād I and the mother of Kaykhusraw II, in Kayseri dated 636/1238 stands within the Khwand complex, having been added later to the corner where the mosque adjoins the medrese. The octagonal mausoleum with its pyramidal roof is built entirely of cut stone and rests on a marble plinth with six rows of stalactites. At each corner there are ornamental pilasters extending as far as the stalactite brackets on the upper end. The building is encircled below these by an inscription in raised *thuluth* script. The central spaces have been left blank, and are surrounded by two rows of pointed arched borders consisting of geometrical entrelacs, whilst the corner insets are worked with various swastika designs and a pattern of small rosettes. The plain surfaces are enlivened by double windows with trefoil arches supported by a central column of white marble (Fig. 72). Inside the building the five-sided mihrab is crowned by a niche with five rows of stalactites, and each facet is decorated with a geometrical composition of 8-pointed stars. Here the tomb is reached by a staircase from one of the cells of the medrese.

The Çifte Kümbed (or Twin Tombs) near Kayseri dated 645/1247 has an octagonal body on a cubic plinth. The pyramidal roof has collapsed revealing the dome underneath. It is essentially a very much simplified and much less ornamented form of the Khwand Mausoleum. The upper edge is encircled by a *thuluth* Koranic inscription band from the Sūrat al-Baqara (the Chapter of the Cow). The niche of the stalactite porch is framed by a wide border of geometrical star entrelacs. A five-line inscription on white marble in the centre of this informs us that the mausoleum was built in 645/1243–4 for al-Malika al-ʿĀdiliyya, the daughter of the Ayyubid al-Malik al-ʿĀdil Abū Bakr and a wife of Kayqubād I. The second tomb that originally stood beside this one has completely disappeared, but the name Çifte (Twin) Kümbed remains.

The Melik Gazi Kümbed at Kırşehir is an octagonal structure with pyramidal roof resting on a square plinth with smoothed corners, and conforms exactly to the form of a tent. Large triangles projecting downwards from the upper edge recall the eaves of a tent covering, and prepare a circular base for the conical roof projecting outwards in the form of a mushroom (Fig. 73). According to an inscription on the richly decorated marble portal with its stalactite canopy it was built by one of the wives of the Mengüjükid Muẓaffar al-Dīn Muḥammad Shāh. In 625/1228 ʿAlā al-Dīn Kayqubād had captured Şebinkarahisar and sent Muḥammad Shāh and his three sons to Kırşehir. The tomb must have been built for them.

The tomb of the vizir Karatay, to whom we owe many priceless works of Seljuk architecture, is in the domed space to the left-hand side of the iwan in his medrese in Konya. It is dated 1251. The tile decoration has completely fallen away, but the herring-bone brick ornament in the dome can still be seen. A geometrical reticulated pattern of turquoise and lapis lazuli tiles on the threshold of the door may be composed of fragments from the cenotaph. In its present state Karatay's tomb is a very modest structure compared to his other magnificent buildings.

The mausoleum adjoining the Gök Medrese Mosque built by Turumtay at Amasya in 1266 has a high octagonal body of brick set on a square substructure of cut stone. It is surmounted by a fluted pyramidal roof, the apex of which has collapsed. The corner insets and the inside of the shallow pointed arched niches on each facet of the octagonal body are filled with geometrical entrelacs and ornament. The upper edge is encircled by a magnificent inscription band of plaited Kufic in turquoise faience, so that the external appearance recalls the tomb of Kaykā'ūs I at Sivas. There are simple tile decorations on the cenotaphs and on the iwan arch opening into the mosque, whilst the façades pierced by pointed arches on the north and east sides of the cubiform substructure of cut stone are enriched with stone decoration of geometrical stars and entrelacs. (Fig. 74.)

The square tomb facing the façade to the left of the entrance iwan in the Burūjirdī Medrese at Sivas (671/1271) is given a very colourful appearance by the fine mosaic decorations on its walls and on the pendentives of the dome. On the upper edge there is a faience mosaic inscription frieze in manganese-purple on a turquoise ground of scrolls with the words: 'This is the tomb of Muẓaffar of Burūjird, the humble servant and homeless stranger. May God forgive him his sins.'

The tomb of the Īl-Khānid governor Jabrā'īl bin Jājā situated on the façade of the Caca Bey Medrese at Kırşehir (671/1272) has the external form of a domed mausoleum. On the drum of the domed interior there is a remarkable faience mosaic inscription frieze in raised white lettering on a lapis lazuli ground.

The Döner Kümbed at Kayseri, the richest centre of Seljuk tomb architecture, is a twelve-sided structure built entirely of cut stone with a conical roof resting on stalactite cornices. The tomb resembles a monumental tent with a cylindrical inner space roofed by a dome. It has a remarkable abundance of figural relief decoration, and between two figures of winged leopards with human heads on the porch façade there would appear to be the much defaced remains of a double-headed eagle. A two-line marble inscription above informs us that it was built for the princess Shāh Jihān Khātūn. There is no date. Each of the facets on the exterior is framed by one of the twelve pointed arches produced by grooved mouldings and is worked in a different type of decoration. Apart from this there is a very much damaged relief to the left of the porch depicting a double-headed eagle on a date palm with a lion at each side, and another relief of a date palm on the right-hand side of the porch. Judging from the similarity of the tomb's style and its approximately cylindrical body to the Ahlat tombs it can be ascribed to about the year 1276. (Fig. 75.)

The general architectural features of the Döner Kümbed can be seen in simplified form in the tombs at Erzurum. The deepened arch mouldings surrounding the body of the tomb attached to the Çifte Minare Medrese, which belongs to the same period, are twisted in the form of a rope (Fig. 76). The facets have been left blank, and the transition to the conical roof is effected by only one row of stalactites. Five other tombs, comprising two of these three tombs together with the Karanlık Kümbed, the Gümüshlü Kümbed and the Rabia Khātūn Kümbed, are poorer and very much simplified versions of the same type dating from the beginning of the 14th century. The Khwāja Yāqūt Mausoleum of 710/1310 attached to the Yakutiye Medrese is built according to the same principles.

Unlike the preceding tombs the Turumtay Türbe at Amasya dated 677/1278 is a rectangular vaulted structure and its windowed façade is richly decorated with rows of palmettes with scrolls and ornamental pilasters. An innovation is the use of stone decoration composed of rows of high-relief palmettes arranged in panels, as the basic decorative composition. A marble inscription above the north window informs us that it was built as a tomb for Turumtay during the reign of Kaykhusraw bin Qılıch Arslan III. (Fig. 77.) Turumtay bin ʿAbd Allāh was a slave of ʿAlā al-Dīn Kayqubād.Later he became his Amīr Akhūr (Master of the Stables).

The Seljuk vizir Sahib Ata, Fakhr al-Dīn Alī, who was known as Abū'l-Khayrāt (the Father of Good Works) on account of the many buildings he erected in various cities, built his family tomb in the complex he founded at Konya (682/1283). The tomb has doors leading both into mosque and *khānqāh*. The spacious interior is roofed with a dome supported on one side by a large pointed arch and on the three other sides by walls, the transition being effected by means of Turkish triangles, and is faced with faience work of the most mature style displaying all the refinements of Seljuk ceramic workmanship. Foliate motifs predominate in this tomb, and the big motifs in high relief on the large arch (Fig. 78) recall the mihrab of the Külük Mosque at Kayseri. Inside there are three cenotaphs, that of Sahib Ata being completely covered with tiles and bearing a raised inscription. At the foot of the cenotaph are the words: 'Al-Ṣāḥib al-Muʿaẓẓam Fakhr al-Dīn passed from this transitory world to the realm of eternity in the month of Shawwāl 684 (1285). May God fill his tomb with radiance.' As the actual date of his death is 687/1289 a mistake must have been made in the inscription. The tiles on the two cenotaphs belonging to his sons are in the same style, but most of them have fallen away. One of the cenotaphs in faience mosaic in the second row belongs to his daughter Melike, who died in 691/1292. The architect of the tomb may have been Kalūk (Kölüg) bin ʿAbd Allāh, whose name appears in this complex only on the porch of the mosque.

Ahlat is second only to Kayseri in the number and variety of its tombs, and is an old centre of art and architecture where architects and master-builders whose signatures are to be found on buildings all over Anatolia were trained. The Turks have left here innumerable examples of tombstones of various composition and ornamentation spread over a wide area, and exhibiting, as in a museum, the age and wealth of their craftsmanship in stone. These are from the 12th to 14th centuries.

Eleven mausolea, some of them ruined, some in perfect condition, but all very regularly built in cut stone, survive from the period before the end of the 15th century. The largest of these is the Ulu Kümbed, which is also the oldest, and is ascribed to the year 672/1273. It has a cylindrical body nearly 7 metres in diameter on a square plinth with chamfered corners and terminating in a pointed conical roof resting on stalactite cornices. (Fig. 79.) Apart from the door on the east side, the body of the tomb is pierced by three windows, one at each of the other quarters of the compass, with round arched niches between, and is decorated with borders of grooved mouldings and round arches (Fig. 80). The conical roof is decorated with mouldings composed of successive rows of ornamental arches. The hexagons arranged in rows under the inscription frieze and joined one to the other at each edge by double arms show that the decorative motif first seen in the side door-frame of the Castle Mosque at Divriği has spread as far as Ahlat.

According to its inscription the half-ruined tomb dated 673/1275 known as the Ḥasan Padishāh Kümbed was built for the Emir Ḥusām al-Dīn Ḥasan Āghā bin Maḥmūd, and is a simplified replica of the Ulu Kümbed.

The two monuments known as the Çifte (Twin) Kümbed, with their conical roofs and cylindrical bodies, are small-scale replicas of the first mausolea. One on the left belongs to the Emir Inal's son Bughatay Āqā and his wife Shīrīn Khātūn, and is dated 680/1281. The other belongs to Bughatay Āqā's son Ḥasan Temir and Ḥasan Āqā's daughter Esen Tekin and is dated 678/1279. The arch mouldings which surround the body of the Bughatay Aqa Kümbed are linked to the rectangular mouldings by a small circle above. (Fig. 81.) This is a Zengid motif, and shows the continued duration of Zengid influence. Here too can be seen once more the fourfold braid motif produced by intersecting octagons.

The basic features of the 13th century mausolea at Ahlat developed, with a few variations, in the traditional form of a conical roof resting on stalactite cornices on a cylindrical body.

In the 13th century too we see the first appearance of tombs in the form of iwans. The oldest of these, the Eyvan Türbe at Seyidgazi, is constructed of cut stone with a crypt underneath, and is traditionally ascribed to the mother of 'Alā al-Dīn Kayqubād. The iwan is reached by staircases rising from either side of the door of the crypt. The iwan was later linked to the arcaded courtyard by the addition of a *tekke* or dervish monastery in front of it.

The Emir Yavtash Bek Türbe at Akşehir, which is constructed in a blend of stone and brick, the Eyvan Türbe at Boyalıköy and the Gömech Khātūn Türbe at Konya are other examples from the second half and the end of the 13th century. The mausoleum of Gömech Khātūn, the lower third of which is constructed of cut stone and the rest completed with bricks, is also of importance in being the most imposing classical structure of this type of tomb, with its façade decorated with crenellations and ornamental tiles. (Fig. 82.)

The mausoleum of the Eshrefoghlu Sulaymān Bek (1301) attached to the eastern wall of the mosque in Beyşehir conforms to the traditional Seljuk style of tomb, being an octagonal structure of cut stone surmounted by a dome within and a conical roof outside. Although the tomb has a very simple exterior the interior of the dome is covered with 12-sided star patterns, combining with scrolls, palmettes and foliate arabesques (*rūmīs*) to form the richest and most spectacular composition of all Seljuk faience mosaic. The drum of the dome is encircled by an ornamental faience mosaic pseudo-Kufic frieze (Fig. 83). The traditional turquoise stars of the Karatay Medrese in Konya, here drowned in the fine detail of the decoration, announce the new taste and style which ushered in the Beylik period of the 14th century.

Seljuk Caravansarais in Anatolia

The high level of Anatolian Seljuk culture is most vividly reflected in the caravansarais that rise up along the roads stretching from Denizli to Erzurum, Kars and Iğdır, from Kütahya to Malatya, Bitlis and Ahlat, and from Antalya to Sinop and Samsun. These monuments bear witness to the greatness of the power of the Seljuk Sultanate and the solidity of its organisation. As in other architectural fields the plans of these buildings and some of their ornamental motifs are based on those of the previous Turkish caravansarais to which the Karakhanids, Ghaznevids and Great Seljuks gave the name *Ribāṭ*, but in Anatolia the caravansarais, called in Turkish *Sultan Han's* or merely *Han*'s, are very monumental works with a highly developed cut stone architecture. Whilst in religious buildings various materials are employed, such as brick or sometimes a mixture of stone and brick, the hans are built entirely of stone, and whereas the religious buildings, apart from a few medreses, are on a modest scale if often with very attractive decoration, the Anatolian Seljuk caravansarais are extremely spectacular large, often palatial, monuments. These great structures, that remind one of the Gothic cathedrals of Italy, were commercial, charitable and at the same cultural institutions on the most important caravan routes of medieval Anatolia; and were all built by the Seljuk sultans or their vizirs during the 13th century. Most of them contained baths, a mosque and a library, as well as doctors and veterinary surgeons to meet the needs of both the travellers and their animals, and craftsmen who could handle every type of repair. Eight Royal caravansarais, one of which has no inscription, survive. The Alay Han was built by Qılıch Arslan II (1156–1192), the Evdir Han by 'Izz al-Dīn Kaykā'ūs I (1210–1219), the two Sultan Hans and the Alara Han by 'Alā al-Dīn Kayqubād I (1219–1236), the Incir Han, the Kirkgöz Han and the Eğridir Han by Ghiyāth al-Dīn Kaykhusraw (1236–1246). Apart from these Royal Hans the plans are known of 59 more, most of which are in ruins, and 35 more have been unearthed in recent excavations and explorations, making up about a hundred still remaining from the hundreds of Seljuk hans. The grandeur of the surviving buildings, with their stone ornament, inscriptions and various architectural innovations, paints a magnificent picture of Seljuk art and culture in Anatolia.

The Alay Han on the Aksaray–Kayseri road is in several respects the first Sultan Han in Anatolia. Qılıch Arslan II (1156–1192) is mentioned in Seljuk chronicles as having built caravansarais in the vicinity of Aksaray. In its plan and architecture the Alay Han combines all the characteristic features of the classical Seljuk caravansarais, with an inner porch with stalactite niche of the type to be found only in the Sultan Hans, a central vault with an open dome and seven perpendicular vaults on either side. The courtyard is in ruins, but the inner façade and the salient porch are in quite a good state of preservation (Fig. 84). The strength and simplicity of the style indicate an early date. On the wide border can be seen the characteristic stone decoration in which geometrical motifs consisting of two concentric octagons are linked together by means of cruciform and diagonal arms. These geometrical designs, which are to be seen on the porch of the Mengüjükid Sitte Melik Mausoleum at Divriği (1195) and on the stone mihrab border of the Seljuk Taş Masjid founded by Hajjī Farrūḥ at Konya (1215), as well as on the old stone mihrab of the Danishmendid Great Mosque at Sivas, first appeared as early as the end of the 12th and the beginning of the 13th century and then disappeared. The fourfold braid motif produced by intersecting octagons on the narrow border and on the ornamental arch surrounding the stalactite niche is a continuation of the old Turkish designs. The stylised figure of a double-bodied lion with the head in profile on the bottom row of stalactites on the porch is symbolic in character. It seems reasonable to suppose that it was placed in so prominent a position as a blazon connected with Qılıch Arslan. Taking all these various features into consideration we may say that the Alay Han was completed by Qılıch Arslan II in the last year of his reign (1192) and, with its highly developed style, became the classical prototype for the great Seljuk hans. The name Alay Han must have been given later. All the Sultan Hans built in the thirty-seven years following the construction of the Alay Han have subsequently disappeared, with the exception of the Evdir Han of 1216–18, so that the next to survive is the Sultan Han (1229) on the Konya–Aksaray road. The dates of other caravansarais extend from the beginning of the 13th century up to 1278, the Çay Han, the last dated structure.

Caravansarais dating from the beginning of the 13th century are built on a simplified plan consisting of courtyard and covered hall of similar dimensions. The han built by the Seljuk statesman and commander-in-chief Shams al-Dīn Altınapa dates from 598/1201. It has no decoration whatsoever. The little mosque added to the left-hand side of the façade is raised on an iwan. (A second han built by Altınapa—the Argıt Han on the Konya–Akşehir road—is in a very ruinous condition.)

The Kuruçeşme Han on the Beyşehir road is built on the same plan but on a somewhat larger scale. The inscription, which is very much damaged, runs as follows: 'This ribāṭ was built by (name illegible) in the reign of Ghiyāth al-Dīn Kaykhusraw and completed in the year 604/1207.' The term *ribāṭ* is still used in connection with this han. The masjid occupies the vaulted chamber on the left of the entrance.

The Kızılören Han was built by the Emir Qutlugh on the same road and during the reign of the same sultan, and was completed one year earlier, in 601/1204. It has a larger covered hall with three aisles. It has an unusual plan, with a large spacious courtyard in front consisting of four porticos on each side in the form of iwans projecting beyond the extremities of the enclosure, a rectangular vaulted room occupying each corner and a salient two-storeyed entrance façade. Other innovations to be seen in this han are the mihrab of the transverse vaulted masjid supported on four arches with a scallop-shaped niche, corner pilasters and a border of simple stone decoration, together with the ornament on the door posts of the other two vaulted rooms beside this. The building is given a decorative appearance by a two-storeyed courtyard façade and the regular construction of the high solid towers and buttressing walls in yellow and red cut stone.

The next caravansarai after the Alay Han to be built by a sultan is the Evdir Han built by 'Izz al-Dīn Kaykā'ūs I on the Antalya–Isparta road. The inscription has been removed from its original position and only the words 'six', 'one' can be read, the 'six' referring to hundreds. It must therefore have been built between 611/1216 and 615/1218. As it is situated in a warm region it has a different type of plan with plain-vaulted double arcades arranged around a spacious courtyard (52 × 71 metres). The arcades in the centre are wider. There is no covered hall. On the outside, however, the magnificent stalactite porch with corner pilasters and side niches, a wide framing border with star-interlacing patterns in low relief, and a frieze on the pointed arch composed of interlocking circles and lozenges continuing on the inside of the niche, has a very monumental appearance. (Fig. 85.) The solid cut stone walls have three buttressing towers on each side, and two at the front and rear. Covering approximately 3800 square metres it approaches the later Sultan Hans in size, and may be put in the third place.

The Hekim Han, also known as the Stone Han (Taş Han), on the Sivas–Malatya road conforms to the normal plan of the Sultan Hans in having a covered hall with three naves and a wider, approximately square courtyard. Although the plain stone architecture is not very striking there is a remarkable inscription written in three languages—Arabic, Armenian and Syriac. According to the Arabic inscription in Seljuk *thuluth* it was built by the physician Abū Sālim bin Abī'l Ḥasan al-Shammās of Malatya and the hall was completed in 615/1218, but the courtyard was added during the reign of Kayqubād I. The Armenian and Syriac inscriptions give the same information. There is also an Ottoman inscription showing that Köprülü Mehmed Pasha had the building repaired by the architect Hasan Agha in 1071/1660. Most of this repair work was carried out in the courtyard section. The han was given the name Hekim Han because it was built by a physician.

The Kadin Han on the Konya–Akşehir road and the Ertokush Han near Gelendost on the Eğridir–Konya road are both plain stone buildings, completely devoid of ornament, built in the year 620/1223. The three-aisled hall section of the first is still standing, but the wider courtyard is in ruins. According to a very much damaged inscription above the portal arch beginning 'Al-Sulṭānī' the han was built by a lady by the name of Raḍiyya or Ruqayya Khātūn. It contains a great deal of material re-used from earlier buildings.

The Ertokush Han on the road from Konya to Eğridir is a stone structure of poor workmanship built by the famous statesman Mubāriz al-Dīn Ertokush, who served three Seljuk Sultans, a year before the Medrese he built on the opposite shore of the lake of Eğridir. The three-aisled hall section is strengthened by triangular towers. The courtyard is slightly wider and consists of a narrow space with various chambers, one of them domed, on each side of the entrance and arcades on both left and right. The hall porch is in stone of two different colours, and on the inscription above the porch arch is written the name Ertokush and the date.

The most magnificent and most highly developed style of Royal han architecture is to be seen in the largest caravansarai (4500 square metres) on the Konya–Aksaray road, the Sultan Han. The masjid, which in the Kızılören Han is placed conventionally on the left-hand side of the façade, is here a kiosk set on a four-bay substructure and is placed in the centre of the courtyard like a monument in a public square, and with the porches made the centre of the whole architectural decoration. Unfortunately a large part of the building is now in ruins. According to its two inscriptions this Royal han, which from the outside resembles a majestic castle strengthened with various towers, was built by 'Alā al-Dīn Kayqubād I, the hall section being completed in 626/1229, and the courtyard at the end of the same year. (Fig. 86.)

In hexagonal medallions on each side of the ornamental arch surrounding the stalactite niche of the outer portal can be seen the partly defaced inscription of a master-builder Muḥammad bin Ḥaw(lā)n (al-Dimishqī). The knotted bicoloured stone entrelacs seen on the porch of the courtyard façade of the ʿAlā al-Dīn Mosque at Konya occupy here the spandrels of the round arches over the side niches in the outer porch. The hand of the architect Muḥammad of Damascus is clearly to be seen in these decorations, which are derived from Zengid architecture in Syria. (Fig. 87.) Obviously ʿAlā al-Dīn Kayqubād entrusted the architect with this prodigious task after he had completed the mosque in Konya. There is another, highly condensed, inscription recording repairs carried out by the governor Sarāj al-Dīn Aḥmad al-Ḥasan in 677/1278, after a fire. The façade, 50 metres in length, with its salient marble porch and corner towers, presents a very imposing appearance. On the outside it is as much as 110 metres long. On entering one can see the decorated arches of the courtyard arcade on the right, rooms and apartments with decorated doors on the left, the kiosk masjid in the centre on a base of four open arches and reached by staircases, and finally, at the far end, the porch of the covered hall section (Figs. 88 and 90). The upper portion of the hall porch, which is plainer in style than the highly ornate and original outer porch, has collapsed. The ornament of the ruined kiosk masjid is in the same style and of the same refinement as the decoration of the outer porch. (Fig. 89.) The hall section consists of a wide central aisle with nine aisles running perpendicular to it on each side, and the open dome in the centre rests on stalactite squinches with decorated arches on pendentives. There is no other decoration of any kind in the hall. The dome, the central part of which has collapsed, was originally covered by an octagonal pyramid as if it were a tomb (Fig. 92). This Sultan Han is a beautifully constructed stone building that served as a model for the great hans of a later date.

According to a badly damaged inscription on the hall porch ʿAlā al-Dīn Kayqubād built his second Sultan Han on the Kayseri–Sivas road (in the village of Palas) between 630/1232–634/1236. It repeats the earlier plan with a few variations and on a slightly smaller scale (3900 square metres). (Plan 28.) Solid walls and various buttressing towers give this building a similar fortress-like appearance. The recess of the porch is developed inwards from the line of the wall and joins with the large semicylindrical flutes of the buttressing towers on either side to form a monumental composition. It is now in a very ruinous condition. There are domed baths in the north-west corner of the courtyard. A kiosk masjid in the centre is in better condition than others of the type. (Fig. 93.) The heads of the serpent-monsters on each side of the faces of the supporting arches are joined together in the middle by their open mouths. This is defined by a border of double knotted entrelacs. Geometrical designs prevail on the marble hall porch, which projects as much as two metres from the line of the wall. In the hall the lofty central aisle, six metres wide, reminds one of an Italian Gothic cathedral with its open dome and seven vaulted arches opening out on each side. (Fig. 91.) The open dome rests on pendentives and was once covered by a conical roof which has now collapsed. In the drum there are four rectangular lobed windows with blind pointed arches, and above this there is a Koranic inscription in raised widely spaced script.

According to an inscription over the porch the Alara Han was built by ʿAlā al-Dīn

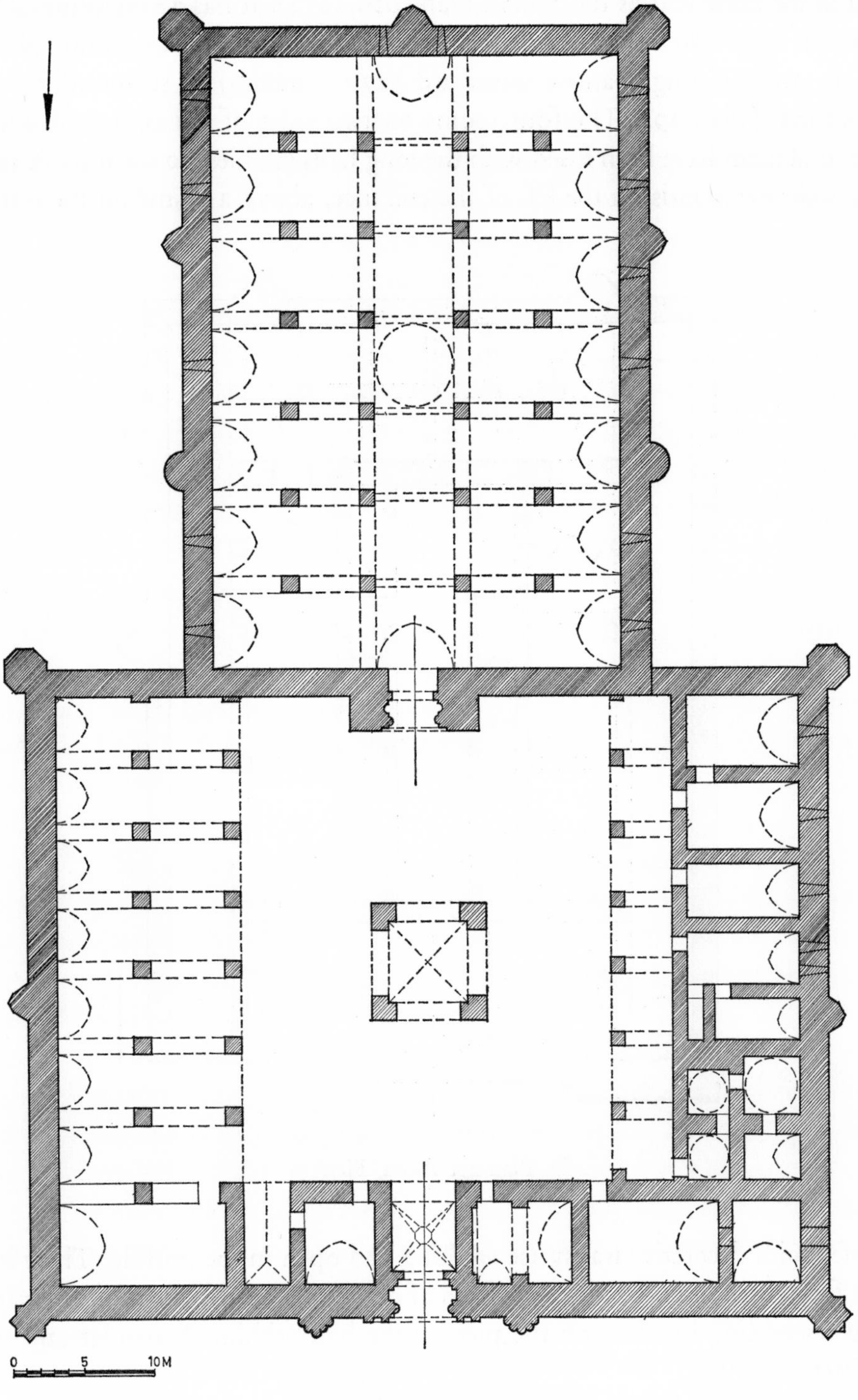

Plan 28. Kayseri, Sultan Han

Kayqubād in the same year as the Sultan Han (629/1232). It has a very unusual type of plan quite unlike the other two Sultan Hans. It stands near Alanya at the beginning of the Antalya–Konya road, and its long, narrow courtyard (27×5 metres) is surrounded by open and closed chambers. (Plan 29.) The four rooms on two sides of the courtyard with one iwan between each of them have been fused with the long halls (stables) to the rear. A small mosque reached by staircases stands on the left of the entrance, above a çeşme on the rear wall of the

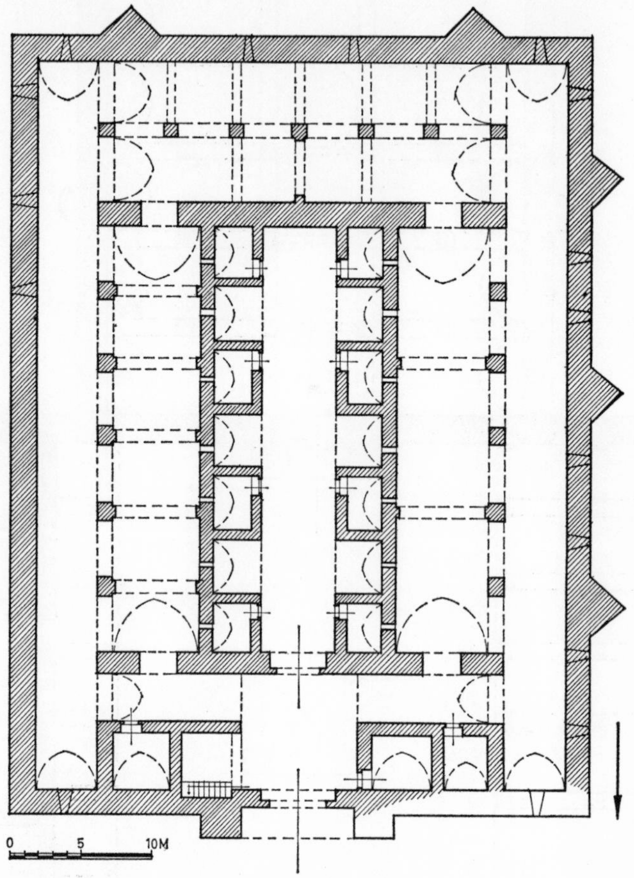

Plan 29. Alara, Han

section roofed with decorative transverse vaulting and open in the middle. There is no decoration except for stylised lions' heads in the form of brackets on the frame of the inscription on the porch, and resembling brackets on the piers of the hall within. A regular and solid type of stone architecture prevails.

The Çardak Han on the Eğridir–Denizli road which is described in its inscription as a ribāṭ was built by Asad al-Dīn Ayāz bin ʿAbd Allāh al-Shahābī, a freed slave and Constable (Amīr Qund al-Isṭabl) of ʿAlā al-Dīn Kayqubād during the reign of that sultan, and completed in 627/1230. Its plan is a simplified form of that employed in the other Sultan Hans, consisting of a square courtyard, of which only the walls are still standing, and five aisles

91 Kayseri-Sivas road, Palas, Sultan Han, interior

92 Aksaray-Konya road, Sultan Han, vaults of hall, central aisle

93 Kayseri-Sivas road, Palas, Sultan Han, Kiosk mosque in courtyard

94 Konya-Aksaray road, Zazadin Han, general view

95 Konya-Aksaray road, Zazadin Han, outer porch

96 Kayseri-Aksaray road, Ağzıkara Han, porch

97 Kayseri-Malatya road, Karatay Han, animal figures on stalactite vaulting of entrance iwan

98 Kayseri-Malatya road, Karatay Han, exterior view of inner porch and hall

99 Incir Köy, Antalya-Isparta road, Incir Han, porch

100 Amasya-Tokat road, Hatun Han, detail of porch

101 Antalya-Isparta road, Susuz Han, angel and dragon figures on side niche of porch

102 Konya-Aksehir road, Horozlu Han

103 Kayseri-Aksaray road, Avanos, Sari Han, outer and inner porches

104 Kayseri-Aksaray road, Avanos, Sari Han, masjid, upper part of entrance iwan

105 Goncali, Ak Han, view of outer and inner porches

106 Goncali, Ak Han, detail of outer porch

107 Aksaray-Nevşehir-Kayseri road, Öresun Han

divided into six sections. The hall porch is in the form of a half vault with pointed arch, and on each side of the pointed arched inscriptions stands a carved lion. (In the Sultan Han at Aksaray a head and a body have been found belonging to two large marble lions.) These are all typical Seljuk lions. Inside, an ox head can be seen in profile on the capital of the first pier of the central aisle, a pair of fish on the third and the head of a man on the fourth. Besides this there appears once more on the borders on the portal the fourfold braid design produced by intersecting octagons, each alternate side being broken, that we have already come across in the Ghaznevid Ribāṭ-i Māhī. (See Design Ib.) There is no obvious architectural decoration apart from these. Outside, the han resembles a fortress with its various buttressing towers and solid cut stone walls.

The Zazadin (Sa'd al-Dīn) Han on the Konya–Aksaray road was begun by the vizir and architect Sa'd al-Dīn Köpek in the last year of 'Alā al-Dīn Kayqubād's reign, and was completed in 634/1237. Its plan is badly proportioned, with a very long courtyard (17 × 54 metres) and a very small hall section (22 × 28 metres). The porch is set to one side and the façade seems to stretch to infinity along the length of the courtyard and hall, both of which have the same alignment. (Fig. 94.) The masjid is above the porch and the richest architectural decoration is to be found on the mihrab wall. Otherwise, there is no ornament apart from the two decorative porches with alternate white and grey courses of stone, the two inscriptions and the ruined dome in the hall with its stalactite squinches. (Fig. 95.)

Two other important caravansarais begun during the reign of 'Alā al-Dīn Kayqubād and approaching the Sultan Hans in richness are the Ağzıkara Han and the Karatay Han. According to its two inscriptions the Ağzıkara Han on the road from Kayseri to Aksaray was built by Khwāja Mas'ūd bin 'Abd Allāh, the hall section being completed in 628/1231 during the reign of 'Alā al-Dīn Kayqubād I, and the courtyard in 637/1237 in the first year of the reign of Ghiyāth al-Dīn Kaykhusraw II. The porch and main façade are at the side, and the powerful mass of the porch and the heavy towers make it resemble a fortress even more closely than do other caravansarais. (Fig. 96.) Its two porchs, kiosk masjid and domed hall are of an architectural quality approaching that of the Sultan Hans. The outer porch is decorated with geometrical designs in low relief, and the brick ornament of the Kharraqān tombs is here repeated in somewhat modified form by a swastika composition that fills the space between the stalactites and the limiting arch. This porch shows the influence of the inner porch of the Sultan Han at Aksaray. The kiosk masjid standing like a cubiform monument in the centre of the courtyard is seen here for the third time after the two Sultan Hans. The low, eight-lobed dome of the masjid is supported on stalactite squinches. The better preserved inner porch is worked with geometrical star-entrelacs and rosettes in bolder relief. The inner porch of the Karatay Han takes this as its model and reproduces it exactly, which is another indication that the inner porch of each was completed together with the hall sections during the reign of 'Alā al-Dīn Kayqubād. The plain stone architecture of the hall is enlivened by the decorations of the dome, supported on stalactite squinches. The conical roof over the dome has collapsed. One of the peculiar features of this building is the complete absence of all figural and foliate decorations, perhaps at the desire of the Khwāja who built it.

The Karatay Han on the Kayseri–Malatya road was built by the Atabek Jalāl al-Dīn Karatay. According to its two inscriptions the hall was completed in the reign of ʿAlā al-Dīn Kayqubād, and the courtyard in 638/1240–1, during the reign of Ghiyāth al-Dīn Kaykhusraw. It is constructed on the traditional Seljuk caravansarai plan, with its buttress towers, some of which have knotted flutes, lending it the appearance of a fortress. The considerably heightened main façade with fluted and knotted pilasters at the corners and on either side of the porch, which project 2.5 metres out from the line of the façade, is the most monumental of all Seljuk architectural creations. Powerfully stylised gargoyles depicting winged lions carrying snakes in their mouths add to the effect, though of these only the one on the left has survived intact. The cubiform capitals of the corner pilasters in the partly ruined porch recess have two lions carved on the right and two bird figures on the left. In the decoration in the border above this, in place of the usual palmettes and arabesques one is struck by figures such as an ox head in profile or a small rounded human head. The high pointed-arched entrance iwan leading into the courtyard has a very majestic appearance. On the right is a domed masjid, on the left a cross-vaulted tomb. The door of the tomb opens into an iwan in the form of a porch, and in the 17 niches under the stalactite cornice above the doorway are rows of various figures such as birds, elephants, gazelles, hares, and two intertwining snakes (Fig. 97). The corner insets and the upper part of the façade of the iwan arch opening into the courtyard are covered with twin figures of monsters developed from the Zengid motif of knotted entrelacs. The door of the masjid also opens into the courtyard in the form of a small porch. The *hammam* (bath) is reached from this corner of the courtyard along a narrow corridor with plain and cross vaulting and domes set upon stalactite squinches. On the left of the courtyard can be seen the arches of the arcades, on the right the doors of the rooms. (Fig. 98.) The hall porch is an exact replica of the composition of the inner porch in the Ağzıkara Han. The hall dome is supported by stalactite squinches and on the exterior is covered by a pyramidal roof, like a domed mausoleum. This han has a wealth of figural decoration, and might well be described as an epitome of Seljuk sculpture.

Although both these hans show the influence of the Sultan Hans in various ways, one is original in its wealth of figures, the other in its severely geometrical ornament.

Like his father ʿAlā al-Dīn Kayqubād, Ghiyāth al-Dīn Kaykhusraw II also built three hans. Today the facing stones have fallen away leaving only the bare walls, the porches have completely disappeared and the roofs have collapsed, but the walls that remain and the traces left by the others show that the Eğridir Han was built on the traditional plan of the Sultan hans, and that it comes fourth in size, its dimensions approaching 3400 square metres. According to the inscription now placed on the main door of the medrese built by Dundar Bek of the Hamidoghulları at Eğridir in 701/1302, this large caravansarai standing 3 km. to the north of the town was built by Ghiyāth al-Dīn Kaykhusraw II and completed in 635/1237–8. Thus we have another Sultan Han built after the time of ʿAlā al-Dīn Kayqubād I by his son. On the lower sections of some of the towers there still remain blocks of the stone facing of fine quality. A considerable number of the carved stones from the marble porch have been re-used in the walls of the castle gate. It is obvious that in the façade and various other parts of his medrese Dundar Bek used stone blocks of the same quality and the same colour that had been removed from this Royal han. It is also possible that in the porch of the medrese Dundar Bek made use of stones from the porch of the Eğridir Han, as well as its inscription. The date in the inscription is confirmed by the style, which is in harmony with the decorations on the porches of other Royal hans. The solidly ordered Seljuk inscription in raised *thuluth* script, which is proved by its name to belong to the han, is here written for the first time on a border block.

A second han built by Ghiyāth al-Dīn Kaykhusraw II is the one known as the Incir Han near the village of Incir Köy on the Antalya–Isparta road. The plan is the one usually employed in Royal hans, but it is on a smaller scale (2750 square metres). The hall section is still in a good state of preservation but the courtyard is in ruins and only a corner of the western wall adjoining the hall is still standing. The salient mass of the porch opens inwards with a recess in the form of a vault with flutes on the upper section, and only on the porch itself can there be seen geometrical designs and rosettes. On each side of the façade, just at the level where the fluting begins, there is a lion carved in high relief with a sun bearing a human face on its back. This was probably the Sultan's device, and can be seen in various forms on his coins. According to its two inscriptions the han was completed in 636/1238–9. It is therefore the fifth Royal han after the Alay Han. (Fig. 99.)

An inscription on the Kırkgöz Han on the Antalya–Isparta road informs us that 'This ribāṭ was built by Ghiyāth al-Dīn Kaykhusraw II'. The section containing the date is illegible. The han is completely devoid of any decoration, even on the monumental salient porch, and it has an unusual plan with a long vaulted horizontal hall (15 × 49 metres), and a very large arcaded courtyard (51 × 49 metres) in front. The building is in a very good state of preservation, but, although built by a sultan, fails to conform to the classical plan of the Sultan Hans. In the courtyard one can see a smaller, simplified copy of the Evdir Han plan scheme with vaulted chambers in place of arcades in the sections adjoining the hall and on either side of the entrance.

As for the other hans constructed during the reign of Ghiyāth al-Dīn Kaykhusraw, the Şarapsa Han near the village of the same name on the Alanya–Konya and Antalya road consists of a long hall (70 × 15 metres) strengthened by frequent towers. A vaulted mosque has been added as a completely separate entity at the left side. Here the hall plan of the Kırkgöz Han has been transformed by the addition of the mosque section into a separate building, longer and narrower in dimensions. The plain stone building has no decoration worthy of note. The salient porch projects as far as the line of the towers, and has an inscription with the name and titles of the sultan but no date. Apart from simple decoration such as the squinch insets in the porch recess on each side of the inscription and the wedge blocks under a Koranic inscription on the masjid, an utterly plain type of architecture prevails. This simple structure could not possibly have been built by a sultan.

The Hatun Han built by the Queen Mother (Malika) Mahperi Khātūn, the mother of Ghiyāth al-Dīn Kaykhusraw II, on the Amasya–Tokat road, is of much greater importance. According to its two inscriptions it was completed in the same year as the Incir Han (Fig. 99)

(636/1238–9), and one year later than the Khwand complex in Kayseri. The plan of the Sultan Hans is here found on a smaller scale and in a simplified form. All the decoration is concentrated on the outer porch, which is in the form of a pointed-arched vault (Fig. 100). A wide border with its geometrical star entrelacs recalls the forms of the mausoleum and west porch from the Khwānd complex in Kayseri. On the other hand the narrow border with the knotted braid design resembles the ornament of the corner tower of the Sultan Han at Palas. A *çeşme* in the form of a niche on the façade on the left-hand side of the porch is an innovation. Mahperi Khātūn also built another four hans on the Sivas and Kırşehir roads, but these are now in ruins.

The Susuz Han on the Antalya–Isparta road has no inscription but it would seem to have been left unfinished in the last year of the reign of Ghiyāth al-Dīn Kaykhusraw II. It has the traditional plan of the Sultan hans, but only the hall section was completed. Work was begun on the courtyard but later abandoned. The richly decorated, monumental marble porch, the upper portion of which has now collapsed, reminds one of the magnificence of the Sultan Hans. The inscription was probably on the section now in ruins. Besides the geometrical star entrelacs that predominate in the wide border we also find palmettes and foliate arabesques on the arch and in the stalactite side insets and other foliate motifs such as acanthus capitals on the double corner pilasters. The symmetrical figures of angels in high relief flying towards the centre in the spandrels of the arches of the side niches of the porch were no doubt holding a heraldic device, but this has been completely destroyed. (Fig. 101.) On the face of the defining arch of the niche there is an exact replica in low relief of the confronted dragons on the kiosk masjid in the Sultan Han at Kayseri, except that here they are holding a small relief of a human head between their mouths. The dome of the hall is in good condition but the roof that had been planned as a fluted cone on an octagonal base was left half finished.

The Horozlu Han, at the beginning of the Konya–Akşehir road, would appear to have been built by an Amir Jāmdār, Asad al-Dīn Rūz-apa, the *atabek* of ʿIzz al-Dīn Kaykā'ūs II (1246–1249), the son and successor of Ghiyāth al-Dīn Kaykhusraw II. It resembles the Susuz Han, but is completely devoid of ornament. The courtyard is completely ruined, but the hall section, which had also fallen into ruins, has been repaired in recent years (1956). The marble inscription stone on the simple vaulted porch recess niche was left blank. (Fig. 102.)

Another han, at Ishaklı on the Akşehir–Çay road, is shown by its inscription to have been built by the vizir Fakhr al-Dīn ʿAlī (Sahib Ata) in the last year of the reign of Kaykā'ūs II (647/1249). This han, which is now in a very ruinous state, was built in accordance with the traditional Seljuk plan with a 5-aisled hall, the central aisle having an open dome, and a large square courtyard with a kiosk masjid in the centre of it, a feature we are now meeting for the fourth time. In order to face Mecca the masjid is set at an angle to the main axis. It is in a reasonably good state of preservation, with arches sunk up to 2 metres in the ground. It is covered by a dome with six rows of stalactites and has a round oculus in the centre. The hall porch is in the shape of a half-dome projecting outwards on two fluted squinches. It is very dilapidated. The upper section of the salient courtyard portal with stalactite decoration has collapsed, and a number of the stones have fallen away. In the upper corners there are simple decorations consisting of a row of geometrical rosettes. There is a three-line *thuluth* inscription under the stalactites.

Another han built by Sahib Ata, of which nothing now remains, once stood near the hot springs at Ilgın Ilıcası (between Akşehir and Konya). This latter (666/1267–8) was the work of the architect Kāluyān al-Qunawī (from Konya). The Seljuk vizir Sahib Ata, Fakhr al-Dīn 'Alī, who was known as Abū'l-Khayrāt (father of good works) on account of his deep love of architecture, also built the Ince Minare Medrese and its associated buildings at Konya, the Taş Medrese at Akşehir (1250), the Sahibiye Medrese at Kayseri (1267) and the Gök Medrese at Sivas (1271).

The Sarı Han (Yellow Han) at Avanos on the Kayseri–Aksaray road, one of the most striking of all Seljuk caravansarais, was built in the reign of 'Izz al-Dīn Kaykā'ūs II and may even be attributed to the sultan himself (Fig. 103). The magnificent architecture of the Sultan Hans is revived here for the last time, and every feature of the plan conforms to the traditional scheme. The masjid (Fig. 104), roofed by a dome on stalactite squinches, is set over the entrance vault, and on the left of the entrance there is an iwan with *çeşme* opening on to the courtyard, whilst on the right there are baths. The decoration shows the continuation of the geometrical designs of the Sultan Hans, and is largely concentrated on the stalactite outer porch, the upper section of which has now collapsed. On the side niches can again be seen a simplified form of the knotted interlacing motifs of the Zengid ornamental tradition. Other spectacular parts of the building upon which the decoration is concentrated are the porch-like doors of two of the cells on the right-hand side of the courtyard, the mosque door opening out on the courtyard, and the hall porch. The building is constructed of regular courses of cut stone of various colours (yellow, reddish and light brown—the dominant colour being yellow) and displays very fine workmanship. The plain pointed arch of the inner porch and the door arches of both porches are composed of bi-coloured roussoirs. The bi-coloration lends the hall arches a highly ornamental appearance. The open dome on pendentives is simple in style.

Although it is on a relatively small scale (2000 square metres) the whole architectural quality of the building together with its traditional type of plan makes one really feel that one is in the presence of a Sultan Han. Thus there is every reason for accepting the Sarı Han as a Sultan Han built by 'Izz al-Dīn Kaykā'ūs II during his first reign which ended in the year 1249. The inscription has disappeared together with the upper portion of the outer portal.

Although there are several important hans dating from the second half of the century no further hans were built by Seljuk sultans.

The Ak Han at Goncalı on the Eğridir–Denizli road is constructed on the traditional plan of the Sultan Hans with a small hall with three aisles and a large courtyard roughly square in shape, but it is quite a small building of no more than 1100 square metres. According to its two inscriptions it was built by the Governor Sayf al-Dīn Qarasunqur bin 'Abd Allāh in 651/1253, and its courtyard was completed one year later in 652/1254. The imperial monogram (Al-Sulṭānī) at the beginning of the inscription indicates a Seljuk Sultan, and the name and titles of 'Izz al-Dīn Kaykā'ūs II are mentioned here. Although in these years he shared the sultanate with his two brothers the inscription is in his name alone. Whilst the hall section is in a very simple style of architecture the courtyard has an extremely spectacular appearance, with two-storeys (a feature here seen for the first time) and an iwan to both right and left, at the corner adjoining the hall, and a masjid with a dome resting on corner triangles. The rich effect of the ornament is enhanced by the courses of bi-coloured stone on the hall porch (Fig. 105), which is in the form of a pointed-arched recess, on the low arched entrance door and hall façade, and on the iwan and arcades. The iwan opens out on to the courtyard through a slightly pointed vault of cut stone, and at the springing of the arch there are to be seen brackets in the form of lions' heads facing inwards. It has been suggested that two rooms of the lower storey to the right-hand side of the iwan, the front walls of which have collapsed, were a bath. But the most important innovation is the figural decoration on the outer porch, which rivals that of the Karatay Han. The outer border of the pointed-arched marble porch, which recalls that of the Hatun Han, is worked with a human head and a row of animal figures in relief in square frames in the empty spaces produced by meanders in a band consisting of a single row of interlinked swastikas. These figures depict various animals, sphinxes and other monsters, birds and wild animals, double-headed eagles, deer, lions and wild goats, and unlike those in the Karatay Han, they are intermingled with foliate motifs such as scrolls, rosettes and arabesques. As in the Karatay Han, figures of pigeons in relief are placed on the capitals of the ornamental corner pilasters (Fig. 106). Whilst this outer border is wholly antique in style the inner border is in the Seljuk decorative tradition with rosettes in the centre of stars produced by octagons and geometrical interlacing patterns.

A second Ak Han, on the Aksaray–Konya road, is in a very ruinous state and only the left corner tower of the courtyard and a few fragments of broken walls remain. The inscription has disappeared.

From the inscriptions bearing the name of Ghiyāth al-Dīn Kaykhusraw III we learn that three hans were built during the twenty years of his reign (663–682/1264–1283). The Durak Han between Boyabad and Vezirköprü was built by the Pervāne Muʿīn al-Dīn Sulaymān bin ʿAlī in 664/1266 on the traditional plan of a Sultan Han, with a hall section with three aisles and a shallow rectangular courtyard surrounded by arcades and rooms. The architect was Jawharbāsh bin ʿAbd Allāh. The first two lines of the inscription of the courtyard porch, now placed on a nearby mosque, give the name of Ghiyāth al-Dīn Kaykhusraw III and all his titles. This han was built on a rather larger scale (1435 square metres) and has a courtyard porch which is now in a very dilapidated condition, and the han is open on the right side. The following year, in 666/1267, the Pervāne Sulaymān built the Great Mosque at Sinop.

The Kesik Köprü Han built by the Vizir and Governor of Kırşehir Nūr al-Dīn Jabrā'īl bin Jājā (Caca Bey) in 667/1268 on the Kırşehir–Aksaray road has the same plan but on a smaller scale (1000 square metres). An inscription on the upper part of the pointed-arched recess of the hall porch mentions the name of Ghiyāth al-Dīn Kaykhusraw III and records that the han was built in his reign. There are two plain lion figures in relief under the arch of the porch recess and on the façade, and outside, on one of the side windows on the left, there is the figure of a bull's head with two snakes. Every stone of the squat door arch resting on brackets in the courtyard porch recess, the upper section of which has collapsed, and which has an opening in the left side, is decorated individually with geometrical braid motifs and rosettes, whilst the walls above the ruined side niches are decorated with geometrical entrelacs. There is a richly decorated stone mihrab and a vaulted mosque to the left of the entrance iwan and another vaulted chamber placed symmetrically on the right.

The Kesik Köprü Han takes its name from the large bridge nearby which had been built over the Kızıl Irmak river in 646/1248 during the first sultanate of ʿIzz al-Dīn Kaykāʾūs II by the Atabek Qāḍī ʿIzz al-Dīn Muḥammad. The Han was built in 1268 by Jājā Bek who also built the Caca Bey Medrese and tomb in Kırşehir in 1271.

The last of the hans bearing an inscription is the rather large (1752 square metres) Çay Han built by Abū'l-Mujāhid Yūsuf bin Yaʿqūb on the Akşehir–Afyon road in 677/1278–9. The hall has a rather unusual space arrangement with five perpendicular aisles intersected by a transverse aisle with a central open dome. Only a few traces remain of the courtyard walls. The composition of the porch is unusual. The transition to the half-dome in the porch recess is effected by means of large triangles with coffering inside. In a circle in the centre is a relief of a lion walking towards the left. Oghulbek bin Muḥammad, who is mentioned in the inscription in the adjoining medrese of the same date, was the architect of this han. Features that recall Mamluk art may indicate Mamluk artistic influences following Baybars's Anatolian campaign of 1277. A long inscription on the upper edge of the porch contains the name and titles of Ghiyāth al-Dīn Kaykhusraw III. Although this is the last Seljuk inscription on a han the two later Seljuk Sultans Ghiyāth al-Dīn Masʿūd II and ʿAlā al-Dīn Kayqubād III continued to be recognised until the last year of the century by the title of Sulṭān al-Aʿẓam, as on the minbar inscriptions dated 689/1290 and 699/1299 in the Arslanhane and Kızılbey mosques at Ankara.

The Öresun Han was built after the Çay Han 6 km. from the Ağzıkara Han and 12 km. from the Alay Han on the Aksaray–Nevşehir–Kayseri road. This small-scale structure (560 square metres) without a courtyard, now in a very ruinous condition, has a mysterious quality of appearing much more spacious than it actually is. (Fig. 107.) It has an unusual plan consisting of five aisles, there being two high cruciform vaults intersecting at the dome on open pendentives, two central vaults on each side that lose height towards the outside and a parallel vault in the entrance and on the rear wall. The plan of the Öresun Han shows a later development and, in K. Erdmann's opinion, should be placed towards the end of the 13th century. The façade and porch are in ruins, and the inscription has disappeared.

Another caravansarai that may be attributed to the end of the 13th century is to be found at Iğdır, which is off the normal caravan routes and is situated on the road that may have come from the south and reached Batum by way of Doğu Bayazid and Kars. It is a fairly large closed structure (52 × 22 metres) without a courtyard and without any inscription. In front of the long hall with its three aisles (the central aisle being higher and wider than the other two) there is a separate vestibule composed of three sections covered by various types of vaulting (Plan 30). The thick rubble walls are faced with stone and buttressed by ten solid semi-cylindrical towers. The plain stone architecture of the hall section has no decoration save stalactite brackets at the springing of the arches. The vaults and arches are almost round. The

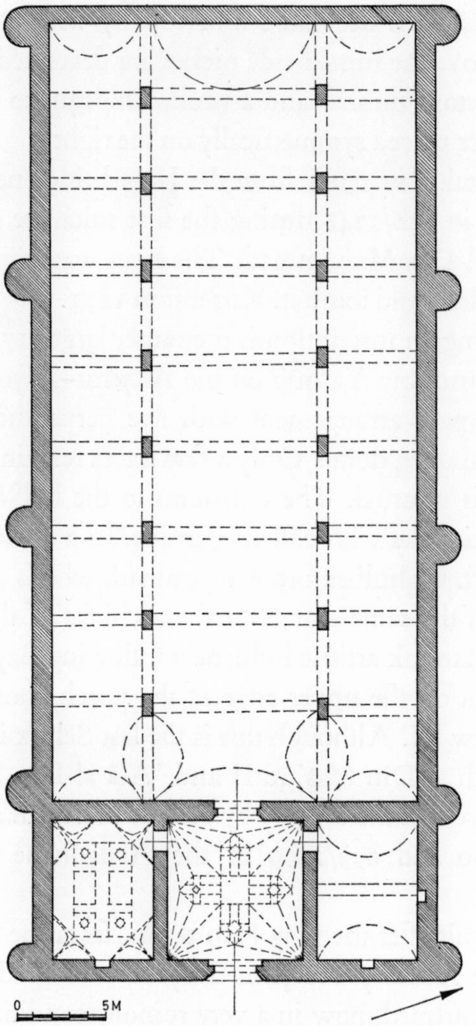

Plan 30. Iğdır, Caravansarai

hall is entered by a door with a sharply pointed arch. The entrance of the vestibule and the vault on the left of this are decorated with ornate stars and ribs, whilst the one on the right is roofed with a vault. Niches cut in the wall in the side sections are not aligned on Mecca and are set high up off the ground. These niches were used as shelves and one of them has a tripartite arch. The richly ornamented porch which still exists up to wall level is the only architectural feature enlivening the monotonous stone façade (Fig. 108). A porch encloses a pointed-arched doorway opening inwards, decorated with powerfully carved *tori* and a wide border of geometrical star interlacing patterns. The upper part of this is closed to form a tympanum and displays an unusual type of decoration to be found nowhere else in Anatolia; it consists of large stars delicately worked with foliate arabesques and scrolls, the spaces between them being filled with diamond patterns. (Plan 30a.) Its three-aisled hall—the central aisle being higher and wider than the other two—and vaulted vestibule with three divisions in front conform to the plan of the Han of Ibrāhīm Shāh on the Elâziğ–Çemişgezek road, which is

108 Kars-Doğu Bayazid-Batum road, Iğdir Han, porch

109 Konya, Kiosk of Qılıch Arslan. (Photographed before 1900)

110 Erkilet, Kayseri, Kiosk of Hızır Ilyas, detail of marble porch

111 Diyarbekir, Artukid Palace, pool with glass and coloured stone mosaics

112 Amasya, porch of Hospital

113 Erzurum, Yakutiye Medrese, blazon with palm, lions and eagle

114 Erzurum, Yakutiye Medrese, interior

115 Niğde, Mausoleum of Khudavend Khātūn

116 Gevaş, Halime Khātūn Mausoleum

117 Ahlat, Erzen Khātūn Mausoleum, detail

118 Hiṣn Kayfā (Hasankeyf), Mausoleum of Zaynāl

119 Ahlat, Bayındır Mausoleum

120 Antalya, Yivli Minare Mosque

121 Kirşehir, Tomb of Ashık Pasha

122 Sivas, Mausoleum of Hasan Bek (Güdük Minare)

123 Niğde, Mosqu
Sunqur Bek, porch

124 Karaman, Hatuniye Medrese, porch

125 Niğde, Ak Medrese, porch

126 Konya, Has Bey Dār al-Huffāz (school for students to memorise the Koran)

127 Karaman, Mausoleum of ʿAlā al-Dīn Bek

128 Kütahya, Imaret of Yakub Bek II, interior

129
Manisa, Great Mosque and
associated buildings,
general view

130 Manisa, Great Mosque,
lobed entrance arch

131 Seljuk, Ephesus, Mosque of ʿIsā Bek, façade

132 Seljuk, Ephesus, Mosque of ʿIsā Bek, general view of courtyard

133 Milâs, Mosque of Firuz Bek, portico

134 Milâs, Mosque of Firuz Bek, rear view

136 Balat (Miletus), Mosque of Ilyās Bek, detail of entrance

135 Balat (Miletus), Mosque of Ilyās Bek

137 Iznik, Yeşil Cami (Green Mosque), portico

138
Peçin, Medrese of Aḥmad Ghāzī,
porch and general view (see page 187)

139
Iznik, Yeşil Cami (Green Mosque),
rear view

140
Iznik, Imaret of Nilüfer Khātūn

141 Bursa, Hudavendigār Mosque, exterior

142 Bursa, Great Mosque, general view

143 Bursa, Great Mosque, Interior

144 Bursa, Yıldırım Mosque, view of portico

145 Bursa, Yeşil Cami (Green Mosque)

146 Bursa, Yeşil Cami (Green Mosque), porch

Plan 30a. Iğdır, Caravansarai porch

thought to date from the end of the 13th century. The courtyard of the Han of Ibrāhīm Shāh, only traces of which now remain, must have been added to the plan at a later date. It seems reasonable to suppose that it was originally a closed han without a courtyard since its plan closely resembles that of the Iğdır Han, except that in the latter the porch projects outwards in the form of a high iwan. Its porch, its geometrical and organic ornament and its closed plan without courtyard would seem to place the Iğdır Han at the end of the 13th century.

The Makit Han near the Ağin Han to the east of Elâziğ is another example of the same courtless plan. This han resembles the Han of Ibrāhīm Shāh in having as its entrance an iwan porch lying flush with the lateral walls in the centre of the façade, and appears to be a type of han peculiar to Eastern Anatolia.

Thus at the very end of the century Seljuk caravansarai architecture comes to an end in a manner worthy of its development, with a large han of the monumental quality of the Iğdır Caravansarai.

Seljuk Palaces and Pavilions (Kiosks) in Anatolia

Compared with the Sultan Hans which the Seljuks built in the form of true palaces constructed wholly of stone, their actual palaces and pavilions are very modest structures. As they were generally built of rubble and brick they quickly fell into ruins. In order to conceal the coarseness of these comparatively plain buildings rich tile and stucco decoration was used. Only the Haydar Bey Pavilion at Argıncık near Kayseri, the Hızır Ilyas Pavilion on a hill at Erkilet in the same area, and the Artukid Palace in the inner citadel in Diyarbekir were constructed in cut stone and of these the first two still stand in a state of good preservation.

Only the east wall remains from the pavilion that Sultan Qılıch Arslan II (1156–1192) constructed by enlarging one of the towers on the wall of the inner citadel in Konya to a height of 10 metres, and which was later named after ʿAla al-Dīn Kayqubād who carried out extensive repairs to it. The pavilion was essentially a square structure set on large protruding brick brackets and surrounded by balconies. The tower was faced with cut stone and a large marble figure of a lion placed in the two niches beneath it. The upper storey was surrounded by a balcony with a pointed-arched door opening on to it bearing an inscription in raised white lettering on a lapis lazuli ground on which Sarre, who published the inscription, read the name Qılıch Arslan in 1896. Both the interior and the exterior of the building were covered with rich and varied tile and stucco decoration. Fragments of these are now in various museums. Large square tiles were used with the figures of a mounted falconer in *mināī* technique, the ground being divided into geometrical sections by means of lines. These are made of local grey clay and recall the difficult ceramic technique employed by the Great Seljuks at Rayy and Kashan. This technique appeared in Konya in 1192 in the last years of the reign of Qılıch Arslan but does not seem to have been continued in Anatolia in the 13th century. Other tiles consisting of 8-pointed stars and diamond patterns covered the walls. The pavilion, about which a great deal of material has been published, consists, apart from the decorations, of an undivided hall. (Fig. 109.) Other pavilions and structures erected on the top of the hills have completely disappeared.

Two Seljuk palaces built by ʿAla al-Dīn Kayqubād and named after him—Keykubādiye and Kubādābād—were discovered by the late Zeki Oral and after the publication of a preliminary report were thoroughly excavated.

ʿAlā al-Dīn Kayqubād's small palace of Keykubādiye near Kayseri consisted of three pavilions disposed along the northern shores of a small lake produced by the waters of a spring, and according to written records it would seem to have been built about ten years before Kubādābād, in 621/1224–6. The pavilion, which is 6 metres square and is set on four arches, may be regarded as a forerunner of the kiosk masjids in the centre of the courtyards of the Sultan Hans. The stone ornament of the two façades has been worn away with the passage of time and only traces of geometrical entrelacs and braid motifs remain.

Excavations have been carried out on another pavilion about 50 metres beyond this consisting of three parallel vaults on a small hill that projects out into the lake. The platform in front of this, composed of seven segments each consisting of a single block of stone, was used as a quay.

The third and most important pavilion was unearthed at the limit of the excavations about 100 metres to the south on the site of the remains of pointed-arched vaults. There is a large rectangular space at the back and a small kitchen in the corner in front. When the ruins were cleared various ceramic fragments were found. These form two separate groups, the first composed of white geometrical braid patterns and entrelacs, with turquoise, dark blue and aubergine insets under a transparent glaze, a type seen before on the cenotaphs in the tomb of Kaykā'ūs I at Sivas and the cenotaphs in the tomb of Qılıch Arslan at Konya. In the second group are to be found the fourfold braid motif of old Turkish brick and stonework produced by intersecting octagons, in the form of wide bands with thick contours and insets of fine spiral scrolls in black under a bright turquoise glaze. It is interesting to note that the fine spiral scrolls filling the enclosed spaces can be seen later in Ottoman blue and white pottery, the so-called Golden Horn wares. Very small lustre tiles were also found but without figural decoration.

According to the historian, Ibn Bībī, when 'Alā al-Dīn Kayqubād was passing through the province of Konya on his way from Kayseri to Antalya he found an extraordinarily beautiful spot on the shores of the lake of Beyşehir and ordered that a town should immediately be built there. In 1236 the sultan's orders were carried out by the Vizir Sa'd al-Dīn Köpek, master of the hunt and head architect, according to a plan sketched by the sultan. A magnificent palace was completed in a short time. In 1949 Zeki Oral, then Director of the Konya Museum, read the name of the palace on an inscription dated 1235 on the mosque built by the Governor of Kubādābād, Badr al-Dīn Sutash. He thereupon discovered the palace itself, drew a rough plan of it, and took the tiles he had collected to the museum. As a result of the excavations begun in 1965 and directed by K. Otto-Dorn, the plan of the complete Seljuk town of Kubādābād, including the palace, was revealed for the first time. The remains of as many as 16 buildings were unearthed, including the town walls, a *Firdaws* (Paradise or *paradeisos*), a park for game and, under the Great Palace, on the shores of the lake, a dockyard with two sections which is a small replica of the dockyard at Alanya. Thorough explorations have been carried out in the Great Palace, which measures 50 × 35 metres, and in the large terrace in front stretching down to the lake.

Through the large courtyard with its regular stone pavement surrounded with rooms on the south and east sides, one enters the actual palace itself containing the large hall, the high brick-faced throne iwan and the harem and guest rooms. (Plan 31.) The plan is asymmetrical. Tile fragments which were found during the excavations, some of them in situ, showed the incredible richness of the ceramic decoration. These tiles date from the year 1236 when the palace was built and form panels in the shape of 8-pointed stars and crosses covering the walls up to a height of 2 metres. There are also various types of square panels. In the star-shaped panels sitting and standing human figures, a portrait very likely that of 'Alā al-Dīn himself, sirens, a double-headed eagle, figures of various birds and animals, and symbolic figures, vividly reflect the original creative power of the Anatolian Seljuks in representational art, unrivalled even by that of the Great Seljuks in Iran. The underglaze multi-coloured tiles seen earlier at Keykubādiye (1224–6) used now at Kubādābād and the use of a lustre technique indicate that the overglaze *mināī* technique was not used after the time of Qılıch Arslan II. There are four underglaze colours employed on the star-shaped panels—turquoise, green, purple and blue. These form a contrast with the cruciform panels with black decoration under turquoise glaze. Stucco reliefs with figures were also found in the Kubādābād excavations.

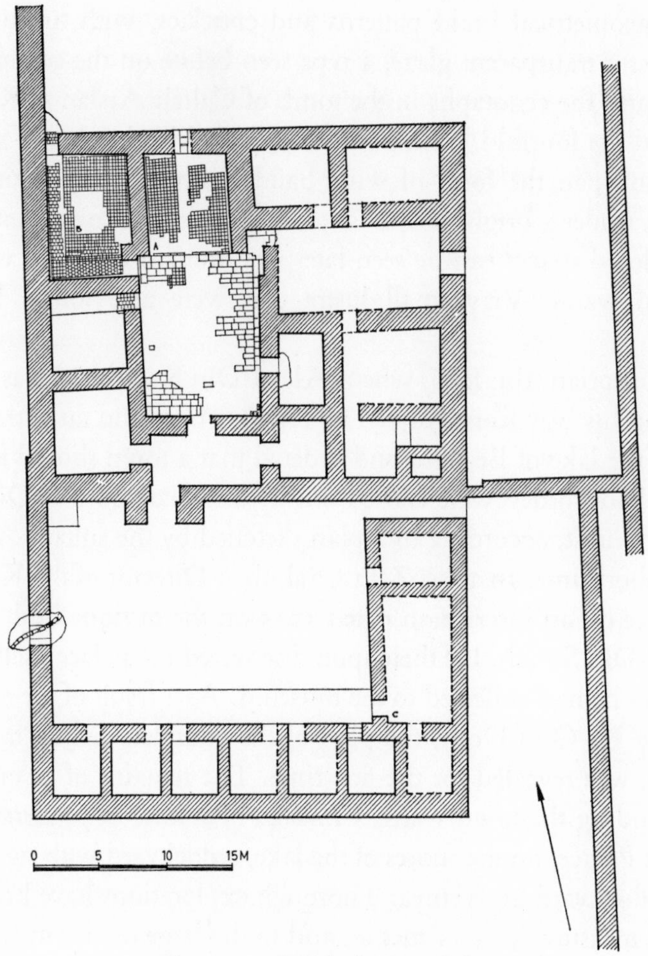

Plan 31. Kubādabād, Great Palace

The second palace is even smaller than the courtyard of the Great Palace and is built according to a symmetrical plan. Parts of the walls and vaulting of this building are still standing but it has not been thoroughly investigated. As ʿAlā al-Dīn Kayqubād died in the year in which Kubādābād was completed his son Ghiyāth al-Dīn Kaykhusraw II was the first to take up residence there.

ʿAla al-Dīn Kayqubād also covered the large staircase tower on the stage of the Roman theatre at Aspendos with figured tiles like those at Kubādābād and converted it into a pavilion. These tiles are now in the Antalya museum.

The ruined Seljuk pavilion known as Hızır Ilyas on a tumulus at Erkilet near Kayseri is a solid structure in dark-coloured cut stone with a richly decorated monumental marble porch. This pavilion, which was first described by Mordtmann in 1850, is a miniature replica of the Seljuk caravansarais, with its strong walls, its solid strengthening towers and its marble porch. On the right of a long corridor there is a mosque with an ornate mihrab, a kitchen opening into a narrow vaulted hall adjoining this and a stairway leading up to the roof, whilst on the left there are two rooms and an anteroom. In its general features the plan resembles the arrangement of the rooms on the left of the entrance iwan in the Karatay Han in the form of private apartments including a tomb—a unique feature to be found in no other han. The courtyard of the Karatay Han was completed in 634/1237 and the Erkilet pavilion (Plan 32) was constructed five years later in 639/1241 on a slightly modified version of the same plan. It is remarkable for the side niches of the marble porch, the ornamental corner pilasters and a wide border with geometrical entrelacs and stars (Fig. 110). An inscription dated 639/1241 which

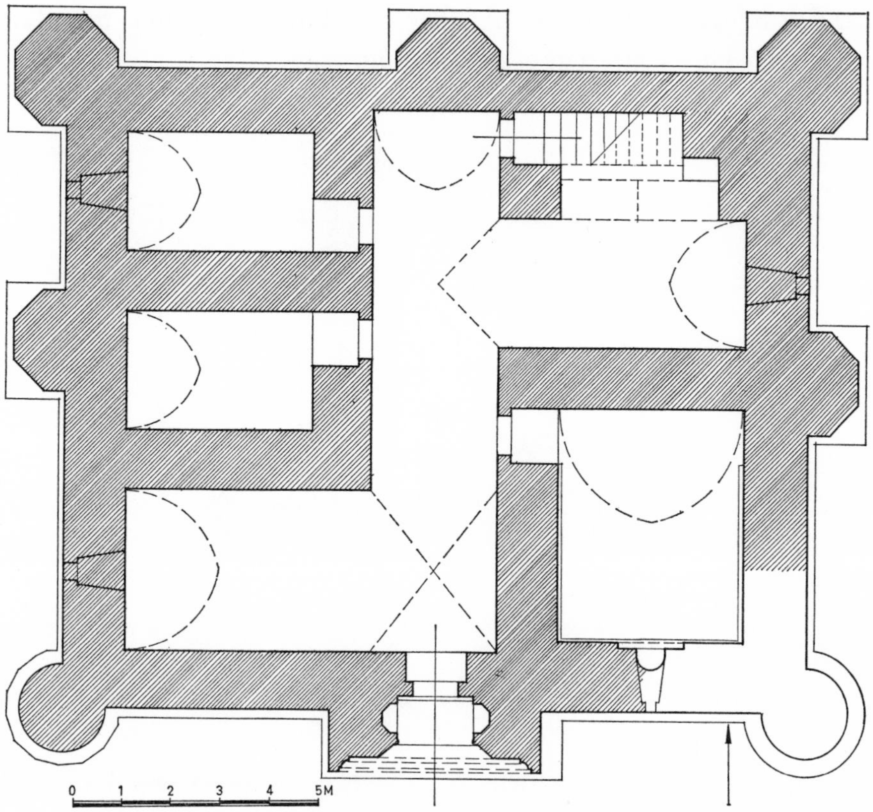

Plan 32. Erkilet, Kayseri, Kiosk of Hızır Ilyas

was read by Mordtmann in 1858 disappeared with the collapse of the upper section of the porch. In 1953 Zeki Oral found two fragments of this inscription, one in the courtyard of the mosque at Erkilet and one in the Kayseri Museum, and was able to read the titles of the sultan and the date 1241. He was unable to discover the third fragment containing the name of the Sultan Ghiyāth al-Dīn Kaykhusraw II. This little pavilion is set on a hill overlooking the whole plain and may also have served as a watch-tower.

A second Seljuk pavilion in the village of Argıncık near Kayseri is known by the name of the Kiosk of Haydar Bey. This building is on a larger scale (17 × 22 metres) and is a large fortress-like structure of regular cut stone with loop-holes. It is entered through a plain door on the western edge of an entrance block that projects 6 metres in the centre of the northern façade. Its stonework is simple in style and both the interior and exterior are monumental in appearance. Through the door one enters an anteroom with a staircase and from this one passes into a long vaulted hall with various rooms arranged along it on both sides. The underside of the landing on the staircase is fluted in the form of a fan. The upper section of the outer door with its pointed-arched pediment and the stone arches of the rooms in the hall are composed of single blocks and resemble the architecture of the nearby Karatay Han. The building is, however, completely devoid of ornament. There is no inscription but it is probable that it was built after the Erkilet pavilion around the year 1252, and that it acquired the name of the Haydar Bey Kiosk at a later date. As they were built of cut stone these last two Seljuk pavilions have survived in a better state of preservation.

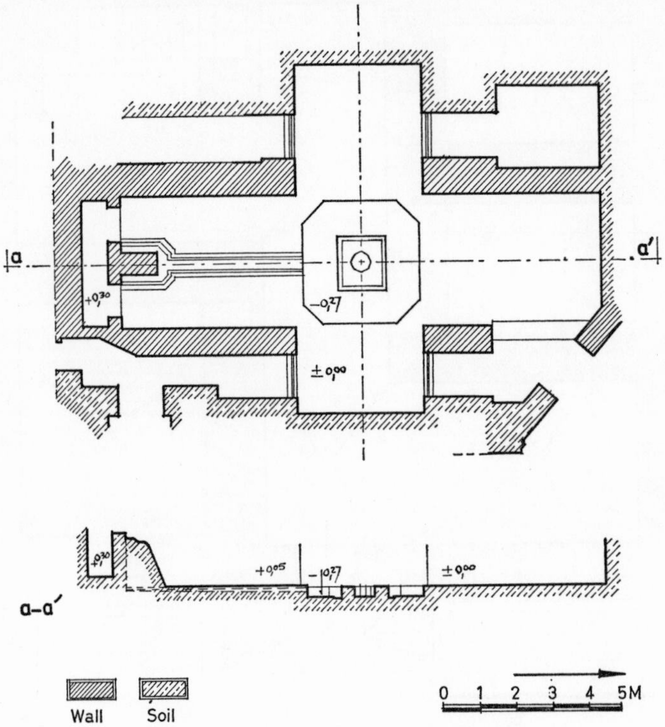

Plan 33. Diyarbekir, Artukid Palace

In addition to these Seljuk palaces and pavilions the remains of an Artukid palace (Plan 33) dating from the beginning of the 13th century were found as a result of excavations carried out on a mound in the inner citadel of Diyarbekir in 1961 and 1962. Here were unearthed and cleaned a fountained pool surrounded by cruciform iwans, waterways linking this to the pool by means of an ornamental selsebil on the south iwan, walls of cut stone and a stone pavement. The pool and ornamental selsebil are richly decorated with glass and stone mosaic and tiles. The pool and ornamental selsebil in the large medrese of Nūr al-Dīn Zengi at Damascus dated 567/1172, and the coloured stone reliefs in his maristan (1154), may both be regarded as prototypes of these. This is the first time that mosaic decoration employing coloured stones and glass cubes is to be seen in Turkish architecture. The decoration consists of geometrical patterns in which are set confronted figures of ducks and fishes. Amongst the ceramic finds were also a number of square tiles with heraldic decoration in the form of double-headed eagles in black under a turquoise glaze. A similar device is also to be found on Artukid coins. In technique the tiles differ in no way from the Seljuk tradition. Another tile was found carved with the figure of a peacock in polychrome glaze technique together with a number of fragments of blue, green, cobalt, manganese-purple and white tiles. The Palace was built during the reign of the Artukid ruler, Malik Nāṣir al-Dīn Maḥmūd (1201–1222), but the exact date of its construction is unknown. (Fig. 111.)

Although Anatolian Seljuk faience mosaic continued to be used in the Beylik (Emirate) and even Ottoman periods up to the last quarter of the 15th century, the tiles used in palaces and pavilions came to an end with the Seljuks.

10

THE ARCHITECTURE OF THE 14TH CENTURY AND THE TURCOMAN EMIRATES

The Anatolian Seljuk state founded in 1077 was severely shaken by the defeat of the weak ruler Ghiyāth al-Dīn Kaykhusraw II by the Mongol armies at the battle of Köse Dağ in 1243, and the subsequent sack and destruction of Erzurum, Sivas and Kayseri. Peace was agreed to in return for tribute and the Seljuk state was able to preserve itself and its administration until 1277. But after the Mamluk Sultan Baybars's Anatolian campaign of that year, in which the Īl-Khān Abaqā invaded Anatolia and massacred the population, the tyranny and oppression of the Mongols were intensified and Anatolia was laid waste. After that the Seljuk Sultans lost all real influence and their position as head of the state became purely symbolic. The Seljuk state was gradually crushed under the power of the Īl-Khānids and in 1308 it finally collapsed. Nevertheless, in the second half of the 13th century Seljuk art still possessed the strength and vigour to produce a number of important works of art. The Turcoman tribes which had settled on the *uj* (the frontiers of Anatolia) began one after the other to declare their independence. Amongst more than twenty Emirates that were created in this way may be mentioned the Karamanids of Ermenak, Karaman and Konya, the Germiyanids of Kütahya, the Hamidoghulları (Hamidids) of Eğridir, the Eshrefoghulları of Beyşehir, the Mentesheids of Muğla, Pacin and Milâs, the Jandarids of Kastamonu and Sinop, the Pervāneoğhulları of Sinop, the Aydinoghulları of Birgi and Seljuk, the Saruhanids at Manisa, the Dhulqadirids at Elbistan, the Ramazanoghulları at Adana, and finally the Ottomans of Söghüt, Bursa and Iznik. Each of these regarded themselves as the heirs of the Seljuk state.

In 1335 the Īl-Khānid Empire broke up and the governor of Anatolia, who was an Uighur Turk by the name of Ertena or Eretna, proclaimed an independent state with its centres at Sivas and Kayseri. After that there appeared the Ottoman state in the west, the Karamanids in Central Anatolia, the Dhulqadirids in the south, the Jandarids or Isfendiyarids in the north, and the Akkoyunlu and Karakoyunlu, descended from the Oghuz tribes, in the east.

After setting up their first capital at Diyarbekir the Akkoyunlu destroyed the Karakoyunlu state in the vicinity of Lake Van and Lake Urmiye, and on taking over the whole of Caucasia and Iran transferred their capital to Tabriz so that their state stretched from Khurasan to the frontiers of the Ottoman and Mamluk kingdoms. The Ottomans had conquered the whole of Rumelia as far as the Danube and in order to bring the whole area under one rule they engaged in a struggle with the Akkoyunlu, whose territory was divided from theirs by the Euphrates, and defeated and expelled them. Although after the fall of the Akkoyunlu Eastern Anatolia remained for a time under the suzerainty of the Safavid Shāh Ismā'īl the area was recaptured by Sultan Selim I, who also destroyed the Dhulqadirids and annexed Southern Anatolia, thus uniting the whole of Anatolia. Anatolia, which had been a single state in the Seljuk period, now formed a single state once more.

Īl-Khānid

At the beginning of the 14th century Seljuk architecture and stone ornamentation had lost nothing of its strength and vitality. This is clearly shown in the works created for the Īl-Khānid rulers. The Dār al-Shifā' (hospital) built in Amasya in 708/1308–9 for Sultan Öljeytü and his wife Yıldız Khātūn by their slave Anbar bin 'Abd Allāh is on the plan of a traditional Seljuk medrese with an arcaded courtyard and two iwans. The façade is well defined with its richly decorated monumental porch, two windows placed symmetrically one at each side, and cylindrical towers at the corners. The porch (Fig. 112) brings together various motifs from Seljuk stonework, such as early Anatolian surface ornamentation, the large high-relief palmettes and arabesques seen at Sivas, and various elements from the north porch at Divriği and the porches at Konya. On the keystone of the door the kneeling figure of a man is carved in relief. In the hospital, operations were demonstrated to the students. Sharaf al-Dīn bin 'Alī, who in 1465 prepared a book of miniatures entitled Kitāb al-Jarrāḥiyya (The Book of Surgery), practised here for 14 years. A number of doctors were trained here until as late as the 19th century.

According to an inscription on the porch the Yakutiye Medrese at Erzurum was built in 710/1310 by Khwāja Yāqūt on behalf of Sultan Öljeytü and Bulgan Khātūn. This comes into the category of Seljuk domed medreses and the central section is roofed by two vaults on four piers and an open transverse vault with oculus. There are three iwans. (Fig. 114.) The influence of the Çifte Minare Medrese is obvious. The domed mausoleum behind the great iwan is exactly the same as the one in the Çifte Minare Medrese. The masjid is in the side iwan on the right. The minarets are set on corner towers and enclose the façade on either side. This is the end of the Twin Minaret type of façade. Of the minarets only part of the one on the right as far as the first balcony is still standing. The composition of the device (Fig. 113) on the strongly projecting porch mass is slightly different from that on the Çifte Minare Medrese, the place of the carving of a double-headed eagle on the top of the date palm being taken by an eagle facing to the right or to the left with symmetrical confronted lions below.

In Niğde, in 712/1312, during the time of the Īl-Khānid governor Sunqur Agha, the Seljuk Princess Khūdavend Khātūn, the daughter of Qılıch Arslan IV, had a mausoleum erected with a 16-sided pyramidal roof on an 8-sided body of cut stone. The east face consists of a spectacular entrance porch, whilst three of the other sides are each pierced by a single window. On the upper portions of each of the facets apart from the portal the transition to the 16-sided roof is effected by two pointed arched lunettes with stalactites above. In one of these lunettes there is the device of a double-headed eagle, and in each of the spandrels of the north window arch the figure of a harpy, all of them being worked in high relief. Apart from these the mausoleum is loaded with symbolism in the reliefs of lions or panthers which decorate it, and the various human heads and figures concealed among the vegetal decorations. The lunettes and windows are surrounded by an exaggeratedly ornate decoration of geometrical star entrelacs, palmettes and arabesques (Fig. 115). These are in the form of untidy, coarsely worked Seljuk stone designs and, as in the hospital at Amasya, these different elements are brought together for the last time, except that here they are enriched by a great number of figural reliefs.

Although the influence of the Seljuk architectural style continued to make itself felt in Anatolia up to the end of the 14th century and even into the beginning of the 15th, original developments began to occur in the several Turkish states that were founded about this time.

Karakoyunlu

The Great Mosque at Van was a richly decorated brick structure showing an important advance in a region of Eastern Anatolia at that time dominated by the Karakoyunlu. The mosque could still be seen in a very ruinous state as late as 1913, but it was subsequently completely destroyed, so that only a fragment of the shaft of the minaret still remains. According to the plan and picture published by W. Bachmann the dome of about 9 metres in diameter in front of the mihrab rested on a transitional zone of stalactite squinches, each with a different style of decoration, and was supported on the mihrab wall and five piers. This was surrounded on three sides by two rows of small transverse vaults and three rows on the north side, all resting on octagonal piers (Plan 34). The excavation started at the great mosque at Van in July 1970 revealed that the mihrab, the dome area and the walls were covered with rich brick and stucco decorations in relief, painted in four colours: yellow, blue, green and red. Apart from this all the vaults were also decorated with different patterns of brick and stucco plugs surrounding them. Contrary to previous assumptions no tile decoration was used at all. These finely detailed decorations form a link with the Great Seljuks and particularly with the Masjid-i Jumʿa at Qazwin in Persia, but the stalactite dome, the vaults and composition of the porch and the stucco decoration point to the 14th century. From the historical point of view the most likely possibility is that this mosque dates from the first sultanate of the Karakoyunlu Qarā Yūsuf (1389–1400) before the arrival of Timur. It may well be that here, as often happened

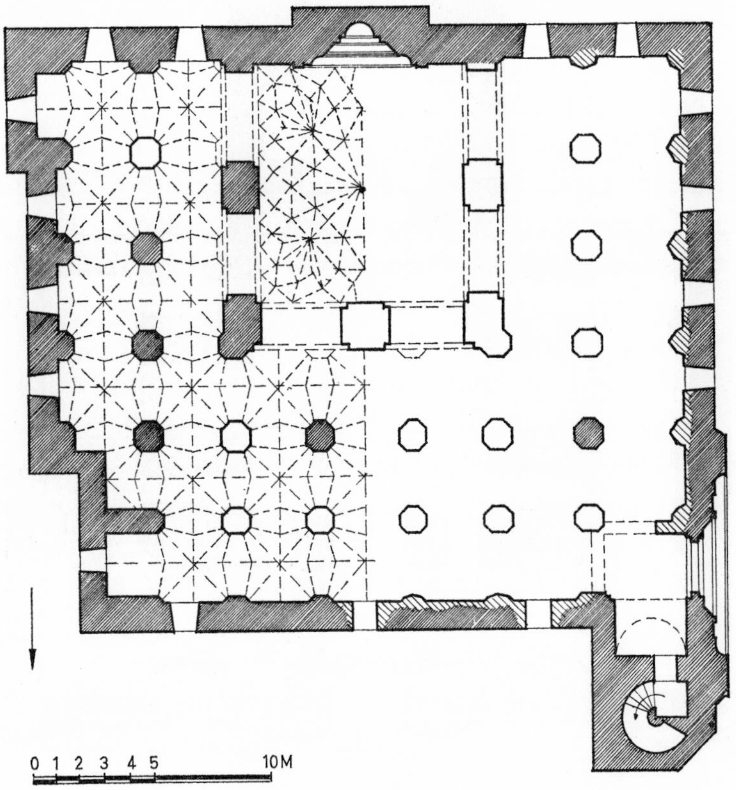

Plan 34. Van, Great Mosque

in other places, the Great Seljuk style of decoration was resuscitated at this late date by a craftsman from Qazwin.

Some light may be shed on Karakoyunlu mosque architecture by the Blue Mosque or Masjid-i Muẓaffariye built at Tabriz in 870/1465 in the period following Timur by another Karakoyunlu ruler Muẓaffar al-Dīn Jihānshāh, which tackles the problem of the dome from an original angle (Plan 35). In each of these mosques one is struck by the concentration of the whole space under a single dome and vault system. The plan of the Tabriz mosque is completely symmetrical. It is more richly decorated than the brick Great Mosque at Van. The name of the architect is given as Himmat Allāh bin Muḥammad al-Bawwāb.

The Halime Khātūn Mausoleum at Gevaş on the southern shore of Lake Van dating from 760/1358 is a 12-sided structure articulated by broken niches recalling the broken arches of Bursa, with a pyramidal roof and mouldings in the form of contoured palmettes. Long narrow vertical niches terminate in a conch, and in one of the wide rectangular borders surrounding them we find once more the fourfold braid motifs produced by intersecting octagons. (Fig. 116.) The structure resembles the 13th-century tombs at Ahlat but the decoration here is much more ornate and in a much more highly developed style. At that date the region around Van was under the domination of the Jalā'irids, but the Karakoyunlu had settled in the same area. The ʿAbd al-Malik ʿIzz al-Dīn whose name is mentioned in the *thuluth* inscription on the porch may have been one of the Karakoyunlu Turcoman Beks.

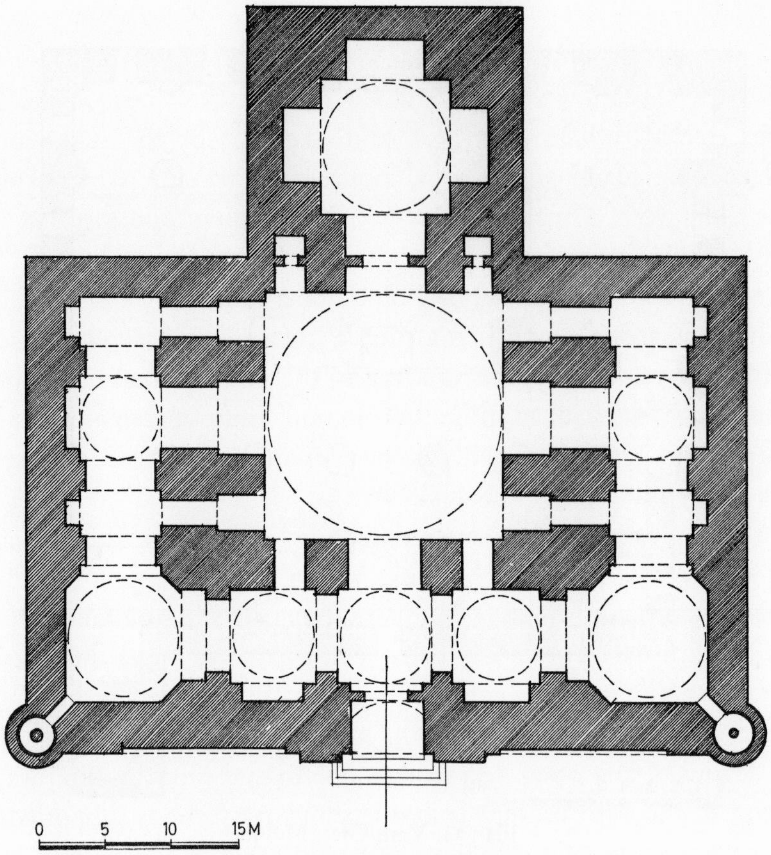

Plan 35. Tabriz, Blue Mosque

The Erzen Khātūn tomb at Ahlat dated 799/1396–7 was built as an almost exact replica of the Halime Khātūn tomb at Gevaş. But instead of the raised palmettes outlined on the pyramidal roof, various types of rosettes are carved on each of the stone tiles. This tomb belongs to the Karakoyunlu period. (Fig. 117.)

The Qādim Pāshā Khātūn tomb dated 863/1458 near Erjiş to the north of Lake Van was built for the mother of a Karakoyunlu Emir in the time of the Karakoyunlu Jihān Shāh. Deep vertical niches decorate the centre of the rectangular profiles surrounding each side of the duodecagonal tomb, though it is absolutely devoid of ornament save for a *thuluth* inscription on the façade of the porch and palmettes, arabesques and braid motifs on the arch of the door.

An anonymous tomb of the same period on the road to Patnos has various figures carved in relief, such as eagles with heads twisted back arranged symmetrically on each side of the portal arch, two decorative reliefs of lions higher up and a double-headed eagle on the upper part of the window, in addition to palmettes, arabesques, large foliate motifs and a Koranic inscription on the upper edge. These tombs of the late Karakoyunlu period have a faint resemblance to the Halime Khātūn and Erzen Khātūn tombs, but they are impaired by inferior workmanship, the proportions are spoilt, and the old architectural quality and style are lost.

Akkoyunlu

Of the buildings erected between 780/1378 and 914/1508 by the Akkoyunlu Turcomans who took the place of the Karakoyunlu a few mosques still remain in their capital, Diyarbekir. The first of these is the Ayni Minare Mosque which according to its *waqfiyya* (deed of endowment) was built by Khwāja Aḥmad in 1489. It is a small plain building of the original type, which may be included in the first category of Ottoman mosques known as *zāwīya* mosques (that is, with adjoining side rooms). It is a simple structure with an elongated barrel-vaulted interior on the two sides and transverse vaulting in the middle, forming an inverted T shape together with the pentagonal vaulted mihrab projection. In front there is a four-part flat-roofed portico and a free-standing minaret with an octagonal body. There is no symmetry in disposition of doors and windows.

The Sheikh Matar Mosque with a dome on squinches built by Sultan Qāsim, the son of the Akkoyunlu Jihāngīr, is a striking building with alternate courses of black and white cut stone and a tripartite portico in front. The square minaret resting on four columns in front of the mosque has an unusual appearance, being constructed as far as the inscription band in black stone, beyond that in alternate course of black and white stone. It recalls the cylindrical minaret supported by four piers attached to the Ottoman Timurtash Pasha Mosque in Bursa. The mosque is devoid of any other decoration. The masjid built by Ibrāhīm, the brother of Qāsim, at the end of the 15th century is divided into six sections supported on two square piers. Of these the section in front of the mihrab and the two on the right are covered with low vaulting, whilst the other sections are covered with cross-vaulting. In front there is a portico having three domes on Turkish triangles.

The Nebi Mosque, which dates from the 15th century and has undergone a good deal of repair, is constructed of black stone and consists of a dome on squinches given extra width by two half vaults on each side. The dome is concealed on the outside by a conical roof. There is a three-domed portico. A minaret of Ottoman construction rises on the left. Here a hesitant step has been taken towards enlarging the single-domed building at the sides.

The Safa or Iparlı Mosque of black and white cut stone attributed to Uzun Ḥasan (1435–1478) also underwent extensive repairs at the hands of the Ottomans in 1531. This also consists of a large hexagonal dome on squinches supported on four piers and two walls, and extended on two sides by one vault in the middle of each side and a small dome in each of the corners. The advance made in the Nebi Mosque is here repeated in a more obvious form. At the entrance there is a five-domed portico. The stone decoration of the tympanum of the outer window, consisting of the fourfold braid motif produced by the intersection of octagons with each alternate side broken and linked to each other by stars with rosettes in the centre, reproduces the Ghaznevid brick decoration of the Ribāṭ-i Māhī (see Design Ib). On the left of the five-domed portico rises a highly spectacular minaret covered with decoration from the base to the cone. The stone decoration of palmettes, lotuses, and foliate and plumed arabesques filling the panels indicates the Ottoman period. There are plain tile facings.

The Akkoyunlu mosques at Diyarbekir are small-scale structures remarkable for their unusual spectacular stone architecture, plan and decorations.

Of an Akkoyunlu mosque dating from the middle of the 15th century in the citadel at Mardin only a fragment 3 metres high of the base of the minaret is still standing, and on the north face of this the device of the Akkoyunlu is worked in relief. This device is also to be found on their coins. But the most monumental of their buildings is the Sultan Qāsim Medrese attributed to Qāsim Bek (893–908/1487–1507), the plan and architecture (fluted domes) of which are similar to those of the Artukid Sultan ʿIsā's Medrese (787/1385). The Akkoyunlu may have completed the half-finished medrese on capturing Mardin and consequently no inscription was placed on the building. The brick-vaulted arcades and dome on squinches given greater width by means of deep vaults may date from this period. In the arcaded courtyard an ornamental selsebil (or fountain) in the large iwan is linked by canals to a central pool. Some of the arcades are roofed by richly carved star vaults. The tomb, mosque and the two-storeyed medrese on two terraces combine to form a single complex. The composition of the porch and façade recall the front of the ʿIsā Bek Mosque at Seljuk from the Aydınid period; and the façade architecture with its coloured stone decoration shows the Syrian Zengid and Egyptian Mamluk influences.

The tomb of Sultan Ḥamza in Mardin (838–848/1435–44), the son of Qarā Yawlāq Arslan, has a dome on squinches, lobed on the exterior and surrounded by four cruciform vaults recalling the tomb of Galla Placidia at Ravenna. It is a plain building completely devoid of decoration.

The tomb of Zaynāl Bek the son of the Akkoyunlu Uzun Ḥasan at Ḥıṣn Kayfā (Hasankeyf) on the left bank of the Tigris has a helmet dome set on a cylindrical body, and, unlike the preceding tombs, is constructed of brick. It is an attractive building faced with glazed bricks in foliate patterns of turquoise, black and yellow faience mosaic on the porch. This original mausoleum built by an architect Pīr Ḥasan dates from the second half of the 15th century and is in a rather ruinous condition. The rich colours of the tiles and foliate motifs show originality of style. (Fig. 118.)

Another Akkoyunlu building that is interesting on account of the originality of its architecture is the mausoleum adjoining a plain mosque built in 890/1492 for the Emir Bayındır, the son of Rüstem Bek, at Ahlat. The cylindrical body is pierced on the south by decorative arches on pillars in the proportion of one to three and is covered by a conical roof with stalactite cornices. (Fig. 119.) The architect Bābā Jān, whose name is mentioned in an inscription, seems to have come from Azerbaidzhan.

In the centre of the audience hall in the form of an arcaded courtyard in the palace of the Shīrvānshāhs at Baku rises a building resembling the Ahlat mausoleum but constructed on an octagonal plan. It is generally accepted that this section was built in the 15th century and it is closely related to Ahlat both in architecture and period. The architect must have come from Azerbaidzhan, since good relations existed between the Shīrvānshāhs at Baku and the Akkoyunlu. The mausoleum of Zaynāl at Ḥıṣn Kayfā also shows influences from Nakhichevan' in Azerbaidzhan.

On the other hand there are obvious points of resemblance between the German Fountain in the Sultan Ahmed square in Istanbul built by Kaiser Wilhelm II in honour of Sultan Abdülhamid II and the Bayındır Mausoleum at Ahlat. Both these structures display features of late Romanesque architecture in Europe.

Hamidid

The Dundar Bek Medrese dated 1302 built by the Hamidids in Eğridir has suffered under repairs, but it was originally a two-storeyed two-iwan structure completely in the Seljuk tradition. The original capitals on the pillars are carved with foliate reliefs and the figure of a bird with outstretched wings in each corner. A porch, dating from 1238, has been removed from a Seljuk caravansarai and re-used here. The Emir Sinān al-Dīn Medrese (1319) built by the Hamidids at Korkuteli in the province of Antalya is another two-iwan building in the Seljuk tradition. Here a great deal of antique fragments have been re-used.

According to an inscription over the south door the Yivli Minare Mosque at Antalya was built in 1373 by Mehmed Bek of the Hamidids. It is built on the walls of a ruined church and has six domes on Turkish triangles set on 12 columns, some of which have Corinthian or Ionic capitals, others having no capitals at all. On the west side there is a section roofed by a vault adjoining the domes. The exteriors of the domes are covered with red roof tiles. This building, which now houses the Antalya Museum, is the earliest example of the multi-domed Great Mosque type of mosque dating from the Hamidid period in Anatolia. The Yivli Minare itself, which has been rebuilt from the balcony upwards, is a Seljuk structure dating, according to both its style and its inscription, from the time of ʿAlā al-Dīn Kayqubād I, and has now become the symbol of the town of Antalya. Nothing remains of the earlier mosque to which this minaret (Fig. 120) belonged. Near that mosque Mehmed Bek built a tomb with a marble porch and a pyramidal roof set on an octagonal body of hewn stone for his son, who died in 1377 four years after the completion of the mosque. It is a simplified form of the Seljuk mausoleum, with frameless windows on each face. Although Mehmed and family are usually known as *Tekeli* on account of the Teke Turcomans who settled in Antalya, they are really only the Antalya branch of the Hamidids.

Eretnid

Two unusual funerary monuments from the period of the Eretnid state established by Eretna (or Ertena), an Uighur Turk, in Central Anatolia show the birth of an original style. Of these the Tomb of Ashık Pasha at Kırşehir dated 733/1322, built entirely of marble, has a long, asymmetrical façade, a dome resembling a Kirghiz tent, and a long, narrow porch set to one side that in no way resemble Seljuk architecture and announce the birth of a completely new style. The inscription is also unusual, being set in front of the dome in a recess formed by the braid mouldings surrounding it. The recess of the porch is surrounded by a border of braid motifs and the plain façade is pierced low down in the centre by a single window with a pointed-arched tympanum (Fig. 121). The tomb consists of a square domed space with a narrow hall to the side of the entrance and is full of original features in which various architectural elements are combined into one harmonious whole.

The Mausoleum of Sheikh Hasan Bek the son of Eretna at Sivas (1347), now known at the Güdük Minare, rises in the form of a cylindrical body with a transitional zone of bold brick triangles on a square base of cut stone. The pyramidal roof has collapsed. (Fig. 122.) A colourful appearance is created by the rows of large turquoise lozenge-shaped tiles placed between the bricks. The tiles arranged alternately on the upper edge display an unusual pattern of white arabesques on a dark blue ground.

Another building dating from the Eretnid period is the Köşk Medrese at Kayseri built by the Emir Eretna in 1339 for his wife Suli Pasha. From the outside it resembles a stronghold entered by a small door. This impression is reinforced by crenellated walls in hewn stone. The building consists of a courtyard with arcades supported on piers, and contains no covered area save for the long vaulted rooms on each side of an entrance iwan. An octagonal mausoleum with pyramidal roof is set on a fairly high square base in the centre of the courtyard. It is obvious that such a massive medrese, closed to the outside and situated outside the town, must originally have been a ribāṭ, and it is probable that Eretna and his wife were buried here. The whole structure gives the impression of being a large funerary monument.

The tombs dating from the middle of the 14th century at Kayseri may also be attributed to the Eretnids. The Sırçalı Kümbed is an absolutely plain cylindrical structure of regular hewn stone. Its conical roof has disappeared revealing a bare stone dome inside. The roof was apparently covered with turquoise tiles, from which the monument got its name. It has a 12-sided interior. The ʿAlī Jaʿfar mausoleum, with a partly ruined pyramidal roof on an octagonal body, is remarkable for a now ruined rectangular entrance hall on the north side. These mausolea differ from earlier Seljuk tombs by their simple geometrical lines. Other mausolea in Kayseri dating from the same period possess similar features.

A mosque from the time of the Eretnids is the mosque of Sunqur Bek at Niğde dated 1335 which was burned down in the 18th century, and was then covered over with a flat wooden roof on wooden columns. It originally consisted of three aisles perpendicular to the qibla, the large central aisle being roofed with four domes, the side aisles with four cross vaults. The porch in the centre of the eastern façade was surmounted by twin minarets. The octagonal mausoleum adjoining the façade on the south side is still intact. From the architectural point of view the Sunqur Bek Mosque is noteworthy for its north-east porch, the stone decoration on its mihrab and its unusual proportions. The heads of animals such as lions and gryphons set amongst scrolls in the decoration of the porch recall the Great Mosque at Bünyan, except that here one finds a more mature style and more meticulous workmanship. The device of a double-headed eagle on the lintel above the arch of the door in the north-east porch, the circular Gothic-like lattice windows in the tympana of both porches and the Gothic capitals on the corner pilasters of the mihrab are all very exotic in appearance. According to A. Gabriel these may have been due to influences from the south, perhaps from Cyprus. An important place in the decoration is taken up by geometrical stars and entrelacs in addition to foliate motifs such as palmettes and lotuses. (Fig. 123.) The mosque is original in having had a porch with twin minarets, seen here for the first time since the Sahib Ata complex in Konya, an unusual composition in its decoration and in displaying Gothic influences. The minbar is at present in the Dişari Mosque in Niğde and its inscription mentions the names of the Īl-khānid Sultan, Abū Saʿīd Baḥādur Khān, Sunqur Agha, and the craftsman who built the minbar, Khwāja Abū Bakr. It is a small, plain minbar with mother-of-pearl inlay. It has no date.

In the buildings of the Eretnid dynasty the birth of a new style different from the Seljuk is to be discerned.

Karamanid

The most powerful and the most long-lived of the Turcoman Emirates after the Ottomans were the Karamanids (1256–1483), and as they put forward the strongest claims to take the place of the Seljuk state they were the ones who kept alive the Seljuk style and tradition. In mosque architecture the Karamanids introduced no definite innovations nor any systematic development. Their mosques were covered with flat roofs supported on piers and arches, and sometimes had a dome over the mihrab. Single-domed mosques frequently occur.

The much repaired Karamanid Great Mosque at Aksaray (1431) has a shallow rectangular plan with five aisles perpendicular to the qibla. Apart from the dome over the mihrab set on fan pendentives and the dome of the second section on the same axis, the five sections in each of the aisles are covered with transverse vaulting. The porch is on the west side. The richly decorated wooden minbar is of Seljuk workmanship and was brought from the ruined mosque of Qılıch Arslan II at Aksaray. The mosque has no courtyard.

The Iplikçi Mosque at Konya, which reached its present form as a result of the restoration in 1332 of a mosque which is thought to have been built in the first half of the 13th century, was rebuilt by Ḥajji Abū Bakr in the Karamanid period. The mosque is in the form of a shallow rectangle with seven aisles perpendicular to the mihrab, the centre aisle being roofed with three domes on pendentives, whilst the side aisles are roofed with two cross vaults each, with one plain vault in front of the mihrab wall. Part of the Seljuk faience mosaic mihrab can be seen buried in the ground under a marble Ottoman mihrab.

In medreses the Seljuk tradition remained most vigorous amongst the Karamanids. The Zinciriye Medrese (1336) at Aksaray is noteworthy for its four-iwan arcaded courtyard and the ovoid domes on each side of the qibla iwan, on which traces of faience mosaic can still be seen. Seljuk features are reproduced in the monumental porch.

The largest of the Karamanid medreses is the very ruined Tol Medrese built by the Emir Mūsā Bek at Ermenak in 1339. It has the traditional plan with a two-iwan, arcaded courtyard. The porch is set inside the entrance iwan. This very high porch with an inscription and a square window under the stalactite canopy differs from Seljuk porches, and contains a doorway with a low arch.

The same two-iwan arcaded courtyard plan is to be seen again in the Hatuniye Medrese at Karaman built by the architect Nuʿmān bin Khwāja Aḥmad in 1382 for Nefise Sulṭan, the daughter of Murad I and the wife of the Karamanid ʿAlā al-Dīn Bek. The fourfold border on the salient monumental white marble porch reproduces the patterns of the Gök Medrese at Sivas and the Çifte Minare Medrese at Erzurum, but in a plain, insipid style (Fig. 124). The porches of the Eshrefoghlu Mosque and the Taş Medrese at Beyşehir also enter this category.

Although the Ak Medrese at Niğde (1409) is a traditional Seljuk medrese with a two-storeyed two-iwan symmetrical plan, the high monumental porch and the façade with open galleries framed by double ogee arches on the second storey remind one of a palace. The obvious resemblances to the façade of the Hudavendigār Mosque at Çekirge in Bursa are due to the years its founder, ʿAlī Bek the Karamanid, had spent with his grandfather Sultan Murad Khān in that city. He himself had strengthened the dynasty by marrying the daughter of the Ottoman Chelebi Sultan Mehmed. Original architectural features of the Ak Medrese include the porch, with an ogee arch surrounding an equilateral triangular stalactite canopy, the pointed arcade arches resting on side walls with braided *tori* and the qibla iwan with a rear window. There is a well in the centre of the courtyard. The form of the façade has been damaged as the result of repairs. It is now a museum. (Fig. 125.)

The plan of the Hatuniye Medrese (1432) at Kayseri follows the scheme of traditional Seljuk medreses with a few modifications but the use of Corinthian and Ionic capitals is an unusual feature. The whole right wing of the façade is occupied by a fountain (*çeşme*).

The mausoleum of Ibrāhīm Bek is contained in the imaret, masjid, medrese, Dār al-Qirā' (Koran School) and tabhane complex completed one year later in 1433 by Ibrāhīm Bek II at Karaman. The spacious central area is roofed by a large dome with fan pendentives simpler and plainer in style than those of the Seljuks, whilst there is an even simpler upper storey. There are no side arcades. The ornament and the three-line *thuluth* inscription on the porch with its pointed arch differ in style from the Seljuks. The ceramic mihrab is now in the Çinili Köşk at Istanbul. In the mausoleum there are three cenotaphs with rich plaster decoration belonging to Ibrāhīm Bek and his two sons. The imaret is one of the finest works of the Karamanids. It was modelled on the Mūsā Pasha Medrese at Karaman dating from the middle of the 14th century, a symmetrical building with a dome over the central area and columned arcades. The minaret rising up on the right of the entrance was identical with the minaret of the imaret. This latter medrese was demolished in 1927. The domed medrese, like the iwan medreses, shows the continuation of the Seljuk tradition.

At Konya the Karamanids built two Dār al-Ḥuffāẓ (schools for prayers and for the study of the Koran). Of these the Has Bey Dār al-Ḥuffāẓ (1421) is roofed with a fairly high dome on Turkish triangles over a square base constructed of brick. The brick walls are faced on three sides with cut stone whilst the façade is covered with marble panels worked with geometrical star entrelacs and braid motifs. Most of the marble panels have fallen away. (Fig. 126.) The rich mihrab in faience mosaic continues the Seljuk tradition. The interior is rather dark.

The date of the Nasuh Bey Dār al-Ḥuffāẓ, a fairly large single-domed Karamanid structure in cut stone, is not known. The three-domed entrance portico has collapsed and only the springing of the arches with an acanthus frieze is still standing. The interior is well lighted by round windows in each facet of the octagonal drum and, between them two pointed-arched windows above the walls. It shows very clearly the influence of 15th century Ottoman architecture.

As for Karamanid funerary monuments, a 12-sided mausoleum in cut stone in Karaman belonging to the Karamanid ʿAlā al-Dīn Bek who was killed in 1397 is a very much ruined building covered by a conical fluted roof. The plain porch occupies one side of the building, its upper part being encircled by a Koranic inscription. This is the most monumental of all the Karamanid tombs and a fragment of the wall linking it to the adjoining mosque is still standing. (Fig. 127.) The whole tomb differs in style from the Seljuk funerary monuments and has a very simple but monumental appearance.

The impressive tomb of Mevlānā Jalāl al-Dīn Rūmī, 25 metres high, in Konya took on its final form in the Karamanid period. Mevlānā died in 1273 and the first tomb in the form of a domed chamber and an iwan founded by his son Sultan Veled and various Seljuk Emirs was constructed by the architect Badr al-Dīn of Tabriz, and the interior decoration carried out by a craftsman called ʿAbd al-Waḥīd. This first tomb was in the form of a stalactite dome supported on four arches, but about 1397 the Karamanid ʿAlā al-Dīn ʿAlī Bek heightened it by the addition of a fluted drum faced with tiles, crowned with a conical roof.

The tomb in Akşehir of Sayyid Maḥmūd Hayrānī who died in 1268 took on its final form in 1409 in the time of the Karamanid Mehmed Bey II. Its fluted cylindrical body with a polygonal brick drum rests on a stone base. The tomb is embellished with glazed brick decoration in three colours and also with cruciform and star-shaped tiles placed between these at a later date. The architect mentioned in the tile inscription, ʿAslī bin ʿAbd Allāh, may also have been the one who gave the tomb of Mevlānā in Konya its final form.

Other 15th-century Karamanid tombs such as the Fakih Dede and Kalenderhane at Konya consist of brick pyramidal roofs on octagonal bodies of cut stone in the Seljuk tradition.

Jandarid

In the Jandarid Emirate 14th century mosques with single domes or in the Ottoman form with side rooms (*zāwīyas* or lodging places for dervishes) can be seen in the Kastamonu region. Of these the Neccar Mosque (1353) with its dome on squinches over a square interior and three-domed portico was destroyed in the 1943 earthquake. The richly ornamented doors were the work of ʿAbd Allāh bin Maḥmūd of Ankara and were made in 1356.

Although the small timber-roofed mosque with columns built by the Emir Maḥmūd Bek in 1366 in the village of Kasaba near Kastamonu is very plain on the outside, the interior, with its polychrome painted ornament and ceiling decorations, is fresh and interesting. The decorations on the stone mihrab recall the mihrab of the Great Mosque at Sinop. The finely carved doors are likewise the work of ʿAbd Allāh bin Maḥmūd of Ankara.

Ismāʿīl Bek (1443–1560), the last of the Jandarids, built a complex at Kastamonu consisting of a mosque, a tomb, a medrese, an imaret, a han and a hammam. The mosque is in the form of an inverted T, with a five-domed entrance portico, the central dome of the portico being fluted. It was completed in 1454 and consists of two domed areas, one behind the other, with symmetrical, vaulted chambers opening through small doors on each side of the front dome on to the central area. The first dome is open in the centre with an oculus and rests on stalactite pendentives, whilst the dome over the mihrab is supported on stalactite squinches. The inscription on the medrese (1475) indicates that it was built well within the Ottoman period. The wooden arcades surrounding the courtyard and the front of the classrooms have collapsed. The attractive tomb with brick dome and fan fluted squinches on massive walls of cut stone was completed before 865/1460. When Mehmed the Conqueror captured Kastamonu he gave Yenişehir, Inegöl and Yarhisar to Ismāʿīl Bek as a *timar* (military fief), but Ismāʿīl Bek was later sent to Filibe where he died and was buried. Consequently his tomb was used for his relations and for some of the scholars that he had patronised. Inside there are as many as ten cenotaphs with meticulously carved *thuluth* inscriptions.

Germiyanid

The mosques built in Kütahya, which was the administrative centre of the Germiyanids, are single-domed structures in the classical tradition with three-domed porticos in front. The oldest of these is the Kurşunlu Mosque built in 1377 by an Akhī (a member of a guild or corporation), Sheikh Mehmed, with dome supported by Turkish triangles over a square base. The portico is open to the front, and consists of a panel vault in the centre with a small dome on each side. The mosque dated 1433 built by the scholar Isḥāq Faqīh, and the mosque built by Yakub Bek II's Subaşı (superintendent of police) Mustafa Bek bin Hisar Bek in 1487, are remarkable for their spectacular façades and meticulous architecture. The walls of all three mosques are faced with cut stone alternating with brick courses, but in the Hisar Bek Mosque a special decorative effect is achieved by surrounding the cut stones in the portico with red bricks. The capitals of the columns are faceted with Turkish triangles. A row of tiles with bi-coloured arabesques surrounding the stone mihrab is a 15th-century feature.

The Vacidiye Medrese built by the Germiyanid Emir ʿUmar bin Savji in 1314 as an observatory comes into the category of domed Seljuk medreses. In a vaulted room to the left of the domed entrance can be seen the places for various astronomical instruments. There is a pool under the large oculus in the centre of the dome built on Turkish triangles. Rooms with similar open domes on both sides of the great iwan are classrooms. On both sides of the central dome are vaulted cells for the students. This medrese is the earliest Germiyanid building, and its plain, salient pointed-arched porch and reduced number of rooms are characteristic of the Beylik period. It now houses the Kütahya Museum.

The date of the medrese, masjid and imaret complex built by the Germiyanid Yakub Bek II (1390–1428) and containing his own tomb, is uncertain. The medrese has an interesting plan with a hall with a *shadırvan* (ablution fountain) under a large open dome, two small domed chambers on each side and a domed iwan in the rear (see Fig. 194). One of each of the side domed rooms opens into the centre in the form of an iwan, the one on the left being a masjid. The tomb is in the form of a small domed chamber behind the mihrab and is enclosed by a grille. Some of the tiles on the cenotaph of Yakub Bek date from the 15th century but the majority date from the most recent repairs. The Yakub Bek imaret has a very interesting and unusual plan with a three-domed iwan opening on three sides into a central hall with *shadırvan* and large dome, and a domed chamber on each side of the entrance in the form of a three-domed vestibule opening outwards through three arches. It is the largest of the Germiyanid buildings and is now used as a library. (Fig. 128.) Its main lines are those of the inverted T type mosque with side rooms (zāwīyas).

Germiyanid buildings were constructed under Ottoman influence, but this observatory dating from the early part of the period is an original work in the Seljuk style.

The Germiyanid Emirs Saruhan and Aydın set up independent Emirates in the regions they conquered.

Saruhanid

The Saruhanids produced in their administrative centre of Manisa what is perhaps the most important and most interesting mosque plan of the whole Beylik period. The Great Mosque built by Isḥāq Bek in 778/1376 as part of a complex containing a medrese and a tomb formed the starting-point of a number of important developments. Here the arcaded courtyard appears once more in a smaller form and the mosque and the courtyard together form two halves of practically a single plan. The mosque consists of four seven-part aisles parallel to the mihrab wall, three of the aisles being intersected by the dome, which is 10.8 metres in diameter on pendentives supported on arches arranged in an octagon formed by the two columns adjoining the mihrab wall and six piers. The courtyard with central pool separated off from the rest of the mosque by a wall is the same size as the dome. The other sections surrounding the dome and the courtyard on three sides are roofed near the dome by small transverse vaults resembling domes and supported on columns (Plan 36). The capitals are a mixture of re-used antique pieces (Corinthian) and original stalactite capitals. The development of the mihrab dome links it with the Artukid Great Mosques at Silvan (1179) and Kızıltepe (Dunaysir) (1204). The same development is to be found in the Great Mosque at Van, which we attributed to the Karakoyunlu period, where we can see a dome on a square plan. In the Great Mosque at Manisa the creation of a large and unified interior by means of a central dome resting on an octagonal base appears as a new development in Western Anatolia. (Fig. 129.) As one enters the mosque, there is a lobed arch in the form almost of a triumphal arch on the mihrab axis, which opens into the large mihrab dome (Fig. 130). The plain mihrab between two columns with Corinthian capitals supporting the piers of the arches on the qibla wall is out of harmony with the architecture of the mosque and would appear to have been constructed later. On the other hand the ebony minbar, with its rich finely detailed ornament and Koranic verses and other inscriptions, is the work of Muḥammad bin ʿAbd al-ʿAzīz al-Dikkī of ʿAyntab. Twenty-four years later the same craftsman built the magnificent minbar of more mature style in the Great Mosque of Bayazid I at Bursa.

The arcaded courtyard is quite separate from the mosque and includes a portico. Like the mosque itself it displays the beginning of a new type of mosque plan that was developing in

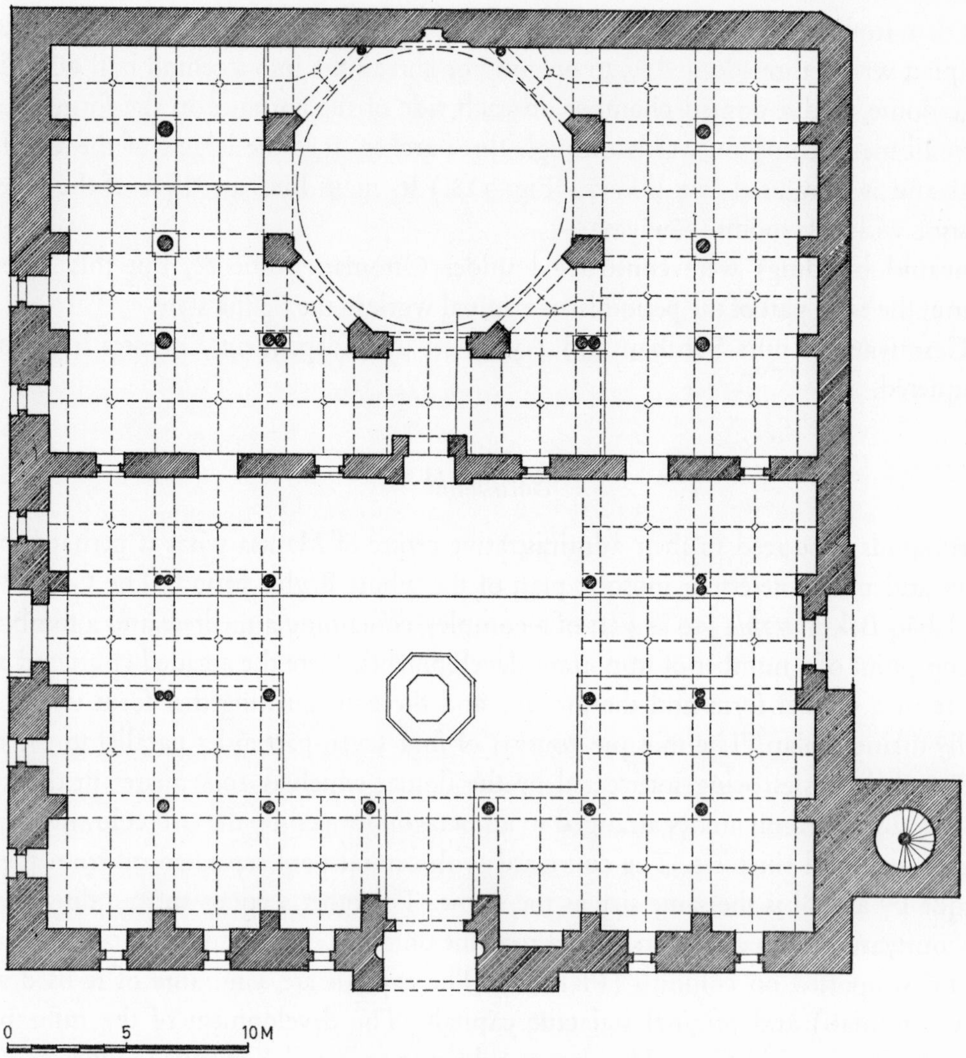

Plan 36. Manisa, Great Mosque

Ottoman architecture. This plan scheme with central-domed prayer hall and arcaded courtyard shows a great advance in the Üç Şerefeli Mosque built by Sultan Murad II at Edirne with two small domes on each side of the large dome and a courtyard with *shadırvan* surrounded by domed arcades.

The north porch is decorated with polychrome stone reliefs and bears an inscription of Isḥāq Bek dated 778/1376. This façade of the courtyard is pierced by two rows of windows. Adjoining the west wall of the courtyard rises the spectacular coloured minaret decorated with unusual arrangements of glazed brick. On the same side the medrese is entered through the western gate and a transverse-vaulted corridor. The two-storeyed asymmetrical single-iwan medrese is noteworthy for the extremely plain long narrow porch facing the north and the fountain on each side of the façade adjoining the mosque. The name of the architect, Emet bin ʿUthmān, may show a connection with Emet, a town in the vilayet of Kütahya. According to the inscription the medrese was built two years after the mosque. According to Evliya

Çelebi the architect of the Saruhanid Emet Mosque at Nif (Kemal Paşa) was also Emet bin ʿUthmān. The tomb of Isḥāq Bek is situated on the left-hand side of the medrese courtyard and opens through a door on to the corridor. This tomb and the vaulted funeral chamber in front of it are square in plan and are covered with a dome on pendentives. Isḥāq Bek, who died in 1388, is buried under the central cenotaph whilst his wife and sons are under the cenotaphs at the side. The inscription on the pointed-arched tympanum of the door is decorated with geometrical star entrelacs. The complex is not directly linked to the plan of the mosque but is added on to the western side.

The Ilyas Bek Masjid (746/1362) is the oldest Saruhanid building with an inscription. It consists of a dome on squinches over a square inner area, approached by a two-domed portico closed in with side walls.

The Revak Sulṭan tomb is an undated Saruhanid structure with a dome on squinches covered on the exterior by a pyramidal roof. Other Saruhanid buildings in Manisa and the vicinity have no outstanding original features.

Aydınid

Although Seljuk influence is very obvious in the earliest buildings constructed by the Aydınoghulları, towards the end of their rule there are several buildings that show original ideas. The Great Mosque of the Aydınid Mehmed Bek at Birgi (712/1312) is a squared stone building with five aisles, the wider central aisle being well defined by the dome on squinches over the mihrab. The other aisles are completely covered by a sloping wooden roof supported on columned arcades. The external façade and the porch are very plain. The minaret is unusual in being set in the south-west corner and is ornamented with turquoise glazed bricks arranged in rows of lozenges and zigzags. The mihrab, which is linked to the Seljuk tradition by the turquoise and dark blue geometrical stars and entrelacs that predominate in the faience mosaic, has only a single border, decorated with double scrolls and foliate arabesques. In the spandrels of the arch supporting the dome facing the nave can be seen a Koranic inscription and geometrical patterns in bi-coloured faience mosaic.

The Seljuk tradition is continued in the magnificent minbar with walnut panels constructed by using smaller interlocking panels without nails. According to the inscription it dates from 1320, eight years after the completion of the mosque, and is the work of Muẓaffar al-Dīn bin ʿAbd al-Waḥīd. It is decorated with geometrical star and entrelac patterns, together with very finely detailed scrolls, arabesques and palmettes. The work of the same craftsman can be seen in the delicate ornament employing different types of motifs on the double shutters of the windows. The portico was added later.

The dome on pendentives and the drum on a square base in the tomb dated 1334, lying on the same axis as the minaret on the western façade of the mosque of the Aydınid Mehmed Bek, was decorated with lapis lazuli glazed bricks, most of which have fallen away. There are decorations in the form of stars in turquoise and lapis lazuli tiles on the edges of the window and a round medallion in faience mosaic can be seen in the very centre of the dome.

The most important work of the Aydınids is the 'Isā Bek Mosque built in 776/1374 (Fig. 131) in their administrative capital of Seljuk near Ephesus. It was built for the Aydınid 'Isā Bek, two years before the Saruhanid Great Mosque at Manisa, by the architect 'Alī ibn al-Dimishqī, whom the inscriptions mention as coming from Damascus. The arcaded courtyard with an octagonal pool in the centre and the arcades with a flat wooden roof are to be seen here before they appeared at Manisa. The arcades have now disappeared, leaving only the twelve columns surrounding the courtyard. In the mosque there are long aisles formerly covered with a flat wooden roof intersected in the middle of the building by two domes (Plan 37). The triangular pendentives of the dome over the mihrab are decorated with geometrical patterns of hexagonal stars with small hexagonal insets in turquoise, dark blue and brown faience mosaic. On the octagonal drum of the dome there are fragments of stalactite fillings in

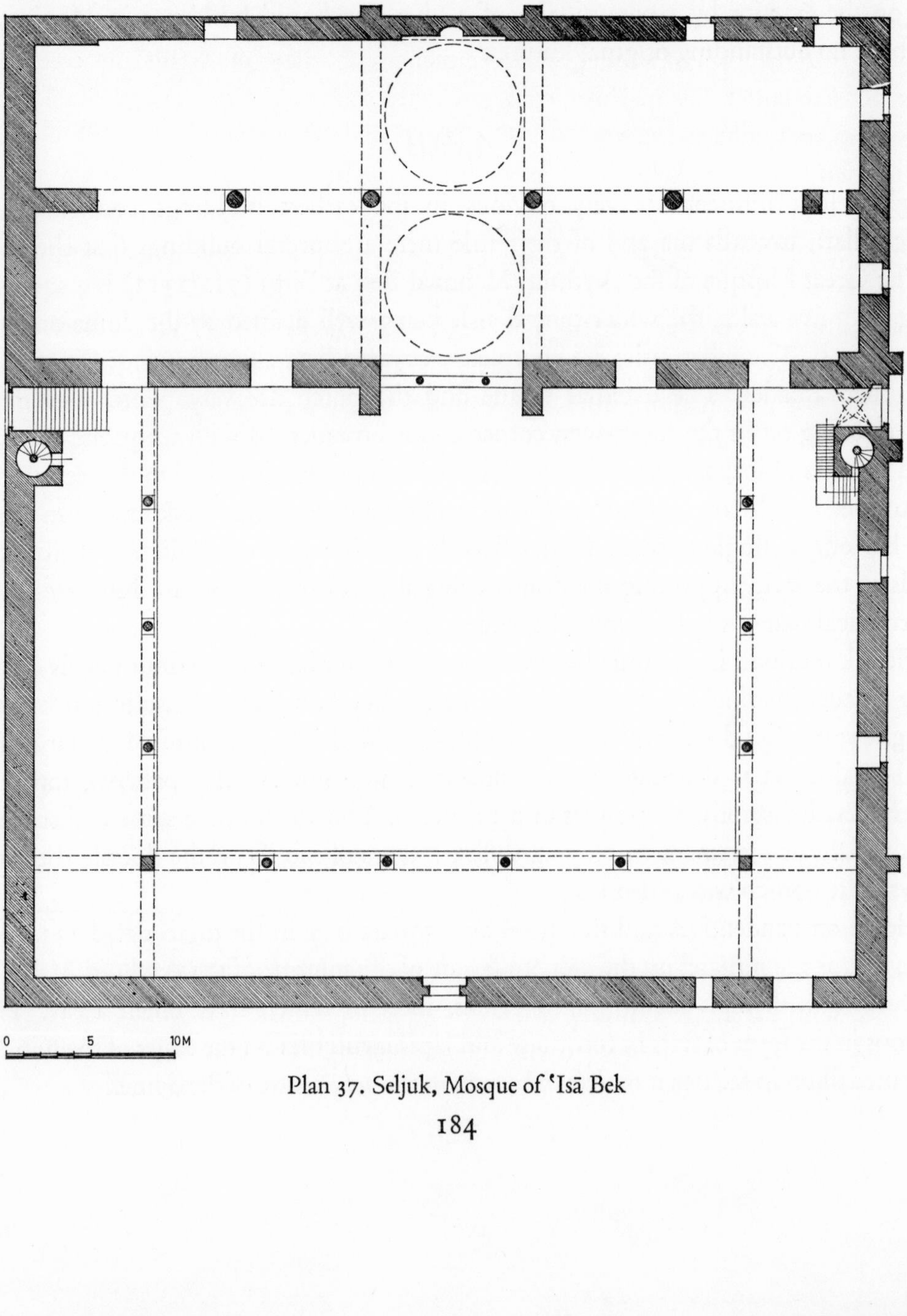

Plan 37. Seljuk, Mosque of 'Isā Bek

turquoise faience, which are in the Seljuk tradition. The plan of the mosque is based on Artukid mosques and the Great Mosque at Diyarbekir, which is based in turn on the 'Umayyad mosque in Damascus. Three of the four granite columns separating the aisles have original stalactite capitals, the fourth has a Roman composite capital. In the last century the mosque was converted into a caravansarai, a door was opened in the place of the mihrab and the upper portion of the mihrab was placed in the Kestane Pazar Mosque in Izmir. There are brick minarets at the east and west porches. The one on the east has collapsed; the one on the west has undergone repairs. This is the second time in the Beylik period that we come across a twin minaret mosque, the first being the Sunqur Agha Mosque at Niğde. The highly impressive and monumental western façade stretching the whole length of the mosque and courtyard is faced with marble and enlivened with two rows of windows. It is on a far larger scale than the other mosques of the Emirate period and is much influenced by the Seljuk tradition. (Fig. 132.) The high narrow porch rising above the façade at the division between the mosque and the courtyard is in the form of a fluted stalactite niche with inlays of marble and coloured stone above rows of stalactites. The marble facings above the arch have fallen away. The low recesses on each side of the staircase leading up to the porch may have been shops. The windows on the monumental front with coloured stone ornament are not arranged according to the interior behind them. Among the different types of stalactite and stone decoration on these one may notice the Zengid knotted entrelac motif. This façade is a prototype of the façade architecture to be found in the large Ottoman mosques in Bursa, Edirne and Istanbul. The originality, the urge towards ever further development that increases in the period of the Turcoman Emirates as one approaches Western Anatolia, achieves its highest expression in the Ottomans. The other Aydınid single-domed mosques with entrance porticos display no special distinguishing features, and this also holds good for the tombs.

Menteşeid

The Menteşeid Turcomans who established an Emirate in the extreme south-west corner of Anatolia displayed a vitality in architecture in no way inferior to their neighbours the Aydınids. The Hacı Ilyās mosque built in Milâs in 1330 in the time of Orhan Bek is a flat wooden-roofed building that owes its importance to the three-domed portico covered with red bricks stretching the whole length of the façade. In this portico, the piers supporting the central dome form double pointed arches in front of the side domes by means of interjacent columns, whilst the large high-pointed arch of the central dome opens out to the front in an unusual rhythm. The minaret in the form of a balcony at the top of an open stairway on the western side is a characteristic feature of Milâs.

The Great Mosque in Milâs built by Aḥmad Ghāzī in 1378 employing a great deal of re-used material has three aisles supported on piers and perpendicular to the qibla. The eastern aisle is roofed with transverse vaulting whilst the western aisle and the wider and higher central aisle with the mihrab dome are roofed with plain vaulting. The plan is in the Seljuk mosque tradition. The dome over the mihrab is supported on pendentives with seven rows of plain stalactite fillings. The minaret is again in the form of a balcony reached by an outer staircase.

The most imposing building in Milâs is the Firuz Bek Mosque built in 1394, the first year of the Ottoman conquest, by Khwāja Fīrūz, the Menteşeid governor appointed by Bayazid I, which thus may properly be considered as Menteşeid architecture. The plan comes into the category of side-roomed (or *zāwīya*) mosques with domes arranged in an inverted T form, which can be seen in the first years of the Ottoman period and, in a more developed form, in the mosque of Orhan in Bursa.

The Nilüfer Khātūn Imaret in Iznik was built on the same plan. In the Firuz Bek Mosque the central section of the portico with five pointed arches on piers stretching the whole length of the north front is roofed with a dome, whilst the two other sections on each side are each covered with a vault. The three arches in the middle have zigzag lobes like the central arch of the portico in the Orhan Mosque in Bursa. The wealth of decoration is increased by the four balustrade grilles with geometrical stars and entrelacs under the side arches and by stalactite brackets on the piers of the arches. (Fig. 133.)

The vestibule is lower than the other sections and is covered with a stone roof in the form of a series of concentric squares corbelled out, a technique that is also to be seen in the Roman funerary monument nearby. On each side of the vestibule there is a chamber with a dome with stalactites and fluted squinches, and in front of it the central space forming a projection roofed with a dome on squinches over the mihrab of a slightly different style. The mihrab niche, which has five rows of stalactites and is surrounded on all four sides by a stalactite border, displays a magnificence of style with its porphyry corner columns, its inscription and the motif of a hanging mosque-lamp inside the niche, and the embossed arabesques and palmettes on its spandrels. The arabesques and palmettes seen here were later to be reproduced in tile and stone in the monuments in Bursa. The signatures of the builder Mūsā bin ʿAbd Allāh and the decorator Mūsā bin ʿĀdil are written perpendicular to the cornice of the mihrab. The minbar is new. The mosque has two rows of windows with different styles of arch and lintel, and is faced on the outside with blocks of grey, green and yellow marble with purple veins and spots, whilst the ornate stalactite-canopied windows are decorated with bi-coloured joggled voussoirs. The windows on the west side are plain. (Fig. 134.) The high, narrow porch is decorated with a stalactite border of polychrome voussoirs. The innovations in the plan and architecture of the Firuz Bek Mosque influenced the early Ottoman mosques of the end of the 14th century. Beside the mosque there is a simple medrese with twelve rooms extending in a single row and roofed by domes, transverse vaulting and barrel vaulting.

The Friday Mosque built at Balat (Miletus) in 1404 by the Menteşeid Ilyās Bek after the re-establishment of their Emirate on the fall of Bayazid I has a dome on squinches 14 metres in diameter and is the most monumental and spectacular of the early single-domed mosques. (Fig. 135.) The transition from the square base to the dome begins with Turkish triangles and terminates in stalactites and squinches in the form of shells. The ornament and fillings in each squinch are different. The interior is dominated by the magnificent mihrab (7.35×5.2 metres) with its varied borders and the six rows of stalactites in the mihrab niche. The iwan-like porch in three sections between bold arches that takes the place of the main façade and portico is Seljuk in feeling, and its marble grilles and coloured voussoirs lend it a very attractive appearance. It opens into the interior through a broken arch. (Fig. 136.) The façades are faced entirely in marble and are articulated by two rows of two windows each, each window being ornamented in a different style. Grooved mouldings running from top to bottom embrace each pair of windows. The stone-carving, which is of the highest quality and most meticulously executed, shows a great advance on that of the Firuz Bek Mosque.

The dome was formerly covered with copper but in 1905 it was covered with roof tiles. Together with a tomb to the north of the mosque and the medrese rooms at the sides the whole formed a complex. The tomb is in ruins, and of the medrese rooms only one on the east side remains. The conception of the complex, the courtyard with open arcades, the two storeys of windows, the marble facing and the coloured stone decoration must have influenced early Ottoman architecture. But the Green Mosque at Iznik (1378) may also be said to have influenced the Ilyās Bek Mosque. The influences were mutual.

A medrese of squared stone and rubble built by Aḥmad Ghāzī in 1375 at Peçin consists of ten plain vaulted cells surrounding a courtyard with a fountain but without arcades, and the domed tomb of Aḥmad Ghāzī, which occupies the place of the large iwan. On the south side staircases on two sides lead up to a flat earthen roof. There is a second storey above the rooms on either side of the tomb. The salient pointed-arched Gothic porch is monumental in appearance (Fig. 138). The tomb, too, opens on to the courtyard through a pointed arch that is somewhat Gothic in style, and which has in its spandrels two reliefs of a lion holding a flag. Aḥmad Ghāzī's name is written on the flag on the right. The Gothic influences to be seen in the northern portal and stone traceries of the Sunqur Agha Mosque (1355) at Niğde thus appear forty years later in the Aḥmad Ghāzī Medrese at Peçin and in the porch of his tomb. These may be associated with the influences of eastern Gothic through the Crusader cathedrals of ʿAqqa and other towns in Palestine, as well as the cathedrals of Cyprus.

Other single-domed mosques built by the Menteşeids in and near Peçin such as the Kepez Yelli Mosque with a transverse-vaulted entrance portico and the Ilyās Bek Mosque in the village of Turgut, the Karapaşa Medrese with vaulted rooms and vaulted iwan standing outside the city walls, and the ruins of a medrese built on a similar plan in the Kepez region introduce no architectural innovations.

The innovations and new developments in style that arose in Anatolian Turkish architecture during the Beylik period and became more pronounced as they moved towards the west were most fully exploited by the Ottomans who, starting as one among several Emirates, rose to dominate all the others, and opened the way for an Ottoman Turkish architecture on a world scale.

11

INTRODUCTION TO OTTOMAN ARCHITECTURE

The Ottoman Turcomans belonged to one of the Oghuz tribes and, like other Turcomans, migrated from Central Asia to Iran with the Seljuks, and from there crossed over into Anatolia. Their leader, Sulaymān Shāh, was drowned near Qal'at Jabr in 1228 while crossing the Euphrates in Mesopotamia, and the Ottomans settled down in Söğüt under the rule of his son Ertughrul Bek. In Söğüt was born Ertughrul Bek's youngest son Osman Bek, who succeeded his father and gave his name to the state he established in 1299. His successor Orhan Bek captured Bursa in 1326, Iznik in 1331, for the first time since its capture by the Seljuks (1078–1147), and the region of Karasī (Balıkesir) in 1336. Murad I captured Edirne in 1361, then Plovdiv and Sofia, and a little later Salonika. The Ottomans made first Bursa and then Edirne their seat of government so that, with the exception of Istanbul and the Byzantine territory of Trabzon, by the end of the 14th century they had established an empire stretching from the Danube to the Euphrates. But just at this time Timur mustered the Asian Turks and descended like a hurricane on Anatolia. Bayazid I, who was the first of the Ottoman rulers to adopt the title of the great Sultan (al-Sulṭān al a'ẓam), was defeated by the armies of Timur at the battle of Ankara, and was taken prisoner. The young Ottoman Empire was dispersed for a time, but was consolidated once more by Chelebi Sultan Mehmed. In 1453 the twenty-one year old Sultan Mehmed the Conqueror, the youngest son of Murad II, captured Istanbul in May after a seven weeks' siege and so put an end to the Byzantine Empire. In 1460 the territory of the Empire of Trabzon was captured, and in 1475 the Crimea. In 1480 a landing was made in Apulia and Otranto was captured. During the eight years of his rule (1512–20) Sultan Selim I defeated the Safawid ruler of Iran, Shāh Ismā'īl, who was himself of Turkish extraction, and united the whole of Eastern Anatolia. He destroyed the Sultanate of the Egyptian Mamluks and so joined Syria, Palestine, Arabia and Egypt to the Empire. He then adopted the title of Caliph. The most brilliant period of the Empire was that of Sultan Suleyman

Kānūnī, whom Europeans nicknamed the Magnificent, and in whose reign an Anatolian Empire was established comparable with the Roman Empire, including the whole of the Balkans, Hungary, Southern Russia and a part of Poland, together with Egypt, the Sudan, Ethiopia and North Africa. The Ottoman admirals, Barbarossa, Piyale Pasha and Turgut Reis, dominated the whole of the Mediterranean. Although Cyprus, Baghdad and Erevan were captured a little later and Crete was taken in 1645 the Empire had lost its old strength, but until the Siege of Vienna (1683) and the Treaty of Karlofça (Karlovač) (1699) it suffered no actual loss of territory. (Map III.)

That the story of its decline should have occupied the 220 years from this first setback in 1699 until its final collapse in 1918 shows the strength of the Empire and the solidity of its foundation. The Ottoman dynasty ruled for 620 years from the foundation of the state. After the First World War the empire was liquidated and in 1923 the Turkish Republic was set up in Anatolia, the old kingdom of the Seljuks, from which the Empire had originally sprung. (Map II.)

Monuments of Iznik (Orhan Bek Period)

Captured by the Turks in 1331, five years after the capture of Bursa, Iznik became the site of the first important Ottoman buildings and thus the cradle of Ottoman architecture. The oldest structure bearing an inscription and a date is the single-domed Hajji Özbek Mosque with its three-vaulted portico dating from 734/1333. The original style of wall construction with one course of hewn stone and three or four courses of brick is continued in Iznik, and particularly in some of the earliest buildings in Bursa, Edirne and Istanbul. This mosque is strongly influenced by the architecture of Seljuk masjids. It has a dome resting on prismatic or 'Turkish' triangles and an entrance portico in the west side with a transverse-vaulted section in front of the door and two sections roofed with a single plain vault. The portico, which dates from three years after the Ilyās Bek Mosque at Milâs and is the oldest portico in a single-domed mosque, was destroyed during road-widening operations in 1959 and a new, closed portico in very poor taste was constructed by demolishing the northern wall.

The first attempts to enlarge the interior area of the traditional single-domed mosque are to be seen in the Green Mosque, which is one of the most important and monumental examples of Ottoman architecture in Iznik. The building was begun by the architect Hajji Mūsā in 1378 for Chandarlı Qarā Khalīl Khayreddin Pasha, but it was only completed 14 years later in 1392 after the latter's death. (Fig. 137.) The rather deep three-vaulted portico opening to the sides through two arches is roofed on the two sides by panelled vaulting and in the centre by a fluted dome resting on a high octagonal drum. There is a vestibule opening on to the large dome through three wide arches, and repeating the plan of the portico in being roofed by panelled vaults at the side and by a dome with a blind lantern in the centre and bold flutes. The central dome, 11 metres in diameter, is in the form of an exact hemisphere on prismatic triangles (Plan 38). Increasing the size of the single-domed interior by extending it towards the front was a new experiment, and gives the mosque architectural qualities both in the

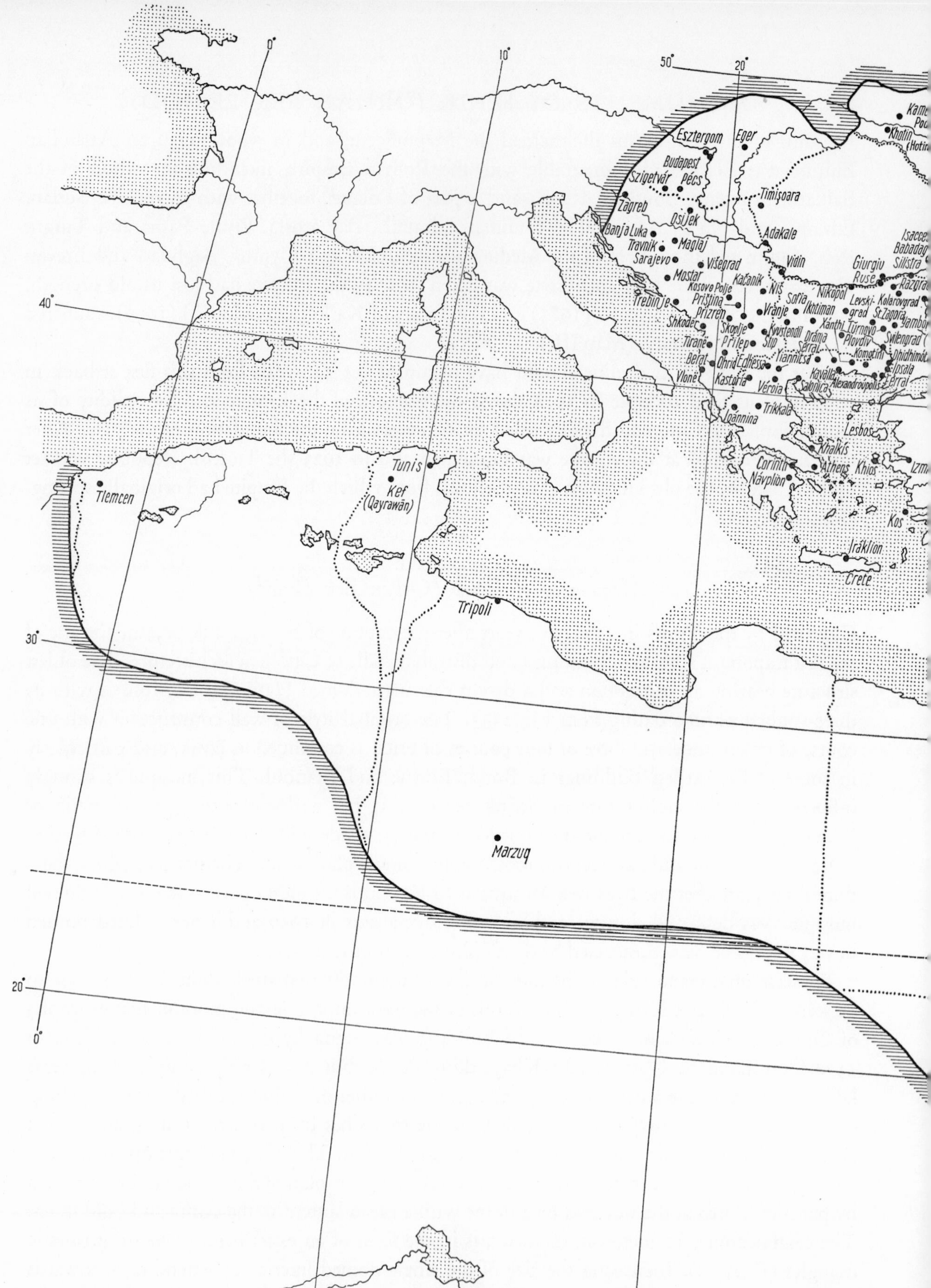

MAP III Ottoman Empire. The modern frontiers of the Successor States of the Ottoman Empire are marked thus . . . . . .

40°
50°
50°
60°
Yevpatoriya
Feodosiya
Stary Krym
Yalta
Sudak
Novorossiisk
Gelendzhik
Derbend
Batumi
Tbilisi
Erevan
Baku
40°
Erzurum
Sivas
Kayseri
Van
Tabriz
Konya
Diyarbekir
Mardin
Aleppo
Kyrenia
Famagusta
Larnaca
Cyprus
Mosul
Kirkuk
Beirut
Damascus
Sidon
Acre
Haifa
Baghdad
Damietta
Jerusalem
Basra
30°
Medina
Jidda
Mecca
20°
60°
Suakin
San'a
40°
50°

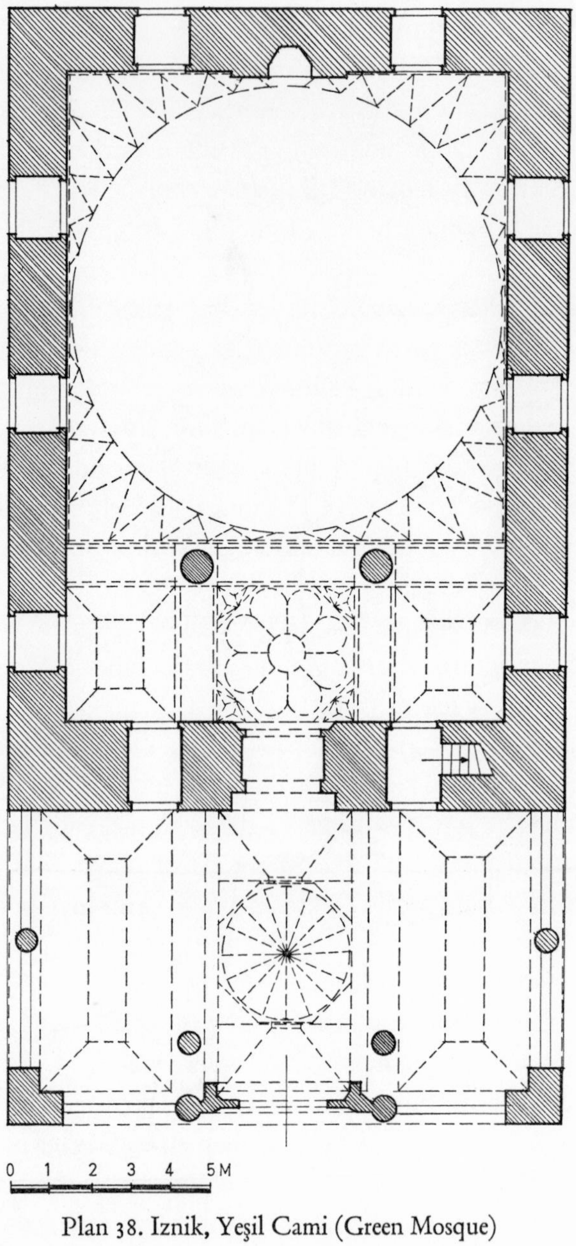

Plan 38. Iznik, Yeşil Cami (Green Mosque)

interior and on the exterior which have an appearance of greater monumental strength than they in fact possess. (Fig. 139.) The walls are faced with marble blocks both inside and outside and are articulated on the east and west sides by two rows of windows, thus foreshadowing the windowed walls of the Bursa mosque. The marble baluster grilles with geometrical designs on each side of the portico have been destroyed. The stalactites surrounding the door are in the Seljuk tradition. The simple mihrab with corner pilasters, a plain stalactite niche and geometrical entrelacs, arabesques and palmettes in relief is the earliest Ottoman example, and heralds the birth of a new style. The brick minaret in the Seljuk style is decorated with the green tiles that give the mosque its name, as well as turquoise, yellow and purple. The knot and star (fourfold braid) motifs produced by the large intersecting octagons on the wide band at the lower edge continues the old Turkish and Seljuk ornamental tradition. Unfortunately this minaret has been very badly restored in recent years. The Green Mosque at Iznik is a transitional structure linking Seljuk architecture to the Ottoman architecture arising from it, and influenced both the Firuz Bek Mosque at Milâs and the Ilyās Bek Mosque at Balat. All the capitals and architectural decorations are original. No ancient fragments have been re-used.

The first development of the single-domed mosque before the Green Mosque is to be seen in the Orhan Mosque at Bilecik, which underwent extensive repairs during the reign of Abdülhamid II (1889) and was converted into a two-minaret mosque. This mosque, which dates from the second half of the 14th century, has a central dome 9.5 metres in diameter supported on pointed arches and extended on all four sides by means of iwans 2.4 metres deep; this may be regarded as a great step forward in the development of the central dome.

The mosque built in Iznik in 1443 by Maḥmūd Chelebi the grandson of Khayreddin Pasha has a single dome resting on prismatic triangles and a portico in front with a dome in the centre and panelled vaults on each side, thus showing a return to the traditional plan. Here the marble baluster grille of the portico has survived. The walls are constructed of one course of hewn stone alternating with three courses of brick, in the Iznik tradition.

During the siege of Iznik a masjid was built by Orhan Ghāzī near the Yenişehir gate, outside the city walls, and excavations have shown that the plan of this mosque displays the inverted T plan of the side-roomed (or zāwīya) mosque for the first time among the Ottomans. But here it is probable that the actual mosque, in the form of a long rectangle in the centre and the rectangular chambers opening into this by means of doors, was originally covered by a flat roof supported on thin curtain walls. The five-vaulted entrance portico can be clearly seen. According to a mutilated and incomplete inscription it was built in the year 725/1325. But the monumental plan of the Orhan Mosque built by Orhan Ghāzī at Bursa in 740/1340 consists of two domes one behind the other with one small dome on each side. The real development of this plan was to be realised in the Bursa mosques.

The impressive imaret in Iznik built by Murad I Hudavendigār in 790/1388 in memory of his mother Nilüfer Khātūn shows the use of this plan in buildings other than mosques. (Fig. 140.) The large open dome resting on prismatic triangles with a high lantern in the centre is extended by a wide arch towards the rear to a depth of two small domes. The plan achieves the complete inverted T form by means of a single-domed chamber on each side. The outer façade is enlivened by an arcade resting on four piers and four columns with two arches at each side and five in front, roofed by a dome in the centre and panelled vaults on the right and the left. The building is lent a very attractive appearance by the alternation of one course of hewn stone and three courses of brick in the walls, and the colourfulness is increased by the red roofing tiles on the domes. Each of the side domes is enlarged by an arch, and a mihrab niche is opened in the chamber by which the central dome is extended in the form of an iwan. The Nilüfer Khatun Imaret is now a museum.

The second-structure resembling this in plan and external appearance is the *zāwīya* built by Yakub Chelebi, the eldest son of Murad I Hudavendigār. After the arcade with five panelled vaults covering the whole length of the front a small entrance dome and wide arch open into the interior off which we find the large dome chamber containing the mihrab. The side rooms have panelled vaults. The walls of the open canopy tomb in front of the arcade consisting of a dome resting on four arches are also constructed of one course of hewn stone alternating with three rows of brick. This is the oldest Ottoman tomb and its style was continued long after the end of the 14th century. There is a tomb of the same type in Iznik known as the Sarı Saltuk Mausoleum

The very much ruined medrese built in Iznik by Sulaymān Pasha, the eldest son of Orhan Ghāzī, consists of domed cells behind columned arcades with one side left open, and a classroom with a large dome on squinches. An asymmetrical plan without an iwan, cell arcades connected to the classroom by a corridor behind and the arrangement of the cells, together with their rectangular and circular windows, herald the birth of a new type of medrese architecture quite different from that of the Seljuks.

In Iznik we find gathered together in one place the domed mosque with an extension towards the front that foreshadows the new Ottoman style of architecture, original stalactite capitals, tiled minarets, marble mihrabs, imarets and tombs, the first development of the inverted T plan scheme and the beginning of Ottoman medrese construction, the first tombs in the Ottoman style, and a type of wall construction with one course of hewn stone and three of brick. Iznik thus was a centre which contained the seeds of the development of subsequent Ottoman architecture.

Monuments of Bursa and Other Cities (Bayazid I, Chelebi Sultan Mehmed I and Murad II)

In Bursa the Ottoman architecture of Iznik underwent a brilliant development and reached monumental proportions. The mosque which would appear to have been built at Hisar in 1326 by ʿAlā al-Dīn Bek, the son of Osman Ghāzī, has survived to our own times only after undergoing a considerable amount of repair. It has a dome resting on large prismatic triangles in the Seljuk style and an entrance portico with Corinthian and Ionic capitals and a dome in the centre and panel vaults on each side. If we accept this portico as forming part of the original plan then it follows that the portico is to be found in Bursa in Ottoman architecture and in a domed mosque four years before it appeared in the Hacı Ilyās Mosque at Milâs. In the period of the Turcoman Emirates the problem of the portico was thus tackled concomitantly, and was not confined solely to any one region. Whilst the ʿAlā al-Dīn Bek Mosque conforms to the traditional single-domed plan scheme with its three-arched portico the inverted T form mosques at Bursa showed a new and brilliant development. This plan derives essentially from the domed medreses of the Seljuks. The plan is to be seen in the domes arranged in T form in the Karatay and Ince Minare Medreses in Konya and in the vaulted iwans surrounding the central dome in inverted T form in the Caca Bey Medrese at Kırşehir; but it was best exploited from the architectural point of view in the five Bursa mosques built by the Ottoman Sultans in their own names.

The first of these is the Orhan Bek Mosque built in 740/1339. The marble and limestone of the portico and entrances were damaged in an attempt to burn the mosque down during the siege of Bursa by the Karamanid Mehmed Bek II in 1413, and in 1417 it was repaired by the vizir Bayazid Pasha on the orders of Chelebi Sultan Mehmed. Although it later underwent several other repairs the plan suffered no essential alteration. The plan of the mosque becomes an inverted T by the addition of two smaller domes on the sides and another larger one (13.5 metres in diameter) to the qibla side, thus surrounding a high central dome (8.45 metres in diameter) on three sides. There is a group of rooms in the front, comprising a room with a very small dome in the centre and beside it small vaulted rooms, and finally at the corner large vaulted rooms. The portico next to this unit is divided into five parts with panel vaults on the sides and three domes in the centre. Composite capitals have been re-used on the twin arches at the sides of the portico whilst the walls of brick and stone patterning are enlivened by the high zigzag arch of the entrance section in the centre, brick sun disks, rosettes and other forms of ornament. In the dome in front of the mihrab the transition is effected by squinches with prismatic fillings, and in the central dome by Turkish triangles in the form of inverted fans. The Orhan Mosque was to show the way for other mosques in Bursa.

The mosque of Murad I Hudavendigār at Çekirge in Bursa was begun in 1366 and completed some time before 1385. It has thick walls constructed of one course of hewn stone and three of brick and is a two-storeyed building of unusual form with a medrese on an upper storey. The basic plan of the lower storey is related to that of the Caca Bey Medrese at Kırşehir in having a high central dome and vaulted iwans surrounding and supporting this on the qibla wall and two other sides. There are vaulted chambers in the corners, and an entrance dome in the centre with staircases on each side leading up to the upper floor. Both storeys are roofed by the central dome and the iwan vault, which is of the same width, whilst along the sides of the upper storey are deployed the rows of vaulted rooms of the medrese. The vaulted corridor completely surrounding the central dome and the qibla iwan opens into the mosque only through a single window in the small domed chamber above the mihrab. A monumental façade is produced by a five-domed portico with piers surmounted by a second storey with three domes in the centre and a panelled vault at each side. The two-storeyed façade with the upper arcade opening out in front and on the sides through double pointed arches with columns in the middle has the spectacular appearance of a Venetian palace. (Fig. 141.) But as there are very few windows on the other sides the exterior produces an effect of massive solidity, whilst the interior is rather gloomy. The faint splashing of the *shadırvan* under the open dome produces a pleasing and harmonious effect. The dome on pendentives 11 metres in diameter and the *shadırvan* under it were reconstructed after an earthquake in 1855. Sixteen small corbels in the drum indicate the position of the old dome. Round arches dominate the interior and pointed arches, the exterior. The character of both interior and exterior together with the peculiarities of certain architectural details set this mosque apart from the other mosques in Bursa. The mosque was constructed in the form of a complex including a public latrine, which is something quite remarkable in Anatolia at that date, a single-domed ablution room adjoining it, the sultan's tomb on the north and an imaret on the west.

The Shahadet Mosque, another mosque built by Murad I Hudavendigār in Bursa in 1365, consists of a wide central aisle with two domes one behind the other supported on two piers and two narrow side aisles, each having two long rectangular sharp-pointed vaults. In front there is a four-domed portico, the place of the fifth dome being taken by the minaret. As a result of various subsequent repairs and alterations it is now reduced to a small mosque consisting of the two-domed central aisle.

The Hudavendigār Mosque built by Murad I at Plovdiv in Bulgaria in 1389 consists of a wide three-domed central aisle and narrow side aisles with three vaults each, a lengthened form of the plan scheme realised in the Shahadet Mosque (40 × 30 metres). There is a pool under the central dome, and in the front there is a portico with a flat roof. The body of the minaret is decorated with turquoise tiles in lozenge patterns. The works of Murad Hudavendigār open the way for the multi-domed Ottoman mosques by his foundations at Bursa and Plovdiv. In all three of Murad I's mosques one is struck by a stylistic unity. There is an interesting resemblance between the plan of the Hudavendigār or Congregational Mosque at Plovdiv and the Sunqur Bek Mosque of the Eretnids at Niğde (1335), which shows the inter-relations of Turkish architecture in the 14th century.

Before becoming Sultan (1382) Bayazid I had built a complex at Mudurnu, a town in the vilayet of Bolu, consisting of a single-domed mosque, a magnificent medrese which was destroyed only quite recently, and a double bath. The dome, 19.5 metres in diameter, resting on pointed arches supported by eight wall piers and rising up from below like a great Kirghiz tent, much wider than it is high, spans a spacious interior. In front, in the middle, there is a recessed arch in the form of an iwan and a portico with a small lobed dome in the entrance and a larger dome at each side. A dome of this diameter, even if low in elevation, was a daring step at the end of the 14th century. Although the mosque has subsequently undergone various repairs it still conforms to its original plan. In spite of its lowness the dome does not produce a squat impression.

According to its inscription the Great Mosque at Bergama was built by Bayazid I in 801/1398. Although it conforms to the plan of the Hudavendigār Mosque at Plovdiv, as the vaults of the side naves are covered over with a plain inclined roof only the three domes in the middle are reflected in the exterior. But the largest of Bayazid's Great Mosques (68 × 56 metres) was built at Bursa between 1396 and 1400. It is the most monumental and traditional of the multi-domed mosques, with twenty domes on pendentives supported by twelve heavy square piers. (Fig. 142.) Although there are two minarets on its north front there is no portico. The walls are articulated by pointed-arched niches reflecting each row of domes, and each niche is pierced by two rows of two windows each. The elevation of the domes increases from the sides towards the centre. The second dome on the main axis has been left open except for its present glass covering, and a large *shadırvan* or fountain is placed beneath it. The doors opening on each of the three sides lead straight to this fountain. (Fig. 143.) Water flows into a 16-sided pool in eight channels from the three basins of the fountain and is distributed through sixteen taps. The rectangular stalactite mihrab with corner pilasters has been spoilt by tasteless painted decoration. The large wooden minbar bearing a dating inscription of Bayazid I and an inscription of a master-craftsman is the work of the same Ḥajjī Muḥammad of ʿAyntab (Gaziantep) who built the minbar of the Great Mosque at Manisa. Here he displays the real mastery of his craft that had developed in the 24 years that had elapsed since his work at Manisa. The minbar with geometrical panels finely worked with arabesques and palmettes, balustrade grilles with geometrical patterns, the inscription above its door and a crown of lattice-work, is a masterpiece in the transitional style linking Seljuk with Ottoman workmanship. After the Great Mosque in Bursa this type of mosque with various numbers of equal domes became a widely cultivated mosque-type, specimens of which are to be seen in various cities from the Balkans to Cairo right up to the end of the 17th century.

The most mature form of the inverted T plan, which first appeared in the mosque of Orhan in Bursa and underwent some modifications in the Hudavendigār Mosque, is displayed in the Yıldırım mosque built by Bayazid I between 1390 and 1395. It is built entirely of hewn stone and rises up in the centre of a large complex in the form of a new district or quarter composed of eight separate buildings outside the city walls. There are two domes one behind the other with small domed iwans at the sides, and on each side of these there is a small room with panelled vaulting. The south walls of the rooms near the dome over the mihrab are entirely occupied with rows of shelves in the form of niches with a fireplace in the centre, and are covered with plaster ornament inset with patches of turquoise tiles between them. There is a second storey only above the rooms beside the entrance. The piers of the magnificent broken arches connecting the domed chambers in the centre rest on finely worked stalactite consoles (Plan 39). The exterior of the mosque is noteworthy for its five-arched portico, without parallel in Ottoman architecture. Here there is a highly monumental entrance façade with five higher and wider broken arches in the centre and two broken arches at each side springing from tall marble piers (Fig. 144). This form of arch is to be seen in the door of the Qılıch Arslan mausoleum in the courtyard of the ʿAlā al-Dīn Mosque at Konya, but it is normally associated with Bursa, where, after the Seljuks, it was most often and most effectively exploited by the Ottomans. Here, as in the Hudavendigār Mosque, the side and rear walls reach a height of two storeys and are enlivened and embellished by rows of windows, most of which are blind. The monumental strength of the mosque depends on the quality of the architectural details and the whole leaves an impression of noble simplicity. Its plan and architecture influenced the later Yeşil Cami (Green Mosque) at Bursa. Although it underwent repairs after the earthquake of 1855 it suffered no essential change. Of the rest of the complex only the tomb and the medrese still stand.

The rapid development of Ottoman architecture at the end of the 14th century was brought to a halt by the shock and confusion following the defeat and capture of Bayazid I by Timur at the Battle of Ankara, but unity was re-established in the ten years following Bayazid's death in 1403 by his son Chelebi Sultan Mehmed. After this, vitality was restored to architecture. The Green Mosque built at Bursa by the architect Hajji Ivaz at the command of Chelebi Sultan Mehmed is in the form of a complex, which has the exceptional feature of a tomb, placed on a higher level than the mosque. The mosque took ten years to build and was completed in 1424 in the reign of Sultan Murad II before the decoration of the outer windows

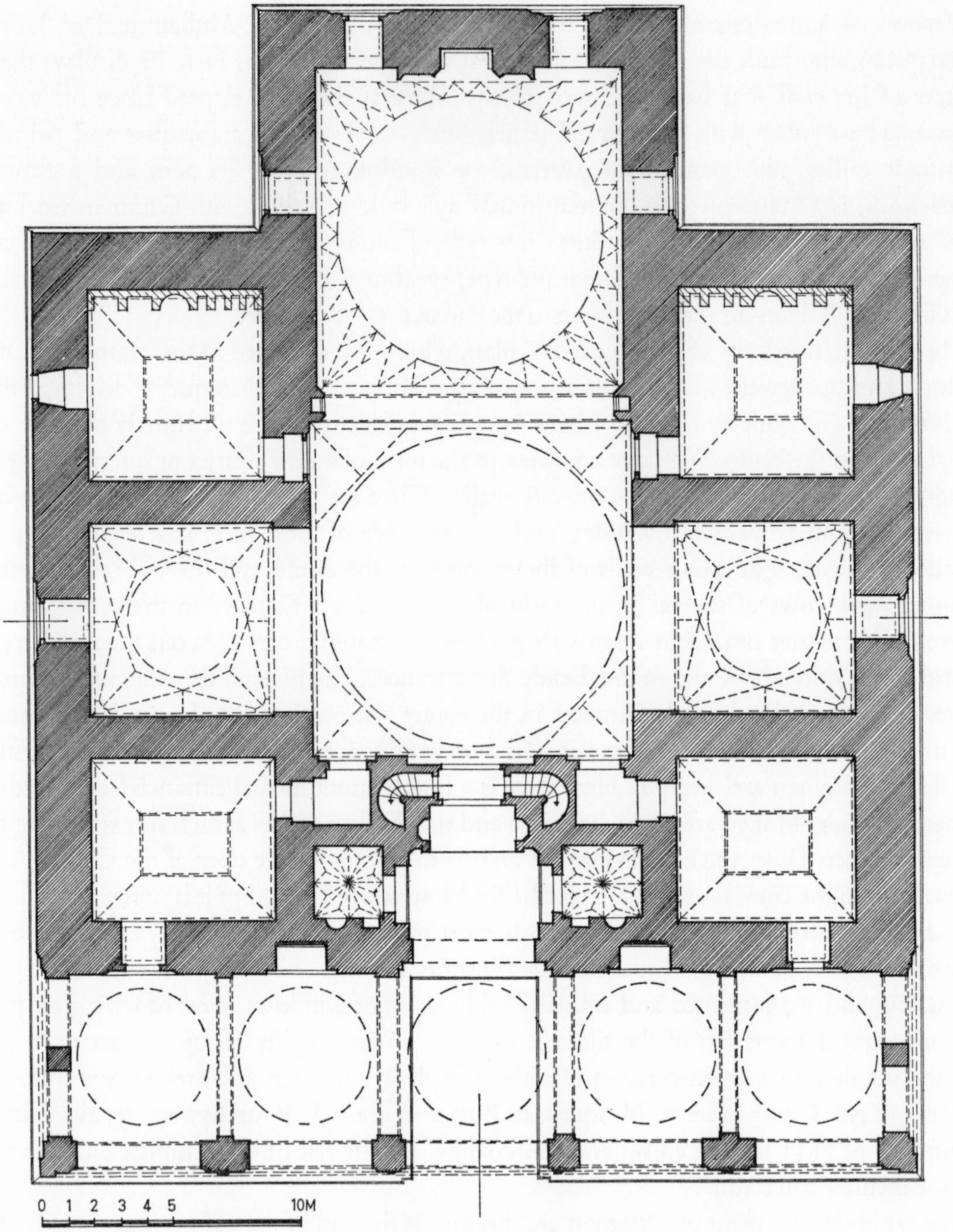

Plan 39. Bursa, Yıldırım Mosque

had been completely finished. (Fig. 145.) From the present state of the piers of the arches it is clear that a five-domed portico had originally been included in the plan but was later abandoned. In the general features of its plan and architecture it resembles the Yıldırım Mosque. It has two domes one behind the other set on prismatic triangles, an iwan with a fluted dome to either side, and in the corners a chamber with a fluted dome on the qibla side and another with transverse vaulting on the entrance side. One wall of each room is adorned with niched shelves and fireplace in plaster as in the Yıldırım Mosque. The first dome was originally open but was later closed in with a lantern and has a large *shadırvan* beneath it at a lower ground level. The vestibule lies at the front between vaulted rooms entirely cut off from the interior of the mosque and is in two storeys with court loggias on each side on the lower storey and an imperial gallery and apartments on the upper storey. There are staircases on each side of the entrance hall and two balconies opening outwards on the first floor. As in the Yıldırım Mosque the section on a lower level containing the *shadırvan* opens into the section under the mihrab dome, which is reached by a number of steps, through a broken arch. The mosque is built entirely of hewn stone, and the porch, the outer mihrabs and the window are richly decorated with meticulously worked stone. (Fig. 146.) The high façades at the sides and the rear are in two storeys with rows of windows (Fig. 147), some of the upper ones being blind, in the style of the Yıldırım Mosque.

Although its architecture is richer and more highly developed than that of the Yıldırım Mosque the Green Mosque owes its name and fame to the tile facings, which are of fine quality and rich design. The art of Ottoman ceramics is here displayed in magnificent style. In complete contrast to Seljuk tiles these are made in the form of *cuerda seca* panels in polychrome underglaze technique, with patterns which resemble faience mosaic and produce a quite marvellous effect. In the contours separating the colours red has been used as well as black. Besides geometrical entrelacs, arabesques and palmettes, new designs can be seen such as *hatayīs* (from the word Hatay, i.e. China, Cathay, and used in Turkish decoration to mean a plumed arabesque), peonies, and rosettes with naturalistically treated flowers and foliate motifs. The colours are also different, the dominant colours being yellow, green, white and purple. The walls are faced with hexagonal green or lapis lazuli tiles up to a height of 2.5 metres, and in the side rooms these are surrounded by triangular tiles of a different colour to form hexagonal stars, in the mihrab section being surrounded by light-coloured contours (Fig. 148). In the Imperial gallery gilt has been used on the tiles. The tile panels with palmettes, *rūmī* and *hatayī* scrolls in polychrome underglaze technique decorating the ceiling and arches are of very high quality, and are as clear and brilliant in colour as faience mosaic. The largest tile mihrab, 15 metres in height, is covered with tiles in which foliate motifs, *rūmī* and *hatayī* scrolls predominate in white, turquoise, lapis lazuli and gold. The magnificence of the Imperial gallery leaves all the other sections in the shade. The walls, ceiling and arches are completely covered with tiles.

In recent years polychrome painted decoration as rich as the tiles has been uncovered by the removal of the plaster on the upper section of the walls and the dome, proving that the mosque was an outstanding monument of decorative art applied to and in conformity with a style of architecture that achieved palatial opulence without ever falling into exaggeration. The name of the craftsman who made the tiles is mentioned on the tiles at the lower edge of the Bursa arch in the Imperial gallery as Muḥammad al-Majnūn (Muḥammad the Mad), but the arrangement of the tiles and all the other decorations into a single stylistic unity was the work of the Naqqāsh (decorator or painter) ʿAlī bin Ilyās ʿAlī, whose signature is carved on one of the stones of the Imperial gallery. ʿAlī bin Ilyās ʿAlī went with Timur to Samarkand in 1402 where he learned various technical refinements and examined specimens of tile-work, after which he returned to Bursa where he produced work of even higher quality than he had seen there. The harmonious stylistic unity displayed in the tiles, decoration, stone and woodwork is his creation. A second inscription mentioning Ustādhān-i Tabrīzī (Tabrīzī craftsmen) refers to the craftsmen whom Naqqāsh ʿAlī brought with him and who worked under his orders. No tiles of this quality and richness were made in Persia until the time of the Safawids. It appears that the tiles employed in the Green Mosque and its complex were manufactured in kilns in the immediate vicinity.

In spite of all its dazzling richness the Green Mosque belongs to the old category of the inverted T form mosques which were being built in Bursa, but in the mosque of Chelebi Sultan Mehmed, the second work of architecture built for the Sultan at Dimetoka, 40 kilometres south of Edirne, by Hajji Ivaz, the great architect of the Green Mosque and its complex, the important innovation of a developed central dome plan is introduced. The mosque at Dimetoka, which is now in a very ruinous condition and is used as a grain depot, is a square, monumental structure 30 metres square with walls 2 metres thick constructed of large hewn stone blocks. The central dome, 13 metres in diameter, rests on four piers and is surrounded by plain vaults, whilst the square spaces in the corners are roofed with transverse vaulting. At the entrance there is a three-domed portico. (Plan 40.) One is struck by the amazing similarity of the plan to that of the small Deggaron Mosque built by the Karakhanids in Khazar. Apart from some minor differences in the Khazar Mosque, which is only half the size, such as a dome at each corner and the transverse vaulting around the dome, the plan scheme of the Ottoman mosque had been realised four centuries earlier at the beginning of the 11th century in this Karakhanid structure of brick and adobe (see Plan Ia). Other noteworthy features of the Chelebi Sultan Mehmed Mosque include the arches of the two porches decorated with chevrons in the manner of the Orhan Mosque in Bursa, an arch decorated with coloured voussoirs, and the bold inscriptions with their very unusual arrangements of the lettering. In the inscription on the southern side door Ivaz's name is given as 'Iftikhār al-muhandisīn wa ikhṭiyār al-muʿāmirīn Ustādh Ivāz bin Bayazid' (the glory of engineers (*or* surveyors) and the venerable old man of architects) and 'al-ustādh al-māhir' (the splendid craftsman) again with the title of muhandis (surveyor or engineer). Hajji Ivaz, the son of an Ahi, Bayazid, was later made a Pasha and was buried at Bursa. He explored new paths leading in quite a different direction from the type of mosque to which the Ottomans were accustomed, and prepared the way for the development of the central-dome type of mosque.

In the reign of Sultan Murad II Ottoman architecture displayed an amazing development and prepared the ground for several innovations. The Muradiye Mosque which he built at Bursa in 1425 and which is named after him, possesses a simplified type of plan. It consists of two domes one behind the other, a domed iwan on each side of the first, an open dome, with a small corner room on the entrance side only, and a portico with three domes in the middle and panelled vaulting at the sides. As the front and side façades are lower in height the structure is dominated by the two large central domes. The mosque was built with two minarets. The

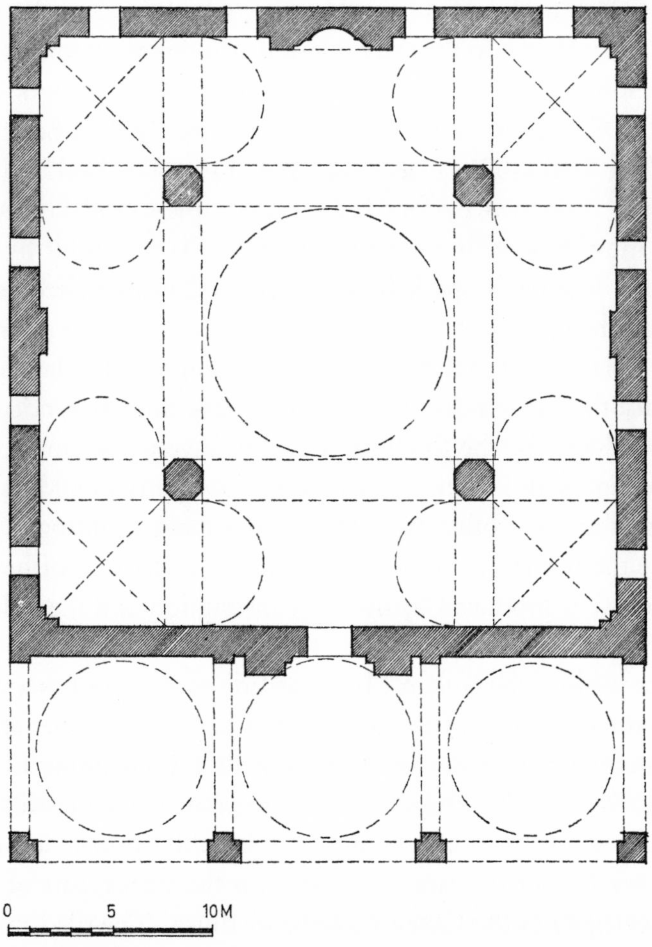

Plan 40. Dimetoka, Mosque of Chelebi Sultan Mehmed

courses of hewn stone and brick on the walls show a return to the tradition of the Hudavendigār mosque at Bursa and the mosques of Iznik. Although the Muradiye Mosque is fairly richly decorated with various geometrical brick patterns between the arches of the portico, and with tiles of various colours, composition and design covering the walls, it is very plain compared with the Green Mosque. The mosque was built as a complex including a tomb and a medrese and is the last work of architecture erected by an Ottoman Sultan at Bursa.

Monuments of Edirne (Murad II and his Period)

The most important buildings erected by Sultan Murad II after 1425 are to be found at Edirne. Edirne had been captured by Murad I Hudavendigār in 1361 and is one of the three centres that demonstrate most vividly the development of early Ottoman art. It replaced Bursa as the capital, and remained the seat of government until the Conquest of Istanbul in 1453. Whilst Iznik and Bursa remained confined to the art of the first period and did not participate in later developments, Edirne stands also as a symbol of the most brilliant period of Ottoman

Imperial art. Here is to be found the Selimiye Mosque, which remains the last word in Turkish mosque architecture and which is in the first rank of European masterpieces of architecture.

The first original monumental structure in Edirne is the Old Mosque (Eski Cami) begun by the Emir Sulaymān Chelebi in 1403 and completed by Chelebi Sultan Mehmed in 1414. The architect was Hajji ʿAlā al-Dīn of Konya. (Fig. 149.) The building is a square structure with nine equal domes supported by four heavy square piers, and belongs to the category of Great Mosques, the most outstanding example of which is that built by Bayazid I at Bursa. The atmosphere of the interior is spoilt by the tasteless Baroque decoration that was added later. Of the domes on the main axis that in front of the mihrab is set upon prismatic triangles, that in front of it on stalactite squinches, and the open dome with a lantern at the entrance on plain squinches, whilst the various domes at the sides have normal pendentives. A rather dark and heavy effect is produced by the thick piers and relatively low dome. The heavy, archaic architecture of the interior is also to be seen in the exterior portico, and in the minarets, one of which has one balcony and the other two. Whilst the main building is constructed of large blocks of hewn stone the portico is built in a decorative patterning of hewn stone and brick. An effect of magnificence is produced by the large inscription and the bold stalactites hanging from the marble porch.

The Muradiye Mosque built by Sultan Murad at Edirne in 1434 has a very much simplified inverted T plan scheme composed of two domes one behind the other and a domed iwan at each side. It has a portico resting on heavy piers with a high dome in the centre and two transverse vaults on each side. The central dome of the mosque is higher than the others, with an open lantern, and rests on prismatic triangles. The old painted decoration that has been uncovered on the inner face of the large arch and on the upper part of the walls place this mosque in the same category as the Green Mosque in Bursa. The tiled mihrab in polychrome underglaze technique in imitation of mosaic patterns is the most magnificent specimen after that of the Green Mosque in Bursa (6.3 × 3.85 metres). It is also related to Bursa from the point of view of technique and style (Fig. 150), except that it exhibits an original feature in the use of hexagonal blue and white tiles, which show the high quality of Iznik blue and white ceramics. Star patterns are formed by hexagonal tiles with various designs in dark and light blue on a white ground with triangular turquoise tiles in the spaces between them. The motifs consist of small flowers, leaves, palmettes, rosettes and delicate scrolls with a small number of geometrical forms (Fig. 151). One theory based on a comparison with the tiles of the Tawrīzī tomb in Damascus and tiles in the Victoria and Albert Museum in London said to have been brought from the ʿUmayyad Mosque there has been put forward linking these tiles with Syria, while another theory suggests that Persian craftsmen were employed, but these theories are completely disproved by the material and the quality of the tiles. The Muradiye Mosque in Edirne is the most attractive of the mosques of the first half of the 15th century from the point of view of Ottoman decoration.

Earlier an innovation had been introduced into the inverted T plan scheme mosque by the now ruined Beylerbey Mosque built by the Beylerbek Yusuf Pasha in 1429. The only difference between the plan of this mosque and that of the Nilüfer Khātūn Imaret at Iznik lies in the placing of a fluted half-dome in front of the mihrab. Between this and the large and more elevated central dome with a lantern there is a shallow rectangular section composed of a small fluted dome extended towards the sides by means of half-star vaults. The mosque has no portico. This is the first example of the use of a half-dome, though here it is not connected to the main dome. A real half-dome appears in the mosque known as the Yeşil (Green) Imaret built by Yahshi Bey, one of Sultan Murad II's commanders, at Tire in 1446. Here, a

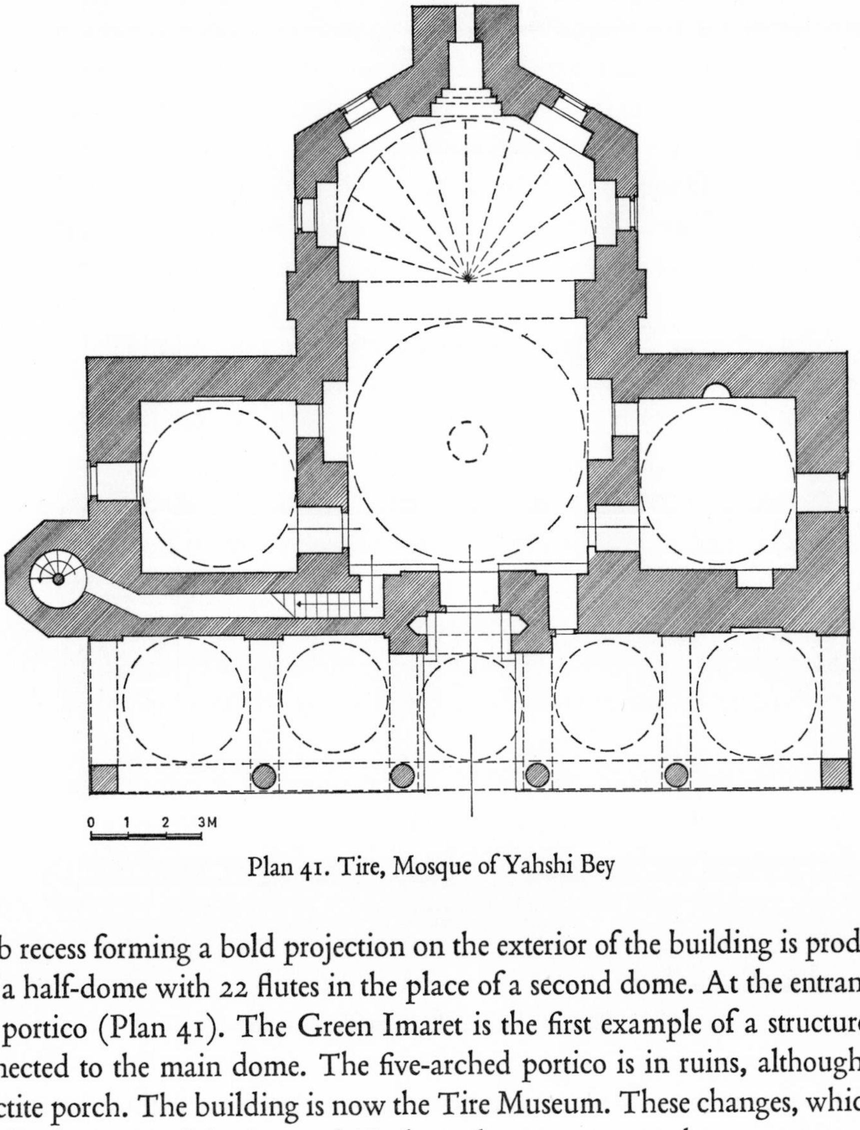

Plan 41. Tire, Mosque of Yahshi Bey

deep mihrab recess forming a bold projection on the exterior of the building is produced by the addition of a half-dome with 22 flutes in the place of a second dome. At the entrance there is a five arched portico (Plan 41). The Green Imaret is the first example of a structure with half-domes connected to the main dome. The five-arched portico is in ruins, although there is an ornate stalactite porch. The building is now the Tire Museum. These changes, which remained within the development of the inverted T plan scheme mosques, the appearance of the half-dome and other single-domed mosques, are architectural features that continued until the middle of the 15th century. But the Üç Şerefeli Mosque built by Sultan Murad II at Edirne in the ten years between 841–51/1437–47 breaks away completely from the previous development of Ottoman architecture and suddenly appears as an unexpected artistic event. It is of extraordinary importance as a prototype already realising the basic idea of a mosque plan that was to be employed by the architect Sinan a hundred years later. The dome, 24.1 metres in diameter, supported at the sides on heavy hexagonal piers and on six pointed arches arranged along the entrance and qibla walls, is extended towards each side by two domes 10.5 metres in diameter and a small dome with stalactite brackets placed in the triangular spaces between them (Plan 42). Such a plan appears here for the first time in Turkish art and shows the

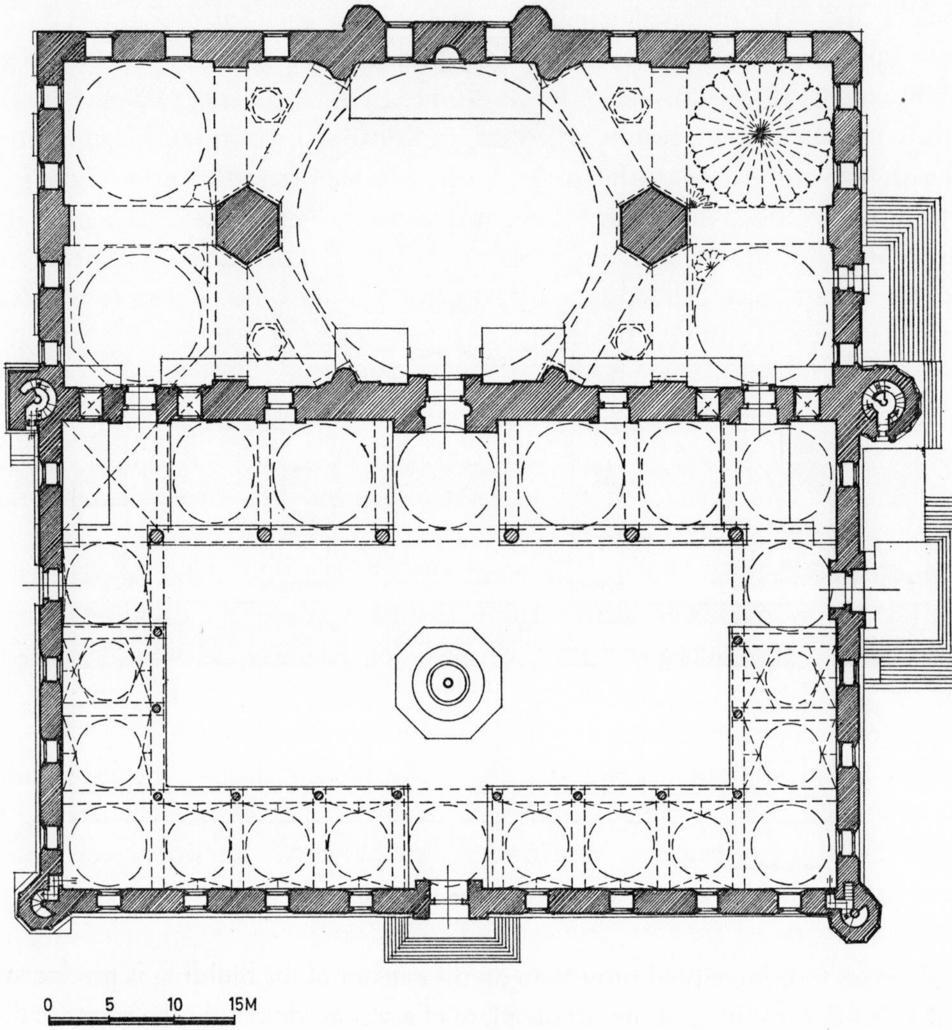

Plan 42. Edirne, Üç Şerefeli Mosque

application of a conception of wide, monumental space ideal for a shallow rectangular type of mosque. Flying buttresses are here used for the first time to support the central dome (Fig. 152). The rectangular arcaded courtyard with a *shadırvan* in the centre is the first monumental example of this type of structure and together with the mosque forms a single architectural whole. The 22 round and ovoid domes of various sizes present an obscure problem that is still the subject of research. On the other hand the vista presented by the harmonious arrangement of the arches certainly possesses great decorative architectural strength. On each of the three sides there are spectacular porches that recall those of the Seljuks, but the higher and larger entrance door opening on to the domed portico surpasses all of them. (Fig. 153.) This is the earliest example of a mosque with four minarets, and each of these, in each of the four corners of the courtyard, are completely different in style, one having spiral flutes, the second vertical flutes, the third lozenge patterns and the fourth three balconies. The Üç Şerefeli (Three Balcony) Minaret from which the mosque takes its name is 6 metres in diameter and 67.75 metres in height, and has a separate internal staircase leading to each balcony. It was the highest minaret built up to that time and its height was exceeded only after 127 years by the 70.89 metres high minaret of the Selimiye Mosque at Edirne. In the lunettes of two of the courtyard windows there are inscriptions bearing the name of Sultan Murad in lapis lazuli and white faience. The original painted decoration, though the paint has been restored, survives in several of the domes of the arcade. These form the oldest specimens of this type of decoration after the Green Mosque in Bursa and the Muradiye Mosque in Edirne. The tasteless blue decoration on the inside of the dome is new. Although the Üc Şerefeli Mosque shows a great leap forward in Ottoman architecture it is still far from completely harmonised as spatial unity, since the low hang of the arches supporting the main dome decreases the effect of space. The piers are 5.5 metres thick, half the width of the squat arches supporting the side domes. The main dome descends to less than half the total height of the mosque. As, in addition to this, there is very little light, the interior produces a heavy and gloomy effect. Nevertheless in this shallow rectangular mosque a completely new conception is realised in the extension of the central domed area towards each of the sides by two small domes half the diameter of the central dome (Fig. 154). The central dome completely dominates the interior of the building (Fig. 155), whilst outside it produces, together with the small domes connected to it, an effect that foreshadows the heaped-up pyramidal effect of the great metropolitan Ottoman mosques. The conception of a compact space extended in width found here in an initial form was developed by the architect Sinan a hundred years later. Although the influence of the Bursa mosques can be seen in the two rows of windows on the external faces the monumental power of the mosque, built entirely of hewn stone and embellished by very restrained polychrome stone decoration, is far greater. The architect who prepared the way for the development of the great Ottoman mosques with all their experiment and innovations was an anonymous paralytic from Konya. In Evliya Chelebi and in the *Risale*'s (or treatises) of Beshir Chelebi mention is made of his being brought on a stretcher. Apart from the Üç Şerefeli Mosque, which was built in the last years of the reign of Sultan Murad II, the Muradiye Mosque (1434) and a Dār al-Ḥadīth (school for the teaching of Muslim tradition) (1475), the city of Edirne was embellished during his reign by the Gazi Mihal Mosque (1422), the Shah Melek Pasha Mosque (1429), the Mezit Bey Mosque (1442), as well as by other buildings connected with these.

Early Ottoman Medreses, Tombs and Hans

Up to the death of Sultan Murad II in 1451 the dynamic development of the new style of Ottoman architecture is clearly to be seen not only in the mosques but also in other types of building such as medreses, tombs, hans, and covered markets (bedestens). In the medreses, the large-scale monumental structures of the Seljuks are replaced by new plans capable of meeting the practical needs of the age, and suited to new educational conditions. In Bursa the only original example is the medrese on the upper storey of the Hudavendigār Mosque. A medrese built by Bayazid I in Bursa in 1400 is a simplified form of Seljuk medrese composed of a long rectangular courtyard (8.5 × 28 metres) with *shadırvan*, and with arcades and cells on both sides, a large domed iwan and an entrance in the form of a domed hall. The walls have spectacular arcading composed of alternating courses of hewn stone and brick. The Hospital of Bayazid I, which we might describe as the first Ottoman hospital, is in a very ruinous condition. It consists of vaulted rooms surrounding a wide, rectangular arcaded courtyard with *shadırvan* and a large domed classroom.

The spectacular Green Medrese of Chelebi Sultan Mehmed, again with courses of hewn stone and brick, is in the traditional medrese plan with domed arcades surrounding three sides of the wide rectangular courtyard with pool, and a large domed classroom, open to the front, on the south side. In the middle of the panel-vaulted cells on each side is a large panel-vaulted iwan. The building is now a museum.

In the medrese dated 1414 built by Chelebi Sultan Mehmed at Merzifon the place of the four iwans is taken by domed classrooms projecting on the exterior, with cells placed between them. Its plan differs from that of Seljuk medreses in having a *shadırvan* in the middle of the arcaded courtyard, and a minaret above its monumental porch. It is a simplified form of the medrese of Sultan Murad II, the Muradiye in Bursa. It is a graceful and impressive building with brick and stone patterning on the walls and brick ornament on the façade of the domed iwan.

Although in the earlier Ottoman period one can see tombs with conical or pyramidal roofs on a square or octagonal body, after the Bursa period simple domed tombs become the prevalent form. The Issız Han dated 1394 built by Bayazid I on the Bursa–Karacabey road on the shore of Lake Apolyont is in the form of a three-aisled hall, 42 × 22 metres. There are two chimneys, each supported on four columns, under the higher middle vault. The sloping earth roof descends towards the lower vaults at the sides. There is a marble inscription over the door which is in the form of a slightly projecting pointed arched porch in the centre of the narrow front. This han is a small structure in the style of a Seljuk caravansarai.

12

MONUMENTS OF THE REIGN OF MEHMED THE CONQUEROR

The thirty years' reign of Sultan Mehmed II, who conquered Istanbul in 1453, saw the construction in Istanbul, Bursa and Edirne and in various other cities of the Empire of some 300 mosques, 85 of them with domes, 57 medreses, 59 baths and 29 bedestens, as well as various palaces, castles, forts, city walls and bridges. Most of these have fallen into ruin with the passage of time. The first mosques to be built after the capture of Istanbul are variations on the side-roomed mosques in the inverted T plan scheme to be seen in Iznik, Bursa and Edirne. The mosque dated 1457 at Karacabey near Bursa, destroyed in an earthquake, the Mosques of Mahmud Pasha (1462) and Murad Pasha (1465) in Istanbul, the Mosque of Gedik Ahmed Pasha (1472) in Afyon, the Isa Bey Mosque (1475) at Skoplje (in Macedonia) may be numbered amongst the early mosques that show no great innovations in either plan or architecture. Of these the Isa Bey Mosque at Skoplje recalls the Bursa mosques with its two domes, 10 metres in diameter, one behind the other, with two vaults on each side, and its walls with one course of hewn stone alternating with three courses of brick. As in Iznik, the blocks of hewn stone are surrounded by bricks, even having a brick placed vertically at the side of each block, but the five-arched portico on piers is constructed entirely of stone and is quite unusual in appearance. According to its inscription it was built during the reign of Sultan Mehmed the Conqueror by the first governor of Bosnia, Ghāzī ʿIsā Bek, son of Ghāzī Isḥāq Bek, in 1475. The plans and façades of the other mosques, however, continue the tradition of Iznik and Bursa architecture. The Ağalar Mosque in the Topkapı Saray in Istanbul, the Mosque of the Conqueror at Köstendil, and the Isḥāq Pasha Mosque dated 1482 at Inegöl, all have the characteristic wall patterning of hewn stone and brick. Some of these monuments, such as the Isḥāq Pasha Mosque at Inegöl, directly recall the Nilüfer Khātūn Imaret at Iznik. Although none of the mosques constructed in the period immediately following the Conquest of Istanbul achieved the fascinating, magical atmosphere of the Bursa and Edirne mosques, either in quality or spatial effect, from the very first years of the Conqueror's reign the tentative first beginnings of a new style can be perceived in some of the monuments. The most important and the most striking of these innovations is the bold handling of the problem of the half-dome. The small Fethiye Mosque in Athens (1488), which is named after the Conqueror, is an amazing structure with a central dome resting on columns and four half-domes. The five-domed portico would appear to be a later addition. The mosque, which lay concealed for a long time inside a military structure, was uncovered on the demolition of the ruined building during excavations in the Agora, and repaired. Here we see the first advance made on the Mosque of Chelebi Sultan Mehmed at Dimetoka in the application on a small scale of the traditional plan of the central plan structure with four half-domes, with a dome added at each of the corners. It has an interesting external appearance with its domes covered with roof tiles and double row of windows.

The incorporation of half-domes into a large-scale building is first seen in the Mosque of the Conqueror built by Sultan Mehmed in Istanbul in the form of a complex. Here there was a large central dome 26 metres in diameter extended towards the qibla by a half-dome, and by three small domes on each side. (Plan 43.) This is a very different development from the modest

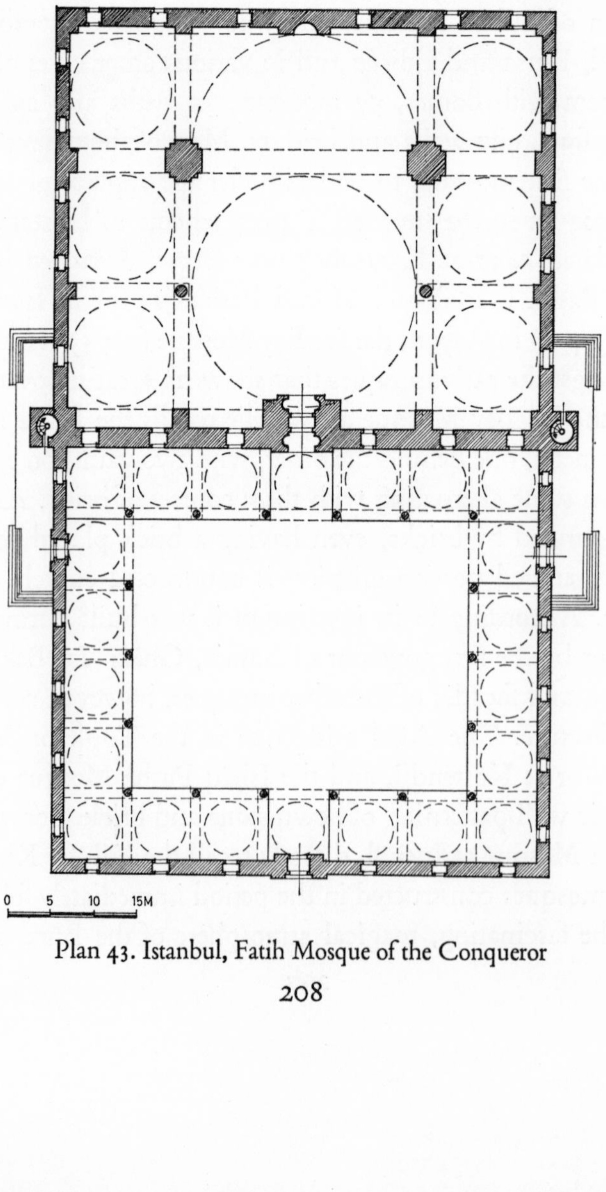

Plan 43. Istanbul, Fatih Mosque of the Conqueror

147 Bursa, Yeşil Cami, detail of north façade

148 Bursa, Yeşil Cami, tiles from vault of lower gallery

149
Edirne, Old Mosque
(Eski Cami)

150
Edirne, Muradiye Mosque,
tiled mihrab

151 Edirne, Muradiye Mosque, detail of hexagonal blue and white tiles

152 Edirne, Üç Şerefeli Mosque, exterior

153 Edirne, Üç Şerefeli Mosque, courtyard porch

154 Edirne, Üç Şerefeli Mosque, general view of dome system

155 Edirne, Üç Şerefeli Mosque, interior

156 Istanbul, Eski Fatih Mosque, courtyard

157 Edirne, Hospital of Sultan Bayazid, rear view

158 Edirne, Foundation of Sultan Bayazid

159 Istanbul, Mosque of Sultan Selim

160 Istanbul, Mosque of Mihrimah Sultan, exterior

161
Istanbul, Mosque of Bayazid,
view from the square. (Photographed before 1960

162 Istanbul, Mosque of Bayazid, interior

163
Diyarbekir, Mosque
of Fatih Pasha

164 Elbistan, Great Mosque,
exterior

165 Gebze, Mosque and Mausoleum of Choban Mustafa Pasha

166 Gebze, Mosque of Choban Mustafa Pasha, interior

167 Istanbul, Shehzade Mosque, exterior

168 Istanbul, Shehzade Mosque, interior

169 Istanbul, view of the Mosque of Mihrimah Sultan with courtyard and medreses

170 Istanbul, Mosque of Mihrimah Sultan, interior

171
Istanbul, Süleymaniye Mosque, distant view

172 Istanbul, Beşiktaş, Mosque of Sinan Pasha, exterior

173 Istanbul, Beşiktaş, Mosque of Sinan Pasha, interior

174 Istanbul, Kadırga, Sokullu Mosque, tiled mihrab

175 Istanbul, Mosque of Rüstem Pasha, interior

176 Istanbul, Mosque of Rüstem Pasha, pilaster with tiles

177 Edirne, Selimiye Mosque, exterior

steps taken in the Green Imaret in Tire. The mosque was built by the architect Sinān al-Dīn Yūsuf between the years 1462–70 and formed the centre of the Fatih complex, an enormous architectural agglomeration composed of the hundreds of domes of the 16 medreses making up the university of that time, the tabhane (refectory), hospital (Dār al-Shifā'), a caravansarai, baths and tombs. The dome of the mosque collapsed in the earthquake of 1765 and the present-day mosque with its four half-domes was constructed by Sultan Mustafa III between 1767 and 1771. However, from the investigations carried out by E. H. Ayverdi it is clear that the dome system which we now see was produced merely by moving the side walls slightly inwards and without making any changes in the courtyard or the mihrab walls. It is obvious from all the stylistic features that the arcaded courtyard has retained its old form and that it has undergone no substantial change. (Fig. 156.) With this mosque, the dome of which is 2 metres larger in diameter than the dome of the Üç Şerefeli Mosque built by his father in Edirne, Sultan Mehmed the Conqueror prepared the way for the great domed mosques of Istanbul. Throughout the whole 900 years of Byzantine architecture following the replacement of the dome of St. Sophia after the collapse of the original dome in an earthquake in 562, none of the domes in any of the churches attained a diameter exceeding 10 metres. This clearly shows the strength of the Ottoman urge towards the creation of a large, unified space, the magnitude of the advance made, and the sure foundations on which the later rapid development was laid. After the Üç Şerefeli Mosque in Edirne the arcaded courtyard attained definitive proportions and assumed the form of a classical model in the Mosque of Fatih in Istanbul. Other parts remaining from the original building besides the arcaded courtyard are the great main door, the lower portions of the minarets and the mihrab. The beautifully ordered *thuluth* inscription on the magnificent marble entrance door resembling the porch of the Üç Şerefeli Mosque is the work of ʿAlī bin Ṣūfī, one of the calligraphers of the period of Mehmed II. Apart from coloured stone inlays the decoration consists of tile panels with white lettering on a blue ground, like those in the Üç Şerefeli Mosque, placed in the lunettes of the windows on the two sides of the portico, but here the inscription consists of the *basmala* and the end of the Ayyat al-Kursī (the Verse of the Throne). In the lunettes of the six windows on the outer face of the west *basmalas* and the *Fātiḥa* are written in white lettering on a green porphyry ground. The minarets have only one balcony and are on a modest scale compared with the Üç Şerefeli minaret. On the southern face of the base of the minaret there is a carved sun-dial attributed to ʿAlī Kushju. The Fatih complex was the first architectural agglomeration on this scale produced by the Ottomans and became a model for the great complexes that followed. At the same time the Conqueror established here the first Turkish university. The strictly symmetrical buildings grouped together to form the Karadeniz and Akdeniz medreses (the Mediterranean and the Black Sea Medreses) on the great square on both sides of the mosques each comprise eight medreses, whilst in front there are a hospital, a guest house (*tabhane*), an imaret and a caravansarai. Most of the wall originally surrounding the complex has collapsed and of the four gates only one, the 'Soup gate', has survived. The hospital is completely ruined. The tombs of the Conqueror and his wife Gülbahar Khātūn behind the mosque would appear to have been reconstructed on the old walls and foundations.

MONUMENTS OF THE REIGN OF MEHMED THE CONQUEROR

The Mosque of Mehmed II Fatih opened a new era in the architecture of Istanbul with its great dome, the largest up to that date, and the half-dome connected to it. Its architectural proportions, its capitals, its arches and, from the point of view of town planning, its handling of a large-scale complex stood as a guide to later periods. The distinguished lay-out of present-day Istanbul was thus initiated by the Conqueror and realised by the other Ottoman sultans who followed in his footsteps.

The development of the great mosques in Istanbul began with the single half-dome in the Mosque of Fatih, and the central dome was for the first time confronted with the problem of reconciling its addition. Towards the end of the 15th century the plan was repeated in Istanbul in the Rum Mehmed Pasha Mosque at Üsküdar (1471) and the Atik Ali Pasha Mosque (1497) at Çemberlitaş, but the scale has been reduced by the removal of the domes on the two sides of the half-dome and the shortening of the side aisles by the length of one dome. The second step was taken a generation later with the double half-dome plan of the mosque built by the architect Khayr al-Dīn for Sultan Bayazid II.

13

MONUMENTS OF THE TIME OF BAYAZID II AND SELIM I

Sultan Bayazid II followed in his father's footsteps by building the second great complex in Istanbul. Its architect, Khayr al-Dīn, had carried out his first preparations for this work outside Istanbul.

His first great work was the Sultan Bayazid complex in Amasya which was completed by his son Shehzade Ahmed, the Governor of Amasya, in 1486. Of this complex on the banks of the Yeşil Irmak, only the mosque and the medrese remain. The plan consists of two large domes one behind the other on heavy piers with three small lower domes to each side, and shows an attempt to unite the interior into one whole by completely opening the side sections towards the centre. The first section with a dome of about 14 metres in diameter is combined at the same level and the same width with a second larger and lighter section with a dome of 15 metres in diameter. At the entrance there is a five-domed portico on columns, and on either side a minaret with a single balcony. In the Bayazid Mosque in Amasya we see an attempt to create a unified space by a masterly simplification of the plan employed in the Mahmud Pasha Mosque at Istanbul, part of a complex built in 1462 by Mahmud Pasha, the well-known vizir of the Conqueror. The plan of the Mahmud Pasha Mosque consists of two domes 12.5 metres in diameter one behind the other with three domes of varying sizes on each side, but it is obscured by the vaulted corridors between these and the five-vaulted vestibule.

The second and more important large-scale complex foundation of Sultan Bayazid was again the work of the architect Khayr al-Dīn and was built at Edirne between 1484 and 1488. The buildings, consisting of a mosque, an imaret, a hospital, a medrese, a bath, a kitchen and food depots, constitute one of the largest socio-religious foundations of the 15th century. (Plan 44.) The architectural agglomeration of more than one hundred domes is dominated by the mosque and its dome 21 metres in diameter, set deep between four walls rising to a height of 19 metres in the form of a cubic block, and strikes the eye even from a distance. The clearly

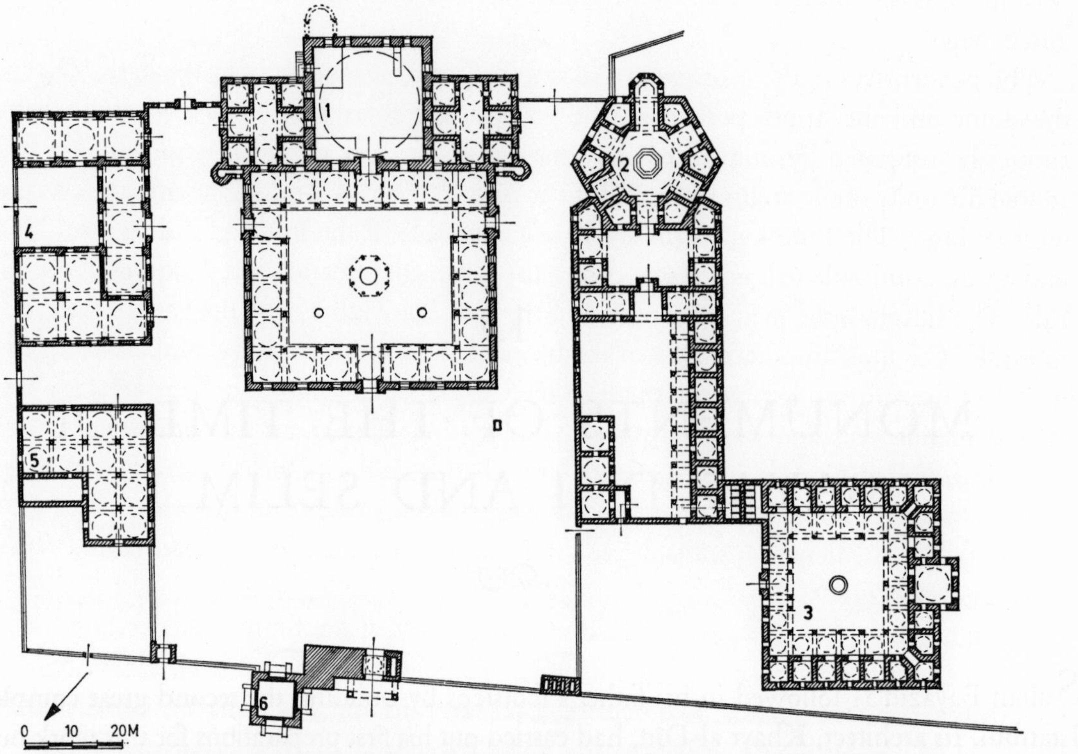

Plan 44. Edirne, Foundation of Bayazid II

defined geometrical lines of the enormous cubic block reflected in the Tunca river leave an unforgettable impression. (Fig. 158.) The low buildings of the *tabhane* (hospice) with nine small domes on each side have no openings into the mosque. There is an arcaded courtyard with *shadırvan* and a minaret with a single balcony at the two outer corners of the *tabhane* buildings. The same plan was repeated 34 years later in the Mosque of Sultan Selim built by Sultan Süleyman the Magnificent for his father in Istanbul in 1522. The architectural maturity of the Bayazid Mosque at Edirne becomes very obvious when compared with the Selimiye Mosque in Istanbul with its much larger dome 24.5 metres in diameter. The four flying buttresses and the numerous props surrounding it deprive the dome of the Selimiye (Fig. 159) of the magnificent tranquillity of the dome at Edirne. The Mosque of Bayazid at Edirne possesses a thoroughly classical repose, while still remaining a massive pile in which nothing of the form and movement of the dome structure is apparent from the outside. From this aspect the Mihrimah Mosque (Fig. 160) built by the architect Sinan in Istanbul in 1555 is of great interest in showing how much architectural style had changed over half a century. Both the Bayazid and the Mihrimah are large-scale single domed mosques, but in the Mihrimah the weight of the dome is balanced by four corner towers. The many-windowed walls between these retain nothing of their original function of support. The trial of strength between the weight of the dome and the corner towers supporting it is enlivened by a Baroque approach, reflected in the treatment of the exterior. The contrast between the Mihrimah Mosque and the

Mosque of Bayazid vividly reflects the great difference between the two architects Khayr al-Dīn and Sinan.

The pendentives in the Mosque of Bayazid at Edirne extend right to the base. The inside of the dome and the upper portion of the walls above the three rows of windows have been ruthlessly disfigured by uninspired Baroque ornament. The complex is surrounded by walls, so that the unity of the architecture and the main silhouette of the complex manifest a contained creative urge. The buildings form a separate ensemble in the midst of a delightful landscape and are an admirable setting for prayer and the treatment of patients in the quiet of the countryside. The hospital, the medical school and the *timarhane* (lunatic asylum) are to the west of the mosque. The most important part of the hospital is the large domed chamber with a *shadırvan* in the centre surrounded by six small domed chambers and an antechamber with six *divans* (raised platforms). The whole is paved with marble. The arcaded courtyard has a lawn in front and domed rooms for the patients on each side. Evliya Chelebi records that music was played under the large dome three times a week by ten singers and instrumentalists as 'a cure for the sick, a medicine for the afflicted, spiritual nourishment for the mad, and a remedy for melancholy'. (Fig. 157.)

In Sultan Bayazid's *waqfiyya* or deed of endowment of the foundation we find among the 167 staff appointed to the whole establishment 21 assigned to the hospital, including one head doctor, two assistant doctors, two oculists, two surgeons and a pharmacist, together with their daily rate of pay. In the north-west corner there are cells for eighteen students arranged around an arcaded garden with *shadırvan*, with a large domed classroom opposite and a medical school.

After experimenting with mosques of very different types of plan at Amasya and Edirne the architect Khayr al-Dīn turned to the Sultan Bayazid complex in Istanbul. According to the magnificent inscription on the main door written by Sheikh Ḥamdullah the mosque was built between 1501 and 1506. Here the architect returned once more to the problem of the half-dome, and by adding a second half-dome on the north side and a small dome on each side he took the plan of the old Fatih Mosque one stage further. The large dome 18 metres in diameter is surrounded by two half-domes of half that diameter and by four small domes at each side (Fig. 161). The five-domed sections that take the place of the *tabhane* of the Bayazid Mosque in Edirne open into the side domes on the north side of the mosque. The connection of the side aisles to the central dome by means of high, wide, pointed arches is executed with strength and energy (Fig. 162). In front there is a square courtyard with *shadırvan* surrounded by domed arcades with two rows of square windows (Plan 45). Two single-balcony minarets are set at the corners at an interval of 87 metres.

The plan of the Mosque of Bayazid has often been linked to that of St. Sophia, but apart from the use of a central dome and two half-domes the two buildings have no resemblance to each other either in plan or in architecture. They are as different as two separate worlds. The Mosque of Bayazid is a natural development of previous Turkish architecture. St. Sophia aroused the great admiration of Ottoman architects, but the ideas and inspiration they received from it were found in their own style and architecture. The Mosque of Bayazid combines all the various elements of classical Ottoman architecture. The façades and the arcaded courtyard

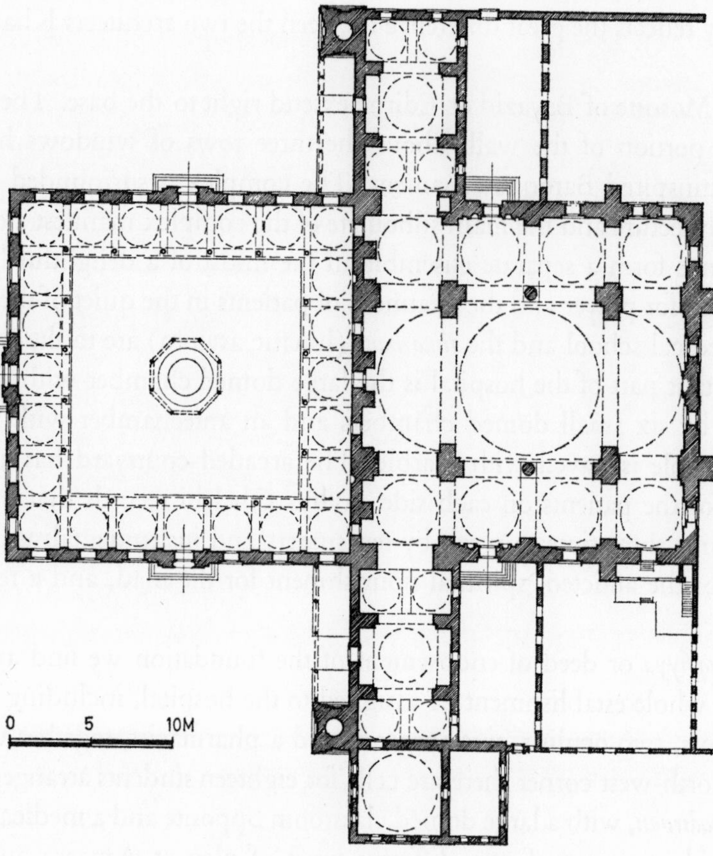

Plan 45. Istanbul, Mosque of Bayazid

are the most successful portions. At first the handling of the large-scale mosque with half-domes presented a great many difficulties and necessitated great architectural skill. As a whole the Bayazid mosque and its complex show that the architect Khayr al-Dīn was able to make the effort demanded of him.

Although according to M. Cevdet's notebook the name of Ya'qūb Shāh has been put forward since 1959 as the architect of the Mosque of Bayazid no conclusive evidence has been offered. On the other hand the Istanbul mosque displays a development of the style employed by Khayr al-Dīn in the Mosques of Bayazid in Edirne and Amasya and thus, although we know nothing of the latter's life, it seems more likely that the mosque is his work.

During the reign of Sultan Bayazid, 'Ātiq 'Alī Pasha built a mosque with six domes at Zincirlikuyu in Istanbul in 1497, and thus provided a model for the multi-domed mosque.

As the eight years' reign of Sultan Selim I (1512–20) were occupied with war and heroic exploits there was no great architectural activity. Nevertheless an experiment with a domed mosque and four half-domes on quite a large scale was made outside Istanbul. The Fatih Pasha Mosque built between the years 1516 and 1520 by Biyikli Mehmed Pasha, who built the first Ottoman mosque in Diyarbekir and was both the conqueror and the governor of that city, shows a successfully executed plan with a central dome resting on four piers, four half-domes, and four small domes on squinches in the corners. Apart from this the half-domes have been extended by double exedras, one large and one small, forming a new feature different from the plain, monotonous style of the half-domes of the Bayazid Mosque in Istanbul. (Plan 46.) The small domed chambers at the sides each opening into the mosque through a separate door recall the inverted T plan type of mosque. No relation has yet been established between the harmony and mature proportions of the interior and the lack of definition in the external appearance of the half-domes. Nevertheless the Fatih Pasha Mosque at Diyarbekir (Fig. 163) served as a preparation for the ideal central plan structure that the architect Sinan was to realise in the Shehzade Mosque at Istanbul 26 years later. The name of the architect of the Diyarbekir Mosque is unknown. We come across another four half-domed mosque in the Great Mosque at Elbistan in Southern Anatolia, which is generally agreed to have been built in 1498 under the Dhulqadirids to whom Selim I finally put an end in 1517. It contains a Seljuk inscription bearing the name Ghiyāth al-Dīn Kaykhusraw II, and the date of 637 (1239 A.D.) at its portal, but this Seljuk inscription belongs to another building. Apparently, when the original Dhulqadirid inscription disappeared in the Ottoman period, this Seljuk inscription was put in its place. (Fig. 164.) There is thus a close connection between the mosques of this type at Diyarbekir and Elbistan.

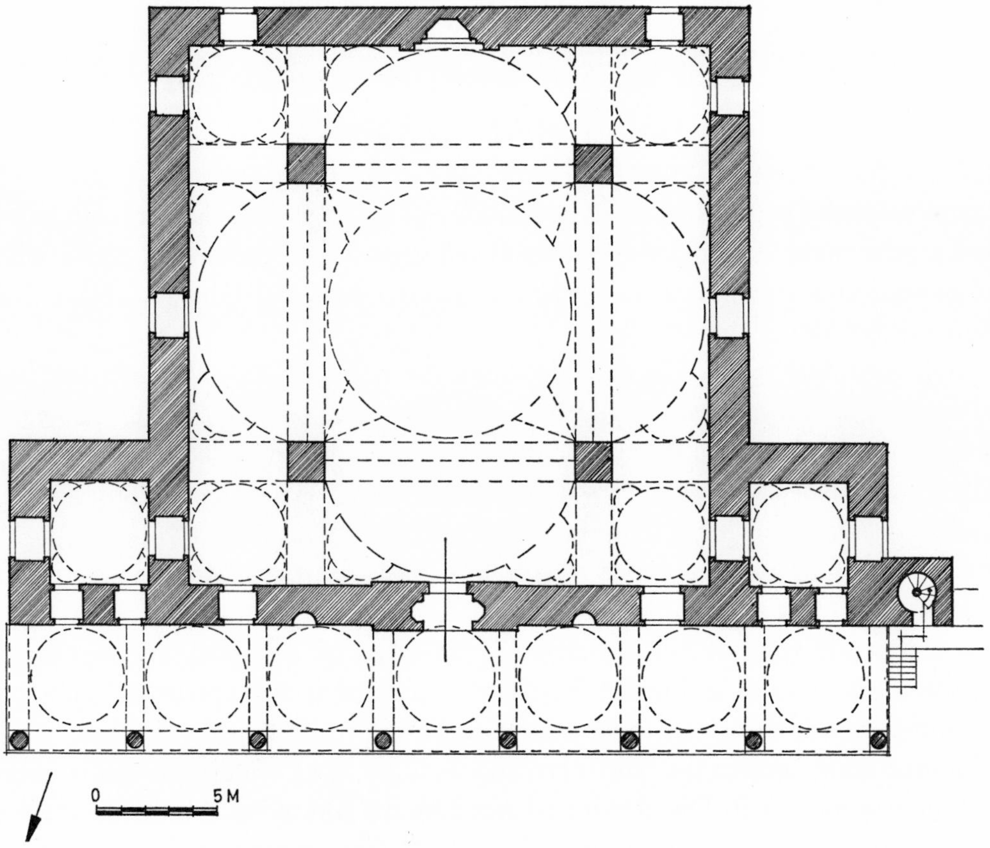

Plan 46. Diyarbekir, Mosque of Fatih Pasha

The mosque that Sultan Selim commenced in Istanbul, on the plan of the Mosque of Bayazid at Edirne, was completed by his son Sultan Süleyman the Magnificent in 1522, after his father's untimely death. Although the large dome 24 metres in diameter is a great success from the technical point of view, in neither the plan nor the spatial arrangement is there any creative fervour or originality. The whole weight of the dome rests on the walls, and, as these are lower, the monumental strength of the Edirne mosque is proportionately weakened. The minarets are of an exaggerated height (38 metres to the balcony), and are placed at the angles formed by the *tabhanes* and the courtyard instead of at the corners of the *tabhanes* themselves. The plain architecture of the mosque is enriched by ceramic decoration in the lunettes of the windows, painted decoration and finely worked marble and wood ornament. The tomb of Sultan Selim is at the side of the mosque. The architect is unknown, though the mosque ought not to be attributed to the architect Sinan, then a young man of only 26 years of age. This error arises from confusion with the Halıcılar Medrese of Sultan Selim built by Sultan Süleyman the Magnificent for his father at Yeni Bahçe in 1562. When Sultan Süleyman the Magnificent ascended the throne conditions were ripe for a great advance in architecture, as in every other field of activity, and experiments and investigations were being made that were to lead to brilliant developments. The Sultan was also very fortunate that an architect of the genius of Sinan should have appeared in his reign, so presenting him with such great possibilities.

14

SINAN AND THE MONUMENTS OF SÜLEYMAN THE MAGNIFICENT AND SELIM II

Sinan, the great architect of the reign of Sultan Süleyman the Magnificent, the most brilliant period of the Ottoman Empire, and a genius of world stature, was born in 1489 in the village of Ağırnas near Kayseri. According to the memoirs of the poet-painter Sai Mustafa Chelebi he was forcibly taken by the *devshirme* as a janissary in 1512 and, after attending the school for the *acemi oğlanlar* (cadets), fought as a janissary in the Belgrade campaign of 1521. It is also known that he took part in Selim I's Persian, Syrian, Iraq and Egyptian campaigns, and that he visited the Balkans, Hungary and Southern Austria. In 1538, during the Moldavian campaign, he won the Sultan's appreciation by constructing a bridge over the river Prut in 13 days, and he also built a bridge across the Danube. Sinan worked as a military engineer and, although by the time he had completed his training and was chosen master-architect he was already 50 years old, he constructed some 364 monuments throughout the Empire in an incredibly short space of time. He closely examined the works he saw in the places he visited and fused the ideas he gained from them with the Turkish architectural tradition. Sinan was a great master of dome construction and of the organisation of space and was able to solve successfully the problems of centralised domed structure which formed the ideal of the Italian architects of the Renaissance.

In his first works Sinan began his explorations of the possibilities of space by continuing in the tradition of the Ottoman architecture of Iznik, Bursa and Edirne. The Hüsreviye complex he built in Aleppo in 1536/7 for Hüsrev (Khusraw) Pasha, then Governor of Damascus, is noteworthy as his first work. Here he combined the plan of the single-dome mosque with the inverted T plan by adding a small, low dome to each of the rear corners of the five-domed portico which projects the width of one section on each side. To the right rises a thick minaret. Although the U-shaped courtyard, the medrese opposite the imaret, the guest-house and the baths at the side are not completely connected, by being kept low they allow the architecture of the mosque to stand out and combine with it to form a unified whole. The small-scale complex has been successfully adapted to the site available.

The mosque and complex built at Gebze in 1523 for the former Governor of Egypt Choban Mustafa Pasha, and attributed to Sinan in the official records, displays decoration reminiscent of Mamluk architecture, with inlay of polychrome stone and marble brought from Egypt. (Fig. 166.) The complex, which is surrounded by a wall, is composed, in front, of a medrese, a *tekke* (dervish monastery), a hospital, an imaret, a library and a caravansarai and, at the side, of a mosque with a large single dome, 14 metres in diameter with fluted scallop-shaped squinches, and an octagonal tomb, the buildings being very skilfully combined with the central tomb and mosque to form a harmonious whole. (Fig. 165.) It seems likely that here Sinan completed a complex that had already been begun or that he worked as an assistant architect, since it is most improbable that he could have created such a large agglomeration single handed at this early date.

Sinan's first work in Istanbul was the Hasseki complex built for Hürrem Sultan. The mosque, completed in 1539, is a single-domed structure with a five-domed portico. Here he employs once more the fluted, scallop-shaped squinches of the Gebze Mosque. In 1612 the Hasseki Mosque was extended by adding a dome to the side and joining it by two columns and two arches. A medrese, primary school, *çeşme*, imaret and hospital form a more or less unified whole, but stand quite apart from the mosque, from which they are separated by a street.

The main stages in the development of Sinan's architectural genius are shown by three great monuments. These are the Shehzade and Süleymaniye Mosques in Istanbul, and the Selimiye Mosque at Edirne.

The Shehzade Mosque, which Sinan later described as a work of his apprenticeship, was begun in 1544, when he was 54 years of age, and was completed in 4 years. Here Sinan took up for the first time the problem of the half-dome and surpassed St. Sophia and the Mosque of Bayazid by creating an ideal central domed structure with four half-domes, thus realising the dreams of the Renaissance architects. Sinan must have seen the Fatih Pasha Mosque in Diyarbekir, and noticed the imperfections in the first experiments in the four half-dome plan, and must have given considerable thought as to how these might be overcome. The influence of the architecture of Bursa is still quite clearly apparent in the Bayazid Mosque in Istanbul but in the Shehzade Mosque Sinan frees himself entirely from these and creates a completely new type of large-scale monumental architecture in his own individual style.

The mosque was built at the orders of Süleyman the Magnificent in memory of his eldest son, the greatly beloved Shehzade Mehmed, who died at Manisa at the age of 21. The square central space, with sides 38 metres in length, is spanned by a dome 19 metres in diameter supported by four piers with four half-domes, and a small dome in each of the corners. The height of the dome from ground level to keystone is 37 metres and the distance between the piers is 16.52 metres. The half-domes are extended by two exedras on each side, as in the Fatih Pasha Mosque at Diyarbekir, and for the first time in Istanbul the half-dome system of St. Sophia is exploited in a different kind of architectural style. An essential innovation in the spatial organisation arises from the base of the half-domes being less than an exact semicircle. The piers, too, are softened by fluting that resembles organ pipes. (Fig. 168.) The courtyard with *shadırvan* in the centre and surrounded by arcades with 16 domes resting on 12 columns form an ensemble equal to the mosque itself, but at the same time forms an organic part of the whole and prepares one for the spatial effect of the mosque. The transfer of the galleries from the interior of the mosque to the exterior gives the interior a feeling of spaciousness and unity, while at the same time relieving the massive construction of the exterior. Instead of the several small turrets surrounding the dome in the Mosque of Bayazid the tops of the piers are covered on the outside by fluted domes to form only four towers, thus producing a more powerful concentration and a stronger cubic effect. (Fig. 167.) The two-balcony minarets 41.5 metres in height stand outside the corners connecting the courtyard with the mosque. Although the walls, which pile up one behind and on top of the other like the steps of a pyramid, have not entirely lost the effect of a massive block, a strong movement towards a new type of development becomes manifest. Here Sinan applied a considerable amount of decoration to the minarets and the architectural details, but later he was to turn to a simplicity in which architecture plays the dominant role. The other buildings in the complex are the tomb of the Shehzade Mehmed (which was completed before the mosque), a medrese, a *tabhane* and an imaret. Whereas the buildings in the Bayazid foundation were scattered around the mosque, here the tombs are arranged in the area behind the mihrab wall, whilst the other buildings are arranged on the east side of the outer courtyard. Only the medrese stands separate from the others, across a street. The Shehzade Mosque is very important both in forming an essential starting-point for later architects and in being the first fairly large-scale complex created by Sinan. (Plan 47.)

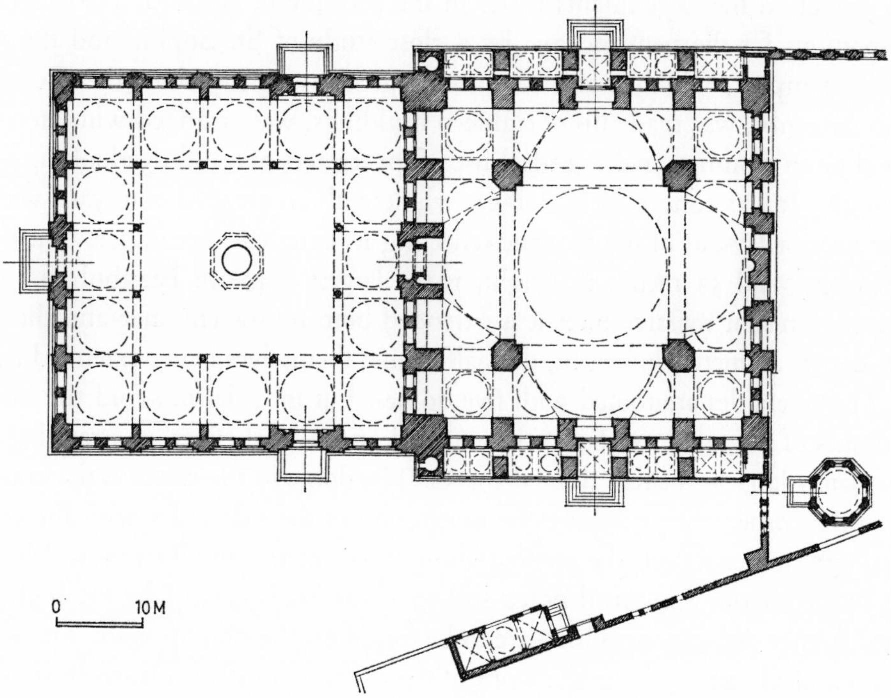

Plan 47. Istanbul, Shehzade Mosque

The Mosque of Mihrimah Sultan, which was completed in the same year (1548), is built on a high terrace beside the landing-stage in Üsküdar and shows Sinan experimenting for the second time with three half-domes, after probably an earlier attempt in the Khādim Süleyman Pasha mosque in Cairo. By replacing the front half-dome and two corner domes by a five-domed portico and placing a slender minaret at each corner, a lofty and harmonious façade has been created. Instead of a courtyard a plain sloping roof is carried out on columned arcades to form an outer portico. A *shadırvan* surrounded by four arches forms a projection forward from the centre open to the landscape on each side. This unusual mosque, with its widened interior, its double portico and architectural façade, dominates the whole of the area. In the mosque and associated buildings built by Sinan on a hill at the Edirnekapı on the death in 1557 of Mihrimah Sultan, the wife of Rüstem Pasha and daughter of Süleyman the Magnificent and Hürrem Sultan, he explores the possibilities of enlarging the interior space created by the large dome 19 metres in diameter resting on four piers by means of three small domes half the height on each side opening into the central space through arches. (Fig. 170.) As the seven-domed portico and the small domes of the arcades are kept fairly low this single minaret mosque dominates the whole surrounding area almost as if it were set on a central height. The mosque, although full of innovations in spatial effect, plan, and exterior architecture, is, however, merely one step forward in Sinan's architectural explorations. (Fig. 169.)

Süleyman the Magnificent waited with patience to build his own mosque and complex, while Sinan continued with his development and experiments. Finally the immense mosque and complex, begun in the very middle of the century, was completed in seven years, in 1557. For this Sinan, at 60 years of age, turned for the first time to the two half-dome scheme and brought to perfection the experiments made in the Mosque of Bayazid. He sought the most mature proportions for the new mosque by a close study of St. Sophia and the Mosque of Bayazid. The complex, which included the first great university since the Conqueror and which, with its tombs, was made up of eighteen buildings, was arranged with an entirely new conception of town planning making ideal use of the terraces of a hill overlooking the Golden Horn. (Plan 48.) It was conceived as a single whole with an arcaded courtyard with *shadırvan* in front, the interior lay-out of the mosque reflecting its external appearance. The dome, 26.5 metres in diameter and 53 metres in height, is the largest dome in Istanbul after that of St. Sophia. Resting on four massive piers it is extended both on the entrance and the qibla sides by two half-domes 40 metres in height, the half-domes themselves being extended by means of an exedra. The side aisles are roofed with five domes, but in order to avoid the monotony of five small domes of the same size Sinan has created an unusual effect by arranging them in a series of alternately large and small domed spaces. The dome in the centre is the same width as the domes in the corner, thus ensuring the integration of the side aisles with the central area. The external appearance reflects the configuration of the interior in all its most delicate details. (Fig. 171.) In the interior a mystical peace and spaciousness is created by the high dome and the restrained faience decorations which are to be found on the mihrab wall. The windows in coloured glass and plaster-work are the work of the craftsman called 'Drunken Ibrahim'. The minarets are at the four corners of the courtyard. In the cemetery behind the mihrab wall stand

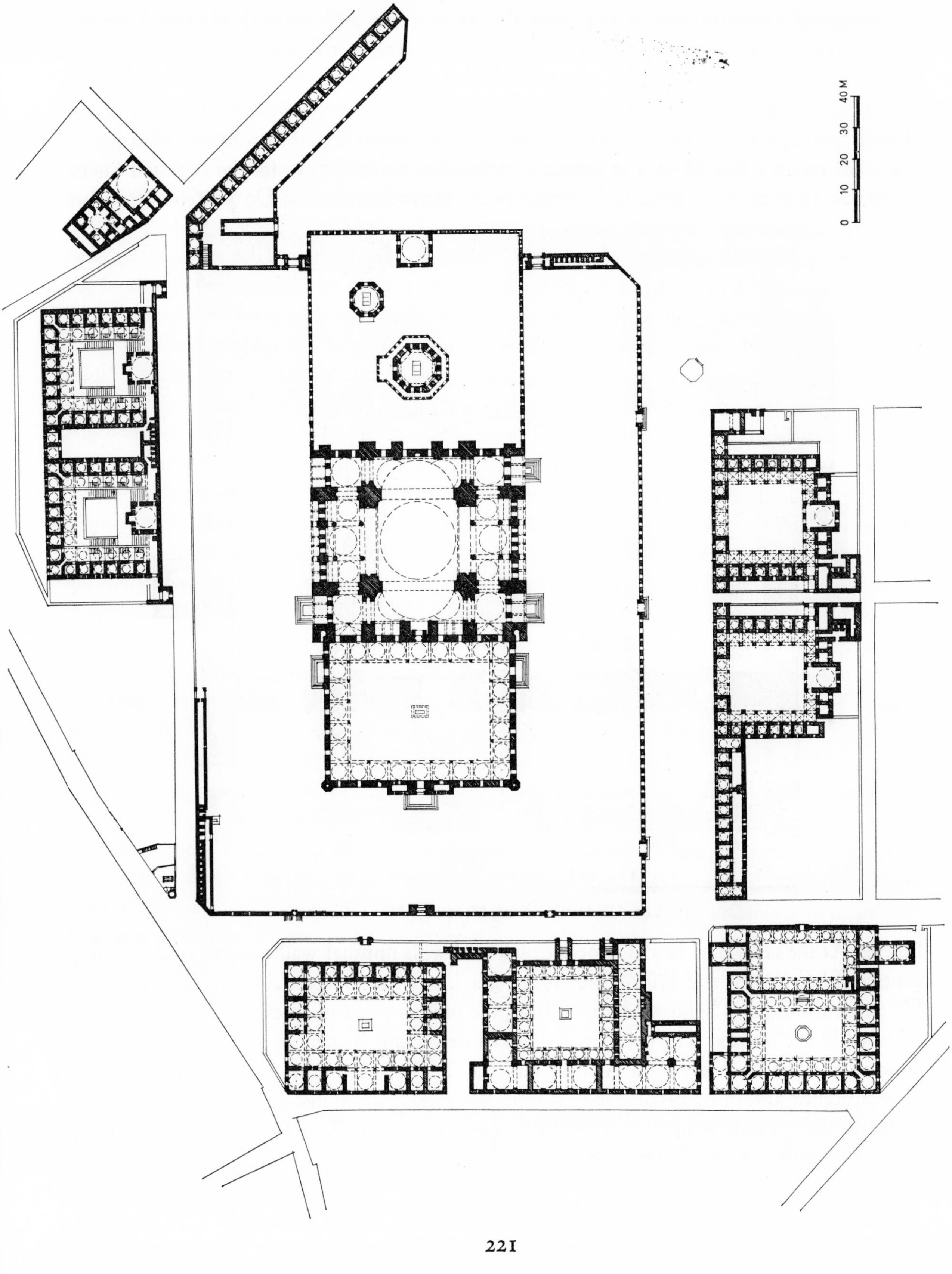

Plan 48. Istanbul, Süleymaniye Mosque

the octagonal tombs of Sultan Süleyman the Magnificent and his wife Hasseki Hürrem. Sinan's own modest tomb is placed unobtrusively outside the north-east corner of the complex.

In the mosque built at Gözleve in the Crimea in 1552 Sinan used the plan scheme of the old Fatih Mosque in Istanbul, though on a smaller scale and without the courtyard (Plan 49).

For the Sinan Pasha Mosque at Beşiktaş, in Istanbul, built in 1555 for the Admiral Sinan Pasha, Sinan employed a small-scale version of the plan scheme of the Üç Şerefeli Mosque in

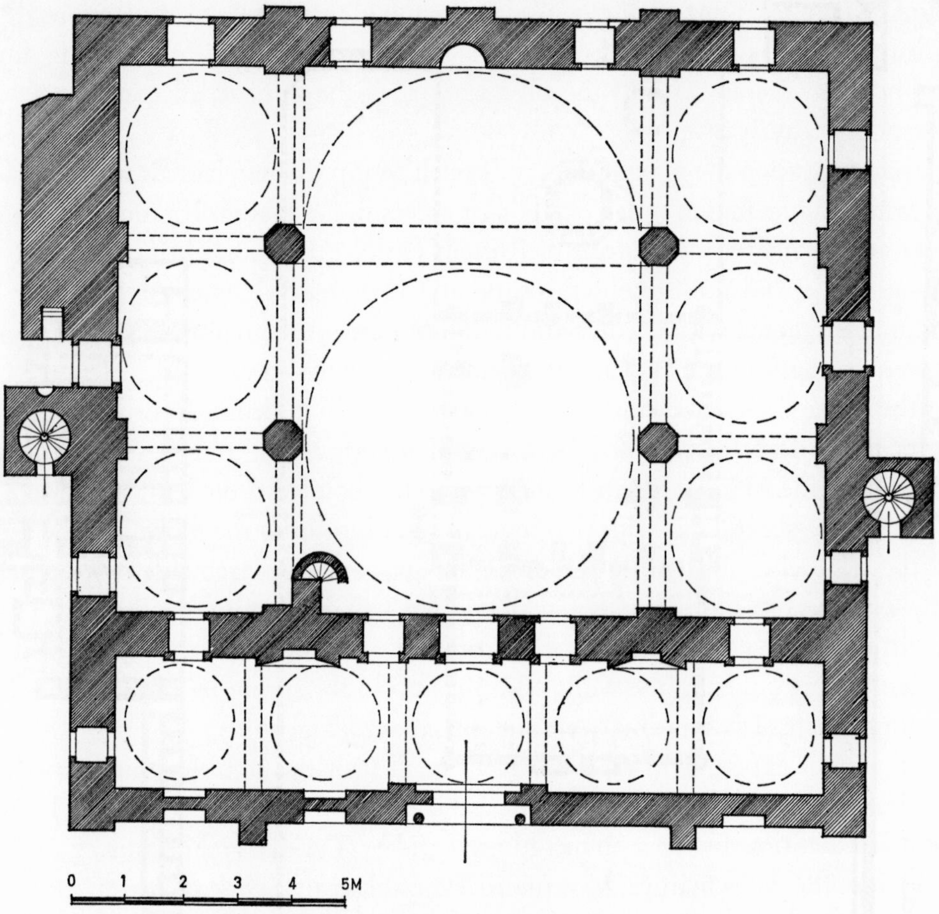

Plan 49. Gözleve, Crimea, Mosque of Mimar Sinan

Edirne. At the same time he has experimented here with unusual wall patterns of alternating courses of hewn stone and brick. (Fig. 172.) The heavy but unforgettable architecture of the Üç Şerefeli Mosque is lightened by modifying the proportions and an effect of spaciousness is achieved in the interior. The over-ornate painted decoration is later work. (Fig. 173.) In the mosque built for the Vizir Kara Ahmed Pasha at Topkapı in Istanbul in the same year this plan is slightly altered by placing the columns supporting the arches which form a hexagon under the dome a little to the front of the walls, removing the two domes on each side and filling the corners with quarter-domes enlarged by exedras, thus leaving only a space the depth of two niches for the side galleries.

In the Sokollu Mosque built just below the Mosque of Sultan Ahmed in 1572 for Esma

Han Sultan, the wife of the Grand Vizir Sokollu Mehmed Pasha, this plan is applied to a single space plan scheme and the exedras are placed in the corners of the walls by connecting the piers in the corners of the hexagonal plan to the walls. The mosque and the medrese with 16 cells and classrooms that takes the place of a courtyard is arranged with great skill on a very awkward site. Sinan here introduces the innovation of employing many-centred pointed arches in the flat-roofed colonnades of the medrese. The system has taken on the form of covering an easily comprehensible ideal space and is an experiment on a small scale for a centralised structure. A central dome and four exedras, with coloured painted decoration, tiles, each more exquisite in detail than the other, covering the mihrab wall up as far as the dome, the pendentives between the arches and the tiled canopy of the minbar, all combine to create a world of legendary beauty. (Fig. 174.)

Before elaborating upon the plan of the Üç Şerefeli Mosque Sinan had already experimented in Istanbul with a dome resting on an octagon of arches in the Hadim Ibrahim Pasha Mosque built in 1551 at Silivrikapı, the Mosque of Rüstem Pasha at Eminönü in 1561 for the Grand Vizir Rüstem Pasha and the Sokollu Mosque at Lüleburgaz (Rumelia). The four corners left by the dome are roofed with exedras and in the Mosque of Rüstem Pasha the interior space has been given greater width by adding three transverse vaults on each side. Here the octagon supporting the dome is clearly defined on the outside by a high drum. In order to insulate the mosque from the din of the crowded bazaars which surround it and to set it in a position dominating the Golden Horn, Sinan built it without a courtyard on a substructure 6 metres in height containing shops, and with two staircases leading up to the mosque. The transverse vaults and the six arches supporting the dome are supported on each side by two octagonal piers and by wall piers set in the entrance-wall and the wall of the mihrab. (Fig. 175.) Galleries are placed at the sides. Apart from this the magnificent tile mihrab and the Iznik and Kütahya tiles of peerless beauty covering the walls and piers up to the springing of the arches lend the mosque an atmosphere of extraordinary wealth and colour. (Fig. 176.)

After these various experiments on a relatively small scale the architect Sinan finally, at the age of 80, created the Selimiye Mosque in Edirne, which combines all the innovations introduced up to that time by the architect himself and by Turkish architecture as a whole. He himself described the Süleymaniye Mosque in Istanbul as the work of his maturity but the mosque at Edirne he built in five years between 1569 and 1574 as his masterpiece. (Fig. 177.) This mosque, the eternal symbol of Edirne and the Ottoman Empire, was built on the orders of Sultan Selim II, and can be recognised from afar by the great dome 31.5 metres in diameter surpassing in size that of St. Sophia, and the four slender minarets surrounding the octagonal body. The silhouette arises directly from the interior construction. The enormous dome, in which the inner space is completely integrated with the outer appearance, may be regarded as the acme of the development of the dome in the whole world. In the *Tezkeret-ül-Bünyan*, which is agreed to have been dictated by Sinan himself, Sinan describes his great masterpiece as follows: 'The four minarets are on the four corners of the dome. The Üç Şerefeli Minaret was as thick as a tower. The difficulty in building minarets as slender as these and at the same time containing three separate stairways is obvious. Those that pass for architects among the

Christians say that they have defeated the Moslems because no dome has been built in the Islamic world that can rival the dome of St. Sophia. It greatly grieved my heart that they should say that to build so large a dome was so difficult a task. I determined to erect such a mosque, and with the help of God, in the reign of Sultan Selim Khān, I made the dome of this mosque

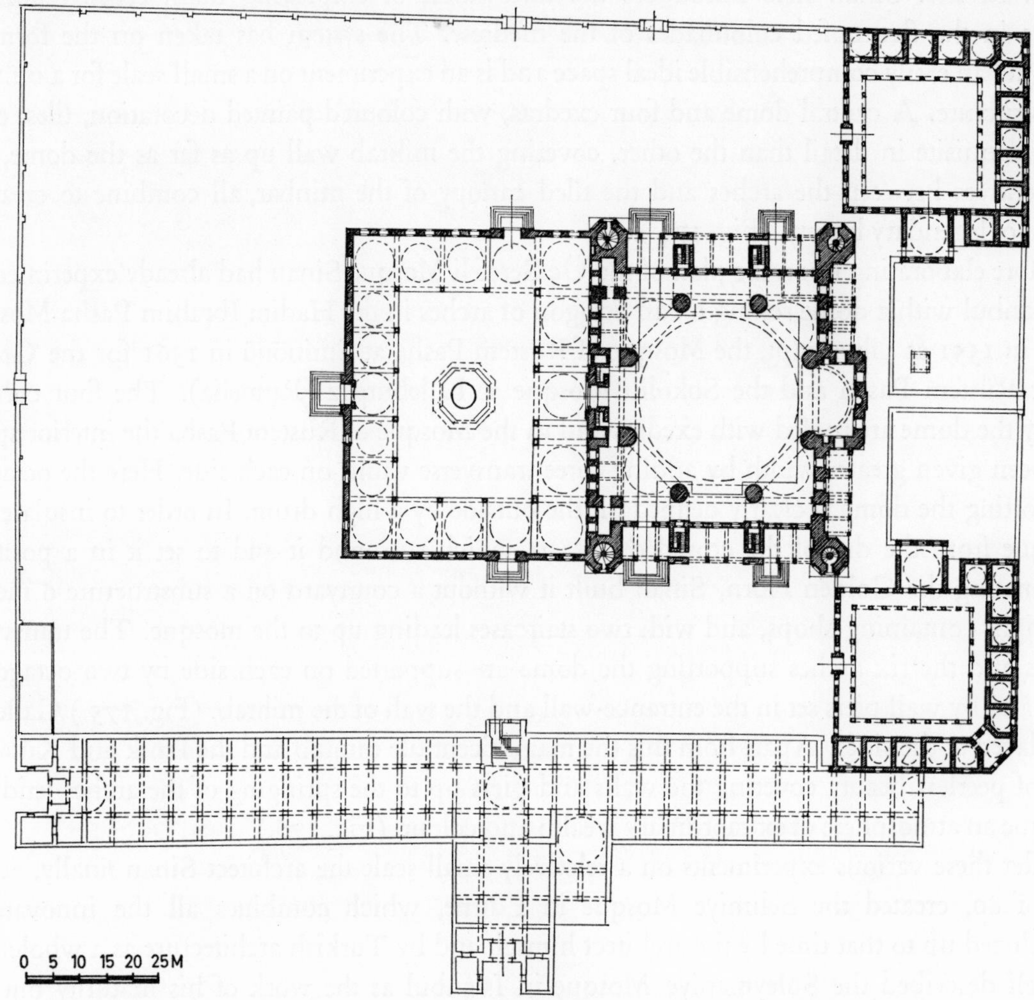

Plan 50. Edirne, Selimiye Mosque

six cubits wider and four cubits deeper than the dome of St. Sophia.' Sinan was probably inspired here by the idea of constructing a colossus,[1] since the system comprising a dome resting on an octagonal base with the weight of the dome being taken by eight piers with flying buttresses between them is here developed to its utmost limits. He must have regarded this octagonal plan as ideal (Plan 50). In the interior, exedras are placed in the corners left by the dome, the arches between the piers are filled with rows of windows and no wall space remains.

[1] The dome of St. Sophia is slightly ovoid in shape, with a diameter of 30.9× 31.82 metres, and a height of 55.92 metres from the floor to the keystone. The dome of the Selimiye has a diameter of 31.5 metres and a height of 43.28 metres. The Selimiye dome owes its superiority to its being built in the much more difficult technique of the first, shallower dome of St. Sophia, which collapsed shortly after its erection.

178 Edirne, Selimiye Mosque, interior

179 Edirne, Selimiye Mosque, mihrab tiles from Imperial gallery

180 Istanbul, Azapkapı Sokullu Mosque, interior

181 Istanbul, Kâsımpaşa, Mosque of Piyale Pasha, exterior

182 Istanbul, Mausoleum of Shehzade Mehmed

183 Istanbul, Mausoleum of Suleyman the Magnificent

184 Istanbul, Mosque of Sultan Ahmed and associated foundations

185 Istanbul, Mosque of Sultan Ahmed, interior

186 Istanbul, Yeni Cami (New Mosque)

187 Istanbul, Üsküdar, Yeni Valide Mosque, interior

188 Istanbul, Nur-u Osmaniye Mosque

189 Istanbul, Laleli Mosque

190
Istanbul, Mosque of Mehmed the Conqueror (Fatih), rear view

191 Istanbul, Mosque of Mehmed the Conqueror, interior

192 Istanbul, Tophane, Nüsretiye Mosque

193 Istanbul, Dolmabahçe Mosque

194 Kütahya, Great Mosque (centre), Imaret of Yakub Bek II (rear), Vacidiye Medrese, dome with oculus (front)

195 Kütahya, Great Mosque, close up

197 Istanbul, Mausoleum of Nakshidil Sultan

196 Istanbul, The Fourth Vakıf Han

198 Istanbul, Türbe of Sultan Mahmud II and façade of the cemetery

199 Istanbul, Çinili Köşk (Tiled Pavilion)

200 Doğu Bayazid, Ishak Pasha complex

201
Istanbul, Sultan Ahmed,
The Hasseki Baths

202 Diyarbekir, The Ulu Beden tower

203 Istanbul, Rumeli Hisar

204 Istanbul, Çeşme (Fountain) of Ahmed III

205 Stucco figure, Persia, Seljuk, 12th century, Worcester Art Museum

206 Three stucco figures, Persia, Seljuk, 12th century

207 Angel relief from the Citadel at Konya

208 Blazon of double-headed eagle from Citadel at Konya

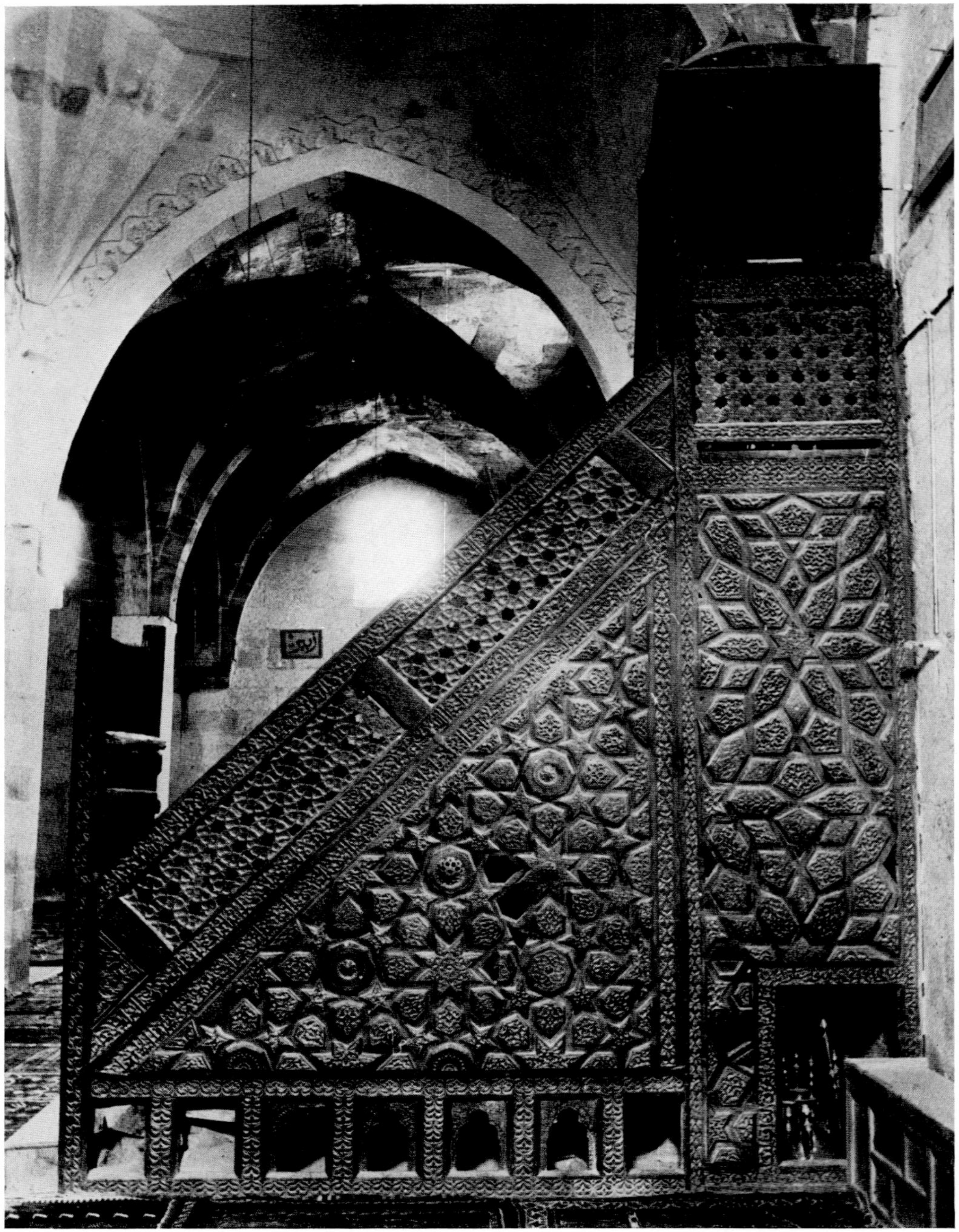

209 Aksaray, Great Mosque, minbar

210 Koran desk, Seljuk, East Berlin, Islamisches Museum

The mihrab recess is 6 metres in depth and is roofed by a half-dome on a lower level. The interior, roofed by a single dome, is extended to the furthest limits on all sides and gives one on entering the feeling of being carried off by some magic force into another world. (Fig. 178.)

From a distance the eye is first struck by the four minarets. On approach they combine with the dome to form a harmonious whole. The building rises up in four bold steps to achieve peace and harmony in the dome. The façades are outstanding for the mature harmony of their proportions, and are enlivened by projecting water-spouts, polychrome stone inlay in the lunettes of the windows and other suitable places, and the coloured stones and varied forms of the arches.

The mosque, in addition to its architectural importance, provides examples of the most brilliant period in each of the other arts. In size, beauty and exquisite workmanship the great minbar carved from a single block of stone is far superior to all other minbars of this type. The sections of wall around the mihrab, the back and conical spire of the minbar, and the lunettes of the lower windows are covered with a most attractive tile decoration. The large tile panels on the mihrab wall are masterpieces of colour and composition. On the upper edge there are Koranic inscriptions written in bold white letters on a cobalt ground (Plate IV). Although the tiles in the Imperial gallery, supported by four columns in the left-hand corner, are richer from the point of view of composition (Fig. 179) they are overshadowed by the monumental size of the tiles on the mihrab wall. The original polychrome ornament of the ceiling under the gallery has remained as fresh as when it was painted. The painted decoration on the inside of the arches was uncovered during the latest repairs. The arcaded courtyard with its very attractive *shadırvan* achieves the ideal form of Turkish architecture in the strength and maturity of its proportions. The outer courtyard is surrounded by walls and the buildings in the south-west corner are now a museum. A row of shops under the terrace of the mosque was built by the architect Davud Agha in the reign of Murad III as an endowment to the mosque.

Sinan continued to work on the plan used in the Selimiye Mosque and applied it once more on a small scale in the Sokollu Mehmed Pasha Mosque built in 1577 at Azapkapı in Istanbul. An unusual feature of the exterior is that the towers corresponding to the eight piers inside are arranged around the dome, and exedras are placed between these. Thus the easy, rhythmic flow of the interior arrangement is reflected in the external dome system. Nevertheless the external appearance of the lower part of the exterior is not successful. Here the whole power is concentrated in creating a highly effective interior of a unity that had not been seen up to that time, and the external appearance, apart from the dome system, plays a secondary role. (Fig. 180.)

In the mosque built by Sinan in 1573 for the Admiral Piyale Pasha at Kâsımpaşa in Istanbul, he returns to the old type of the Great Mosque and employs six equal domes. Inside, in addition to one of the finest tile mihrabs of the period, there are rich decorations including a tile inscription band and painted decorations in the lunettes of the windows. The mosque is surrounded on three sides by two-storeyed arcades and the minaret rises from the wall in the middle of the entrance façade. (Fig. 181.) The tomb of Piyale Pasha is in the cemetery on the qibla side.

Before this, in the mosque he erected for the Beklerbek Hüsrev Pasha at Van in 1567, Sinan had returned to the traditional single-domed plan scheme with a five-domed portico and dome on squinches, and sought decorative effect by the unusual patterning of two-colour squared stone in the minaret to the right-hand side of the façade and in the walls. The octagonal mausoleum of Hüsrev Pasha, which was added to the eastern end of the mosque in 1583, is however, clearly not the work of Sinan.

The mosque of the Admiral Qılıch Ali Pasha at Tophane in Istanbul is one of Sinan's last works. Here he takes up the plan of St. Sophia and by removing the walls separating the side aisles he creates an interior in which the width is almost equal to the length. The galleries are placed over the transverse vaulted side aisles to form the women's galleries. In the graveyard behind the projecting mihrab recess there is the *türbe* (mausoleum) of the Admiral Qılıch Ali Pasha. The mosque is remarkable for its tile and stone decoration and its inscriptions.

The architect Sinan lived through the reign of four Ottoman Sultans and towards the end of his life, from 1583 to 1585, he constructed the Muradiye Mosque at Manisa on the orders of Sultan Murad III. Sinan prepared the plans of the mosque but as he was now very old the building was begun under the supervision of the architect Mahmud Agha; then, on the latter's sudden death, Mehmed Agha, one of the Hassa architects, was sent to Manisa and the work completed in 1585. The plan of the mosque is very simple, without a courtyard, and is on a much smaller scale than Sinan's other royal mosques. It is in an old mosque tradition with three half-domes, the one on the south side being salient. In front there is a five-arched portico with a panel vault in the middle and two domes on each side. The central dome is 10.8 metres in diameter and is surrounded by half-domes that are really in the form of half transverse vaults. The front façade with its high stepped arch is far from satisfying. Where, however, Sinan was not able to supervise the whole building himself it is obvious that there would be imperfections and deficiencies. On the east is to be found a medrese and an imaret, which make up the complex.

Sinan built another similar mosque at Karapınar on the Konya–Ereğli road. In 1572 Sultan Selim II founded a town to serve as a halting-place in this deserted region. Here Sinan built the complex foundation the Sultan had endowed. The single-domed mosque has a simple plan with two minarets in front and a five-domed portico. The fairly large dome on pendentives 15 metres in diameter on the exterior is strengthened by stepped projecting wall piers. The marble porch with its shell-shaped tympanum and the mihrab with its stalactite niches are decorated in traditional style and form the richest sections of the building. A ruined bath and a *çeşme* (public fountain) near the mosque also form part of the complex. Although the simple but harmonious architecture of the mosque and complex may be attributed to its style it is much more likely that the building was constructed by assistants following Sinan's plans and his directions than that Sinan himself should have supervised the whole construction in this remote region.

The architect Sinan explored the possibilities of many other types of building besides mosques. The octagonal Kapı Ağası medrese built in Amasya in 1488, two years after the Mosque of Bayazid, must have attracted his attention with its arcaded courtyard and the classroom on the qibla side extended by a small half-dome on each side to form an inverted T type plan. In Istanbul, in constructing a medrese for Rüstem Pasha in 1550, Sinan employed a variation of this form. 22 cells are deployed behind an arcade of 14 domes around an octagonal courtyard, the large domed classroom forming a projection on the outside and the whole outer structure being made to form a square by filling in the four corners. (Plan 51.)

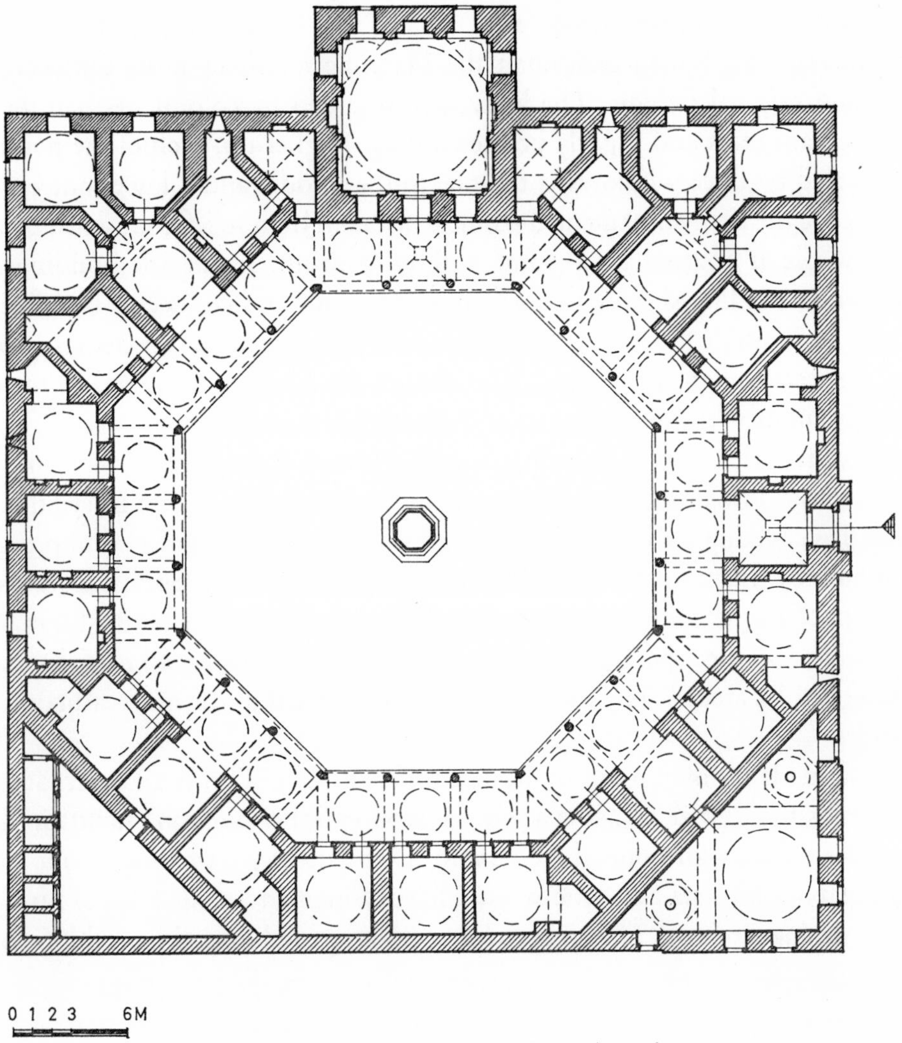

Plan 51. Istanbul, Medrese of Rüstem Pasha

But it was in his tombs that Sinan created the most original of his works after his mosques. The tomb of Shehzade Mehmed, which was completed before the mosque, is Sinan's earliest but at the same time one of his finest creations. (Fig. 182.) It is roofed by a fluted dome on an octagonal body and with its polychrome inlay of stone on the exterior and the matchless beauty of its tile-work within it created a corner of paradise for the dead prince.

Although in the tomb built in Istanbul in 1545 for Hüsrev Pasha, the founder of a complex at Aleppo, Sinan again uses a dome set on an octagonal body, here the proportions and style of architecture are completely changed and the result would seem to form a simplified copy in stone of the brick mausolea of Maragha and Nakhichevan. It is a very simple style of architecture completely devoid of ornament save for the stalactite cornice around the upper edge of the body, the geometrical patterns on the octagonal drum and the palmettes arranged in high relief along its edge. The vizir Hüsrev Pasha was dismissed after entering into an argument in the council of state in the presence of Süleyman the Magnificent and was later driven by grief to commit suicide by starving himself to death.

In the tomb built for Sultan Süleyman the Magnificent Sinan treats the octagonal plan scheme in a most original fashion. The body is surrounded by colonnades half the height of the walls, with plain roofs and slightly pointed arches. Higher up, each of the pointed-arched lunettes are pierced by three windows, a tall one in the middle and a lower one on each side. On the upper edge the richly ornamented palmette frieze in high relief is crowned by a stalactite cornice. The whole is covered by a dome without a drum. Inside the building the dome rests on 8 columns standing slightly to the front of the walls and connected by arches. The 33 columns inside and outside the building resemble sentinels with spears on eternal guard around the tomb of the great Sultan. (Fig. 183.) The tiles on the entrance front and in the interior of the dome greatly augment the magnificence of the rectangular niches in it.

The octagonal marble tomb of Süleyman's wife, Hürrem Sultan, has a very simple exterior and is roofed with a low dome on a drum ornamented with a Koranic inscription in raised lettering. The tiles covering the inside walls conjure up the atmosphere of a fresh spring day.

The tomb built by Sinan for Sultan Selim II in the cemetery of St. Sophia towards 1577 has the exterior form of a square with slightly softened corners and a dome resting on massive walls faced with marble. On the other hand the inner dome is supported on an octagon formed by 8 columns connected by arches. The inner octagon is connected to the outer structure in a most original manner.

Finally Sinan made his own tomb on quite a different plan. This is an open tomb with the surrounding walls meeting at an acute angle. A sebil (public fountain) stands in the corner. The tomb opens off through pointed arches and is crowned by a small symbolic dome. The poet and calligrapher Mustafa Sai, who wrote a life of Sinan and made a list of his works, was responsible for the inscription: 'The great architect Sinan passed from this world in 996/1588.'

15

17TH AND 18TH CENTURY MOSQUES

Sinan's style of architecture dominated his period and continued to exert its influence long after his death. The skyline of Istanbul, which began to take shape towards the end of the 16th century with the construction of mosques and various other buildings, together with the characteristic type of Turkish city that had already developed in Bursa and Edirne, spread in this characteristic form even to very distant environments. Thus, a similar townscape is clearly visible in a number of old cities such as Skoplje, Sarajevo, Shumnu, Rhodes, Aleppo and Cairo. After Sinan his assistants who were trained at his side continued his tradition as master-builders, but they took as their starting-point not the later experiments of the master but his first great work the Shehzade Mosque which he had described as the work of his apprenticeship. The plan of the Shehzade Mosque was adopted by the master-builder Davud Agha fifty years later when preparing the plans for the Yeni Cami (the Valide Mosque or Mosque of the Sultan's mother). In 1598 Davud Agha, who had been commissioned by Safiye Sultan, the mother of Sultan Mehmed III, to build a great mosque complex, began the enormous building by boldly sinking the foundations under water on firm sections of the shore of the Golden Horn, but a year later he died in an outbreak of plague. His place was taken by the Diver Ahmed Chavush who completed the building as far as the first row of windows, but when, on the death of Mehmed III in 1603, the Queen Mother was sent to the Old Palace, all work on the building was suspended. The building was finally completed by Hatije Sultan, the mother of Mehmed IV, in 1663, but half a century before this the Mosque of Sultan Ahmed had already been completed.

This mosque, built by Sedefkar Mehmed Agha for Sultan Ahmed I, is the largest complex in Istanbul and the first great work to be completed after the death of Sinan. Mehmed Agha, who had had his training under Sinan and Davud Agha, had begun his career as a musician and inlayer skilled in using mother-of-pearl. The influence of these crafts is very obvious in his work. The Mosque of Sultan Ahmed, the largest of all the royal mosques, with six minarets, was begun in 1609 and completed in 1617. It resembles the Shehzade Mosque and Davud Agha's Yeni Cami in adopting the four half-dome plan scheme. It measures 64×72 metres and the dome has a diameter of 23.5 metres and a height of 43 metres. The dome rests on four marble piers 5 metres in diameter known as 'elephants' legs'. The harshness of the interior is removed by extending the half-dome towards the mihrab by two exedras and the others by three. The possibilities which Sinan had left in an embryonic state are here developed in an entirely new spirit. The interpenetration of spherical forms lends the interior a feeling of fluidity. (Fig. 185.) The large, spacious, brilliantly illuminated interior is the work of Mehmed Agha, and has a most expressive effect. The exterior shows a completely new approach in its windows, its system of arches and its proportions. The fluidity of the interior reveals itself on the exterior in the harmonious agglomeration of the domes. (Fig. 184.) The brilliantly lit interior resembles a palace in the richness of its ornament. 21,043 tiles in over fifty different designs covering the walls of the upper galleries were supplied by the tile-maker Hasan and are the richest collection still in place after those in the Topkapı Saray. The turquoise tiles with gilded Koranic inscriptions in the richly decorated Imperial gallery and the coloured painted decorations beneath it are quite unrivalled.

The painted decoration covering every part of the building from the fluted piers to the domes spreads a blue atmosphere throughout the interior. The inscriptions are the work of the calligrapher Ahmed Gubari. In the mother-of-pearl inlay work in the doors and window shutters Mehmed Agha created masterpieces of his old art. The bronze doors resembling these are of especial interest.

The mosque is surrounded on three sides by a large outer courtyard, and in front of the mosque there is a courtyard with *shadırvan* surrounded by a colonnade of 26 granite columns and thirty domes. The mosque is set in the middle of a complex consisting, apart from the tomb of Sultan Ahmed, of a medrese, an imaret, a hospital, a bazaar and a row of tradesmen's shops. Most of these are partially or completely ruined.

The Yeni Cami (the New Mosque) (Fig. 186) which was completed between the years 1661 and 1663 by the master-builder Mustafa Agha at the orders of the Queen Mother Turhan Sultan nearly sixty years after work on its construction had been discontinued in 1603, is the last large-scale Ottoman complex. The dome system of the Mosque of Sultan Ahmed is again applied here using different proportions. The dome, 17.5 metres in radius and 36 metres in height, is rather more pointed than those of the other mosques. As the half-domes are much lower in height the central dome has a higher and more dominating appearance. The four piers supporting the dome are defined on the outside by octagonal, lobed buttress towers. There are two minarets, each with three balconies. The courtyard is surrounded by colonnades with 25 domes on 20 columns, the *shadırvan* in the middle consisting of a dome set on arches. The interior of the mosque is embellished by the richest tile-work of the second half of the 17th century and by painted decoration of the same period covering the dome and the arches. The interior decoration, together with the rhythmic arrangement of large and small arches on the two-storeyed side façades, the bi-coloured voussoirs of the courtyard arcades, the coloured stone columns and the delicate ornament on the *shadırvan*, reflects the sensitive mind of Turhan Valide Sultan. The Yeni Cami was created by the combined efforts of the three greatest architects to succeed Sinan.

The complex which the Yeni Cami comprised includes the tomb of Turhan Sultan, a Koran school, a primary school, 86 shops, the Mısır Çarşısı (the Egyptian Market), a *çeşme* and a spectacular sebil. It was originally surrounded by walls. A bath was also added. Nothing now remains apart from the shops, the sebil and the tomb, but the royal pavilion adjoining the wall of the mosque and connected to the Imperial gallery within is one of the most original works of classical kiosk architecture after the Çinili Köşk. The pavilion, which is reached by a long ramp and is set on a high vault with pointed arches, looks out over the Bosphorus and the Golden Horn. The tiles and painted decoration covering the interior prove that the traditional decorative arts had not yet lost their power.

The plan, construction and ornament of the Yeni Valide Mosque and complex built in Üsküdar at the beginning of the 18th century between 1708 and 1710 by Gülnüsh Sultan, the mother of Sultan Ahmed III, remain in the classical tradition and are completely unaffected by European influence. The plan is based on the eight pier scheme of the Mosque of Rüstem Pasha. (Fig. 187.) The decorations are also in the classical tradition, but there is an obvious decline in the proportions, the quality of the architecture and the materials used. The courtyard is larger than the mosque, and there is no harmony between the three disproportionately large domes of the portico and the small domes of the arcades.

It is clear that no large-scale mosque was built on an original plan after the Mosque of Sultan Ahmed. Mosques of a six or eight pier plan were built in Istanbul and other cities by pupils of Sinan and the architects who succeeded them, but in the course of time these lost their architectural strength and became nothing more than small, unpretentious, worthless copies of the originals.

The Ottoman armies were routed at Vienna in 1683, and in 1689, as a result of the harsh terms imposed by the treaty of Karlofça (Karlovač), Hungary too was lost to the Empire. This was the beginning of a gradual movement towards Europe and France. New artistic developments begin to appear during the reign of Sultan Ahmed III (1703–30) as a result of the efforts of the Grand Vizir Damat Ibrahim Pasha of Nevşehir. In October 1720 Yirmisekiz Chelebi Mehmed Efendi was sent to Paris at the head of a delegation of 80 and was given a brilliant reception. Their reports to the Saray on what they had seen in France aroused great interest and they brought back with them plans of French palaces and gardens. The desire to build similar pavilions and gardens at Kâgıthane (on the Golden Horn) and on the Bosphorus led to the introduction of Baroque and Rococo influences from France, and all eyes turned to Europe. In the thirty years known as the Tulip Period the construction of large monumental buildings gave way to the embellishment of several parts of Istanbul with villas, pavilions and fountains in which the new European influence was applied. Later the Mosque of Nur-u Osmaniye was begun by Sultan Mahmud I in 1748 and completed by Sultan Osman III in 1755, the first large-scale building in which the new style was powerfully displayed. Here the Baroque development indicated in the Mihrimah Mosque of Sinan at Edirnekapı is brought to conform to the new style in its decoration and peculiar plan. (Fig. 188.)

According to a written account of the construction of the Mosque of Nur-u Osmaniye the Sultan summoned his supervisor of works, Dervish Efendi, and ordered him to prepare a plan for a large single-domed mosque in which there was no emphasis upon columns, giving special attention to the construction of storeys and galleries. A picture of the mosque was drawn on a large panel, and after the Sultan had approved it, it was decided that work should begin. Ali Agha, the superintendent of works, and Simeon Kalfa were made responsible for the supervision of the work. The large dome, 25.75 metres in diameter and supported by four large arches and four corner towers, is built over a high basement foundation and dominates the whole district. The mihrab section forms a projection on the outside roofed by a low small half-dome. The exterior side galleries are in two storeys with undulating Baroque arches resting on columns in the lower storey and on piers in the upper. The mosque is approached by a flight of 11 steps and the arcaded courtyard on the same level is in the form of a half oval. There is no *shadırvan*. (Plan 52.) The nine domes of the arcade with its eighty porphyry columns and Baroque capitals is connected to the five-domed portico, and on each side there is a two-balcony minaret.

The mosque is completely faced with marble, and very much space has been allotted to applied decoration. Apart from inscriptions in the dome, a Koranic inscription band which contains the Surat al-Fatḥ (the Sura of Victory) starting from the left of the mihrab, an inscription course and compositions by well-known calligraphers in oval medallions in the lower section, all the decoration is in the Baroque style. The undulating arches, the shell ornaments, the acanthus scrolls and the peculiar capitals are treated in a different manner from the European and indicate the birth of a new Turkish Baroque style. Though there is a great number of windows the interior does not produce an effect of spaciousness and light.

The Imperial pavilion and royal gallery are decorated in an exaggerated and ostentatious style, and are approached by a ramp adjoining the eastern side of the outer courtyard wall wide enough to be negotiated on horseback. There is a very fine sebil to the right-hand side of the gate opening from the outer courtyard into the covered bazaar, and a *çeşme* to the right. The other buildings composing the complex comprise an oval library, the tomb beside it, a medrese by the qibla wall, an imaret adjoining it, and 142 shops.

All in all, the special features of the Mosque of Nur-u Osmaniye—the great dome over 25 metres in diameter, the unusual plan of the complex and its peculiar type of decoration—reflect the capacity of Turkish architecture to create a new style in the middle of the 18th century.

The Laleli Mosque, and its associated buildings, based on the eight pier plan scheme Sinan had employed in the Mosque of Rüstem Pasha, is the second great work to show the assimilation of the Baroque style. It was built between 1759 and 1763 by the architect Tahir Agha on the orders of Sultan Mustafa III, but was destroyed in the earthquake of 1765. The mosque remained in a ruinous state until 1783, during the reign of Abdülhamid I, when repairs were undertaken by Seyid Mustafa Agha. Like Nur-u Osmaniye this mosque is built up on a high substructure broken by bold cornices and developing upwards in a series of steps. This weakens its monumentality and fails to ensure the effect of a harmonious upward movement. (Fig. 189.) The mihrab section forms a projection on the exterior, where it is roofed by a low half-dome. The side galleries are placed on the outside, thus creating an

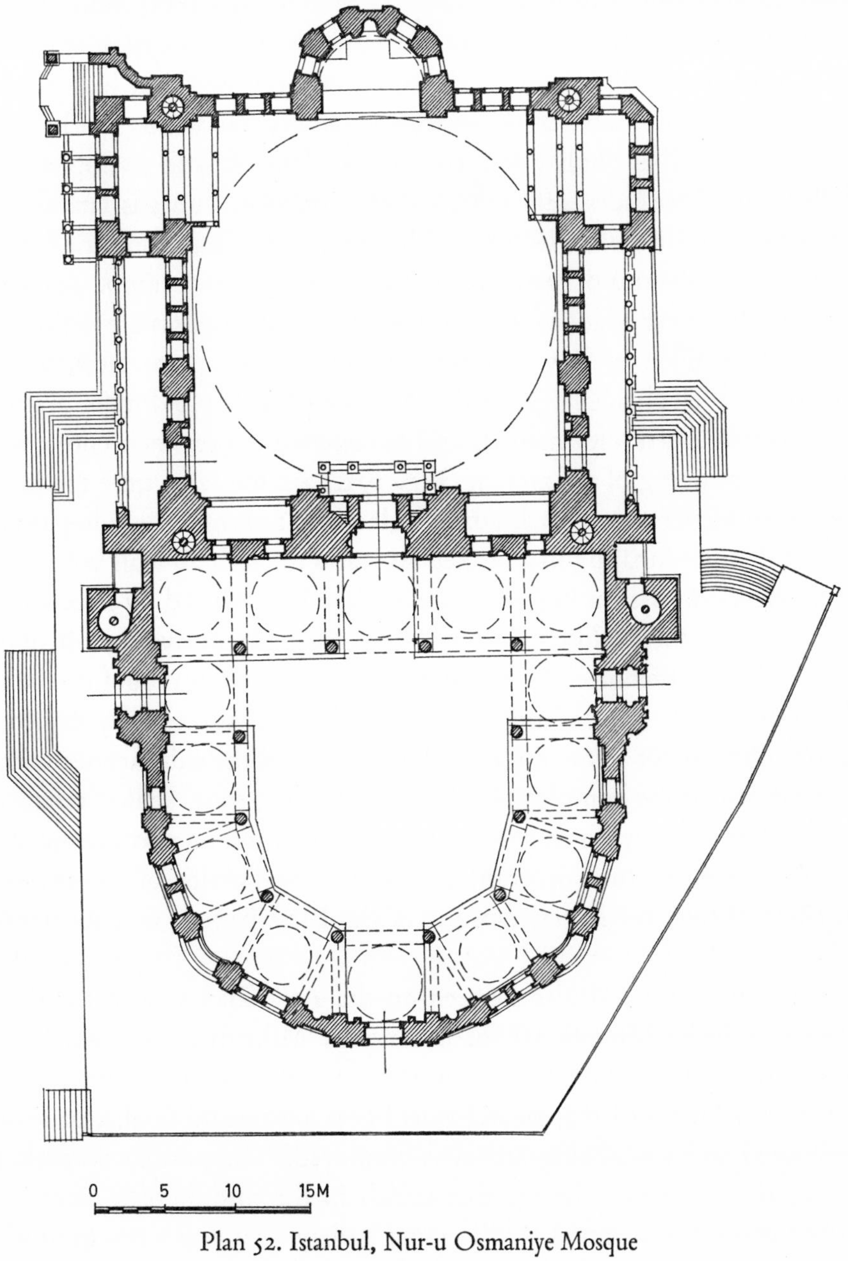

Plan 52. Istanbul, Nur-u Osmaniye Mosque

interior in the shape of an elongated rectangle that is spacious, well lit and full of life and movement. The outer walls are also lively in construction. There is a square courtyard with arcade and *shadırvan*. The complex includes a sebil on the street, a tomb beside it, an imaret behind the mosque, medreses and other buildings. The royal gallery is reached from the courtyard by means of a ramp. A high-vaulted bazaar in the basement had been filled with earth but has been cleaned out in recent years and is being used once more.

After the collapse of its dome in the earthquake of 1766 Mustafa III ordered the architect Tahir Agha to carry out repairs on the Mosque of Fatih, and between the years 1767 and 1771 the present mosque was constructed in a Baroque style based on the plan of the Mosque of Sultan Ahmed, the side walls of the original mosque being brought slightly inwards. The central dome is 19 metres in diameter and rests on four piers with four half-domes and corner domes. Each of the half-domes at the sides have three exedras whilst the half-domes on the entrance and mihrab sides have only two each. The Mosque of Fatih resembles Sultan Ahmed in having galleries on three sides, and outer galleries on two, but it is far from approaching the size and magnificence of Sultan Ahmed. The royal gallery stands on the left of the mihrab and is approached from the rear of the building by means of a wide ramp. The stepped broken cornices encircling the lower edges of the half-domes and the exedras are defined in relief, and the corners have been filled by low, Rococo cushions. The square piers, which are rather more slender than the 'elephants' legs' in the Mosque of Sultan Ahmed, are softened at the corners and completely faced with marble, and are noteworthy for their cornices that conform more closely to the springing of the arches. (Fig. 191.) At the same time the large arches and some of the window arches are pointed, whilst stalactites appear on the side piers. The portico, the large entrance door terminating in a broken arch and the mihrab wall belong to the original building, whilst the dome system and the interior have been altered by making the side walls narrower and bringing them closer together. The arcaded courtyard with a *shadırvan* also belongs to the period of Mehmed the Conqueror, but the conical roof of the fountain was erected in the 17th century. The architect Tahir Agha thus successfully united the Baroque style prevailing in the interior of the mosque, the domes and the side façades with the classical architecture of the rest of the complex. The minarets (Fig. 190), which retain their original form as far as the first balcony, form a bond between the mosque and the arcaded courtyard. The tasteless black 19th-century decoration covering the interior of the mosque spoils the monumental effect of this, the largest mosque of the latest period, and so greatly reduces its charm.

Works in the new style are also to be seen on the Anatolian side of the Bosphorus. The Ayazma Mosque built by Mustafa III for his mother Mihrishah in 1760, before the Laleli Mosque, stands on a hill dominating the surrounding country. The exterior is based on the same principles as the Nur-u Osmaniye Mosque, but is diffuse and smaller in scale. A mixture of pointed, rounded and undulating arches is employed. The portico is reached by a semi-circular flight of marble steps. The mosque stands in the middle of a courtyard entered by three gates. On the right is the royal pavilion and gallery. Although it was originally built in the form of a complex now only a *çeşme* remains along with the mosque.

The large complex built by Sultan Abdülhamid I in Istanbul is a scattered collection of buildings comprising a small mosque surrounded by a large medrese, a library, a tomb, a *çeşme*, a sebil, an imaret and a row of shops. The imaret was demolished when the 4th Vakıf Han (Fig. 196) was being built, and the sebil and *çeşme* were removed and reconstructed at the corner of the small Baroque mosque in hewn stone and brick built by Ahmed III for his daughter Zeyneb Sultan in 1769 in front of the gates of Gülhane Park.

The largest of Abdülhamid I's mosques is the one he built in 1778 at Beylerbey on the Anatolian shore of the Bosphorus for his mother Rabia Sultan. The mosque has a single dome on squinches and the mihrab section forms a bold projection roofed with a low half-dome. The royal pavilion is placed on a second storey above the portico. The interior of the mosque is spacious and well lit, but an unusual effect is created by the contrast between the Baroque style of the architecture and tiles from an earlier period that cover the walls.

Sultan Selim III built a mosque on the Anatolian side beside the Selimiye barracks which had been named after him. Like the Ayazma Mosque, the Selimiye Mosque resembles Nur-u Osmaniye in having a large dome supported on four large arches and corner towers. The royal apartments are placed along the sides. The exterior, with its two slender single-balconied Baroque minarets, achieves a more peaceful and harmonious effect than the Ayazma Mosque.

16

MOSQUES OF THE LAST OTTOMAN PERIOD

By the time the Baroque style entered Istanbul the Empire style was already dominant in Europe, though it was not introduced into Istanbul until the reign of Sultan Mahmud (1808–1839). The Nüsretiye Mosque built by Mahmud II between the barracks at Tophane and completed in 1826 is most successful as a first experiment in the Empire style. Here the Empire style has been modified to suit Turkish taste and outlook and differs markedly from the European original. All Baroque elements have completely disappeared. The plan is reminiscent of Nur-u Osmaniye with its dome on four arches and the semicircular projection formed by the mihrab, but the dome is supported by a high drum and surrounded by turrets. (Fig. 192.) It contains calligraphic compositions, the work of Mustafa Rakim Efendi. The royal pavilion looks on to Tophane Square, and its four corner windows, mouldings and metal balustrade grilles are typical of the Turkish Empire style.

The school built on the Divan Yolu in the corner overlooking the Hippodrome and dedicated to Jevri Kalfa, who saved Mahmud II's life, is in a more highly developed form of Empire style with marble façade, wide windows, sebil and *çeşme*. The Ortaköy and Dolmabahçe Mosques were built in 1854 during the reign of Abdülmejid. They also are in Empire style with a single dome supported by four arches and corner towers. The Dolmabahçe Mosque was built for Bezmi Alem Valide Sultan and is like a brilliantly illuminated palace with two minarets in the form of Corinthian columns. Although very ornate in style the quality of both the architecture and the materials employed is very poor. (Fig. 193.)

The mosque at Ortaköy is built on a jetty surrounded on three sides by the sea. The quality of the architecture is so poor and the materials so inferior that it is in continual danger of collapse.

During the reign of Sultan Abdülaziz (1867–76) the whole of Europe was dominated by an eclectic style made up of a mixture of all sorts of styles from Indian to Gothic. This is vividly portrayed in the Aksaray Valide Mosque built by the Queen Mother Pertevniyal Kadin in 1871. The Aziziye Mosque that Sultan Abdülaziz planned to build on the slopes at Maçka remained unfinished after his dethronement and only the foundations now remain.

One of the strangest examples of this eclectic style is the excessively ornate Hamidiye Mosque built by Sultan Abdülhamid II in 1886 within the grounds of the Yıldız Palace.

It is surprising to see that while such confusion reigned in Istanbul large monuments of traditional Turkish architecture still appeared in Anatolia. The Great Mosque at Kütahya is a good example of this. A wooden mosque on 57 timber columns begun by Bayazid I and completed by Musa Chelebi in 1410 was replaced in 1889–91 by the present-day Great Mosque of the same dimensions as the original, 46 × 26 metres. Here the two domes are placed one behind the other and are surrounded by six half-domes with a small dome in each corner. (Fig. 194.) The mihrab recess takes the form of a pentagonal projection on the outside, and is covered with a low half-dome. The portico, with its four panel vaults and the dome in the centre, may belong to the original mosque. Each of the side façades has two rows of windows and an entrance door, and is articulated by the marble pillars supporting the dome. (Fig. 195.) The interior, with its slender columns supporting the arches and the domes, imparts a powerful feeling of spaciousness and strength, and the whole building displays an architectural conception of real genius.

After the four Armenian architects of the Balyan family, who were active during the reigns of Abdülmejid and Abdülaziz, architects of Italian origin like Darenco and Valaury erected, during the reign of Abdülhamid II (1876–1909), a number of worthless buildings in a style utterly alien to Turkish taste, such as the Military Hospital (now the Haydarpaşa Lycée) on the Asiatic shore of the Bosphorus, the Public Debts building (now the Istanbul Lycée) and the buildings of the Ottoman Bank at Eminönü and Galata.

Finally the nationalist movement under the leadership of Ziya Gökalp instilled new life and vigour into art and architecture, and Turkish architects, turning their attention to the innumerable works of Turkish architecture, began a renaissance that finally brought about the birth of a Neo-classic style.

The well-known architect Kemaleddin (1870–1927), who had studied architecture in Germany, built the magnificent Vakıf Hans in Istanbul (Fig. 196), the Bostancı Mosque, the Bebek Mosque and the Kamer Khatun Mosque at Tarlabaşı, all displaying a pure, uncorrupted taste, the tombs of Sultan Mehmed V Reshad at Eyüb, the open tomb of Mahmud Shevket Pasha at Hürriyet Tepe, the Laleli apartment blocks, all in Istanbul, and the old National Assembly building and Gazi Terbiye Institute in Ankara.

The architect Vedat, who studied in Paris, built the Central Post Office at Sirkeci in Istanbul, the Deniz Bank at Karaköy (now demolished), his own house at Nişantaş, and the quay buildings at Haydarpaşa and Moda. Although several young architects have followed in the footsteps of Kemaleddin and Vedat the excessive use of old classical elements taken from religious buildings, such as pointed arches, stalactite capitals, domes and tile decoration has resulted in a degeneration of the style. With the advent of reinforced concrete the traditional forms have been abandoned and their place has been taken by a modern architectural outlook.

17

OTTOMAN TOMBS

The most characteristic development of the second half of the 14th century is the open canopy tomb, consisting of a dome resting on four arches. At the same time the Hajji Hamza Türbe in Iznik dated 1349 and built by the architect Hajji Ali, the Lala Shahin Pasha Türbe at Kırmastı dating from the last quarter of the 14th century, the türbe of Devlet Shah Khatun, the mother of Chelebi Sultan Mehmed, at Bursa dated 1412, and the Jariyeler Türbe at Muradiye are all in the form of domed structures with pyramidal conical roofs in the Seljuk tradition. The Yakub Chelebi and Saltuk Dede Türbes in Iznik are the first open tombs consisting of four arches surmounted by a dome. The Kırk Kızlar Türbe in Iznik, also dating from the 14th century, is a square structure with high walls having an unusual patterning of stone and brick, and with a dome on squinches topping a high cylindrical drum, presenting the external appearance of a low domed mausoleum. Inside there is painted decoration composed of foliate arabesques. In this tomb and the Kırmastı Lala Shahin Pasha Türbe there is a vaulted chamber in the front section. The türbe built at Iznik for Chandarlı Hayreddin Pasha, who died in 1387, and his family, is a two-domed structure.

Up to the time of Mehmed the Conqueror all the Ottoman Sultans were buried in Bursa. The türbes built in 1863 by Abdülaziz to take the place of the demolished tombs there, of Osman and Orhan Ghāzī at Tophane, have no architectural value. Similarly, in the case of the türbe of Murad I Hudavendigār, nothing of the original structure remains. The first original Ottoman royal mausoleum is the tomb of Bayazid I, which consists of a dome of 10.5 metres in diameter with prismatic triangles resting on comparatively low walls in alternate courses of two rows of brick and one of stone, and has a three-domed arcade in front with two columns and two corner piers. According to the inscription it was built by his son the Emir Süleyman Chelebi in 1406. Although it was destroyed by the Karamanids in 1414 and damaged by an earthquake in 1855 it has been repaired since and its original form restored.

The türbe of Chelebi Sultan Mehmed was completed forty days before his death in 1421, and has since undergone a number of repairs. It is an octagonal structure 20 metres in height, each side measuring 8.2 metres, with a slightly tapering dome 15 metres in diameter resting on a high drum. It takes its name—the Green Tomb—from the turquoise tiles covering the sides on the exterior. The tiles on two of the sides are original. Hajji Ivaz Pasha, the architect responsible for the whole complex, must also have been the architect of the tomb. The interior is remarkable for the magnificent tiled cenotaph of the Sultan and the other more simply tiled cenotaphs. The walls are faced up to a height of 3 metres with dark green tiles, and the tiled mihrab, one of the masterpieces of Turkish art, is to be included in the same category as the magnificent mihrabs of the Green Mosque in Bursa and the Muradiye Mosque in Edirne. All the faience decoration was the work of Naqqāsh Ilyas Ali, who was responsible for the decoration of the Green Mosque, and the master-craftsman, Muḥammad al-Majnūn. Here, as in the Green Mosque, the addition of new colours prepares the way for the development of the later naturalistic style, and the techniques of underglaze painting introduce fresh life into Turkish tile revetments. The colour and wealth of design of the tile mosaic are here reflected with great success in the tile panels. According to the inscription the walnut doors, with their richly ornamented geometrical sections, were the work of Hajji 'Alī bin Aḥmad of Tabriz.

The tomb of Sultan Murad II, situated in a garden with plane trees behind the mosque, is a very simple, modest structure with an open dome with stalactite squinches on four columns and four piers, surrounded by a low vaulted corridor. In accordance with his will the tomb was left open to the rain and to the sky, and the top of the cenotaph is covered with earth. Broken Corinthian capitals have been employed as bases for the columns. The interior of the tomb is completely devoid of decoration, but on the outside the magnificent eaves over the salient marble portal niche display woodwork of unparalleled craftsmanship, with circles and geometrical entrelacs in green, red and dark blue. A smaller tomb for the princes, again with a dome on stalactite squinches, was later added on the east side. There are eleven more tombs among the trees and flowers in the same garden, all combining to produce a calm and romantic whole. Nine of these belong to Shehzades and Sultans, whilst the tomb of Ebe Khatun, the nurse of Mehmed the Conqueror, is open with a plain dome on pillars built of alternating courses of brick and stone, and the tomb of the Saraylılar (palace servants) or Jariyeler (concubines) is an open mausoleum with two pointed arches in each face.

The plan and decoration of the octagonal tomb built for the Shehzade Ahmed, the son of Chelebi Sultan Mehmed, who died in 1429, would point to a date in the reign of Murad II. Until recent years this tomb was wrongly attributed to Shehzade Mustafa, son of Mehmed the Conqueror, and was known as the Mustafa-i Atik Türbe. The walls of the tomb are patterned in hewn stone and brick, and in front there is a three-arched marble arcade with broken arches and low eaves. The turquoise and cobalt hexagonal tiles on the walls, and the border tiles decorated with symmetrical *rūmī* and *hatayī* arabesques and scrolls in light blue on a white ground, are of high quality. The upper part of the walls is encircled by a broad Koranic inscription with scrolls and leaves on a blue ground.

The tomb known as the Jem Türbe was originally built for the Conqueror's son Shehzade Mustafa, who died in 1479. The name of the prince has even been written as 'Sultan Mustafa' in the small medallions in the painted decoration in the dome, which rests on prismatic triangles. Jem Sultan died at Naples in 1495 and it was only in 1499 that he was buried here, but as he was perhaps more famous the tomb came in time to be called after him. The exterior of the building is very plain but the interior is decorated with very rich painted ornament and rare tiles. The walls are covered with brilliant turquoise and dark blue hexagonal tiles decorated in gilt, and with borders of blue, white and turquoise *rūmī* arabesques, palmettes and interlacing scrolls on a dark blue ground. Above this the walls and the dome were adorned with *thuluth* and Kufic inscriptions in bright red, dark blue, yellow and brown, and painted decoration with palmettes, *rūmī* arabesques and foliate motifs. At a later date these decorations, having been ruined during an attempt at restoring them with dark colours, were removed altogether to reveal decorations of the end of the 15th century in azure and white on a bright scarlet ground.

The türbe of Shehzade Mahmud was built on the orders of his mother between 1505 and 1506 by the architect ʿAlī bin ʿAbd Allāh for Mahmud, the son of Sultan Bayazid II, who died in Manisa. It is an octagonal structure with a marble arcade in front, and resembles the Shehzade Ahmed Türbe in plan. The walls are richly decorated with tiles below and painted decoration above. Cobalt and turquoise hexagonal tiles framed in gilt cover the walls up to a height of 2.5 metres and the borders have *rūmī* and *hatayī* arabesques in white on blue. The painted decoration on the upper section of the walls and in the dome has been partly restored in recent centuries.

The fourth tomb with faience decoration is known as the Mustafa-i Jedid Türbe. According to the written records the tomb was built a little after 1513 for Ahmed, Shahinshah and Korkud, the three brothers of Selim I. The tomb was given its present name when Shehzade Mustafa, the son of Süleyman the Magnificent, was buried here in 1552. To differentiate between the tombs of Mustafa the son of the Conqueror and Mustafa the son of Süleyman the Magnificent the former was known as the Mustafa-i Atik Türbe and the latter as the Mustafa-i Jedid Türbe. It is identical with the others in style, and is octagonal in plan with brick and stone patterning on the walls and without an arcade. The transition to the dome is effected by arches and pendentives on flattened wall piers. According to an inscription on the door the tiles covering the walls up to a height of three metres were added by Sultan Selim II in 1574. These are amongst the finest specimens of 16th-century faience, with completely naturalistic representation of hyacinths, tulips, carnations, peonies and pomegranate blossoms in red, blue and green on a white ground. The designs on the borders are on a dark blue ground. A wide inscription band encircles the upper edge with the Ayyat al-Kursī (the Verse of the Throne) in white on a dark blue ground. In recent years the white plaster has been removed to reveal old painted decoration. The other tombs in the Muradiye Cemetery are in the same style but although some of them have a richer external appearance they have no faience decoration. In some of them old painted decoration has been uncovered.

The decagonal tomb of Sultan Mehmed the Conqueror and the octagonal tomb of his wife Gülbahar Khatun stand behind the mihrab wall of the mosque among the other buildings of the Fatih complex in Istanbul. These were destroyed in the earthquake of 1765 and rebuilt in 1766 on what remained of their lower portions according to the original plan but with

Baroque influences clearly seen in the windows. The wide eaves of the tomb of the Conqueror were added at the end of the 18th century. Three of the tombs dating from the reign of Mehmed and the later 15th century are noteworthy from the architectural point of view. These are the tombs of Mahmud Pasha and Davud Pasha in Istanbul and the tomb of Rum Mehmed Pasha at Üsküdar. The tomb of Mahmud Pasha, which was erected by the side of his own mosque in 1473, is an octagonal structure in hewn stone with a very striking exterior of tile inlay of cobalt and turquoise. This decoration is a continuation of the inlaid tile decorations in the marble frames of the windows of the Green Mosque in Bursa, and the ornamental motifs include intersecting duodecagons as well as eight-, five- and four-pointed stars. Apart from the mouldings on the edges there are mouldings surrounding the lower and upper windows in the form of a long rectangle. The entrelacs resemble those in the mihrab of the Great Mosque at Sinop and continue the Seljuk tradition. In the latest repairs these have been replaced by a plain door.

The tombs of Davud Pasha and Rum Mehmed Pasha are plain octagonal structures of hewn stone set behind their mosques. In the Davud Pasha Türbe (1485) the centre of the lunettes of the lower windows resembles a broken arch in the form of a multicentric pointed arch. The upper windows have pointed arches. In front there is a single-domed arcade with two columns and lozenge-patterned capitals.

The Rum Mehmed Pasha Türbe (1471) has a very plain exterior with slightly pointed arches on the lower windows and squat pointed arches on the windows above.

The türbe of Sultan Bayazid II, who died in 1512, was erected on the south side of the Mosque of Bayazid by his son Selim I. The türbe is octagonal in plan, built of hewn stone and, as in the Bursa türbes, the dome rests on a blind octagonal drum. Each of the eight sides is surrounded by mouldings of green marble and there are windows in both the lower and upper sections. As a result of its harmonious proportions the türbe achieves a very simple, noble architectural effect and must have been the work of the architect Khayr al-Dīn. The eaves in front of the building and the painted decoration in the interior are later additions. The tomb of his daughter Seljuk Khatun at the side is a smaller and plainer octagonal structure in the same style.

The tomb of Sultan Selim I was built behind the Mosque of Sultan Selim by his son Sultan Süleyman the Magnificent. The türbe is a marble octagonal building with a squat fluted dome on a low drum resembling the türbes of Sinan (the dome of the Shehzade Türbe is also fluted), but it is less mature and developed in style than these. It has a portico in front with three round arches supported on three columns. The faience panels adorning the walls on each side of the door show a return to Seljuk motifs with geometrical star entrelacs on wide borders. In the centre there is a yellow, white and pale red design in polychrome underglaze technique with large *rūmī* and small *hatayī* arabesques, palmettes and lotus motifs on a cobalt ground. In the narrow borders fine Chinese cloud motifs can be seen for the first time. In the inscription on the panel on the right the date 929/1523 can be seen written in words.

The Shehzadeler Türbe nearby built by Süleyman the Magnificent for the princes of his family consists of a squat dome with round drum on an octagonal body. In front there is a low portico with plain eaves on four columns, and tiles with hexagonal star patterns arranged alternately side by side and one above the other have been sunk into the walls on each side of the door. The side of the octagon carrying the portico is slightly salient.

Sultan Süleyman the Magnificent is buried in a türbe built by Sinan in the Süleymaniye complex. By means of various innovations the architect Sinan attempted to reflect the individual personality of the Sultan or Vizir in the architecture of their türbes, but a very difficult situation arose in the case of the Royal tombs, as their relatives and other sultans were buried in the same tomb. Sometimes, as in the cemetery of St. Sophia, three marble tombs belonging to three sultans, father, son and grandson, stand side by side. The architects responsible for these also succeeded one another as master, journeyman and apprentice. In the middle tomb built by Sinan in 1577 for Selim II the son of Süleyman the Magnificent, the dome rests on an inner octagon composed of eight columns and arches, whilst on the outside it is placed on a solid pile in the form of a square with truncated corners. It was constructed as a double-domed building with the inner dome resting on columns and the outer on the walls. Inside, the walls are entirely covered with Iznik tiles of the highest quality, with naturalistic flower and leaf patterns, verse inscriptions and a band of *thuluth* inscription. It has a three-arched portico with a dome in the centre and low eaves at the sides. Forty-four people were later buried in this tomb. The tile panel on the left-hand side of the door was later removed and is now in the Louvre.

The hexagonal tomb built by Sinan's apprentice Davud Agha for Murad III in 1599 stands to the west of this. It has a double dome, the inner dome resting on six columns and the outer dome on the exterior walls. Both sides of the door and all the walls inside are covered with rich tiles. Inside, the designs consisting of palmettes, *rūmī* and *hatayī* arabesques and naturalistic flowers in cobalt and turquoise, with red and green as the dominating colours, are bordered above the windows by an inscription course in white letters on a cobalt ground. The dome still preserves the original painted decoration. Forty-nine people have been buried in this tomb, 6 under large cenotaphs, 43 under small. There is a portico in front. A small Princes' Tomb has been added to the west edge of the portico.

The türbe of Mehmed III, to the east of these, was begun by the Diver Ahmed Agha and completed by Sedefkar Mehmed Agha in 1608. Both the interior and the exterior of the mausoleum are octagonal in form, the inner dome resting on eight columns and the outer dome on the walls. Thus, although all three türbes start off from the same basic principles in each of them the architect has employed different forms to produce his own distinctive style. In this last tomb there is no ceramic decoration outside in the portico, but inside, as in the other türbes, the walls are covered with tiles, though their quality is very poor, and the colours are pale. Painted decoration is more sparingly used and differs from the other tombs in employing foliate motifs.

The large tomb built within the Sultan Ahmed complex in 1619, three years after the completion of the mosque, is a square structure entirely faced with marble, and roofed with a high dome on a blind drum. There is a three-arched portico extending the whole length of the front façade. On entering the door with its mother-of-pearl inlay one is struck by the tiles adorning the intervals between the windows, and a Koranic inscription course on a blue ground. The architect Mehmed Agha has conceived a well-lit, spacious chamber with many windows. Here, thirty-six people are buried, including the Ottoman Sultans Osman II and Murad IV, as well as the founder Ahmed I and his wife Hasseki Kösem Sultan. The domed structure behind the tomb is a Dār al-Qirā' (a building for readers of the Koran).

The türbe built beside the Yeni Cami for the Valide Turhan Sultan at the end of the century (1682) is a square structure with a dome resting on eight arches, and with a fine three-arched portico in front with a dome in the centre and one panel vault on each side. The walls of the portico and the interior of the tomb are covered with tiles, the colours of which have now faded. The walls of the exterior are faced with marble and pierced by three rows of windows. Apart from Turhan Hatije Sultan five Ottoman Sultans are buried in this tomb—Mehmed IV, Mustafa II, Ahmed III, Mahmud I and Osman III. Two small türbes have been built adjoining this and Murad V is buried in one of these türbes entered by a door at the side. At the beginning of the 18th century the traditional style was continued both in türbes and the mosques (e.g. the Yeni Valide Mosque at Üsküdar, 1710, and the Hekimoghlu Ali Pasha Mosque, 1734) but towards the middle of the century mausolea began to be built in a Baroque style. The one built together with the Mosque of Nur-u Osmaniye in 1755 is the earliest of these. It has a square plan with the corners softened in the form of towers and a three-arched portico in front with round arches. The dome on pendentives rests on round Baroque arches with an outward projection in the form of eaves. The walls are of marble but as a result of their bad workmanship are now in a much ruined condition. The tomb was intended for Mahmud I, who began the mosque, and for Osman III, who completed it, but as they were both buried in the Yeni Cami türbe, it was finally used for the burial of Shehsuvar Sultan, the mother of Osman III. Inside there is a broad inscription band above the windows, and, above this, Baroque painted decoration as far as the dome.

The Koja Raghib Pasha türbe, dated 1762, and standing in the courtyard of his own library at Laleli, was built as an open tomb on a hexagonal plan with low round arches on columns, but the original form has been altered during subsequent repairs.

The tomb of Mustafa III beside the Laleli Mosque, dated 1773, is a decagonal structure with a wide, three-arched portico in front embracing three sides of the building. The interior and exterior of the tomb is decorated with acanthus leaves in a Baroque style. Inside, a broad inscription band encircling the upper part of the wall, tapering oval medallions in 16th-century style covering the walls between the windows, brightly coloured naturalistic carnations and tulips, and border tiles with Chinese clouds, *rūmī* arabesque and palmette designs form a strange contrast with the Baroque decoration. Selim III was later buried here by the side of his father.

The türbe of Abdülhamid I was built at Bahçekapı in 1789 by the architect Mehmed Agha in a corner of the complex, several parts of which have now been demolished. It is a square, marble structure with slightly chamfered corners. The dome rises from an octagonal drum and inside is set up on arches. Apart from small, delicate Baroque *çeşmes* adorning two sides of the softened angles, the façade of the mausoleum, with its two rows of windows, is dominated by pure, classical lines. The architectural details of the grand three-arched portico in front, with its eight columns and capitals, display a restrained Baroque style. Inside there is a broad inscription band and Baroque painted decoration in the dome. Mustafa IV was buried in this tomb beside his father.

The marble türbe standing in the complex at Eyüb consisting of a medrese, *çeşme*, sebil and library, and built for Selim III's mother Mihrishah Sultan in 1792, is a duodecagonal—almost circular—structure. It has a harmonious style with Baroque features, such as double-storeyed colossal columns at the corners, two rows of windows with undulating arches, cornices and the voluted flying buttresses surrounding the dome. Inside, at the corners there are white marble pilasters, and, above these, a broad inscription band, broken, stepped cornices and Baroque acanthus ornament. At the entrance there is a portico. The Tomb of Mihrishah displays a pure, harmonious, mature Baroque style.

The circular türbe of Selim III's sister Shah Sultan built at Eyüb in 1800, together with a sebil and a school, by the architect Ibrahim Kamil Agha, is inharmonious and ungainly in its proportions. With its four large external arches and its four decorative corner towers it has a deceptive, square shape that conceals the form of the interior. But here the lively façades with their convex and concave lines, the large arches which lean slightly forward like light eaves, and the whole building, with its long oval windows on the upper storey and undulated arch windows on the lower, displays a powerfully developed Baroque style. The Baroque *çeşme* on the façade facing the street, with its acanthus decoration and inscription, resembles the *çeşme* in the türbe of Abdülhamid I. In front there is a portico roofed by three small domes set on eight columns, whilst inside there is a broad inscription band and Baroque painted decoration.

The marble türbe built together with a school, a sebil and courtyard in 1817 in the cemetery in the Fatih Mosque for Nakshidil Sultan, the wife of Abdülhamid I and the mother of Mahmud II, is a two-storeyed building on a circular plan. There is a column between each of the lower windows and a pier between each of the oval windows on the upper storey, whilst the lightly fluted dome resting on a high drum is surrounded by buttresses and turrets. Although the türbe possesses a harmonious Baroque style, with its curved lines, broken cornices and double acanthus leaves on the capitals, indications of the advent of the Empire style are to be seen in the swags over the oval windows. (Fig. 197.) In front there is a portico with a dome in the centre and transverse vaults on each side, all supported on eight columns. Inside there is a broad inscription band on the drum of the dome, and Baroque and Rococo ornament covers the whole dome from above the oval windows. The inscriptions on the türbe and the *çeşme* are the work of the celebrated calligrapher Rakim and his elder brother Ismail Zühtü Efendi. In the tomb, in addition to Nakshidil Sultan, are buried Jevri Kalfa, who saved Mahmud II's life, and the Sultanas Mihrimah, Adile, Munire and Fatma, together with princes and favourites.

The tomb of Sultan Mahmud II, which was built by the Sultan himself on the Divan Yolu in 1840, is a marble-faced structure entirely in Empire style. There is also a cemetery façade with round arched doors and windows along the street side and a sebil in the centre. (Fig. 198.) The octagonal tomb has a very spectacular interior. Besides Mahmud II, Abdülaziz and Abdülhamid II were also buried here.

The tomb of Abdülmejid is in the cemetery of the Mosque of Sultan Selim, whilst the tomb of Mehmed V Reshad is a small domed building in Neo-classical style built by the architect Kemaleddin.

The octagonal tomb of Fuad Pasha near Sultan Ahmed, dated 1869, is in a mixed style resembling that of the Valide Mosque at Aksaray in Istanbul. The horseshoe arches and the plaster decoration covering the whole of the walls are in a sort of Moroccan style completely alien to Turkish architecture. The tomb built by Kemaleddin at Hürriyet Tepe in Istanbul in 1909 for Mahmud Shevket Pasha is an open tomb with a dome and four arches on four columns with stalactite decoration on the outside, and shows a return from the mixed style, which had never become assimilated, to the pure classical Turkish style.

18

OTTOMAN PALACES AND KIOSKS

From the information given by Hammer and Texier it appears that the first palace was built in Bursa. In 1832 Texier visited the ruins of this palace which had taken the form of a number of pavilions set amidst gardens. This palace at Bursa was burned to the ground by the armies of Timur.

The buildings of the Edirne Palace and Topkapı Palace were scattered over a wider area, but as there was no change in the court ceremonies the distribution of the buildings was kept the same. The palace at Edirne consisted of kiosks or pavilions, harem apartments and various offices grouped around large courtyards entered through wide gates. Today the site of the palace is a field and apart from the bridges only four ruins remain as melancholy relics of the past. These consist of fragments of the walls of the Cihannuma Pavilion, the most spectacular of all the buildings of the Old Palace, the remains of the single-domed bath of the Kum Pavilion beside it, and the large, round-arched gate to the left known as the Bab al-Saʿāda or Gate of Felicity. A ruin with eight domes is the Matbah-i Amire (the Palace Kitchens). Another ruin consists of the towers from the Adalet Köşk (pavilion of justice) built by Süleyman the Magnificent.

This palace, which began with the kiosk built by Sultan Murad II in the Sarayiçi (Inner Palace) on the banks of the river Tunca, developed in the course of time into a congeries of buildings that was to be taken as the model for the Topkapı Palace in Istanbul. Various kiosks and pavilions were added to the palace by every Sultan in every period and finally, in 1828, during the reign of Mahmud II, it underwent extensive repairs, only to be sacked during the Russian invasion of the same year. In 1873 the Governor Hajji Izzet Pasha had it repaired for the occasion of Abdülaziz's return from Europe and had photographs taken of it. During the Russian War of 1878 the ground floor of the Cihannuma Pavilion and the apartments surrounding the square on which the Divanhane (audience chamber) stood were converted into ammunition depots, and later, as the Russian armies were approaching Edirne, on an order given as a result of a misunderstanding between the Governor, Jemil Pasha, and the Commander, Ahmed Eyüb Pasha, the depot was set on fire and blown up, with the result that the palace apartments burned for days afterwards. Attempts to restore the remaining sections of the palace were without result, and the pavilions were demolished one by one and the materials used in the construction of barracks and other buildings.

As the first palace built by Sultan Mehmed the Conqueror on the site of the main buildings of the present-day Istanbul University in Bayazid Square has completely disappeared, it is possible to get only a very slight idea from 16th- and 17th-century engravings, and from a map of the water conduits of the city in the 19th century.

The Conqueror later constructed a few kiosks on the Zeytinlik Hill in Istanbul at the present-day Seraglio Point, and in the course of time, between 1474 and 1479, these buildings were gathered together into an architectural composition based on the lay-out of the Edirne Palace to form the basis of the present-day Topkapı Saray. The palace area covers 700,000 square metres and is protected on the land side by the Sur-i Sultani (imperial wall) 1400 metres in length joining the Byzantine sea walls on the Marmara to the Golden Horn, and strengthened by 28 towers. The Topkapı Saray consists of pavilions or kiosks, mosques, audience chambers, state apartments, libraries, barracks and other buildings surrounding four courtyards arranged one behind the other, and has assumed its present form by the addition of various groups of buildings such as kitchens, harem apartments, *çeşmes* and gardens at various different periods. It has thus become a living museum gathering together in itself the richest collection of Ottoman ceramics and decorative arts of every period from the time of the Conqueror onwards. The Çinili Köşk (the tiled pavilion), dated 877/1472, which occupies the first courtyard, and the Kiosk of the Conqueror, the present-day Hazine or treasury of the palace, are among the oldest and the most important architectural monuments in the style of Mehmed the Conqueror's reign. In the Tiled Pavilion the lay-out of a traditional Turkish house is translated into the monumental scale of a palace. It is a two-storeyed palace with four iwans opening into the large domed central chamber, and a room with a dome of the same diameter in each of the four corners. Four successive domed chambers are arranged on the main axis leading from the entrance, that at the far end being defined on the exterior by a five sided projection. The façade opens on to the exterior in the form of a portico with high pointed arches on slender columns extending the whole length of the front. (Fig. 199.) The large iwan in the centre of the entrance façade is entirely covered with faience mosaic, and displays the full magnificence of the Seljuk tradition. One cannot help noticing the obvious resemblance to the Great Iwan of the Sırçalı Medrese in Konya (see Plate I). The extremely intricate *thuluth* inscription is written in white lettering on a cobalt ground. A verse inscription of four couplets above this is in yellow. Other colours of the faience mosaic are turquoise, cobalt, green and white, varied here and there with brown. This is the last occurrence of faience mosaic in Ottoman architecture. (Plate II.) The hexagonal tiles, fireplaces and book-niches covering the walls of the rooms show the influence of the architecture of Bursa and Edirne. The hexagonal turquoise tiles are decorated with various delicate motifs in gilt, including Chinese cloud-scrolls, palmettes, *rūmī* and *hatayī* arabesques, whilst the interstices are filled with triangular cobalt tiles.

Here, however, the triangular tiles are arranged in a circular form surrounding each hexagon:

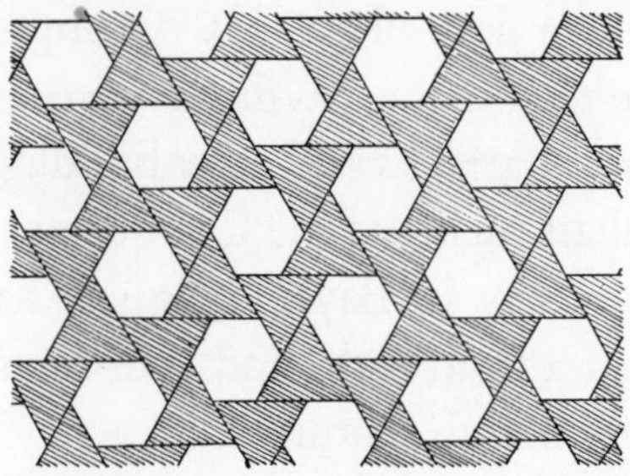

The dome of the room at the far end, which forms a five-sided projection, is entirely covered inside with embossed *rūmī* arabesque and palmette decoration, and the dome of the corresponding room in the lower storey is decorated in the same way. The side façades, each of which has an iwan in the centre, also have tile courses, and the rear façade has glazed brick and tile decoration. The plan of the lower storey is an almost exact replica of the plan of the upper storey. Every part of the Çinili Köşk points to the influence of Seljuk and old Turkish architecture, though the building remains unique in Ottoman architecture. The structure of the central dome with its stalactite decoration and the squinches heightened in the form of towers suggests influence from Central Asia, of Karakhanid and Timurid architecture. It is now the Museum of Turkish Ceramics.

The Kiosk of the Conqueror or the Treasury on the east side of the third courtyard is in a simpler, more dignified style. It is constructed against the length of the courtyard, consisting of a chamber with a fireplace and a section with two domes side by side, a portico 41×9 metres with nine rounded arches on columns extending the whole length of the front, a loggia on the left opening out through two arches on each of two sides, and a room in front of this occupying a corner of the portico. The loggia in the centre has a lobed pool carved from a single block of marble with a fountain in the centre, and the view of the Marmara from it must be one of the most beautiful in the world. A door in the left corner opens into lavatories. The rear façade is comparatively plain with very few windows, though its monotony is relieved by the arches of a loggia together with a marble bay window resting on four boldly projecting brackets with decoration in high relief in the corner of the room containing a fireplace, with three broken arches in front and one on each side. The large stone brackets of the bay window derive from the projecting upper storeys of wooden Turkish houses. The domed chamber to the far right was built as the tepidarium of the adjoining bath, the door into which was blocked up at a later date. A door in the right-hand corner of the first domed room leads down to a basement beneath the kiosk by a staircase in the thickness of the wall. (Plan 53.) From outside, at first, the rounded arches and their Ionic capitals produce a strange impression, but then, on passing under the portico, there is a change initiated by the porch niches with their broken arches and their pointed arched windows, and a familiar atmosphere begins to make itself felt. Turkish architects, however, never again employed this combination of Ionic capitals and rounded arches in a portico. The kiosk is the expression of a youthful mind investigating the possibilities

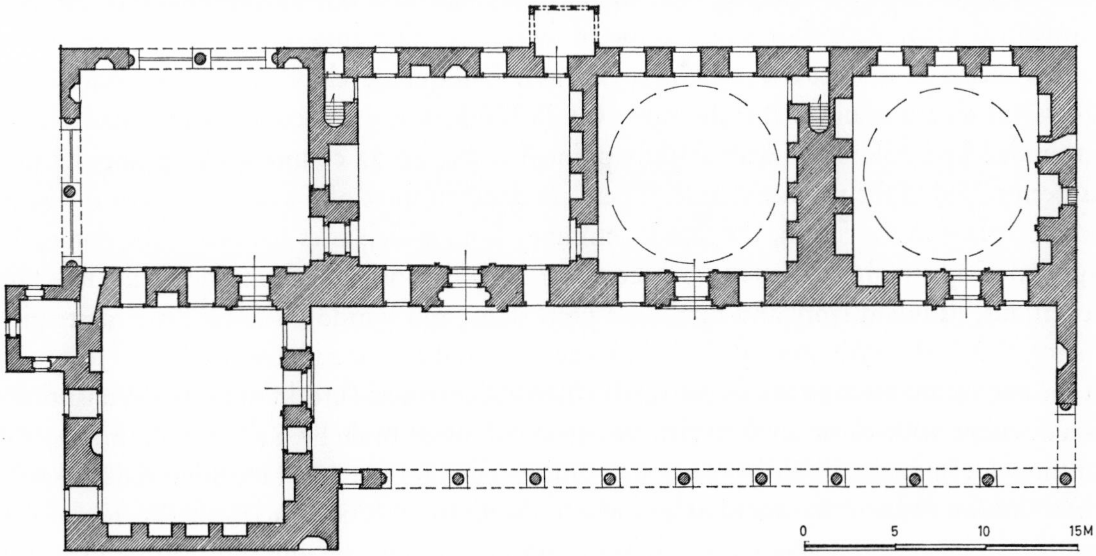

Plan 53. Istanbul, Fatih Köşk (Pavilion of the Conqueror)

of various forms with confidence and mastery. The age of the Conqueror was one in which various influences were mixed and blended.

After the other sections of the palace had been built this kiosk was converted into a treasury by Selim I, and it is now used as the treasury section of the Topkapı Saray. The two-domed Divanhane or Council Chamber where meetings of the council of state were held was built in the reign of Süleyman the Magnificent. The harem which consists of more than 200 rooms, reception rooms and baths deployed around a number of courtyards, is a separate section, and the original parts remaining from the 15th and 16th centuries have undergone considerable modifications. The apartments of Murad III, the Royal Bath and the high vaulted basement on piers with a large pool in the centre were the work of the architect Sinan, but were later altered.

In addition to the harem, the great palace kitchens were also the work of Sinan. The Revan and Baghdad kiosks dating from the 17th century are noteworthy from the architectural point of view. The Revan Köşk was built by Murad IV as a memorial of his capture of the fortress of Erevan in 1653 and the building was completed in 1636. The kiosk has an octagonal plan and is surrounded by three wooden roofed iwans opening into a central domed chamber. In the fourth corner there is a fireplace 15 metres in height. Tiles on the walls from the windows up to the eaves, and marble decoration below and the arched portico, lend the kiosk a rich external appearance, whilst inside a magnificent effect is produced by tiles covering the entire walls from the floor to the dome, embossed plaster work in the ceilings, and cupboard and window shutters inlaid with mother-of-pearl. The painted decoration in the dome, however, dates from the middle of the 19th century.

As a memorial to his second capture of Baghdad in 1638 Murad IV built a larger kiosk beside the Revan Köşk known as the Baghdad Köşk. The Sultan gave orders for the construction of the kiosk on setting out on his campaign and it was completed in 1639. Its symmetrical plan, with four wooden-roofed iwans opening into a central chamber with a dome 9 metres in diameter, can be regarded as a Baroque development of the principle that was begun on a monumental scale in the Çinili Köşk. On the outside the Baghdad Köşk is surrounded by a colonnade with slightly pointed arches on 22 columns. A rectangular room has been added to the south-east side. There are doors in three of the sides between the iwans, and a fireplace in the fourth, the slender chimney from which rises up beside the dome. The Baghdad Köşk, with its faience work covering both the inside and outside walls, its ceiling decorations, its inlaid ivory and mother-of-pearl doors and window shutters, is a masterpiece, proving that in the 17th century Turkish kiosk architecture had still lost nothing of its quality. At the edge of the terrace there is the small Iftariye Kemeriyesi (breakfast arbour) consisting of a small dome with eaves on four slender metal columns, built by Sultan Ibrahim in 1640. But the most important building erected by Sultan Ibrahim is a small room on the left known as the Sünnet Odası (circumcision chamber), dated 1641. The large tile slabs in one piece with their long verse eulogies dating from the 16th century in the windows, and on the small *çeşmes* and walls, make this room one of the most attractive corners of the Topkapı Palace.

Finally, the Mecidiye Kasrı, with its magnificent view, was built by Abdülmejid (1839–1861). This was built in the European style in the same courtyard on the side overlooking the Marmara, using as substructure an old kiosk that is thought to date from the time of the Conqueror.

The large palaces built by Abdülmejid and Abdülaziz in various parts of Istanbul were spectacular structures on the scale of European palaces totally alien to Turkish taste, and completely outside the architectural tradition that had developed in the old Turkish kiosks, mansions and villas. The largest of these is the Dolmabahçe Palace built by Abdülmejid in 1835. This was the work of the architects Hajji Emin Pasha and Serkis Balyan Usta and shows a mixture of Baroque and Empire styles. The plan of the building, which is a large-scale architectural complex, was prepared by Hajji Emin Pasha. There are spacious harem apartments, a large domed throne room, various apartments in the side wings, kitchens, a park and an Alay Köşk (parade pavilion or saluting base), as well as a theatre and a boathouse that were later demolished. The Dolmabahçe Palace was built as the Sultan's residence.

The Beylerbey Palace built by Abdülaziz in 1865 was a summer palace. The Çirağan Palace built by Abdülaziz in 1871 on the site of the old half-finished palace of Mahmud II was burned down in 1910. The Yıldız Palace, which consisted of various kiosks built throughout the course of the 19th century, was enlarged by Abdülhamid II with the addition of the Chalet, Chadır, and Malta Köşks, and was used as his residence. Abdülhamid II, who was himself a very keen and skilful carpenter, had workshops added, as well as a theatre and a rich library.

Another building, outside Istanbul, that conforms to the traditional arrangement of an Ottoman palace is a palace of 360 rooms and halls, including an audience chamber, barracks, a medrese, an arsenal, food depots, a bakery, baths, a prison, harem apartments, living quarters for the court retinue and a mosque, built on a hill at Doğu Bayazid near the Persian–Russian frontier by the son of Hasan Pasha of the Çıldıroghulları, the Vizir and commander-in-chief of Georgia in 1789, and a descendant of the Ishak Pasha who was the Ottoman governor of Georgia in 1724. Before this time the Çıldıroghulları had already built a similar place at Ahiska. The audience hall is a room 30 × 20 metres in size, with an inscription showing that the building was a summer palace, and giving the date as 1199/1784. The whole palace is dominated by the mosque, with its dome and minaret. The great porches with their pointed arches and stalactite decoration are more reminiscent of Seljuk than of Ottoman architecture. The bold naturalistic carved stone foliate decoration in high relief is, however, foreign to Turkish art and shows Caucasian influences. (Fig. 200.)

The general characteristics of old Turkish houses are more or less accurately represented by a house at Muradiye in Bursa dating from the end of the 17th century, and the Meşruta Yalı built by Amjazade Hüseyin Pasha of the Köprülü family in 1698 at Kanlıca on the Bosphorus. The house at Muradiye is a two-storeyed one with basement, set in a garden and consisting of a *selâmlik* (public rooms), harem apartments, a kitchen and two halls opening on to the garden through arches. The ceilings are decorated with geometrical entrelacs and painted decoration, and there is also painted decoration in the book-niches and cupboards. In Turkish houses the only furniture consists of low, wide divans. The floors are covered with carpets, and there are cushions on the divans. Only one room of the Meşruta Yalı remains. It has an inverted-T plan scheme with one of the arms projecting into the water, and having a wooden dome in the middle. The *divanhane* (hall) has a pool and an exquisite marble fountain in the centre, and opens out on to the Bosphorus through wide windows at hall level. The doors of the room and of the cupboards are decorated with ivory and mother-of-pearl inlay, whilst the walls have the most exquisite and harmonious painted decoration, the ceiling being richly decorated in the same style. Although it is now in a much ruined condition the Meşruta Yalı remains the finest example of old Turkish domestic architecture to have survived to the present day.

19

HAMMAMS (TURKISH BATHS) OF THE OTTOMANS

The Ottomans also made great advances in spa and *hammam*[1] architecture. The Orhan baths, the early 15th-century Hajji Hamza Hamam, and the baths of Ismāʿīl Bek with domes ornamented on the inside with stars and spiral lobes dating from the same century, are all typical in the various forms of their domes. The tepidarium of the Demirtaş Hamam in Bursa, which is generally agreed to have been built in the reign of Bayazid I, has a dome 16 metres in diameter supported on prismatic pendentives, the only example on such a large scale. The Yıldırım Hamam at Mudurnu and the *hammams* at Bolu and Bergama have spacious, richly decorated interiors. The Eski Kaplıca (an old spa or hot springs) was built by Murad I on the site of a ruined Byzantine spa at Çekirge in Bursa. Although columns, capitals and other materials from the Byzantine building were used in its construction the architect was a Turk. The Turkish spa consists of a dressing-room (apoditarium) in the form of a vestibule with two domes one behind the other, the chamber being extended by two half-domes on the east and west sides of the second dome, a cool room (tepidarium) adjoining this, with a dome on eight columns resting against the walls, and a hot room (calidarium) containing the pool of hot water. Here the dome rests on an octagon produced by columns and rounded arches in the middle of a square chamber, and the corners are filled by means of exedras. There are lanterns in the centre of all the domes which admit light, and beneath the domes of the tepidarium and the adjoining apoditarium there are pools with fountains in the centre.

The Yeni Kaplıca (new spa) erected, according to an inscription in the interior, in 960/1553 by Rüstem Pasha, the Grand Vizir of Süleyman the Magnificent, shows a more highly developed plan. After a two-domed apoditarium and a tepidarium, consisting of a dome extended on each side by two half-domes, one passes through a connecting chamber with three small domes side by side into a calidarium, containing a large pool of hot water. Here the dome is supported on eight niches in the form of pointed arched iwans arranged in a star pattern,

[1] In Arabic, ḥammam; in modern Turkish, hamam.

whilst the chamber is surrounded on the outside by four thick walls. The marble pavement is decorated with coloured stone mosaic set in geometrical star entrelacs, whilst the walls are covered with hexagonal tiles, there being seven different patterns in each niche. Amongst the tiles in the niche opposite the entrance there is an inscription in white on a cobalt ground stating that the *hammam* was built by Rüstem Pasha.

In Istanbul almost every one of the Royal foundations or 'complexes' contains a *hammam*. Of these the Mahmud Pasha Hamam was originally built as a double bath with separate accommodation for men and women, but only the men's section has survived. It consists of a monumental *apodyterium* with a large dome on stalactite squinches, and an octagonal *calidarium* surrounded by several small domes, each with a separate type of decoration. The inscription gives its date as 871/1466, which, as no Byzantine baths have survived, makes it the oldest *hammam* in Istanbul.

The baths of Bayazid were originally built as a double *hammam* and are a monumental building dating from the 16th century with a dome in the men's apoditarium over 15 metres in diameter.

Hammams leave the architect little scope for variation, so that he is obliged to follow the accepted norms, arranging the various sections in accordance with a preconceived plan. In spite of this Turkish architects managed to create original forms by finding diverse solutions to the perennial problems.

The largest *hammam* built by the architect Sinan is the Hasseki Hamam, which he built for Hürrem Sultan near the Mosque of Sultan Ahmed in 1553. Here an unusual type of double *hammam* 75 metres in length has been achieved by joining the men's and women's calidaria together by a single partition wall. Another innovation is the brick and stone patterning in the walls. The columned portico facing St. Sophia in front of the men's apoditarium is very attractive. The pavement of coloured marble in the calidarium is decorated in rich patterns of geometrical star entrelacs. (Fig. 201.) Of the various other *hammams* built by Sinan in the Topkapı Saray and in other parts of Istanbul, the Çinili Hamam (tiled *hammam*) endowed by Barbarossa (Hayreddin Pasha) at Zeyrek is noteworthy for the wooden roof of its apoditarium, its *shadırvan*, decorated in coloured marble, and the tile decoration covering the walls of the calidarium. The Çifte Hamam built by Sinan at Edirne on the orders of Sokollu Mehmed Pasha is a double *hammam* with apoditaria in the form of two large domes resting on the outer walls with bi-coloured stone patterning. The portico and the front arcades would appear to have been added later. It was normally regarded as preferable, however, to have a large number of small *hammams* in each town and quarter, rather than large central *hammams*. Most of the *hammams* built in the various parts of the Empire are still in use today. One of these is the Rudas Hamam built by Sokollu Mustafa Pasha, the Governor of Buda, in the Hungarian capital in 1566, in which the large dome 10 metres in diameter over the pool of the *hammam* rests on arches arranged in an octagon on eight green porphyry columns. Evliya Chelebi called it the 'Bath with the green columns' because of these. The Rudas Hamam, which is still in use today, is the work of a period in which the type of plan and architectural characteristics commonly shown by Turkish *hammams* had reached maturity.

20
TURKISH FORTIFICATIONS AND CASTLES IN ANATOLIA

As the cities of Anatolia, from the east westwards, were extended and improved, their walls and castles underwent extensive repairs or were completely rebuilt. The walls of Diyarbekir are among the oldest of these, and form a veritable museum with their countless inscriptions and figural relief decoration. The original walls date back to Roman times, but after the capture of the city by the Great Seljuks in 1088 they were embellished with innumerable Turkish additions and were given a predominantly Turkish character. The floriated Kufic inscriptions on the four towers built by Malik Shāh, and the restoration inscriptions on the walls of Tutush, date from this first period. On the inscription written on behalf of Malik Shāh dated 481/1088 there is a man seated cross-legged in the centre, with two kneeling bulls arranged symmetrically on each side, two quadrupeds on the outer edges and reliefs of two birds of prey with outspread wings below. On the same level as the birds there can also be seen a relief of two confronted rams. The greatest towers, however, are the work of the Artukids, who made this their capital. From 1183 onwards Muḥammad, the son of the Artukid Qarā Arslan, gave the Urfa gate its final form, whilst the Ulu Beden and Yedi Kardeş towers built by the Artukid al-Malik al-Ṣāliḥ Maḥmūd in 1208 are the finest and most spectacular of all. The enormous tower of the Ulu Beden, 25.5 metres in diameter, with a broad inscription band half way up its sides, a lion with human head on either side of a double-headed eagle above and another pair of lion reliefs below, constitutes an unforgettable monument that has come to form the symbol of the city. The inscriptions inform us that it was built by the architect Ibrāhīm bin Ja'far at the orders of the Artukid Sultan al-Malik al-Ṣāliḥ Maḥmūd. (Fig. 202.)

The Yedi Kardeş Tower (Tower of the Seven Brothers) is a tower of even greater dimensions, 27.8 metres in diameter, built by the architect Yaḥyā bin Ibrāhīm Ṣūfī on plans prepared by the Artukid Sultan al-Malik al-Ṣāliḥ Maḥmūd himself. The upper section, however, is very much ruined. It, too, is encircled half way up by a wide inscription band and here again we find the Artukid crest of a double-headed eagle with a lion on either side, above the inscription in the centre of the tower. As the tower contains seven rooms, each one lit by a loophole, it is known as the *Yedi Kardeş* (Seven Brothers). On both the right and the left of an Artukid inscription dated 1183 on the Urfa Gate there are dragon figures and on the keystone a bull's head with a ring, placed beneath the figure of a bird of prey with outspread wings worked in high relief.

The position occupied by the wall and two gates of the fortress dating from the time of the Mengüjükids, at Divriği, is more or less clear. According to their inscriptions one of the gates dates from 634/1236 and the other from 640/1242. A relief of two lions on a high polygonal tower in the inner castle is most noteworthy. Of the inner keep, however, which according to its inscription, was built in 650/1252 by Ḥusām al-Dawla wa'l-Dīn, only a few fragments of the wall attached to this tower have survived.

The citadel of Kayseri dates from the Seljuk period and is in a comparatively good state of preservation. The Yoğun Burc and the walls and towers on the south side were built by 'Izz al-Dīn Kaykā'ūs I between 1210 and 1229. The three towers of very finely squared stone were, according to the inscription that was formerly to be found there, built by 'Alā al-Dīn Kayqubād I in 1224. The city walls, which are now completely ruined, were no doubt in perfect condition in his day. Mehmed the Conqueror carried out extensive repairs to the citadel of Kayseri and in 1466 built the mosque there that bears his name.

Nothing now remains of the city walls of Konya, which were originally of a magnificence to rival the walls of Diyarbekir, save for a few sculptures and reliefs now in the museum. Von Moltke, who saw the walls in 1838, tells of the wealth of antique and Seljuk decorations and inscriptions. Figures of winged angels (Fig. 207) from either side of a gate of the city no doubt formed part of a threefold composition completed by another central figure on the centre of the arch. These walls were also decorated by a magnificent relief of a double-headed eagle, the device of 'Alā al-Dīn Kayqubād.

Of the many hundreds of castles built during the Ottoman period the most spectacular and the most advanced from the architectural point of view are the two castles of Anadolu Hisar and Rumeli Hisar on the Bosphorus. The keep of Anadolu Hisar, built by Bayazid I in 1395, is of special importance as being the first Turkish building work at Istanbul. This keep, which is known as Güzelce Hisar, was strengthened and enlarged by Mehmed the Conqueror, who surrounded it with walls and towers. The Conqueror also built the castle of Rumeli Hisar, known as Boğazkesen (the castle built to shut up the Bosphorus), immediately opposite. Rumeli Hisar, which both enhances and enlivens the shores of the Bosphorus with its architecture, covers an area of 250 × 125 metres and consists of three great towers, one of them twelve-sided and the other two cylindrical, bearing the names of Halil Pasha, Saruja Pasha and Zaghnos Pasha, and connected by outer walls 7 metres in thickness. The twelve-sided tower of Halil Pasha standing on the edge of the Bosphorus is 23.3 metres in diameter and rises to a height of 35.35 metres above sea-level. Of the two towers on the hill behind, the tower of Saruja Pasha on the right is 23.8 metres in diameter and 28 metres in height, whilst the tower of Zaghnos Pasha on the left is 26.7 metres in diameter and 21 metres in height. Of the 12 small towers arranged between these three, six are polygonal and the other six cylindrical. This magnificent work of architecture, which dominates the Bosphorus and commands one of the finest views in the world, was begun in August 1452, on the eve of the capture of Istanbul, and completed in the incredibly short space of time of four and a half months. (Fig. 203.)

Yedi Kule Hisar (the fortress of the seven towers), which might be regarded as the keep of Istanbul, was constructed by Mehmed the Conqueror in 1458 to an unusual half-star plan by adding three cylindrical towers and four connecting walls to the two towers of the triumphal arch known as the Golden Gate and two other towers in the walls built by Theodosius II in the middle of the 5th century on each side of these. The walls are 12 metres high and 5 metres thick. It is not known for exactly what purpose the Castle of the Seven Towers was constructed. For a time it was used as a treasury, and then for a long period it was used as a prison.

21

ÇEŞMES AND SEBILS

Most of the *çeşmes* and sebils built into the façades of Anatolian mosques and medreses from Seljuk times onwards still remain *in situ*. The *çeşme* of the Gök Medrese at Sivas (1272) is decorated with two-coloured stones in a trefoil niche and the corners are filled with heavy interlacing patterns in high relief. The whole is surrounded by a double border. Above there is a two-line inscription in Seljuk *naskhī*. Other examples surviving from Seljuk times are the sebils on each side of the porch of the Sahib Ata complex in Konya, built by Kalūk (Kölük) bin ʿAbd Allāh in 1258. On one of these the name of the craftsman is written in two round medallions (ʿAmal Kalūk (Kölük) bin ʿAbd Allāh, the work of Kalūk).

The simplest *çeşmes* takes the form of pointed-arched wall niches in hewn stone closed in front with an ornamental stone of marble slab decorated with reliefs or sometimes an inscription. The water flows from a spout in the middle of this slab into a trough in front. Of the innumerable *çeşmes* of this simple type that supply drinking water and water for household purposes in streets and at street corners in every town in Anatolia only a limited number possess an inscription and a date, but there is no doubt that the Turks built hundreds of these in every period. A large number of the 800 or so inscribed *çeşmes* that were known to have existed in Istanbul up to recent times have unfortunately been demolished for various reasons, though some have been removed to new sites. In the records of the Tahrir-i Emlâk (Land Registry) at the time of Murad IV 10,390 *çeşmes* are declared to have existed.

The oldest surviving Ottoman *çeşme* today is that of Davud Pasha (1485) consisting of a marble trough under a pointed-arched niche. The style of *çeşmes* changed, however, together with the buildings to which they were attached. The four-sided *çeşmes* rising up like small kiosks in the middle of public squares are monumental in appearance. These have fountains and decorations on one or several of the façades. Two-sided fountains are sometimes known as *çatal çeşmes* (double or forked *çeşmes*).

Innumerable fountains in Istanbul are connected to the water conduit built by Sinan on the orders of Süleyman the Magnificent. In the course of time the conduits and arches of the aqueducts that had brought water from considerable distances into the city from the time of Valens (364–78) onwards had fallen into ruin. As the population of the city had greatly increased since the Roman period Sinan ensured a plentiful water supply by building, in the course of ten years (1554–64), a reservoir and a number of aqueducts—the Bend Aqueduct, the Uzun Aqueduct, the Muğlava Aqueduct, the Güzelce Aqueduct and the Müderris Köy Aqueduct, which together cost the treasury as much as the whole of the Süleymaniye complex. The Muğlava Aqueduct is 35 metres in height and 257 metres in length. The old aqueduct, which had been destroyed in a hurricane, was rebuilt by Sinan, and is a masterpiece from the point of view of technique and architecture. The water installations were supplied from several dams. The water in the Kırkçeşme (forty fountains) network is brought from the Forest of Belgrade and Kemerburgaz and taken to Eğrikapı by way of the slopes of Eyüb. The water for the Beyoğlu district was brought from dams built by Sultan Mahmud I at Bahçeköy by way of Maslak, and distributed from the large waterworks at Taksim (it was from this that Taksim (partition or division) Square took its name). The most recent installation was the Hamidiye (Kağıthane) network constructed with iron pipes by Abdülhamid II in 1904, to meet the requirements of Beyoğlu and the European shores of the Bosphorus.

The number of *çeşmes*, sebils, *shadırvans* and cisterns increased rapidly together with these supply networks. The *shadırvans* in the courtyards of mosques and medreses were elegant, attractive little square or polygonal kiosks covered with a dome or a roof and surrounded with columns or piers with marble or metal grilles between them. The first specimens were the 14th-century sebils known as *sabīl kuttābs*, combinations of a public fountain and a small Koran school, to be seen in Cairo and dating from the Mamluk period. These are in the form of windows in arched pavilions surrounded by metal grilles enlivening the architecture of the façades of various buildings or complexes. Water and, on certain days, sherbet were distributed to passers-by from copper bowls. Another richly ornamented type of *çeşme*, known as a selsebil, was used to embellish parks and gardens. In the selsebil, rows of small troughs are arranged one above the other, and the water flows from one to the other like a small waterfall into the pool or large trough in the foreground of view. Selsebils were particularly popular in the Baroque period, and assumed various attractive forms amidst trees and flowers in the gardens of the *yalıs* and kiosks on the Bosphorus.

Sebil architecture in Turkey did not make its appearance until the second half of the 16th century but its most brilliant development is to be seen at the end of the 17th century, from the Lâle (Tulip) Period onwards. Then sebils assumed a variety of forms and were to be found on façades, at street corners or as independent structures, but most of them have now completely disappeared. A typical example of a simple style 16th-century sebil is the corner sebil with five rectangular windows and a dome with wide eaves above, which Sinan built adjoining the lower corner of his own tomb. After that built by Sinan we find the Koja Sinan Pasha Sebil built by the architect Davud Agha in 1594 at Çarşıkapı, a fully developed classical example, the main lines of which prevailed for a very long time, practically up to the Lâle (Tulip) Period. Of other sebils in a similar style we may mention the Gazanfer Agha Sebil (1613) at the foot of the Bozdoğan (Valens) Aqueduct, the Kuyuju Murad Pasha Sebil in the quarter of Vezneciler (1606), the Bayram Pasha Sebil at Hasseki (1635), the sebil attributed to Sultan Ibrahim in the corner of the tombs at St. Sophia (1648), the Merzifonlu Kara Mustafa Pasha Sebil at Çarşıkapı (1684) and the Amjazade Hüseyin Pasha Sebil at Saraçhanebaşı. The projecting corner sebil with five windows of the Nevşehirli Ibrahim Pasha complex at Şehzadebaşı (1720) is a magnificent piece of work reflecting the rich and distinctive style of the Tulip period and later came to be accepted as a model for other sebils.

A new development in *çeşme* and sebil architecture is to be seen in the reign of Sultan Ahmed III. The monumental fountain with a sebil at each of the four corners and a *çeşme* on each of the four sides built by Sultan Ahmed III behind St. Sophia and in front of the outer gate of the Topkapı Saray is a masterpiece of fountain architecture. (Fig. 204.) At the sides of the *çeşme* on each face there are seating recesses resembling mihrab niches, whilst the sebils on the corners are screened by metal grilles. The whole is covered by a roof resembling a truncated pyramid with five small domes and wide eaves. Amongst the ornament completely covering the walls and the eaves can be seen several new motifs imported from Europe. Apart from gilt decoration, coloured stone inlay, tiles and stone relief work, there are verse eulogies written by the poet Seyyid Vehbi. The chronogram composed by Ahmed III himself—'Open with a *basmala*, drink the water, and say a prayer for Ahmed Khan'—gives the date as 1141H., i.e. 1728 A.D.

Sultan Ahmed built another large public fountain, richly decorated in the same style, at the landing-stage in Üsküdar, but here the corner sebils are replaced by small, elegant *çeşmes*. The magnificent public fountain beside the landing-stage at Tophane, covered all over with decorative stone reliefs, was built by Mahmud I in 1731 as a successor to these.

Although the public fountain built by Saliha Sultan, the mother of Mahmud I, at Azapkapı in 1733 is another work belonging to the same group, it has a sebil jutting out from one side only with a *çeşme* on each side. The other three faces are plain.

The Bereket Zade Çeşme built by the Minister of Finance Mehmed Efendi at Galata in 1732 during the reign of Sultan Mahmud I is a single façade fountain remarkable for the wealth of its decoration and for its long inscription. There are two small and very elegant *çeşmes* higher up on each side of the large central fountain.

The most spectacular examples, however, in Istanbul are the three-sided sebils in Baroque style. Amongst these may be counted the Hajji Emin Agha Sebil dated 1644 at Dolmabahçe, in which Corinthian columns are used for the first time. The Koja Yusuf Pasha Sebil dated 1787 at Kabataş, which was removed from its original position and set up first against the façade of the Molla Chelebi Mosque at Fındıklı, and finally in its present position in front of a terrace wall, is an original example with two small windowed sebils on each side of a central *çeşme*. The Valide Mihrishah Sebil at Eyüb, dated 1796, can also be included in this group.

The Nakshidil Valide Sultan Sebil dating from 1809, at Fatih in Istanbul, is in very animated style. The semicircular sebil with metal grilles and a dome resting directly on columns without any arches in the centre of the façade of the cemetery where the *türbe* of Mahmud II is situated is one of the most successful examples of the Empire style.

22

ENGRAVED AND RELIEF DECORATION, FIGURAL RELIEFS, IN TURKISH ART

The palmettes and *rūmī* arabesques, and the various geometrical patterns produced by the intersection of octagons and hexagons that appeared in Karakhanid, Ghaznevid and Great Seljuk architecture of the 11th and 12th centuries, continued, as we have seen, to be employed in Seljuk and Ottoman art in Anatolia until the beginning of the 16th century. In the Ghaznevid Ribāṭ-i Māhī dated 1019 the spaces between the octagons and other geometrical patterns in the fourfold braid motifs produced by intersecting octagons, each alternate octagon having one side broken, are filled by slender scrolls, and the decorative use of Kufic script adorned with palmettes, foliate arabesques, and scrolls displays a sound brick and terracotta technique as early as the beginning of the 11th century (see Design Ib). As for the Karakhanids, the brick decorations on the porch of the tomb of Nāṣir bin ʿAlī, dated 1012, at Uzgend display the almost contemporary use of the fourfold braid motifs produced by the intersection of half octagons and palmettes, lotus and foliate arabesque compositions, and, in the squinches, of a bevelled style recalling that of Sāmarrā (Design Ia). In other Karakhanid tombs dated 1152 and 1186 at Uzgend a rich and brilliant development can be observed in Kufic and *naskhī* script, and in the now very much more varied geometrical and foliate ornament in brick and terracotta. In Karakhanid monuments of the 12th century at Bukhara the same geometrical decorative patterns were employed in brick and terracotta.

On the other hand, the embossed lettering and carved arabesques joined by fine scrolls between human and animal figures, the palmettes, arabesques and lotus flower reliefs on the marble slabs covering the brick walls of the palace, and the Kufic friezes in the Ghaznevid style, which are all to be seen on the marble slabs unearthed during the Bombaci–Scerrato excavations carried out on the 12th-century palace of Sultan Masʿūd III at Ghazne, all display the working in marble of more highly developed, intricate forms. At Ghazne during the same period, as in the minaret of Sultan Masʿūd III for example, brick and terracotta also continue in even more finely detailed forms.

Fourfold braid motifs produced by intersecting octagons and other geometrical patterns produced by intersecting hexagons in the Great Seljuk monuments of the 12th century were plentifully used in the Kharraqān mausolea dated 1067 and 1093, together with rich brick and terracotta decorations consisting of Kufic and *naskhī* script in compositions of stars, swastikas and various geometrical forms (see Design Ic). These were later used as a continual source in the stone, brick, woodwork and faience decorations of the Anatolian Seljuks.

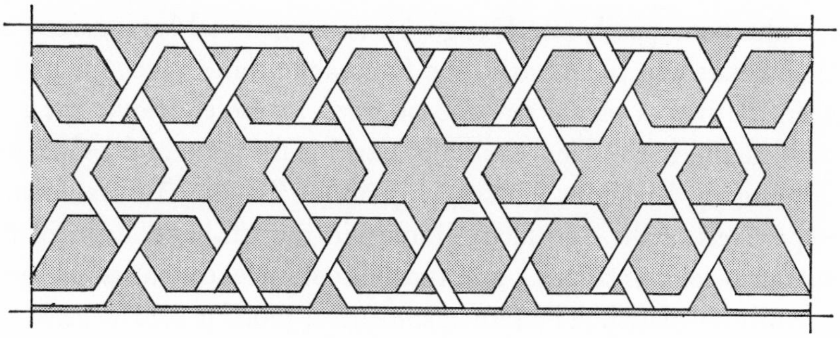

Design Ic. Kharraqān Tomb, 1067–8, porch façade

The stucco decoration of the Seljuk mosques built in the towns of Gulpayagan, Qazwin, Zaware and Ardistan in Iran in the first half of the 12th century, and the decoration in mausolea and other structures, particularly in the Ribāṭ-i Sharaf Caravansarai, led the way, after a brilliant development, to Seljuk decoration in Anatolia. The geometrical designs produced in brick and terracotta by various combinations of hexagons and octagons in the Yūsuf bin Kuthayyir (1162) and Mu'mine Khātūn (1186) tombs at Nakhichevan show that these made their way into Anatolia by the northern road (see Design Ie). In the south other Seljuk motifs passed from the Atabeks of Iraq into Anatolia by way of the Zengids. Geometrical designs worked in stone on the porch of the Mengüjükid mosque, dated 1180, in the castle of Divriği in Northern Anatolia take the form of braid motifs produced by the intersection of elongated hexagons (see Design 3). In the niche arch of the side entrance, on the other hand, there is a pattern composed of horizontal and vertical rows of octagons bound one to the other by double arms extending from each side (see Design 4).

Geometrical designs composed of two concentric octagons joined by two arms extending from each side form the basis of the border decoration of the old stone mihrab dated to the end of the 12th century in the Great Mosque at Sivas, the capital of the Danishmendids (see Design 1). The border of the stone mihrab, also dating from the end of the 12th century, from the Great Mosque at Erzurum, displays a fourfold braid motif produced by intersecting octagons, but here the larger octagons are bound together in groups of four (see Design 2). In the Great Mosque at Divriği, erected by the Mengüjükids in 1228, the predominantly foliate motifs of the stone decoration can be seen as a continuation of the stucco ornament in monuments of the Great Seljuks at Hamadhān, Abarqūh and Ardistan. The geometrical pattern produced by two concentric octagons joined by two arms extending from each side on the wide border of the mihrab in the Seljuk Taş (stone) Masjid in Konya, dated 1265, follows the design of the

Danishmendid stone mihrab in the Great Mosque at Sivas. We find a similar design on the outer border of the porch in the Mengüjükid Sitte Melik Mausoleum in Divriği, dated 1195. The ornament of the mouldings surrounding the door, moreover, is connected to earlier Karakhanid and Great Seljuk designs by the fourfold braid motif produced by intersecting octagons.

In the Seljuk hospital of Kaykā'ūs at Sivas, dated 1218, designs bringing together various Great Seljuk motifs are revived in stone, brick and faience. (Design 7.) Here the use of motifs from the mausolea at Kharraqān and Nakhichevan can be seen in the intersecting hexagons on the upper edge of the stone porch (see Design 5). A geometrical composition composed of a mixture of octagons, stars and swastikas in the Kharraqān tomb (1067) is repeated here with slight variations in the niches of the ten-sided domed mausoleum over the roof. The same composition is to be found in the faience mosaic adorning the iwan of the Gök Medrese (1271) at Sivas. The intersecting hexagons (Design Id) on the Kharraqān mausoleum (1093) are repeated in the spandrels of the two facing niches in the left-hand iwan of the hospital of Kaykā'ūs in alternate hexagons of brick and turquoise faience, the interstices being filled with arabesques and scrolls on plaster. The same geometrical motif is seen worked in stone in the ornament of an angle column in the courtyard of the Çifte (Twin) Minare Medrese at Erzurum. A fourfold braid motif with intersecting octagons appears frequently in the ornament of the pointed arch and the inner border of the porch niche of the Alay Han, a Seljuk caravansarai dating from the end of the 12th century, and in early stone decoration such as the double borders of the long pointed arched niches on both sides of the porch of the Mama Khātūn tomb at Tercan. A geometrical motif produced by vertical rows of concentric octagons connected by double arms projecting from each side in the wide outer borders of the Alay Han is identical with the stone ornament in the border of the mihrab in the Taş Masjid in Konya and the portal of the Sitte Melik tomb at Divriği, and may thus be regarded as evidence for attributing the Alay Han to a date around 1192. The most characteristic motifs borrowed by the Anatolian Seljuks from the Zengids are knotted entrelacs in coloured or plain stone in the spandrels of arches of porches or niches. This decorative motif, which appears for the first time in the porch of the 'Alā al-Dīn Mosque at Konya, is also seen on the side niches of the porch of the great Sultan Han on the Aksaray road, and in a simplified form, on the east porch of the Great Mosque at Divriği, on the porch of the Karatay medrese in Konya and, with slight variations, in a number of other Seljuk monuments.

Stalactite decoration, geometrical star entrelacs and braid motifs are used with great skill and taste; but apart from such geometrical compositions, foliate motifs also underwent a very considerable development among the Seljuks. Besides exuberant forms in high relief like those depicting a naturalistic artichoke stem on the porch of the Ince Minare Medrese at Konya we find everywhere arabesques, palmettes, lotus flowers and scrolls in forms and shapes that are constantly changing in an inexhaustible joy of creation.

Another important element that is exploited to the full in architectural decoration is epigraphy. Although various forms of Kufic script (plain, plaited, floriated and geometrical) are employed from time to time the most prevalent script in Anatolian Turkish architecture is *naskhī* (Seljuk *thuluth*).

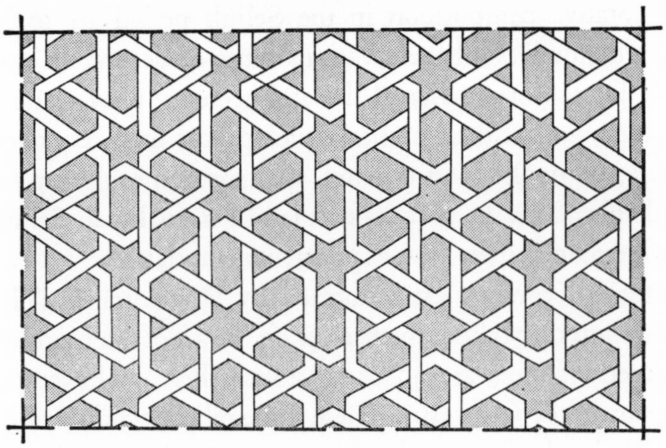

Design 5. Sivas, Hospital of Kaykā'ūs, decoration of porch

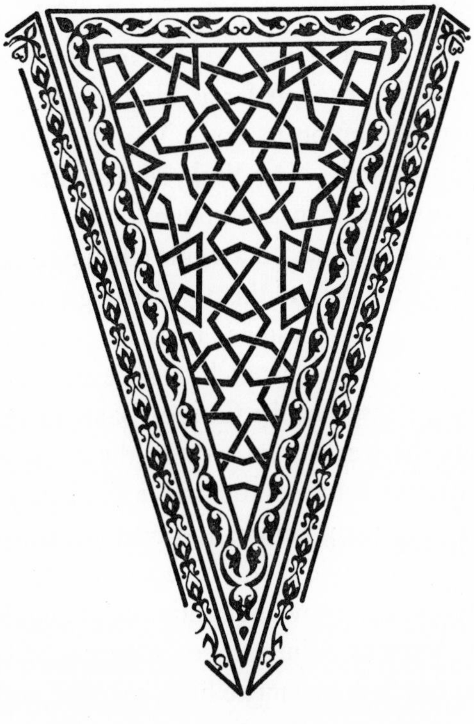

Design 6. Konya, ʿAlā al-Dīn Mosque, ceramic mosaic covering transitional zone of dome over mihrāb

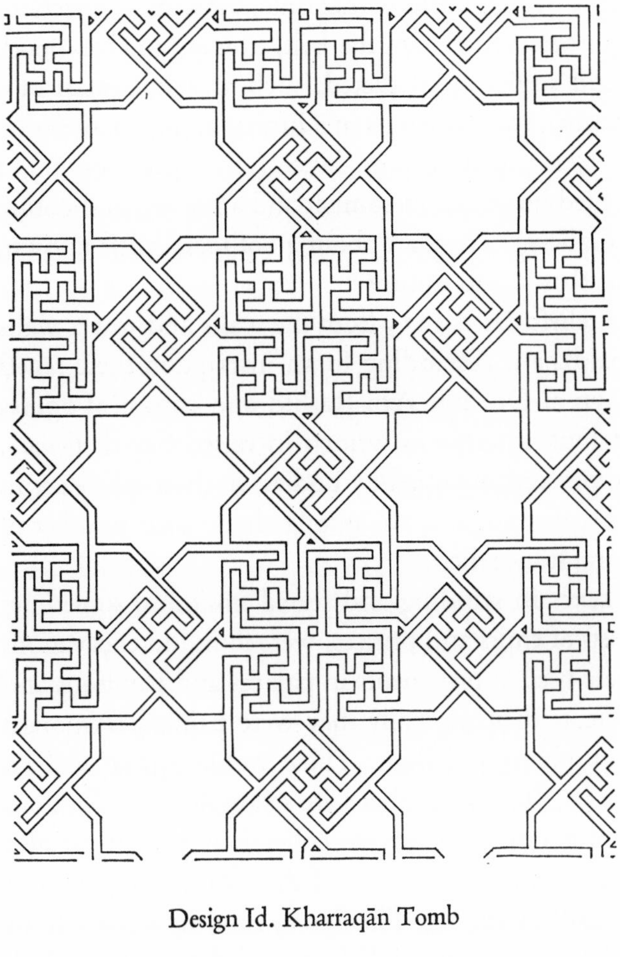

Design Id. Kharraqān Tomb

The most successful examples of decorative composition in the Seljuk period are to be found on porches, which incorporate in themselves all these various types of decoration and are very often the sole factor responsible for the originality of the architecture. They reach a monumental scale of decorative art in stone, and at their highest development they very often completely outshine the architectural base, while the twin minarets that sometimes rise up on each side add greatly to the monumental effect. It is the porches that lend personality to Seljuk mosques, medreses and caravansarais and remain as their most expressive memorials.

Another category of Seljuk architectural decorative art is formed by figural reliefs. The Anatolian Turks revived the art of figural sculpture basing themselves on the art of the Uighurs and of the Great Seljuks. The forerunners of these are 40 or so stone reliefs, architectural decoration found at Kubachi in Daghestan in the Caucasus. These stone reliefs, worked with great skill and rich artistry, were first made by the Turks when they conquered this region at the end of the 11th century, and the tradition was continued by the Turkish Atabeks of Azerbaidzhan until the middle of the 13th century. They are also particularly valuable in that they depict the everyday life and costumes of the Seljuk Turks of that time, showing connections reaching back as far as Uighur art. The short-sleeved caftan, the belt, trousers and top boots, were common to both. Various subjects and scenes are depicted, such as a horseman in a lunette arch (New York, Metropolitan Museum), two horsemen in a lunette arch, a man sitting cross-legged in a Baroque frame, two men about to wrestle or dance (all in the Louvre), a boar hunt and, on a single relief, two confronted horsemen in combat and a horseman shooting an arrow behind them (Washington, Freer Gallery). There are about 40 of these reliefs known, the rest being scattered in various museums in Russia and Europe.

The nearest parallels to these are the stone reliefs dated 1235 from the walls and tower walls of the castle in the Gulf of Baku in Azerbaidzhan. According to an inscription these reliefs are the work of an artist of the name of Zayn al-Dīn bin Abī Rashīd and consist of figures inserted between and above the letters of a long inscription written in raised Seljuk *thuluth*. The human, animal and bird heads, sometimes accompanied by bodies, in these reliefs are in the same style as the Kubachi reliefs from Daghestan, and are among the limited number of works that show the continuity of Seljuk figural stone reliefs.

Various Seljuk stucco statuettes of both sexes in standing and seated positions, sometimes as much as one metre high, together with busts of emirs and princes, were found in excavations carried out at Rayy in Iran. These figures were used as ornaments in palaces and pavilions and fragments of colour remaining on them indicate that originally they were painted. Amongst them were also found figures of sphinxes, gryphons and lions. These would appear to be a continuation of the Uighur art of sculpture in Turkestan; there are examples in collections in Teheran and Baghdad and in various museums and private collections in Europe and America. A statue of a standing man in the Worcester Museum of Art (Massachusetts) is a fine specimen of the archaic style of Great Seljuk plastic art. The figure, carrying a mace in its right hand and a handkerchief (?) in its left, is portrayed full face, and depicts the Seljuk type with conventional features devoid of all individual expression. It has long hair, and is wearing a skullcap, with a necklace round its neck. A caftan is tied at the waist with a sash with two ends hanging down, and is ornamented with a decorative design of stars and crosses which is very commonly found in Turkish art. The *ṭirāz* bands on the arms have abstract ornament instead of an inscription. (Fig. 205.) The legs of the statue are broken.

Three stucco statues in the same style in the Victoria and Albert Museum in London are portrayed full face, head-dresses richly decorated in front and hanging down at the sides in the form of a veil. The caftans are bound at the waist with a sash with the two ends hanging down, and both the figures have *ṭirāz* bands with a Kufic inscription on their arms. (Fig. 206.)

A smaller statue in the Metropolitan Museum, New York (Cora Timken Burnett Bequest), may well depict a Seljuk Emir, with his ornate and sumptuous head-dress and necklaces, a long sword hanging from his waist and rich caftan with a Kufic *ṭirāz* band. Other stucco reliefs of the Great Seljuks show very fine workmanship and are more finely detailed than these statues, and display a different kind of style in which decorative elements are very keenly stressed. A very well preserved head in the Metropolitan Museum, New York, displays a Seljuk type in all its characteristics. The main facial features are very finely modelled and the long wavy hair under the ornate head-dress is highly stylised.

Stucco relief panels found in the excavations at Rayy depict various scenes in a highly characteristic style. In an inscription on the upper edge of a panel in the Pennsylvania Museum we find the name and titles of Sultan Tughrul II, who was the Sultan of the Seljuks of Iraq in 1195. Beneath this can be seen symmetrically arranged standing figures to either side of a ruler seated on a high throne in the centre of a façade decorated with crosses and stars filled with palmettes and foliate arabesques. The Sultan is holding a glass in his right hand, while his left is resting on his knee. At the foot of the throne can be seen small elephants, dishes full of fruit, and tables. The palace scene is enlivened by cup-bearers, servants and dancers. The caftans worn over their inner garments and tied at the waist with a sash with the ends hanging down, and the short boots, are typical elements of Turkish costume. Here the style of decoration of Mosul inlaid metalwork has been translated into stucco on a large scale.

Another stucco relief found at Rayy (Stora Collection) is painted in brilliant colours deriving from ceramic decoration. The design is composed of large 8-pointed stars. In two of these there are seated figures of a man and a woman, with smaller standing and seated figures in the empty spaces behind. Above, in the centre, there is another throne scene with figures of musicians and dancers at the sides. In the top right and left corners can be seen a small piece of inscription in plaited Kufic.

In a third stucco relief in the Boston Museum containing a large composition, the figures are set in large decorative medallions arranged side by side. Three of these medallions contain a horseman, whilst the second medallion from the left contains two male dancers. On the lower edge there is a row of small reliefs forming very narrow borders with figures of leopards and greyhounds walking one behind the other. A wide border of floriated Kufic extends along the upper edge. As the background in each of the three panels is carved in the form of a fine net, the figures and motifs are very strongly defined. One can easily imagine the magnificence of the Great Seljuk palaces that were decorated with these reliefs.

In the rich art of sculpture that arose among the Anatolian Seljuks as a result of influences derived from the Uighurs and the Great Seljuks stucco was little used on account of the harsh and rainy climate, and was replaced by stone. The figural reliefs of two winged angels with ornate crowns and long tresses adorning both sides of a gate of the old city walls in Konya are now at Konya in the Ince Minare Medrese Museum. (Fig. 207.) The city walls of Konya were decorated with white marble sculptures, reliefs, verse inscriptions, talismans and fabulous beasts, together with a number of antique statues and reliefs. Amongst these one frequently comes across reliefs of a double-headed eagle, which was the device of ʿAlā al-Dīn Kayqubād and other Seljuk Sultans. (Fig. 208.)

A number of figural reliefs now in the Ince Minare Medrese Museum in Konya display important examples of figural plastic work of the Seljuk period. Of these, a relief depicting a dragon with knotted body, wings in the forms of arabesques and a tail terminating in a monster's head, together with a fabulous beast with arabesque-like wings pursuing an elephant with harness and ornamental headgear decorated with tassels, come from the citadel of Konya. The style shows a very close affinity with the figural stone reliefs of the Ghaznevids.

In the same museum there is a further relief of a man sitting cross-legged holding a round object in his hand. In this relief, which is said to have been brought from the Citadel of Konya, it would seem that the conception of the ruler is portrayed in symbolic fashion.

Another relief, in the Islamisches Museum in East Berlin, depicts a man sitting cross-legged in the same manner, playing a lute. In the lines of the face, which depict in realistic fashion a man carried away by the harmony of the music, one can perceive the influence of an art of portraiture reaching back to the time of the Uighurs.

On a figural tombstone in the Ince Minare Museum in Konya an elderly, bearded figure is portrayed sitting on a stool holding a falcon in his gloved hand, and caressing with his other hand the chin of a smaller figure who is holding on to the sash at his waist. This composition obviously has a symbolic significance, but at the same time possesses a powerfully graphic quality. The costumes of the figures are typical in reflecting old Turkish attire.

Very fine examples of figural decoration are to be found adorning various works of Turkish architecture in Anatolia, such as medreses, tombs, fortress towers and even mosques. As far as statues are concerned the only one to survive from the Anatolian Seljuk period is the statue of the couched lion in a niche under the Kiosk of Qılıch Arslan in Konya, which is now in the Museum of Turkish and Islamic Art (Türk ve Islâm Eserleri Müzesi) in Istanbul. There are also stylised figures of a lion of the Mengüjükid period on each side of the main tower in the castle of Divriği. Lions, snakes with the heads of monsters, eagles and human figures are to be found separately or combined with other decorations in various works of architecture as reliefs in the form of gargoyles or set amongst scrolls.

Figures were used in architecture as devices, symbols or as pure decoration. Although strongly decorative, figural relief in Anatolia never attained the quality of the Great Seljuk stucco statuary nor of the Great Seljuk and Daghestan stone reliefs. Anatolian stone decoration showed its real strength in the development and use of lettering together with geometrical and foliate motifs.

Although the stucco decoration used on the inner walls of palaces and kiosks introduced little that was new in subject matter, the greater facility of the medium permitted the use of more lively forms. Compared with the truly magnificent stucco decoration of the Great Seljuks, Anatolian stucco work seems very plain and insipid. Most of it occurs in the Seljuk palace in Konya. A number of the pieces of figural stucco found there are now displayed in the Museum of Turkish and Islamic Art in Istanbul. Of these only a single relief depicts a large scene. In this two horsemen are seen confronting each other against a decorative background of symmetrical scrolls, arabesques, lotus flowers and palmettes. The horseman on the left is thrusting his sword into the mouth of a monster lying beneath his rearing horse. The other is turning round in an attempt to kill a lion that is leaping upon him. (The combat of a horseman and a lion is reminiscent of the marble reliefs of the Ghaznevids.) All the figures are executed in a very superficial and insipid style.

Other smaller fragments are between 15 and 20 centimetres in length and contain geometrical designs, animal figures, devices, fishes, birds, winged monsters and mythological creatures. Other important representational elements in these decorative fragments are horsemen, seated or standing figures and various types of script. Some of the figures and motifs on the marble reliefs found in the excavations at Ghazne, although they do not appear in the works of the Great Seljuks, are to be seen in a simplified form in the stucco decorations of the Anatolian Seljuks. Although poor in execution, the human and animal figures and the wealth of subject matter in these stucco decorations show that in spite of the amazing abundance of antique Classical sculpture around them the Turks remained faithful to their old art and traditions.

In the Ottoman period non-figural stucco decoration was used in the side chambers of mosques to cover wall surfaces, including fireplaces and shelf niches. This type of decoration has survived in its original form in early Ottoman mosques at Bursa, Edirne and Amasya. Fragments of a very fine stucco niche probably belonging to the mihrab of an early 15th-century mosque were found in recent excavations at Iznik and have been transferred to the Iznik museum. In these a meander border, geometrical star entrelacs, peonies and rosette flowers are found in addition to the usual arabesques and palmettes, and floriated Kufic and *naskhī* inscriptions are all meticulously executed in fine detail. But the most remarkable thing is the appearance among various geometrical motifs of fourfold braid motifs and intersecting octagons, providing evidence of the continuation of ancient Turkish motifs in the Ottoman period. These fourfold braid motifs which are to be seen in Edirne at the beginning of the 14th century in the decorations on the fireplace recess of the Yıldırım Mosque, and on a plaster mihrab of 1429 in the Mosque of Shah Melek Pasha, appear from time to time in various decorations in later Ottoman art.

The fourfold braid motif is also frequently seen in woodwork. A spirited example of this is the wooden minbar (or pulpit), an Artukid work of the 12th century from the Great Mosque at Harput, now in the Sare Khatun Mosque there. The fourfold braid motifs produced by intersecting octagons in the large triangular side panels of this minbar are embellished with fine arabesques and scrolls which fill the interstices. Other examples showing the continuation of this motif amongst the Seljuks are the balustrade grilles on the minbar of the late 13th-century Great Mosque at Ayaş, and the side balustrade grilles of the upper part of the minbar of the

Great Mosque at Sivrihisar. Minbars are the most monumental of all works in wood and from the 12th century onwards they occupy, by reason of their extraordinary brilliant development, a very special place in Anatolian Seljuk art. In the earliest minbars of the 12th century the framework was constructed of very hard wood and the spaces were filled by separate pieces of wood fitting into each other by tongue and groove joints, and with surfaces decorated with stars and geometrical forms containing foliate arabesques and scrolls. Later, in the 13th and 14th centuries, a technique of revetment developed by which these small mosaic pieces were nailed on to thick wooden blocks. In the decoration space is principally given to script, geometrical and foliate motifs. The surfaces are dominated by various geometrical designs in the form of stars and polygons, and the same designs are used in the balustrade grilles. In the Ottoman minbars the decorations were generally carved directly on to large, thick wooden blocks.

In Seljuk minbars inscriptions in floriated Kufic and Seljuk *thuluth* are very commonly used . Although it is undated and has undergone repairs the large minbar of the Great Mosque at Aksaray would seem to be the oldest of these. In the inscriptions the name of Sultan Mas'ūd is given and his son appears as Alp Inanch, Qutlugh Bilge, Qılıch Arslan. The name of Zayn al-Ḥajj Khwāja Nushtekin al-Jamālī is also mentioned in the inscription as the architect of the mosque and the minbar. The other inscriptions on the minbar are Koranic. (Fig. 209.) It must have been constructed some two years before the Konya minbar dated 550/1155. The minbar of the 'Alā al-Dīn Mosque at Konya is a little smaller, of medium size, though the soundness of its style and high quality of its decoration make it the most magnificent monument of Seljuk craftsmanship in wood. The fact that the master-craftsman came from Ahlat, an ancient centre of Turkish art, shows how Seljuk woodwork springs from very deep roots. (Fig. 20.)

Koran lecterns (*rahles*) dating from the Seljuk period form a group of small but very attractive wooden objects. These have interlocking tongues in the centre that allow them to open and close. (Fig. 210.) A lectern of this type from Konya made of a single piece of walnut wood and now in the Museum of Turkish and Islamic Art in Istanbul is inscribed in the name of the Seljuk Sultan 'Izz al-Dīn Kaykā'ūs II. Symmetrically arranged lines of closely spaced arabesques are carved in relief on both sides of an axis formed by a row of palmettes placed one above the other. The decoration of each face is identical and the *thuluth* inscriptions on the upper sides form an unbroken continuity. In another Seljuk lectern dated 678/1279 in the Mevlânâ Museum in Konya there is a single line of *thuluth* inscription placed between two faces carved with arabesques and scrolls. Another lectern in the same museum differs in having a *thuluth* inscription border surrounding both the upper and lower faces with veined arabesques and palmettes in the centre. The legs are turned up at the ends in the form of half palmettes, the spaces between them being filled with openwork palmettes and arabesques, encompassed by an arch in the form of a knotted entrelac that forms a link with the architectural decoration of the Zengids. A lotus-palmette frieze extends along the upper edge of the reading-stand.

The Seljuk lectern 1 metre in height in the Islamisches Museum in East Berlin is of a delicacy and richness of ornament that far surpass all these others, however. The space between the legs is in the form of a poly-lobed decorative arch with spandrels of openwork palmettes and arabesques, the base of the spandrel on one face being broken. The surfaces remaining on the two sides are surrounded by veined arabesques whilst the central space in the square moulding is inscribed with the word Allāh in plaited Kufic, in two different styles, the spaces between the letters being filled with arabesques and scrolls (see Fig. 210). The name of the craftsman—'Abd al-Waḥīd bin Sulaymān al-najjār—is written on two of the tongues in the centre. A carved walnut chest belonging to Mevlânâ (Jalāl al-Dīn Rūmī) in his tomb at Konya, a masterpiece of Seljuk art, was constructed by the same craftsman. It would appear that in later times lecterns of this quality could no longer be made. Although wooden objects requiring very delicate workmanship and embellished with ivory, mother-of-pearl and tortoise shell are to be found in the 15th and 16th centuries, the mastery which the Seljuks showed in these lecterns came to an end with the dynasty. The large number of minbars (pulpits), Koran boxes and lecterns made in the Ottoman period conform to the general development of Classical, Baroque, Empire and Neo-classical styles. The minbar in the Mosque of Süleymaniye may be regarded as the most mature and successful example of an Ottoman wooden grille (see Fig. 250).

23

CERAMICS

Seljuk and Pre-Ottoman Tiles

Turkish ceramics have had a long history stretching back as far as the Uighurs. It became clear from the excavations and explorations carried out in the ruins of Karakhocho (in the Turfan oasis) in 1902–3 that grey-blue glazed bricks and square glazed tile panels, with designs consisting of a rosette in the centre and a quarter rosette in each corner, were used as a pavement in the temples there.

That tiles were used in architecture in the Karakhanid period is shown by the blue tiles remaining at the base of the arch of the porch recess of the tomb of Jalāl al-Dīn Ḥusayn at Uzgend (1152) and on the porch of the Maghāk-i ʿAṭṭārī Mosque at Bukhārā.

The Italian excavations at Ghazne have brought to light a large quantity of small square moulded tiles with raised designs in green, yellow, blue and brown, monochrome glaze. The tiles in the form of stars are plain, whilst on the embossed tiles are to be seen rosettes like those on the Uighur tiles at Karakhocho, as well as double-headed eagles, walking animal figures, arabesques and epigraphic motifs. They show a close resemblance to Ghaznevid marble and stucco reliefs. Although the carved inscription in turquoise tiles on the magnificent minaret, from the site of Jam, built by Ghiyāth al-Dīn Maḥmūd at the beginning of the 13th century has been used as evidence that Ghaznevid faience is really Ghurid, the style of relief is Ghaznevid and must have been executed by Ghaznevid workmen. The resemblance between the single reliefs on the square Ghaznevid tiles and the stone relief figures carved on the Ak Han in Anatolia has already been pointed out.

The regular use and development of ceramic decoration in architecture begins with the first faience produced by the Great Seljuks in Iran. Most of the buildings decorated in this way were destroyed during the Mongol invasion, however, and few specimens have survived.

The earliest example is a turquoise glazed inscription (dated 450/1058) in raised Kufic on square panels on the Seljuk minaret of the Masjid-i Jumʿa at Damghan. Small tile fragments are also inserted between the bricks to form a narrow border above the broad stucco inscription in the Friday Mosque (1115) at Qazwin. In the Masjid-i Ḥaydariye there, ceramic fragments of two different colours have been inlaid in the plaster above a stucco border with a plaited Kufic inscription. On the Sīn minaret (1131) in the vicinity of Isfahan there is an inscription band in which the upper faces of the letters are in turquoise. Tiles were also used at Isfahan in the inscriptions and borders on the Ziyar, Rehrevan and Masjid-i ʿAlī minarets. But actual ceramic decoration employing mosaic technique is first to be seen in the concentric and intersecting polygonal interlacing patterns set in hard plaster in the porch lunette of the Gunbādh-i Surkh (1147), built by Bendāne bin Bakr Muḥammad at Maragha in Persian Azerbaidzhan. Geometrical patterns produced by intersecting hexagons can be seen in the spandrels. Blue faience mosaic was also used in the porch lunette of the Round Tomb at Maragha (1167), as well as in the inscriptions under and above the lunette. On the tomb of Mu'mine Khātūn (1186) at Nakhichevan in Soviet Azerbaidzhan the whole structure is covered with patterns of light blue tiles combined with unglazed bricks, and most of the inscriptions are in faience mosaic. Besides these simple tile decorations dating from the Great Seljuk period the tradition can also be seen continued in a magnificent mosaic tile panel from the rear wall of the palace mosque of the Khwārizmshāhs at Zawzan in Khurasan built during the reign of Sultan Tekesh in 1219. This large panel measures 13 × 15 metres and contains medallions of cobalt and turquoise tiles, Kufic and *thuluth* inscriptions and various other decorations. In a *naskhī* inscription which concludes the panel we find the date 616/1219. This early 13th-century mosque of the Khwārizmshāhs is the only work in Iran which can be compared with Seljuk ceramics in Anatolia and is of very great importance in providing a clue to the development of the use of faience in architectural decoration.

The conical roofs of the early 13th century mausolea of Sultan Tekesh and Fakhr al-Dīn Rāḍī at Urgench, the capital of the Khwārizmshāhs, are faced with turquoise glazed tiles. The lustre tile panels made in Persian cities of Rayy and the magnificent early lustre tile mihrabs now exhibited in various museums throughout the world are attributed to the first half of the 13th century. *Mīnāī* technique was first employed by the Seljuks in the workshops of Rayy and Kashan, and came to an end in the Īl-Khānid period, which was followed by a period of 50 or 60 years of stagnation resulting from the destructive invasion of the Mongols.

Throughout the whole of the 13th century the greatest and most brilliant development of ceramics is to be seen in Anatolian Turkish art. From the outset ceramic decoration in architectural forms created by the Turks themselves displays a wealth of design and a technical maturity far in advance of Persia. The designs are derived from the Great Seljuks and are to be found in all the arts of decoration, but in ceramics, as in other decorative arts, there was a remarkably rapid advance in colour and technique. So much so, that by the introduction of ceramic panels and mosaic patterns into the basic forms of Seljuk architecture it attained the status of monumental art. The first examples are in the form of turquoise complements to brick decoration. In buildings of the middle of 13th century, as, for example, in the Sırçalı, Medrese at Konya, one of the first large-scale tiled structures, the whole of the interior is dominated by the faience mosaic decoration, whilst in the Karatay Medrese the most magnificent monument of this art has been created by facing practically the entire interior surface of the walls, dome, and vaults with tiles. Nevertheless the technique always remained a means of enlivening and adding colour to the architecture to which it was subordinate, and never attempted to oust the architecture from its primary position. The number of colours employed was increased to four—turquoise, dark blue, green and purple, and in addition to mosaic and panel tiles, embossed tiles were also manufactured.

The brick and turquoise ceramic decorations of the mausolea at Maragha and Nakhichevan were the inspiration of the first tiles in Anatolia, but the brilliant development in 13th-century Anatolia left these other regions far behind. The technical excellence, the wealth and quality of colour and design in Anatolian ceramics of the 13th century were attained nowhere else.

In the 12th century seven different colours were produced in *mīnāī* ceramics by double firing, once under and once over the glaze, but later these gave way to lustre wares. The tiles, from the Kiosk of Qılıch Arslan II (1156–92) in Konya, belong both in technique and design to the Persian Great Seljuk tradition and were manufactured in the *mīnāī* overglaze technique. The spandrels of the entrance arch of the kiosk had a design composed of octagons linked by 4-pointed stars and made up of square tiles 24 cm. in size. Inside one of the octagons from the centre of the square panels can be seen a mounted falconer holding a hawk in his hand, and in the other a very small fragment of another figure. On another star-shaped tile there is a standing figure, broken off above the shoulders, with a caftan and top boots. Apart from these examples, now in the Museum of Turkish and Islamic Art in Istanbul, there are also pieces in the Berlin and Stockholm Museums. The kiosk was enlarged during the reign of ʿAlā al-Dīn Kayqubād I when it became known as the ʿAlā al-Dīn Kiosk, but there can be no doubt that the very high-quality *mīnāī* tiles belonged to the original building, for no *mīnāī* tiles have been discovered in any Seljuk building in Anatolia dating from after the period of Qılıch Arslan II.

Other early tiles from Seljuk kiosks discovered during excavations in Konya are at present in museums in Berlin and Paris. The overflow of the glaze on the sides of the pieces clearly shows that the body was first of all cut into the shape of stars, lozenges, crosses and deltoids and then glazed. On star-shaped tiles can be seen decoration in *mīnāī* enamels depicting figures of a horseman, a cross-legged figure playing a musical instrument, three figures standing side by side, and others. Other tiles surrounding the stars or filling in the spaces between them have predominantly foliate motifs. Gilt tiles, and tiles with black decoration under a turquoise glaze, have also been found. These panels are composed of large octagonal compositions or of rows of star and cross tiles. The great number of very fine specimens of *mīnāī* tiles that have been found in these kiosks testifies to the short but brilliant development of this very difficult faience technique in Anatolia at the end of the 12th century. Although a considerable quantity of Seljuk pottery of the late 12th century at Rayy and Kashan was made by the *mīnāī* technique, which was originally invented by the Seljuks, very few tiles are known to have been made in this way. In Anatolia, on the other hand, this process was never used in pottery.

Excavations at the Palace of Kubādābād, erected by ʿAlā al-Dīn Kayqubād I in 1236, revealed a large number of tile fragments in both lustre and underglaze technique. The star-shaped tiles display a wealth of human and animal figures. These are linked by cruciform

211 Konya, Mausoleum of Sahib Ata, detail of ceramic decoration

212 Konya, Mausoleum of Sahib Ata, window with glazed grille

213 Konya, Mausoleum of Sahib Ata, view of great arch and door

214
Bursa, Yeşil Türbe, mihrab and cenotaph faced with ceramic tiles

215 Bursa, Jem Sultan Mausoleum, mihrab with tiles

216 Istanbul, Mosque of Rüstem Pasha, mihrab with tiles

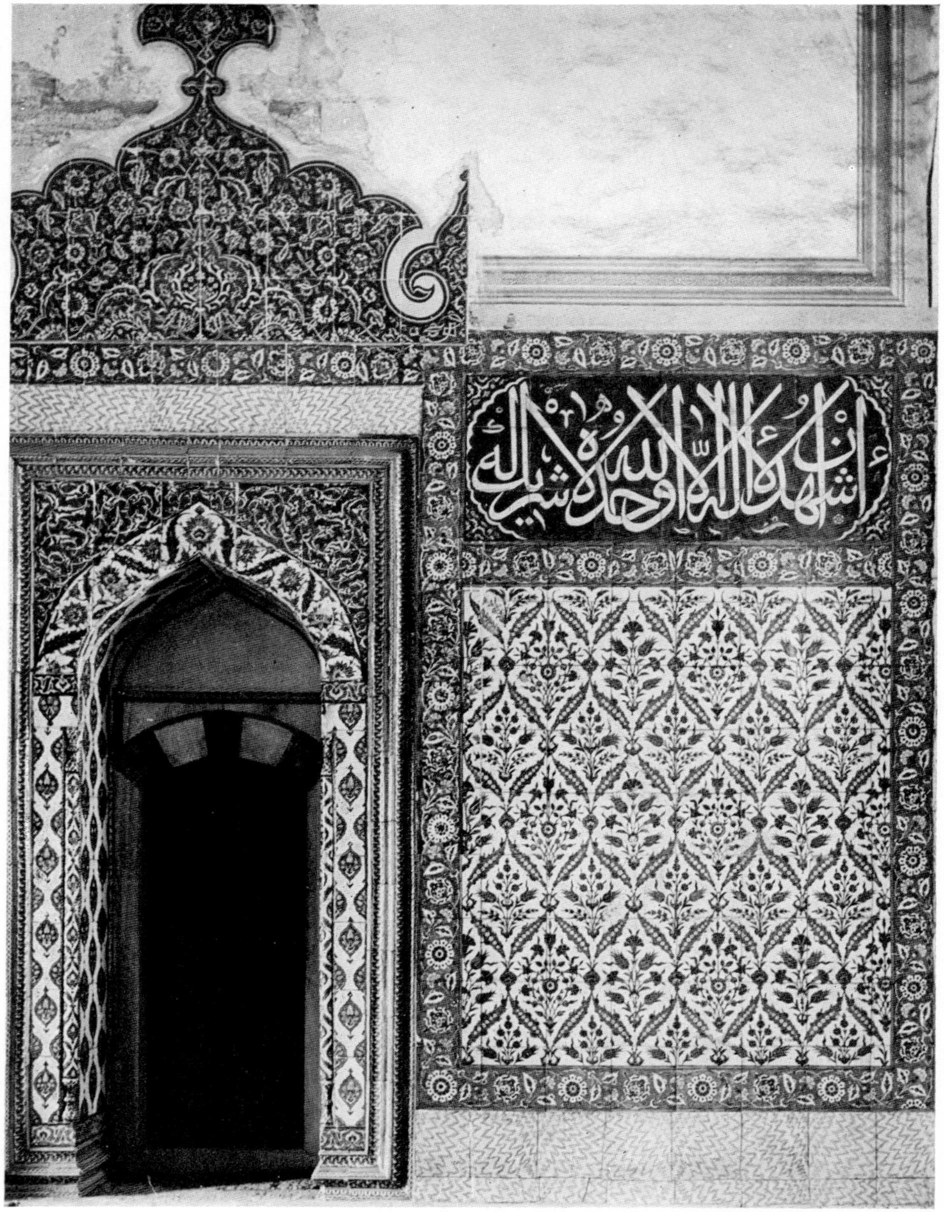

217 Edirne, Selimiye Mosque, Imperial gallery

218 Bowl with deep foot, Golden Horn ware, Victoria and Albert Museum

219 Silver tray with inscription in the name of Sultan Alp Arslan. Courtesy, Museum of Fine Arts, Boston

220 Silver candlestick with inscription in the name of Sultan Sanjar. Courtesy, Museum of Fine Arts, Boston

221 Metal sphinx, Artukid

222
Bronze mirror with mounted huntsman, Istanbul, Topkapı Saray Museum

223 Striped-glass mosque lamp with enamelled decoration (*Çeşm-i bülbül*)

224 Striped-glass bottle with handle and stopper

225 Holbein carpet with pseudo-Kufic border (sometimes known as a Lotto carpet), Philadelphia Museum of Art

226 Ushak carpet with star pattern, Philadelphia Museum of Art

227 Gördes prayer rug, Seattle Art Museum

228 Prayer rug in the form of an animal skin, Istanbul, Museum of Turkish and Islamic Art

229 Woven silk textile, Seljuk, Persia, Victoria and Albert Museum

230 View of Paradise, from a Chaghatay Miʿrājnāme (Book of the Ascension of Muhammad) in Uighur script, Paris, Bibliothèque Nationale

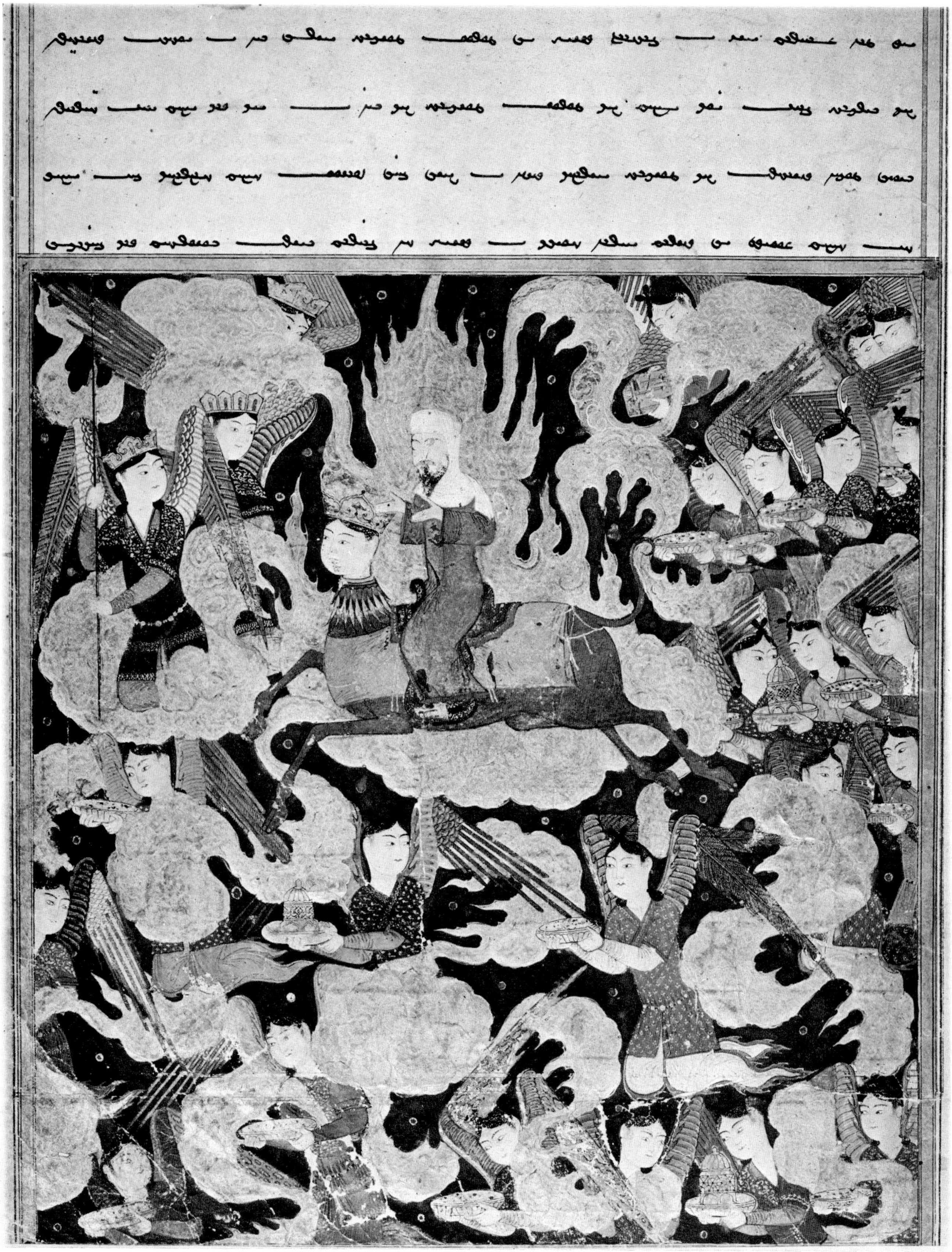

231 View of the heavens, from Chaghatay Miʿrājnāme in Uighur script, Paris, Bibliothèque Nationale

232 Dervishes, 'Siyah Kalem', Topkapı Saray Museum, Fatih Album

233 Demons, 'Siyah Kalem', Topkapı Saray Museum, Fatih Album

234 Portrait of Mehmed the Conqueror (Fatih) by Sinan Bek, Topkapı Saray Museum

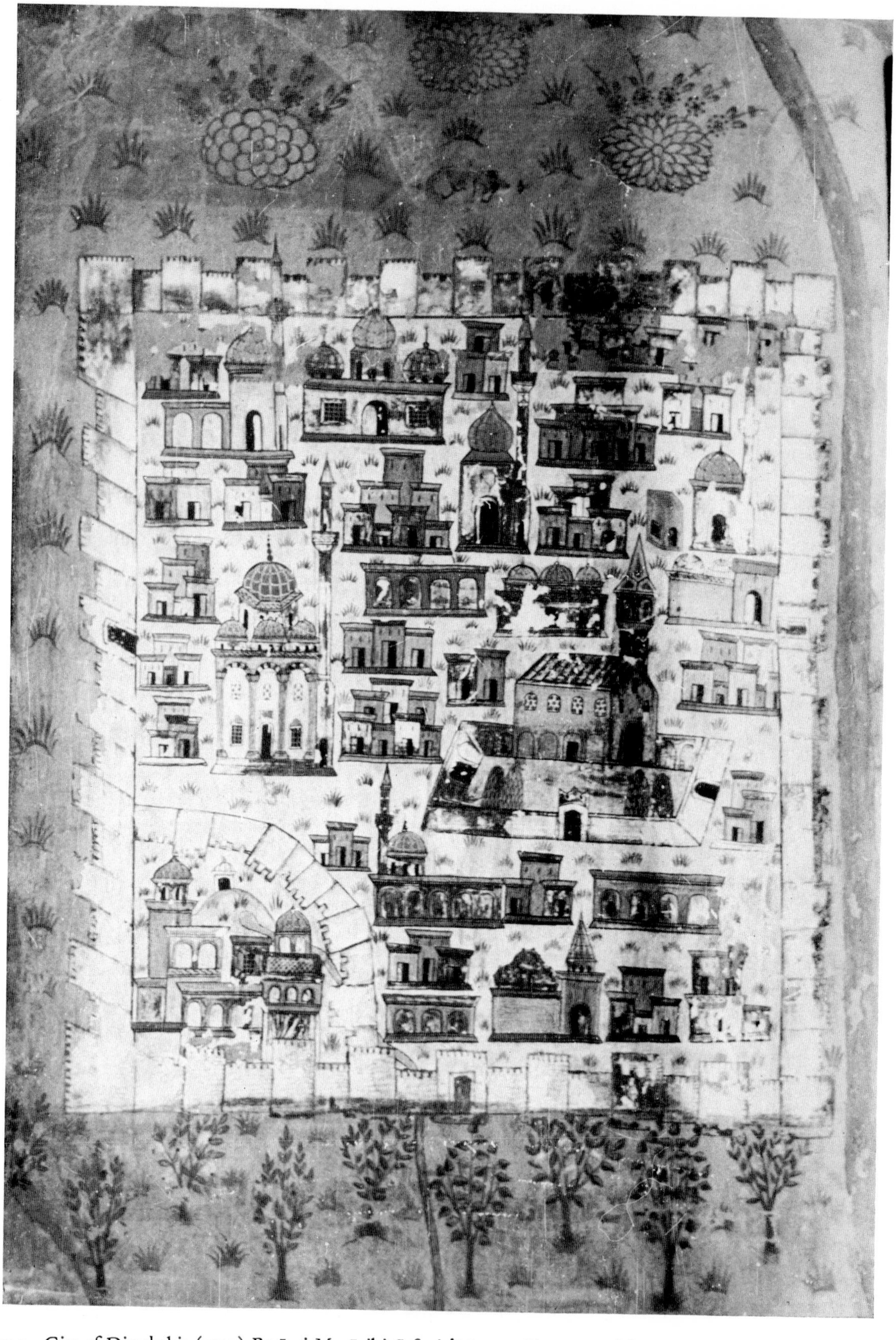

235 City of Diyarbekir (1537) Beyān-i Menāzil-i Sefer-i ʿIrāqayn (Account of the stages of the campaign in the two Iraqs), Nasūh al-Matrakī (Matrakçı Nasuh), Istanbul University Library

236a Battle of Mohacs, Süleymānnāme, 219 b Topkapı Saray Museum

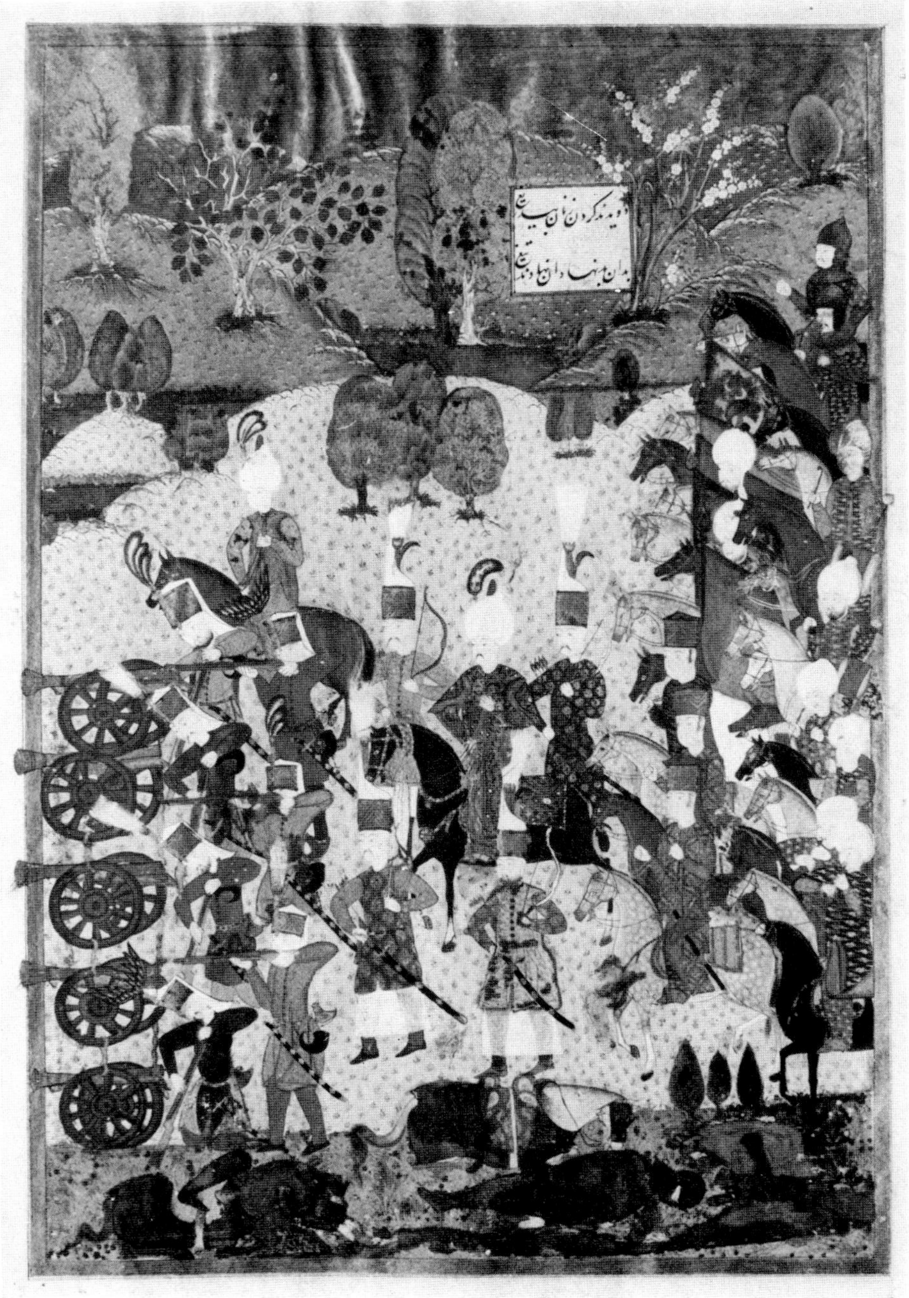

236b Battle of Mohacs, Süleymānnāme, 220 a Topkapı Saray Museum

237 Circumcision of Shehzade Bayazid and Jihangir, Süleymānnāme, Topkapı Saray Museum

238 Taking away of Jam-i Jihannūma by Ishak Pasha to the palace, Topkapı Saray Museum

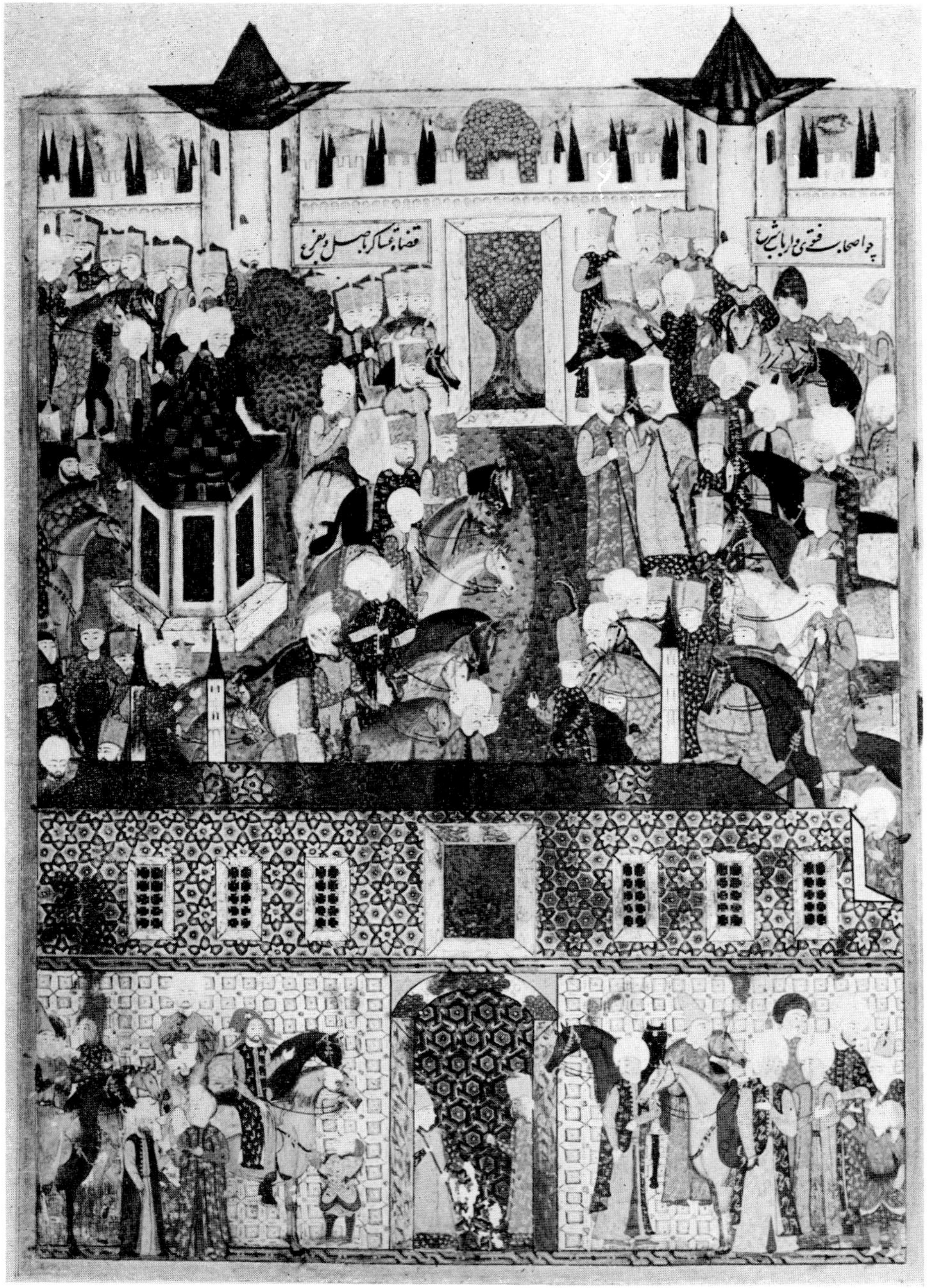

239 The Bāb al-Saʿāda and the Bāb al-Salām, two of the gates of the Topkapı Palace, Süleymānnāme, Topkapı Saray Museum

240 Reception of the son of the King of Erdel and his mother by Suleyman I, Hünernāme, Topkapı Saray Museum

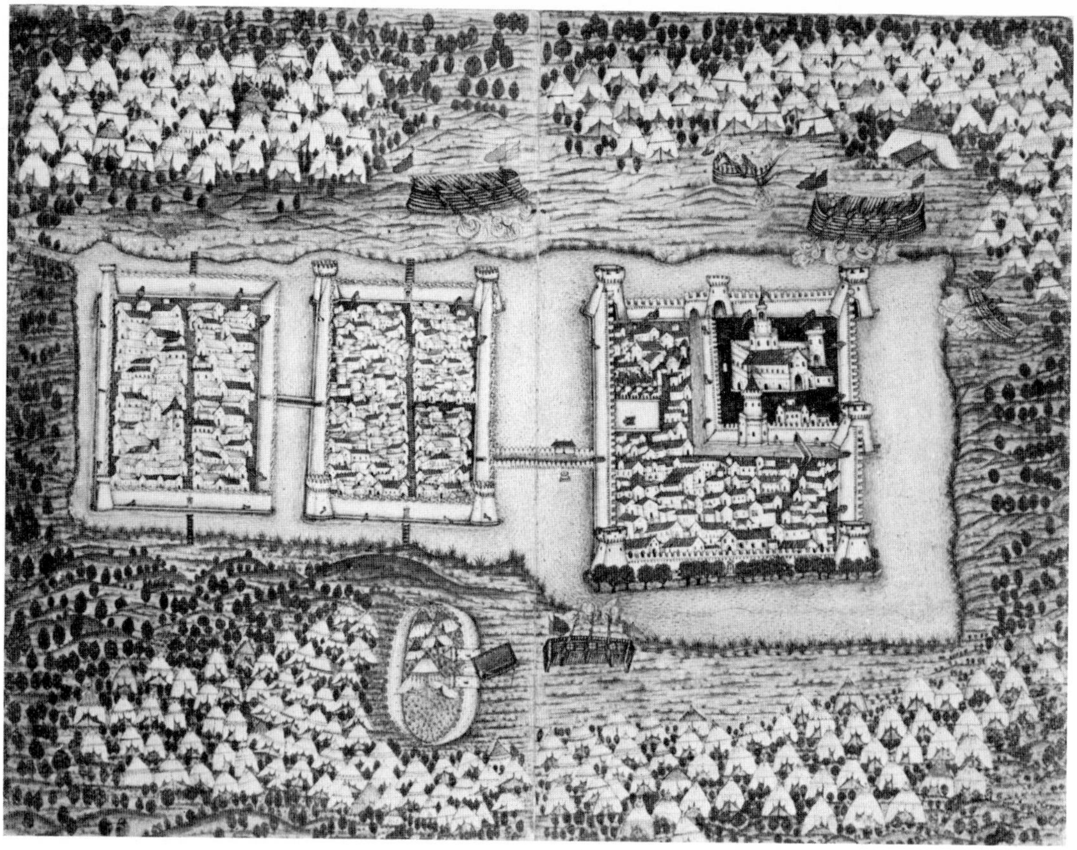

241 Szigetvár Castle, Nüzhet al-Akhbār der Sefer-i Sigetvar, Topkapı Saray Museum

242 Siege of Szigetvar, Hünernāme, Vol. II. Topkapı Saray Museum

243 Musicians by Levni, Topkapı Saray Museum

244 13 Basmalas from various Turkish manuscripts:
(Basmala is the conventional term for the customary Muslim invocation 'In the name of God, the merciful, the compassionate')

1	T.I.A.M. 2487	Muraqqaʿ	*Riḥānī*	Finest period	Sheikh Hamdullah
2	T.I.A.M. 2465	Muraqqaʿ	*Thuluth*	Finest period	Sheikh Hamdullah
3	T.Pal. E.H. 2112	Muraqqaʿ	*Thuluth*	In the style of Yāqūt (947/1540)	Ahmed Karahisarî
4	T.I.A.M. 1443	Anʿam-i Sharīf	*Thuluth*	Gilt Basmala	Ahmed Karahisarî
5	T.I.A.M. 1443	Anʿam-i Sharīf	*Thuluth*	Free style	Ahmed Karahisarî
6	T.I.A.M. 1443	Anʿam-i Sharīf	*Thuluth*	Linked Basmala	Ahmed Karahisarî
7	T.Pal. III. A (3657)	Muraqqaʿ	*Jeli* in	Specially careful	
8	T.I.A.M. 2473	Muraqqaʿ	*Thuluth*	Fine period (1690)	Hafız Osman
9	T.I.A.M. 2469	Muraqqaʿ	*Thuluth*	Middle period (1671)	Hafız Osman
10	T.Pal. II. A (3655)	Muraqqaʿ	*Riḥānī*	Finest period (1685)	Hafız Osman
11	T.Pal. Hz. 2244	Muraqqaʿ	*Thuluth*	Fine hand (1731)	Yedikuleli Seyyid Abdullah
12	T.Pal. G.Y. 325/77	Hilye	*Riḥānī*	Fine period (1800)	Mahmud Jelâleddin
13	T.Pal. G.Y. 309/89	Muraqqaʿ	*Thuluth*	Fine period (1876)	Mehmed Shevki

(T.Pal. = Topkapı Palace Museum. T.I.A.M. = Museum of Turkish and Islamic Art)

1

2

3

4

5

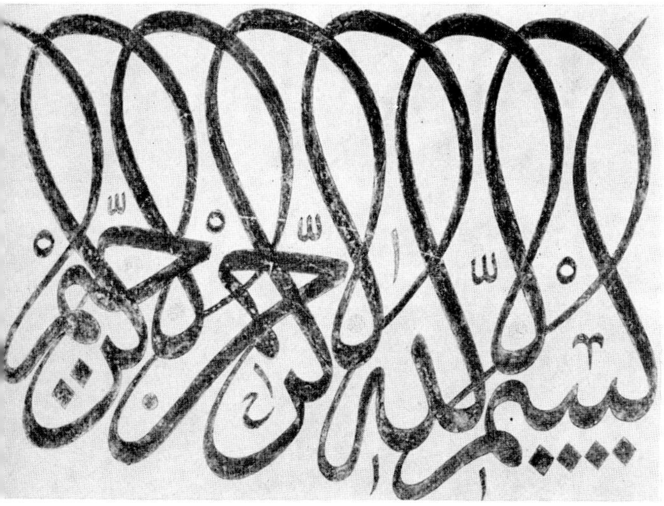

6

7

8

9

10

11

12

13

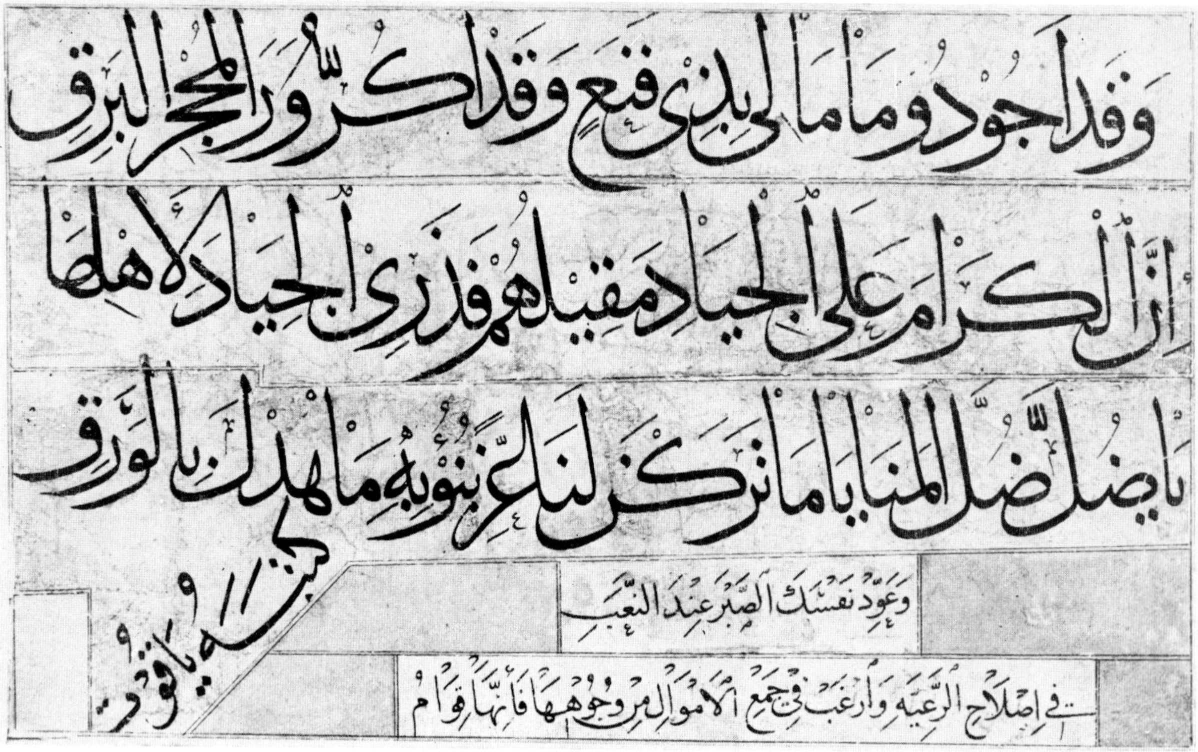

245 Calligraphy, Muraqqaʿ (album leaf), *Thuluth*, signed by Yāqūt, Topkapı Saray Museum

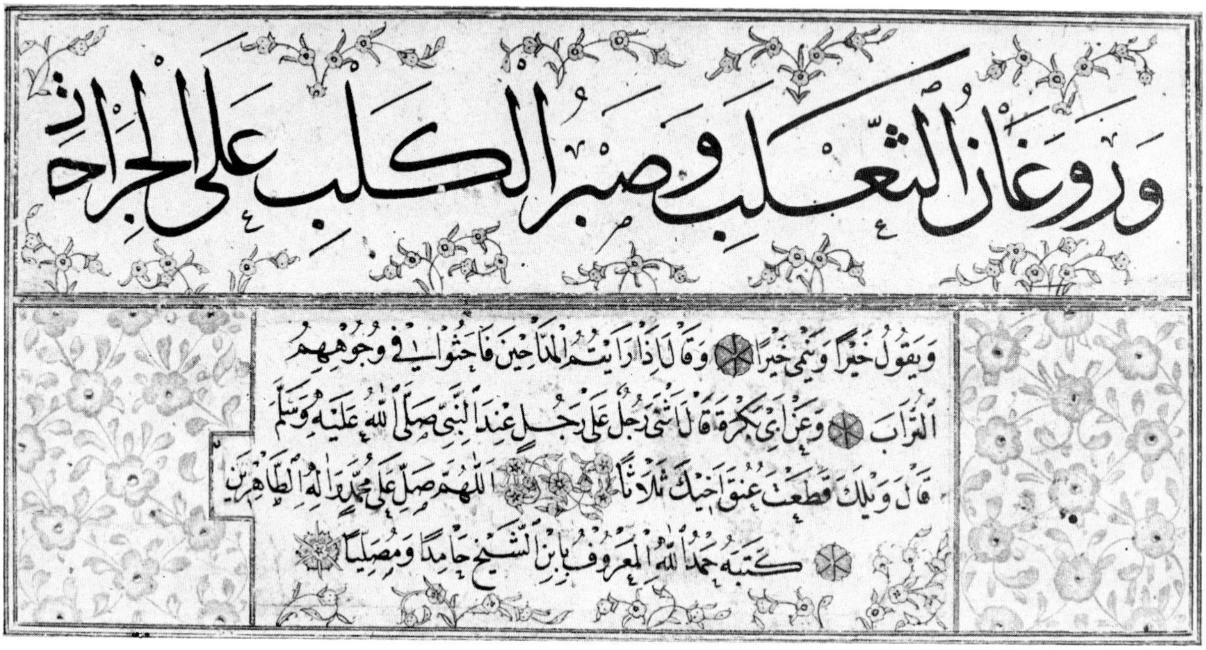

246 Calligraphy, Muraqqaʿ, *Thuluth* and *Naskhi*, signed by Sheikh Hamdullah, Topkapı Saray Museum

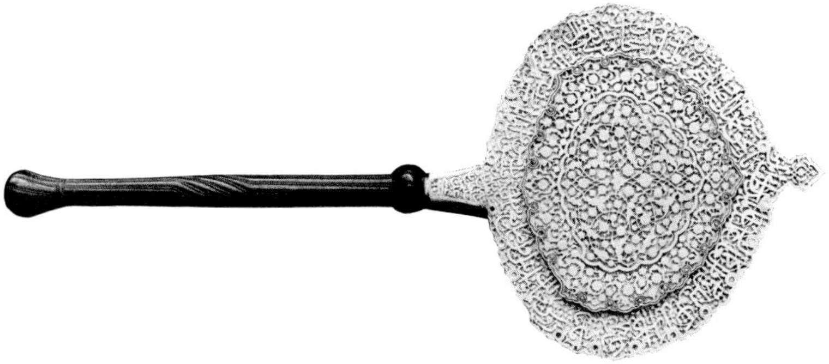

247 Ivory-backed mirror, Topkapı Saray

248 Bursa, Muradiye, Tomb of Sultan Murad II, detail from eaves of porch

249 Bursa, Muradiye, ceiling

250 Istanbul, Mosque of Süleymaniye, wooden minbar

tiles. On the former are depicted seated and standing figures, various animals such as peacocks, water birds, fish, double-headed eagles, bears, donkeys, goats and dogs, mythological creatures such as sphinxes, harpies and gryphons, bird figures on either side of a tree, and symbolic figures, in underglaze turquoise, green, purple, and blue with greenish-blue contours. Two of these tiles, now in fragments, depict a young bearded man, and may very probably be a portrait of ʿAlā al-Dīn Kayqubād I. Very fine specimens of lustre tiles in the form of octagonal stars were found in situ. There are underglaze tiles with 'Sarāi-yi Jihān' and other inscriptions in *naskhī*, and the words 'Al-Sulṭān' are inscribed on the breast of a double-headed eagle. All the tiles were produced in local kilns. Tiles with black decoration under a turquoise glaze were also found. In these a whole new world of representational art was created, peculiar to Anatolia.

Tiles from the Palace at Keykubadiye built by ʿAlā al-Dīn Kayqubād near Kayseri some time before, in 1224–6, are completely devoid of figural decoration. Among these are to be found square tiles with turquoise underglaze painting between thick black contours with a design of fourfold braid motifs produced by intersecting octagons in the old Turkish decorative tradition. The slender spiral scrolls filling the interstices will be seen again in a group of Ottoman blue and white pottery known as Haliç (Golden Horn) ware. Another group of tiles has geometrical interlacing patterns, stars and braid motifs painted in turquoise, cobalt blue and dark purple underglaze on a white ground. Gold and silver lustre overglaze tiles with a turquoise or cobalt blue ground were also found.

Tiles from the kiosk in the Roman theatre at Aspendos now in the Antalya Museum are similar in style to the Kubādābād tiles but inferior in quality.

While in the palaces we find a rich, wordly, cheerful and vivacious figural type of tile decoration, in religious buildings a more serious style of tile mosaic prevails. In these the stiff angularity of the Kufic script and geometrical patterns and the soft, flowing curves of *naskhī* or *thuluth* form a harmonious contrast that is very often sharpened by the use of colours.

The most monumental work employing a mixture of brick and tile mosaic is the hospital and tomb of 'Izz al-Dīn Kaykā'ūs I at Sivas (1217). Only the tile decorations on the façade of the tomb and in the left-hand iwan of the hospital have survived (see Design 7). The oldest examples of decoration consisting entirely of faience mosaic are to be seen in the mihrab borders and dome triangles of the ʿAlā al-Dīn Mosque at Konya, completed in 1220 (see Design 6). Here there suddenly appear rich and mature specimens of inscriptions with geometrical and foliate motifs. In the Sırçalı Medrese even richer examples of mosaic faience can be seen. Foliate and geometrical motifs are set side by side, without any intermingling, to form a harmonious whole. In the Karatay Medrese, on the other hand, foliate motifs and epigraphy prevail. The geometrical interlacing patterns of the inner filling of the iwan arch are made of embossed tiles.

Subsequently, the tiles of the Sahib Ata Mosque (1258), tomb (1280) and *khānqāh* (monastery) form a very rich collection. (Fig. 211.) In the mosque only the faience mosaic mihrab remains. The window grille of the *khānqāh* is covered with embossed glazed tiles (Fig. 212), whilst the dome is faced with turquoise, purple and brown glazed bricks in zigzag patterns. The türbe is the most spectacular work of its age, with the richest and most perfect

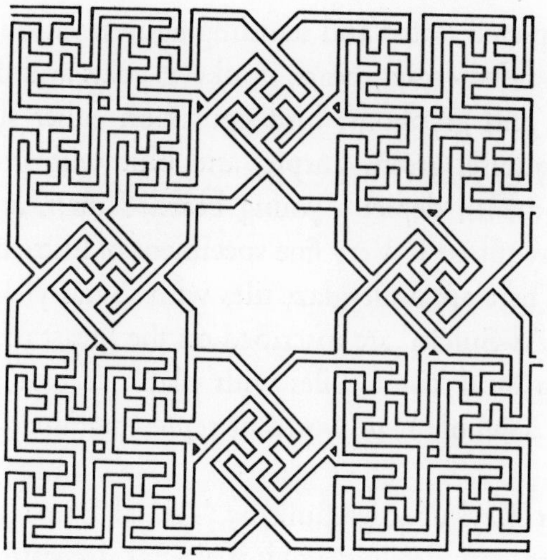

Design 7. Sivas, Tomb of Kaykā'ūs in the Hospital he endowed, section of decoration on exterior of drum

tile mosaic that Seljuk art had yet produced. (Fig. 213.) The six cenotaphs in this tomb belonging to Sahib Ata and his relations are all faced with tiles.

The Gök Medrese (1271) built by Sahib Ata at Sivas is a very fine work with faience mosaic in the masjid adjoining the entrance iwan and in the two side iwans. In the faience mosaic on the rear wall of the iwans the decorative brick motifs of the Kharraqān Mausolea are translated into colour (see Design Id). The mosaic tile mihrabs from the second half of the 13th century of the Sırçalı Masjid and the Mosque of Ṣadr al-Dīn Qunawī (1274) at Konya are also amongst the finest specimens of Seljuk art. (Fig. 26.)

The monumental inner porch of the Eshrefoghlu Mosque built at Beyşehir at the very end of the century (1297–9) has mosaic tile-work covering the whole of its surface, and is a magnificent example of the Konya style of Seljuk tile decoration. (Fig. 27.) In front of the equally splendid faience mihrab rises the dome, also covered with tile mosaic. The large geometrical stars of the mihrab niche resemble the dome decorations of the Karatay Medrese at Konya. The inner dome of the mausoleum of the Eshrefoghlu Süleyman Bek dated 1301 is one of the very few other examples of this type of tile decoration.

During the Beylik period in the 14th century the Seljuk ceramic tradition was carried on by the Aydınids. The faience mosaic mihrab in Seljuk style in the Great Mosque at Birgi (1312) is a monumental example of the type. The spandrels of the arches of the dome opening into the central nave are also decorated with faience mosaic. Other ceramic decoration of the Aydınid period can be seen in the 'Isā Bek Mosque at Seljuk and the Mehmed Bek Türbe at Birgi. The rich tile mosaic mihrab in the Karamanid Great Mosque at Gaferyat in the vicinity of Karaman is also linked with the Seljuk tradition. Although other tile works are to be found, on the whole the 14th century was a period of inactivity from the point of view of ceramic revetment; but this inactivity was at the same time a preparation for the birth of a completely new period in the art of tile decoration.

Ottoman Tiles

The combination of the art of Seljuk tile mosaic with the technique of polychrome glaze laid the foundations of the art of Ottoman tiles.

Although the minaret of the Green Mosque at Iznik (1378) was still in the Seljuk tradition it was the first work in which turquoise, blue and green were varied with light yellow and white. Unfortunately the minaret was recently demolished and re-erected with new tiles.

The magnificent tradition of Ottoman ceramics begins with the Green Mosque (Yeşil Cami) and Türbe, at Bursa (1421–4). This is, in effect, a collection of tiles of very diverse techniques. Here are to be seen examples of faience mosaic of the highest quality and technical perfection side by side with examples of Ottoman polychrome technique quite outside the Seljuk tradition. But the delicate patterns of the tile mosaics on the ceilings of the court galleries, the inside of the window niches, the door arches of the rooms on the upper storey, the soffit of the broken arch of the Imperial gallery, and, in the türbe, the lower section of the door arches and window niches, are drowned in the wealth of the tile panels produced in polychrome technique. In these the turquoise and purple of the Seljuks are enriched by the addition of an attractive yellow, green and white. Another innovation is a matt red applied in hardened clay to the spaces between the designs. The yellow tiles are also ornamented with gilt. The colours as well as the designs have become richer, and the large white *hatayī* arabesques are especially typical of the 15th century (see Fig. 148). Raised turquoise stems and large yellow *rūmī* arabesques inserted among these and enriched with attractive yellow tiles and matt red clay join at the corners to form a closed pattern. Tiles covered entirely with foliate motifs with very fine details and soft contours are another innovation differentiating Ottoman from Seljuk faience.

As for the polychrome tile panels in *cuerda seca* technique, these indicate the rise of a type of art quite different from that of the Seljuks. The finest examples of these tiles are to be seen in the Green Mosque and Türbe and the appearance of red as well as black in the contours separating the coloured glazes is of very great importance. This prepares the way for the innovations such as the use of naturalistic flowers, *hatayī* arabesques, peonies and rosettes together with other foliate motifs in tile panels imitating Seljuk faience mosaic; and for the attainment of the same artistic excellence.

The flowers springing from a vase in the mihrab of the Yeşil Türbe (the Green Tomb) herald the approach of such a naturalistic style. The prevailing colours in these tiles are yellow, green, white and purple, and in the mihrab of the Green Türbe and the ceramic cenotaph several shades of purple and blue are very skilfully applied without contours in this polychrome technique (Fig. 214).

Polychromy is the first great innovation introduced by Ottoman art. These tiles were manufactured in Bursa, and in excavations carried out in Iznik not a single tile in this technique has been discovered. Although there is, at first glance, a certain resemblance between these Ottoman tiles and the tiles used in Timurid constructions at Samarkand at the beginning of the 15th century the colours of Samarkand tiles are of very poor quality and the glaze has cracked.

Turquoise glaze predominates. The colour and composition of the clay is also different. However, the black and red contours isolating the various coloured glazes of the tiles in the Bibi Khanum Mosque (1399–1404) and the Ulugh Bek Medrese (1420) at Samarkand are meticulously executed and show a very advanced technique.

Tile mosaic with a darker yellow is used in the Muradiye Mosque in Bursa in the window lunettes and the spandrels of the door arch in the portico.

Another innovation in early Ottoman tile-work is underglaze-painted blue and white. These blue and white tiles are employed as a border in two of the tombs at the Muradiye in Bursa. (Fig. 215.) The hexagonal tiles in 37 different patterns on the side walls of the Muradiye Mosque in Edirne are amongst the finest examples of these (see Fig. 151). But the most remarkable feature of this mosque (1436) is the magnificent mihrab in polychrome glazed tiles measuring 6.3 × 85 metres—the largest tile mihrab after the mihrab in the Green Mosque in Bursa, to which it has a very close resemblance. No red is to be seen in the contours, but in the mihrab niche can be found an unusual design of finer quality than the Bursa tiles. Another feature is the employment of *cuerda seca* tiles together with blue and white tiles (see Fig. 150).

In a fourth mihrab in this group originally belonging to the Imaret of Ibrahim Bek (1432) at Karaman and now in the Çinili Köşk in Istanbul there are red contours separating the coloured glazes.

The entrance iwan of the Çinili Köşk (1472) built for Sultan Mehmed the Conqueror in Istanbul is a final masterpiece of tile mosaic. Although in technique and general effect it is in the Seljuk tradition, its naturalistic flowers, arabesques and attractive turquoise colouring recreate the atmosphere of the Bursa tiles (see Plate II).

The first examples of polychrome glazed tiles in Istanbul are to be seen in the *türbe* and mosque of Sultan Selim (1522), but the finest examples are those decorating the *türbe* of Shehzade Mehmed (1548). These tiles are superior to the Bursa ones in technique, colour and wealth of design, and turn the interior of the *türbe* into a sort of fairy-tale world (Plate III). As, from the middle of the 16th century, this *cuerda seca* technique was completely abandoned in the ceramics replaced by underglaze painting, the second and greatest of Ottoman ceramic styles made its appearance. This new style of tiles was employed in the Süleymaniye Mosque on either side of the mihrab and on the walls on the upper sections of these (1557). A more ornate variety of these is to be seen in the mausoleum of Hürrem Sultan (frontispiece). After that there is one important innovation after another in both colour and design. One indication of this is the 41 varieties of tulip to be seen amongst other refinements in the tiles of the Mosque of Rüstem Pasha (1561). (Fig. 216.) In the Türbe of Süleyman the Magnificent (1566) the whole décor is dominated by a similar style of tiles in rich colours and designs. The tiles in the Mosque of Sokollu Mehmed Pasha, near Sultan Ahmed (1572) (see Fig. 174), and in the mosque of Piyale Pasha at Kâsim Paşa also in Istanbul (1574) show an advance in colour and quality. In these there appears a brilliant coral red standing out in relief which continued in use for forty years and then suddenly disappeared. It would appear that this very great technical achievement was a discovery of the Iznik workshops. The production of seven different colours—turquoise, blue, an attractive dark green, red, light blue, white and sometimes

VI Istanbul, Topkapı Saray Museum, tile panel from exterior of Sünnet Odası (circumcision room) (see page 277)

VII Dishes (so-called Damascus ware), British Museum (see page 281)

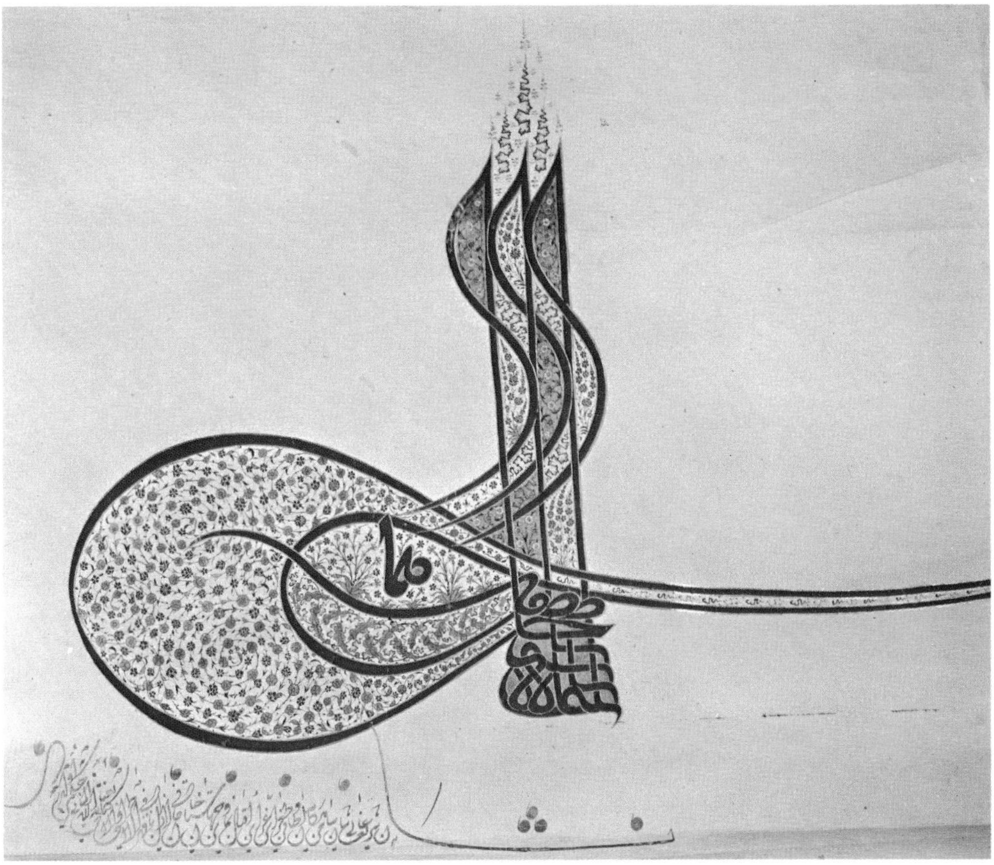

VIII Tughrā (the Imperial calligraphic emblem) of Süleyman I, Topkapı Saray Museum (see page 328)

black—in this underglaze technique constituted a technical advance unparalleled anywhere else in the world. The designs consist predominantly of completely naturalistic specimens of tulips, hyacinths, carnations, pomegranate flowers, peonies, and spring branches of plum and cherry blossom. The spaces between the flowers are filled with large green leaves shaped like curved daggers. By the second half of the 16th century these naturalistic flowers had permeated all the various Turkish decorative arts.

The Topkapı Saray contains a collection of the finest of the tiles in which coral red is abundantly used.

The colour and composition of the large tile panels decorating the walls on either side of the mihrab of the Selimiye Mosque at Edirne (1574) are most harmonious (Plate IV). But the tiles decorating the Imperial gallery are richer in variety and more meticulous in workmanship. (Fig. 217.) An original feature is the addition of branches of plum and apple blossom (Plate V). In Istanbul tiles of the brilliant coral red are to be seen in the Eski Valide Mosque at Üsküdar (1583), the Takkeji Ibrahim Agha Mosque outside the walls at Topkapı (1592) and in all the important buildings up to the end of the 16th century, after which this great stylistic period is brought to an end with the türbe of Sultan Murad III in 1600.

The finest tiled structure after the Topkapı Saray is the Mosque of Sultan Ahmed, in which some 70 different designs and 20,413 separate tiles were used. Obviously, after 1600, the strength and creative vitality of the art were by no means exhausted, but, although the designs show a great mastery of composition, they have become schematised and stylised, and the less pronounced use of red results in a loss of brilliance and vigour.

After this begins a period of increasing retrogression and degeneration. The Circumcision Room (Sünnet Odası) built by Sultan Ibrahim in the Topkapı Palace in 1640 is faced with tiles from various periods. Of these, panels with stags measuring 126 × 48 cm., and panels with vases measuring 123 × 34 cm., each made of one large glazed slab, are especially remarkable on account of their large size, and their light and dark blue colouring on a brilliant white ground (Plate VI). These panels must have remained from the most brilliant period of the art of Turkish faience in the 16th century. In the Baghdad Köşk, dated 1639, there are exact replicas of these stag and vase panels, each of which is composed piece by piece by placing seven shallow rectangular slabs one above the other. In these, red has been used in the form of red berries in the birds' beaks.

In the tiles in the Yeni Cami and the Türbe attached to it completed in 1669 both the quality and the colours have much deteriorated. After 1725 a workshop was set up for the manufacture of tiles in the Tekfur Palace in Istanbul, and the Fountain of Sultan Ahmed and the Mosque of Hekimoghlu Ali Pasha are both decorated with these tiles. They are of very poor quality, with green, blue, faded red and yellow (a colour abandoned after the early Ottoman period, which now reappears) on a dirty bluish ground, and this lack of success soon led to the closure of the workshops.

The Ottoman tiles decorating the Green Mosque at Bursa must have been manufactured in workshops established in the vicinity of the monuments. In the 16th century the largest centre of tile manufacture was Iznik, under the close control of the Topkapı Saray in Istanbul.

Kütahya and Istanbul were simultaneously production centres, but whilst the art of tile-making completely died out in Iznik the fact that the Kütahya factories are still turning out tiles at the present day shows its continuing vigour.

Turkish Pottery

Anatolian pottery, like all the other arts, developed on foundations laid down in earlier Turkish periods.

From the 11th century onwards the Karakhanids developed polychrome glazed pottery in a technique that can be regarded as native to Samarkand (so-called Afrasiyab wares) alongside other high-quality wares in which the possibilities of calligraphy are exploited to the full. Pottery of this type with slip decoration continued to be manufactured in the vicinity of Samarkand up till quite recent times, and there are examples dating from the 19th century in the Victoria and Albert Museum in London.

During the Great Seljuk period a polychrome technique was used in Iran in the pottery known as *laqabī*. The Seljuks successfully developed a completely new style of the lustre technique which had originated in Samarra. But the really great innovation introduced by the Seljuks in their centres of Rayy and Kashan was their discovery of the use of overglaze enamels, the *mīnāī* technique. In the scenes depicted on these many-figured *mīnāī* wares we can see the costumes, physical types and the whole life of the Seljuks of that time.

The *mīnāī* technique is sometimes used together with lustre, but the most delicate productions are the gilt lustre *mīnāī* wares. Dishes in the Freer Gallery in Washington and in the Berlin Museum depicting battle scenes show the very close connection with the art of the miniature. The Seljuks discovered and applied this *mīnāī* technique in Iran; in Iraq, Syria and Egypt it was completely unknown. That it should have passed from Iran into Anatolia together with the Seljuks plainly shows the role they played in its development. Yet although a large quantity of lustre and *mīnāī* tiles of the Seljuk period has been recovered in Anatolia no pottery has been found. In excavations carried out at Kalehisar near Alacahüyük, kilns and pottery fragments were found dating from the beginning of the 13th century, but very little real information can be gleaned from the single small fragment of lustre pottery, brown on the outside and yellow inside, which was found amongst them. The fragments of real, local, characteristic Seljuk pottery found at Kalehisar are of colour glazed slip wares. A great many fragments in *sgraffiato* technique were also found with predominantly figural scenes. Apart from this it would seem that pottery with black decoration under a turquoise glaze was very popular with the Anatolian Seljuks.

Excavations at Iznik have shown that the first Ottoman pottery was made from red clay; the biscuit after being treated with a slightly raised white slip was dipped into a coloured glaze and fired for a second time. Thus the first Iznik wares were linked to the Seljuk slip pottery known from Kalehisar. The first Ottoman Turkish slip-painted wares produced in Iznik from the middle of the 14th century onwards were manufactured in a monochrome glaze in either blue, green, or light or dark brown. These are without figures, with designs consisting of scrolls, arabesques and stylised flowers. Brilliantly coloured fragments, of very high quality, of this type of pottery together with unglazed fragments and remains from the kilns have been found in excavations.

As a result of these excavations it was also proved that the type of pottery, also made from red clay, belonging to the second period and generally known as 'Miletus ware' originated in Iznik. Its underglaze-painted, coloured designs were drawn on a white slip base and then covered with a transparent lead glaze. The predominant colour is a dark cobalt blue, but light blue, turquoise, purple and green are also used. Besides these, pottery with black decoration under a turquoise glaze in the Seljuk tradition has also been found. In these examples of the earliest original Anatolian Turkish pottery one is struck by the very advanced decorative feeling and bold style shown in the simplified naturalistic designs, with motifs developed from the simple forms of the stems, leaves, flowers and buds of wild flowers, fan-shaped leaves, sprays of carnations, vine-clusters and various types of rosette. Two principal design schemes are to be observed in these decorations: wide bands drawn one inside the other, and a pair of large motifs repeated alternately. The decoration was carried out in three different ways: the designs could be drawn and painted within thick contours, they might be engraved with a fine point and then painted (*sgraffiato*), or they might be painted freely with a brush without any contours at all. Other important types of decoration include thick radial leaves and striations, and geometrical ornament with thick bands. The decoration might also include decorative bird figures.

Although it was influenced in some ways by the tradition of Seljuk pottery the most brilliant period of Iznik art began with the creation of a very advanced pottery style by means of a very simple technique and designs employing only one or two colours. The skill displayed in drawing innumerable different designs with a light brush testifies to an amazing creative power. This pottery, which was a purely local, hastily decorated artistic creation, had a compelling influence that transcended frontiers and centuries. Apart from the thousands of fragments with colours and designs unknown until the present day, the excavations in Iznik have also revealed various kiln wasters that had fused with one another or stuck to their spurs, together with a quantity of kiln material and unglazed pottery. It would appear that this type of pottery was manufactured on a large scale in Iznik and exported from there to other regions. It was thus that in Iznik, in the second half of the 14th century and the first half of the 15th, the Ottomans gave birth in Anatolia to an art of pottery full of creative vitality.

Towards the end of the 15th century in Iznik the rough red clay is replaced by a hard white clay, and a magnificent, completely new type of blue and white pottery appears, closely resembling porcelain. Dark blue continues to be used in this third period of Ottoman pottery. The white ground is very clean and hard, and the transparent, colourless glaze is very thin, brilliant and absolutely pure. Although the designs are composed of the *rumis*, 'Chinese' arabesque and stylised cloud motifs to be seen in the tiles of the 15th century, they are treated here in quite a different fashion and in such a way as to give the effect of relief. At first dark blue remains the dominant colour, but later gives way to a lighter, warmer, more delicate blue. These light blue colours can be seen in a ewer with an Armenian inscription mentioning the name Abraham of Kütahya and the date 1510, now in the Godman collection. Taking this ewer as a standard a number of pottery pieces of the same type have been grouped together as belonging to the style of Abraham of Kütahya. The only colour used besides blue was a pale turquoise, and this only in later pieces. Like the colours, the designs were at first very heavy and overloaded but gradually became lighter. There is a candlestick belonging to this group in the British Museum. Among the very varied selection of blue and white pottery discovered during the 1963 excavations in Iznik are to be seen small pieces decorated with fishes, hares and other quadrupeds, and even some scenes showing animals attacking one another. On a blue and white decanter in the E. H. Ayverdi collection in Istanbul there is a random arrangement of hares, dogs, foxes, deer and birds, side by side or pursuing one another. In the mosque lamps made in this series a great deal of space is given up to epigraphy. Kufic or *naskhī* (*thuluth*) script reserved in white on a blue ground, or simply in blue on a white ground, is very frequently seen. Although the colours and designs in this third period of Ottoman pottery are obviously influenced by Ming blue and white porcelain, motifs from the Seljuk period also play a very important role in its development, and although the main centre of this pottery was Iznik, Kütahya was also a very important, though apparently secondary centre. As it is impossible to carry out excavations under the houses in Kütahya the position remains obscure. There is also another group of pottery which has come to be known, misleadingly, as Haliç (Golden Horn) ware. This pottery is of the same style and quality as the blue and white pottery but is differentiated from it by designs composed of very small leaves and flowers, and extremely fine spiral scrolls resembling calligraphy. This is really a further development of Iznik blue and white pottery. At first long delicate leaves and dark-coloured medallions of fine *rūmī* arabesques can be seen among the spiral scrolls. Later, at the beginning of the 16th century, we see lighter and simpler designs composed only of spiral scrolls, small leaves and flowers. An Armenian inscription on the base of a broken-necked decanter with very delicate designs of spiral scrolls in the Godman collection mentions that it was made to order in Kütahya in 1529. Sometimes these patterns are combined with other designs in blue and white, whilst we find unusual forms with the inside of the bowl decorated with spirals and the outside with *rūmī* and *hatayī* arabesques. Earlier tiles and book illumination had made remarkable use of fine spiral scrolls, as, for instance, the tiled cenotaph of the Green Türbe at Bursa, the window lunette in the courtyard of the Üç Şerefeli Mosque at Edirne, and the türbe of Choban Mustafa Pasha at Gebze. This is a type of decoration stretching back to the Seljuk period, and is to be seen in the tiles from Keykubadiye near Kayseri. The so-called Golden Horn wares occupy a special place in the history of ceramics on account of their high quality and fine, graceful ornament. (Fig. 218.)

Turquoise was used together with blue in a large quantity of pottery that may be approximately dated to the years 1530–40. On these plates we find for the first time the tulip, hyacinth and carnation designs that were to play such a large part in later pottery. The tulip had long been known among the Turks and had occupied an important place in the decorative arts. In 1554, the ambassador of Ferdinand I secretly smuggled some tulip bulbs out to Europe.

The fourth period of Iznik pottery begins with a very rich and original decoration that appeared in large quantities in the middle of the 16th century. This pottery is mistakenly known as Damascus ware on account of the fact that some examples of it now survive in the tile-work of various monuments in Damascus. It quite obviously belongs to the blue and white group of pottery and is of great importance as a transition to the coral red group, the fifth and last period of Iznik pottery. Besides tulip, hyacinth and carnation designs we find rosebuds and full-blown roses, artichokes, fish scales, rosettes and sometimes vases or metal ewers. The colours too become richer and besides turquoise and the three shades of blue there now appear olive green, and violet, with contours of greenish black. In place of the brilliant colours of the earlier pottery we now find matt, misty, smoky colours, whilst the white ground is replaced by a bluish ground with slightly corrugated nuances. Examples of this type are amongst the most original specimens of the art, with a magnificent decorative blend of naturalistic and stylised flowers (Plate VII). A considerable number of large and small fragments of this type of pottery was found in the excavations in Iznik. A lamp belonging to this group from the Dome of the Rock at Jerusalem and now in the British Museum has an inscription surrounding the circular base giving the signature of Naqqāsh (decorator) Muslu, together with Iznik and the date 956/1549.

As a result of the increasing quantity of tiles produced in the workshops of Iznik and Kütahya from the second half of the 16th century onwards there was a rapid decline in the production of pottery, which was continued now merely as a side line. As matt, misty colours were not suitable for architectural decoration they sought to produce a tile and pottery design with more vivid and brilliant colours. Thus the Turkish art of pottery in Iznik entered its last and most brilliant period.

This pottery is to be found among the most precious collections in all the museums of the world; the colours consist of a cobalt blue, a soft green, turquoise and, for a space of about fifty years, a brilliant raised coral red on a brilliant white ground. We also find other colours such as pink, brown and grey, which may be laid in relief sometimes on a coloured ground. The colours are prevented from running by black contours. Rich decoration composed of carnations, tulips, daisies, hyacinths, roses, violets, lilies, pomegranate and plum blossoms, vines and cypresses produces an impression of eternal spring. Large green leaves in the shape of curved daggers and classical borders on the plates in imitation of Chinese rock- and wave-scrolls lend these designs a characteristic appearance (Plate IX). Other Chinoiserie motifs, clouds, fish-scale motifs, flowered medallions and sailing boats are frequently to be seen.

Long-necked pottery decanters with various types of designs were also very commonly used. Their brilliant white and coral red colours and attractive, elegant lines are very pleasing to the eye (Plate X). Another group consists of ewers with handles and wide mouths. Goblets resembling beer-mugs with handles were also manufactured. On the plates can be seen various decorations composed of clusters of grapes and vine leaves, peacocks and birds amongst flowers, standing figures of men and women and animal combats. Unfortunately, as a result of a fanciful theory that has now long been disproved but was originally based on the fact that the Musée de Cluny in Paris happened to buy a large quantity of these wares on the island of Rhodes, these works belonging to the most brilliant period of Turkish pottery were long stamped as Rhodes or Lindos ware. Several pieces of this ware were discovered in recent excavations at Iznik. At the end of the 17th century work in the Iznik workshops ceased entirely, and the demand was met by the tiles and pottery produced at Kütahya.

We have very little information concerning the kilns set up on the Golden Horn in the 17th century. Evliya Chelebi records that 250 kilns were established at Eyüb. Pieces now known as Golden Horn ware were found in sondages there, and accordingly were given this name.

In the 18th century a new, very attractive type of pottery, possessing a very forceful style and very modern in outlook, began to be produced at Kütahya. Small vessels such as cups, bowls, ink-pots and flasks bear the stamp of a local type of art, with designs applied with light, free brush-strokes, quite different from classical Turkish pottery decoration. They are decorated with designs composed of small flowers and medallions in blue, red, yellow, purple and green. This was the last original style created by Turkish pottery. In the 19th century work of very low quality imitating classical Turkish wares (as well as European potteries such as Sèvres) began to be produced, and thus the great historical periods of Turkish ceramic art drew to a close.

24

TURKISH METALWORK

An art of metalwork differing entirely from that of the Sasanids appeared in Khurasan under the Great Seljuks. The oldest specimen of this extremely fine Seljuk metalwork is a splendid silver salver, 43 cm. in diameter, in the Museum of Fine Arts in Boston. According to its inscription it was made by the craftsman Ḥasan al-Kashānī in 459/1066 at the orders of the wife of the Great Seljuk Sultan Alp Arslan, to be presented to her husband. The tray is round, with slightly raised edges. In the centre there is the inscription 'Al-Sulṭān al-aʿẓam Alp Arslan' in large, beautifully composed Kufic script. Below there are two confronted winged goats, and above two birds resembling storks with their necks twisted backwards, all engraved on a highly ornate ground of spiral scrolls, palmettes and arabesques. This central composition terminates on each side in a palmette. A Kufic inscription band on a ground of similar spiral scrolls, palmettes and arabesques completely surrounds the inner edge of the raised border. Its sound technique and highly effective style make it a work worthy of so great a sultan. (Fig. 219.) It has sometimes been regarded as a forgery, but fits its period according to its inscription and the style of writing.

A silver candlestick in the same museum bears the name of Sanjar, the last Seljuk Sultan, with the date 532/1137. The identical reproduction 25 years later of the tri-lobed arches seen in the marble revetments on Sultan Masʿūd III's palace at Ghazne (1112) in the composition of the central band and the neck of this candlestick clearly indicates the link between Sanjar and Ghazne. Although an interval of 70 years had intervened, the style of the Kufic script is in exactly the same tradition as that of the silver salver of Alp Arslan. The complete absence of figures is typical, and may be taken as an indication that the candlestick was made for a mosque. These two rare works show the close interest taken by the Great Seljuk Sultans in metalwork. (Fig. 220.)

Although we find examples of silver and even gold vessels during the Seljuk period, which was the most brilliant period in the development of metalwork, the most popular medium in this art was bronze, with brass coming second.

The art of decorating bronze objects by engraving was already very advanced in Khurasan in the 11th and 12th centuries. The most important types of objects produced were incense burners, jugs, ablution ewers, mortars, candlesticks and mirrors. One can see a highly developed feeling for sculpture in the incense burners in the form of hunting animals or birds and adorned with highly stylised open-work decorations. In the earliest works in bronze we can see engraved designs consisting of inscriptions, scrolls and arabesques. A very important innovation introduced by the Seljuks was the development of silver inlay in bronze or brass objects. This technique had previously been known in a primitive form employing copper wires on bronze, and simple objects had been produced in this way. With the Seljuks this technique entered upon a brilliant development as a completely new type of art. Apart from copper, we also find very rich silver, and even gold, inlay. After the designs had been cut out in rough outline in the bronze very thin plaques of copper, silver or gold were placed in the grooves and hammered into position. After this they were embellished with very fine engraved decoration. The technique was carried to the utmost refinement of that time in Khurasan in the 12th century. The oldest specimen of this work is a pen-case now in the Hermitage Museum bearing the signature of ʿUmar bin Faḍl and the date 542/1148. It bears Arabic and Persian inscriptions written in silver inlay, together with engravings of small birds and arabesques with scrolls. The best-known work in this technique, however, is a small bronze bucket (or 'kettle') with handle and feet in the same museum. As it was formerly in the collection belonging to Prince Bobrinsky it is now known by his name. It is 18 cm. in diameter and, according to its inscription, it was made for the merchant Rashīd al-Dīn ʿAzīzī bin Abī'l Ḥusayn of Zenjan by Muḥammad ʿAbd al-Waḥīd in Herat in 559/1163, and the inlay work was carried out by Masʿūd bin Aḥmad. The body is divided into five horizontal bands. Each band contains a different design, beginning with a narrow frieze along the upper edge consisting of a row of birds (ducks). The next band consists of an inscription broken by round medallions composed of a figure seated between two dragons and written in a form of *thuluth* known as 'talking script' in which the letters terminate in a human head and body. This type of script in which the letters terminate in a human head or body was developed in Central Asia and Khurasan in the 12th century, and must have passed from there to Iran. Below this inscription band there is a frieze of musicians, acrobats and dancing girls, then, in the central band, a decorative inscription in plaited Kufic. Below there is a frieze of horsemen, followed by a *thuluth* inscription interrupted by cross-legged figures and finally a border with braided designs and several pairs of running animals. The handle is cast in the form of a large circle attached to the bucket and terminating in lions couchant. This bucket is a masterpiece of inlay work.

Another bucket closely resembling the above is to be found in the same museum. It is 25.5 cm. in height and bears the signature of Muḥammad bin Nāṣir bin Muḥammad al Ḥarāwī. This bucket, however, is divided into vertical rectangular strips decorated by two alternate designs. One design consists of a rosette in the form of a circle with a filling of geometrical stars and two birds above and below, and with two running animals at the bottom and an inscription at the top, whilst the second design consists of a tapered Kufic inscription ribbon with figures on camels and on horseback filling the spaces.

IX Iznik dishes, Victoria and Albert Museum (see page 281)

X Iznik bottle, Victoria and Albert Museum (see page 281)

We have here another example of how Seljuk metalwork excelled in inlay work with continually varying designs. The figures, motifs and epigraphic decoration to be seen in *mīnāī* and lustre tiles and pottery and in other Seljuk decorations re-appear in metalwork in a form adapted to the special features of that art. A footed brass bowl with silver inlay work 16.5 cm. in diameter and 10.5 cm. in height, thought to have been made around 1200 at Herat or Nishapur in Khurasan and now in the Cleveland Museum of Art, has a broad inscription band on the upper edge in which the letters of the 'talking script' assume an exaggerated form that might be called 'animated script' in which the letters take on the appearance of human figures in action. At the foot, in contrast, there is a simpler form of inscription in which the shafts of letters merely terminate in human heads. The whole outer surface of the bowl is entirely covered with inlaid designs, which have fallen out in some places. Other motifs used are running animals, signs of the zodiac, sphinxes, fishes and a Kufic inscription on the inner edge. The decoration of a central boss inside the bowl consists of a circular medallion with four sphinxes and fishes swimming around it. This valuable brass bowl may be said to illustrate the high quality and refinement attained by Seljuk metalwork before the destruction of the cities of Herat and Nishapur in Khurasan by the Mongols.

The brilliant art of metalwork that developed in Khurasan under the Seljuks, who were responsible for outstanding developments in every kind of art, spread to Mosul with the Zengids at the beginning of the 13th century, and it was here that the inlay technique produced its finest works of that century. A larger quantity of fine-quality metal objects has been preserved from this period, and in these the Seljuk tradition of inscribing the object with the craftsman's name is still continued. Progress can be seen in the refinement of the gold and silver inlay technique. There is a plentiful use of braid-work and meander designs. There are lively scenes of everyday life, the court, hunting and music, with original costumes. In contrast to the very lively hunting scenes of the Sasanids these scenes are static and symbolic, with only now and again a flying bird or a duck. No roughness is perceptible on the surface of these. These Mosul bronze or brass objects, most of which have *Mosul* inscribed in addition to the craftsman's name, reflect an entirely new conception. The technique spread from here back to Iran, and to Baghdad, Aleppo, Damascus and Cairo, and a number of objects have survived bearing the names of these cities. A large basin in the Museum für Völkerkunde in Munich and a tray in the Victoria and Albert Museum in London are two Mosul metal objects ordered by the Zengid ruler Badr al-Dīn Lu'lu' (1231–59), whose name they bear. Like the footed brass bowl in Cleveland Museum each of them has a round interior medallion with four sphinxes on the central boss, which may be evidence of a link with Khurasan. A basin and ewer with domed spout, both Mosul work of the middle of the 13th century, now in the Berlin Museum of Islamic Art, are in gold and silver inlay, with medallions containing figures, animal designs, a frieze of running animals and inscriptions. The ewer bears the name of the craftsman, ʿAlī bin ʿAbd Allāh al-ʿAlawī from Mosul.

A brass ewer 28 cm. in height in the Victoria and Albert Museum, with a handle but no foot, and having very rich engraved designs in addition to silver and copper inlay work, was made in Mosul in 629/1232 and bears the signature of Shujāʿ bin Manʿa. Figural decorations arranged in a wide band in the centre and other figures and inscriptions inside the medallions are in inlay work, whilst the engraved designs are composed of geometrical patterns and rosettes. A characteristic feature of these designs is the re-appearance in various forms of old Turkish geometrical architectural decorations employing intersecting hexagons. This motif was widely used by the Mamluks. A footed brass vase with silver inlay in the Bargello Museum in Florence bears the date 657/1259 and the signature of another craftsman ʿAlī bin Ḥamūd, whilst a brass spouted ewer with gold and silver inlay bearing the date 673/1274 and the signature of the same craftsman is to be found in the Archaeological Museum in Teheran.

On the other hand recent investigations have proved that the well-known Baptistère de Saint Louis in the Louvre which was formerly thought to be Mosul work of the beginning of the 13th century is actually from the Mamluk Palace and dates from the beginning of the 14th century. M. Ağaoğlu was the first to assign this object to Syria and the Mamluks, and to place it at the beginning of the 14th century. This bronze basin is 50 cm. in diameter and 24 cm. in height, and has inlay both inside and outside. More light has been thrown on the problem by the researches of D. S. Rice. Judging from the figure of an emir on horseback within a large circular medallion on the exterior Rice assigned it to the Emir Salar and the period 1290–1310, that is, during the reigns of al-Ashraf Khalīl and his brother al-Nāṣir Muḥammad, whilst R. Ettinghausen has dated it to before 715/1315. On the interior there are battle and hunting scenes and on the exterior scenes depicting the Emir hunting with his retinue, with a frieze of running animals both above and below. The Bourbon fleur-de-lis was later engraved in alternate medallions, and the inscriptions giving the date and the name of the person for whom it was made may have been destroyed at this time. Nevertheless the name of the craftsman Muḥammad bin al-Zayn was not damaged, and is to be found repeated six times. After its acquisition, probably from the Lusignans, the basin was long used for the baptism of the Kings of France.

Another brass object bearing the signature of Ustādh Muḥammad bin al-Zayn is a bowl 21.5 cm. in diameter with silver inlay and engraved decoration, formerly in the Vasselot collection and now in the Louvre. A great deal of metalwork has been preserved from the Mamluk period, and the technique of inlay in metal was eventually carried to Venice in the 15th century by Moslem craftsmen.

Although the centre of the art of metalwork in the 13th century was Mosul there was also a development of the art in Anatolia under the Artukids and Seljuks based on Great Seljuk metalwork. The objects that have survived show that engraving, repoussé, relief, inlay and enamel techniques were applied to metalwork. The most common objects were oil-lamps, candlesticks and incense burners. The oldest specimen of known date is a four-handled bronze drum in the form of a broad truncated cone (diameter 47 cm., height 50 cm.) which was discovered in Diyarbekir and is now in the Museum of Turkish and Islamic Art in Istanbul. It is Artukid work of about 1200 and the outer face is decorated as far up as the handles with a broad engraved band of bold Kufic lettering against an engraved design of arabesques with spiral scrolls. The shafts of each of the Kufic letters are knotted once and terminate in a human head in adjacent double shafts, and in a dragon's head in the single shafts. This type of 'talking'

Kufic script with human heads in the Seljuk style is different from the metalwork of Khurasan and Mosul and is peculiar to Anatolia.

Another object that has survived from the Artukid period is a two-handled copper cup in the Ferdinandeum in Innsbruck. According to its inscription it was made for the Emir Sökmen (Sukman) bin Dā'ūd (1114–49) of the Artukids of Ḥiṣn Kayfā, and it is decorated in seven-coloured cloisonné enamels, a technique very rarely found in Turkish or Islamic art. Apart from a *naskhī* inscription band surrounding the edges, the main Alexander figure in the centre and the other figures in and between the medallions surrounding this show very clearly the influence of Byzantine art. Both the technique and the design are alien to Turkish metalwork, and it is thus quite untypical.

A small sphinx 12.5 cm. in height clearly dating from the time of the Artukids in Anatolia was discovered in a cemetery, and having been bought at Dunaysir (Kızıltepe) was taken to the museum in Diyarbekir. The sphinx is sitting on four legs, and has a human head with plaited hair and threefold crown that is in every respect an exact copy of the Seljuk type. Each of the curving wings ends in a dragon's head. This sphinx was probably made as an ornamental finial for the lid of an incense burner. Incense burners are often seen in open-work or pierced inlay work in the shape of wild animals, horses, ducks or birds. They are sometimes made with a lid with a moulded figure placed on it, or their handles or legs may be decorated with such figures. The metal sphinx in Diyarbekir may have belonged to an incense burner of this type. (Fig. 221.)

A bronze lamp 20 cm. in height and 60 cm. in body diameter which was taken from the Eshrefoghlu Mosque at Beyşehir in 1942 and placed in the Ethnographical Museum at Ankara is a typical specimen of Anatolian metalwork. The body is entirely covered with scrolls, palmettes and arabesques in filigree, and the mouth, which gradually widens towards the top, consists of extremely intricate *thuluth* inscriptions in open work. Thirty-five verses of the *Surat al-Nūr* (the Sura of Light) are written here. From the *naskhī* inscription on the foot we learn that the lamp was made at Konya in 699/1299 by 'Alī ibn Muḥammad of Nusaybin. That is, the craftsman was from Nusaybin but the lamp was made at Konya. The Eshrefoghlu Süleyman Bek ordered the lamps at the same time as the mosque was being built, but unfortunately only one of these has survived.

Candlesticks were among the finest specimens of Seljuk metalwork, and these continued to be produced in Zengid and Mamluk times. They averaged a height of about 21 cm. and were made of copper, bronze or brass, with various types of decoration. Mamluk candlesticks resemble the Seljuk style very closely, and can only be distinguished by their inscriptions and blazons. Diyarbekir, Konya and Sivas were well-known centres during the Seljuk period, and Mosul, Damascus and Aleppo during the Zengid period. Freely worked designs of hunters on horseback and groups of three emirs set unframed on a background of scrolls are very commonly seen on Mosul work. The whole surface is entirely covered with ornament. A copper candlestick with gold and silver inlay in the Museum of Turkish and Islamic Art in Istanbul is of interest in showing the influence of several different styles. A large central design below the fine Kufic border on the lower edge depicts the signs of the zodiac in a series of cartouches. These figures derive from European art but are worked in Seljuk style. The interstices are decorated with scrolls and arabesques in silver inlay. Figures are also shown engaged in various occupations according to the various months of the year. There is a further Kufic inscription on the upper edge, a *naskhī* inscription on the neck section, and, at the very top, a *naskhī* inscription embellished with flowers on the holder. Gold inlay is used only in the details. Judging from the script and decoration the candlestick may be assigned to Mosul and the second half of the 13th century.

Metal mirrors form another category of Seljuk art. Their forms and decoration were adopted by the Ottomans. Their decoration consisted of engraved or inlaid designs, with or without figures.

A bronze mirror decorated in relief work (diameter 20 cm.) in the Topkapı Saray Museum has decoration consisting of a narrow surrounding frieze of arabesques and palmettes, then an inscription band in broad Kufic script adorned with arabesques setting forth a prayer beginning with the *basmala*. The central part of the mirror contains a symmetrical design of five-veined arabesques and palmettes. It is thought to be Anatolian Seljuk work of the middle of the 13th century.

A second mirror in this museum is decorated by a very interesting figural relief in inlay on steel. In the centre there is depicted a symbolic hunting scene with a horseman holding a falcon. A design composed of a wild duck flying in front of a mounted horseman with hunting-dog and fox, and a snake or a dragon attacking the horse, is arranged with great skill in the circular space. The hunter holding a falcon is a figure used in the *mīnāī* tiles from the Qılıch Arslan Kiosk in Konya. The same figure is also to be seen in *mīnāī* pottery. The presence of the same figure of a hunter worked in relief on two bronze mirrors of the Karakhanid period in the Hermitage Museum shows that this was a very old motif and one that was widely used among the Turks. The Topkapı mirror has a wide border with two interlaced dragons at the very top with figures of a stag, a centaur, a bull and a gryphon arranged symmetrically on either side. The hunter's dress, his features, and the horse trappings are all entirely Seljuk. This richly figured mirror must date from the beginning of the 13th century, and is a rare specimen of Anatolian Seljuk metalwork. (Fig. 222.)

Another magnificent mirror in gold and silver inlay on iron preserved in the Topkapı Saray Museum is one of the very fine works of high quality produced in Aleppo around 1320. Here again we find depicted the twelve signs of the zodiac. In the *naskhī* inscription in gold inlay in the centre we find the titles of the owner together with the name of the craftsman: ' 'Amal ustādh Muḥammad al-Wazīrī [the work of the craftsman, Muḥammad al-Wazīrī]'. In the small circle in the centre we find the name of the owner, 'Alā al-Dīn. This must probably be a Turkish emir of the name of 'Alā al-Dīn Altinbughā who was governor of Aleppo between 1314 and 1326 during the Mamluk period. Apart from the sign Leo all the signs of the zodiac are represented by human figures. In the central inscription the shafts of an inscription are arranged to form a small circular sun symbol. In the band surrounding this sun inscription there is a design consisting of animals pursuing each other against a background of foliate motifs. The animals include a lion, a stag, a goat, a sphinx and an unidentifiable creature.

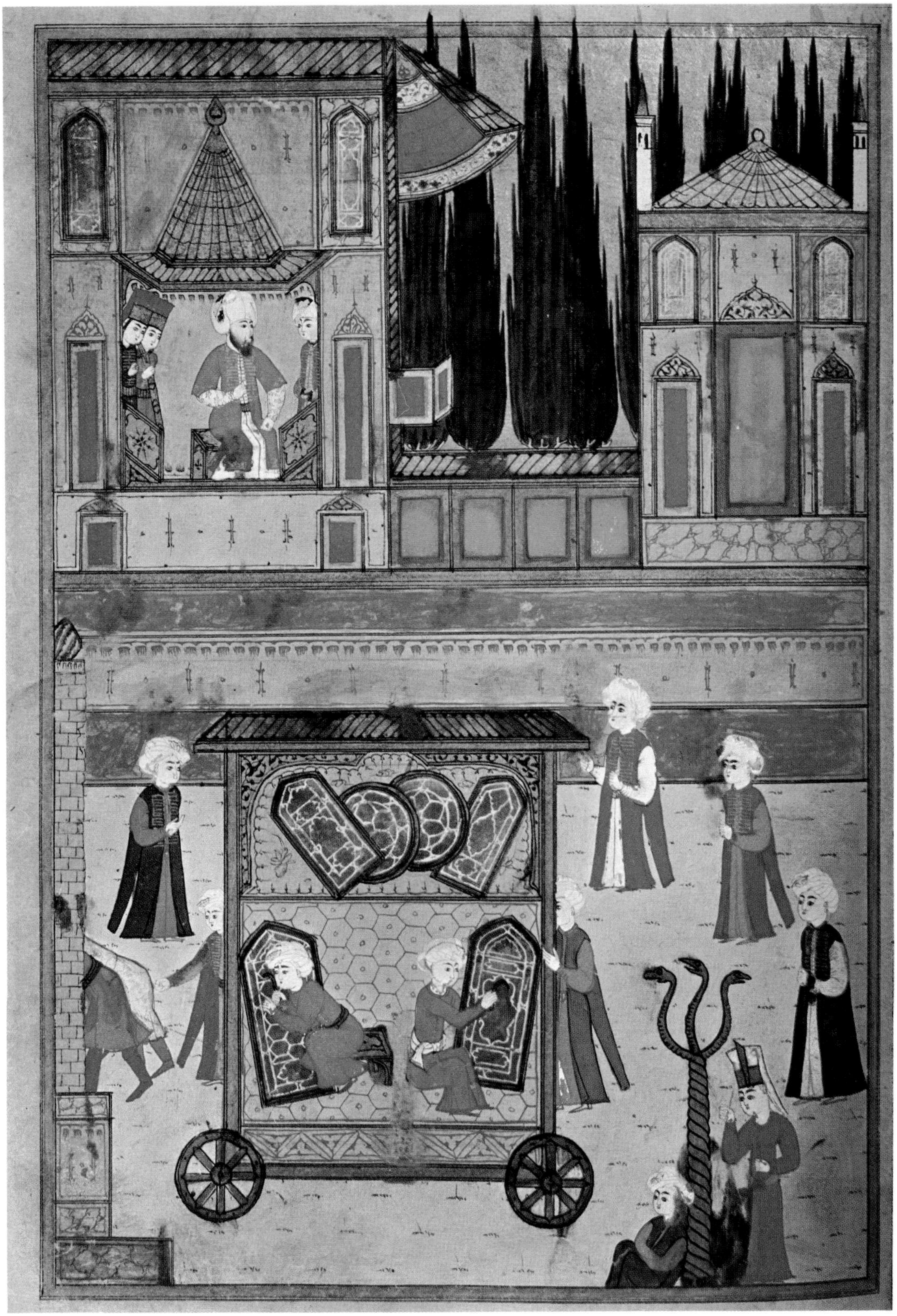

XI The glaziers, Sūrnāme, Istanbul, Topkapı Saray Museum, Hazine Library (see page 290)

25

TURKISH GLASS

The beaker had a symbolic meaning for Turkish rulers and emirs. In miniatures, pottery, tiles and other figural arts, they are often shown sitting cross-legged with a beaker in their hands. As Kühnel very aptly pointed out, the use of glass vessels decorated with enamel and gilt became established in Syria, Aleppo and perhaps Iraq under the influence of the Great Seljuks from the 12th century onwards. Bottles, beakers, decanters and dishes of various shapes continued to be produced in the Zengid period and, as happened in every branch of art, the Seljuk tradition passed on to the Ayyubids. The decorations used in Rayy and Kashan pottery are found repeated in glassware. There are also some beakers completely devoid of decoration save for a band of lettering or ornament. The beaker known as the Luck of Edenhall decorated with enamelled arabesques and palmettes in five colours, produced in Aleppo in the middle of the 13th century and now in the Victoria and Albert Museum, became famous enough to find a place in both English and German literature. Glass lamps with inscriptions and a very restrained use of ornament were made in Egypt during the Turkish Mamluk period for use in mosques.

Various types of glassware known as *shemsiye* made from glass manufactured in Anatolia in the Artukid and Seljuk periods for use in mosques and medreses are worthy of special note. A number of plain, round or slightly convex glass plaques of various colours, some of them buried in plaster, were unearthed during the Kubādābād excavations. These had adorned the windows of the palace of ʿAlā al-Dīn Kayqubād. A gilt glass plate 30 cm. in diameter was restored from fragments found there. The name of Sultan Ghiyāth al-Dīn Kaykhusraw II (1237–47) is mentioned in a clearly arranged *thuluth* inscription in the form of a wide border to it.

In the Ottoman period a large quantity of candlesticks, vases for tulips and other flowers, rose-water flasks, glass and crystal bowls, decanters, cooling vessels, travelling-flasks, glasses, cups, sugar bowls, glass bombs used in the army, naval lanterns, lamp glasses and stained-glass windows were manufactured. The glass-blowers and the craftsmen fitting glass into plaster windows who can be seen taking part in the procession in front of the bakers in the *Sūrnāme* miniatures present a living record of the 16th century (Plate XI). Glass bombs used by the Ottoman army during the siege of Rhodes have been recovered during excavations carried out there. The stained-glass windows made for the Süleymaniye Mosque by Ibrahim the Drunkard are well known. The Ottoman glass industry was centred in Istanbul in the vicinity of Eğrikapı and the Tekfur Palace. Near the Baruthane-i Amire (or Imperial Powder Factory) at Bakırköy there were large highly decorative wheels driven by draught animals, mortars for polishing, glass workshops, saltpetre cauldrons and kilns. In the reign of Mustafa III (1757–74) all the glass and bottle workshops were gathered together in the precincts of the Tekfur Palace and it was forbidden to open any such workshops elsewhere. Very fine, white sand suitable for glass manufacture is found at Kum Burgaz near Yedikule, and was even exported. There were completely separate corporations for the manufacturers of glass bottles, spun glass and mirrors, and glass itself was divided up into three types—plain glass, coloured glass and crystal. Products known as 'false' or 'vile' work which did not conform to certain standards and weights were broken and the craftsman responsible punished. At the beginning of the 19th century a workshop near Çubuklu won the approval of the Sultan by its manufacture of luxury, high-quality, glass and crystal ware. This factory was later bought by the State and in 1846 Tahir Efendi, the superintendent of the mint, was appointed director. The great variety and very high quality of the plain glassware and *çeşm-i bülbül* produced here was held in high esteem. This *çeşm-i bülbül* was a type of glass manufactured in the Çubuklu workshops that was given this name because the colours used were thought to resemble a nightingale's eye. (Fig. 223.)

In 1848, in the reign of Abdülmejid, a dervish known as Mehmed Dede who had studied glass-making in Italy opened a workshop at Beykoz, which produced gilt crystal bowls, dishes, glasses, bottles, tulip vases etc. in an original style which came to be known as 'Beykoz ware'. Coloured spiral *çeşm-i bülbül* ware was also manufactured here. (Fig. 224.)

In 1899 a glass factory was established at Paşabahçe on the initiative of a Jewish manufacturer, Saul Mediano, and by 1902 there were five hundred workers in this factory. It could not, however, compete with the glassware imported in large quantities from Europe free of customs duties. There was a revival, nevertheless, with the opening of a glass and bottle factory at Paşabahçe in 1935. This factory produces every type of clear, coloured and opaline glass, and in recent years a few experiments have been made with types of glass resembling *çeşm-i bülbül*.

There is a rich collection of old Ottoman glassware in the Topkapı Saray Museum. There we find displayed in a separate showcase 57 pieces of various kinds of *çeşm-i bülbül* originally belonging to Hawland Shaw and presented to the museum in 1937.

26

SELJUK AND OTTOMAN CARPETS

The art of carpet-making is one of the most valuable contributions of the Turks to world civilisation and one of the most original creations of Turkish art.

Leaving aside the Pazyryk Carpet, which probably dates from the Asiatic Huns of the 3rd or 2nd century B.C. but has little connection with later carpet-making, the oldest examples of knotted carpets known are fragments found by Sir Aurel Stein in East Turkestan in 1906–8. Further pieces were unearthed in the Le Coq Turfan explorations of 1913. The oldest of these carpets, now preserved in the museums of London, Berlin and Delhi, date from the 3rd century, and the most recent from the 6th. Although the knotting is still rather coarse, lozenge and stylised flower designs are clearly defined by clipping the ends of coloured wools. The colours are bright and strong, and consist of dark blue, brown, red, matt green and three shades of yellow. To have reached such an advanced technique, carpet-making must have begun as far back as the 1st century. After that the art spread eastwards with the Seljuks in the 11th century, though no carpets of the Great Seljuk period in Iran have survived.

In 1905 the German Consul Löytved discovered eight 13th-century carpets of the Anatolian Seljuk period in the 'Alā al-Dīn Mosque in Konya. Three of these are complete, although in a very worn condition, and five of them in fragments. These are now in the Museum of Turkish and Islamic Art in Istanbul, which houses the richest collection of Turkish carpets in the world, consisting of more than a thousand fine carpets. These Seljuk carpets sometimes measure as much as 15 square metres, and display an incredible wealth of colour and ornament. The field is usually dark blue and light red. A striking feature is the use of light and dark yellow and, occasionally, of light green. Although only a limited number of different colours is employed a very rich effect is produced by the use of various shades of the same colour. The designs consist of geometrical patterns of lozenges arranged in horizontal and vertical rows, eight-pointed stars, and octagons surrounded with hooks, together with foliate forms that have been adapted to fit into a geometrical scheme; but their most monumental and characteristic feature is the bold Kufic script in a wide border. At first one finds a type of Kufic with very upright lettering and pointed triangular tips resembling arrow-heads, but later various changes are introduced. These Seljuk carpets were no doubt presented to the mosque by ʿAlā al-Dīn Kayqubād after he had had the mosque enlarged.

CARPET I

Pattern 1 (*above*). Arrow-head (Konya)

Pattern 2 (*right*). Arrow-head (Fusṭāṭ)

In 1930 an American Professor, R. Riefstahl, found fragments of three more Seljuk carpets in the Eshrefoghlu Mosque at Beyşehir and presented them to the Konya museum. As the mosque was built at the end of the 13th century the carpets must also date from that period. The fourth carpet found by Riefstahl at Beyşehir dates from the 15th century.

In 1935–6 fragments of about a hundred Anatolian carpets of the 13th, 14th and 15th centuries were unearthed at Fusṭāṭ in Egypt. Most of these were taken by C. Lamm to Sweden, whilst others were acquired by the Benaki museum in Athens. Of the 29 fragments published by Lamm, 7 date from the Seljuk period. Thus of the eighteen Seljuk carpets, three of them complete and fifteen in fragments, which have survived to the present day, only two are identical, giving seventeen different patterns in all, and that there should be such a wealth of variety in so small a number of specimens testifies to creative fertility. On the Konya carpet, which is the largest of these, dark red designs recalling arrow-heads and resembling the shafts of Kufic letters are arranged in rows, one overlapping the other, on a light red ground (Pattern 1). A similar design and colours are to be found in one of the Fusṭāṭ fragments (Pattern 2). The monumental border of the Konya carpet composed of a large pseudo-Kufic design in light blue on a dark blue ground produces an unforgettable and monumental effect (Plate XII). The narrow border consists of stars set in squares.

On a second Konya carpet the ground consists of 8-pointed stars in light on dark blue with a red star in the centre of each. The points of these are joined by light blue double ribbons decorated with hook designs (Pattern 3). The wide border has a light red pattern on a dark red ground, whilst the narrow border has a yellow pattern on a brown ground (Patterns 4–5; Plate XIII).

The third, large Konya carpet has a pattern of filled octagons known as 'camels' feet' arranged in horizontal and vertical rows in red on cream yellow with a border consisting of interwoven pairs of fine white Kufic letters on a red pattern (Pattern 6).

CARPET 2

Pattern 3. 8-pointed stars joined by ribbons (Konya)

Pattern 4. Border design (Konya)

Pattern 5. Border design (Konya)

On the fourth Konya carpet there is a pattern of stylised flowers in the form of octagons with swastikas in the middle and ornamented with hooks and stems, in light red on a dark purple (Pattern 7). In the border there are two patterns in turquoise on a brown ground. The border across the width resembles the second Konya carpet, whilst the border along the length consists of delicate lines with stars and hooks (Patterns 8–9; Plate XIV).

A fifth Konya carpet has a pattern of light blue octagons on a dark blue ground; each octagon is surrounded with hooks and has one end terminating in an arrowhead. The centre of the octagon is occupied by a red, rectangular letter S known as a 'flint' (Pattern 10). The border of white Kufic lettering on a red ground is ornamented with broken lines and fillings of coloured stars (Plate XV). On the inner border there is a row of angular floral patterns known as 'goose feet'. The same design is to be found in different colours and a more naturalistic form in the Fusṭāṭ fragments (Patterns 11–12). The same design appears on a Beyşehir carpet of the 15th century.

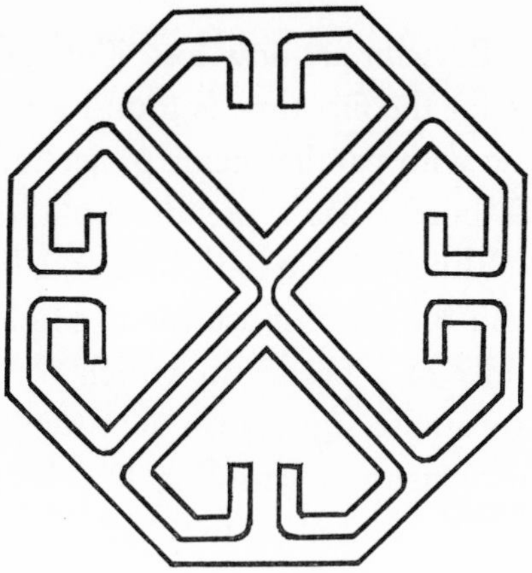

CARPET 3. Pattern 6. 'Camel's foot' (Konya)

The sixth Konya carpet has rows of lozenges with hooks, known as 'Elibelinde' (torso with arms akimbo), in dark blue on a yellow ground. At the bottom edge the colour of the ground suddenly changes to give yellow patterns on dark blue (Pattern 13). The border consists of dark red Kufic script on a light red ground, enlivened by a green crescent pattern produced by joining two of the letters together. The same border is repeated on one of the Fusṭāṭ fragments in yellow Kufic letters (Pattern 14). This sixth Konya carpet has a twin measuring 2.26 × 1.23 metres (Plate XVI).

CARPET 4

Pattern 7. Stylised flowers with hooks or stems (Konya)

Pattern 8. Border design (Konya)

Pattern 9. Border design (Konya)

The seventh Konya carpet, which is a smaller piece, has a pattern of lozenges with hooks surrounded in the form of an octagon by long, narrow lozenges with 'flints' in the centre, all in light blue on a dark blue ground (Pattern 15). The border resembles the fifth Konya carpet with some differences in colour.

In the Seljuk carpet from Beyşehir there is a pattern of light blue lozenges with hooks on two sides and red and dark blue stars in the centre on a dark blue ground. (Pattern 16.) Only a small fragment of the border remains, with white Kufic lettering on a red ground (Plate XVII).

Two of the fragments found at Beyşehir are now lost. Two of the remaining pieces are from a carpet 5 metres in length. Here for the first time is found a pattern composed of an angular flower motif in light on dark blue with parallel stems projecting to the left in one row and to the right in the other. The wide border has a pseudo-Kufic decoration embellished with a stylised figure with arms akimbo (Elibelinde) in dark blue on a light ground, whilst the narrow border has a pattern of small reddish-brown Kufic script on a light yellow ground.

The third fragment consists only of a border in which the border pattern of the second Konya carpet is repeated with turquoise squares on a brown ground (Pattern 17). On the inner and outer borders there are patterns resembling fine Kufic in cream yellow on a red ground. A rather larger fragment of the central portion of the same carpet has been found in the store-rooms of the Konya Museum. Here the main pattern of the second Konya carpet is repeated in light brown red. This carpet may be one of a number of lost fragments.

From the 14th century onwards we find a decorative use of highly stylised animal figures in Anatolian carpets. These are inserted as fillings in geometrical forms. The most popular design consists of birds perched on both sides of a tree. Towards the end of the century we find lively scenes of groups of animals, or animals attacking one another. As the first carpets with animal or bird figures appear in paintings by European artists in the 14th century the prototypes may well go back as far as the 13th century. Representations of these in Italian and Flemish painting continue until the middle of the 15th century. No original carpets have survived from the 14th century.

CARPET 5

Pattern 10. S-shaped pattern 'flint' (Konya)

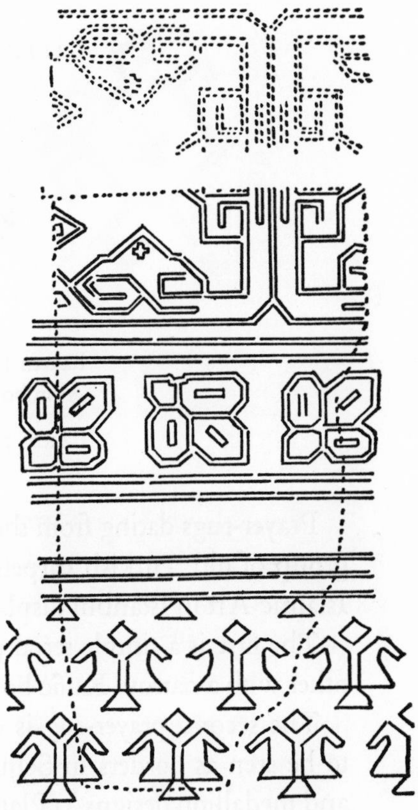

Pattern 11 *(right)*. Floral pattern, goose feet and 'akimbo' (Fusṭāṭ)
Pattern 12 *(above)*. Kufic border (Fusṭāṭ)

On a carpet purchased by Bode in Rome and now in the East Berlin Museum a pattern representing a combat between a phoenix and a dragon is twice repeated. This is an Anatolian carpet dating from the second half of the 15th century.

Another Anatolian carpet with stylised bird figures on each side of a tree was found in the Swedish village of Marby in 1925. But here we find a late variation of the end of the 15th century in which the filling is completed by repeating the branches of the trees below as if reflected in water (Plate XVIII).

Three of the fragments found at Fusṭāṭ have bird or animal figures. Another carpet dating from the end of the 15th century with a pattern consisting of ten rows of four cockerels each, is now in the Konya Museum.

Towards the end of the 15th century carpets with animal figures are replaced in European painting by carpets with geometrical designs. These are to be found after 1451 first in Italian and then in Flemish and Dutch painting, but as they are found particularly frequently in the works of Holbein they have come to be known by his name. A 15th-century carpet, a fragment of which was found by Riefstahl at Beyşehir, is the oldest of all known Holbein carpets and is of very large dimensions. Ten squares of the pattern were completed by the find of pieces of this carpet in summer 1968 in the store-rooms of the Konya Museum (Plate XIX). The extremely ornate and spectacular border and the purple colour here seen for the first time are both characteristic of the 15th century.

CARPET 6

Pattern 13. Torso with Arms Akimbo 'Elibelinde' (Konya)

Pattern 14. 'Elibelinde' (Fusṭāṭ)

Prayer-rugs dating from the 15th century—the oldest prayer-rugs yet known—form a separate group of old Turkish carpets. Of these the three prayer-rugs in the Museum of Turkish and Islamic Art in Istanbul display three totally different patterns.

The first is a simple serial prayer-rug consisting of two rows of eight mihrabs one above the other with a narrow Kufic border (Plate XX).

The second prayer-rug is composed of a row of mihrabs decorated with the Kufic motifs to be seen as borders in Seljuk carpets. (The inside of the mihrabs is ornamented with lamp and medallion designs.) (Plate XXI.)

The third prayer-rug has fillings consisting of three medallions one above the other between

CARPET 7. Pattern 15. Border design (Konya)

three looped ribbons and a traditional Seljuk border of fine Kufic script. The designs are in blue, yellow and green on a purple ground, whilst the border is green on yellow.

We can find other types of 15th-century prayer-rug in paintings of the Renaissance, particularly in the works of Gentile and Giovanni Bellini, Carpaccio and Lorenzo Lotto. A prayer-rug of this kind is set beneath the feet of a table in a painting by Giovanni Bellini of the Venetian Doge Loredano dated 1507 in the Munich Pinacotheca. A prayer-rug in the Islamic Museum in West Berlin is the exact replica of this. The plain mihrab with angular apex and parallel sides has an octagonal inward projection from the base. The whole pattern is completed by a design in the middle consisting of a large medallion and hanging lamp, with a

CARPET 8

Pattern 16. Lozenges and stars (Beyşehir)

Pattern 17. Border design of a carpet fragment (Konya)

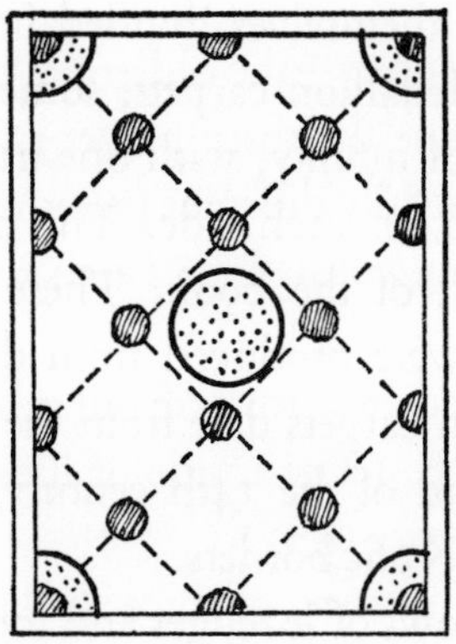

Pattern 18. Ottoman Palace carpet

Kufic border. (Plate XXII.) In addition to this magnificent 15th-century prayer-rug there are two prayer-rugs in the same museum of a similar pattern.

A special feature of the 15th century, as we have said, was the appearance of the carpets now associated with the name of Holbein. Some of these were represented earlier in the works of Italian painters, others were never included in any of Holbein's paintings, but although the attribution of his name to these carpets is both surprising and misleading, it has persisted. The oldest of the Holbein carpets belongs to the 15th century and they are rarely found after the 16th century. The patterns consist of octagons with indefinite outlines, and rows of overlapping lozenges or rows of octagons in small variously coloured squares arranged side by side. The borders very often have a pseudo-Kufic pattern.

Patterns consisting of a smaller version of the lozenge-octagon design on the Beyşehir carpet are also included in this category.

Other Holbein carpets composed of scattered designs in the form of rich cross-like lozenges produced by joining various foliate motifs together, and octagons without outlines, preserve the same general patterns. These carpets always consist of a yellow pattern on a red ground, but the Kufic border is sometimes replaced by the cloud motifs of the traditional Uşak border. Of the great many original carpets depicted in paintings between 1500 and 1800, that have survived to the present day, some attain a length of six metres and others display coats of arms. As these are very often seen in the paintings of Lorenzo Lotto they are also known as Lotto carpets. (Fig. 225.) Plain Holbein carpets consisting of rows of large squares one above the other with octagonal fillings developed throughout the 15th century and continued until recent years.

A different type of Holbein carpet displays pattern-grouping for the first time, with two octagons above and below large squares. These Holbein carpets all fall into the four categories above, and were manufactured in Uşak, or elsewhere in Western Anatolia.

Another brilliant period begins with the carpets made in the same district in the 16th century. Holbein carpets prepared the transition from the Seljuk to the Ottoman art of carpet-making that developed throughout the 16th century. Uşak carpets make up a very rich and varied group, which has not yet been extensively studied. Uşak carpets developed from the second group of Holbein carpets, and are themselves divided into two main categories—those with stars and those with medallions. Medallion carpets, some of which are as long as 10 metres, have a pattern expressing the idea of infinity, with one truncated medallion above and below a large central medallion, and two on each side. The medallion is a motif imported from Tabriz and borrowed from the art of the book. These latter, however, were finite, closed patterns. Uşak medallion carpets were produced from the 16th century until the middle of the 18th century. The oldest Persian carpets date from the end of the 15th century, but carpets depicted in miniatures from the end of the 14th century onwards are in the Turkish carpet tradition with octagon patterns and Kufic borders.

Uşak star carpets with alternate rows of lozenges and medallions arranged in the form of stars the endless pattern is more conspicuous. These disappear after the 17th century, and there is a very limited number of original specimens. (Fig. 226.) In the painting by Paris Bordone in the Accademia at Venice dated 1533 entitled 'A fisherman bringing the ring of St. Mark to the Doge', the Doge's throne is set on a magnificent Uşak star carpet, but the oldest originals are three carpets now in the possession of the Duke of Buccleuch bearing the Montagu coat of arms in the border and dated 1584 and 1585. The 1584 carpet is a very rare specimen with an arrangement of alternately three stars and two lozenges.

Uşak carpets with a white field mentioned in written documents of the middle of the 16th century and depicted in later paintings are known as Kushlu (Bird) Carpets, and are to be found as late as the 18th century. This type of carpet originally got its name because the pattern composed of two symmetrically arranged leaves with a variously coloured ground between gives the impression of the shape of a bird. Some of the white Uşak carpets have *çintemani* (Chinoiserie) patterns. Those with a red ground have *çintemani* patterns in dark-blue and yellow. These various types of Uşak carpet had a brilliant development lasting for over three centuries but at the end of the 18th century a period of degeneration and retrogression set in.

Another type of carpet that developed from the large patterned Holbein carpets is the Bergama carpet. These usually have geometrical patterns, with sometimes highly stylised forms adapted to conform to the same pattern. The oldest of these carpets date from the 16th century, and they have continued to use the Kufic border and a number of the Seljuk patterns up to the present day.

In the second half of the 16th century there appears side by side with the traditional Anatolian carpets another group known as Ottoman Palace carpets, that are completely different from them in both technique and colour. The naturalistic leaf and flower designs of the Ottomans are here combined with the Persian (*Sine*) knot. In contrast to the other Turkish carpets, all of which employ the Ghiordes (*Gördes*) knot, these use a very tight knot that produces a soft effect like that of velvet. In 1514 the Ottomans conquered Tabriz, and in 1517 Cairo. Both these dates are of great importance in the history of Turkish carpet-making. The Palace carpets were greatly influenced by the technique, materials and colours employed in Mamluk carpets of the early 16th century. In Palace carpets, unlike Uşak carpets, the medallion pattern plays only a very secondary role. The basic pattern is a type of endless design (Pattern 18). The sound artistic sense of the Turks rejected any kind of close connection with the art of the book and remained faithful to laws of textile manufacture. Here we have the basic reason for the superiority of Turkish carpets over Safawid carpets. It has recently been suggested that the Palace carpets were manufactured in Cairo in accordance with patterns sent from Istanbul. A document exists showing that craftsmen were summoned to the Palace from Cairo in 1685, but there is also evidence that carpets and prayer-rugs of this quality were manufactured in private workshops in Istanbul and Bursa. The tradition of Palace carpets has continued up to our own time in both Istanbul and Anatolia.

From the middle of the 16th century prayer-rugs in the style of Ottoman Palace carpets were made as luxury articles for the palace. The mihrabs have undulating contours, whilst the central space is sometimes left blank, sometimes filled with flowers. These constitute the most successful and the most satisfying designs of the Palace carpet group. A prayer-rug of this type with mihrab and plain green field presented to the Mosque of Sultan Ahmed as an example of 'Istanbul work', was transferred in a very worn condition to the Museum of Turkish and Islamic Art where it was put on display with the same label. A well-preserved carpet of the same pattern in the Islamic Museum in West Berlin gives a very good idea of its original appearance. The date 1610 is inscribed in two square panels on the upper border. (Plate XXIII.) There is also another, very worn palace prayer-rug in the Topkapı Saray known as the prayer-rug of Sultan Ahmed I. At the end of the 16th century small prayer-rugs with mihrabs at either end can be seen in addition to the medallion Uşak carpets. Here, a medallion design has been placed in the centre. This type of prayer-rug continued to be manufactured as late as the eighteenth century.

From the 17th century onwards large quantities of simple serial prayer-rugs based on Palace carpets begin to be manufactured in a large variety of designs. The search for novelty evident in them results in a number of attractive patterns in various colours and designs. These are completely dominated by the naturalistic flower and leaf design to be found in all Ottoman art. A spring atmosphere is sometimes created by the use of plum blossoms, tulips, carnations, roses and hyacinths, so that one feels as if one were praying in a flower garden.

Towards the end of the 17th century prayer-rugs gradually increase in wealth and variety, and of these the Ghiordes (*Gördes*) prayer-rugs are particularly noteworthy on account of their mihrab designs with undulating contours and the decorative columns to be seen on each side. Those with the decorative columns on each side are known as Marpuçlu Gördes. There are also different types of these known as 'pipe' and 'ewer'. The field of the mihrab is dark blue, pale blue, red or green. (Fig. 227.) Those with the dark blue field are very valuable, and Gördes prayer-rugs with a white field in the mihrab are very rare. Those with two mihrabs one at the top and the other at the bottom are known as Kız (maiden) Gördes, probably because they were prepared as trousseaux for brides. They are in cream, red and blue with a short, dull pile. (Plate XXIV.)

Of all the various groups of prayer-rugs the Gördes rugs have the closest affinity to those made in the style of the Ottoman Palace carpets, and they may well have been produced under their influence. They possess a rich variety of design.

As Kula prayer-rugs were manufactured in the vicinity of Gördes there is a resemblance between the two types. In Kula carpets, however, the mihrab niche is plainer and consists of a plain or stepped triangle. Above the mihrab niche there is a shallow rectangular inscription panel. The borders are filled with various types of fine ribbons. There may be as many as ten of these borders, sometimes all of the same width, sometimes with one wider border taken as the essential border. The colours in the Kula prayer-rugs are duller than those in the Gördes, and there is considerable use of yellow, blue and red. Some of them have a very wide border section. The most remarkable of the Kula prayer-rugs, however, are those in which the centre of the mihrab is filled with landscape patterns. In these rugs designs composed of small houses with a kind of cypress and a tree are arranged in rows one above the other on each side of the field of the mihrab. The mihrab triangle is double-sided and has steps leading up to it. The centre is defined in the form of an axis with large flower motifs placed one on top of the other. Prayer-rugs from Lâdik near Konya are remarkable for the softness of their wool and the brilliance of their colours, though in quality they are inferior to the Gördes and Kula rugs. A characteristic feature is the line of tulip, flower or tree motifs arranged side by side in the form of a long stalk on the upper or lower side of the mihrab. The mihrab may have either one or three niches, the central niche of the three being higher and wider than the other two. The niches are supported on very slender decorative columns. In Lâdik prayer-rugs of the later periods a mihrab niche with steps can be seen. The colours are very bright, with red or dark blue in the mihrab field and yellow, purple and occasionally green in the borders.

Prayer-rugs from Kırşehir, again in Central Anatolia, are quite well known. Their mihrabs have two or three contours and a characteristic feature is the use of two or three different shades of red. The most commonly used colours are red, blue, green and cream. Prayer-rugs from Mucur, which is a town in the province of Kırşehir, closely resemble Kırşehir rugs except for their use of purple.

Milâs prayer-rugs are remarkable for their lively, brilliant colours. In these the mihrab often forms a lozenge in its upper portion. Sometimes the mihrab field is only half as wide as the border section. The field is most commonly apricot red, and the borders a yellowish-green. Besides white and purple, dark blue also occurs. Another conspicuous feature of them is the brilliant yellow in the border ribbons. Milâs prayer-rugs continue the Gördes designs but at the same time show influence of Uşak and Bergama. They generally display a hybrid type of pattern, and hence have come to be known as 'hybrid' carpets.

Other types of prayer-rug to be seen in Anatolia—e.g. the Bergama prayer-rugs—are no more than variations on the types mentioned above. Ewer, comb and hand motifs can also be seen on prayer-rugs. Some of them are inscribed with the date of manufacture. Prayer-rugs with an animal skin design constitute a very characteristic category in the art of Turkish carpet-making. In these the whole of the field of the carpet is covered with a stylised representation of a stretched, spotted leopard skin. As the use of an animal skin for the performance of prayers was an ancient and widespread custom it is quite natural that such a motif should have been employed in prayer-rugs. The oldest specimens of this type of prayer-rug date from the 17th century. (Fig. 228.)

27

TURKISH TEXTILES

In Iran under the Great Seljuks developments took place in textiles as well as in the other arts, but examples of this work have disappeared with the passage of time.

A silk fragment dating from the end of the 11th century now in the Victoria and Albert Museum in London is one of the very rare examples still extant (Fig. 229). The design consists of large circles with octagons between them. In the large circles we find figures of falcons and gryphons on each side of a tree, in a border of small circles eagles with outstretched wings, gryphons and small birds, and in the interstices pairs of confronted doves and other figures.

After the time of the Great Seljuks rapid progress continued to be made under the Anatolian Seljuks. Their silks were highly praised by Arab chroniclers, who described them as Rūmī (i.e. Anatolian). In the museum at Lyons there is a fragment of gold brocade from this period. The material itself is red, with the patterns woven in gold thread. At the edge is woven the name of ʿAlā al-Dīn Abu'l-Fatḥ Kayqubād bin Kaykhusraw. This cloth must have been woven for ʿAlā al-Dīn Kayqubād I on the palace looms at Konya. Here also we find a design consisting of large circles. The circles contain the stylised figures of two lions set back to back with the ends of their tails terminating in an arabesque. Between the lions' heads there is a filling composed of palmette and half-palmette motifs. The spaces between the circles are filled with a 4-pointed star motif consisting of lotus palmettes. A second piece of gold brocade from the Anatolian Seljuks has as design the Seljuk device of a double-headed eagle. This figure is surrounded by a border in the form of a shield. The triangular spaces between these are filled by two arabesques the stems of which curl downwards to terminate in two confronted dragons' heads. This piece of embroidery is to be found in the Cathedral of Siegburg in the Shrine of St. Apollinaris.

From the examples still extant it is clear that bird and animal figures formed the most prevalent type of design in Turkish textiles of both the Great Seljuk and the Anatolian Seljuk periods.

It is very difficult to obtain any very clear idea of the textiles of the Anatolian Beylik period, which was one of transition between the Seljuks and the Ottomans, but from the 15th century onwards it is possible to follow the development of Turkish textiles step by step. It was the custom to preserve the clothes worn by the Sultans very carefully in bales. These bales all have labels showing their date, and constitute a most valuable collection of Turkish textiles and velvets. The collection, which was preserved in the Topkapı Saray, is the richest collection of Turkish textiles and velvets in the world. Other valuable collections, however, are to be found in the Mevlânâ Museum in Konya, the Victoria and Albert Museum in London, the Royal Scottish Museum in Edinburgh and museums in Paris, Lyons, Moscow and Bucharest.

There are several references to 14th-century textiles in written sources. In these we frequently come across the names of various types of cloth, 'kızıl efladı' or 'vale', 'denizli bezi', 'ak alemli Denizli bezi' and 'kızıl kemha'. From this it is obvious that in the Anatolian Beylik and early Ottoman periods there existed a highly advanced art of textile manufacture together with a large variety of different kinds of cloth, even though it is not always possible to provide precise identifications for the names we have. Ibn Baṭṭūṭa describes the magnificence of the Lâdik textiles.

The Anatolian Seljuk textiles had laid the foundations for the production of the finest Ottoman textiles in the 15th century, though the latter have no figural decoration, and the predominant designs consist of symmetrical arrangements of geometrical and vegetal forms together with lozenge patterns.

In the bale of clothing supposed to have belonged to Osman Bey (1299–1326) now in the Topkapı Saray have been found nine caftans very probably made from the 'ak alemli bez' of Denizli. The ground is woven from white cotton thread, and the design consists mainly of a pomegranate motif in dark yellow framed by two long leaves with another filling. The design is very large and the whole caftan can accommodate only two complete patterns. In the 15th century similar caftans of an even higher quality continued to be manufactured. During this period the textile industry concentrated in Bursa showed a very great advance and various types of cloths and velvets began to be manufactured on a large scale. Bursa velvets, silk brocades, silk velvets, satins, and taffetas are known all over the world. This rapidly developing textile industry very probably spread to Edirne, but after the Conquest of Istanbul it developed especially and on a very large scale in Istanbul.

Very fine workmanship is shown in a caftan of the 15th century manufactured in an ancient technique and with old designs. The warp is of silk thread, the woof of a mixture of silk and cotton with fine silver threads. There are two large designs in dark yellow on a white ground. These consist of a pineapple or artichoke motif framed by two large, broad leaves. The motifs have contours of green silk.

A second specimen is a short-sleeved caftan belonging to Mehmed the Conqueror. The ground is cream. A large lozenge pattern is produced by four bold cloud motifs in gold thread, with large red wave forms in the centre and red and bright blue lines on the contours. In the centre of this there are two 'seals of Solomon' or 6-pointed stars in gold thread one inside the other, with carnations rising from a highly ornamental vase below, and a large tulip with roses springing from it set between two roses beneath. The centre of the seal is filled with a rosette with tulips and hyacinths arranged radially around it.

The quality of the textiles began to deteriorate at the beginning of the 16th century, and to counteract this a law was issued in 1502 entitled '*Qānūnnāme-i iḥtisāb-i Bursa*' (Code of statutes for the Bursa Guilds). In the section relating to textiles it points to the superior quality of the textiles manufactured 25 years previously and urges the weavers to be more diligent. The various paragraphs of the law deal in detail with the number of threads, size and quality of the various textiles and clearly point out the various deficiencies and imperfections. Apart from this it lays down the dimensions of the cloths and velvets, the number of weft threads, knots and the combinations of gold and silver required. The fact that the law mentions that there were as many as a thousand workshops in Bursa turning out imperfect cloth and that a hundred master-weavers had given witness, shows the scale on which the manufacture of cloth and velvet was carried on in Bursa.

In the list of plunder taken during the Çaldıran campaign of 1514 under Sultan Selim I we find 91 garments of Bursa cloth listed among the goods taken from the *Hesht Bihisht* (the Eight Paradises) Palace at Tabriz. This proves that Turkish cloth was widely used in the Safawid Palaces of Iran at the beginning of the 16th century. The various types of cloth presented on the occasion of a circumcision feast are listed in a gift ledger dated 1582 in Topkapı Palace. The list includes *serengi* (literally tricoloured) from Istanbul, *kutni* from Baghdad, *diba* from Damascus, *seraser* from Istanbul, *chatma* and *beneki* from Istanbul, Bursa and Amasya, silk velvets from Bursa, Hasanpaşa and Damascus, satins from Chios, *seraser* brocades from Istanbul, and *mukaddem* brocades from Damascus, Derviş Paşa and Hasan Paşa. This proves that textiles were being manufactured at that time in various centres of the Ottoman Empire. *Seraser* brocade was the best-known and most popular of Ottoman textiles. This cloth was woven of gold and silver thread and used for robes of honour. Written records show that there were five different kinds of *seraser* brocade. *Zerbaft* is a type of brocade in which the patterns were woven in gold thread and which went also under such different names as *altınlı kadife* (gold velvet) and *müzehheb kemha* (gilt brocade). There is also a kind of cloth known as Istanbul *diba*, the name given to very fine-quality satin. In Ankara, and also in Tosya, a very popular type of cloth known as '*sof*' (literally, woollen cloth) was manufactured. At Soma and Bergama *kutni*, *alaja* and *kırpas* cloth was produced.

The magnificent caftan of Sultan Bayazid II is a very fine illustration of the polychrome cloths of the 16th century made from heavy gold brocade. The pattern consists of peonies and pomegranate blossoms set between long branches and leaves woven in gold thread and red, blue, pink and green silk on a cream ground. No patterns are repeated, each flower and leaf being a separate colour and design. The long leaves shaped like curved daggers and the large, full pomegranate blossoms produce an effect of magnificence well suited to the greatness of the 16th-century Ottoman Sultans. (Plate XXV.)

A robe of fine silk belonging to Süleyman the Magnificent is simpler in appearance. The pattern consists of repeating patterns of a tulip or a carnation on widely spaced parallel branches stretching from one extreme to the other on a cream ground. The carnations are in chestnut, pink and yellow, the tulips in pink and blue.

A caftan belonging to Sultan Murad III bears a repeating pattern of two circles one inside

XII Seljuk carpet from the Mosque of ʿAlā al-Dīn, Konya, 13th century, Istanbul, Museum of Turkish and Islamic Art (see page 292)

XIII Seljuk carpet from the Mosque of ʿAlā al-Dīn, Konya, 13th century, Istanbul, Museum of Turkish and Islamic Art (see page 292)

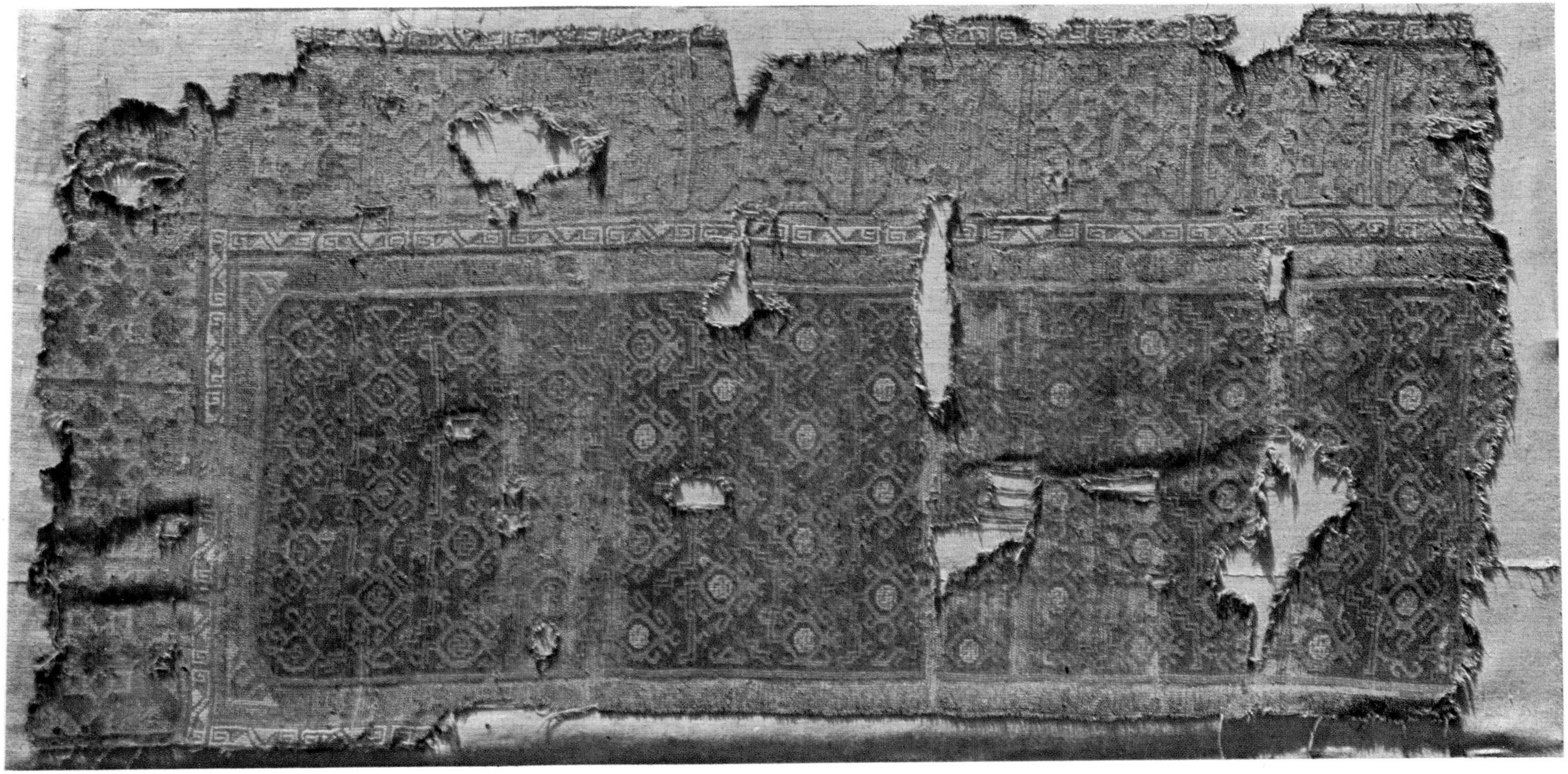

XIV Seljuk carpet from the Mosque of ʿAlā al-Dīn, Konya, 13th century, Istanbul, Museum of Turkish and Islamic Art (see page 293)

XV Seljuk carpet from the Mosque of ʿAlā al-Dīn, Konya, 13th century, Istanbul, Museum of Turkish and Islamic Art (see page 293)

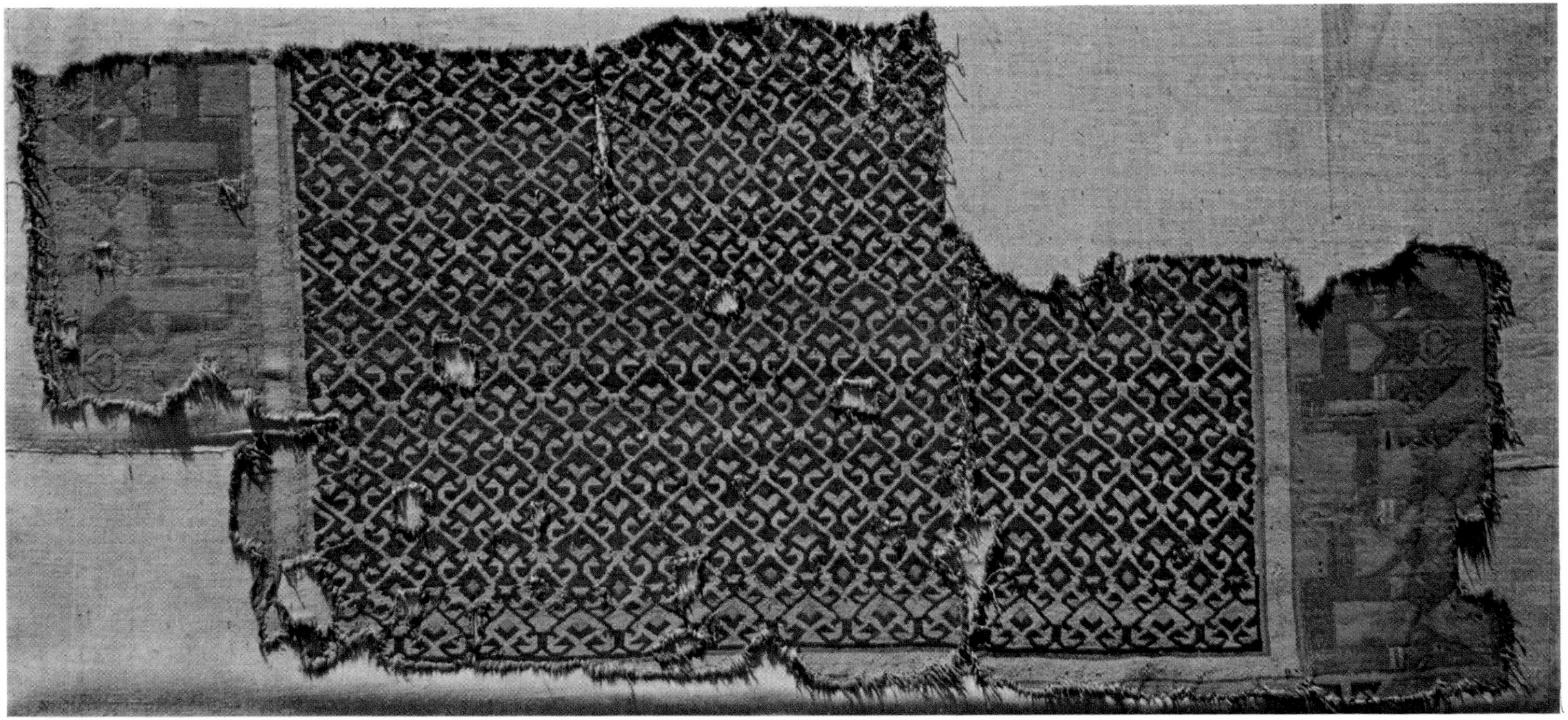

XVI Seljuk carpet from the Mosque of ʿAlā al-Dīn, Konya, 13th century, Istanbul, Museum of Turkish and Islamic Art (see page 294)

XVII Seljuk carpet, Konya, Mevlânâ Museum (see page 294)

XVIII Marby rug, Stockholm, Statens Historiska Museet (see page 295)

XIX 'Holbein' carpet, 15th century, Konya, Mevlânâ Museum (see page 296)

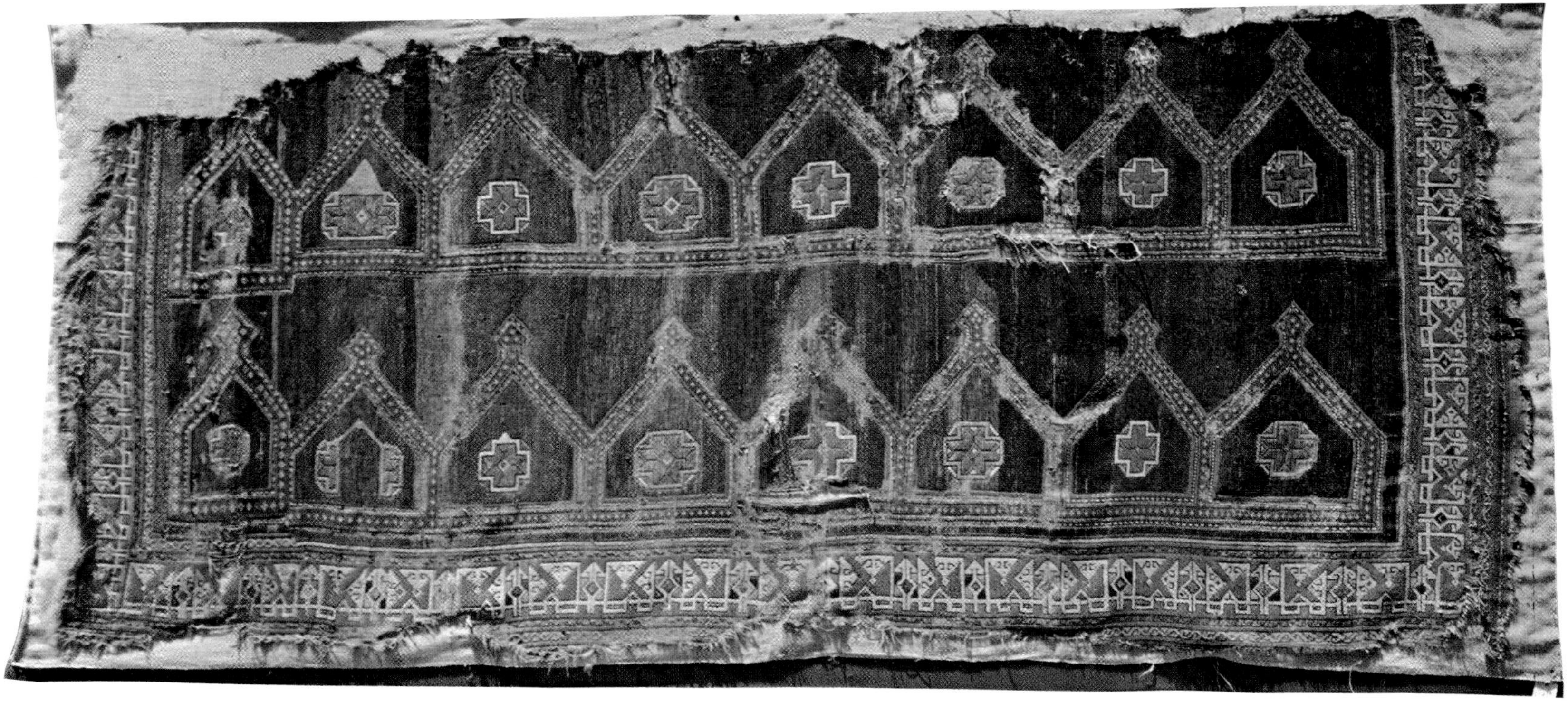

XX Serial prayer-rug, 15th century, Istanbul, Museum of Turkish and Islamic Art (see page 296)

XXI Serial prayer-rug, 15th century, Istanbul, Museum of Turkish and Islamic Art (see page 296)

XXII 'Bellini' prayer-rug, Berlin State Museum, Islamic Department (see page 297)

XXIII Palace prayer-rug, Berlin State Museum, Islamic Department (see page 299)

XXIV Prayer-rug, 18th century, Konya, Mevlânâ Museum (see page 300)

XXV Caftan of Bayazid II, Istanbul, Topkapı Saray Museum (see page 304)

the other in green on a white ground. In the inner circle there is a large half-moon and star, and beneath this a cloud motif. The space between the two circles is decorated by a carnation and leaf pattern, and a carnation is set both above and below the large circle.

On another silk fabric of the 16th century we find a richer repeating pattern. Here large pointed ovals are arranged in vertical and horizontal rows, each oval containing a design of tulips and carnations springing from a long bough. The ovals have dark-coloured contours, and are surrounded by scrolls stretching the whole length of the intervening spaces. Above this are arranged widely spaced rosette flowers.

As for the 17th century, a code of laws dated 1050/1640 makes it clear that at this period the greatest quantity and variety of cloth was produced in Istanbul. Other important centres were Bursa, Aleppo, Damascus, Menemen and Chios. The code gives a list of the colours and types of these textiles, together with designs such as plane leaves, pomegranates, crescents, peacocks' tails, roses, pistachio flowers, rosebuds and tendrils.

From the entry for the year 1631 in the tailors' notebooks in the Topkapı Palace we find that Murad IV had 133 costumes made by the head tailor in seven months of that year. They were of various materials including satin, silk, broadcloth, cotton and *sof*, and only some ten of them were decorated with designs. This proves that the manufacture of plain, undecorated textiles was increasing and becoming more widespread.

There was a great decline in the manufacture of gold and silver cloth, and as a result the number of colours employed decreased and designs changed in form.

A child's caftan in gold brocade from the tomb of Sultan Ahmed I (1603–17) gives some idea of the design used in the textiles of this period. In this there is a design composed of long broad leaves embroided in gold thread filled with black and blue pomegranate flowers, and plane leaves with red centres set between broad interlacing boughs. The spaces between these are filled with large plane leaves ornamented with tulips in the centre, long leaves, plum blossoms and tulips.

A caftan of gold brocade belonging to Sultan Murad IV (1623–40) has an entirely different type of design. Here we find a pattern composed of tiger skin and leopard spots. The motifs are woven in gold thread with blue silk contours and silver thread in the centre of the spots.

Another caftan of the 17th century has a design composed of large pine cones (or pine-apples) and pomegranates emerging from thick branches woven in gold thread on a red ground. The centres of the motifs are enlivened with small white and blue flowers.

Another gold brocade of the 17th century has designs consisting of a large fan in the form of a carnation on a red ground, surrounding by pointed ovals. The fans are woven in yellow thread, with raised red borders and white centres. The handles of the fans and the pointed ovals surrounding them have white edges and red centres on a blue ground.

In the Museum at Lyons there is a silk brocade cushion dating from this period. It has red tulips, carnations and hyacinths with green stems or large carnations in the form of fans woven in yellow thread on a red ground. At each end of the cushion there are large stylised rose motifs with green leaves set inside niches arranged serially. In the Topkapı Saray there is another specimen very closely resembling this.

In the 18th century there was a notable deterioration and retrogression in the manufacture of textiles and velvets. Nevertheless various cloths and velvets of good quality were still produced in the reigns of Ahmed III (1703–30) and Mahmud I (1730–54). In order to cut down the consumption of silver Ahmed III forbade the use of silver thread in textiles. As Turkish textiles deteriorated the market was captured by European textiles, with the result that the old harmonious, sound artistic taste became corrupted and the high quality of the old fabrics was completely forgotten.

A short-sleeved caftan belonging to Ahmed III has a silver ground with a large pomegranate motif between two long, wide leaves resembling half-moons woven in gold thread with pomegranate flowers joining these beneath the leaves. Here we can see the reappearance in a degenerate form of the bold motifs of the 14th and 15th centuries. A few cloths of this type were manufactured in the 18th century, but in these few colours were used apart from yellow and white, and the old red degenerated to a sort of pale pink.

The *shalwar* or baggy trousers belonging to Mahmud I are moiré on a cream ground. On this are woven stylised cypress trees in light red with leaf fillings, again in cream, showing very strong Baroque influence. On each side of the cypress motifs there are Rococo style interlacing stems terminating in rosebuds.

The art of Turkish embroideries and velvets subsequently declined still further, and continued throughout the first half of the 19th century in a very degenerate form. There are documents showing that Üsküdar *chatmas* (brocades) and Selimiye cloths were purchased in order to be sent to the Paris Exhibition of 1855. In 1843 a factory was set up at Hereke for the manufacture of silks. When it was first established the factory had 25 silk looms producing fabrics used in furnishing the royal palaces. In 1849 a three-storeyed building was added for the manufacture of silk velvets.

A special place among Turkish embroideries is occupied by battle standards, and the magnificent Turkish tents that were used in Ottoman campaigns.

A standard on which the name of Sultan Selim I is embroidered in the silver border does not actually date back as far as his reign. It is made of red stuff measuring 400 × 250 cm., with designs and writings in gold thread. A decorative two-bladed sword (the sword of ʿAlī) stretches the whole length of the standard with a star and crescent at the end of the hilt, and two dragons' heads joining the guard to the body of the sword. The medallion in the centre is divided into eight segments containing eight times *Yā Burhān* (O Proof) and once *Yā Allāh* (O God), whilst on each of the sword blades is inscribed once the *Basmala* and once *Inna fataḥnā laka* (that we have conquered for thee) (Koran, *Sūrat al-Fatḥ*). On the upper edge is sewn a piece of embroidery inscribed with verses from the same *Sura*. There are three half-moons on the right and on the left (four of them having suns in the centre) with *Naṣr min Allāh wa fatḥ qarīb* (Victory is from God and conquest is nigh) inscribed on the edges, *Yā Muḥammad* in the centre and the *Kalimat Tawḥid* (the assertion that God is one) below. Between them there are sun symbols set in circles. Embroideries with the name *Allāh* or decorated with sun and moon symbols are sewn to the triangular-shaped point. The standard is surrounded by a border of half-moons and stars.

An Ottoman tent now in the Karlsruhe Museum gives some idea of the magnificence of the military tents of the 17th century. The whole of the interior is lined with brightly coloured embroideries. The tents of vizirs and sultans were much larger and more magnificent. When the Sultan set out on a campaign the Imperial Tent was erected. There are similar large tents in the Vienna Arsenal and the Topkapı Saray.

From the examples we have dealt with up to now it is clear that red was a predominant colour in Turkish textiles. Red has been the national colour for a very long time, and it has various shades. After red the most popular colours were blue, green, black, white, beige and gold. A honey colour called '*aselî*' was also used and a dark brown called '*surmayî*'. At first only two colours were used in textiles, but at Bursa, from the 15th century onwards, cloth began to be woven in seven different colours. In the 16th century various types of cloths were imported from Iran and Europe, and particularly from Venice, but these were distinguished from the others under the names of 'frankish brocade' and 'Frankish velvet'.

As a result of the close relations between the Ottomans and Amalfi, Pisa and the Republics of Venice and Genoa, we find some cloths inspired by Italian textile designs but manufactured in the Turkish fashion; though it was the naturalistic flower and leaf motifs that appeared in characteristic form in all the various Turkish arts that dominated Turkish textiles and velvet manufacture. However, the crown motifs in Ottoman velvets derive from Italian designs, whilst the pineapple and artichoke motifs were also widely used in Italian silks and velvets.

At their most brilliant period Turkish textiles were known all over Europe and were found as far afield as Sweden. In the Armoury in the Kremlin in Moscow there are seven heavy silver satin surplices of Turkish cloth. In the 17th century the Metropolitans or the Patriarchs of Moscow always wore ornate surplices of Turkish embroidery on ceremonial occasions. Magnificent caftans of Turkish cloth found in a number of monasteries in Roumania are now in the Bucharest Museum.

As with Chinese textiles, although the fine designs and motifs in these cloths were closely modelled on nature the total effect is abstract. The contrast between dark and light colours lends vitality to the designs, yet they still remain a surface ornament most suitable for this type of medium.

28
TURKISH MINIATURE PAINTING

It would appear, from the limited works and records that have survived, that a very advanced art of miniature-painting and book-production had been reached by the Uighur Turks as early as the 8th century. These miniatures, together with the Bezeklik and Sorchuk frescoes that were brought to light in the Turfan excavations, show that there existed a characteristic Central Asian Turkish style of painting that, even at first glance, is quite distinct from Chinese art. Some of these Uighurs came to Baghdad as early as the beginning of the 9th century, during the caliphate of al-Ma'mūn, and received a warm welcome there. On the foundation of Samarra in the reign of al-Muʿtaṣim, the Uighurs also settled in that city, where they very quickly formed the predominant ethnic group, and engaged in artistic activity. A painting 85 × 20 cm. on a flask of unglazed pottery portrays one of the local Turks in original costume, carrying a gazelle on his shoulders. Later, one can see the influence of Uighur painting in frescoes from the Ghaznevid Palace of Lashkari Bazar dating from the beginning of the 11th century, as well as in frescoes from the Seljuk centre of Rayy and in *mīnāī* and lustre ceramics and tiles from Rayy and Kashan dating from the end of the same century. The first Islamic miniatures produced during that period have completely disappeared. However, as Grube has very aptly pointed out, in spite of a number of changes in style, the basic principles of Uighur fresco and miniature painting continued unchanged into the 15th century. The Turks brought the Uighur style of painting from Central Asia to the west, and planted it in Ghazne, Rayy, Kashan, Mosul and, ultimately, Anatolia. The entry of Tughrul Bek, the founder of the Great Seljuk state, into Baghdad in 1055 and his assumption of the title of Sultan marked the beginning of the spread of Seljuk art and culture in that area. A few paintings remaining on decorated pottery and on the very limited number of early Seljuk tiles known to us give a very clear idea of Great Seljuk style. Its most outstanding quality is the realistic portrayal of physical types, the everyday life of the Seljuks of that time and even battle scenes. But no works showing the Seljuk art of miniature-painting have survived from before the end of the 12th century. The best examples of these are then to be found in the manuscript of the Kitāb al-Tiryāk, a book of antidotes written by the Pseudo-Galen. One of these manuscripts, which is dated 1199 and is now in the Bibliothèque Nationale in Paris, contains very fine miniatures and was very probably written at the command of the Zengid Nūr al-Dīn Arslan Shāh I at Mosul. Here, in a miniature depicting a prince's palace and garden, against a red background we see, in the middle of a group of the ladies of the harem, a bearded figure sitting cross-legged with a glass in one hand, whose costume, features and various characteristics are in the Uighur–Seljuk style. The women around him are all types that we have encountered in Seljuk pottery.

A Book of Automata, the Kitāb fī Ma'rifat al-Ḥiyal al-Handasiyya, written at the command of the Artukid Sultan al-Malik al-Nāṣir Maḥmūd at Diyarbekir in 1205, deals only with mechanical toys and thus throws little light on the Uighur–Seljuk style.

The frontispiece of the Kitāb al-Aghāni, Vol. XVII, dated 1219 (Istanbul, Millet Library) consisting of a full-face portrait of the Seljuk Atabek Badr al-Dīn Lu'lu' bin 'Abd al-Raḥmān seated amongst the ladies of the harem and holding a bow and arrow in his hand, shows the continuation of the Uighur style in lapis lazuli, red, and various shades of blue on a gold ground.

In another manuscript of the Kitāb al-Tiryāk (Pseudo-Galen) of the 13th century from Mosul, now in the National Library in Vienna, a miniature consisting of three different scenes one above the other—the central scene being a realistic portrayal of palace life on a red ground, the upper a hunting scene with horseman, and the lower a group of men and women travelling on horseback—is quite clearly in the Seljuk artistic tradition.

The small miniatures in the Warka and Gulshāh manuscript dating from the first half of the 13th century, now in the Treasury Library (Hazine) of the Topkapı Palace, have been attributed to an Azerbaidzhani artist from the town of Khoy and belong to the same stylistic tradition. The text of the poem in the form of a love romance was originally written for the Ghaznevid Sultan Maḥmūd. The name Muḥammad al-Khoyī al-Naqqāsh written on the 58th page of the manuscript is connected with the town of Khoy in the immediate vicinity of the present Turkish–Persian border. The calligrapher and writer 'Abd al-Mu'min bin Muḥammad al-Khoyī, whose name shows that he was the son of Muḥammad al-Naqqāsh, is known to have come to Kastamonu in the time of Arghūn Khan and to have dedicated a book to Muḥammad bin Yawlāq Arslan. Thus the Warka and Gulshāh miniatures have a very close and obvious connection with Anatolia. Theories connecting them with Iraq from the stylistic point of view are far from convincing.

This style was continued by the Turkish Mamluks in Egypt at the beginning of the 14th century. On the title-page of a manuscript of the Maqāmāt dated 1334 in the National Library in Vienna we find similar Turkish types on a gold ground, with a prince seated on a throne with a glass in his hand and surrounded by musicians, acrobats and ladies of the palace. The figures in the foreground, however, have foreign features with slanting eyes.

As 13th-century miniature-painting was by no means confined to Baghdad but developed in various other cities, such as Mosul, and various other countries, such as Syria, Egypt and Anatolia, E. Kühnel has suggested that it would be preferable to describe the period as the Seljuk Period rather than the Baghdad Period of Muslim painting.

With the supremacy of the Īl-Khānids at the end of the 13th and the beginning of the 14th century, Uighur artists entered upon a new and brilliant period of miniature painting. Most of the state officials and scribes of the Mongols were Uighur. Masterpieces of miniature-painting were produced by the Uighurs in new centres such as Maragha and Tabriz. Most of the miniatures of the world history, the Jāmiʿ al-Tawārīkh, commissioned by the Īl-Khānid vizir and historian Rashīd al-Dīn may be attributed to Uighurs. In the copies of parts of the work dated 1306 (Edinburgh), 1314 (London) and 1314 (Istanbul) colour is subordinated to line, a distinguishing feature of the work of Uighur artists.[1] That the Jāmiʿ al-Tawārīkh was originally written in Turkish and later translated into Persian and Arabic is shown by the use of a number of Turkish words and terms for which no Persian or Arabic equivalent could be found. The Waqfnāme-yi Rashīdī mentions that some Turkish painters (Ghılāmān-i Turk) together with others took part in the artistic activities in the Rabʿ-i Rashīdī,[2] for the names of some Turkish artists employed there are written in Turkish but we do not know in what type of activity they took part.

The close resemblance between a miniature from the fragment of the work dated 1314 in the possession of the Royal Asiatic Society in London and one of the Bezeklik Uighur frescoes of the 8th or 9th centuries in the State Museum in West Berlin indicates a connection between them. Each of these depicts a lake surrounded by mountains, but in the miniature there are fish in the lake, whilst in the fresco there is a monster. Diez and Kühnel connect some of the miniatures in this manuscript of the Jāmi-ʿal-Tawārīkh with Central Asia, and Diez agreed that the artist was an Uighur Turk.

Thus Persian miniature-painting began under the influence of Far Eastern and Central Asian painting introduced by Uighur artists working in the Īl-Khānid palaces. In later periods too Turkish artists played a predominant role. The Uighur artists at the court of Shāhrukh in Herat in the first half of the 15th century showed great skill and understanding in blending together Chinese, Uighur and Persian styles of painting. A miniature from a manuscript of the romance of Humay and Humayun by the painter Ghiyāth al-Dīn, now in the Musée des Arts Décoratifs in Paris, is one of the masterpieces of this time. It is very probable that the Uighur artist Ghiyāth al-Dīn played a part in the later development of the Persian miniature. A miniature depicting an armed standing Turkish warrior[3] painted in Herat around 1425 bears many of the qualities of a portrait and is another indication of the Turkish artistic outlook. A new period opened when Ḥusayn Bayqarā succeeded Abū Saʿīd as ruler of Herat, and at the end of the 15th century the style developed along different lines in the Uzbek centre of Bukhara. The portrait quality to be seen in a miniature of the beginning of the 16th century by Shaybanī Khan, now in the Metropolitan Museum in New York, is repeated in another miniature depicting a single figure belonging to the middle of the 16th

[1] In Istanbul there are two MSS of the Jāmi ʿal-Tawārīkh: Hazine 1653, dated 1314, bound into a manuscript of Ḥāfiẓ-i Ābrū from 1425 and Hazine 1654, dated 1317. This manuscript was written during the year when Rashīd al-Dīn was put to death. The following year the Rabʿ-i Rashīdī was plundered. Only three miniatures are contemporary with the text, the rest are from the late 14th and early 15th centuries.

[2] The quarter which Rashīd al-Dīn endowed at Tabrīz in the early years of the 14th century.

[3] Private Collection, ref. Grube, *The Classical Style in Islamic Painting*, 1968, fig. 25.

century. The most important quality distinguishing Turkish from Persian art is the realism that has always prevailed among the Turks.

The *Mi'rājnāme* in the Bibliothèque Nationale in Paris (Supp. Turc 190) is written in the Uighur alphabet and in Chaghatay Turkish and contains 58 miniatures depicting the legend of the *Mi'rāj* or the Ascension of Muḥammad in a narrative style. These miniatures, and the use of the Uighur alphabet, show that Uighur artistic influences were still very much alive in Herat at the beginning of the 15th century. In the colophon it is stated that the book was copied by Malik Bakhshi in Herat in 840/1436. At that time Shāhrukh was trying to revive Chaghatay and Uighur literature and patronised these artists. On the pages decorated with miniatures there are explanations in Ottoman and Arabic. The manuscript may have been brought by Bādi' al-Zamān, who sought refuge in Istanbul after the death of his father Ḥusayn Bayqarā in 1507. In 1672 it was bought by Antoine Galland on behalf of the French ambassador and presented to Colbert.

There are very obvious signs of Uighur artistic influence in the costumes, physical types, and the portrayal of the *Mi'rājnāme* figures. These are depicted, especially in scenes representing Paradise, in a very lively, realistic style with various types of movement. The same style is applied to the few animals (e.g. camels) depicted. (Fig. 230.) Scenes portraying the Prophet Muḥammad with the angel Gabriel among angels greeting them and presenting them with gifts are comparatively calm and static. (Fig. 231.)

Although, in the hands of Riẓā-i 'Abbāsī and other artists, the Persian miniature-painting, which developed in the 15th and more especially from the beginning of the 16th century at the court of the Safawids, who were themselves Turks, came under the influence of Western painting, it developed at the same time a new style of very delicate naturalism. As was usual in the Middle Ages the subjects of paintings are normally drawn from the national literature. Everyday life is very rarely portrayed. A limited number of scenes were employed, and various figures were inserted into the same composition. For example, in the scene depicting Khusraw seeing Shīrīn bathing in a mountain pool, once a satisfying composition had been established this composition was faithfully adhered to by subsequent painters, with only minor changes and refinements aimed at enhancing the quality, until a master like Sultan Muḥammad produced a definitive masterpiece. Ottoman miniatures depicted real events, battle scenes and everyday life. All scenes of historical importance were portrayed once only.

A limited number of characteristic manuscripts relating to the beginnings of Turkish miniature painting in Anatolia has survived. There is a very interesting manuscript (Paris Bib. Nat. Persan 174) of 146 pages in *naskhī* script which is stated to have been produced in Kayseri and Aksaray in the years 1271–2 and in which the writer and painter indicates that he belonged to Sivas. The work is in three parts and was written throughout by the same scribe, Ibn al-Sijistānī, who declares in the first part that he had travelled all over the Islamic world, and had occupied himself with astrology, sorcery, geomancy and magic pictures. The second part, entitled Kitāb Daqā'iq al-Ḥaqā'iq (The Book of the Minutiae of Truth), was written in Aksaray in 670/1271, and in one part the writer's name is given as Nāṣir al-Dīn Muḥammad ibn 'Ali al-Sijistānī. In the last section of the work entitled Mu'nis al-Ḥawārid, written in Kayseri in 671/1272, the writer, whose name is given here as Nāṣir al-Rammāl al-Sa'ātī al-Sīwāsī, dedicates this section to the Sultan Ghiyāth al-Dīn Kaykhusraw III. The writer, who came from Seistan and settled in Sivas, was also a miniature-painter. It is clear from the style that all the miniatures are from the same hand, nor is there any change in the composition from beginning to end. At the beginning there are various pieces of lore from astrological manuscripts, magical procedures, paintings of the wonders of nature (a well-known text, the Ajā'ib al-Makhlūqāt), and cabbalistic signs in various alphabets. Various miniatures portraying such subjects as angels with many heads and many arms, an angel on horseback attacking a dragon, an angel riding a lion, a man with a flag in his hand riding on the back of a white bird, and various imaginary birds, together with the style of painting, suggest Buddhistic art, and even perhaps, as Blochet has pointed out, the Byzantine wall paintings at Göreme, in the vicinity of Kayseri. The costumes, and crowns on the angels' heads, are Turkish. There are forerunners of most of these astrological images in old Uighur painting. Rubruk[1] mentions in his account of his journeys that Uighur monks made talismans of statues, pictures and letters. The figures in the Turkish 12-animal calendars were also a continuation of these. Finally some resemblances between the illustrations of the Sijistānī-Sīwāsī manuscript and the Warka and Gulshāh miniatures allow us to link this manuscript with Anatolia. The two angel reliefs (Fig. 207) on the city walls in Konya also indicate that this type of figure entered Anatolia along with the Turks.

Although we do not possess complete information concerning the art of painting in Anatolia after the fall of the Seljuks, these early works may be regarded as a preparation for the style of classical Ottoman miniature-painting. The nickname 'Black Pen' (Mehmed Siyah Kalem) was later ascribed to a substantial group of miniatures in colour or black and white displaying a complete unity of style to be found in the album attributed to Fatih (The Conqueror) now in the Topkapı Saray in Istanbul (Hazine 2153). That Black Pen's pictures should have been carefully collected together in one album shows that he was a well-known and greatly admired artist. Kühnel states quite categorically that 'there is no doubt whatsoever that these miniatures of the 15th century are of Turkish origin. They are quite clearly distinct from Persian'. They show a naturalistic style with certain influences from the painting of Central Asia. An atmosphere of pitiless ridicule prevails in subjects portrayed by rapid strokes of the brush. (Fig. 232.) Although these works, which might well be regarded as the extremely original beginning of Turkish painting in Anatolia, failed to produce a tradition of quite the same strength and vigour, the ironical, mocking, grotesque character that is so apparent in later Turkish miniatures may be regarded, as Kühnel pointed out, as a continuation of this. The connection between the pictures attributed to Black Pen and the pictorial art of the Uighurs is clearly shown by the resemblance in their portrayal of demons. (Fig. 233.) The portrait of an Uighur demon (9th century) in Chinese ink on paper, which was found at Khocho, now in the West Berlin Museum, is a remarkable analogue. Other miniatures in the style of 'Siyah Kalem' are thoroughly realistic representations of the Turkish types and costumes of Central Asia.

A Turkish manuscript of the Alexander romance completed in 1416, in the reign of

[1] The 13th century Franciscan traveller.

Chelebi Sultan Mehmed, in Amasya, an important cultural centre of Anatolia at that time, shows the high quality of Ottoman miniature-painting at the beginning of the 15th century. This Iskandarnāme by the poet Aḥmadī written by a Sivas calligrapher known as Hajji Baba, and now in the Bibliothèque Nationale in Paris, contains 20 miniatures. A miniature portraying a reception and conversation scene with five figures on a red ground continues the Uighur-Seljuk style. The principal figure sitting cross-legged with a crown on his head and wearing a gold caftan displays all the qualities of a portrait. Unfortunately the identity of the painter is not known.

Another work which, although inferior in quality, enters the same stylistic category is a book of tales that was dispersed in Paris. One miniature from this manuscript, which is dated 843/1439 and was prepared for a vizir of the name of Fakhr al-Dīn ʿAbd al-Raḥmān, was bought for the Museum of Islamic Art in Berlin. It depicts two rows of mounted horsemen arranged in a horizontal composition between hills, with pack camels below. In the upper section the leading horseman is preceded by two armed foot soldiers. The costumes and the facial features are completely Turkish, and the composition, which is quite alien to Persian style, shows qualities that were to be repeated in Ottoman miniatures. It may be attributed to an Anatolian artistic centre.

A Turkish book of surgery entitled Kitāb-i Jerrāhīye-i Īlkhāniye was written in 1465 by Sherefeddin, the head doctor of the hospital at Amasya, better known as Sabunjuoghlu, and dedicated to Sultan Mehmed the Conqueror. This manuscript, which is now in the Bibliothèque Nationale in Paris and was published in 1960, contains 140 miniatures illustrating how operations should be performed for various complaints. These miniatures depict scenes with simple figures in the clearest and most vivid style, and are dominated by a wholly realistic educational character. Because of this educational character no importance was given to the quality of the miniatures, and the subject is portrayed by the use of schematic figures. A simpler copy of this manuscript containing 47 miniatures is to be found in the Fatih Library (Ali Emiri Library) in Istanbul.

During the reign of the Conqueror there was a very considerable advance in the art of portraiture. First Matteo di Pasti in 1465 and then Costanzo di Ferrara between 1478 and 1481 came from Italy to Istanbul at the Conqueror's request to work for the Sultan. More than a hundred medals were produced by these artists, together with relief portraits of the Conqueror, who is sometimes shown on horseback. There is also a portrait of the Conqueror (26×22 cm.) in the Topkapı Saray Museum which is thought to be the work of Costanzo di Ferrara. In response to a letter from the Conqueror to the Doge, Gentile Bellini arrived in Istanbul from Venice in September 1479 and remained until the end of 1480. His portrait of the Conqueror is in the National Gallery in London. It is quite impossible that a painter of the stature of Bellini should have worked so long at the court of the Conqueror without exerting any influence. A miniature in the Freer Gallery in Washington, thought to be a portrait of Prince Jem (Jem Sultan) at the age of 21, was long regarded on the authority of the forged signature of Bihzad beneath it as a copy made by Bihzad of a portrait by Bellini. The sitter is portrayed in a sitting position drawing a picture on a piece of paper on his knee.

It was E. Kühnel who first asked how Bihzad could have copied the Bellini portrait when the original must necessarily have been in Istanbul. R. Ettinghausen has since stated categorically that this picture had no relation whatsoever to the style of Bihzad, and that it could at best only have been the work of a Turkish follower of Bellini. (Plate XXVI.)

During the same period a Turkish painter, Sinan Bek, went to Venice, where he worked for a time, and on his return he trained a pupil known as Ahmed of Bursa. A well-known portrait by Sinan Bek of the Conqueror sitting smelling a rose, now in the Topkapı Saray, delineates the powerful personality of the Sultan in restrained colours and with very great persuasive power. (Fig. 234.)

It is a great misfortune that no illustrated manuscripts should have come down to us from a period which saw so great an advance in the pictorial arts. However the two full-page miniatures which form the frontispiece of a manuscript of the Süleymānnāme dating from the time of Bayazid II and written by Sherefeddin of Bursa, who was known as Uzun (Tall) Firdawsī (Dublin, Chester Beatty Library MS. number 406, dated circa 1500), may show the beginning of the classical Ottoman art of miniature-painting, which was just developing at that time. In the first miniature Solomon is portrayed with seven rows of figures, whilst in the second, Belkis, Queen of Sheba, is portrayed with 6 rows of figures. Solomon is portrayed above as a young man with a moustache, and with the costume and appearance of an Ottoman Sultan, seated on a throne beneath a small dome. He is surrounded by attendant *jinns* or *peris* and various kinds of birds. Below there are four central arches and a flight of stairs leading up to a kiosk at the back. On the first and second rows stand the other prophets of Islam, and on the third kings and rulers, with youthful figures standing on the right-hand side of each of the three rows. On the right of the fourth row we find Zāl and other heroes, soldiers and angels, while on the left are demons. At the very bottom of the composition there are various figures, on the right a fountain with birds and beasts arranged on both sides. The prophet Muḥammad sits above to the right of the arches, his face covered with a veil. The horizontal arrangement is an old Turkish form of composition going back as far as the Uighurs. The bright but slightly matt colours are utterly different from those used in Persian painting of the period, and the demons painted by Mehmed Siyah Kalem here appear in a simpler style. A marvellous wealth of symbolism and content has been concentrated within one single miniature. (Plate XXVII.) In the miniature facing we see Belkis seated on a throne surrounded by angels and a retinue of attendants. Here the demons fill the whole of the bottom three rows. On the right of the bottom row are a wild boar and a lion, whilst on the left there are two grooms holding a horse. The style of these two miniatures suggests the character of the art of miniature at the court of the Conqueror, and is of better quality and has finer nuances than later Ottoman miniatures. It possesses, however, nothing of the realism of the earlier miniatures. The use of a slight perspective in the dome of Solomon's pavilion may indicate the influence of European painting.

The brilliant development of the first years of the reign of Süleyman the Magnificent led up to the most splendid period of the classical Ottoman art of miniature, in which a great many works were produced. The first of these is the Selimnāme, a Turkish poem in the form of *mesnevi* (a classical Persian metre used for epics), with 24 miniatures, relating the conquests of

Sultan Selim I. The facial features are stylised, but the costumes are realistically rendered. The designs on the dresses and textiles, and the details of architectural decoration, are shown with great exactitude; from the point of view of composition it is obvious that this forms the first hesitant step in a period of exploration. The technique differs from Persian miniatures in that the unknown artist blends matt, pale colours in a stylistic unity.

Later, in the second half of the century, we find a large number of miniatures connected with the artist Naṣūḥ al-ṣilaḥī al-Matrakī (Matrakçı Nasuh) and depicting, very often with the most astonishing realism, views of various cities, castles and harbours, without figures. The first and most important of his works is the Beyān-i Menāzil-i Sefer-i ʿIrāqayn (Account of the stages of the campaign in the two Iraqs) in the University Library in Istanbul, which was both written and illustrated by Naṣūḥ al-Matrakī. Nasūḥ accompanied Süleyman the Magnificent on his Persian and Iraq campaigns of 1534–5 and depicted the various stopping-places on the journey out from Istanbul to Tabriz and back by way of Iraq, in a series of 128 miniatures. Great cities such as Istanbul, Tabriz, Baghdad, Aleppo and Diyarbekir were portrayed as they were at that time, with very great skill. Some of the halting-places and important centres in which they spent only a short time are represented only by rough sketches. Architectural features such as city walls and castles, and the characteristic features of the cities, are very vividly depicted. Mountains, trees, and animals such as hares, deer, stags and ducks are painted in bright colours with a deep love of nature that gives a lively, cheerful quality to the miniatures. (Fig. 235.) Two other of his works are the Tarīkh-i Sultan Bayazid and the Süleymānnāme (a history of the conquest of the Balkans and Hungary). Although the miniatures are partly in the nature of maps, important and necessary details have been dwelt upon with great care.

The Tarīkh-i Sultan Bayazid, with 10 miniatures depicting the wars between Bayazid II and Jem Sultan, including pictures of the castles and harbours of Gülek, Inebahti and Methóni, dates from the middle of the 16th century. The lively sketches show the various castles and harbours in schematic form.

The Süleymānnāme contains 32 miniatures depicting cities, castles and harbours connected with Süleyman the Magnificent's Hungarian campaign of 1543 and Barbarossa's Mediterranean campaign of the same year. In the first section depicting the Mediterranean campaign the ships are portrayed against a background of the towns, city walls and buildings of Nice, Toulon and Genoa, whilst in the second section we see Budapest, Esztergom, Stuhlweissenburg (Székesfehérvár) and the stages and halting-places between these cities embellished with various refinements such as trees, flowers and hills closely resembling the miniatures of the account of Süleyman the Magnificent's Iraq campaign. Miniatures in all three manuscripts completely lack human figures. The colours—blue, green, yellow, orange, red and sometimes gold—contrast and enliven the forms of the objects represented. The forerunner of this type of map-miniature is the atlas of Pirî Reis (Kitāb al-Baḥriye) of 1525–6 in the Museum of the Topkapı Saray (Hz. 642). The harbours of Nice, Koróni, Methóni and Genoa in this work served as a model for later map-miniatures in composition and topography. Naṣūḥ al-Silāḥī was thus able to sketch the stages, halting-places and castles of campaigns in which he did not participate by referring to these pictorial records. It is also possible that other artists working with him may have assisted him in some of the miniatures, for although they are all in the same style the miniatures of the latter two manuscripts, the Tarīkh-i Sultan Bayazid and the Süleymānnāme, in which we find neither the date nor the writer and artist's name, reveal a considerable difference in quality. The sound composition of later Ottoman miniatures treating of historical events, and the realistic portrayal of architectural monuments, forts and castles, are based on the realism of the style established by Naṣūḥ.

The Süleymānnāme, dated 965/1558, is a very important work in *mesnevi* form written in Persian by a calligrapher from Azerbaidzhan named ʿAlī bin Emir Bek of Shirvan, and depicting in 69 miniatures various events from the reign of Süleyman the Magnificent, state receptions, hunting and recreation scenes, battles and victories. The very fine miniatures produced in various styles by both native and foreign artists, together with the binding and illumination, herald the birth of historical Ottoman miniature-painting. Various influences from both East and West are assimilated into a vivid, predominantly realistic style. One is struck by the determined effort to develop the most suitable style by means of lively and creative exploration. Various scenes in which Hungarians, Persians and Turks are portrayed together show remarkable observation in the delineation of costumes and weapons. In the Battle of Mohacs (Fig. 236a), in which Süleyman the Magnificent and one of his sons took part, armour, flags, weapons and costumes are portrayed with the most meticulous realism, and the composition of the battle scene was to be repeated in a number of later miniatures. The encounter between the heavily armed knights and the light cavalry is very vividly rendered (Fig. 236b). In the hunting scenes the lively and intricate composition formed by the hunters and the animals vividly reflects the excitement of the chase. The importance given in the delineation of receptions and scenes of pleasure to the details of the ancient Turkish geometrical ornament in all its richness and delicacy was to be continued in later miniatures (Figs. 237–9). Scenes of pleasure, however, are still dominated by an artificial atmosphere utterly divorced from any attempt at realism, and they remain very jejune and lifeless beside the spectacular compositions of the later Sūrnāmes.

That Hungarian and Persian artists worked under the direction of Turkish masters and according to their designs is apparent from the prevalent style, as well as from a number of the details, of these miniatures.

The development of this style came to a halt during the last years of Süleyman the Magnificent's reign. However, the 20 minatures in the Turkish Nüzhet al-Akhbār der Sefer-i Sigetvar (an account of the Szigetvár campaign), written by Ahmed Feridun Pasha in 976/1568–9 for Sokollu Mehmed Pasha, show that the miniaturists trained during the time of Süleyman the Magnificent were able to continue in this style until the end of the century.

The art of portaiture that developed during the reign of Süleyman the Magnificent can be linked with the name of a single artist, Haydar Reis, better known under the name of Nigârî, who was born in Istanbul and died in 1572 at the age of eighty. He was originally a sailor. His large miniatures in the Topkapı Saray, some of which measure as much as 30×45 cm., are painted on very dark backgrounds and display a truly amazing expressiveness and realism in the faces, though feet, hands and lines of the body are neglected. One of the most characteristic of these is a miniature portraying Süleyman the Magnificent in his old age. The Sultan is shown walking in the garden followed by two armed guards. Nigârî also produced a very vivid portrait of the Kapudan Derya (Admiral) Barbaros Hayreddin Pasha (Barbarossa), who had made the whole of the Mediterranean tremble. He is shown with a grey beard, with a precious sceptre presented to him by the sultan in one hand, and a carnation, which he is sniffing, in the other. Although a final portrait miniature showing Sultan Selim II shooting an arrow, with a guard behind him and his head falconer holding the target in front, is executed in a richer and more flamboyant style the expressive quality is weaker. Nigârî's style displays original and purely personal qualities quite unlike that of the other manuscript miniatures of the period.

The classical style of the historical miniature assumes definitive form in the miniatures depicting the conquest of Szigetvár and the last campaign of Süleyman the Magnificent. (Fig. 241.) In these miniatures, most of which cover a whole page and some double pages, we find a well-balanced and harmonious relation between the figures and the setting. Figures are given a small but definite place in these miniatures, though in some of them we come across scenes completely without human figures recalling those of Matrakī. As for the composition, the scene showing the reception of the King of Erdel by Süleyman the Magnificent formed the basis for later depictions of coronation scenes. Here we find a detailed delineation of the costumes and the great tents and pavilions. It is interesting to note the geometrical ornament of intersecting hexagons from ancient Turkish architecture on the background and the throne. (Plate XXVIII.) In a scene representing the reception of the Persian ambassador by Selim II in his palace these geometrical architectural decorations are displayed in greater variety.

The 25 miniatures in the Süleymānnāme of 1579 written by Luqmān (Lokman) bin Sayyid Ḥusayn al-ʿAshūrī al-Urmāwī and now in the Chester Beatty Library in Dublin, show scenes from the last years of Süleyman's reign, such as the conquest of Szigetvár. Two miniatures showing the Janissaries and cavalry soldiers taking part in the funeral of the Sultan very finely express a sense of mourning by means of a schematic composition and a relatively dry style.

The colophon of another work written by Lokman and entitled Shāhnāme-i Selim Khan (The Shāhnāme of Selim Khan), with 43 miniatures illustrating the battles of Selim II's reign and the castles and cities he captured, is dated 1581. This work, which is written in Persian in *mesnevi* form, shows a further development of the Ottoman style. In the full-page miniatures the figures are reduced in size, and the composition is dominated by the galleons, the sea and the architectural forms. Full-page minatures were also made depicting Haghia Sophia and the Mosque of Selimiye. The two different styles in these miniatures indicate that two different artists worked on the manuscript. That Naqqāsh Osman and other artists worked on this book is shown in a document in the Ottoman Archives. Another work by Lokman, the Shāhanshāhnāme (The Book of the King of Kings) of 1581 (Istanbul University Library), contains miniatures depicting events during the reign of Sultan Murad III and shows the continuation of the classical style of historical miniature-painting. The fact that in these historical miniatures none of the names of the artists are given makes it very difficult, however, to trace the development of the genre.

In the Hünernāme (or Book of Accomplishments), another work written by Sayyid Lokman, there is a change in the situation. The finest miniatures in this and several other works are linked with the name of the master painter Osman, an artist about whom we have very little information, and his atelier. These works, in order of their conjectured dates of publication, are the Sūrnāme of Murad III 1582, the Maṭāliʿ-i Saʿādet 1582 (a Turkish translation of a work of astrology and fortune-telling, Bibliothèque Nationale, Paris), the Hünername I 992/1584, the Hünernāme II 1587, and the Shāhanshāhnāme 1592. Although the more than 700 miniatures decorating the pages of these books possess a general stylistic unity they differ very greatly in quality. But with the historical miniatures produced by Osman and his atelier the art suddenly comes to life and produces works of the finest quality. In the Hünernāme, the first volume relates the lives and battles of the Sultans from Osman Ghāzī up to Selim I in a series of 45 miniatures. The 95 miniatures of the second volume are devoted entirely to Süleyman the Magnificent. Other important illustrated works include the Sūrnāme, with 437 miniatures depicting the Circumcision Feast of Murad III's son, Shehzade Mehmed, and the two-volume Shāhnāme (Vol. 1, Istanbul, University Library) with 137 miniatures describing the reign of Murad III. We may also add to this the 68 miniatures in the Maṭāliʿ al-Saʿāda wa Yanābiʿ al-Si-yāda (a book of fortune-telling and astrology by Muḥammad al-Suʿūdī) translated into Turkish for Fatma Sultan, the daughter of Murad III (Bibliothèque Nationale, Paris). The writer came from a noble family of Niksar (i.e. from Anatolia).

Some examples may give us some idea of the style of the miniatures in the Hünernāme (or Book of Accomplishments). One of these portrays Sultan Murad II practising archery in the presence of ambassadors. The spectators and palace officials have taken up their positions on horseback behind a hill, leaving the centre free for the Sultan, who is riding his horse at full gallop and shooting an arrow at a small target at the top of a high pole. This type of composition, in which the picture is divided into separate planes and the spectator's interest is immediately drawn to a desired point, was very widespread in Persia.

In enthronement scenes the same composition scheme is repeated with alterations made merely in the figures. The enthronement of a sultan was always portrayed with special meticulousness, and that of Selim I, surrounded by the vizirs and palace officials, is depicted with great magnificence.

Another miniature portraying Selim I hunting leopards in the province of Zulkadir (a territory composed of the Maraş, Elbistan, Malatya and Harput regions) breaks away completely from any type of schematised composition and creates a scene of great dynamism. The Sultan is riding at full gallop after a leopard. Two greyhounds, one black and one white, are chasing other animals. Falconers with hunting-birds on their wrists wait on the other side of the hill. A stream flows past on the right. The hunting scene is treated very realistically, and with a simplicity unknown in Persian miniatures. The figures are arranged at the sides of the pictures leaving ample space for the landscape. It is obvious that both landscape features and the movements of animals had been closely studied.

In the sieges and battles depicted in the second volume of the Hünernāme we find historically accurate representations of the siege technique and buildings and tents of the period in a completely naturalistic composition. One of these miniatures depicts the siege of Vienna by Süleyman the Magnificent. Above is written 'Withdrawal owing to wintry weather after the capture of the outskirts of the city'. The state tent, defence towers, and buildings are portrayed in conformity with the outlook and military technique of the period. The siege of Szigetvár in Hungary (Fig. 242) is typical in showing how the same composition was handled by Osman 20 years after the Nüzhet al-Akhbār (Fig. 241).

Another miniature portraying Süleyman the Magnificent hunting in his palace at Plovdiv in Bulgaria depicts the palace buildings with trees in blossom in the background and the hunting scene in the foreground. This miniature demonstrating Süleyman's skill in archery presents a vivid picture of an arrow piercing a tree after passing through a wild boar and of three boars falling lifeless to the ground. Architecture is shown in the minutest detail, without the use of any stereotyped patterns.

The great battle in the Mohacs plain at which Süleyman the Magnificent defeated the King of Hungary is depicted in a type of composition quite different from those employed in other miniatures. Here an attempt has been made to recreate the horror, noise and confusion of battle. The hills and mountains are covered from top to bottom with Janissaries, cavalry soldiers and cannon. The Sultan is distinguished from the others by being drawn on horseback on a larger scale.

A miniature depicting the horse-races held at the Circumcision Feast of the princes, on the other hand, depicts a peaceful, joyful gathering. The Sultan is seated on a throne in front of the tent with palace officials and princes at each side. The movements of the horsemen and the galloping horses have been closely studied and accurately reproduced. The foreground of the picture is left entirely free for the galloping horses, and the figures are gathered together at the back, in front of the tent. A scene depicting the reception of the son of the King of Erdel and his mother by Sultan Süleyman is one of the most successful compositions of the manuscript and is shown in very fine detail. (Fig. 240.)

One of the miniatures depicting scenes from the life of Süleyman the Magnificent shows the Sultan being helped down from his horse by the Grand Vizir Sokollu Mehmed Pasha and being conveyed to a waiting litter, on being taken ill during the campaign of Szigetvár. The army that had formerly sped from one victory to another is suddenly plunged into deep mourning. In deep reverence, they pay their silent respects to their sultan who had remained at the head of his army until his last breath. The atmosphere of tragedy blended with love and respect is portrayed with the greatest skill by means of a very simple composition and slight head movements.

In the miniatures of the Sūrnāme Osman acts with greater freedom, choosing a separate composition for each group and resolving the problems each one of them poses with the greatest skill. The illustrations reproduce with great exactness the life and work of craftsmen of the period.

In these double-page miniatures we find depicted the pageants in which the various craftsmen's guilds exhibited their skills, together with the banquets and revelry that continued throughout the whole of the 40 days of the great Circumcision Feast held in the Hippodrome. The palace of Ibrāhīm Pasha, with boxes for the Sultan and the palace officials, forms the background to every scene. By his portrayal of the life of the people of Istanbul, the manner in which the tradesmen and artisans carried on their work, and the costumes of the time, Osman created a completely new genre of miniature painting. By bringing out the peculiar characteristics of each scene, such as that of craftsmen making coloured glass (see Plate XI), or craftsmen blowing bottles in a glass furnace, and by means of a separate composition for each, he gives a superlative rendering of the whole ceremony and display (Plate XXIX). On looking at these pictures we seem to breathe the gay, cheerful atmosphere of the celebrations, and to recapture the excitement of the period (Plate XXX). According to researches carried out by N. Atasoy a new name, Intiẓāmī, from Foça in the province of Hersek, appears in place of Lokman, the writer of all the Books of Kings, as the writer of the Sūrnāme. Although a Sūrnāme is mentioned among the works of Lokman this must merely be the single chapter from the second volume of his Hünernāme.

The historical miniature style was taken up again towards the end of the century in the Shāhanshāhnāme, a manuscript with 95 miniatures in two volumes. The first volume, now in the Istanbul University Library, contains 42 miniatures depicting the reign of Sultan Murad III and the circumcision feast of Prince Mehmed in the style of the Sūrnāme miniatures. These must have been the product of the atelier of Osman. We also find full-page miniatures in which the Ottoman army setting out on a campaign and the ensuing battle are brilliantly depicted by means of crowds of small figures on the field and in front of the castle. A book of fortune-telling together with an anthology dated 1582 now in the Bibliothèque Nationale (Supp. Turc.) in Paris made for Murad III's daughter Fatma Sultan is a manuscript containing 68 miniatures. The portrait of Murad III and the figures of the 12 signs of the zodiac are from Osman's own hand, and are miniatures of meticulous workmanship and the finest quality. These miniatures are arranged as cameos in four columns of seven figures each, and although small, display a very refined technique. Starting with the planets, the sultan and his Beks, a series of amusing and original pictures portray the masters of various arts and crafts performing their work, with the names of the crafts written in witty fashion beside them. These would appear to be products of Osman's atelier, produced under his own direction. The same book contains several other miniatures of inferior quality and insipid style.

Another manuscript illustrated with historical Turkish miniatures from the end of the 16th century is the Nüsret-nāme (or Book of Victory), dated 1584, depicting the campaigns in Georgia and Azerbaidzhan of the conqueror of Cyprus, Lala Mustafa Pasha, in a series of 41 miniatures, most of them full-page. In a full-page miniature showing the chronicler Mustafa Ali, who recorded the events of the campaign day by day, presenting his work to Lala Mustafa Pasha, with musicians and dancing dervishes below, we once more find geometrical architectural decoration.

The Shejāʿatnāme of Āṣafī Pasha (Istanbul University Library) dated 1586 containing 77 miniatures depicting the Persian campaign of Özdemir Oghlu Osman Pasha and the Turco-

XXVI Portrait of Jem Sultan, Washington, Freer Gallery of Art (see page 314)

XXVII The Court of Solomon, Süleymānnāme, Dublin, Chester Beatty Library (see page 314)

XXVIII Reception of the King of Erdel by Süleyman I, Nüzhet al-Akhbār der Sefer-i Sigetvar (an account of the Szigetvár campaign), Istanbul, Topkapı Saray Museum, Hazine Library (see page 320)

XXIX Glass furnace and glass-blowers, Sūrnāme, Istanbul, Topkapı Saray Museum, Hazine Library (see page 320)

XXX The carrying of the festival devices (Nakhl), Sūrnāme, Topkapı Saray Museum, Hazine Library (see page 320)

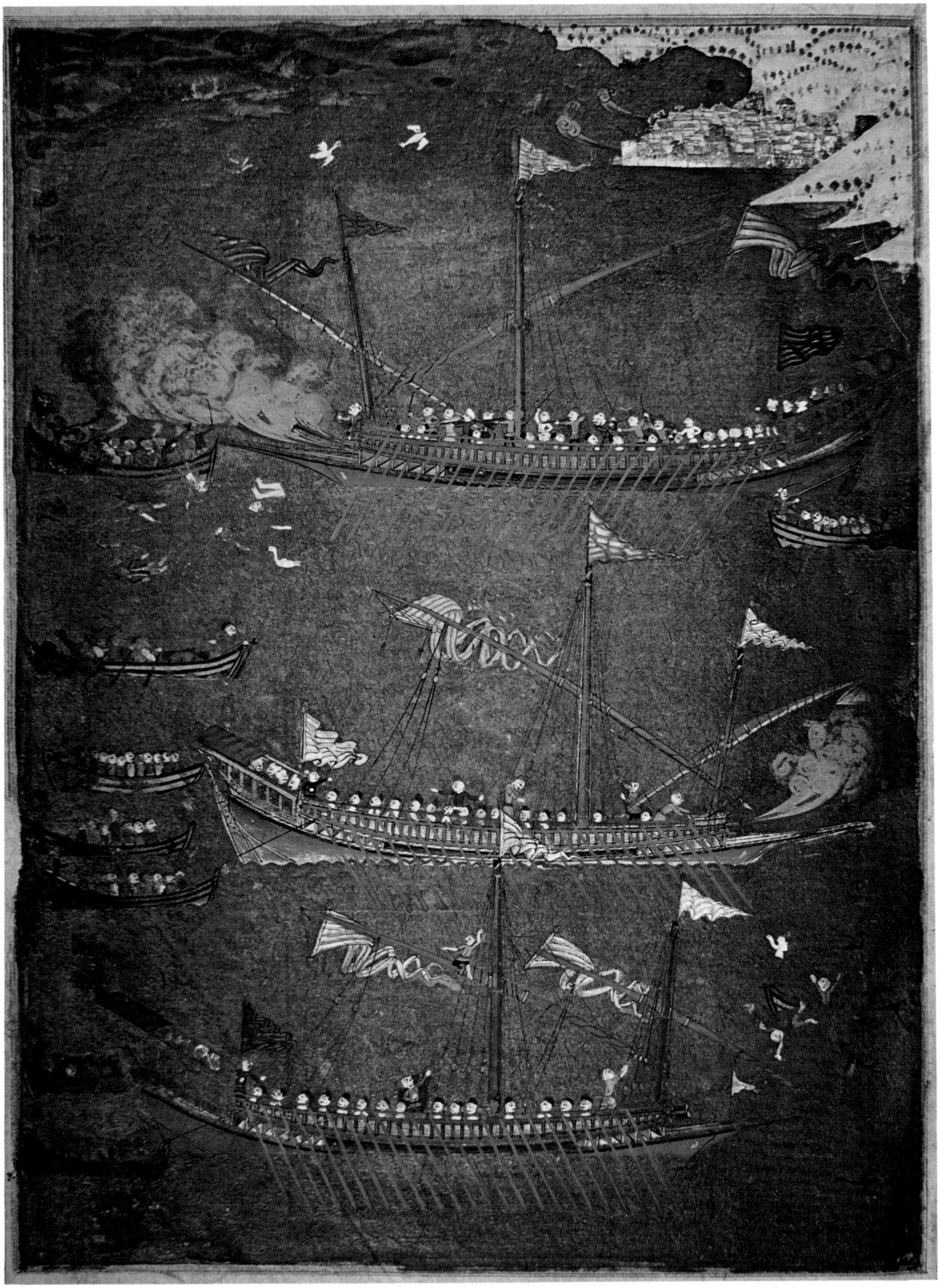

XXXI Kenan Pasha's Galleons, 1630, Pāshānāme, London, British Museum (see page 321)

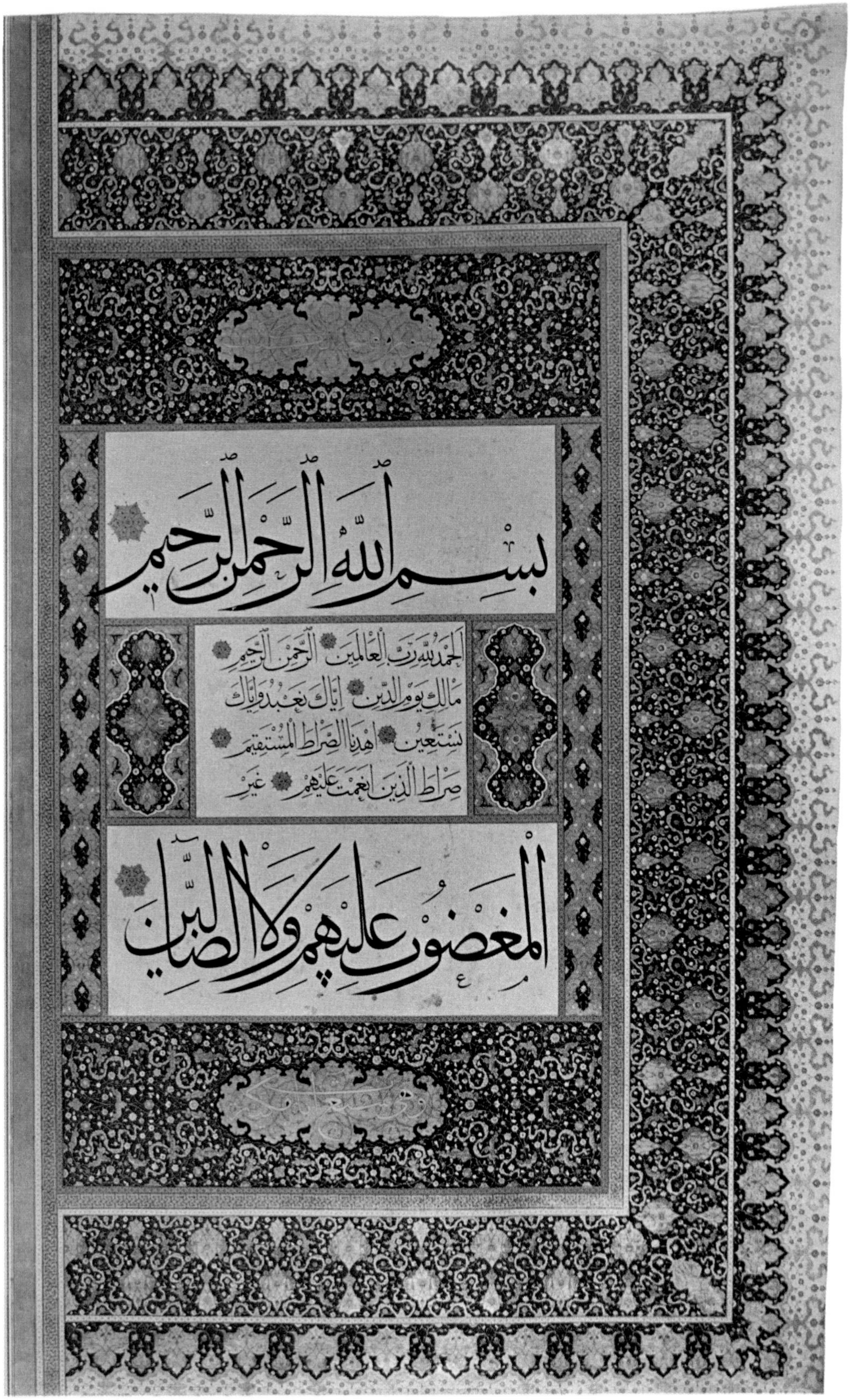

XXXII Illuminated title-page from Koran written by Ahmed Karahisarî, Istanbul, Topkapı Saray Museum, Hazine Library (see page 325)

Russian war is a Turkish manuscript prepared by a number of artists engaged on the production of historical Turkish miniatures, the illustrations of which vary greatly in style and quality.

The Genjine-yi Feth-i Genje, that relates the conquest of Gandzha in Azerbaidzhan by Ferhad Pasha, is a manuscript dated 1589 containing 20 miniatures. These miniatures display very fine workmanship and a lavish use of gold leaf, whilst their unity of style would suggest they are all from the same hand. A manuscript entitled Tarīkh-i Fatḥ-i Yaman recounting the Arabian and Tunis campaigns of Sinan Pasha was begun in the reign of Selim III and completed in 1594, in the reign of Murad III. It is now in the Istanbul University Library. Its 104 miniatures display the same fine quality and the same lavish use of gold leaf, and prove that the historical miniature style of the palace ateliers had lost none of its vitality. A single miniature in the Turkish manuscript Ghazawāt-i ʿUthmān Pashā, an account of the Erevan campaign of Özdemir Oghlu Osman Pasha, is in the same style.

Another miniaturist, Hasan Pasha, appears at the very beginning of the 17th century. The four miniatures from the Egri (Eger) Fetiḥnāme (an account of the Conquest of Eger in Hungary) of Sultan Mehmed III (circa 1600), three of which occupy double pages, are in the naturalistic style of the palace atelier. There is a definite deterioration in composition and colour. The figures in the portrait of Mehmed III are very lively.

Similarly, in the Turkish Hotin Fetiḥnāme in epic style with 20 full-page miniatures, most of which are arranged on double pages, depicting the 1621–2 Hotin campaign of Sultan Osman II the cities, castles and the movements of the army continue to be delineated in classical historical miniature style but there are changes in the colour scheme and the composition. The Divān containing the poems of Nādirī, who was the writer of the Hotin Fetiḥnāme and whose real name was Muḥammad bin ʿAbd al-Ghānī (died 1626), also contains 9 miniatures depicting events in the reigns of Mehmed III and Osman II. We find in these, side by side with the classical historical miniature style, successful innovations in colour and in the use of realistic details and unusual perspective in the delineation of architectural forms.

A very important illustrated manuscript of the first half of the 17th century, now in the British Museum in London, entitled the Pashānāme, contains the poems of Tului Ibrahim Efendi of Kalkandelen together with a number of miniatures. These were written in 1630 in honour of Kenan Pasha's restoration of order to the provinces of Rumelia. From there Kenan Pasha proceeded to the Crimea. At the end of the poem we find an account of the sea-battle he won against Cossack pirates in the Black Sea. Of the miniatures in the Pashānāme all but two have been ruined by damp. The miniature depicting the battle waged by Kenan Pasha's galleons against the pirates in the Black Sea is drawn in fine detail and unusual colours with very great care and precision, and constitutes a most valuable document concerning the navigation of that period (Plate XXXI).

In another illustrated manuscript of the period we find a very great change. The Shaqāyīq-i Nuʿmānīye is a translation made in the reign of Osman II with 49 miniatures by Ahmed Mustafa, better known as Nakshi, of a work illustrating the lives of various Turkish notables, sheikhs and scholars and their relations with the Ottoman rulers. The miniatures are very simple in composition with very unusual colours, whilst the figures are in a dry but very meticulous style. The very close resemblance between the interesting perspective employed in the delineation of architectural forms and that in the Divān-i Nādirī suggest that the miniatures in the latter may also have been the work of Nakshi.

In the 18th century very great fame was achieved by Levni, the master-miniaturist of Sultan Ahmed III. Levni, whose real name was ʿAbd al-Jalīl Chelebi, was a native of Edirne and died in 1732. Unlike the other miniaturists he also produced miniatures on separate sheets of paper. His greatest work consists of the 137 miniatures illustrating the Sūrnāme written by the poet Vehbi for the Circumcision Feast of Ahmed III's son, Prince Süleyman.

Levni's portraits of Ahmed III and other characters of his age are photographic in quality, and show no distinction of style or artistic perception. The facial features in these single-sheet miniatures are all more or less similar, the only difference being in the costumes.

A miniature portraying four women playing musical instruments has greater warmth of feeling. It also provides information concerning the type of instruments played by the women of that period. It produces the immediate impression that one is about to hear a light and delicate piece of music. (Fig. 243.) A dancing girl, too, moves in harmony with the music. She dances with graceful movements, striking together the bells in her hands. Her face, however, has a dull, lustreless expression.

Levni's works show the steadily increasing influence of European artists during the reign of Ahmed III.

A painting showing Selim III together with his vizir Koja Yusuf Pasha dating from the beginning of the 19th century has lost all the qualities of a miniature painting and is completely in line with the perspective drawing of the West. Painting subsequently developed parallel to European styles.

In Ottoman miniature-painting, besides portraits and scenes relating to historical events and court life, works of original quality were produced by the treatment of scenes of siege and war, and views of castles and cities. Although in their composition and in the use of landscape backgrounds these miniatures are still partly bound to several of the traditions that had taken root in Iran, they were treated in a basically realistic manner. The artists employed the limited means at their disposal to give as accurate a pictorial representation as possible of real events. Besides this, one is often struck by the amazingly successful delineation of nature, especially in the horse-races and battle scenes the Ottomans loved so much. On the other hand the fact that historical events were portrayed uniquely rendered the creation and development of character types impossible, though it also had the merit of eliminating stereotypes. The same reason prevented the creation of a definite style in Ottoman miniature-painting. In miniatures of the period one encounters a cheerful atmosphere with bright, lively colours in which red plays a dominant role, an atmosphere that now and then verges on ridicule.

29

TURKISH CALLIGRAPHY

Writing in Islam occupies as important a place in architecture as it does in stone carving, brick decoration, tiles, woodwork, metalwork and textiles. It thus became an element that was exploited to the full in every branch of Turkish art, and which gave added vitality to architecture. An angular cursive script is known as Kufic, while a rounded cursive is called *naskhī* and an early subdivision of this is called *thuluth*. Ornate styles of lettering known as floriated and braided Kufic were widely used in the Seljuk period.

Kufic, with its thick, angular letters, was used on parchment. Although there is no definite proof, it is thought by some to have originated in the city of Kūfa in Iraq.

In the early years of the Hejira Kufic was used as much as *naskhī*, or *thuluth*. Kufic may be said to have died out of general use in the 16th century.

We have so far mentioned two forms of rounded cursive, *naskhī* and *thuluth*. *Naskhī* formed the basis of *thuluth* and it was used for the Koran and other books that are to be read in the hand. *Thuluth*, the long straight shafts of which contrast with its generally rounded letters, did not begin to reach its finest development until the 16th century. *Naskhī* and *thuluth* were followed by a large type of cursive script called *jeli*. *Jeli* is not merely an enlarged version of *thuluth*, for its structure and anatomy are quite different. This is a form of writing particularly used for the decoration of religious edifices.

When the Turks were converted to Islam in the 10th century they took over Arabic as a script together with the Koran, but they transformed it into an art form of their own.

Yāqūt of Amasya, a Turkish calligrapher who acted as secretary to al-Mustaʿṣim (1242–58) the last of the ʿAbbāsid Caliphs, made use of an obliquely cut pen in writing *naskhī*, *thuluth* and *jeli* script and so gave rise to a new style. *Naskhī*, at the hands of Yāqūt, found the essence of what was eventually to become its classical form. *Thuluth*, too, which continued to be written in the same style for hundreds of years without any perceptible change, was subjected by Yāqūt to a sort of anatomical investigation and given, with its finest details, a most suitable and satisfying form. (Fig. 245.) By the formulation of all the rules and peculiar characteristics of the six different varieties of script later known as the Aqlām-i Sitta Yāqūt created a solid basis for the art of Turkish calligraphy.

After this advance, no very important change took place until the Ottoman period. Calligraphy was made a fine art by the Turks in Istanbul. In the 15th century the six types of lettering were taken in hand by Sheikh Ḥamdullah, also from Amasya, who laid down rules according to certain principles recalling the portrayal of the human body in accordance with the principles of anatomy. In consequence Ḥamdullah became the master of all the calligraphers of the Islamic world, and was given the title of 'the *qibla* of the calligrapher'. He was Sultan Bayazid II's teacher while Bayazid was still a prince. One day the Sultan, who felt so great a respect for the Sheikh that he would hold his inkpot for him, asked him if it was not possible to create a special style of writing quite different from any known in Arabia or Persia. Thereupon Sheikh Ḥamdullah spent forty days without talking to anyone, and produced six different new styles of writing, that were to comprise the new Aqlām-i Sitta (or Six Scripts), *naskhī, thuluth, rīḥānī, muḥaqqaq, tawqīʿ* and *riqʿa*.

Naskhī continued to be used in religious works. It has fine and broad varieties. The very fine ones are known as *hurda* and *gubarî*. The kind known as *naskhī kırması* is a type of writing employing no vowel points. *Gubarî* is an extremely fine style of writing. Apart from chapters of the Koran written in *gubarî* on a grain of rice we also find the whole 300 pages of the Koran squeezed into a space of 3 cm. square.

Thuluth was the ancestor of all the later forms of script and from it these other styles are descended. Its large size, however, makes it unsuitable for texts. It is used for the titles of books, or invocations such as the *Basmala*, at the beginning of a work, the *Muraqqaʿ* sections of the Koran, and some inscriptions and epitaphs. The greatly enlarged variety used in sacred architecture is, as we have seen, known as *jeli*.

With Sheikh Ḥamdullah, *nashkī* reached maturity. Whereas in Yāqūt it had been grouped in single words, it now gained a fluency and organic unity embracing whole lines. *Thuluth*, which owed its form to Yāqūt, was completely Turcicised in the hands of Sheikh Ḥamdullah and given a rich aesthetic quality. The *jeli* script first created by Yāqūt was also brought to classical perfection by Ḥamdullah. Sheikh Ḥamdullah died in Istanbul in 1519 and was buried in the cemetery of Karaja Ahmed. The inscription on the main door in the Mosque of Bayazid in Istanbul and the *jeli* lettering above the door of the *shadırvan* courtyard, as well as the inscription on the Mosque of Sultan Bayazid at Amasya, are examples of his work. He produced several Korans together with hundreds of other manuscripts. The Sheikh gave the Ottoman art of calligraphy its classical form and his influence has continued without any loss of vitality through the centuries down to our own day. (Fig. 246.)

Although ʿAlī bin Yaḥyā Ṣūfī, who had grown up in the reign of the Conqueror, was an older calligrapher he cannot be compared with the Sheikh. He was responsible for the inscription on the Fatih Mosque in Istanbul and the inscription of the Bāb-i Hūmayūn in the Topkapı Saray, and was particularly successful in the symmetrical style of writing known as *musanna* (*muthanni*, doubled).

Ahmed Karahisarî developed the *jeli* script in the same century as Sheikh Ḥamdullah, but he built upon the values created by Yāqūt and Sheikh Ḥamdullah and made no changes save in the proportions of the forms; using thick strokes instead of the tapering ends of other Turkish calligraphers. From his signatures it appears that Karahisarî was the pupil of Asad Allāh of Kirman though Yaḥyā Ṣūfī is said also to have been his first master. Karahisarî was responsible for the *jeli* lettering in the dome of the Süleymaniye Mosque in Istanbul, and by working in *rīḥānī* and *muḥaqqaq*, two of the six forms of lettering, he produced a new style of his own. Though his style partly derives from Yāqūt of Amasya, he may be said to have written more beautifully than Yāqūt. He had a bold style in both *naskhī* and *thuluth*. A great illuminated Koran written for Sultan Süleyman is a monument of 16th-century art. (Plate XXXII.) (Istanbul, Topkapı Saray Museum.) The various forms of its *Basmalas* are like separate pictures. Linked *Basmalas* are here seen for the first time in the art of Turkish calligraphy. (Fig. 244.)

He died at the age of 90 in 1556, the year in which the Mosque of Süleymaniye was completed, and was buried in the cemetery of the *dergâh* (dervish convent) at Sütlüce where he had spent his peaceful life.

Of the six pupils trained by Karahisarî the most important was Hasan Chelebi. The long dating inscription on the Süleymaniye Mosque and the *jeli* writing in the Mosque of Piyale Pasha are examples of his work. On his death in 1594 he was buried by the side of Karahisarî. However, the extraordinary style adopted by Ahmed Karahisarî remained as a completely separate, isolated episode in the development of Turkish calligraphy, and apart from a few pupils was to find no followers. Turkish calligraphers were particularly influenced by Sheikh Ḥamdullah and it is from him that the distinctively Ottoman style of writing derives.

In the 17th century Turkish calligraphy reached new heights of achievement in the work of Hafız Osman, who was born in Istanbul in 1642. He received a diploma in *thuluth* and *naskhī* calligraphy from Suyoljuzade Mustafa Efendi of Eyüb. Hafız Osman developed and simplified *naskhī* script, and organised it on the lines of greater legibility. His mature *naskhī* is so rapid and dynamic in its flow that it is known as 'spark' *naskhī*. By their advances Yāqūt, Sheikh Ḥamdullah, and Hafız Osman in his turn, form the main periods of *naskhī* and *thuluth* script.

Hafız Osman introduced a new freedom into the art of calligraphy by breaking the old classical moulds. He thus became the greatest master of the art after Sheikh Ḥamdullah and his style of writing was adopted by other masters. (Fig. 244.) In 1695 he became a teacher of calligraphy to Sultan Mustafa II and Prince Ahmed III. He died in 1698 at the age of 56 and was buried in the cemetery of the Sünbül Efendi Tekke at Koca Mustafa Paşa. He wrote 25 Korans, a considerable number of separate *sūra*-headings, a large number of calligraphic collages, and countless couplets and calligraphic exercises. He was also the first of all Turkish calligraphers to compose a *Hilye*, a calligraphic portrait of the Prophet in the form of a panel. Lithographic prints of his Korans carried his fame throughout the whole of the Islamic world as far as India and Indonesia. A facsimile of a Koran he wrote in 1682 when he was 40 years of age was printed in Istanbul in 1967. Of his many pupils the most important are Seyyid Abdullah of Yedikule (died 1731), Mehmed of Crete (died 1751) and Yusuf Mehdi (died

1721), who continued his manner and style with vigour and vitality into the middle of the 18th century and passed it on to succeeding generations. Later calligraphers have recognised Sheikh Ḥamdullah and Hafiz Osman as two great masters of the art.

At the end of the 18th century Ismail Efendi of Ünye achieved such a reputation that some of his writings have been attributed to Sheikh Ḥamdullah. Yet his greatest service to the art lies in his having taught his younger brother Mustafa Rakim Efendi. Rakim, who was also a painter, was a calligrapher of genius who revolutionised the *jeli* script. He regarded *jeli*, which depends on distance for its effect, as a kind of picture, and invented a style of writing employing checkered lines. The new development of *thuluth* and *naskhī* introduced by Hafız Osman attained its final culmination in the *jeli* of Rakim.

The innovations introduced by Mustafa Rakim gave *jeli* writing a new vitality. In his *jeli* script we find different forms and letters that are continually changing in stance and feature. His *jeli* style achieved very high artistic perfection with a minimal use of vowel points and decoration, and freed the lettering from the stereotyped formalism of the classical period. In every piece of calligraphy he invented original forms for the letters. Rakim was also a genius in *istif*, that is, the harmonious arrangement on a given surface of letters, words and lines. By choosing those forms that would blend most harmoniously together he created a pure flow of perfection. To fit an inscription into a given space in architectural constructions is a difficult problem demanding very great artistic ability. An imperfect arrangement is as disturbing as music played out of tune. *Jeli* achieved its characteristic form amongst the Ottomans in the work of Rakim and succeeding calligraphers. Such inscriptions were sometimes produced, like paintings, after many months of work.

As the great representative of a dynamic understanding of beauty, Rakim became the most imitated of calligraphers, and an increasing number of artists followed his lead. Unlike him, Mahmud Jelâleddin (died 1829) and his wife and pupil Esma Ibret, who was as skilled as himself, created a new style, but apart from a few other pupils he had no followers. In his work the vitality of Hafız Osman became fixed and immobile. Instead of the vigorous, lively writing of Rakim we find a static type of beauty. In his *thuluth*, and particularly in his *jeli* compositions, we perceive a harsh and severe style that recalls the solitude of rugged rocks. In composition his attitude is completely different from that of Rakim. Although several calligraphers after Rakim created works of flawless beauty, they were not able to capture his genius. But of these Mustafa Izzet Efendi, a distinguished musician and Kazasker of Anatolia, deserves more detailed treatment. The tenseness of Rakim's *jeli* lettering acquires a certain softness in his hands. The large round cartouches which still hang in St. Sophia are examples of his work. But he followed Jelâleddin rather than Rakim. The calligrapher Sami, who excelled in *jeli*, followed successfully in Rakim's footsteps.

A script known as *ta'līq* made great progress amongst the Ottomans. It seems to have first appeared in the 12th century and achieved its classical form at the hands of an Azerbaidzhani Turk, Mīr 'Alī of Tabriz. Later it spread among the Ottomans and gave rise to a very graceful style known as Turkish *ta'līq*. It was in this style that 'Imād al-Husaynī most excelled and, though he did not possess the creative genius of Mīr 'Alī, within his own limits, he lent Persian *ṭa'līq* its most fitting style. But Katibzade Mehmet Refi' Efendi, who was brought up in Istanbul and died in 1769, rightfully adopted the title 'Imād al-Rum and, without impairing its essential features, adapted *ṭa'līq* script to Turkish taste. Mehmed Esad Yesari, another great 18th-century master of *ṭa'līq*, made further progress in the art and created works of matchless beauty. His inscriptions can be seen in every corner of Istanbul and there are plaques of his on a number of private houses. His son and pupil Yesarizade Mustafa Izzet followed in his father's footsteps and raised Turkish *ṭa'līq* to its highest pitch of perfection. Succeeding calligraphers in this style were content to imitate his works.

Ṭa'līq became the chosen style of writing of scholars in Istanbul, and works of literature, court poetry and books of poems were written in this medium. Until the 18th century monumental inscriptions had been written in *thuluth* or *nashkī*, but they then began to be written on various buildings, sebils, *çeşmes* and gravestones in fine or broad *ṭa'līq*.

Dīvānī script was an entirely Turkish script used by the Ottomans only for orders of the Sultan, such as firmans, patents and warrants. These would normally be written very closely so as to prevent any subsequent alterations being made to the text.

The Ottomans also used Kufic. We can see it used in 15th-century wood-carving, in the painted decorations in mosques and as a decoration in the centre of illuminated title-pages. In the 16th century one of the calligraphers who used Kufic script most originally and successfully was Karahisarî. In the later Ottoman empire Kufic script gradually fell into disuse.

Besides being an art in itself calligraphy also played an important role in architectural decoration and in the enrichment of the decorative arts. If we were to remove all writing from buildings and works of art they would present a very jejune appearance.

Calligraphers as well as architects have demonstrated their skill in the great buildings of Islam throughout the centuries. From the 10th century onwards Turkish architectural monuments of every period have acquired greater meaning and magnificence, as a result of the employment of calligraphy.

30

VARIOUS ARTS

Ṭughrās

The *ṭughrā* or Sultan's monogram is an ancient Turkish tradition which continued from the Great Seljuk and Anatolian Seljuk periods right up to Ottoman times. The well-known author Mu'ayyad al-Dīn Abū Ismā'īlī 'Āmidī Jawzaqānī was one of the most famous writers of these monograms in the Great Seljuk period. It is known from written records that in this period the monogram was in the form of a bow, and that the Sultan's name was written beneath this bow. In the Anatolian Seljuk period the historian Ibn Bībī actually speaks of the *bow* of the Sultan's *ṭughrā* ('kemanja-i ṭughrā-i Salṭānat').

During the Ottoman period all firmans and other important documents were headed by the monogram of the Sultan. This was a distinct skill practised by an artist known as a *tughrakesh*. These monograms contained the Sultan's name together with his patronymics and various titles such as Shāh, Khān, or al-Muẓaffar (the victorious). The official, the *nishanji*, who was responsible for these either drew the monograms himself or had them prepared by a *tughrakesh* working under his supervision. Two documents bearing the monogram of Orhan Ghāzī show that these monograms were used as early as 1324, in the first years of the Ottoman period. Thereafter individual monograms were created for each sultan in turn, some sultans having several. In the course of time these monograms assumed a great wealth and variety of forms. Some of them were large and conspicuous, and were richly decorated in gilt and various colours according to the style of the period. Some of the monograms had no ornament apart from the script itself, others were decorated with lotus, palmette, *rūmī* and *hatayī* arabesques, carnations and cloud motifs. The *ṭughrā* of Süleyman the Magnificent on a *Tamlīknāme* (deed of property) issued in the month of Ramaḍan 963 (1555) allotting lands from the fiefs of the Sanjak Bek (Governor) of the Sanjaks of Jerusalem and Nablus and from the military fiefs (*timars*) and arable lands of the Renk Sanjak for the *waqf* (pious foundation) of Hürrem Sultan is a classical example of a *ṭughrā*, dating from the middle of the 16th century (Plate VIII). The decoration with spiral scrolls, small flowers, *rūmī* arabesques and cloud motifs shows a development parallel with that of the other arts. *Ṭughrās* assumed their classical form in the 16th and 17th centuries, but in the 18th century they display further change and development. At the beginning of the 19th century Rakim created a masterpiece in his monogram for Sultan Mahmud II.

Illumination

The art of illumination occupies an important place alongside the art of the *ṭughrā*. The title-pages of books and the edges of the other pages were tastefully decorated with designs of foliate motifs. Innumerable specimens of illumination in various colours and styles were produced from the Seljuk to the end of the Ottoman period. Most of these are in the form of patterns which show a matchless harmony of colour and nobility of design which one can never grow tired of looking at. The art of illumination, in combination with calligraphy, performed a very great cultural service in creating good taste in books and the desire to read.

Bookbinding

Bindings display both very good taste and extremely fine workmanship. Turkish bookbinding has a history going back as far as the Uighurs. Two fragments of bindings from the 9th century were unearthed in the excavations carried out at Karakhocho. The Turkish word *cild* (binding) is derived from the Arabic word for leather (*jild*). Several leather bindings of the Seljuk period dating from the 13th and 14th centuries are preserved in the Museum of Turkish and Islamic Art and the Topkapı Saray Museum. The 15th and 16th centuries constituted the most brilliant period of the development of the art of Turkish bookbinding, and in the 16th century Turkish work was even imitated by the Persians. Both the inner and outer leather surfaces of the cover are decorated. In design and choice of motifs they very often show close affinities with the art of illumination. In the centre there is a round or oval medallion known as a *shemse*, and in the corners a decoration known as *köshebend*. If the *shemse* is extended at both ends this is known as a *salbekli shemse*. In the Seljuk and early Ottoman periods the *shemses* were generally round, but from the 17th century onwards they began to be made oval. The cover was cardboard covered with leather or sometimes cloth, and had engraved, embossed or coloured decoration. The Ottomans used chiefly goat skin, and, to a lesser extent, ordinary sheepskin. The quality of the leather was of great importance.

In Turkish bookbinding only foliate and floral motifs were used, and the landscapes and human and animal figures of Persian art find no place. Among the most commonly used motifs are stylised *rūmī* arabesques, water-lilies, geranium leaves, clouds and, in the 16th century, pomegranate flowers and tiger skin and leopard spots.

When compared with the Turkish leather binding of Mahmud Chelebi, one of the great bookbinders of the reign of Süleyman the Magnificent in the 16th century, and of Süleyman Chelebi and Mustafa Chelebi, who belonged to the same family, Persian bookbinding appears very insipid. Although there was some deterioration of quality in Turkish work in the 17th century there was a certain revival in the 18th, as a result of the efforts of Sultan Ahmed III and Ibrāhīm Pasha, and from that time on lacquer bindings were also produced.

Weapons, Shields and Helmets, Flasks, Mirrors

In the Ottoman period very little work was done in bronze, and silver inlay or engraving was little used. On the other hand the Ottomans made great progress in the manufacture of arms. European museums contain collections of the finest specimens of Turkish weapons. Turkish swords are famous for the high quality of their steel, and were taken as models by European cavalry soldiers. The method of producing the high-quality steel that ensured Turkish weapons their superiority, and the decorative techniques known as *menevish* (terebinth) and *hale* (halo) have remained a secret to the present day. The various pieces of armour made for the cavalry and the trappings of their horses were sometimes richly ornamented in inlay work. The reins were adorned with engraved silver and gilt bronze plates.

Ottoman helmets became famous as a result of the long wars waged in Europe, and their style was adopted in Hungary and Poland. Some helmets resemble the caps of the Janissaries and are in the form of dervish head-dresses with spoon-cases at each side, others are conical in shape. Shields are in very decorative shapes and are very attractively ornamented. The most striking of the designs are cloud motifs and naturalistic flower compositions.

A 16th-century wicker shield, 53 cm. in diameter, in the Topkapı Saray Museum is made of silver thread wound on willow, and is ornamented with rows of cloud and three spot (leopard spot) motifs in black and white silver thread on a purple ground. The four cartouches between the rows are inscribed with the words 'Yā Allāh', 'Yā Muḥammad', 'Ya Abū Bakr' and 'Ya 'Umar' on a black ground. Between these are placed nails with metal rosettes for hanging up the shield. Black and white silver threads are used in the borders. The iron boss of the shield is 20 cm. in diameter and still preserves traces of inlaid foliate designs. The inside of the shield is covered with black velvet.

Another wicker shield in the Topkapı Saray Museum made of silver thread wound on willow is 56 cm. in diameter and is decorated with a repeat pattern of stylised tulip, rosebud and vervain (verbena) designs in beige, light blue and light green silver thread on a purple ground. Between are to be seen nails with metal rosettes for hanging up the shield. In the borders black and white silver thread is used. The boss is 22 cm. in diameter and is adorned with pairs of lilies in very fine gold inlay. The inside of the leaves and the tulips are filled with *rūmī* arabesque designs, and rosettes and Chinese cloud motifs can be seen between the bouquets of lilies. The inside of the shield is covered with red velvet.

Leather flasks with foliate motifs in coloured appliqué are products of a very fine taste.

Ottoman craftsmen ornamented the backs of hand mirrors with *rūmīs* and naturalistic floral designs. These are sometimes surrounded by a *naskhī* inscription. These mirrors are made of ivory or metal, the metal ones being decorated with gilding or gold or silver inlay. The centre of an ivory mirror 30 cm. in diameter presented to Süleyman the Magnificent is decorated with clouds, *rūmīs* and other vegetal motifs, surrounded by a verse inscription and the name

Sulṭān Sulaymān Shāh bin Sulṭān Salīm. At the end of the handle we find the signature of the craftsman, 'amal Ghānī' (the work of Ghānī), and the date 950/1549. (Fig. 247.) The handle is of ebony and is spirally fluted. Another ivory mirror, again 30 cm. in diameter, is engraved with *rūmī* and *hatayī* arabesques and palmettes with fine scrolls and a turquoise in a gold setting in the very centre.

Metal Grilles, Jade, Ivory, Tortoise-Shell and Mother-of-Pearl

Metal grilles of wrought iron or cast bronze or brass in sebils, *shadırvans*, tombs and windows produce a very attractive appearance by means of the play of light. In the 15th and 16th centuries simple geometrical forms and traditional arabesque patterns prevailed. The most common forms are concentric hexagons and circles, intersecting hexagons, and hexagons arranged in rows with adjacent sides. In later periods there was an increasing use of foliate motifs. In the 18th century metalwork resisted the European influences that had permeated other fields of art and long continued to preserve its traditional forms.

Objects made from jade occupy a special place in Ottoman art. Of these mirrors, ewers and cups are particularly remarkable. One of two green jade mirrors in the Topkapı Saray has very graceful arabesques in fine gold plate. On the other the surface is fluted and worked with gold wires, whilst the ground is decorated with medallions in green jade inlaid with emeralds and rubies. In the Topkapı Saray there is a very rich collection of objects made from green jade.

The art of wood-carving was well advanced in Ottoman times, and we also find this enriched with ivory, mother-of-pearl and tortoise-shell. Doors, window shutters, lecterns and Koran chests were also made with this type of ornament.

The throne of Ahmed I in the Topkapı Saray, faced with mother-of-pearl and tortoise-shell and decorated with precious stones including emeralds and rubies, is a most magnificent example of woodwork worthy of a sultan. Naturalistic flowers such as tulips, hyacinths and carnations springing from a vase are cut entirely from mother-of-pearl and set on a ground of brown tortoise-shell. Precious stones of various colours are set in mother-of-pearl and contained within gold frames. The finest examples of wood-carving are the 17th-century ceiling of a house, the Muradiye at Bursa, and the minbar or pulpit in the Süleymaniye Mosque in Istanbul (Figs. 249 and 250).

Decorative Painting

Decorative painting is another art that took its place beside tiles in interior decoration. This was done in coloured plaster, and there is a form in relief known as *malakârî*. The richest painted decoration was that done on wood to lend colour to ceilings and domes. Painted decoration had a very wide field of use in Ottoman art in accordance with the style of every period.

Painted decoration consisting of slender and graceful undulating *rūmī* arabesques in the tomb of Hajji Jamaza, the Kırk Kızlar or Forty Maidens at Iznik, is in the same style as the motifs of contemporary blue and white tiles and pottery. The decorative painting enriched with braided knots in the Muradiye Mosque in Edirne shows a resemblance to the patterns of the polychrome glazed tile mihrab. There is also a resemblance between the painted decorations in the Selimiye Mosque in Edirne and the designs used in the materials of the same period. A decorative painting of the Kaʿba at Mekka in the Haznedar Mosque in Sivrihisar is unique.

The decorations that have survived inside the arch of an old imaret at Bilecik are the oldest known examples of the *malakârî* technique. The *malakârî* decorations in the dome of the Çinili Köşk in Istanbul are richly coloured, flamboyant compositions. Among examples of painted decoration on wood we find instances where they have been applied to a ground that has been prepared by sticking a thick cloth on to the wood. Gilt is also very often employed. Decorative painting uncovered in the course of the recent repairs to the domes of the Green Mosque is amongst the richest and most spectacular specimens of this art, and it also has a peculiar importance as decoration dating from the beginning of the 15th century. In the eaves of the tomb of Murad II in Bursa we have a valuable example of the genre enriched with mother-of-pearl inlay. (Fig. 248.) Various types of painted ornament in the other tombs in the Muradiye cemetery form a decorative element that combines with the tile decorations to increase the appearance of colour and richness. A monumental example of decorative painting embellished in this manner with mother-of-pearl inlay is the dome of the Uftade zāwīya in Bursa, dating from the reign of Süleyman the Magnificent.

Decorative painting in the Muradiye Mosque in Manisa displays the richest and most highly coloured examples of painted decoration on wood and also on plaster. Written records inform us that these were made by the *Hassa nakkash* (court decorator) Mehmed Halife and his assistants.

In Istanbul rich and varied examples of painted decoration can be found on the gallery ceilings of the mosques of Kara Ahmed Pasha, Sokollu Mehmed Pasha, and Qılıch Ali Pasha, the Atik Valide Mosque at Üsküdar, the Mosques of Takkeji Ibrahim Agha and Sultan Ahmed, and in the ceilings of the Revan and Baghdad Kiosks in the Topkapı Saray. The naturalistic flowers, medallions, Chinese cloud-scrolls, and arabesques of the tiles of the period are repeated in the painted decorations.

The newly exposed dome in the apartments of the *Veliahd* (heir to the throne) in the Topkapı Saray is a spectacular example of painted decoration on cloth stretched over wood.

The naturalistic motifs such as spring trees in blossom, tulips, hyacinths and carnations on the cupboard doors and window shutters of the apartments of Murad III are in the same style as the tile decoration.

The decoration of the dining-room of Ahmed III in the Topkapı Saray with plates full of fruit and vases full of naturalistic flowers such as roses and lilies is in harmony with the purpose for which the room was designed and at the same time heralds the beginning of a new style.

Although the garlands, landscapes and architectural forms adorned with draped curtains characteristic of Baroque and Rococo painted decoration are for the most part tasteless and tiring, successful examples can be found in several buildings.

GLOSSARY

AKHĪ (Tk. Ahi)

Groups of tradesmen, in some respects comparable to mediaeval guilds, particularly characteristic of 14th century Anatolia. To judge from the contemporary traveller, Ibn Baṭṭūṭa, they tended to live, as well as work, together in communities, but whether these were comparable to present-day clubs or to the houses of a religious order is very difficult to say.

Cf. *Encyclopaedia of Islam,* 2nd Edition: Akhī.

ARABESQUE

A sinuous unbroken interlacing pattern of foliate scroll-work, normally held to be characteristic of all Islamic decoration, but not in fact fully developed until the 12th century. To be contrasted with so-called 'geometrical' ornament, that is, interlacing patterns composed of angular strapwork enclosing polygons or stars. Earlier scroll-work in Islam tends to rely upon derivatives of the Classical acanthus scroll extended in straight rather than curved lines. In Ottoman Turkey arabesques are often divided into *rūmī* (literally 'Greek' or 'Anatolian') and *hatayī* (literally 'Chinese'), the distinction applying more to the types of motifs used than to the way in which they are combined.

Cf. *Encyclopaedia of Islam,* 2nd Edition: Arabesque.

ATĀBEG (Tk. Atabek)

The post of tutor to the young prince held by an Emir of the Seljuk court. Since the holders were also often generals they sometimes used their position to make themselves independent, as at Mosul and Damascus. The Atabeg Jalāl al-Dīn Qarāṭay (Karatay), founder of the sumptuous Büyük Karatay Medrese at Konya, was one of the great statesmen of the Anatolian Seljuks.

Cf. *Encyclopaedia of Islam,* 2nd Edition: Atābak.

BASMALA. *See* BESMELE.

BATHS (Ar. ḥammam; Tk. hammam)

An essential part of Islamic public architecture which supplies the Koranic requirements of ritual purification, and tends to be built in close adjunction to the principal mosques or the large *madrasas* of a town. The construction with latrines, a *calidarium*, *tepidarium* and *frigidarium* and heating by hypocausts in the manner of a Roman bath, is now somewhat misleadingly called a 'Turkish' bath, though the baths of the Turks do not differ sensibly from those of other Muslim dynasties. Although no Islamic baths on the scale of the great Roman municipal baths are known, in the 'Umayyad period the palace baths were also audience and feasting places (e.g. at Khirbat al-Mafjir in Palestine). No court baths of the Seljuk period have survived and in the Ottoman period their function as places of entertainment seems to have been abandoned.

Cf. *Encyclopaedia of Islam,* 2nd Edition: Ḥammam.

BEDESTEN. *See* QAYṢARIYYA and KÜLLIYE.

BESMELE (Ar. basmala)
Bi-ismi'llahi'l-raḥmani'l-raḥīm (In the name of God, the Compassionate, the Merciful), the opening phrase of the first chapter of the Koran (the *Fātiḥa*), which has become a pious invocation and which appears subsequently in many formal documents and inscriptions. Traditionally the page on which it occurs is one of the most splendidly illuminated.

BLAZON (Ar. rank; Tk. renk)
In Mamluk Egypt and Syria the symbol of the Court office held by an individual (a cup for the *sāqī*, or cup-bearer, a napkin for the *jāmdār*, or butler etc.) and which appears frequently on objects made for him and on the buildings he founded. The position is complicated by the fact that since all the high officials had many Mamluks in their employ, all of whom used the sign of their master's office, it cannot be seen as exactly equivalent to the coats of arms of contemporary European heraldry, though composite blazons known from 14th century Syria and 15th century Egypt may have been a way of tying a blazon to an individual owner and not just to his office. It is possible that the frequent representations of eagles, or other birds of prey, lions and dragons etc. in Seljuk Anatolia may have had an heraldic significance, though, again, these may be only generalised symbols of Royal authority.

Cf. L. A. Mayer, *Saracenic Heraldry,* Oxford, 1932.

CARAVANSARAI (Ar. khān; Tk. han; Pers. ribāṭ, rubāṭ)
Two types may be distinguished, firstly, those in country areas away from towns, normally about 25 km. apart on the main trade-routes and which were primarily lodging places for caravans, though also to a certain extent meeting places and trading centres for the merchants who lodged there. A second type, within towns, was frequently a market for a particular commodity or a selling place for merchants from a particular country (which often came to the same thing), and not primarily a lodging place, since it came fully under the control of the supervisors of the markets. Although the institution in at least one of its forms certainly goes back to the *pandokheion* of Classical Antiquity and Byzantium (which gave the word *funduq* to Arabic), the archaeological material for the pre-Seljuk period is very scanty and indecisive.

CENOTAPH (Ar. tābūt; Tk. lâhid)

A boxlike construction, often of carved wood, marking a burial place inside a mausoleum, sometimes, as in the great Shīʿī shrines, having a largely symbolic importance. Muslims are not normally buried in coffins, and the Classical sarcophagi occasionally to be found in the mausolea of Seljuk Anatolia served not for burial but as cenotaphs, standing for the body, which is normally buried in a vault below the tomb-chamber.

ÇEŞME. *See* under SABĪL.

ÇIFTE MINARE

A building with two minarets over the main entrance porch. The form appears to have originated in Seljuk Iran (the Mosque of Ṭabās), but it was particularly exploited in the architecture of Seljuk Anatolia.

DĀR AL-SHIFĀ' (Tk. şifahane, timarhane; Pers. bīmāristān)

Hospitals, sometimes for the treatment of mental illness only, sometimes for the treatment of a wider variety of diseases. Their importance in the Seljuk period is often ascribed to the influence of the medical school of Jundaishāpūr in Southern Persia which, from the Sasanian period onwards, had been famous for its medicine. However, it is also possible that, in Anatolia at least, their form was to some extent influenced by the Asklepion of Classical Antiquity; architecturally at this period they are indistinguishable from *madrasas* or *khānqāhs*. In Ottoman Turkey they came to occupy an important position as teaching institutions.

DĪWĀN

In the Seljuk and pre-Seljuk periods the *dīwāns* were the great Ministries of State concerned with its administration, their work being largely legal and financial. Only in the Ottoman period is the word regularly used to designate the High Council of State composed of the Grand Vizir and other ministers.

FĀTIḤA. *See* under ILLUMINATION.

GUNBADH. *See* MAUSOLEUM.

ḤADĪTH (Tradition). *See* under MADRASA, SUNNĪ Muslims and MIʿRĀJ.

ḤAMMAM (Tk. HAMMAM). *See* BATHS.

HAN. *See* CARAVANSARAI.

HATAYĪ. *See* under ARABESQUE.

ILLUMINATION

Decoration composed of arabesques or complicated interlacing patterns of angular strapwork ('geometrical ornament'), freely enhanced with gold and silver. This is normally characteristic of Koran decoration, since the Koran is never illustrated by miniatures. In such cases various elements are traditionally singled out for decoration, the first page (the *'unwān,* literally, 'title', though it is not usually considered necessary to give the title of the Koran), and the opening verses of the first chapter (the Fātiḥa), as well as the opening verses of each succeeding chapter, generally in a less elaborate way. Colophons are as a general rule not illuminated.

IMARET

A public soup-kitchen or restaurant, which was an essential part of the *külliye* or complex Royal foundation. The word, derived from the Arabic *'imāra* (*any* construction), by its very specificity suggests that the *imaret* was an Ottoman invention and so far, indeed, no analogues have been found in the architecture of earlier dynasties.

IWAN (Ar. līwān; Tk. eyvan)

An open porch with a vaulted ceiling, sometimes leading to a domed chamber, used in Sasanian architecture for the ceremonial reception and audience halls of the palace (cf. the great *iwan* at Ctesiphon, near Baghdad). Fully developed in Islamic architecture under the Ghaznevids and the Seljuks it retained its function in palace architecture and was soon widely employed for the prayer halls of mosques, the classrooms of *madrasas,* the wards of hospitals and in caravansarais, in the latter case largely with the purpose of emphasising the axes of the courtyard. Although widely regarded as essentially Iranian in character the *iwan* was in fact employed by almost all the Islamic dynasties of the High Middle Ages from Khurāsān and Central Asia to Mesopotamia and Egypt.

JĀMI'. *See* MOSQUE.

KA'BA

The shrine at Mecca towards which Muslims turn when praying. Cubic in form it stands at the centre of a vast arcaded courtyard and contains built into the walls a celebrated black stone, which is a relic of the pre-Islamic animistic cults of Arabia. The *Ka'ba* is normally covered by a veil, the *kiswa.*

KHĀN. *See* CARAVANSARAI.

KHĀNQĀH (Tk. haneġâh, dergâh; Pers. khānegāh)

Dervish convent, where members of the Ṣūfī orders assembled or lived together. The architecture follows that of the *madrasa* (q.v.), though the institution, in Seljuk and Ottoman Turkey, is frequently more intimately associated with a tomb, either that of a founder or of some illustrious Sheikh of the order. The word *zāwīya* (Tk. zâviye) is also used for such institutions, though it is not clear that there is any substantial difference involved in the nomenclature.

KHUṬBA (Tk. hütbe)

The Friday sermon, delivered from the *minbar* of the Congregational Mosque (*Jāmiʿ*), attendance at which is compulsory in Sunni Islam. The *khuṭba*, when not pronounced by the Caliph himself, contained an invocation in his favour. This was required as a recognition of his sovereignty, and omission of it constituted an act of rebellion.

KÖŞK (Ar. kushk)

English, kiosk. Small pavilions, often consisting of a set of reception rooms only, generally serving for feasts and only intended for living quarters for short times. Their small scale lends them an intimate character which is lacking from the grand ceremonious constructions of the Sasanians and the palaces of the early Islamic dynasties. Particularly favoured in Anatolia (for example, in the Kayseri area) and by the Ottomans, who took advantage of the possibilities afforded by the site of Istanbul to line the shores of the Bosphorus with elaborate wooden constructions which served as summer houses. It is thought that the Venetian painter, Gentile Bellini, may have decorated a kiosk for Mehmed II at Istanbul, within the enceinte of the Topkapı Saray, on his journey there in 1479.

KUFIC (Ar. Kūfī)

Angular style of Arabic script with carefully formed, regular letters, the invention of which is attributed by legend to the town of Kūfa in Iraq. First used in monumental inscriptions under the ʿUmayyads it was then developed in the writing of Korans from the 9th to the 11th centuries. In the Seljuk period it occurs universally in a wide variety of forms, foliated, floriated, plaited and, occasionally, with the shafts of some letters terminating in human torsos. With the appearance in the late 11th century of *naskhī* (q.v.) as a monumental script Kufic goes into a decline. In 13th century Anatolia and 14th to 15th century Egypt it occurs side by side with *naskhī*, though rarely used except for Koranic texts. In Ottoman Turkey it is completely replaced by *thuluth* and, later, by *taʿliq* (q.v.) or *nastaʿlīq* in the decoration of architecture.

KÜLLIYE (Ar. kulliyya)

A complex foundation, consisting normally of a Great Mosque (*jāmiʿ*), one or more *madrasas*, a hospital, khans, covered markets (*bedestens*), a tomb, a guest house (*tabhane*) and a soup kitchen or *imaret*. Although such complex foundations are known from 14th century Egypt and may, indeed, have originated in Seljuk Khurāsān, the type is essentially characteristic of the Ottoman period in Istanbul.

KÜMBED. *See* MAUSOLEUM.

MADRASA (Tk. medrese)

An official institution for the teaching of Muslim theology (the study of the Koran and of *ḥadīth,* Tradition), with a special emphasis upon canon law. The institution, which became a favourite form of pious foundation, normally contained in its endowments stipends for a number of professors and living expenses for their students. Architecturally, it comprised living accommodation for the students and professors, usually arranged in the form of one or two storeys of cells round a courtyard, the axes of which were often emphasised with 2 or 4 *iwans,* which served as classrooms or prayer halls, or, in Ottoman Turkey, students' rooms and special ranges of classrooms. It is probable that the *madrasa* originated in the small private classes given by eminent theologians to small numbers of students, either in their own homes or in the local mosque, though the institution was not canonised until the Seljuk period, when the vizir Niẓām al-Mulk founded State *madrasas* (Niẓāmiyyas) in some of the principal cities of the Seljuk Empire. None of these buildings, with the possible exception of buildings excavated by Godard at Khārgird and Rayy, has survived, but from the late 11th century onwards the *madrasa* was devoted to the teaching of Orthodoxy and remained invariably under strict State supervision. The great Imperial *madrasas* of Ottoman Istanbul were in many ways the equivalent of our modern universities, serving for the education and training of the higher civil service of the Ottoman Empire. Smaller, less comprehensive institutions of this type are known from Seljuk Anatolia and elsewhere, distinguished architecturally chiefly by their smaller proportions, notably the *Dār al-Ḥadīth,* a school for the teaching of Muslim Tradition, and the *Dār al-Ḥuffāẓ* (*ḥāfiẓ,* plu. *ḥuffāẓ,* is the title given to a Muslim who has memorised the Koran). And a good deal of the less advanced teaching continued to be given in mosques.

MAMLUK (Tk. Memlük)

From the Arabic *mamlūk,* owned possessed. The name is given to slaves often of Turkish extraction educated at a number of Islamic courts to form the Sovereign's personal guard and who, after some more or less formal ceremony of manumission, came to form a military aristocracy, occupying high offices at Court and in the administration. The Mamluk Sultans of Egypt and Syria, who supplanted the Ayyubids, originated mainly from Turkish-speaking areas of the Crimea and the Northern Caucasus (the Dasht-i Qipchāq). The institution has analogues in the *ghulāms* of the Anatolian Seljuks and, later, in the *kapıkulları* at the Ottoman Court.

Cf. *Encyclopaedia of Islam,* 2nd Edition: Ghulām.

MAQṢŪRA (Tk. maksure)

The place set apart in the Great Mosque of a town for the Caliph or his representative during Friday prayers, serving partly as a way of protecting him against assassination but also playing an important part in Court ceremonial. Although sometimes composed of a movable wooden screen in Seljuk Iran it seems to have assumed architectural form in a series of splendid domed chambers in mosques of the period, each enclosing the main *miḥrāb* (q.v.) of the mosque and approached by a monumental *iwan* from the courtyard, as in the Great Mosque (q.v.) at Iṣfahān.

MASHHAD (Tk. Meşhed)

Literally, a place of witness, a martyrium, commemorating the burial place of a *shahīd* or martyr, that is, of anyone who has died fighting for the Muslim faith. Such constructions are not connected with any one type of architecture, though their function as shrines or oratories, particularly for Shīʿī Muslims, tends to favour an open interior space with room to circumambulate the cenotaph contained there. The term is now used for other places of witness, for the tombs of the 12 Shīʿī Imams, for example (as at Meshhed in North-Eastern Iran), or where a Prophet is traditionally believed to have appeared.

MASJID (Tk. mescid)

An oratory or place of worship which did not satisfy the requirements of the Koran that the Faithful should assemble there to listen to the Friday sermon, hence usually of a small or local character (though the 9th century Mosque of Ibn Ṭūlūn is described in its foundation inscription merely as a *masjid*). In the later Seljuk period mausolea were often built as oratories and contained a *miḥrāb*, while caravansarais and even palaces, e.g. Lashkari Bazar, were often furnished with *masjids* of a considerable size, which architecturally are indistinguishable from mosques. However, although the congregational mosque (*jāmiʿ*) has often been associated in the Islamic town with the ruler's palace, there are no examples known where it was actually contained within the palace walls.

MAUSOLEUM (Ar. qubba, turba; Tk. kümbed, türbe; Persian gunbadh)

The alternative terms are used more or less interchangeably in modern Arabic and Turkish, though originally *qubba* and *kümbed* were applied to a square domed chamber, *turba* or *türbe* being used for other types of funerary construction, in particular the tomb-towers which are such a characteristic feature of Seljuk Iran and Anatolia. Mausolea were unknown in the early centuries of Islam and, indeed, were discouraged (the earliest known is the 9th century Qubbat al-Ṣulaybiyya at Sāmarrā in Iraq). Very often the precise functions of the early Islamic mausolea have not yet been established and their relationship to traditional non-Islamic Turkish forms of burial remains unclear. In the later Seljuk period and in some Ottoman buildings a tomb or *türbe* was often attached to a larger complex, not just as a memorial to the founder, but as a sort of small oratory.

MEDRESE. *See* MADRASA.

MEŞHED. *See* MASHHAD.

MIḤRĀB

A niche in the *qibla* wall of a mosque indicating the direction of Mecca and the *Kaʿba* where the Imam now stands when leading congregational prayers. Probably derived from the apses of Roman throne-rooms and taken over by the ʿUmayyads when the Caliph was still as much a political as a religious figure, the *miḥrāb* rapidly became an essential feature of Muslim religious architecture and is, traditionally, the most highly decorated area inside a mosque.

MINARET (Ar. ma'dhna, ṣawmaʿ; Tk. minare; Persian manār)

Tower for the giving of the call to prayer (*adhān*) either part of, or close by to, a mosque. The origins of the construction are still dubious, but the Persian word for minaret, *manār* (derived from Ar. *nār*, fire) suggests that, in Iran at least, it may be derived from the pre-Islamic fire-towers, signs of the Sasanian royal cities, and that they may have served the purpose of signalling towers as well as their liturgical role. The double or multiple minarets of Anatolian Seljuk, and Ottoman architecture show that their value as vertical elements in a building scheme often consisting of spreading domes was well appreciated; this profusion does not appear, however, to indicate any difference of function.

MINBAR (Tk. mimber)

The stepped pulpit in a mosque placed next to the *miḥrāb* from which the Friday sermon (*khuṭba*) is preached by the Imam. Originally a throne from which the Caliph as chief of the Muslim community delivered a politico-religious discourse, the *minbar* was in the early centuries of Islam restricted to one mosque in a town, the Congregational or Great Mosque, and the word *minbar* in the Muslim geographers is thus used to describe towns sufficiently important to have the Friday prayers said there (in Seljuk Anatolia there were only seventeen such towns). *Minbars* became more widespread in the later Middle Ages as it soon became clear that one mosque could not be sufficient for all the Faithful to congregate in. They are almost all of wood, panelled and deeply carved, and bear the inscription of the Sultan in whose reign they were made. However, in Ottoman Turkey there are a number of *minbars* in stone, or even incorporating ceramic revetment, and in Seljuk Iran they sometimes take the form of a bare flight of brick steps with a landing placed beside the *miḥrāb* and devoid of all decoration.

MIʿRĀJ

A journey from Mecca to Jerusalem which Muḥammad is believed to have accomplished in the space of one night and during which he was transported to the seventh heaven. The Koranic indications are somewhat ambiguous, and it is to Muslim Tradition (*ḥadith*) that we owe the complete accounts. These seem to have been popular among various Turkish cultures of the 14th and 15th centuries, and two finely illustrated manuscripts from this early period have survived in the form of *Miʿrājnāmes*.

MOSQUE (Ar. jāmiʿ; Tk. Ulu Cami; Pers. Masjid-i Jāmiʿ, Masjid-i Jumʿa)

The English word is derived from the Arabic verb *sajjada,* to prostrate oneself, which gives rise to the word *masjid,* a place for prostrations. Although in recent times the distinction between the mosque and the *masjid* has become less sharp the *jāmiʿ* was originally the place of worship where the Faithful were bound in law to attend Friday prayers, and its sense, assembly, is roughly equivalent to that of the Latin *ecclesia.* The necessity of accommodating enormous numbers of worshippers led to the early development of imposing large-scale architecture in Islam, and an excellent example of this is the Masjid-i Jumʿa at Iṣfahān (present buildings dating mainly from the 12th century). From the 12th century onwards, with the relaxation of the requirements of general assembly on Fridays in one building, we find *madrasas* also serving as mosques—in Seljuk Anatolia, Ayyubid and Mamluk Egypt and in Ottoman Turkey. However, architects still continued to build large Friday mosques.

MUQARNAS

Stalactite vaulting. Angular or spherical squinches arranged in steadily diminishing horizontal registers and used to effect the transition from the angular base of a building to the circle of the dome, as a filling to the canopy over the entrance to a building and, in a non-structural context, as a cornice or as decorative relief to the bareness of a façade. They first appear in the architecture of Iran and Central Asia in the mid-11th century, but it is possible that they were used independently in other parts of Islam about this time.

MUṢALLA (Tk., Pers. namāzgāh)

A large open area, enclosed only by low walls, often outside the walls of a city and furnished only with a *miḥrāb* (often portable) and a *minbar* where it is the custom for the Muslim population to assemble for prayers on the two great feasts of the Muslim calendar. Architecturally, these institutions are of little interest, since their simplicity and vast extent gave no scope to builders. However, in later periods these praying places were sometimes enclosed, as in the Namāzgāh Mosque at Bukhara (12th century with later additions).

NASKHĪ

The elegant, rounded, cursive script of Islam, developed in Iran by the 11th century for the writing of fine, non-Koranic manuscripts and then, at the end of the century, used in architectural decoration in the form of monumental inscriptions (the Mosque at Dandanaqan in the Merv oasis, dated to the 1090s, is perhaps the earliest example known), when it rapidly came to supplant Kufic. A form with specially elongated shafts of the vertical letters (*alifs, kāfs* and *lams*) is known as *thuluth* (Tk. *sülüs*) and was particularly employed in Ottoman epigraphy.

Cf. Stern in *Paintings from Islamic Lands,* Oxford/London, 1969.

QĀḌĪ

Judge in a Muslim court of law. In Ottoman Turkey the *qāḍīs* formed the corps of the higher civil service. Educated in the great Imperial *medreses* of Istanbul they were then appointed governors of provinces of the Ottoman Empire or even ministers of state.

QALAM (plu. AQLĀM)

Pen, also style of writing (cf. the *Aqlām-i Sitta,* or Six Scripts). The flexibility of Muslim writing materials, in reed or in bamboo, played an essential part in the development of Muslim calligraphy in the 10th and 11th centuries which was not without its effect upon calligraphy as used in architecture. Indeed, it is highly probable that the rise of monumental calligraphy associated with the Seljuk period in Iran was inspired by the achievements or experiments of the masters of penmanship.

Cf. D. S. Rice, *The unique Ibn al-Bawwāb Manuscript,* Dublin, 1955.

QAYṢARIYYA (equivalent to Tk. bedesten; Persian bazzāzistān)

Lock-up market contained within the bazar quarter, normally built on a basilical plan and normally designed for commerce in valuable goods, particularly silks. It was widely believed by Arab authors that the institution was invented by some Imperial ruler at Antioch, hence the name, which means Caesarian, but the archaeological evidence does not appear to go back further than the Mamluk period in Egypt and Syria. The functions of the *qayṣariyya* were fulfilled by the *bedesten* of Ottoman Turkey, the name of which suggests that it was a cloth market also (cf. the English word *baize*).

QIBLA

The direction of Mecca, more precisely of the *Kaʿba,* normally indicated in a mosque by the *miḥrāb,* which is placed in the *qibla* wall which is at right angles to the direction. Strictness of orientation has varied from period to period, and it is not uncommon to find serious errors in mediaeval monuments which have survived uncorrected up to the present day. In Seljuk Anatolia *madrasas* were often not oriented; but in Ottoman Turkey it is usual for *madrasas, khānqāhs* and even hospitals, not just mosques, to contain *miḥrābs* precisely oriented.

RIBĀṬ

An institution arising from the obligation recognised in early Islam as incumbent upon Muslims to fight the Holy War (*jihād*). It consists of a fortress with watch-towers containing permanent living quarters and a communal praying place for the inhabitants, normally young men who would spend a certain time there (*ghāzīs*). Bartold has suggested that in Khurāsān such *ribāṭs* were of importance in the development of Muslim towns there, forming nuclei round which the town later grew up. However, none of these fortresses have survived in Iran, nor are any known from the frontiers of Seljuk and Ottoman Turkey with Byzantium, on which a more or less permanent war was waged between 1071 and the middle of the 15th century. The position is somewhat complicated by the fact that in Iran *ribāṭ* is now generally used in the sense of *khān,* or caravansarai (q.v.).

RŪMĪ. *See* under ARABESQUE.

SABĪL (Tk. sebil)

A public fountain. The term is applied to fountains providing drinking water which are not independent constructions, that is, usually in the walls of mosques. These installations appear, apparently for the first time, in the mosque architecture of Seljuk Anatolia and become in the Ottoman period an essential and varied element of town architecture. The type should be distinguished from the *çeşme*, a construction peculiar to the chief towns of Ottoman Turkey, which is a large, independent structure, devoted entirely to the provision of drinking water, not necessarily in proximity to a mosque or any other building, and often of considerable Baroque elegance. It is possible that in more recent terminology, however, the distinction between *çeşme* and sebil has become somewhat eroded.

SALSABĪL (Tk. selsebil)
The Koranic name for one of the rivers of Paradise. The term is applied to the ornamental fountains, weirs and canals which decorated the chief reception rooms of many Islamic palaces, for example, the Artukid palace at Diyarbekir.

SARAY
A palace, especially in the Ottoman period. 'The Saray' normally refers to the Topkapı Saray at Istanbul, which dominates the point overlooking the Sea of Marmara and the Golden Horn and occupies the site of the Great Palace of the Byzantine Emperors. The Sublime Porte of so much European diplomatic history is merely a metonymical description of the Saray, being the Bāb-i ʿAlī (the High Gate) which led to the Palace archives. In the Ottoman provinces 'the Saray' is used for the residences and offices of the Pasha or viceroy.

SEBIL. *See* SABĪL

SELSEBIL. *See* SALSABĪL

SHADIRVAN (Ar. Shādurwān)
The Arabic word, which appears to be derived from a Persian original, means simply 'a weir', though it was used particularly to mean that part of a *salsabīl* across which water flowed in a thin sheet and by its evaporation produced a cooling effect. In Ottoman architecture the term is applied to the pool in the centre of the courtyard of a mosque at which ritual ablutions are performed, doubtless because, at least in early cases, the water was designed to overflow the edges and fall into a trough, thus satisfying the prescription of the Ḥanafī rite, to which the Ottomans mainly belonged, that ablutions should be performed in running water.

SHAHĀDA
The Muslim profession of faith, 'There is no God but God and Muḥammad is his Prophet', utterance of which in the presence of witnesses is sufficient to signify conversion to Islam. The formula is supplemented by Shīʿī Muslims with the phrase, ʿAlī walī Allāh (ʿAlī is the vicar of God).

SHĪʿĪ Muslims (Shiʿites)
Partisans of ʿAlī and his descendants who refused to admit the legitimacy of the ʿUmayyad and ʿAbbāsid Caliphates, replacing their authority by a series of Imams, or spiritual leaders,

usually twelve in number. The Shī'ī gave birth to a number of sects, of which the Ismā'īlīs, now under the authority of the Agha Khan, are perhaps the best known. In matters of religion they are not considered by Sunnī Muslims to be orthodox. The great Turkish dynasties, with the single exception of the Safawids of Iran, have been generally strongly Sunnī, Shī'ism being limited geographically pretty well to Iran and Iraq.

STALACTITE VAULTING. *See* MUQARNAS.

SUNNĪ Muslims (Sunnites)

The major sect of Islam, which believes that the revelation of the Koran must be supplemented by the reported sayings or gestures of Muḥammad, these latter constituting *ḥadīth* or Tradition, which is preserved within the body of the Faithful (*umma*) and is an essential basis for the clarification of Islamic law and theology. Sunnī lawyers are divided into four schools or rites, the Shāfi'ī, Hanbalī, Malakī and Ḥanafī, many *madrasas* of the Middle Ages being adapted to the teaching of two of these schools, or to all four of them. However, although their teaching on points of law may differ, there is a general presumption that on matters of dogma they all agree.

ṬABKHĀNE (Tk. Tabhane)

A guest house, normally attached to the large Imperial *külliyes* (q.v.), or complex foundations at Istanbul or Edirne.

ṬA'LĪQ, NASṬA'LĪQ

Scripts characteristic of Iran developed, chiefly in manuscripts of the early 14th century onwards, where the letters are less well formed than in *naskhī* and *thuluth,* and a greater smoothness, without over-prominent vertical strokes, gives emphasis to the word rather than to the letters which make it up. This lack of clarity militated against its being used in architecture, and it is only in the late Ottoman period that it appears in the form of monumental inscriptions. A particularly bold form of this script, used in later Persian and Ottoman poetry, is known as *shekaste* (literally, Persian, *broken*).

THULUTH (Tk. SÜLÜS). *See* under KUFIC, NASKHĪ and ṬA'LĪQ.
TIMARHANE. *See* under DĀR AL-SHIFĀ'.
TÜRBE. *See* MAUSOLEUM.

12-ANIMAL CALENDAR

A calendar which reckons lunar years in cycles of twelve, each having the name of an animal, borrowed from the Chinese and used by the pre-Islamic Turks in Central Asia. Certain reminiscences of this may appear in the animal sculpture of the Anatolian Seljuks.

ULU CAMI. *See* MOSQUE.

WAQF (Tk. vakıf)

Pious foundations (that is mosques, masjids or mausolea, or works of public utility, such as baths, fountains or hospitals) endowed in perpetuity and governed by a trust. Such foundations cannot be sold, given away or otherwise disposed of, and replace quite adequately the municipal architecture of Western Europe in the Middle Ages and the Renaissance which is otherwise lacking in Islam.

WAQFIYYA (Tk. vakfiye)

Document in which the terms of a *waqf* bequest are stipulated. The rare examples which have survived from the Seljuk and Ottoman periods are of great value, not only as giving the details of the foundation of important buildings and the minute details of their organisation and the trusts which governed them, but also for the information they give on income and expenditure, which are an unequalled source for the social and economic history of the periods.

ZĀWĪYA (Tk. zâviye). *See* KHĀNQĀH.

SOME DYNASTIC TABLES

The chronological information in these few tables is extracted from *The Islamic Dynasties* by Clifford Edmund Bosworth, by permission of the publishers, the Edinburgh University Press. Professor Bosworth is not responsible for the form in which the names are printed here.

The Karakhanids

382-607/992-1211

Transoxania and eastern Turkestan

1. Great Qāghāns of the united kingdom

?	ʿAlī b. Mūsā
388/998	Aḥmad I Arslan Qarā Khan or Toghan Khan
406/1015	Manṣūr Arslan Khan
415/1024	Aḥmad II Toghan Khan
417–24/1026–32	Yūsuf I Qadır Khan

2. Great Qāghāns of the western kingdom (Transoxania, including Bukhara and Samarkand and western Ferghana)

433/1041	Muḥammad ʿAyn-al-Dawla
444/1052	Ibrāhīm I Böritekin Tamghach Khān
460/1068	Naṣr
472/1080	Khiḍr
?473/?1081	Aḥmad I
482/1089	Yaʿqūb
488/1095	Masʿūd I
490/1097	Sulaymān
490/1097	Maḥmūd I
492/1099	Jibrā'īl
495/1102	Muḥammad II
?523/?1129	Naṣr
?523/?1129	Aḥmad II
524/1130	Ḥasan
?526/?1132	Ibrāhīm II
526/1132	Maḥmūd II (later, ruler of Khurasan after the Seljuk Sanjar)
536/1141	Ibrāhīm III

551/1156 ʿAlī
556/1161 Masʿūd II
574/1178 Ibrāhīm IV (before 574/1178 in Ferghana only, thereafter in Samarqand also)
600–7/1204–11 Osman (ʿUthmān)
Occupation of Transoxania by the Khwārizmshāhs

3. Great Qāghāns of the eastern kingdom (Talas, Isfījāb, Shāsh, Semirechye, Kāshghar and usually eastern Ferghana)

423/1032 Sulaymān
448/1056 Muḥammad I
449/1057 Ibrāhīm I
451/1059 Maḥmūd
467/1074 ʿUmar
467/1075 Ḥasan or Hārūn
496/1103 Aḥmad or Hārūn
522/1128 Ibrāhīm II
553/1158 Muḥammad II
? Yūsuf II
607/1211 Muḥammad III
Occupation by Küchlüg

The Ghaznevids
366–582/977–1186
Khurasan, Afghanistan and northern India

366/977 Nāṣir-al-Dawla Sebük Tekin (governor on behalf of the Sāmānids)
387/997 Ismāʿīl
388/998 Yamīn-al-Dawla Maḥmūd
421/1030 Jalāl-al-Dawla Muḥammad, *first reign*
421/1031 Shihāb-al-Dawla Maʿsūd I
432/1041 Muḥammad, *second reign*
432/1041 Shihāb-al-Dawla Mawdūd
441/1050 Masʿūd II
441/1050 Bahā'-al-Dawla ʿAlī
441/1050 ʿIzz-al-Dawla ʿAbd-al-Rashīd
444/1053 Qiwām-al-Dawla Toghrıl, usurper
444/1053 Jamāl-al-Dawla Farrukhzād
451/1059 Ẓahīr-al-Dawla Ibrāhīm
492/1099 ʿAlā'-al-Dawla Masʿūd III
508/1115 Kamāl-al-Dawla Shīrzād
509/1115 Sulṭān-al-Dawla Arslan Shāh

512/1118 Yamīn-al-Dawla Bahrām Shāh
547/1152 Muʿizz-al-Dawla Khusraw Shāh
555–82/1160–86 Tāj-al-Dawla Khusraw Malik
Ghūrid conquest

The Seljuks
429–590/1038–1194

1. Great Seljuks (Iraq and Persia) 429–590/1038–1194

429/1038 Rukn-al-Dunyā-wa'l-Dīn Toghrıl I (Tughrul)
455/1063 ʿAḍud-al-Dawla Alp Arslan
465/1072 Jalāl-al-Dawla Malik-shāh
485/1092 Nāṣir-al-Dīn Maḥmūd I
487/1094 Rukn-al-Dīn Berk-yaruq (Barkiyāruq)
498/1105 Muʿizz-al-Dīn Malik-Shāh II
498/1105 Ghiyāth-al-Dīn Muḥammad I
511–52/1118–57 Muʿizz-al-Dīn Sanjar (ruler in eastern Persia 490–552/1097–1157; after 511/1118 supreme Sultan of the Seljuk family)

In Iraq and western Persia only:

511/1118 Mughīth-al-Dīn Maḥmūd II
525/1131 Ghiyāth-al-Dīn Dā'ūd
526/1132 Rukn-al-Dīn Toghrıl II
529/1134 Ghiyāth-al-Dīn Masʿūd
547/1152 Muʿīn-al-Dīn Malikshāh III
548/1153 Rukn-al-Dīn Muḥammad II
555/1160 Ghiyāth-al-Dīn Sulaymān Shāh
556/1161 Muʿizz-al-Dīn Arslan
571–90/1176–94 Rukn-al-Dīn Toghrıl III
Khwārizmshāhs

2. Seljuks of Syria 471–511/1078–1117

471/1078 Tāj-al-Dawla Tutush
488–507/1095–1113 Riḍwān (in Aleppo)
488–497/1095–1104 Duqāq (in Damascus), succeeded by his Atabeg Tughtekin
507/1113 Alp-Arslan al-Akhras } in Aleppo
508–11/1114–17 Sulṭān Shāh } in Aleppo
Line of Tughtekin, the Börids or Būrids, in Damascus; the Artukid Il Ghāzī in Aleppo

3. Seljuks of Kirman 433–582/1041–1186

433/1041 ʿImād-al-Dīn Qāwurd
465/1073 Kirmān Shāh

467/1074 Ḥusayn
467/1074 Rukn-al-Dawla Sulṭān Shāh
477/1085 Muḥyī-al-Dīn Tūrān Shāh I
490/1097 Bahā'-al-Dīn Irān Shāh
495/1101 Muḥyī-al-Dīn Arslan Shāh I
537/1142 Mughīth-al-Dīn Muḥammad I
551/1156 Muḥyī-al-Dīn Shāh Toghrıl
565/1170 Bahrām Shāh
570/1175 Arslan Shāh II
572/1176 Tūrān Shāh II
579–82/1183–6 Muḥammad II
Ghuzz occupation

The Khwārizmshāhs

1. Line of Anūshtekin c. 470–628/c. 1077–1231, originally as governors for the Seljuks, latterly as independent rulers in Central Asia and Persia

c. 470/c. 1077 Anūshtekin Gharcha'ī
490/1097 Turkish governor Ekinchi b. Qochqar
490/1097 Quṭb-al-Dīn Muḥammad
521/1127 ʿAlā-al-Dīn Atsız
551/1156 Il-Arslan
567/1172 ʿAlā-al-Dīn Tekesh
567–89/1172–93 Sultān Shāh b. Il-Arslan, rival ruler in northern Khurasan
596/1200 ʿAlā-al-Dīn Muḥammad
617–28/1220–31 Jalāl-al-Dīn Mingburnu (? The exact form of this Turkish name, especially the second component, is uncertain)
Mongol conquest

The Zengids

521–619/1127–1222

al-Jazīra (that is, Mesopotamia) and Syria

1. Principal line in Mosul and Aleppo

521/1127 ʿImād-al-Dīn Zengī b. Aq Sunqur
541/1146 Sayf-al-Dīn Ghāzī I
544/1149 Quṭb-al-Dīn Mawdūd
564/1169 Sayf-al-Dīn Ghāzī II
572/1176 ʿIzz-al-Dīn Masʿūd I
589/1193 Nūr-al-Dīn Arslan Shāh I
607/1211 ʿIzz-al-Dīn Masʿūd II
615/1218 Nūr-al-Dīn Arslan Shāh II
616–19/1219–22 Nāṣir-al-Dīn Maḥmūd
Power seized by the Vizir Badr-al-Dīn Lu'lu'

2. Line in Damascus and then Aleppo

541/1146	Nūr-al-Dīn Maḥmūd b. Zengī
569–77/1174–81	Nūr-al-Dīn Ismāʿīl
	United again with Mosul, then conquered by Saladin

The Artukids

495–811/1102–1408

Diyarbekir

1. Ḥiṣn Kayfā and Āmid (Diyarbekir) branch 491–629/1098–1232

491/1098	Muʿīn-al-Dīn Sökmen I
498/1105	Ibrāhīm
c. 502/c. 1109	Rukn-al-Dawla Dā'ūd
539/1144	Fakhr-al-Dīn Qarā Arslan
562/1167	Nūr-al-Dīn Muḥammad
581/1185	Quṭb-al-Dīn Sökmen (Sukman) II
597/1201	Nāṣir-al-Dīn Maḥmūd
619/1222	Rukn-al-Dīn Mawdūd
629/1232	al-Malik al-Masʿūd
	Ayyūbid conquest

2. Mardin and Mayyafāriqīn branch 497–811/1104–1408

497/1104	Najm-al-Dīn Il Ghāzī I
516/1122	Ḥusām-al-Dīn Temür Tash
547/1152	Najm-al-Dīn Alpī
572/1176	Quṭb-al-Dīn Il Ghāzī II
580/1184	Ḥusām-al-Dīn Yülük Arslan (Yawlāq)
c. 597/c. 1201	Nāṣir-al-Dīn Artuk Arslan
637/1239	Najm-al-Dīn Ghāzī I
658/1260	Qarā Arslan al-Muẓaffar
691/1292	Shams-al-Dīn Dā'ūd
693/1294	Najm-al-Dīn Ghāzī II
712/1312	ʿImad-al-Dīn ʿAlī Alpī
712/1312	Shams-al-Dīn Ṣāliḥ
765/1364	Aḥmad al-Manṣūr
769/1368	Maḥmūd aṣ-Ṣāliḥ
769/1368	Dā'ūd al-Muẓaffar
778/1376	Majd-al-Dīn ʿIsā al-Ẓāhir
809–11/1406–8	al-Ṣāliḥ
	Karakoyunlu conquest

SOME DYNASTIC TABLES

The Danishmendids

c. 464–573/c. 1071–1177

Central and eastern Anatolia

1. Sivas branch c. 464–570/c. 1071–1174

c. 464/c. 1071	Melik Danishmend Ghāzī
477/1084	Amir Ghāzī Gümüshtekin
529/1134	Melik Muḥammad
536/1142	Melik ʿImād-al-Dīn Dhu'l-Nūn, *first reign* (in Kayseri)
537/1142	Melik Niẓām-al-Dīn Yaghıbasan
560/1164	Melik Mujāhid Jamāl-al-Dīn Ghāzī
562/1166	Melik Shams-al-Dīn Ibrāhīm
562/1166	Melik Shams-al-Dīn Ismāʿīl
564–70/1168–74	Melik Dhu'l-Nūn, *second reign* (now with the honorific title Nāṣir al-Dīn)
	Seljuks of Rūm

2. Malatya branch c. 537–573/c. 1142–78

c. 537/c. 1142	ʿAyn-al-Dīn b. Gümüshtekin
547/1152	Dhū'l-Qarnayn
557/1162	Nāṣir-al-Dīn Muḥammad, *first reign*
565/1170	Fakhr-al-Dīn Qāsim
567/1172	Afrīdūn
570–3/1175–8	Nāṣir-al-Dīn Muḥammad, *second reign*
	Seljuks of Rūm

The Seljuks of Rūm

470–707/1077–1307

Anatolia

470/1077	Sulaymān b. Qutalmısh
479/1086	*interregnum*
485/1092	Qılıch Arslan I
500/1107	Malikshāh
510/1116	Rukn-al-Dīn Masʿūd I
551/1156	ʿIzz-al-Dīn Qılıch Arslan II (division of territories amongst his sons during the latter part of his reign)
588/1192	Ghiyāth-al-Dīn Kaykhusraw I, *first reign*
592/1196	Rukn-al-Dīn Sulayman II
600/1204	ʿIzz-al-Dīn Qılıch Arslan III
601/1204	Ghiyāth-al-Dīn Kaykhusraw I, *second reign*
607/1210	ʿIzz-al-Dīn Kaykā'ūs I

616/1219	ʿAlā-al-Dīn Kayqubād I
634/1237	Ghiyāth-al-Dīn Kaykhusraw II
644/1246	ʿIzz-al-Dīn Kaykā'ūs II
646/1248	Kaykā'ūs II and his brother Rukn-al-Dīn Qılıch Arslan IV jointly
647/1249	Kaykā'ūs II, Qılıch Arslan IV and ʿAlā-al-Dīn Kayqubād II jointly
655/1257	Qılıch Arslan IV
663/1265	Ghiyāth-al-Dīn Kaykhusraw III
681/1282	Ghiyāth-al-Dīn Masʿūd II, *first reign*
683/1284	ʿAlā-al-Dīn Kayqubād III, *first reign*
683/1284	Masʿūd II, *second reign*
692/1293	Kayqubād III, *second reign*
693/1294	Masʿūd II, *third reign*
700/1301	Kayqubād III, *third reign*
702/1303	Masʿūd II, *fourth reign*
704/1305	Kayqubād III, *fourth reign*
707/1307	Ghiyāth-al-Dīn Masʿūd III
	Mongol occupation

The Karakoyunlu

782-873/1380-1468

Azerbaidzhan and Iraq

782/1380	Qarā Muḥammad Ṭurmush
791/1389	Qarā Yūsuf
802/1400	*Tīmūrid invasion*
809/1406	Qarā Yūsuf (reinstated)
823/1420	Iskandar
841/1438	Jihānshāh
872–3/1467–8	Ḥasan ʿAlī
	Akkoyunlu conquest

The Akkoyunlu

780-914/1378-1508

Diyarbekir, eastern Anatolia, Azerbaidzhan

780/1378	Qarā Yawlāq (Yülük) Arslan
839/1435	Ḥamza, in dispute with his brother ʿAlī till 842/1438
848/1444	Jihāngīr
857/1453	Uzun Ḥasan
882/1478	Khalīl
883/1478	Yaʿqūb

896/1490 Baysonqur
898/1493 Rüstem (Rustam)
902/1497 Aḥmad Gövde
903/1497 Murād (in Qum)
903/1498 Alwand (in Azerbaidzhan, later in Diyarbekir till his death in 910/1504)
903/1498 Muḥammad Mīrzā (in Jibāl and Fārs till 905/1500)
907–14/1502–8 Murād (latterly sole ruler)
Safavid conquest

The Karamanids
c. 654–888/c. 1256–1483
Central Anatolia

c. 654/c. 1256 Karaman b. Nūra Ṣūfī
660/1261 Muḥammad I
677/1278 Badr-al-Dīn Maḥmūd
? Burhān-al-Dīn Mūsā
? Fakhr-al-Dīn Aḥmad
750/1349 Shams-al-Dīn
753/1352 ʿAlā-al-Dīn Khalīl
783/1381 ʿAlā-al-Dīn b. Khalīl
792–805/1390–1403 Ottoman occupation
805/1403 Muḥammad II
822–4/1419–21 Mamlūk occupation
824/1421 Muḥammad II (reinstated)
827/1424 ʿAlā-al-Dīn ʿAlī
827/1424 Tāj-al-Dīn Ibrahim
868/1463 Isḥāq
869/1464 Pīr Aḥmad
874/1479 Pīr Aḥmad and Qāsim jointly
879–88/1474–83 Qāsim
Ottoman conquest

The Ottomans or Osmanlıs
680–1342/1281–1924
Anatolia, the Balkans, the Arab lands

680/1281 Osman I b. Ertughrul
c. 724/c. 1324 Orhan
761/1360 Murad I
791/1389 Bayazid (Bayezit) I Yıldırım ('the Lightning-flash')

804/1402	*Timurid invasion*
805/1403	Mehmed (Mehmet) I Chelebi (at first in Anatolia only, after 816/1413 in Rumelia also)
806/1403	Süleyman I (in Rumelia only till 813/1410)
824/1421	Murad II, *first reign*
848/1444	Mehmed II Fatih ('the Conqueror'), *first reign*
850/1446	Murad II, *second reign*
855/1451	Mehmed II, *second reign*
886/1481	Bayazid II
918/1512	Selim I Yavuz ('the Grim')
926/1520	Süleyman II Kānūnī ('the Law-giver', also called in western usage 'the Magnificent')
974/1566	Selim II
982/1574	Murad III
1003/1595	Mehmed III
1012/1603	Ahmed I
1026/1617	Mustafa I, *first reign*
1027/1618	Osman II
1031/1622	Mustafa I, *second reign*
1032/1623	Murad IV
1049/1640	Ibrahim
1058/1648	Mehmed IV
1099/1687	Süleyman III
1102/1691	Ahmed II
1106/1695	Mustafa II
1115/1703	Ahmed III
1143/1730	Mahmud I
1168/1754	Osman III
1171/1757	Mustafa III
1187/1774	Abdülhamid I
1203/1789	Selim III
1222/1807	Mustafa IV
1223/1808	Mahmud II
1255/1839	Abdülmejid I
1277/1861	Abdülaziz
1293/1876	Murad V
1293/1876	Abdülhamid II
1327/1909	Mehmed V Reshad
1336/1918	Mehmed VI Vahidüddin
1341–2/1922–4	Abdülmejid II (as Caliph only)
	Republican régime of Mustafa Kemāl

BIBLIOGRAPHY

I. GENERAL

A. *General History of Turkish Art*

Aga-Oglu, Mehmet: 'About one of the "Two Questions in Moslem Art"', *Ars Islamica*, III, 1936, pp. 116–23.

Arseven, Celâl Esad: *L'Art turc depuis son origine jusqu'à nos jours.* Istanbul, 1939.

Arseven, Celâl Esad: *Türk sanatı tarihi.* (History of Turkish Art.) Vols. I, II, III. Istanbul, 1954–9.

Aslanapa, Oktay: 'Ortaçağın en eski yatılı ilim ve kültür Müesseseleri' (The Oldest Residential Scientific and Cultural Foundations of the Middle Ages), *Türk Kültürü* 12, Ankara, 1963.

Creswell, K. A. C.: *Early Muslim Architecture. I. 'Umayyads.* Oxford, 1932.

Creswell, K. A. C.: *Early Muslim Architecture. II. Early 'Abbāsids.* Oxford, 1940.

Creswell, K. A. C.: 'Fortification in Islam Before A.D. 1250', *Proceedings of the British Academy* Vol. 38, 1952.

Creswell, K. A. C.: *A Bibliography of the Architecture, Arts and Crafts of Islam.* Cairo and Oxford, 1961.

Diez, Ernst: *Die Kunst der islamischen Völker.* Berlin, 1915; 2nd ed. Potsdam, 1928.

Diez, Ernst: *Türk Sanatı.* Istanbul, 1946.

Diez, Ernst and Aslanapa, Oktay: *Türk Sanatı.* (Turkish Art.) Istanbul, 1955.

Diez, Ernst: *Islamische Kunst.* Berlin, 1964.

Dimand, Maurice, S.: 'Turkish Art of the Muhammadan Period', *Bull. Metropolitan Museum of Art* New Series II, 1944, pp. 211–17.

Erdmann, Kurt. 'Türkische und islamische Kunst', *Atlantis* XXV, 1953, pp. 187–8.

Erdmann, Kurt: *Der Aufstieg des Islam.* Darmstadt, 1961. (Weltkunstgeschichte.)

Gabriel, Albert: 'Note sur un voyage en Haute-Mésopotamie par MM. A. Gabriel et Sauvaget', *Syria* XIII, 1932, pp. 315–16.

Glück, Heinrich: 'Türkische Kunst', *Mitt. d. ungarischen Wissen. Ins. in Konstantinopel* Vol. 1, Budapest–Konstantinopel, 1917.

Glück, Heinrich: 'Türk Sanatı', (Turkish Art), *Yeni Mecmua* Nos. 59–60, 1918.

Glück, Heinrich: 'Die Weltstellung der Türken in der Kunst', *Wiener Beiträge zur Kunst und Kultur Asiens*. Vienna, 1920.

Glück, Heinrich: 'Türk Sanatının dünyadaki mevkii', (The Position of Turkish Art in World (Art)), *Türkiyat Mecmuası* III, 1935.

Glück, Heinrich and Diez, Ernst: *Die Kunst des Islam*. Berlin, 1925. (*Propyläen Kunstgeschichte* V.)

Godard, A.: *L'Art de l'Iran*. Paris, 1962.

Goetz, Hermann: *India. 5000 years of Indian Art*. Baden Baden, 1950, 1960, 1964.

Grabar, Oleg: 'The Earliest Islamic Commemorative Structures', *Ars Orientalis* VI, 1966, pp. 1–46.

Grabar, O. and Hill, D.: *Islamic Architecture and its Decoration A.D. 800–1500*. London, 1964; 2nd ed. 1967.

Herzfeld, E.: *Die Ausgrabungen von Samarra*. I. Berlin, 1923. III. Berlin, 1927.

Hoag, J. D.: *Western Islamic Architecture*. New York, 1963.

Kühnel, E.: 'Die Islamische Kunst', in A. Springer, *Handbuch IV, Die Aussereuropäische Kunst*. Leipzig, 1929.

Kühnel, E.: *Die Kunst des Islam*. 2nd ed. Stuttgart, 1962.

Kühnel, E.: 'Türkische und islamische Kunst', *Halil Edhem hatıra kitabı*. Ankara, 1947, pp. 201–9.

Kühnel, E.: *Die Moschee*. Berlin, 1949.

Kühnel, E.: *Islamic Art and Architecture*. (Trans. Katherine Watson.) London, 1966.

Marçais, G.: *L'Art de l'Islam*. Paris, 1947.

Mayer, L. A.: *Islamic Architects and Their Works*. Genève, 1956.

Migeon, Gaston: *Les Arts Musulmans*. Paris and Bruxelles, 1926.

Migeon, Gaston: *Manuel d'Art Musulman*. 2nd ed. Paris, 1927.

Mongait, A.: *Archaeology in the U.S.S.R.* Moscow, 1959. (Pelican Books, London, 1961.)

Ögel, Bahaeddin: *Islâmiyetten önce Türk kültür tarihi*. (Cultural History of the Pre-Islamic Turks.) Ankara, 1962.

Otto-Dorn, K.: *Die Kunst des Islam*. Baden-Baden, 1964.

Pearson, J. D.: *Index Islamicus. 1906–1955*. Cambridge, 1958.

Pearson, J. D.: *Index Islamicus. Supplement. 1956–1960*. Cambridge, 1962.

Pope, A. U. and Ackerman, P.: *A Survey of Persian Art*. Oxford, 1938–9.

Rice, D. S.: 'Medieval Harran: Studies on its Topography and Monuments', *Anatolian Studies* II, 1952, pp. 36–84.

Rice, Tamara Talbot: *The Seljuks*. London, 1961.

Rumpler, M.: *La Coupole dans l'architecture byzantine et musulmane*. Strasbourg, 1956.

Saladin, H.: *Manuel d'Art Musulman. I. L'Architecture*. Paris, 1907.

Schacht, J.: 'Ein archaischer Minaret-Typ in Ägypten und Anatolien', *Ars Islamica* V, 1938, pp. 46–54.

Smith, E. B.: *The Dome*. Princeton, 1951.

Sourdel, D. et J.: *La Civilisation de l'Islam Classique*. Paris, 1968.

Söylemezoğlu, H. N. K.: *Islam Dini, Ilk camiler ve Osmanlı camileri.* (The Earliest Mosques in Islam and Ottoman Mosques.) Istanbul, 1955.

Wilson, Arnold: *A Bibliography of Persia.* Oxford, 1930.

Yetkin, Suut Kemal: *Islâm Sanatı.* (Islamic Art.) Ankara, 1954.

Yetkin, Suut Kemal: *Islâm Mimarisi.* (Islamic Architecture.) Ankara, 1965.

B. *Problems of Turkish Art*

Aslanapa, Oktay: 'Türk sanatının bütünlüğü ve devamlılığı', (The Integrity and Progressiveness of Turkish Art), *Konferanslar I*, 1964. Ankara, 1965, pp. 58–87. (*Türk Kültürünü Araştırma Enstitütüsü yayınları*: 13, Series I, Vol.: a 1.)

Atabinen, R. S.: *Les caractéristiques de l'Architecture Turque.* Paris, 1938.

Ayverdi, Ekrem Hakkı: 'Türk ve Bizans mimari unsurları', (The Principles of Turkish and Byzantine Architecture), *Istanbul Enstitütüsü Dergisi* II, 1956, pp. 25–36.

Batur, S : 'Osmanlı camilerinde sekizgen ayak sisteminin gelişmesi üzerine', (On the Origins of the Octagonal Ground Plan in Ottoman Architecture), *Anadolu Sanatı Araştırmaları* I. Istanbul, 1968, pp. 139–64.

Çetintaş, Sedat: *Yeşil cami ve benzerleri cami değildir.* (The Uniqueness of the Green Mosque Type.) Istanbul, 1958.

Eyice, Semavi: 'Ilk Osmanlı devrinin dini-içtimai bir müessesesi: Zaviyeler ve Zaviyeli camiler', (A Socio-theological Institution from the Early Ottoman Period: the Zāwīya and the Mosque-Zāwīya), *Iktisat Fakültesi Mecmuası* Vol. XXIII, 1962–3, pp. 1–80.

Gabriel, Albert: 'Türk sanatı ve tarih-i sanattaki mevkii' (Trans.: A. Vahid), (Turkish Art and Its Place in the History of Art), *Hayat* Vol. 40, 1927.

Gabriel, Albert: 'Bursada Murat I Camii ve Osmanlı Mimarisinin Menşei Meselesi', (The Mosque of Murad I, and the Problem of the Source of Ottoman Architecture), *Vakıflar Dergisi* II, 1942, pp. 37–43.

Gabriel, Albert: 'Mimarlık bakımından Türkler Istanbul'a neler getirdi?', (What Did the Turks Bring to Istanbul from the Architectural Point of View?), *Resimli Hayat ilavesi*, 1953.

Gebhard, David: 'The Problem of Space in the Ottoman Mosque', *The Art Bulletin* XIV, 1963, pp. 271–5.

Glück, Heinrich: 'Türk sanatının dünyadaki mevkii', (The Place of Turkish Art in World Art), *Türkiyat Mecmuası* Vol. III, 1935, pp. 119–28.

Godard, A : 'Origine de la Madrasa, de la Mosquée et du Caravansérail à quatre iwans', *Ars Islamica* Vols. XV–XVI, 1951, pp. 1–9.

Grabar, Oleg: 'The Islamic Dome, Some Considerations', *Journal of the Society of Architectural Historians* Vol. XXII, No. 45, pp. 191–8.

Kuban, Doğan: *Osmanlı dini mimarisinde iç mekân teşekkülü.* (The Formation of Interior Space in Ottoman Religious Architecture.) (Rönesansla bir mukayese.) Istanbul, 1958.

Kuban, Doğan: *Anadolu-Türk mimarisinin kaynak ve sorunları.* (The Origins and Development of Anatolian–Turkish Architecture.) Istanbul, 1965.

Martiny, G.: 'Zur Entwicklungsgeschichte der Osmanischen Moschee', *Ars Orientalis* IV, 1961, pp. 107–12.

Riefstahl, Rudolf M.: 'Persian Influence in Seljuk Art', *Parnassus* III, No. 5, 1931, p. 24.

Schneider, A. M.: 'Sophienkirche und Sultansmoschee', *Byzantinische Zeitschrift* Vol. 44, 1951, pp. 509–16.

Strzygowski, J.: *Altai-Iran und Völkerwanderung*. Leipzig, 1917.

Strzygowski, J.: Türkler ve Ortaasya sanatı meselesi, (The Turks and the Problem of Central Asian Art), *Türkiyat mecmuası* II–III, Istanbul, 1930–5, pp. 1–80.

Ülgen, Ali Saim: 'Le caractère philosophique et esthétique de l'architecture turque', *First International Congress of Turkish Arts: Communications Presented to the Congress*, Ankara, 1961, pp. 343–9.

C. *Technical and Decorative Details*

Aslanapa, Oktay: 'Mukarnas', (Stalactite Vaulting), *Islâm Ansiklopedisi* Vol. VIII, pp. 566–7.

Berry, B. Y.: 'The Development of the Bracket Support in Turkish Domestic Architecture in Istanbul', *Ars Islamica* Vol. V, 1938, pp. 272–82.

Binan, Muhittin: *Türk saçak ve kornişleri; Ilk çağlar, Selçuk ve Osmanlı devirleri.* (Turkish Eaves and Cornices: The Earliest Periods, the Seljuk and Ottoman Periods.) Istanbul, 1952.

Deri, M.: 'Das Seldschukische Ornament', in *Denkmäler Persischer Baukunst von Konia.* Berlin, 1901–10.

Diez, E.: 'Mukarnas', (Stalactite Vaulting), *Islâm Ansiklopedisi* Vol. VIII, pp. 564–6.

Pauty, E.: 'Contribution à l'Etude des Stalactites', *Bulletin de l'Institut Français d'Archéologie Orientale du Caire* Vol. XXIX, 1929, pp. 129–53.

Rosintal, J.: *Pendentifs, Trompes et Stalactites dans l'architecture orientale.* Paris, 1928.

Rosintal, J.: *L'origine des stalactites de l'architecture orientale.* Paris, 1938.

D. *Sources*

1. General

Aktepe, Münir: 'Abide ve sanat eserlerimize ait Türk tarihlerinde mevcut bilgiler', (Literary Sources in Turkish for the History of Turkish Art and Architecture), *Ist. Üniv. Ed. Fak. Sanat Tarihi Yıllığı* II, 1966–8, pp. 169–83.

Aslanapa, Oktay: 'Archivalien zur Geschichte der osmanischen Baukunst im 16. und 17. Jahrhundert im Topkapı Serail-Archiv zu Istanbul', *Anatolia* III, 1958, pp. 18–20.

Babinger, F.: 'Quellen zur osmanischen Künstlergeschichte', *Jbb. Asiat. Kunst* I, 1924, pp. 31–41.

Barkan, Ömer Lutfi: 'Osmanlı Imparatorluğunda bir iskân ve kolonizasyon metodu olarak vakıflar ve temlikler', (The Use of Deeds of Endowment or Title as a Method of Settlement or Colonisation in the Ottoman Empire), *Vakıflar Dergisi* II, 1942, pp. 279–386.

Berki, Ali Himmet: *Vakıflar.* (Waqfs.) Istanbul, 1946.

Berki, Ali Himmet: *Vakıflar 2.* Ankara, 1950.

Ekrem, Cemal: *Vakıflar.* (Waqfs.) Istanbul, 1935.
Erdmann, Kurt: *Ibn Bibi als Kunsthistorische Quelle.* Istanbul, 1962. (Nederlands Historisch-Archeologisches Institut.)
Erdoğan, Muzaffer: 'Osmanlı mimarisi tarihinin otantik yazma kaynakları, (Authentic Sources for the History of Ottoman Architecture), *Vakıflar Dergisi* VI, 1965, pp. 111–36.
Ergin, Osman: *Bizde Vakıflar.* (Waqfs in Turkey.) Istanbul, 1936.
Evliya Çelebi Seyahatnamesi. (The Travels of Evliya Çelebi.) Istanbul, 1314 (1908)—1938, 10 vols.
Evliya Çelebi Seyahatnamesi. (The Travels of Evliya Çelebi.) (Edited by Reşad Ekrem Koçu.) Istanbul, 1949. (Türk Tarihi Serisi: 4.)
Hommaire De Hell, Xavier: *Voyage en Turquie et en Perse pendant les années 1840, 1847, 1848, 1844–60.* 4 vols. and atlas. Paris, 1853–60.
Jerphanion, Guillaume de: *Mélanges d'archéologie anatolienne.* Beirut, 1928. (*Mélanges de l'Université Saint-Joseph, Beyrouth,* Tome XIII.)
Köprülü, M.Fuad: 'Vakıf müessesesinin hukukî mahiyeti ve tarihî tekâmülü,' (The Legal Character of Pious Foundations and Their Historical Development), *Vakıflar Dergisi* II, 1942, pp. 1–36.
Kunter, Halim Baki: 'Türk vakıfları ve vakfiyeleri üzerine mücmel bir etüd', (A Concise Study of Turkish Waqfs and Waqfiyyas), *Vakıflar Dergisi* I, 1938, pp. 103–29.
Kunter, Halim Baki: *Türk vakıflar ve vakfiyeleri.* (Turkish Waqfs and Waqfiyyas.) Istanbul, 1939.
Marco Polo: *Le livre de Marco Polo citoyen de Venise.* Paris, 1886.
Oral, M.Ziya: 'Aksaray'ın tarihi önemi ve vakıfları', (The Historical Importance of Aksaray and the Pious Foundations There), *Vakıflar Dergisi* V, 1962, pp. 223–40.
Orgun, Zarif: *Sinan'a ait yeni bir vesika.* (A New Source Concerning Sinan.) Istanbul, 1941. (Arkitekt Neşriyatı: 6.)
Öz, Tahsin: *Risâle-i mimariye hülasâsı.* (A Short Architectural Treatise.) Istanbul, 1946.
Piri Reis: *Kitab-ı Bahriye.* (The Book of the Navy.) Istanbul, 1936. (Türk Tarihi Araştırma Kurumu, Series I, No. 2.)
Rubruquis: *Travels in Tatary and China in 1253.* The Hague, 1735. (ed. De Bergeron.)
Taeschner, Franz: *Das Anatolische Wegenetz nach Osmanischen Quellen.* 2 vols. Leipzig, 1924–6.
Tarih-i Cami-i Şerifi Nur-u Osmaniye. (History of the Nur-u Osmaniye Mosque.) Istanbul, A. H. 1335–7. (Tarih-i Osmani mecmuası neşriyatından.)
Turan, Osman: II. *Izzeddin Keykâvus'a ait bir Temliknâme.* (A Title Deed of 'Izz al-Dīn Kaykā'ūs II.) Istanbul, 1955. (Zeki Velidi Togan Armağanı.)
Uluçay, M.Ç.: *Saruhanoğulları ve eserlerine dair vesikalar.* (Sources for the Saruhanids and Their Monuments.) Istanbul, 1940.

2. Waqfiyyas (Deeds of endowment of charitable foundations)

Ayverdi, E. H.: 'Mudurnu'da Yıldırım Bayezid manzumesi ve Taş vakfiyesi', (Yıldırım Bayazid's Foundation at Mudurnu and the Taş Waqfiyya), *Vakıflar Dergisi* V, pp. 79–86.

Cevdet, M.: *Sivas Darüşşifası vakfiyesi ve tercemesi.* (The Waqfiyya of the Hospital at Sivas and a Commentary upon it.) Istanbul, 1938.

Ergin, Osman: *Fatih imareti vakfiyesi.* (The Waqfiyya of the Imaret of Mehmed the Conqueror.) Istanbul, 1945. (Istanbul Belediyesi Istanbul Fethinin 500. yıl dönümü Kutlama Yayınları I.)

Fatih Mehmet II Vakfiyeleri. (Waqfiyyas of Mehmed the Conqueror.) Istanbul, 1938. (Vakıflar Umum Müdürlüğü neşriyatı I.)

Turan, Osman: 'Selçuklu Devri Vakfiyeleri I, II, III', (Waqfiyyas of the Seljuk period), *Belleten* XI, 1947, pp. 197–235, pp. 415–429; XII, 1948, pp. 17–158.

Turan, Osman: 'Celâleddin Karatay vakıfları ve vakfiyeleri', (The Waqfs and Waqfiyyas of Jalāl al-Dīn Karatay), *Belleten* Vol. XII, 1948.

Uzunçarşılı, I.Hakkı: *Karamanoğlu Ibrahim Bey vakfiyesi.* (A Waqfiyya of Ibrahim Bek, the Karamanid.), Istanbul, 1937.

Uzunçarşılı, I.Hakkı: *Gazi Orhan Bey vakfiyesi.* (A Waqfiyya of Ghāzī Orhan Bek.) Istanbul, 1941.

3. Epigraphy

Ahmed Tevhid: 'Antalya Surları kitabeleri', (Inscriptions from the Walls of Antalya), *Türk Tarih Encümeni Mecmuası* Vol. 86, pp. 171 et seq.

Berchem, Max van: 'Epigraphie des Danishmendides', *Zeitschrift für Assyriologie* XXVII, 1912, pp. 85–91.

Berchem, Max van: 'Arabische Inschriften', in Sarre and Martin, *Die Ausstellung von Meisterwerken muhammedanischer Kunst I.* Munich, 1912.

Berchem, M. van and Halil Edhem: *Asie Mineure, Sivas-Divriği.* (Corpus Inscriptionum Arabicarum, III.) Cairo, 1910.

Beygü, A. Ş.: *Ahlat kitabeleri.* (Inscriptions of Ahlat.) Istanbul, 1932.

Gronbeck, K.: 'Iç Mogolistan'da Türk yazıtları', (Turkish inscriptions from Inner Mongolia), *Belleten* 31, 1944, pp. 457–60.

Halil Edhem: 'Anadolu'da islâmî kitabeler', (Muslim Inscriptions from Anatolia), *Tarih-i Osmanî Encümeni Mecmuası* XXVII, pp. 149–51. *Tarih-i Osmanî Encümeni Mecmuası* XXVIII, p. 516.

Hilmi, Hüseyin: *Sinop Kitabeleri.* (Inscriptions of Sinop.) Sinop 1339–41/1920–2.

Kadri, Hafız: 'Muğla Ulu camii kitabesi', (The Inscription of the Great Mosque at Muğla), *Tarih-i Osmanî Encümeni Mecmuası* VIII, 1913, p. 16.

Konyar, Basri: *Diyarbekir kitabeleri.* Vol. II. (Inscriptions of Diyarbekir.) Ankara, 1936.

Kunter, Halim Baki: 'Kitabelerimiz,' (Inscriptions of Turkey), *Vakıflar Dergisi* II, 1952, pp. 431–56.

Löytved, J.: *Konia, Inschriften der seldschukischen Bauten.* Berlin, 1907.

Mantran, Robert: 'Les Inscriptions Arabes de Brousse', *Bulletin d'Etudes orientales* XIV, 1954, pp. 87–114.

Mustafa, Cavit: *Akşehir kitabeleri ve tetkikatı.* (The Inscriptions of Akşehir and Researches Upon Them.) Muğla, 1934.

Sauvaget, Jean: 'Inscriptions arabes,' in Albert Gabriel, *Voyages archéologiques dans la Turquie Orientale,* I, Paris, 1940, pp. 287–356.

Uzunçarşılı, I.Hakkı: *Kitabeler* I, II, Istanbul, 1927–9.

II. RESEARCHES on ANATOLIAN TURKISH ART

A. *General*

Akok, Mahmut: *Ankara'nın eski evleri.* (Old Houses of Ankara.) Ankara, 1951.

Akok, Mahmut: XIII–XVII. yüzyıllarda yapılmış Türk camilerinin iç mimarisi', (The Interior Construction of Turkish Mosques from the 13th to the 17th Centuries), *Milletlerarası Birinci Türk sanatları Kongresi: Kongreye sunulan tebliğler.* (First International Congress of Turkish Arts: Communications Presented to the Congress) Ankara, 1959, pp. 12–16.

Akok, Mahmut: 'Architecture intérieure de mosquées turques construites entre les XIIIe et XVIIe siècles', *First International Congress of Turkish Arts: Communications Presented to the Congress.* Ankara, 1961, pp. 13–18.

Akozan, Feridun: 'Türk Han ve Kervansarayları', (Turkish Khans and Caravansarais), *Türk Sanatı Araştırmaları.* Istanbul, 1963, pp. 133–67. (Güzel Sanatlar Akademisi Yayınlarından.)

Aslanapa, Oktay: 'Bir doğu Anadolu gezisinden notlar', (Notes on a Trip to Eastern Anatolia), *Milletlerarası Birinci Türk sanatları Kongresi: Ankara, 1959; Kongreye sunulan tebliğler.* (First International Congress of Turkish Arts, Ankara 1959: Communications Presented to the Congress) Ankara, 1962, pp. 26–27.

Bachmann, Walter; *Kirchen und Moscheen in Armenien und Kurdistan.* Leipzig, 1913.

Bittel, Kurt: 'Kleinasiatische Studien', *Istanbuler Mitteilungen* Vol. 5, Istanbul, 1942.

Cuda, A.: 'Stadtaufbau in der Türkei', *Die Welt des Islams* 21, 1939, pp. 16–48.

Çetintaş, Sedat: 'Minarelerimiz', (Turkish Minarets), *Güzel Sanatlar mecmuası* 4, 1942.

Dilaver, Sadi: 'Bünyan Ulu camii—Erbaa/Akçaköy (Fidi) Silahdar Ömer Paşa camii', (The Great Mosque at Bünyan and the Mosque of Ömer Pasha Silahdar at Akçaköy), *Ist. Üniv. Ed. Fak. Sanat Tarihi Yıllığı* II, 1966–8, pp. 184–99.

Erdmann, Kurt: 'Beobachtungen auf einer Reise in Zentralanatolien im Juli 1953', *Archäologischer Anzeiger des Deutschen Archäologischen Instituts* LXIX, 1955, cols. 160–207.

Erdmann, Kurt: 'Weitere Nachträge zu den-Beobachtungen auf einer Reise in Zentralanatolien', *Archäologischer Anzeiger des Deutschen Archäologischen Instituts* LXXI, 1957, cols. 361–72.

Erdmann, Kurt: 'Anatolien, ein Neuland der islamischen Kunstgeschichte', *Akten des vierundzwanzigsten internationalen Orientalisten Kongresses: München, 1957,* Wiesbaden, 1959, p. 377.

Erdmann, Kurt: 'Zur türkischen Baukunst seldschukischer und osmanischer Zeit', *Istanbuler Mitteilungen* 8, 1958, pp. 1–39.

Erdmann, Kurt: 'Vorosmanische Medresen und Imarets vom Medresentyp in Anatolien', Studies in Islamic Art and Architecture in Honour of K. A. C. Creswell 1965, pp. 49–62.

Gabriel, Albert: *La Turquie Terre d'Histoire et d'Art.* Istanbul, pp. 53–71.

Gabriel, Albert: 'Les Antiquités turques d'Anatolie', *Syria* X, 1929, pp. 257–70.

Gabriel, Albert: *Monuments turcs d'Anatolie.* I–II. Paris, 1931–34.

Gabriel, Albert: *Voyages archéologiques dans la Turquie Orientale. Avec un recueil d'inscriptions arabes par Jean Sauvaget.* Paris, 1940.

Gabriel, Albert: *En Turquie.* Paris, 1953.

Halil Edhem: 'Anadolu Selçukları devrinde mimarî ve tezyinî sanatlar', (Architecture and the Decorative Arts of Anatolia in the Seljuk period), *Halil Edhem Hatıra kitabı* Ankara, 1947, pp. 279–97.

Sarre, Friedrich: *Reise in Kleinasien—Sommer 1895. Forschungen zur seldjukischen Kunst und Geographie des Landes.* Berlin, 1896.

Taeschner, Franz: 'Anatolische Forschungen', *Zeitschrift der Deutschen Morgenländischen Gesellschaft* LXXXII, 1928, pp. 83–118.

Taeschner, Franz: 'Beiträge zur frühosmanischen Epigraphik und Archäologie', *Der Islam*, XX, 1932, pp. 109–86.

Texier, C.: *Description de L'Asie Mineure* II. Paris, 1849

Ünsal, Behçet: *Turkish Islamic Architecture in Seljuk and Ottoman times 1071–1923.* London, 1959.

Yetkin, Suut Kemal: 'The Evolution of Architectural form in Turkish Mosques (1300–1700)', *Studia Islamica* XI, 1959, pp. 73–91.

Yetkin, Suut Kemal: *L'Architecture Turque en Turquie.* Paris, 1962.

Yetkin, S. K.; Özgüç, T.; Sümer, F.; Ülken, H. Z.; Çagatay, N. and Karamağaralı, H.: *Turkish Architecture.* Ankara, 1965.

B. *Monographs on regions and cities*

Akarca, A. and Akarca, T.: *Milâs.* Istanbul, 1954.

Aslanapa, Oktay: *Edirne'de Osmanlı devri abideleri.* (Ottoman Monuments of Edirne.) Istanbul, 1949.

Balin, R.: *Diyarbakır.* Istanbul, 1966.

Banoğlu, N.: 'Şaheserleri ile Ahlat', (Ahlat and Its Masterpieces), *Tarih-Coğrafya Dünyası* 11/8, 1959, pp. 81 et seq.

Bayatlı, Osman: *Bergama tarihinde Türk-Islâm eserleri.* (Turkish-Islamic monuments in the history of Bergama.) Istanbul, 1956.

Baykal, K.: *Bursa ve anıtları.* (Bursa and Its Monuments.) Bursa, 1950.

Beygü, Abdürrahim Şerif: *Erzurum: Tarihi, Anıtları, Kitabeleri.* (Erzurum, Its History, Its Monuments, Its Inscriptions.) Istanbul, 1936.

BIBLIOGRAPHY

Beysanoğlu, Ş.: *Kısaltılmış Diyarbakır tarihi ve abideleri.* (Brief History of Diyarbekir and Its Monuments.) Istanbul, 1963.

Çetintaş, Sedat: *Bursa: tarihî yerler, müze, camiler ve türbeler.* (Bursa, Historical Monuments, Museums, Mosques and Mausolea.) Istanbul, 1934.

Dursunkaya, Ziya: *Kırklareli vilayetini tarih, coğrafya, kültür ve eserler yönü ile tetkik.* (Researches in the fields of the History, Geography, Culture and Monuments of the Vilayet of Kirklareli) Vol. I. Kırklareli, 1948.

Erdmann, Kurt: 'Die Grabkirche von Seyitgazi', *Istanbuler Mitteilungen* 8, 1958, pp. 11 et seq.

Erten, S. Fikri: *Antalya vilayeti tarihi.* (History of the Vilayet of Antalya.) Antalya-Istanbul, 1940–48.

Eyice, Semavi: 'Sultaniye-Karapınar'a dair', (On Sultaniye-Karapinar), *Tarih Dergisi* XV, 1965, pp. 117–40.

Gabriel, Albert: 'Mardin ve Diyarbekir vilayetlerinde icra olunmuş bir arkeologya seyahati hakkında rapor', (Report on an Archaeological Excursion in the Vilayets of Mardin and Diyarbekir), *Türk Tarih, Arkeologya ve Etnografya Dergisi* I, 1933, pp. 134–49.

Gabriel, Albert: *Une Capitale turque, Brousse, Bursa.* Paris, 1958.

Gökoğlu, A.: *Paflagonya, Kastamonu, Sinop, Çankırı, Safranbolu, Bartın, Bolu, Gerede, Mudurnu, Iskilip, Bafra, Alaçam ve civarı, gayrımenkul eski eserleri arkeolojisi.* (The Archaeology of the Indigenous Ancient Monuments of Paphlagonia, Kastamonu, Sinop, Çankırı, Safranbolu, Bartın, Bolu, Gerede, Mudurnu, Iskilip, Bafra, Alaçam and their surroundings) Kastamonu, 1952.

Grenard, M. F.: 'Notes sur les Monuments de Sivas', *Journal Asiatique* 9, Series XVI, 1900, pp. 451–8.

Grenard, M. F.: 'Note sur les Monuments du Moyen age de Malatia, Divrighi, Siwas, Darendeh, Amasia et Tokat', *Journal Asiatique* 8, Series XXVIII, Paris 1901.

Gurlitt, Cornelius: 'Die Bauten Adrianopels', *Orientalisches Archiv* I, 1910–11.

Gurlitt, Cornelius: 'Die islamischen Bauten von Isnik (Nicaea)', *Orientalisches Archiv* III, 1912–13, pp. 49–60.

Günkut, Bedri: *Diyarbakır Tarihi.* (History of Diyarbekir.) Diyarbekir, 1936. (Diyarbakır Halkevi: 3.)

Halil Edhem: *Kayseriye Şehri.* (The Town of Kayseri.) Istanbul, 1915.

Halil Edhem: *Niğde Kılavuzu.* (Guide to Niğde.) Istanbul, 1936.

Hüseyin, Hüsamettin: *Amasya Tarihi.* (History of Amasya.) Istanbul, 1927–35.

Kadı, H. M.: 'Aksaray'daki Türk eserleri', (Turkish Monuments at Aksaray), *Hasandağ Gazetesi,* Aksaray, 1966.

Kafesoğlu, Ibrahim: 'Ahlat ve çevresinde 1945 de yapılan tarihi ve arkeolojik tetkik seyahati raporu', (Report on an Archaeological Excursion to Ahlat and the Surrounding Area), *Tarih Dergisi* 1, 1949, pp. 167–90.

Konyalı, I. H.: *Akşehir.* Istanbul, 1945.

Konyalı, I. H.: *Alanya.* Istanbul, 1946.

Konyalı, I. H.: *Abideleri ve kitabeleri ile Erzurum tarihi.* (The Monuments, Inscriptions and History of Erzurum.) Istanbul, 1960.

Konyalı, I. H.: *Konya Tarihi.* (History of Konya.) Konya, 1964.

Konyalı, I. H.: *Karaman, Ermenak, Mut.* Istanbul, 1967.

Konyar, Basri: *Diyarbekir Tarihi.* Vol. I. (History of Diyarbekir.) Ankara, 1936.

Koyunoğlu, A. Memduh Turgut: *Iznik ve Bursa Tarihi.* (History of Iznik and Bursa.) Bursa, 1935. (Bursa Halkevi: 8.)

Lloyd, Seton and Rice, D. Storm: *Alanya* ('Alā'iyya). London, 1958.

Mamboury, E.: *Ankara. Guide touristique.* Ankara, 1934.

Mehmet Behçet: *Kastamonu Asar-ı kadimesi.* (Ancient Monuments of Kastamonu.) Istanbul, 1341/1925.

Mübarek, Galip: *Ankara.* Istanbul, 1928.

Niemann, Georg: 'Die seldschukischen Bauwerke in Ajasoluk', *Forschungen in Ephesos* I 1906, pp. 111–31.

Otto-Dorn, Katharina: 'Islamische Denkmäler Kilikiens', *Jahrbuch für Kleinasiatische Forschung* II, 1952, pp. 113–26

Otto-Dorn, Katharina and Anhegger, Robert: *Das islamische Iznik.* Berlin, 1941.

Önder, Mehmet: *Tarihi-Turistik Konya Rehberi.* (Historical and Touristic Guide to Konya.) Konya, 1956.

Önder, Mehmet: *Mevlânâ Şehri Konya.* (Konya the City of Mevlânâ.) Konya, 1962.

Önder, Mehmet: 'Romanya'da sulara gömülecek olan bir Türk Kasabası, Adakale', (A Turkish site in Rumania in danger of submersion—Adakale), *Türk Kültürü* No. 54 (1966), pp. 427–34.

Özalp, T.: *Sivrihisar Tarihi.* (History of Sivrihisar.) Eskişehir, 1961.

Özdoğan, Kâzım: *Kayseri tarihi. Kültür ve sanat eserleri.* Vol. I. (History of Kayseri. Culture and Art.) (Alimler-Şairler-Sanatkârlar.) Kayseri, 1948.

Özgüç, Tahsin and Akok, Mahmut: 'Develi abideleri', (Monuments of Develi), *Belleten* XIX, 1955, pp. 377–84.

Peremeci, Osman Nuri: *Edirne Tarihi.* (History of Edirne.) Istanbul, 1939.

Ridvan, Nâfiz and Ismail Hakkı: *Sivas Şehri.* (The Town of Sivas.) Istanbul, 1928.

Riefstahl, Rudolf M.: *Cenubi Garbi Anadolu'da Türk mimarisi.* (Turkish translation of the foregoing) Istanbul, 1941.

Riefstahl, Rudolf M. and Wittek, Paul: *Turkish Architecture in Southwestern Anatolia.* Cambridge, 1931.

Ruben, Walter: 'Kırşehir'in dikkatimizi çeken sanat abideleri', (Noteworthy Monuments at Kırşehir), *Belleten* XI, 1947, pp. 603–40.

Sayılı, Adnan: 'Tire'de bir araştırma', (Researches at Tire), *Belleten* XII, 1949, pp. 683–7.

Sayman, F. and Tongur, I.: *Konya eski eserler kılavuzu.* (Guide to the Ancient Monuments of Konya.) Konya, 1944.

Strzygowski, J. and Berchem, M. van: *Amida.* Heidelberg, 1910.

Sungurluoğlu, I.: *Harput yollarında.* I. (On the roads to Harput.) Istanbul, 1958.

Süslü, Memduh Yavuz: *Eşrefoğulları tarihi. Beyşehir kılavuzu.* (History of the Eshrefoghulları. Guide to Beyşehir.) Konya, 1934.

Tarım, C. H.: *Tarihte Kırşehri-Gülşehri.* (Kırşehir-Gülşehir in History.) Istanbul, 1948.

Tokluoğlu, F.: *Tire ve Turistik değerleri.* (Tire and Its Touristic Treasures.) Istanbul, 1957.

Tokluoğlu, F.: *Tire.* Tire, 1964.

Totaysalgir, G.: *Karaman-Lârende.* Konya, 1944.

Turan, Osman: 'Selçuklular zamanında Sivas şehri', (Sivas in the Seljuk period), *Dil ve Tarih Coğrafya Fakültesi dergisi* Vol. IX, No. 4, 1951, pp. 447–57.

Uzluk, Şahabettin: *Konya Abideleri.* (Monuments of Konya.) Konya, 1939.

Uzunçarşılı, I. Hakkı: *Sivas Şehri.* (The Town of Sivas.) Istanbul, 1928.

Uzunçarşılı, I. Hakkı: *Kütahya şehri.* (The Town of Kütahya.) Istanbul, 1932.

Ülgen, Ali Saim: 'Iznik'te Türk eserleri', (Turkish Monuments at Iznik), *Vakıflar Dergisi* I, 1938, pp. 53–69.

Ülgen, Ali Saim: 'Kırşehir'de Türk eserleri', (Turkish Monuments of Kırşehir), *Vakıflar Dergisi* II, 1942, pp. 235–62.

Ünal, Rahmi Hüseyin: 'Monuments Saltūqides de Kemah (Anatolie Orientale)', *Revue des Etudes Islamiques*, Paris, 1967, pp. 149–72.

Ünal, Rahmi Hüseyin: *Les monuments islamiques anciens de la ville d'Erzurum et de sa région.* Paris, 1968.

Wilde, H.: *Brussa, Eine Entwicklungsgeschichte türkischer Architektur in Kleinasien unter den ersten Osmanen, (Beiträge zur Bauwissenschaft* 13), 1909.

Wulzinger, Karl: *Drei Bektaschi-Klöster Phrygiens.* Berlin, 1913.

Wulzinger, Karl; Wittek, Paul and Sarre, Friedrich: *Das Islamische Milet.* Leipzig, 1935.

Yeşil, Mustafa: *Kütahya ilinin kısa tarihi.* (A Short History of the Kütahya Area.) Istanbul, 1937.

C. *Istanbul*

Altınay, Ahmet Refik: *Hicrî Onikinci asırda Istanbul hayatı.* (Life in 18th Century Istanbul.) Istanbul, 1930.

Altınay, Ahmet Refik: *Hicrî onbirinci asırda Istanbul hayatı.* (Life in 17th Century Istanbul.) Istanbul, 1931.

Altınay, Ahmet Refik: *Hicrî XIII. asırda Istanbul hayatı.* (Life in 19th Century Istanbul.) Istanbul, 1932.

Altınay, Ahmet Refik: *16. asırda Istanbul hayatı.* (Life in 16th Century Istanbul.) Istanbul, 1935.

Eyice, Semavi: *Istanbul, petit guide à travers les monuments byzantins et Turcs.* Istanbul, 1955.

Eyice, Semavi: 'Istanbul,', *Islâm Ansiklopedisi* 1967, pp. 1135–214.

Gurlitt, Cornelius: *Die Baukunst Konstantinopels.* Berlin, 1907–12.

Kühnel, Ernst: 'Die türkische Kunst', in Baedeker's *Konstantinopel, Balkanstaaten,* etc., 2nd ed. Leipzig, 1914; 3rd ed. 1921.

Mamboury, Ernest: *Constantinople. Guide Touristique.* Constantinople, 1925; New ed. Istanbul, 1951, (English 1953).

Ülgen, Ali Saim: *Fatih devrinde Istanbul.* (Istanbul in the Reign of Mehmed the Conqueror.) (Vakıflar Umum Müdurlüğü neşriyatı: 2.)

III. ARCHITECTURE

A. Central Asia

1. Pre-Islamic

Appelgren-Kivalo, Hjalmar: *Alt-Altaische Kunstdenkmäler.* Helsingfors, 1931. (Reisen in Sibirien und der Mongolei 1887–89.)

Belenitsky, A. M.: 'Neue Denkmäler der vorislamischen monumentalen sogdischen Kunst', *XXIV. Int. Orient. Kong. vortrag* Moscow, 1957.

Esin, Emel: 'Eurasia göçebelerinin sanatının ve Islâmiyetten evvelki Türkistan sanatının Türk plâstik ve tersimî sanatları üzerindeki bazı tesirleri', (Various Influences from the Art of the Euro-Asiatic Nomads and the Art of pre-Islamic Turkestan on Turkish Graphic and Plastic Art), *Milletlerarası I. Türk Sanatları Kongresi: Kongreye sunulan tebliğler.* (First International Congress of Turkish Arts, Ankara 1959: Communications Presented to the Congress) Ankara, 1962, pp. 152–74.

Gabain, Annemarie v.: 'Das Uigurische Königreich von Chotscho, 850–1250', *Sitzungsbericht der Deutschen Akademie der Wissenschaften zu Berlin; Klasse für Sprachen, Literatur und Kunst,* Berlin, 1961, No. 5.

Grünwedel, A.: *Altbuddhistische Kultstatten in Chinesischen Turkistan.* Berlin, 1912.

Härtel, Herbert: *Turfan und Gandhara. Frühmittelalterliche Kunst Zentralasiens.* 2nd ed. Berlin, 1964.

Inan, A.: 'Altay dağlarında bulunan eski Türk mezarları', (Ancient Turkish Tombs in the Altay Mountains), *Belleten* XI, 1947.

Le Coq, A. von: *Chotscho.* Berlin, 1913.

Le Coq, A. von: *Bilderatlas zur Kunst und Kulturgeschichte Mittelasiens.* Berlin, 1925.

Le Coq, A. von: *Auf Hellas Spuren in Ost Turkestan.* Leipzig, 1926.

Le Coq, A. von: *Die Buddhistische Spätantike in Mittelasien I–VII.* Berlin, 1922–28.

Masson, V. M.: *Srednyaya Aziya v Epokhu Karun'ya i Bronzy.* (Central Asia in the Karun and Bronze Ages.) Moscow, 1966.

Phillips, E. D.: 'New Light on the Ancient History of the Eurasian Steppes', *American Journal of Archaeology* 61/3, 1957, pp. 268–80.

Rudenko, S. I.: *Kultura Naseleniya Gornogo Altaya v Skifskoye Vremya.* (The Culture of the Population of the Altay Mountains in the Scythian Period.) Moscow, 1953.

Stein, A.: *Ruins of Desert Cathay.* London, 1912.

Stein, A.: *Innermost Asia.* Oxford, 1928.

Tolstov, S. P.: *Po stopách dávného Chorezmu.* (On the Tracks of Ancient Khorezm.) Prag, 1951.

Tolstov, S. P.: *Auf den Spuren der altchoresmischen Kultur.* (German translation of the foregoing) Berlin, 1953.

Tolstov, S. P.: *Po drevnim del'tam Oksa i Yaksarta.* (Through the Ancient Deltas of the Oxus and the Jaxartes.) Moscow, 1962.

Yakubovsky, A. Y. and D'yakonov, M. M.: *Zhivopis' Drevnego Pyandzhikenta.* (The Painting of Ancient Pyandzhikent.) Moscow, 1954.

2. Islamic

Basenov: *Ornament Kazakhstana v arkhitekture.* (Kazakhstan Decoration in Architecture.) Alma Ata, 1957.

Bussagli, Mario: L'Influsso classico ed iranico sull'arte dell'Asia Centrale', *Rivista dell'-Instituto Nazionale d'Archeologia e Storia dell'Arte* N.N., II, 1953, pp. 171–262.

Cohn-Wiener, E.: *Turan. Islamische Baukunst in Mittelasien.* Berlin, 1930.

Cohn-Wiener, E.: 'Ruin Sites in Turkistan', *Asia* XLI, 1941.

Denike, B.: 'Quelques Monuments de Bois Sculpté au Turkestan Occidental', *Ars Islamica* II, 1935, pp. 69–83.

Diez, Ernst: *Churasanische Baudenkmäler.* Berlin, 1918.

Diez, Ernst: 'Zentralasien und der eurasische Kunstkreis', *Atlantis-Buch der Kunst,* Zurich, 1952, pp. 602–15.

Diez, Ernst: 'Das Erbe der Steppe in der turco-iranischen Baukunst', *Symbolae in honorem Zeki Velidi Togan,* Istanbul, 1950–55 pp. 331–8.

Esin, Emel: *Türkistan Seyahatnamesi.* (Account of a Journey to Turkestan.) Ankara, 1959.

Field, H. and Prostov, E.: 'Archaeological Investigations in Central Asia 1917–37', *Ars Islamica* V, 1938, pp. 233–271.

Field, H. and Prostov, E.: 'Excavations at Khwarezm, 1937–38', *Ars Islamica* VI/2, 1939, pp. 158–166.

Field, H. and Prostov, E.: 'Excavations in Uzbekistan, 1937–39', *Ars Islamica* IX, 1942, pp. 143–159.

Field, H. and Prostov, E.: 'Recent Excavation at Khwarezm', *Ars Islamica* XIII–XIV, 1948, pp. 139–48.

Gerasimov: *Pamyatniki arkhitektury doliny reki Kara Kengir v Tsentral' nom Kazakhstane.* (Monuments of the Kara Kengir Valley in Central Kazakhstan.) Moscow, 1957.

Godard, A.: 'Khorasan', *Athar-é Iran* IV, 1949.

Haase, C. P.: 'Temuridische Baukunst', *Westtürkestan Referate zur Turkologischen Exkursion 1966* Vol. 1, Hamburg, 1968, pp. 120–59.

Hrbas, Milos and Knobloch, Edgar: *Die Kunst Mittelasiens.* Prague, 1965.

Lechner, E.: 'Die Kunst der turanischen Völker', *Turan, Zeitschrift der turanischen Gesellschaft* 1922, pp. 179–92.

Les Monuments historiques de l'Islam en U.R.S.S. Tashkent, 1963.

Liele, Harkot: 'Das Observatorium Ulugh Begs in Samarkand', *Westtürkestan Referate zur Turkologischen Exkursion 1966* Vol. 1, Hamburg, 1968, pp. 160–4.

Meinecke, Michael: 'Vortemüridische Baukunst in Türkestan', *Westtürkestan Referate zur Turkologischen Exkursion 1966* Vol. 1, Hamburg, 1968, pp. 91–119.

Nilsen, A.: *Monumental'naya Arkhitektura Bukharskogo Oazisa XI–XII vv.* (Monumental Architecture of the Bukhara Oasis, XI–XII centuries.) Tashkent, 1956.

Polupanov: *Arkhitekturniye Pamyatniki Samarkanda.* (The Architectural Monuments of Samarkand.) Moscow, 1948.

Pribytkova, A. M.: *Pamyatniki Arkhitektury XI veka v Turkmenii.* (Monuments of the 11th Century in Turkmenia.) Moscow, 1955.

Pugachenkova, G. A.: *Puti razvitiya arkhitektury yuzhnogo Turkmenistana.* (The Architectural Development of Southern Turkmenistan in Antiquity and the Middle Ages.) Moscow, 1958.

Pugachenkova, G. A.: 'Mazar Arab-Ata v Time', (The Arab Ata Mazar at Tim), *Sovetskaya Arkheologiya*, 1961/4.

Pugachenkova, G. A.: *Iskusstvo Zodchikh Uzbekistana.* (The Art of Uzbek Architects. (The Mausoleum of Arab Ata.)) (*Mavzolei Arab-Ata 977/8—IX–X.*) Tashkent, 1963.

Pugachenkova, G. A.: *Iskusstvo Turkmenistana.* (The Art of Turkmenistan.) Moscow, 1967.

Pugachenkova, G. A. and Rempel, V. I.: *Istoriya Iskusstva Uzbekistana.* (History of the Art of Uzbekistan.) Moscow, 1965.

Pugachenkova, G. A. and Rempel, V. I.: *Zodchestvo Uzbekistana.* (The Architecture of Uzbekistan.) Tashkent, 1959.

Rempel, V. I.: *Arkhitekturny ornament Uzbekistana.* (Architectural Ornament of Uzbekistan.) Tashkent, 1961.

Yaralov, Youri, 'Architectural Monuments in Middle Asia of the VIII–XIIth Centuries', *First International Congress of Turkish Arts: Communications Presented to the Congress.* Ankara, 1961, pp. 364–70.

Yuldashev, A. A.: *Arkhitekturny Ornament Tadzhikistana.* (The Architectural Ornament of Tadzhikistan.) Moscow, 1957.

Zasypkin, B.: *Pamyatniki arkhitektury v srednei Azii i ikh restavratsiya.* (Architectural Monuments of Central Asia and Their Restoration.) Off-print, 1927.

Zasypkin, B.: *Arkhitekturniye Pamyatniki Srednei Azii.* (Architectural Monuments of Central Asia.) Moscow, 1928.

Zasypkin, B.: *Arkhitektura Srednei Azii.* (The Architecture of Central Asia.) Moscow, 1948.

B. *Caucasus and Azerbaidzhan* (Transcaucasia)

Baklanov: *Arkhitekturniye Pamyatniki Dagestana.* (Monuments of Dagestan.) Makhachkale or Moscow, 1935.

Bretanitsky, L. S.: *Zodchestvo Azerbaydzhana XII–XV vv.* (Monuments of Azerbaidzhan XII–XV centuries.) Moscow, 1966.

Useinov, M. A.: *Pamyatniki Azerbaydzhanskogo Zodchestva.* (Monuments of Azerbaidzhan.) Moscow, 1951.

Useinov, M.; Bretanitsky, L. S. and Salamzade, A.: *Istoriya arkhitektury Azerbaydzhana.* (History of the Architecture of Azerbaidzhan.) Moscow, 1963.

C. *Ghaznevids*

Ahmad Ali Kohzad: 'Premiers échantillons de la peinture Ghaznévide', *Afghanistan* IV, No. 2, 1949, pp. 48–51.

Bombaci, A.: 'Introduction to the Excavations at Ghazne', *East and West* New series Vol. 10, Nos. 1–2, Rome, March–June, 1959.

Bombaci, A.: 'Gazne'deki kazılara giriş', (Turkish translation of above), *Türk sanatı tarihi araştırma ve incelemeleri,* Istanbul, 1963, pp. 537–60.

Bombaci, A.: 'Les Turcs et l'art ghaznévide', *First International Congress of Turkish Arts: Communications Presented to the Congress,* Ankara, 1961, pp. 65–70.

Bombaci, A. and Scerrato, Umberto: 'Summary Report on the Italian Archaeological Mission in Afghanistan', *East and West* New series Vol. 10, Nos. 1–2, Rome, March–June, 1959.

Flury, S.: 'Le décor épigraphique des monuments de Ghazne', *Syria,* 1925, pp. 61–90.

Maricq, A. and Wiet, G.: *Le Minaret de Djam.* Paris, 1959.

Ögel, Semra: 'Anadolu Selçuklu tezyinatının önemli bir kaynağı: Gazne sanatı, (An Important Source for the Decoration of the Anatolian Seljuks, the Art of Ghazne), *Türk Kültürü Araştırmaları Dergisi* II, 1964, pp. 197–205.

Schlumberger, Daniel: 'La Mosquée (de Lashkari Bazar)', *Afghanistan* II, 1949, pp. 34–44.

Schlumberger, Daniel: 'Les Fouilles de Lashkari Bazar', *Afghanistan* VI, No. 4, 1950.

Schlumberger, Daniel: 'The Ghaznevid Palace of Lashkari Bazar', *The Illustrated London News,* London, 1950.

Schlumberger, Daniel: 'The Great Palace of Mahmud in Afghanistan', *The Illustrated London News,* London, 1951.

Schlumberger, Daniel: 'Le Palais Ghaznévide de Lashkari Bazar', *Syria* XXIX, 1952, pp. 251–70.

Schlumberger, Daniel: 'La Grande Mosquée de Lashkari Bazar', *Afghanistan* VII, 1952, pp. 1–4.

Sourdel-Thomine, J.: 'Deux minarets d'époque seljoukide en Afghanistan', *Syria* XXX, 1953, pp. 108–36.

D. *The Seljuks in Iran*

Bivar, A. D. H.: 'Seljūqid *zıyārats* of Sar-i Pūl (Afghanistan)', *Bulletin of the School of Oriental and African Studies, University of London* Vol. XXIX, Part 1, 1966, pp. 57–63.

Cohn-Wiener, E.: 'Die Ruinen der Seldschukenstadt von Merv und das Mausoleum Sultan Sandschars', *Jahrbuch der asiatischen Kunst* II, 1925, pp. 114–22.

Gabriel, Albert: 'Le Masdjid-i Djum'a d'Isfahan', *Ars Islamica* Vol. II, Part 1, 1935.

Godard, André: 'Historique du Masdjid-é Djum'a d'Isfahan', *Athar-é Iran* I, 1936, pp. 213–38.

Godard, André: 'Isfahan', *Athar-é Iran* II, 1936, 7, 8, pp. 3–176.

Godard, André: 'Ardistan et Zawaré', *Athar-é Iran* I, 1936, pp. 285–309.

Godard, André: 'Les anciennes mosquées de l'Iran', *Athar-é Iran* I, 1936, pp. 187 et seq.

Pope, A. U.: 'Note on the Aesthetic Character of the Masjid-i Jāmi' of Isfahan', *Studies in Islamic Art and Architecture in Honour of K. A. C. Creswell*. Cairo, 1965, pp. 179–93.

Sauvaget, J.: 'Observations sur quelques mosquées Seldjoukides', *Annales de l'Ins. d'Études Orientales d'Alger* Vol. 4, 1938, pp. 81–120.

Sourdel-Thomine, J.: 'L'architecture islamique de l'Iran', *Art et lit. en Iran,* pp. 77–94.

Stronach, D. and Cuyler-Young, T.: 'Three Octagonal Seljuq Tomb Towers', *Iran* Vol. IV, 1966, pp. 1–28.

Wilber, D.: *The Architecture of Islamic Iran: the Il-Khanid Period*. Princeton, 1955.

E. *Tulunids, Fatimids, Ayyubids, Mamluks, Zengids*

Berchem, M. van: 'Une mosquée du temps des Fatimites an Caire', 1889. (*Mémoires de l'Institut Français d'archéologie Orientale au Caire.*)

Creswell, K. A. C.: 'Some Newly Discovered Tûlûnide Ornament', *Burlington Magazine* XXXV, 1919, pp. 180–8.

Creswell, K. A. C.: 'The Origin of the Cruciform Plan of Cairene Madrasas', *Bulletin de l'Institut Français d'archéologie orientale au Caire,* 1922.

Creswell, K. A. C.: *Muslim Architecture of Egypt: I. Ikhshids and Fatimids*. Oxford, 1952.

Creswell, K. A. C.: *Muslim Architecture of Egypt: II. Ayyubids and Early Mamluks*. Oxford, 1959.

Hautecoeur, Louis and Wiet, Gaston: *Les mosquées du Caire*. Paris, 1932.

Herzfeld, E.: 'Damascus: Studies in Architecture', *Ars Islamica* IX, 1942, pp. 1–53; X, 1943, pp. 13–70; XI–XII, 1946, pp. 1–72; XIII–XIV, 1948, pp. 118–38.

Müller, K.: *Das Karawanserail im vorderen Orient*. Berlin, 1920.

Sarre, F. and Herzfeld, E.: *Archäologische Reise im Euphrat-und Tigris-Gebiet*. 4 vols. Berlin, 1911–20.

Sauvaget, J.: Architecture musulmane en Syrie, *Revue des Arts asiatiques,* 1937.

Sauvaget, J.: *Les Monuments Ayyoubides de Damas*. 4 parts. Paris, 1938–50.

F. *The Seljuks and the first Turkish States in Anatolia*

Akok, Mahmut: 'Melik Gazi türbesi ve kalesi', (The Tomb and Citadel of Melik Gazi), *Belleten* XVIII, 1954, pp. 331–6.

Akok, Mahmut: 'Kayseri Huand mimarî külliyesinin rölövesi', (Plan of the Foundation of Huand at Kayseri), *Türk Arkeoloji Dergisi* XVI/1, 1967, pp. 5–44.

Arel, Hilmi: 'Divriği Ulu camisi tekstil kapısı ve diğerleri', (The West Porch of the Great Mosque at Divriği and Others), *Vakıflar Dergisi* V, 1962, pp. 113–25.

BIBLIOGRAPHY

Arel, Hilmi: 'Divriği Ulu camii kuzey portalının mimarî kuruluşu', (The Architectural Origins of the North Porch of the Great Mosque at Divriği), *Vakıflar Dergisi* V, 1962, pp. 99–111.

Artuk, Ibrahim: 'Dunaysır'da Artukoğulları Ulu Camisi', (The Artukid Great Mosque at Dunaysir), *Belleten* 1946, pp. 167–9.

Aslanapa, Oktay: 'Selçuk devlet adamı Mübarizeddin Ertokuş tarafından yaptırılan âbideler', (Monuments Erected by the Seljuk Statesman Mubāriz al-Dīn Ertokush), *Islâm Tetkikleri Dergisi* I, 1957, pp. 97–113.

Aslanapa, Oktay: 'Diyarbakır sarayı kazısı, ilk rapor, (Excavations at the Palace at Diyarbekir, Preliminary Report), *Türk Arkeoloji Dergisi* XII/2, 1961–2, pp. 10–18.

Aslanapa, Oktay: Erster Bericht über die Ausgrabungen des Palastes von Diyarbakır, (German translation of above), *Istanbuler Milteilungen* 12, 1962, pp. 115–28.

Aslanapa, Oktay: 'Kayseri'de Keykubadiye köşkleri kazısı', (Excavations in the Palaces of Keykubadiye at Kayseri), *Türk Arkeoloji Dergisi* XIII/1, 1964, pp. 19–40.

Aslanapa, Oktay: 'Kalehisar'da bulunan mimari eserler', (Architectural Remains at Kalehisar), *I. Ü. Ed. Fak. Sanat Tarihi Yıllığı* II, 1966–8, pp. 1–14.

Berliner, Rudolf: 'Die grosse Moschee von Diyarbekir', *Monatshefte für Kunstwissenschaft* XV, 1922, pp. 161–72.

Çetintaş, Sedat: *Türk Tarih Kurumu tarafından Sivas şifahanesinde yaptırılan mimarî hafriyat.* (The Excavations of the Türk Tarih Kurumu at the Hospital in Sivas.) Istanbul, 1939.

Çetintaş, Sedat: *Sivas darüşşifası.* (The Hospital at Sivas.) Istanbul, 1953.

Erdmann, Kurt: 'Notizen zum inneranatolischen Karavansaray: Beobachtungen auf einer Reise im Juli 1953', *Kunst des Orients* II, 1955, pp. 5–29.

Erdmann, Kurt: 'Zum Vierbogenbau von Keykubadiye', *Ilâhiyat Fakültesi Yıllık Araştırmalar Dergisi* II, Ankara, 1957, pp. 93–5.

Erdmann, Kurt: 'Serailbauten des 13. und 14. Jahrhunderts in Anatolien', *Ars Orientalis* III, 1959, pp. 77–94.

Erdmann, Kurt: 'Der Kargi Han bei Alanya', *Kunst des Orients* III, 1959, pp. 1–13.

Erdmann, Kurt: 'Das seldschukische Karavansaray', *Institut für Auslandsbeziehungen* Vols. 2–3, 1962, pp. 163–9.

Erdmann, Kurt: *Das anatolische Karavansaray des 13. Jahrhunderts, I–II.* Berlin, 1962.

Erdmann, Kurt: 'Die Sonderstellung der anatolischen Moschee des XIII. Jhdts.', *First International Congress of Turkish Arts: Communications Presented to the Congress.* Ankara, 1961, pp. 94–101.

Erdmann, Kurt: 'Vorosmanische Medresen und Imarets vom Medresentyp in Anatolien', *Studies in Islamic Art and Architecture in Honour of K. A. C. Creswell.* Cairo–London, 1965, pp. 49–62.

Eyice, Semavi: 'Sivas'ta Keykâvus I. Darüşşifası', (The Hospital of Kaykā'ūs I at Sivas), *Bilgi Dergisi* No. 130–1, Istanbul, 1958.

Ferit, M. and Mesut, M.: *Selçuk veziri Sahip Ata ile oğullarının hayat ve eserleri.* (The Life and Works of the Seljuk Vizir, Sahib Ata, and His Sons.) Istanbul, 1934.

Ferrero, D.: 'Il caravanseraglio di Ak Han presso Denizli', *Palladio* III–IV, (Uglio-Dicembre) 1959, pp. 1–16.

Gabriel, Albert: 'Dunaysir', *Ars Islamica* IV, 1937, pp. 352–68.

Gabriel, Albert: 'L'architecture seldjoukide', *II. Türk Tarih Kongresi.* Ankara, 1937.

Gabriel, Albert: 'Mosquées et medressés ortokides', *Halil Edhem Hatıra Kitabı.* Ankara, 1947, pp. 211–18.

Glück, Henrich: *Die Kunst der Seldschuken in Kleinasien und Armenien.* Leipzig, 1923.

Glück, Henrich: 'Küçük Asya'da Selçuk sanatı', (Seljuk Art of Asia Minor), (Trans. Köprülüzâde Ahmet Cemal), *Hayat* 23, 1927.

Gürkan, K. I.: 'L'hôpital-école de Kayseri', *Pagine di Storia della Medicina* VIII, 1964.

Halil Edhem: 'Anadolu'da Selçuklu harabeleri', (Seljuk Ruins in Anatolia), *Halil Edhem Hatıra Kitabı* Ankara, 1947.

Inan, A.: 'Kayseri'nin 749 yıllık Şifaiye Tıp medresesi', (A hospital and medical school at Kayseri, seven hundred and forty-nine years old), *Belleten* XX, 1956, pp. 217–22.

Karamağaralı, Hâluk: 'Mevlânâ'nın türbesi', (The Tomb of Mevlânâ), *Türk Etnografya Dergisi* VII–VIII, 1947, pp. 38–42.

Karamete, K.: 'Develi Ulu Camii', (The Great Mosque at Develi), *Erciyes Kayseri Halkevi Dergisi* No. 81, 1949, pp. 18–19.

Katoğlu, M.: '13. yüzyıl Konyasında bir câmi gurubunun plân tipi ve son cemaat yeri', (A Type of Mosque Plan with Portico from 13th-Century Konya), *Türk Etnografya Dergisi* IX, 1966–7, pp. 81–100.

Klinghardt, Karl: 'Vom Geist türkischer und seldschukischer Kultbauten', *Deutsche Bauzeitung* LXI, 1927, pp. 681–8.

Kuban, Doğan: 'The Mosque and Hospital at Divriği and the Origin of Anatolian Turkish Architecture', *Anatolica* II, 1968, pp. 122–30.

Kuran, Aptullah: 'Tokat ve Niksar'da Yağı-Basan medreseleri', (The Medreses of Yaghıbasan at Tokat and Niksar), *Vakıflar Dergisi* VII, 1968, pp. 39–44.

Kuran, Aptullah: *Anadolu medreseleri.* (Medreses of Anatolia.) Vol. I. Ankara, 1969.

Lamb, Dorothy: 'Notes on Seljuk Buildings at Konia', *Annual of the British School at Athens* XXI, 1914–16, pp. 31–61.

Mendel, Gustave: 'Les monuments seldjoukides en Asie Mineure', *Revue de l'Art Ancien et Moderne* XXIII, 1908, pp. 9–24, 113–27.

Meriç, Rıfkı Melûl: 'Tombeaux et turbés d'Akşehir', *Türkiyat Mecmuası* V, 1936.

Oral, M. Z.: 'Kubadabad nasıl bulundu?', (How Was Kubādābād Found?), *Ilâhiyat Fakültesi Dergisi,* Ankara, 1953, pp. 171 et seq.

Oral, M. Z.: 'Kayseri'da Kubadiye Sarayları', (The Palaces of Keykubadiye at Kayseri), *Belleten* XVII, 1953, pp. 501–17.

Oral, M. Z.: 'Konya'da Alâeddin camii ve türbeleri', (The 'Alā al-Dīn Mosque and its Tombs at Konya), *Yıllık Araştırmalar Dergisi* I, 1956, pp. 45–62.

Oral, M. Z.: 'Konya'da Alâ üd-din Camii ve Türbeleri', (The 'Alā al-Dīn Mosque and its Tombs at Konya), *Ilâhiyat Fakültesi Dergisi* V, Nos. I–IV, 1956, pp. 144–64.

Oral, M. Z.: Sırçalı Medrese, (The Sırçalı Medrese at Konya), *Belleten* XXV, 1961, pp. 355–96.

Oral, M. Z.: 'Le sarcophage et le mausolée d'Ahi Şeref-üd-din', *First International Congress of Turkish Arts: Communications Presented to the Congress,* Ankara, 1961, pp. 276–8.

Otto-Dorn, Katharina: 'Seldschukische Holzsäulenmoscheen in Kleinasien', *Aus der Welt des Islam, Festschrift für Ernst Kühnel* Berlin, 1959, pp. 59–88.

Otto-Dorn, Katharina: 'Der seldschukische Moscheenbau in Kleinasien', *Institut für Auslands-Beziehungen, Stuttgart, Zeitschrift für Kulturaustausch* 2–3, 1962, pp. 158–63.

Otto-Dorn, Katharina: 'Die Ulu Dschami in Sivrihisar', *Anadolu* IX, 1965, pp. 160–70.

Otto-Dorn, K. and Önder, M.: 'Bericht über die Grabung in Kobadabad', *Archäologischer Anzeiger* 2, 1965.

Önder, M.: 'The excavation at the Kubâdâbâd Palace', *Turkish Art: Seljuk and Ottoman Periods,* Plaistow, 1967, pp. 9–10.

Önder, M.: 'Konya'da Alevî Sultan mescidi ve mihrabı', (The Masjid of Alevi Sultan at Konya and Its Mihrab), *Vakıflar Dergisi* IV, pp. 241–4.

Önder, M.: 'Konya'da Bilinmeyen Bir Selçuklu Devri Eseri', (An Unknown Monument of the Seljuk Period at Konya), *Vakıflar Dergisi* VII, 1968, pp. 127–8.

Öney, Gönül: 'Akşehir Ulu Camisi', (The Great Mosque at Akşehir), *Anadolu* IX, 1965, pp. 171–84.

Öney, Gönül: 'Kayseri'de Hacı Kılıç Camii ve medresesi', (The Hacı Kılıç Mosque and Medrese at Kayseri), *Belleten* XXX, 1966, pp. 377–87.

Önge, Yılmaz: 'Çankırı Hasbey Darüşşifası', (The Hospital of Has Bek at Çankırı), *Vakıflar Dergisi* V, Ankara, 1962.

Özergin, M. K.: 'Anadolu'da Selçuklu Kervansarayları', (Seljuk Caravansarays in Anatolia), *Tarih Dergisi* XV, 1965.

Özgüç, T.: 'A Mengüdjük Türbeh', *First International Congress of Turkish Arts: Communications Presented to the Congress,* Ankara, 1961, pp. 283–4.

Özgüç, T. and Akok, M.: 'Melik-Gazi türbesi ve kalesi', (The Tomb and Citadel of Melik Gazi), *Belleten* XVII, 1953.

Özgüç, T. and Akok, M.: 'Sarı Han', (The Sarı Han), *Belleten* XX, 1956.

Özgüç, T. and Akok, M.: 'Ağzıkara Han', *Yıllık Araştırmalar Dergisi* I, 1957.

Özgüç, T. and Akok, M.: 'Alayhan, Öresun Han ve Hızırilyas Köşkü', *Belleten* XXI, 1957.

Özgüç, T. and Akok, M.: 'Üç Selçuklu âbidesi: Dolay Han, Kesik Köprü Kervansarayı ve Han Camii', (Three Seljuk Monuments, the Dolay Han, the Kesik Köprü Han and the Han Mosque), *Belleten* XXII, 1958.

Özgüç, T. and Akok, M.: 'Afşin yakınındaki Ashabı Kehf Külliyesi', (The Foundation in the name of the Seven Sleepers near Afşin), *Yıllık Araştırmalar Dergisi* II, 1958, pp. 77–87.

Riefstahl, R.: 'New types of Seljuk Hans in Anatolia', *Parnassus* 1/3, 1929, pp. 21–9.

Rogers, J. M.: 'The Çifte Minare Medrese at Erzurum and the Gök Medrese at Sivas', *Anatolian Studies* XV, 1965, pp. 63–85.

Sarre, Friedrich: *Denkmäler persischer Baukunst IV: Die seldschukischen Baudenkmäler von Konia.* Berlin, 1910.

Sarre, Friedrich: *Konia, seldschukische Baudenkmäler.* Berlin, 1921.

Sarre, Friedrich: *Der Kiosk von Konia.* Berlin, 1936.

Sayılı, Aydin and Ruben, Walter: 'Türk Tarih Kurumu adına Kırşehir'de Cacabey medresesinde yapılan araştırmanın ilk kısa raporu', (Preliminary Summary Report on the Researches of the Türk Tarih Kurumu on the Cacabey Medrese at Kırşehir), *Belleten* IX, 1947, pp. 673–91.

Schneider, Gerd.: 'Rekonstruktionen Seldschukischer Moscheen', *I. Ü. Ed. Fak. Sanat Tarihi Yıllığı* II, 1966–8, pp. 134–41.

Sözen, Metin: 'Anadolu'da Eyvan Tipi türbeler', (Iwan Tombs in Anatolia), *Anadolu Sanatı Araştırmaları* I, Istanbul, 1968.

Strzygowski, Josef: 'Der Kiosk von Konia', *Zeitschrift für Geschichte der Architektur* I, 1907, pp. 3–9.

Sümer, Faruk: 'The Seljuk türbehs and tradition of embalming', *II Congresso Internazionale di Arte Turca, Venezia, 1963* Napoli, 1963.

Taeschner, M. F.: 'Die Grosse Moschee (Ulu Cami) in Sinop', *Atti del Secondo Congresso Internazionale d'Arte Turca* Venezia, 1963, pp. 249–52.

Turan, Osman: 'Selçuk Kervansarayları', (Seljuk Caravansarays), *Belleten* 1946, pp. 471–95.

Uğur, M. F. and Ferit, M. M.: *Selçuklu büyüklerinden Celâlettin Karatay ve Kardeşlerinin hayat ve eserleri.* (The Life and Works of the Seljuk Notable Jalāl al-Dīn Karatay and his Brothers.) Konya, 1940.

Ülgen, Ali Saim: 'Siirt Ulu Camisi', (The Great Mosque at Siirt), *Vakıflar Dergisi* V, 1962 pp. 153–5.

Ülgen, Ali Saim: 'Divriği Ulu camisi ve Dar-üş-Şifası', (The Hospital and Great Mosque at Divriği), *Vakıflar Dergisi* V, 1962, pp. 93–8.

Ülkütaşır, M. Şâkir: 'Sinop Selçukîler zamanına ait tarihî eserler', (Monuments of the Seljuk Period at Sinop), *Türk Tarih, Arkeoloji ve Etnografya Dergisi* V, 1949.

Ünver, A. Süheyl: 'Sıvas'ta Birinci Keykâvus hastahanesi, 1217 (614)', (The Hospital of Kaykā'ūs I at Sivas), *Abbotempo* III, Holland, 1965, pp. 24–9.

Ünver, A. Süheyl: *Divriki'de Prenses Turan Malik hastahanesi.* (The Hospital of the Princess Turan Malik at Divriği.) Istanbul, 1934. (Offprint.)

Ünver, A. Süheyl: *Amasya darüşşifası, (1308).* (The Hospital at Amasya.) Istanbul, 1935. (Tedavi Seririyatı ve Laboratuvarı, Vol. 5, No. 17, Offprint.)

Ünver, A. Süheyl: 'Büyük Selçuklu imparatorluğu zamanında vakıf hastahanelerinin bir kısmına dair', (A Type of Endowed Hospital from the Period of the Empire of the Great Seljuks.) *Vakıflar Dergisi* I, Ankara, 1938, pp. 17–23.

Ünver, A. Süheyl: 'Konya'da Ikinci Çift Şerefeli Minare', (The Second Mosque with double 'Şerefe' at Konya), *Konya Mecmuası* 1947, pp. 105–7.

Yalvaç, C.: 'Eski Malatya Ulu camii', (The Great Mosque at Eski Malatya), *Türk Yurdu* Vol. V, No. 5, 1966, pp. 22–9.

Yetkin, Suut Kemal: 'The Twin Minaret Medreseh of Erzurum', *Annales de l'Université d'Ankara* IV, 1954, pp. 255–9.

Yetkin, Suut Kemal: 'Beylikler devri mimarisinin klâsik Osmanlı sanatını hazırlayışı', (Reminiscences of the Architecture of the Beylik Period in Classical Ottoman Art), *Ilâhiyat Fakültesi Dergisi* III–IV, 1955, pp. 39 et seq.

Yetkin, Suut Kemal: 'The Mausoleum of Mama Hatun', *The Burlington Magazine* XCIX, No. 650, 1957; *Yıllık Araştırmalar Dergisi* I, 1957.

Yetkin, Suut Kemal: 'The Turbeh of Gumaç Hatun, a Seljuk Monument', *Ars Orientalis* IV, 1961, pp. 357–60.

Yetkin, Suut Kemal: 'Les caractéristiques des caravanserails seldjoucides', *First International Congress of Turkish Arts: Communications Presented to the Congress* Ankara, 1961, pp. 371–4.

Yetkin, Şerare: 'Anadoluda Selçuklu Şifahaneleri', (Hospitals of the Anatolian Seljuks), *Türk Kültürü* 10, Ankara, 1963.

Yınanç, M. H.: 'Yakutiye Medresesi', (The Yakutiye Medrese), *Tarih Yolunda Erzurum* Nos. 8–9, Erzurum, 1961.

G. *The Turcoman Emirates in Anatolia*

Akçay, I.: 'Yakutiye medresesi', (The Yakutiye Medrese), *Vakıflar Dergisi* VI, 1966, pp. 146–52.

Akok, Mahmut: 'Kastamonu'nun Kasaba köyünde Candaroğlu Mahmut Bey camii', (The Mosque of the Jandarid Mahmud Bek at Kasaba in the Vilayet of Kastamonu), *Belleten* X, 1946, pp. 293–301.

Akok, Mahmut: 'Uşak Ulu camii', (The Great Mosque at Uşak), *Vakıflar Dergisi* III, 1956, pp. 69–72.

Akyurt, Y.: 'Beyşehir Kitabeleri ve Eşrefoğlu Camii ve Türbesi', (Inscriptions at Beyşehir, and the Eshrefoghlu Mosque and Mausoleum), *Türk Tarih, Arkeoloji ve Etnografya Dergisi* IV, 1940.

Arel, Ayda: 'Menteşe Beyliği Devrinde Peçin şehri', (The Town of Peçin in the Period of the Menteşe Emirate), *Anadolu Sanatı Araştırmaları* I, Istanbul, 1968, pp. 69–98.

Arel, Mehlika: Muttaki Karamanoğulları devri Eserleri', (Karamanid Monuments at Mut), *Vakıflar Dergisi* V, 1962, pp. 241–50.

Aslanapa, Oktay: 'Doğu Anadolu'da Karakoyunlu türbeleri', (Karakoyunlu Mausolea in Eastern Anatolia), *Yıllık Araştırmalar Dergisi*, 1956, pp. 105–13.

Diez, Ernst; Aslanapa, Oktay and Koman, Mahmut Mesut: *Karaman devri sanatı.* (Art of the Karaman Period.) Istanbul, 1950.

Kadri (Hafız): 'Menteşe Beyliği asâr-ı kadimesi', (Ancient Monuments of the Emirate of Menteşe), *Tarihi Osmanî Encümeni Mec.* 25, 1914, pp. 57–60.

Kızıltan, Ali: *Anadolu Beyliklerinde cami ve mescitler.* (Mosques and Masjids in the Time of the Anatolian Emirates.) Istanbul, 1958.

Ogan, Aziz: 'Aydın oğullarından Isa Bey camii', (The Aydinid Mosque of 'Isā Bek), *Vakıflar Dergisi* III, Ankara, 1956, pp. 73–81.

Otto-Dorn, Katharina: 'Die Isa Bey Moschee in Ephesus', *Istanbuler Forschungen* XVII, Berlin, 1950, pp. 115–31.

Özgüç, Tahsin: 'Monuments of the Period of Taşkın Paşa's Principality', *First International Congress of Turkish Arts: Communications Presented to the Congress,* Ankara, 1961.

Şakir, M.: *Sinop'ta Candaroğulları zamanına ait tarihî eserler.* (Historical Monuments of the Jandarid Period at Sinop.) Istanbul, 1934.

Sayılı, A.: 'Vâcidiye medresesi', (The Medrese at Vacidiye), *Belleten* No. 12, Ankara, 1948.

Sözen, Metin: 'Oba Pazarı çevresi ve Oba Medresesi', (The Market area and the Medrese at Oba), *Ist. Ü. Ed. Fak. Sanat Tarihi Yıllığı* I, 1964–5, pp. 143–54.

Taeschner, F.: 'Die Türbe der Isfendiyaroğlu in Sinop', *Beiträge zur Kunstgeschichte Asiens, In Memoriam Ernst Diez,* Istanbul, 1963, pp. 31 et seq.

Uzunçarşılı, I. H.: 'Ibrahim Bey'in Karaman imareti', (The Imaret of Ibrāhīm Bek at Karaman), *Belleten* I, 1937.

Ülgen, Ali Saim: 'Niğde'de Akmedrese', (The Ak Medrese at Niğde), *Vakıflar Dergisi* II, 1942, pp. 81–2.

Ülkütaşır, Ş.: 'Sinop'ta Candaroğulları zamanına ait tarihî eserler', (Historical Monuments of the Jandarid Period at Sinop), *Türk Tarih, Arkeoloji ve Etnoğrafya Dergisi* V, 1949, pp. 112–51.

Wulzinger, Karl: 'Die Piruz Bey Moschee in Milâs', *Festschrift der Technischen Hochschule* Karlsruhe, 1925.

H. *Ottomans*

1. General

Anhegger, Robert: 'Beiträge zur frühosmanischen Baugeschichte', *Symbolae in Honorem Zeki Velidi Togan* Istanbul, 1950–5, pp. 301–30.

Anhegger, Robert: 'Zur Stellung einiger Städte innerhalb der osmanischen Baugeschichte vor Sinan', *Mélanges Fuad Köprülü* Istanbul, 1953, pp. 5–16.

Anhegger, Robert: *Beiträge zur frühosmanischen Baugeschichte.* Istanbul, 1953.

Anhegger, Robert: 'Beiträge zur frühosmanischen Baugeschichte II', *Istanbuler Mitteilungen* 8, 1958, pp. 40–56.

Anhegger, Robert: 'Beiträge zur osmanischen Baugeschichte III., Moscheen in Saloniki und Serne. Zur Frage der T-Planmoscheen', *Istanbuler Mitteilungen* 17, 1967, pp. 312–30.

Anon.: 'Islamic Monuments in Yugoslavia', *Islamic Review* XLVI, September, 1958, pp. 22–6.

Aru, Kemal Ahmet: *Türk Hamamları Etüdü.* (A Study of Turkish Hamams.) Istanbul, 1949.

Aslanapa, Oktay: 'Fatih Devri Abideleri', (Monuments of the time of Mehmed the Conqueror), *Türk Sanatı Tarihi Araştırma ve Incelemeleri* 1963, pp. 1–20.

Ayverdi, Ekrem Hakkı: *Fatih devri mimarisi.* (Architecture in the Reign of Mehmed the Conqueror.) Istanbul, 1953.

BIBLIOGRAPHY

Ayverdi, Ekrem Hakkı: 'Yugoslavya'da Türk âbideleri ve vakıfları', (Turkish Monuments and Waqfs in Yugoslavia), *Vakıflar Dergisi* III, Ankara, 1956, pp. 151–223.

Ayverdi, Ekrem Hakkı: 'Orhan Gazi Devrinde mimarî', (Architecture of the Time of Orhan Gazi), *Yıllık Araştırmalar Dergisi* I, 1957, pp. 136 et seq.

Ayverdi, Ekrem Hakkı: *Osmanlı mimarisinin ilk devri 630–805 (1230–1402)*. (The First Period of Ottoman Architecture.) Istanbul, 1966.

Bajraktarević, Fehim: 'Turski spomenici u Ohridu', (Turkish monuments at Ohrid) *Prilozi* V, 1955, pp. 100–32; French summary, pp. 132–4.

Balducci, Hermes: *Architettura Turca in Rodi*. Milano, 1932.

Bejtić, Alija: 'Spomenici Osmanlijske arhitekture u Bosni i Hercegovini', (Monuments of Turkish Architecture in Bosnia and Herzegovina), *Prilozi* III–IV, 1953, pp. 229–97.

Charles, M. A.: 'Hagia Sophia and the Great Imperial Mosques', *Art Bulletin* XII, No. 4, 1930.

Çetintaş, Sedat: *Osmanlı Türk mimarisi*. (Ottoman Turkish Architecture.) (Türk Tarihinin Ana Hatları, II, 5) Ankara, 1934.

Çetintaş, Sedat: *Türk mimari anıtları. Osmanlı Devri*. (Monuments of Turkish Architecture: Ottoman Period.) Istanbul, 1946–52, 2 vols.

Çulpan, Cevdet: Köprülerde tarih köşkleri', (Pavilions Containing Inscriptions on Bridges), *I. Ü. Ed. Fak. Sanat Tarihi Yıllığı* II, 1966–8, pp. 24–35.

Duda, Herbert, W.: *Balkantürkische Studien*. Vienna, 1949.

Eyice, Semavi: 'Istanbul'da bazı cami ve mescid minareleri', (The Minarets of Various Mosques and Masjids at Istanbul), *Türkiyat Mecmuası* X, 1953, pp. 247–68.

Eyice, Semavi: 'Yunanistan'da Türk mimari eserleri I', (Turkish Architecture in Greece), *Türkiyat Mecmuası* XI, 1954, pp. 57–182.

Eyice, Semavi: 'Yunanistan'da Türk mimari eserleri II', (Turkish Architecture in Greece), *Türkiyat Mecmuası* XII, 1955, pp. 205–30.

Eyice, Semavi: 'Cami', *Türk Ansiklopedisi* Part 69, 1957, pp. 255–79.

Eyice, Semavi: 'Iki Türk âbidesinin mahiyeti hakkında notlar. Iznik'te Nilüfer Hatun imareti ve Kayseri'de Köşk Medrese', (Notes on the Characteristics of Two Turkish Monuments, the Imaret of Nilüfer Khatun at Iznik and the Köşk Medrese at Kayseri), *Yıllık Araştırmalar Dergisi* II, 1958, pp. 107–12.

Eyice, Semavi: 'Anadoluda ve Rumelide Türk mescit ve camileri', (Turkish Mosques and Masjids in Anatolia and Rumelia), *Islâm Ansiklopedisi* Vol. VIII, pp. 101–18.

Eyice, Semavi: 'Istanbul minareleri I', (Minarets of Istanbul), *Türk Sanatı Tarihi Araştırma ve Incelemeleri* I, 1963, pp. 31–132.

Eyice, Semavi: 'Ohri'nin Türk devrine ait eserleri', (Monuments at Ohrid from the Turkish Period), *Vakıflar Dergisi* VI, Istanbul, 1965, pp. 137–45.

Eyice, Semavi: 'Anadoluda Türk minareleri', (Anatolian Turkish Minarets), *Islâm Ansiklopedisi* Part 83, pp. 329–35.

Fekete, Louis: 'Souvenirs turcs en Hongrie', *Nouvelle revue de Hongrie*, Budapest, 1943.

Gabriel, Albert: 'Les mosquées de Constantinople', *Syria* VII, 1926, pp. 353–419.

Gerö, Gy.: 'Beiträge zur Geschichte der türkischen Bautätigkeit in Ungarn', *Acta Historiae Artium* XIV/3–4, Budapest, 1968, pp. 235–54.

Glück, Heinrich: *Die Kunst der Osmanen*, Leipzig, 1922.

Glück, Heinrich: 'Osmanlılarda mimarî', (Architecture of the Ottomans), *Hayat Mecmuası* 11, 1927.

Halil Edhem: *Camilerimiz*. (Turkish Mosques.) Istanbul, 1932.

Halil Edhem: *Nos mosquées de Stamboul*. Istanbul, 1934.

Jacobson, A. L.: *Srednevekovy Krym*. (The Mediaeval Crimea.) Moscow, 1964.

Kresevljakovic, Hamdiya: 'Kazandžijski obrt u Bosni i Hercegovini', *Glasnik Zemalskog Muzeja u Sarajevu* N.S. VI, 1951, pp. 191–240.

Kuban, Doğan: *Türk Barok mimarisi hakkında bir deneme*. (A Study of Turkish Baroque Architecture.) Istanbul, 1954.

Kuban, Doğan: 'Influences de l'art européen sur l'architecture ottomane au XVIII ème siècle', *Palladio* (N.S.) V, 1955, pp. 149–57.

Kuban, Doğan: 'Les mosquées à coupole à base hexagonale', *Beiträge zur Kunstgeschichte Asiens, In Memoriam Ernst Diez,* Istanbul, 1963, pp. 35–48.

Kuran, Aptullah: 'Basic Space and Form Concept in Early Ottoman Architecture', *II. Cong. Int. di Arte Turca, Communicazioni,* Venezia, 1963, pp. 71–8.

Kuran, Aptullah: *Ilk devir Osmanlı mimarisinde cami*. (The Mosque in the First Period of Ottoman Architecture.) Ankara, 1964.

Kuran, Aptullah: *The Mosque in Early Ottoman Architecture*. Chicago, 1968.

Mijatev, Petâr: 'Les monuments osmanlis en Bulgarie', *Rocznik Orientalistyczny* XXIII, 1959, pp. 7–28.

Minetti, Henry: *Osmanische provinziale Baukunst auf dem Balkan*. Hanover, 1923.

Parvillé, L.: *Architecture et décoration Turque au XV siècle*. Paris, 1875.

Rasony: *Ortaçağda Erdelde Türklüğün izleri*. (Remains of the Turkish Occupation of Erdel.) Istanbul, 1937.

Rudloff, Hille and Rudloff, O.: 'Die Stadt Plovdiv und ihre Bauten', *Bulletin de l'Institut Archéologique Bulgare* VIII, 1934.

Şehsuvaroğlu, Bedi N.: 'Edirne Fatih devri eserlerine kısa bir bakış ve Sitti Hatun camii', (A Short Account of the Monuments of the Time of Mehmed the Conqueror at Edirne, and the Mosque of Sitti Khatun), *Vakıflar Dergisi* V, 1962, pp. 199–204.

Vogt-Göknil, Ulya: *Türkische Moscheen*, Zürich, 1953.

Vogt-Göknil, Ulya: *Osmanische Bauten,* Munich, 1965.

Zdravković, Ivan: *Le choix des matériaux pour l'étude des monuments de l'architecture islamique en Yougoslavie*. Belgrade, 1964.

2. Buildings

Aga-Oglu, Mehmet: 'Die Gestalt der alten Mohammedije in Konstantinopel und ihr Baumeister', *Belvedere* IX–X, 1926, pp. 82–94.

Aga-Oglu, Mehmet: 'The Fatih Mosque at Constantinople', *The Art Bulletin* XII, 1930, pp. 179–95.

Anhegger, Robert: 'Die Römerbrücke von Mostar', *Oriens* VII, 1954, pp. 87–107.

Anhegger, Robert: 'Eski Fatih Camii meselesi', (The Problem of the Original Mosque of the Conqueror), *Tarih Dergisi* VI, 1954.

Aslanapa, Oktay: 'Iznik'te Sultan Orhan imaret camii kazısı', (Excavations at the Imaret of Sultan Orhan at Iznik), *I. Ü. Ed. Fak. Sanat Tarihi Yıllığı* I, 1964–5, pp. 16–38.

Ayverdi, Ekrem Hakkı: *Hüsrev Paşa Türbesi.* (The Mausoleum of Khusraw Pasha.) Istanbul, 1955.

Ayverdi, Ekrem Hakkı: 'Dimetoka'da Çelebi Sultan Mehmed camii', (The Mosque of Chelebi Sultan Mehmed at Dimetoka), *Vakıflar Dergisi* III, 1956, pp. 13–16.

Ayverdi, Ekrem Hakkı: 'Bursa Orhangazi Camii ve Osmanlı mimarisinin menşei meselesi', (The Mosque of Orhan Ghāzī at Bursa and the Problem of the Origins of Ottoman Architecture), *Vakıflar Dergisi* VI, 1965, pp. 69–85.

Ayverdi, Ekrem Hakkı: 'Ilk Fatih camii hakkında yeni bir vesika', (A New Source Relating to the original Mosque of the Conqueror), *Vakıflar Dergisi* VI, 1965, pp. 63–9.

Baykal, Kâzım: *Bursa Kozahanı ve mescidi.* (The Koza Han at Bursa and its Masjid.) Bursa, 1946.

Baykal, Kâzım: *Bursa'da Ulu Cami.* (The Great Mosque at Bursa.) Istanbul, 1950.

Baykal, Kâzım: *Bursa ve anıtları.* (Bursa and its Monuments.) Bursa, 1950.

Bierbauer, V.: 'Les bains turcs en Hongrie', *Revue Europa* I, Budapest, 1943.

Çetintaş, Sedat: *Saray ve kervansaraylarımız arasında Ibrahim Paşa sarayı.* (Palaces and Caravansarays: the Palace of Ibrahim Pasha.) Istanbul, 1939.

Çetintaş, Sedat: *Türk mimari anıtları, Osmanlı devri Yıldırım darüşşifası.* (Monuments of Turkish Architecture: the Hospital of Yıldırım.) Istanbul, 1952. (Bursa da Hüdavendigâr Murad ve Yıldırım Bayezit binaları eserinden ayrıbasım.) (Off-print from the author's monograph on the buildings of Hüdavendigâr Murad and Yıldırım Bayazid at Bursa.)

Erdmann, Kurt: 'Die Moscheen Istanbuls', *Die Karawane* IV, 1963, pp. 3–12.

Erdoğan, Abdülkadir: *Silivrikapı'da Hadım Ibrahim Paşa camii.* (The Mosque of Khadim Ibrahim Pasha at Silivrikapı.) Istanbul, 1938.

Erdoğan, Muzaffer: 'Son incelemelere göre Fatih camiinin inşası meselesi', (The Problem of the Construction of the Mosque of the Conqueror in the Light of Recent Researches), *Vakıflar Dergisi* V, 1962, pp. 161–92.

Eyice, Semavi: 'Istanbul 'da Koca Mustafa Paşa camii ve onun Osmanlı-Türk mimarisindeki yeri', (The Mosque of Koja Mustafa Pasha at Istanbul and Its Place in Turkish-Ottoman Architecture), *Tarih Dergisi* 8, 1953, pp. 153–82.

Eyice, Semavi: 'Le château des Sept tours et le Mescid de Fatih', *Annual of the arch. Mus. of Istanbul,* Istanbul, 1962, pp. 147–52.

Eyice, Semavi: 'Türk hamamları ve Bayazıt hamamı', (Turkish Baths and the Baths of Bayazid), *Türk Yurdu* 244, 1955, pp. 849–55.

Eyice, Semavi: 'Demirciler ve Fatih Darüşşifasi Mescitleri' (Demirciler and the Masjids of the Fatih Hospital) *Tarih Dergisi,* I, 1950, pp. 358–376.

Eyice, Semavi: 'Demirciler ve Fatih Darüşşifası mescitleri hakkında yeni bazı notlar' (Recent notes on the Demirciler and the masjids of the Fatih Hospital) *Tarih Dergisi* IV, 1954, pp. 358–76.

Eyice, Semavi: 'Istanbul'un kaybolan bir eski eseri: Kazasker Ebu'l-Fazl Mahmud Efendi Medresesi' (The ruined medrese of the Qāḍī ʿAskar Abū'l-Faḍl Maḥmūd Efendi in Istanbul) *Tarih Dergisi* X, 1959, pp. 147–162.

Eyice, Semavi: 'Die Medrese des Kazasker Ebû'l Fazl Mahmud Efendi in Istanbul', *Istanbuler Mitteilungen* VIII, 1958, pp. 57–64.

Eyice, Semavi: 'Kosova 'da Meşhed-i Hüdavendigâr ve Gazi Mestan türbesi', (The Mashhad -i Khudavendigar at Kosova and the Tomb of Ghāzī Mestan), *Tarih Dergisi* XII, 1962, pp. 71–82.

Eyice, Semavi: 'La mosquée-zaviyah de Seyyid Mehmed Dede à Yenişehir', *Beiträge zur Kunstgeschichte Asiens, In Memoriam Ernst Diez,* Istanbul, 1963, pp. 49–69.

Eyice, Semavi: 'Bursa'da Osman ve Orhan Gazi türbeleri', (The Tombs of Osman and Orhan Ghāzī at Bursa), *Vakıflar Dergisi* V, 1962, pp. 131–47.

Eyice, Semavi: 'Atik Ali Paşa camiinin Türk mimari tarihindeki yeri', (The Place of the Atik Ali Pasha Mosque in Turkish Architectural History), *Tarih Dergisi* 19, 1964, pp. 99–114.

Eyice, Semavi: 'Iznikte büyük hamam ve Osmanlı devri hamamları hakkında bir deneme'. (The Great Baths at Iznik and a Study of Ottoman Baths), *Tarih Dergisi* XI, pp. 99–120,

Eyice, Semavi: 'Başçık ile Varna arasında Akyazılı Sultan tekkesi', (The Akyazılı Sultan Tekke Between Başçık and Varna), *Belleten* XXXI, 1967, pp. 551–600.

Eyice, Semavi: 'Yunanistan'da unutulmuş eski bir Türk eseri: Narda'da Faik Paşa camii', (A Forgotten Turkish Monument in Greece, the Fā'iq Pasha Mosque at Narda), *Belgelerle Türk Tarihi Dergisi* I, Vol. 5, February 1968, pp. 67–73.

Eyice, Semavi: 'Les Bedestens dans l'architecture turque', *Atti del II. Cong. Int. di Arte Turca,* pp. 113–117.

Eyice, Semavi: 'Svilengrad'da Mustafa Paşa köprüsü (Cisr-i Mustafa Paşa)', (The Mustafa Pasha Bridge in Svilengrad), *Belleten* XXVIII, 1964, pp. 729–56.

Eyice, Semavi: 'Işkodra'da Kurşunlu Cami', (The Kurşunlu Mosque at Skutari) *Belgelerle Türk Tarihi Dergisi* 17, Istanbul, 1969, pp. 73–6.

Eyice, Semavi: *Galata ve kulesi.* (Galata and its tower.) Istanbul, 1969.

Eyice, Semavi: 'Hanköyü'nde Husrev Paşa camii', (The Husrev Pasha Mosque at Hanköy), XXIII, 1969, pp. 179–204.

Eyice, Semavi: 'Çorum'un Mecidözü'nde Aşık Paşa oğlu Elvan Çelebi zâviyesi', (The *zāwīya* of Elvan Chelebi son of ʿĀshiq Pasha at Mecidözü, Çorum) *Türkiyat Mecmuası* XV, 1969, pp. 211–46.

Eyice, Semavi: 'Elçi Hanı' (The Ambassadors' Han) *Tarih Dergisi* XXIV, 1970, pp. 93–130.

Gabriel, Albert: 'Bursa'da Murad I. camii ve Osmanlı mimarisinin menşei meselesi', (The Mosque of Murad I at Bursa and the Problem of the Origin of Ottoman Architecture), *Vakıflar Dergisi* II, 1942, pp. 37–46.

Gabriel, Albert: *Chateaux Turcs du Bosphore.* Paris, 1943.

Glück, Heinrich: *Die Bäder Konstantinopels.* Vienna, 1921.

Glück, Heinrich: 'Türkische Brunnen in Konstantinopel', *Jahrbuch der Asiatischen Kunst* I, 1924, pp. 26–30.

Güler, Hamza: *Kütahya camileri.* (The Mosques of Kütahya.) Kütahya, 1964.

Halil Edhem: *Topkapı Sarayı.* (The Topkapı Palace.) Istanbul, 1931.

Halil Edhem: *Yedikule Hisarı,* (The Fortress of Yedikule.) Istanbul, 1932.

Hüseyin Ayvansarayi: *Hadikatü'l-cevami.* 2 vols. Istanbul, 1281.

Karahasan, Ponsu: 'Istanbul Sultan Selim camii hakkında', (The Mosque of Sultan Selim at Istanbul), *I. Ü. Ed. Fak. Sanat Tarihi Yıllığı* I, 1964–5, pp. 183–187.

Kepecioğlu, K.: *Bursa hanları.* (The Hans of Bursa.) Bursa, 1935.

Klinghard, Karl: *Türkische Baeder.* Stuttgart, 1927.

Koçu, Reşad Ekrem: *Istanbul Camileri.* (The Mosques of Istanbul.) Vol. I Part I. Istanbul, 1948.

Konyalı, Ibrahim Hakkı: *Istanbul Sarayları.* (The Palaces of Istanbul.) Vol. I. Istanbul, 1942.

Kumbaracılar, Izzet: *Istanbul sebilleri.* (Fountains of Istanbul.) Istanbul, 1938.

Kunter, H. B. and Ülgen, A. S.: 'Fatih camii', (The Mosque of the Conqueror), *Vakıflar Dergisi* I, 1938, pp. 91–103.

Lloyd, S.: 'Old Waterside Houses on the Bosphorus. Safvet Paşa Yalısı at Kanlıca', *Anatolian Studies* 7, 1957, pp. 163–70.

Martiny, G.: 'Die Piale Pascha Moschee', *Ars Islamica* III, 1936, pp. 131–72.

Ogan, Aziz: 'Les fontaines d'Istanbul', *Türkiye Turing ve Otomobil Kurumu Belleteni* 68, 1947.

Orgun, Zarif: 'Boğaziçinde eski bir Türk yalısı', (Old Turkish Yalıs on the Bosphorus), *Arkitekt Mecmuası,* Istanbul, 1939.

Orgun, Zarif: *Tophane çeşmesi.* (The Fountain at Tophane.) Istanbul, 1940. (Arkitekt Neşriyatı: 4.)

Orgun, Zarif: *Çinili Köşk.* (The Çinili Köşk.) Istanbul, 1943. (Arkitekt Neşriyatı II.)

Osman Rıfat; *Edirne Sarayı.* (The Palace of Edirne.) Ankara, 1957.

Öz, Tahsin: 'Sultanahmet camii', (The Mosque of Sultan Ahmed.) *Vakıflar Dergisi* I, 1938, pp. 25–8.

Öz, Tahsin: *Istanbul camileri.* (The Mosques of Istanbul.) Ankara, 1962.

Penzer, N. M.: *The Harem.* London, 1936.

Reynolds, Edwin F.: 'Imperial Mosques at Constantinople', *Architectural Review* XXV–XXVIII, 1909–10.

Riefstahl, Rudolf M.: 'The Selimiyeh in Konya', *Art Bulletin* XII, 1930, pp. 311–18.

Su, Kâmil: *Mimar Sinan'ın eserlerinden Muradiye camii.* (The Muradiye Mosque, One of Sinan's Buildings.) Istanbul, 1940. (Manisa Halkevi Neşriyatı: 7.)

Taeschner, F.: 'Die Yeşil Camii in Brussa', *Der Islam* 20, 1932.

Tanışık, Ibrahim Hilmi: *Istanbul çeşmeleri I.* (Fountains of Istanbul I.) Istanbul, 1943, II, 1945. (Maarif Vekilliği Antikite ve Müzeler Müdürlüğü Yayınları. Seri II, 3.)

Tansuğ, Sezer: '18. yüzyılda Istanbul çeşmeleri ve Ayasofya şadırvanı', (18th Century fountains in Istanbul and the Shadırvan at Aya Sofya), *Vakıflar Dergisi* VI, Istanbul, 1965, pp. 93–111.

Texier, Ch.: 'Fontaine turque à Constantinople', *Revue générale de l'Architecture et des Travaux Publics* I, 1840, cols., 129–33.

Tomsu, Leman: *Bursa evleri.* Istanbul, 1950. (Istanbul, Teknik Üniversite Yayınları.)

Toy, Sidney: 'The Castles of the Bosphorus', *Archaeologia* LXXX, 1930, pp. 215–28.

Uludağ, Osman Şevki: *Haseki darüşşifası.* (The Haseki Hospital.) Istanbul, 1937, pp. 753–760. (Offprint.)

Ülgen, Ali Saim: 'Köprülü konağı', (The Mansion of the Köprülü Family.) *Mel. Köprülü* 1935, pp. 565–80.

Ülgen, Ali Saim: 'Yenicami', (The New Mosque.) *Vakıflar Dergisi* II, 1942.

Ünver, A. Süheyl: *Fatih darüşşifası, 875 (1470).* (The Hospital of Mehmed the Conqueror.) Istanbul, 1932.

Ünver, A. Süheyl: *Edirne Sarayında Kum Kasrı* (The 'Sand Castle' in the Edirne Palace.) Istanbul, 1940. (Arkitekt Neşriyatı, 5.)

Ünver, A. Süheyl: *Edirne Darüşşifası tarihi 891 (1486).* (The Hospital at Edirne Dated 1486.) Istanbul, 1941.

Ünver, A. Süheyl: *Fatih külliyesi ve zamanı ilim hayatı.* (The Foundation of the Conqueror and Contemporary Scientific Life.) Istanbul, 1946. (Istanbul Üniversitesi Yayınları 278.)

Ünver, A. Süheyl: *Edirne Murâdiye câmii.* (The Muradiye Mosque at Edirne.) Istanbul, 1952. (Tege Laboratuarı Yayınları 4.)

Ünver, A. Süheyl: *Anadolu Hisarında Amuca Hüseyin Paşa yalısı.* (The Yalı of Amuja Hüseyin Pasha at Anadolu Hisar.) Istanbul, 1956. (Türkiye Anıtlar Derneği Istanbul Şubesi Yayınlarından No.3.)

Ünver, A. Süheyl and A. Fehmi: *Selçuk Türkleri zamanında Anadolu kaplıcaları.* (The Medicinal Springs of Anatolia in the Seljuk Period.) Istanbul, 1934.

Ünver, A. S. and Pakalın, M. Z.: *Mustafa ve Sultan Cem türbeleri.* (The Tombs of Mustafa and Jem Sultan.) Bursa, 1946.

Yücel, E.: 'Manisa Muradiye Camii ve Külliyesi', (The Muradiye Mosque at Manisa and its Associated Buildings), *Vakıflar Dergisi* VII, Istanbul, 1968.

3. Individual Architects

Akurgal, Ekrem: 'San'at tarihi bakımından Sinan', (Sinan, in the Light of Art-History), *Dil, Tarih, Coğrafya Dergisi* II/3, 1944, pp. 373–384.

Altınay, Ahmet Refik: *Mimar Sinan.* (Sinan the Architect.) Istanbul, 1929.

Altınay, Ahmet Refik: *Türk mimarları.* (Turkish Architects.) Istanbul, 1936.

Altınay, Ahmet Refik: *Türk mimarları (Hazine-i evrak vesikalarına göre).* (Turkish Architects in the Light of Treasury Documents.) Istanbul, 1937.

Anhegger, Robert: 'Probleme der osmanischen Architectur bis Sinan', (Summary) *22. Cong. Or. 1951*, 1957, p. 643.

Babinger, F.: 'Die türkische Renaissance. Bemerkungen zum Schaffen des grossen türkischen Baumeisters Sinân', *Beiträge Zur Kenntnis des Orients* XI, 1914, pp. 67–88.

Corbett, S.: 'Sinan, Architect in Chief to Suleiman the Magnificent', *The Architectural Review* 113, No. 677, May, 1953.

Diez, Ernst: 'Der Baumeister Sinan und sein Werk', *Atlantis* XXV, 1953, pp. 183–6.

Egli, E.: *Sinan. Der Baumeister osmanischer Glanzzeit.* Zürich, 1954.

Glück, Heinrich: 'Neues zur Sinân-Forschung. Die bisherige Forschung über Sinân', *Orientalische Literatur-Zeitung* 29, 1926, cols. 854–8.

Inan, Afet: *Mimar Koca Sinan,* (Sinan the Architect.) Ankara, 1955.

Konyalı, Ibrahim Hakki: *Mimar Koca Sinan'ın eserleri.* (The Works of Sinan.) Istanbul, 1950.

Konyalı, Ibrahim Hakkı: *Fatih'in mimarlarından Azadlı Sinan (Sinan-ı Atik); Vakfiyeleri, eserleri, hayatı ve mezarı.* (Azadlı Sinan, an Architect of Mehmed the Conqueror (Sinan the Elder). Istanbul, 1953.

Kuban, Doğan: 'Mimar Sinan ve Türk mimarisinin klasik çağı', (Sinan and the Classical Age of Turkish Architecture), *Mimarlık* II, Istanbul, 1967, pp. 13–44.

Orgun, Zarif: *Mimar Dalgıç Ahmet.* (The Architect Dalgıch Ahmed.) Istanbul, 1939.

Orgun, Zarif: 'Hassa mimarları', (The Court Architects.) *Arkitekt* XII, Istanbul, 1938, pp. 333–342.

Öz, Tahsin: *Mimar Mehmet Ağa ve risale-i mimariye.* (Mehmed Agha and His Treatise on Architecture.) Istanbul, 1944. (Arkitekt yayınları, 16.)

IV. ARTS AND CRAFTS

A. *General*

Arseven, Celâl Esad: *Les arts décoratifs turcs.* Istanbul, 1952.

Aslanapa, Oktay: 'Täbriser Künstler am Hofe der osmanischen Sultane in Istanbul', *Akten des vierundzwanzigsten internat. Orientalisten-Kongresses, München, 1957*, Wiesbaden, 1959, pp. 344–5.

Aslanapa, Oktay: *Turkish arts: Seljuk and Ottoman carpets, tiles and miniature paintings.* (Trans. Herman Kreider.) Istanbul, 1961.

Aslanapa, Oktay: *Türk sanatı. Selçuklu ve Osmanlı halıları, çini ve minyatür sanatı.* (Turkish original of the above), Istanbul, 1961.

Aslanapa, Oktay: 'Türklerde arma sanatı', (Turkish Weapons), *Türk Kültürü* 16, Ankara, 1964.

Baer, Eva: *Sphinxes and Harpies in Medieval Islamic Art.* Jerusalem, 1965.

Butak, Behzad: *XI., XII., XIII. yüzyıllarda resimli Türk paraları.* (Turkish Coins (10th–13th Centuries) with Figural Decoration.) Istanbul, 1947.

Butak, Behzad: *XI., XII. ve XIII. yüzyıllarda resimli Türk paralarına, ek.,* (Supplement), Istanbul, 1948.

Dimand, M. S.: *A Handbook of Muhammadan Decorative Arts.* New York, 1930.

Esin, Emel: 'The Hunter Prince in Turkish Iconography', *Die Jagd bei den altäischen Völkern, Altäische Forschungen*', Vol. 26, Wiesbaden, 1968, pp. 18–77.

Ettinghausen, Richard: 'Die bildliche Darstellung der Kaʿba im islamischen Kulturkreis.' *Zeitschrift der Deutschen Morgenländischen Gesellschaft* LXXXVII, 1934, pp. 111–37.

Ettinghausen, Richard: '*Studies in Muslim Iconography,*' '*The Unicorn*' Washington, 1950.

Ettinghausen, Richard: 'The "Bevelled Style" in the Post-Samarra Period', 1952, p. 81. *Archaeologia Orientalis, In Memoriam E. Herzfeld,* Ed. by G. C. Miles. New York, 1952, pp. 72–83.

Ettinghausen, Richard: *Art Treasures of Turkey. The Islamic Period.* Washington (D.C.), 1966, pp. 47–66.

Glück, Heinrich: 'Türkische Dekorations-Kunst', *Kunst und Kunsthandwerk* XXIII, 1920, pp. 1–46.

Grube, Ernst; 'Islamic Sculpture, Ceramic Figurines', *Oriental Art* XXIII, No. 3, New Series, Autumn 1966, pp. 165–75.

Halil Edhem and Migeon, Gaston: 'Les collections du vieux Serai à Stamboul', *Syria* XI, 1930, pp. 91–102.

Hancar, F.: 'The Eurasian Animal Style and the Altai Complex', *Artibus Asiae* VI, 1/2.

Hartner, W. and Ettinghausen, Richard: 'The Conquering Lion, the Life Cycle of a Symbol', *Oriens* 17, Leiden, 1964.

Herzfeld, E.: *Der Wandschmuck der Bauten von Samarra und seine Ornamentik,* (*Ausgrabungen von Samarra.* Vol. I.) Berlin, 1923.

Herzfeld, E.: *Die Malereien von Samarra.* Berlin, 1928.

Horvath, T.: *The Art of Asia.* Budapest, 1954.

Kühnel, Ernst: *Islamische Kleinkunst.* Berlin, 1925; 2nd ed. Braunschweig, 1963.

Kühnel, Ernst: *Die Sammlung türkischer und islamischer Kunst im Tschinili Köschk.* Leipzig, 1938.

Kühnel, Ernst: *Die Arabeske, Sinn und Wandlung eines Ornaments.* Wiesbaden, 1949.

Lamm, C. J.: 'Studien über die Weinornamentik in der reifen islamischen Kunst', *Svenska Orientallskapots Arzbok,* 1926–7.

Landau, R.: 'The Arabesque: the Abstract Art of Islam', *The American Academy of Asian Studies,* San Francisco, 1955.

Lechler, G.: 'The Tree of Life in Indo-European and Islamic Cultures', *Ars Islamica* IV, 1937, pp. 369–416.

Meriç, Rıfkı Melûl: *Türk tezyini san'atları ve son üstadlardan altısı.* (Turkish Decorative Arts.) Istanbul, 1937.

Norbert, E.: 'Islamische Sternflechtornamente', *Forschungen und Fortschritte,* Berlin, 1956.

Otto-Dorn, Katharina: 'Osmanische ornamentale Wandmalerei', *Kunst des Orients* I, 1950, pp. 45–54.

Otto-Dorn, Katharina: 'Der Mihrab der Arslan Hane Moschee in Ankara', *Anatolia* I, 1956, pp. 70–75.

Oygar, Ismail Hakkı: 'L'art et l'industrie', *La Turquie Kémaliste* 6, 1935, pp. 16–22.

Ögel, Semra: 'Der Wandel im Programm der Steinornamentik von den seldschukischen zu den osmanischen Bauten', *Anatolica* II, 1968, pp. 103–11.

Önder, Mehmet, *Konya müzesi taş ve ahşap eserler seksiyonu (Inceminare) rehberi.* (Guide to the Stone and Wooden Objects in the Konya (Ince Minare) Museum.) Istanbul, 1962.

Öney, Gönül: 'Anadolu Selçuk sanatında balık figürü, (The Fish Motif in Anatolian Seljuk Art), *I. Ü. Ed. Fak. Sanat Tarihi Yıllığı* II, 1966–8, pp. 142–168.

Öney, Gönül: 'Anadolu Selçuklu sanatında hayat ağacı motifi', (The Tree of Life in the Art of the Anatolian Seljuks), *Belleten* XXXII, 1968, pp. 25–50.

Öz, Tahsin: 'Sultan Ahmet camii tezyinî hususiyetleri', (Decorative Peculiarities of the Mosque of Sultan Ahmed), *Vakıflar Dergisi* I–II, 1938–9, pp. 25–9, 209–13.

Öz, Tahsin: 'Tavanlarımız', (Ceilings), *Güzel Sanatlar Mecmuası* 5, 1944, pp. 29–38.

Öz, Tahsin: *The Topkapi Sarayı Museum. 50 Masterpieces.* Istanbul, 1952.

Öz, Tahsin: *Topkapı sarayında Fatih Sultan Mehmet II. ye ait eserler.* (Objects in the Topkapı Saray Associated with Mehmed the Conqueror.) Ankara, 1953.

Pope, Arthur Upham: '*Architectural Ornament*', in *Survey of Perisan Art* II, London, 1939, pp. 1258–1364.

Pope, Arthur Upham and Ackerman, Phyllis: '*A Survey of Persian Ornament*', in *Survey of Persian Art* III, London, 1939, pp. 2678–765.

Ritter, Hellmut: *Karagöz Türkische Schattenspiele.* Wiesbaden, 1953.

Rostovtzeff, M.: *The Animal Style in Southern Russia and China.* Princeton, 1929.

Sarre, Friedrich: *Seldschukische Kleinkunst.* Berlin, 1909.

Sarre, F. and Martin, F. R.: *Meisterwerke muhammedanischer Kunst.* Munich, 1912.

Soustiel, J.: *L'art Turc, la céramique, les tapis etc.* Paris, 1952.

Sözer, Mihriban: *Sırçalı medrese süslemeleri hakkında,* 640 (1242). (On the Decoration of the Sırçalı Medese at Konya.) Istanbul, 1943. (Arkitekt Neşriyatı 10.)

Strzygowski, Joseph: *Asiens bildende Kunst.* Augsburg, 1930.

Tayanç, Muin Memduh: *Fatih devri güzel sanatları.* (The Fine Arts in the Reign of Mehmed the Conqueror.) Istanbul, 1953.

Tuncay, Rauf: 'Die türkische Dekorations-Kunst im XIII–XVIII Jahrhundert', *Cultura Turcica* Vol. I, No. 2, Ankara, 1964, pp. 274–80.

Türkische Kunst: *Historische Teppiche und Keramik, Eine Ausstellung des deutschen Kunstrates* Darmstadt, 1965.

Ünver, A. Süheyl: 'Türk tezyinatında halkâriye dair', (Turkish Freehand Gilt Book Illuminations.) *Arkitekt* 1938, pp. 301–9.

Ünver, A. Süheyl: 'Les arts décoratifs turcs sous le règne de Fatih', *Türkiye* 2, 1954, pp. 28–33.

Yetkin, Şerare: 'Anadolu Selçuklularının mimari süslemelerinde büyük Selçuklulardan gelen bazı etkiler', (Motifs of Great Seljuk Provenance in Anatolian Seljuk Architectural Decoration), *I. Ü. Ed. Fak. Sanat Tarihi Yıllığı* II, 1966–1968, pp. 36–48.

Zieck, J.: 'Osmanischer Dekorationsstil', *Bustan* 4, Vienna, 1964, pp. 35–46.

B. *Ceramics*

Anhegger, Robert: '*Quellen zur osmanischen Keramik*', in K. Otto-Dorn, *Das islamische Iznik* Berlin, 1941. (Istanbuler Forschungen, 3.)

Aslanapa, Oktay: *Osmanlılar devrinde Kütahya çinileri.* (Kütahya Faience in the Ottoman Period.) Istanbul, 1949.

Aslanapa, Oktay: *Anadoluda Türk çini ve keramik sanatı.* (Ceramic Art of the Anatolian Turks.) Istanbul, 1965.

Aslanapa, Oktay: *Türkische Fliesen und Keramik in Anatolien.* Istanbul, 1965.

Aslanapa, Oktay: 'Antalya müzesinde bulunan Selçuklu çinileri', (Seljuk Tiles in the Antalya Museum,) *Raşit Rahmeti Arat için,* Ankara, 1966.

Brocklebank, R. H. R.: 'Anatolian Faience from Kutiyeh', *Burlington Magazine* LX, 1932, pp. 246–52.

Dayıgil, Feyzullah: 'Istanbul çinilerinde lâle', (The Tulip in the Tiles of Istanbul), *Vakıflar Dergisi* II, 1942, pp. 223–233.

Dayıgil, Feyzullah: articles: 'Türk çiniciliği', (Turkish ceramics); 'Çini', (ceramics) in *Islâm Ansiklopedisi* Vol.3, 1945, pp. 430–5.

Dussaud, R.: 'La faïence de Damas', *Syria* XVIII, 1937.

Erdmann, Kurt: 'Noch einmal die Scherben von Kalehisar', *Istanbuler Mitteilungen* 8, 1958, pp. 142–3.

Erdmann, Kurt: 'Die Fliesen am Sünnet Odası des Topkapı Saray in Istanbul', *Aus der Welt des Islam, Festschrift für Ernst Kühnel* Berlin, 1959, pp. 144–53.

Erdmann, Kurt: 'Ka'ba Fliesen', *Ars Orientalis* III, 1959, pp. 193–7.

Erdmann, Kurt: 'Neue Arbeiten zur türkischen Keramik', *Ars Orientalis* V, 1963, pp. 191–219.

Frantz, Alison: 'Turkish Pottery from the Agora', *Hesperia. Journal of the American School of Classical Studies* XI, 1942, pp. 1–28.

Hobson, R. L.: *Guide to the Islamic Pottery of the Near East.* London, 1932.

Izzet Hakkı: 'Caractéristiques techniques de la manufacture de faïences anatoliennes non étudies à ce jour', *First International Congress of Turkish Arts: Communications Presented to the Congress,* Ankara, 1961, pp. 210–12.

Jakobsen: *Islamische Keramik.* Hamburg, 1959.

Kiefer, Charles: 'Les céramiques musulmanes d'Anatolie', *Cahiers de la Céramique* 4, 1956, pp. 15–30.

Kiefer, Charles: 'Les céramiques silicieuses d'Anatolie et du Moyen Orient', *Bulletin de la Société française de Céramique* 30, 1956, pp. 3–24; 31, 1956, pp. 17–34.

Koechlin, R.: *La céramique.* Paris, 1928. (*Musée des arts décoratifs, l'art de l'Islam.*)

Migeon, Gaston: *Islamische Kunstwerke.* Berlin, 1928.

Lane, Arthur: 'Turkish Peasant Pottery from Chanak and Kutahia', *The Connoisseur* CIV, 1939, pp. 232–37.

Lane, Arthur: *Early Islamic Pottery.* London, 1947.

Lane, Arthur: *Guide to the Collection of Tiles.* (Victoria and Albert Museum.) London, 1957.

Lane, Arthur: 'The Ottoman Pottery of Isnik', *Ars Orientalis* II, 1957, pp. 247–81.

Lane, Arthur: *Later Islamic Pottery (Persia, Syria, Egypt, Turkey)* London, 1957.

Lucius, Ervin: 'Neue verzierte seldschukische Keramik aus Anatolien', *I. Ü. Ed. Fak. Sanat Tarihi Yıllığı* II, 1966–8, pp. 122–33.

Martin, F. R.: 'The True Origin of So-Called Damascus Ware', *Burlington Magazine* XV, 1909, pp. 29.

Maysuradze: *Keramika Afrasiyaba.* (Ceramics of Afrasiyab.) Tbilisi, 1958.

Meinecke, M.: 'Die Keramiköfen von Afrāsiāb—Samarkand', *Westtürkestan Referate zur Türkologischen Exkursion 1966* Vol. 1, Hamburg, 1968, pp. 81–9.

Meinecke, M.: 'Mnhammed b. Mnhammed b. Utmān al-Bannā' at-Tūsī. Eine Fayencedekor-Werkstätte des 13. Jahrhunderts in Konya', *Türk Etnografya Dergisi* XI, 1968, pp. 75–93.

Migeon, Gaston and Sakisian, A.: 'Les faïences d'Asie-Mineure du XIIIe au XVIIIe siècle', *Revue de l'Art Ancien et Moderne* XLIII, 1923, pp. 241–52, 353–64; XLIV, 1923, pp. 125–41.

Mohammed Mostafa: 'La céramique d'Anatolie', *La Femme Nouvelle* 2, Cairo, 1947.

Mohammed Mostafa: 'Isnik Ceramics', *Egypt Travel Magazine* No. 6, January, 1955, pp. 20–25.

Oral, Zeki: 'Kubadabad çinileri', (Pottery from Kubādābād), *Belleten* XVII, Ankara, 1963.

Otto-Dorn, Katharina: *Türkische Keramik.* Ankara, 1957.

Oygar, I. H.: 'Les origines de la céramique Seldjoukide et Ottomane', *Türk Sanatı Tarihi, Araştırma ve Incelemeleri,* Istanbul, 1963, pp. 583–606.

Önder, Mehmet: *Konya müzesi çini eserler seksiyonu (Karatay Medresesi) rehberi.* (Guide to the Department of Ceramics in the Konya Museum (Büyük Karatay Medrese).) Istanbul, 1961.

Önder, Mehmet: 'Kubâd-âbâd Sarayları kazılarında yeni bulunan resimli dört çini', (Four Tiles with Figural Decoration Recently Found in Excavations at the Palace of Kubād-ābād), *I. Ü. Ed. Fak. Sanat Tarihi Yıllığı* II, 1966–68, pp. 116–21.

Öz, Tahsin: 'Les faïences Turques', *Transactions of the Oriental Ceramics Society,* London, 1933–4.

Öz, Tahsin: 'En nadir Türk çinileri', (The Rarest Turkish Ceramics), *Türk Tarih, Arkeoloji, Etnografya Dergisi* IV, 1940, pp. 131–8.

Öz, Tahsin: 'Çinilerimiz', (Turkish Ceramics), *Güzel Sanatlar Dergisi* 2, 1940.

Öz, Tahsin: *Turkish Ceramics.* Ankara, 1957.

Paker, Mükerrem: 'Anadolu Beylikler Devri Keramik sanatı', (Ceramic Art of the Period of the Turkoman Emirates), *I. Ü. Ed. Fak. Sanat Tarihi Yıllığı* I, 1964–5, pp. 155–182.

Poulsen, Vagn: *Tyrkisk Keramik I. C. L.,* København, 1958.

Rackham, Bernard: 'Turkish Pottery', *Transactions of the Oriental Ceramics Society 1934–5,* London, 1936, pp. 35–48.

Raymond, Alexandre M.: *Alttürkische Keramik in Kleinasien und Konstantinopel.* Munich, 1922.

Riefstahl, Rudolf M.: 'Early Turkish Tile Revetments in Edirne', *Ars Islamica* IV, 1937, pp. 249–81.

Sakisian, A.: 'Les questions de Kotāhya et de Damas dans la céramique de Turquie', *Journal Asiatique* CCXXVIII, 1936, pp. 257–79.

Sakisian, A.: 'Les faïences du bain de Selim II, au Harem du vieux Serail', *Mélanges Syriens offerts a Monsieur R. Dussaud. Bibliothèque Archéologique et Historique* XXX, Paris, 1939.

Sarre, Friedrich: *Die Keramik von Samarra.* Berlin, 1925. (Die Ausgrabungen von Samarra, 2.)

Sarre, Friedrich: 'The Seljuq and Early Osmanli Pottery of Miletus', *Transactions of the Oriental Ceramics Society 1930–1*, pp. 20–3.

Sarre, Friedrich: 'Die Fayencen von Nicaea und ihr Export nach dem Abendland', *Pantheon* XXIV, 1939, pp.341–5.

Scerrato, U.: 'Islamic Glazed Tiles with Moulded Decoration from Ghazni', *East and West* 13, 1962.

Schmidt, I. H.: *Islamische Baukeramik.* Berlin, 1933.

Shelkovnikov, B. Alexandrovich: *Polivnaya keramika iz raskopok goroda Ani.* (Glazed Pottery from the Ani Excavations.) Erevan, 1957.

Soustiel, J.: 'Le décoration "aux quatre fleurs" des céramiques turques', *Faenza* 39, 1953.

Staude, W.: 'Le caractère Turc dans l'ornamentation des fayences Osmanlies', *Syria* XV, 1934.

Tamer, Hadi H.: 'Quelques analyses, observations et comparaisons à propos de la technique et de la composition des faïences turques', *First International Congress of Turkish Arts: Communications Presented to the Congress,* Ankara, 1961, pp. 320–9.

Ünver, A. Süheyl: *Yeşil türbe mihrabı.* (The Mihrab of the Green Tomb at Bursa.) Istanbul, 1951.

Wilber, D. N.: 'The Development of Mosaic Faience in Islamic Architecture in Iran', *Ars Islamica* VI/1, 1939, pp. 16–47.

Yatman, Nurettin: *Eski Türk çinileri.* (Ancient Turkish Ceramics.) Ankara, 1942.

Yetkin, Şerare: 'Türk çini sanatında bazı önemli örnekler ve teknikler', (Some Important Patterns and Techniques in Turkish Pottery), *I. Ü. Ed. Fak. Sanat Tarihi Yıllığı* I, 1965, pp. 60–102.

C. *Rugs*

Beattie, May H.: 'Antique Rugs at Hardwick Hall', *Oriental Art* V, 1959, pp. 52–61.

Beattie, May H.: 'Britain and the Oriental Carpet', *Leeds Arts Calendar* No. 55, 1964, pp. 4–15.

Bell, Hamilton and Riefstahl, Rudolf M.: *Special Loan Exhibition of Carpets and Other Textiles from Asia Minor.* Philadelphia, 1919.

Bellinger, Louisa: *Cairene Rugs and Others Technically Related. 15th–17th centuries.* Washington (D.C.), 1957. (The Textile Museum: Catalogue raisonné.)

Bidder, Hans: *Carpets from Eastern Turkestan Known as Khotan, Samarkand and Kansu Carpets.* London, 1964.

BIBLIOGRAPHY

Bode, von W. and Kühnel, Ernst: *Vorderasiatische Knüpfteppiche aus alter Zeit.* Leipzig, 1914, Leipzig, 1922; Braunschweig, 1955.

Ellis, Ch. G.: 'A Soumak-woven Rug in a 15th Century Style', *Textile Museum Journal* Vol. 1, No. 2, Washington, Dec. 1963, pp. 3–21.

Erdmann, K.: 'Ein neuerworbener Holbeinteppich', *Berliner Museen* LI, 1930, pp. 140–5.

Erdmann, Kurt: *Ausstellung Orient-Teppiche.* Hamburg, 1950.

Erdmann, Kurt: 'Zu einem anatolischen Teppich fragment aus Fostat', *Istanbuler Mitteilungen* 6, 1955, pp. 42–52.

Erdmann, Kurt: *Der orientalische Knüpfteppich.* Tübingen, 1955, 1960, 1965.

Erdmann, Kurt: *Der Türkische Teppich des 15. Jahrhunderts* (15. asır Türk halısı. Trans. H. Taner). Istanbul, 1957.

Erdmann, Kurt: 'Neuere Untersuchungen zur Frage der Kairener Teppiche', *Ars Orientalis* IV, 1961, pp. 65–105.

Erdmann, Kurt: *Europa und der Orientteppich.* Berlin–Leipzig, 1962.

Erdmann, Kurt: *Oriental Carpets. An Essay on Their History.* (Trans. Charles Grant Ellis.) New York, 1962.

Erdmann, Kurt: *Siebenhundert Jahre Orientteppich.* Wiesbaden, 1966.

Erdmann, Kurt: 'Weniger bekannte Uschak-Muster', *Kunst des Orients* IV, pp. 79–97.

Ettinghausen, Richard: 'New Light on Early Animal Carpets', *Aus der Welt der Islamischen Kunst, Festschrift für Ernst Kühnel,* Berlin, 1959, pp. 93–116.

Hein, Wilhelm: 'Türkische Mihrabteppiche', *Alte und Moderne Kunst* III, No. 3, 1958, pp. 23–5.

Işilksaçan, Güngör: *Batı Anadolu halılarının desen ve kaliteleri.* (Designs and Qualities of Western Anatolian Carpets.) Izmir, 1964.

Kühnel, Ernst: *Cairene Rugs* (*Textile Museum*). Washington, 1957.

Lamm, Carl Johan: 'The Marby Rug and Some Fragments of Carpets Found in Egypt', *Orientallskapets Arsbok* 1937, pp. 51–130.

McMullan, Joseph V.: *Islamic Carpets.* (Foreword by Ernst J. Grube.) New York, 1965.

Mohammed Mostafa: *Turkish Prayer Rugs.* Cairo, 1953.

Özbel, Kenan: *Anadolu seccadeleri.* (Anatolian Carpets.) Ankara, 1949.

Riefstahl, Rudolf M.: 'Turkish "Bird" Rugs and Their Design', *The Art Bulletin* VII, 1925, pp. 91–5.

Riefstahl, Rudolf M.: 'Some Travel Notes on Turkish Rugs', *Good Furniture Magazine* XXVI, 1926, pp. 13–20.

Riefstahl, Rudolf M.: 'Primitive Rugs of the "Konya" Type in the Mosque of Beyşehir', *The Art Bulletin* XIII, 1931, pp. 177–220.

Sarre, Friedrich: 'The Hittite Monument of Ivriz and a Carpet Design of Asia Minor', *Burlington Magazine* XIV, 1908, pp. 143–7.

Sarre, F. and Trenkwald, H.: *Altorientalische Teppiche.* Vol. I, Vienna—Leipzig, 1926; Vol. II, Vienna—Leipzig, 1928.

Schmutzler, Emil, *Altorientalische Teppiche aus Siebenbürgen.* Leipzig, 1933.

Vegh, J. de and Layer, Ch.: *Tapis Turcs provenant des églises et collections de Transylvanie.* Paris, 1925.

Yetkin, Şerare: 'Yurdumuzdaki müzeler ve camilerde bulunan değerli halılar', (Important Carpets in Turkish Mosques and Museums), *Türk Kültürü* 4, 1963, pp. 21–8.

Yetkin, Şerare: 'Istanbul Türk ve Islam Eserleri Müzesinde bulunan bazı halılar ve rönesans ressamlarının eserleri', (A Number of Carpets in the Museum of Turkish and Islamic Art at Istanbul and the Works of Renaissance Painters), *Türk Kültürü Araştırmaları* 2, Ankara, 1964, pp. 208–22.

Zieck, Johanna: 'Eine Gruppe von Gebetsteppichen und ihre Datierung', *Berliner Museen* N.F. Vol. III, No. 11, 1962, pp. 6–14.

D. *Textiles*

Ahmad Ali Kohzad: 'Uniformes et armes des gardes des sultans de Ghazna', *Afghanistan* 1951, No. 1, pp. 48–53.

Celâl, Melek: *Türk işlemeleri.* (Turkish Embroideries.) Istanbul, 1939.

Corina, Nicolescu: 'Quelques tissus orientaux dans les collections Roumaines', *Centre d'études des textiles anciens* 29, Lyon, Jan. 1969, pp. 27–31; English summary pp. 32–5.

Dietrich, Bernhard: *Kleinasiatische Stickereien.* Plauen i. V., 1911.

Ettinghausen, Richard: 'An Early Ottoman Textile', *First International Congress of Turkish Arts: Communications Presented to the Congress,* Ankara, 1961, pp. 134–41.

Öz, Tahsin: 'La broderie turque', *La Turquie Kémaliste* 44, 1941, pp. 9–16.

Öz, Tahsin: *Turkish Textiles and Velvets, XIV–XVI Centuries.* Ankara, 1950.

Öz, Tahsin: *Türk Kumaş ve kadifeleri II. XVII–XIX. yüzyıl ve kumaş süslemesi.* (Turkish Textiles and Velvets, 17th–19th Centuries, and their Patterns.) (Table of contents and list of reproductions in English, French and German.) Istanbul, 1951.

Özbel, Kenan: *El sanatları* (Minor Arts.) Fasc. 1–16, Ankara, 1945–49.

Palotay, G. von: 'Turkish Embroideries', *CIBA Review* No. 102, Basel, 1954, pp. 3661–87.

Şehsuvaroğlu, Halûk: 'Les costumes de Mehmet le Conquérant', *Türkiye* No. 2, 1954, pp. 38–44.

Wace, A. J. B. and Tattersall, C. E. C.: *Brief Guide to the Turkish Woven Fabrics.* (Victoria and Albert Museum.) London, 1931.

Yatman, Nurettin: *Türk kumaşları.* (Turkish Textiles.) Ankara, 1945.

Yetkin, Şerare: 'Zwei türkische Kilims', *Beiträge zur Kunstgeschichte Asiens, In Memoriam Ernst Diez,* Istanbul, 1963, pp. 182–92.

E. *Miniatures and Painting*

Adıvar, A. Adnan: *La science chez les Turcs Ottomans.* Paris, 1939.

Ahmet, Tevhit: '*Hünername*', (The Book of Accomplishments), *Tarih-i Osmani Encümeni Mecmuası* 2/1, Istanbul, 1328, p. 103.

Akalay, Zeren: 'Tarihî konuda ilk Osmanlı minyatürleri', (The Historical Place of the Earliest Ottoman Miniatures), *I. Ü. Ed. Fak. Sanat Tarihi Yıllığı* II, 1966–8, pp. 102–15.

BIBLIOGRAPHY

Ali, Gelibolulu: *Künhülahbar.* Ist. Üniversite Library MS. 5959, Istanbul, 1277.

Anafarta, Nigâr: *Hünernâme minyatürleri ve sanatçıları.* (The Miniatures and Artists of the Hünername). Istanbul, 1969.

And, Metin: *Kırk gün kırk gece.* (Forty Days and Forty Nights.) Istanbul, 1959.

Anon.: 'A Miniature of the Turkish School', *Rupam* No. 31, July, 1927, p. 95.

Arnold, T. and Grohmann, W.: *The Islamic Book.* Florence–Paris, 1929.

Arnold, T. W.: *The Court Painters of the Grand Mongols.* Oxford, 1921.

Arnold, T. W.: *Painting in Islam*, Oxford, 1928; New York, 1965.

Arseven, Celâl Esad: Article: 'Minyatür', *Sanat Ansiklopedisi* Vol. III, Istanbul, 1950, pp. 1415–27.

Aslanapa, Oktay: 'Türkische Miniaturmalerei am Hofe des Eroberers in Istanbul', *Ars Orientalis* I, 1954, pp. 77–84.

Atasoy, Nurhan: 'Türk minyatüründe tarihî gerçekçilik', (Verisimilitude in the Turkish Miniature), *I. Ü. Ed. Fak. Sanat Tarihi Yıllığı* I, 1964–5, pp. 103–9.

Atasoy, Nurhan: '1510 tarihli Memlûk şehnamesinin minyatürleri', (The Miniatures of a Mamluk Shāhnāme Dated 1510), *I. Ü. Ed. Fak. Sanat Tarihi Yıllığı* II, 1966–8, pp. 49–69.

Baer, Eva: 'Representations of Planet-Children in Turkish Manuscripts', *Bulletin of the School of Oriental and African Studies* XXXI/3, London, 1968, pp. 526–33.

Berk, Nurullah: 'Türkiyede resim', (Painting in Turkey), *Güzel Sanatlar Mecmuası* I, 1939.

Berk, Nurullah: *La peinture Turque.* Ankara, 1950.

Blausteiner, Kurt: 'Die Ausstellung "Türkische Kunst aus sieben Jahrhunderten" in der Wiener Secession', *Belvedere* XI, 1932, pp. 78–80.

Blausteiner, Kurt: 'Beispiele osmanischer Buchkunst aus der Zeit Sultan Selims II. und Sultan Murads III', *Wiener Beiträge zur Kunst- und Kulturgeschichte Asiens* X, 1936, pp. 34–55.

Blochet, E.: *Peintures de manuscrits arabes, persans et turcs de la Bibliothèque Nationale.* Paris, 1910.

Blochet, E.: *Les peintures des manuscrits orientaux de la Bibliothèque Nationale.* Paris, 1914–20.

Blochet, E.: *Catalogue des manuscrits turcs.* Paris, 1922–3.

Blochet, E.: *Les enluminures des manuscrits orientaux turcs, arabes, persans de la Bibliothèque Nationale.* Paris, 1926.

Blochet, E.: 'Mazdeism'in Türk kavimlerinin itikatları üzerindeki tesiri', (Trans. M. F. Köprülü), (The Influence of Mazdeism on the Beliefs of the Turkish Tribes), *Milli Tetebbular Mecmuası* Mart-Nisan 1331, pp. 273–305.

Blochet, E.: *Catalogue des manuscrits turcs de la Bibliothèque Nationale de Paris.* Paris, 1932.

Brockelmann, C.: *Verzeichnis der arabischen, persischen, türkischen und hebräischen Handschriften der Stadtbibliothek zu Breslau.* Breslau, 1903.

Brockelmann, C.: *Catalog der orientalischen Handschriften der Stadtbibliothek zu Hamburg.* Hamburg, 1908.

Bussagli, Mario: *Die Malerei in Zentralasien.* Genève, 1963.

Cochran, Alex Smith: *A Catalogue of the Collection of Persian Manuscripts, Including Also Some Turkish and Arabic, Presented to the Metropolitan Museum of Art.* New York, 1914.

BIBLIOGRAPHY

Coomaraswamy, Ananda K.: 'Miniatures from Turkish and Persian Books of Fables', *Bulletin of the (Boston) Museum of Fine Arts* XXVI, 1928, pp. 89–91.

Creswell, K. A. C.: *A Bibliography of Painting in Islam*. Cairo, 1953.

Çığ, Kemal: 'Türk ve Islam Eserleri Müzesindeki minyatürlü kitapların kataloğu', (Catalogue of the Illustrated Manuscripts in the Museum of Turkish and Islamic Art at Istanbul), *Şarkiyat Mecmuası* III, 1959, pp. 50–90.

Diez, Ernst: 'Maler der Steppe', *First International Congress of Turkish Arts: Communications Presented to the Congress*, Ankara, 1961, pp. 94–101.

Dimand, M. S.: 'Turkish Art of the Muhammadan Period', *Bulletin of the Metropolitan Museum of Art* New Series II, 1944, pp. 211–17.

Dimand, M. S.: *A Handbook of Muhammadan art*. New York, 1947, 3rd ed. 1958.

Edhem, H. and Migeon, Gaston: 'Les collections du Vieux Serai à Stamboul', *Syria* XI, 1930.

Edhem, H. and Sachau, E.: *Catalogue of Persian, Turkish, Hindustani and Pushahamu Scripts in the Bodleian Library*. Oxford, 1890.

Esin, Emel: *Turkish Miniature Painting*. Tokyo, 1960.

Esin, Emel: 'Quelques aspects des influences de l'art des anciens nomades eurasiens et de l'art du Turkestan pré-islamique sur les arts plastiques et picturaux turcs', *First International Congress of Turkish Arts: Communications Presented to the Congress*, Ankara, 1941, pp. 102–28.

Esin, Emel: 'Selçuk devrine ait bir Anadolu yazması', (An Anatolian Manuscript of the Seljuk Period), *Türk Sanatı Tarihi Araştırma ve incelemeleri* I, Istanbul, 1963, pp. 561–74.

Esin, Emel: 'An Angel Figure in the Miscellany Album H. 2152 of Topkapı', *Beiträge zur Kunstgeschichte Asiens, In Memoriam Ernst Diez*, Istanbul, 1963, pp. 264–82.

Ettinghausen, Richard: 'Some Paintings in Four Istanbul Albums', *Ars Orientalis* I, 1954, pp. 91–105.

Ettinghausen, Richard: 'Chinese Representations of Central Asian Turks', *Beiträge zur Kunstgeschichte Asiens, In Memoriam Ernst Diez*, Istanbul, 1963, pp. 208–22.

Ettinghausen, Richard: *Turkish Miniatures from the Thirteenth to the Eighteenth Century*. New York, 1965.

Ettinghausen, Richard: *Arab Painting*. Skira, 1962.

Gabriel, Albert: 'Les étapes d'une campagne dans les deux 'Irak d'après un manuscrit turc du XVIe siècle', *Syria* IX, 1928, pp. 328–49.

Gray, Basil: 'Two Portraits of Mehmet II', *Burlington Magazine* LXI, 1932, pp. 4–6.

Gray, Basil: *Persian Painting*. Skira, 1961.

Gray, Basil: 'Unpublished Miniatures from Illuminated Turkish Manuscripts in the British Museum', *First International Congress of Turkish Arts: Communications Presented to the Congress*, Ankara, 1961, pp. 144–9.

Grube, Ernst: 'A School of Turkish Miniature Painting', *First International Congress of Turkish Arts: Communications Presented to the Congress*, Ankara, 1941, pp. 176–209.

BIBLIOGRAPHY

Grube, Ernst: 'Miniatures in Istanbul Libraries', *Pantheon* III, 1962.

Grube, Ernst: *The Classical Style in Islamic Painting*. Germany, 1968.

Ipşiroğlu, Mazhar Ş.: 'Das Buch der Feste', *Du (Zürich)* 23, 1963, pp. 57–89.

Ipşiroğlu, Mazhar Ş.: 'Das Hochzeitsbuch Murats III', '*Deutsch-Türkische Gesellschaft*' Bonn, 3, 4 June, 1960.

Ipşiroğlu, Mazhar Ş. and Eyüboğlu, S.: *Fatih Albumuna bir bakış, Sur l'Album du Conquérant*. Istanbul, 1955.

Ipşiroğlu, Mazhar Ş. and Eyüboğlu, S.: 'Ein Beitrag zur türkischen Malerei im 15. Jahrhundert. Sultan Mehmet II und seine Zeit. Das Album des Eroberers. Üstad Mehmed Siyah Kalem, genannt "Die Schwarze Feder" ', *Du (Zürich)* Vol. 19, 1959, pp. 8–36.

Ipşiroğlu, Mazhar Ş. and Eyüboğlu, S.: *Turkey. Ancient Miniatures*. (Preface by Richard Ettinghausen.) New York, 1961.

Kappert, Petra: 'Innenräume, dargestellt auf timuridischen und spaeteren Miniaturen' *Westtürkestan Referate zur Türkologischen Exkursion 1966* Vol. 1, Hamburg, 1968, pp. 63–80.

Karabacek, J. von: *Abendländische Künstler zu Konstantinopel im XV. und XVI. Jahrhundert: Italienische Künstler am Hofe Muhammeds II des Eroberers. 1451–1481*. Vienna, 1918. (Kaiserl. Ak. der Wiss. in Wien, Philos.-Hist. Kl., Denkschriften 62/1.)

Karatay, Fehmi Ethem: *Topkapı Sarayı Müzesi Türkçe yazmaları kataloğu*. (Catalogue of the Turkish MSS. in the Topkapı Saray Museum.) Istanbul, 1961.

Karatay, Fehmi Ethem and Stchoukine, Ivan: *Les manuscrits orientaux illustrés de la Bibliothèque de l'Université de Stamboul*. Paris, 1933. (Mémoires de l'Institut Français d'Archéologie de Stamboul, I.)

Kühnel, Ernst: *Doğu islam memleketlerinde minyatür*. (The Miniature in the Eastern Lands of Islam.) (Trans. S. K. Yetkin and M. Özgü.) Ankara, 1952.

Kühnel, Ernst: 'Der türkische Stil in der Miniaturmalerei des 15. und 16. Jahrhunderts', *First International Congress of Turkish Arts: Communications Presented to the Congress*, Ankara, 1961, pp. 246–50.

Kühnel, Ernst: *Miniaturmalerei im islamischen Orient*. Berlin, 1922.

Lamm, C. J.: 'Miniatures from the Reign of Bayazid II. in a Manuscript Belonging to the Uppsala University Library', *Orientalia Suecana* I/3–4, 1952, pp. 95–114.

Loehr, Max: 'The Chinese Elements in the Istanbul Miniatures', *Ars Orientalis* I, 1954.

Martin, F. R.: 'A Portrait by Gentile Bellini Found in Constantinople', *Burlington Magazine* IX, 1906, pp. 148–9.

Martin, F. R.: 'New Originals and Oriental Copies of Gentile Bellini Found in the East', *Burlington Magazine* XVII, 1910, pp. 5–6.

Martin, F. R.: *The Miniature Painting and Painters of Persia, India and Turkey from the 8th to the 18th century*. London, 1912.

Martinovitch, Nicholas N.: 'The Funeral of Sultan Murad III. of Turkey', *The Art Bulletin* X, pp. 263–5.

BIBLIOGRAPHY

Meredith-Owens, G. M.: *Turkish Miniatures.* (The British Museum.) London, 1963.

Meriç, Rıfkı Meriç: *Türk nakış sanatı tarihi araştırmaları, Vesikalar I.* (Researches on the History of Decorative Painting in Turkey, Documents I.) Ankara, 1953.

Miller, Barnette: *The Palace School of Muhammad the Conqueror.* Cambridge, 1941.

Minorsky, V. and Wilkinson, J. V. S.: *The Chester Beatty Library. A Catalogue of the Turkish Manuscripts and Miniatures.* Dublin, 1958.

Ögel, Bahaeddin: 'Topkapı Sarayı Müzesinde bulunan iki minyatür albumu hakkında notlar', (Notes on Two Albums in the Topkapı Saray Museum), *Tarih Vesikaları Dergisi* I, 1955, pp. 135–40.

Öğütmen, Filiz: *XII–XVIII yüzyıllar arasında minyatür sanatından örnekler* (*Topkapı Sarayı Minyatür Bölümü rehberi*). (Examples of the Art of the Miniature 12th–18th Centuries.) Istanbul, 1966.

Öz, Tahsin: 'Barbarosun otantik resmi', (An Authentic Portrait of Barbarossa), *Türk Tarih, Arkeologya ve Etnografya Dergisi* III, 1936, pp. 155–8.

Öz, Tahsin: 'Hünername I', (The Book of Accomplishments), *Journal of the Palestine Oriental Society* 18, Jerusalem, 1938, pp. 67–171.

Öz, Tahsin: 'Türk el işlemeleri ve resim dairesi', (Turkish Handicrafts and Picture Frames), *Güzel Sanatlar Mecmuası* 4, Istanbul, 1942, pp. 29–52.

Öz, Tahsin: 'Türk minyatür kaynaklarına bir bakış', (A Glance at the Origins of the Turkish Miniature), *Ilâhiyat Fakültesi Dergisi* I, 1952.

Öz, Tahsin: *Topkapı Sarayında Fatih Sultan Mehmet II. ye ait eserler.* (Objects in the Topkapı Saray Relating to Mehmed the Conqueror.) Ankara, 1953.

Pertsch, W.: *Catalogue des manuscrits Turcs.* Vienna, 1864.

Rieu, C.: *Catalogue of the Turkish manuscripts in the British Museum.* London, 1888.

Sakisian, Armenag: 'The Portrait of Mehmed II', *Burlington Magazine* LXXIV, 1939, pp. 172–81.

Sakisian, A.: 'Turkish Miniatures', *Burlington Magazine* LXXXII, 1945, pp. 224–32.

Sarre, Friedrich: 'Eine Miniatur Gentile Bellinis gemalt 1479–1480 in Konstantinopel', *Jahrbuch der K. Preussischen Kunstsammlungen* XXVII, 1906, pp. 302–6.

Sarre, Friedrich: 'The Miniature by Gentile Bellini Found in Constantinople, Not a Portrait of Sultan Djem'. *Burlington Magazine* XV, 1909, pp. 237–8.

Serjeant, R. B.: 'A Rare Ottoman Manuscript with Two Contemporary Portraits of Murad III', *Islamic Culture* XVIII, 1944, pp. 15–18.

Sevin, Nureddin: 'Human Figures as the Chief Element in the Traditional Turkish Painting', *First International Congress of Turkish Arts: Communications Presented to the Congress,* Ankara, 1961, pp. 299–305.

Sevin, Nureddin: 'Turkish Artists Illustrating Festival Play', *First International Congress of Turkish Arts: Communications Presented to the Congress,* Ankara, 1961, pp. 306–7.

Siren, Oswald: 'Central Asian Influences in Chinese Painting of the T'ang Period', *Arts Asiatiques* III, 1956.

Stein, M. A.: *Wall Paintings from Ancient Shrines in Central Asia.* London, 1948.

Strzygowski, Joseph: *Asiatische Miniaturmalerei im Anschluss an Wesen und Werden der Mongolmalerei.* Vienna, 1933.

Strzygowski, Joseph: *Asiatische Miniaturmalerei.* Klagenfurt, 1933.

Tansuğ, Sezer: *Şenlikname düzeni.* (The Book of the Festival.) Istanbul, 1961.

Thuasne, L.: *Gentile Bellini et Sultan Muhammed II. Notes sur le séjour du peintre Vénetien à Constantinople (1479–80).* Paris, 1888.

Togan, Zeki Velidi: 'Topkapı Sarayında dört cönk', (4 Albums in the Topkapı Saray), *Islâm Tetkikleri Dergisi* I, 1953–4, pp. 73–89.

Togan, Zeki Velidi: *On the Miniatures in Istanbul Libraries.* Istanbul, 1963.

Tornberg, C. J.: *Codices arabici, persici et turcici bibliothecae Regiae Universitatis Uppsalensis.* Lund, 1849.

Uran, H.: *Üçüncü Sultan Mehmedin sünnet düğünü.* (The Circumcision Feast of Sultan Mehmed III.) Istanbul, 1942.

Uzluk, Şahabettin: *Mevlananın ressamları.* (Painters of Mevlânâ.) Konya, 1945.

Uzluk, Şahabettin: *Mevlananın resimleri.* (Portraits of Mevlânâ.) Konya, 1953.

Ünver, A. Süheyl: 'Türk ressam ve içtimai hayatı', (Turkish Painters and Social Life), *Güzel Sanatlar Dergisi* I, Istanbul, 1939.

Ünver, A. Süheyl: *Istanbul'da Dioscorides eserleri.* (The Dioscorides MSS. at Istanbul.) Istanbul, 1944.

Ünver, A. Süheyl: *Ressam Nigari, hayatı ve eserleri.* (The Painter Nigâri, His Life and Works.) Ankara, 1946.

Ünver, A. Süheyl: *Ressam Levni, hayatı ve eserleri.* (The Painter Levni, His Life and Works.) Istanbul, 1949.

Ünver, A. Süheyl: *Turkish Designs.* Istanbul, 1951.

Ünver, A. Süheyl: *Levnî.* Istanbul, 1951.

Ünver, A. Süheyl: *Fatih Sultan Mehmed ve babası ile oğlu, Resimlerini yapan ressam Levni ve bibliyografisi.* (The Paintings of Mehmed the Conqueror, His Father and His Son Done by Levni, and a Bibliography.) Istanbul, 1953.

Ünver, A. Süheyl: 'L'album d'Ahmed Ier', *Annali dell'Instituto Universitario Orientale di Napoli* New series, Vol. 13, 1963, pp. 127–62.

Walsh, John R.: 'The Turkish Manuscripts in New College, Edinburgh', *Oriens* Vol. 12, Nos. 1–2, 1959, pp. 170–89.

Wiet, Gaston: *Miniatures Persanes, Turques et Indiennes. Collection de Son Excellence Chérif Sabry Pacha.* Cairo, 1943.

Yetkin, Şerare: 'Sultan I. Alâeddin Keykubat'ın Alara Kalesindeki Kasrının Hamamındaki Freskler', (The Wall-Paintings from the Baths of Sultan 'Alā al-Dīn Kayqubād in the fortress of Alara), *Sanat Tarihi Yıllığı III,* Istanbul, 1970, pp. 69–88, English summary pp. 291–8.

Yetkin, Suut Kemal: 'Türk resim sanatının menşei hakkında', (On the Origins of Turkish Pictorial Art), *Ilâhiyat Fakültesi Dergisi* XI, 1963, pp. 5–11.

Yörükhan, Beyhan: 'Topkapı Sarayı Müzesinde bulunan dört album üzerindeki çalışmalara toplu bakış', (A General View of Work on 4 Albums in the Topkapı Saray Museum), *Türk Etnografya Dergisi* VII–VIII, 1964–5, pp. 50–8.

Yörükhan, Beyhan: 'Topkapı Sarayı Müzesinde bulunan bazı rulo parçaları', (Various Painted Scrolls in the Topkapı Saray), *Sanat Tarihi Araştırmaları Dergisi* I, 1965, pp. 188–90.

Yurdaydın, Hüseyin: *Matrakçı Nasûh.* (Nasūḥ al-Matrakī.) Ankara, 1963.

F. *Stone and Plaster*

Baer, Eva: 'A Group of Seljuq Figural Bas Reliefs', *Oriens* 20, 1967, pp. 107–24.

Diez, Ernst: 'The Zodiac Reliefs at the Portal of the Gök Medrese in Siwas', *Artibus Asiae* XII, 1949, pp. 99–104.

Erdmann, Kurt: 'Die beiden türkischen Grabsteine im Türk ve Islâm Eserleri Müzesi in Istanbul', *Beiträge zur Kunstgeschichte Asiens, In Memoriam Ernst Diez,* Istanbul, 1963, pp. 121–130.

Eyice, Semavi: 'Kırşehir'de H. 709 (1310) tarihli tasvirli bir Türk mezartaşı', (A Turkish Gravestone Dated 1310 from Kırşehir with Figural Decoration), *Reşit Rahmeti Arat için,* Ankara, 1966, pp. 208–43.

Glück, Heinrich: 'Eine seldschukische Sphinx im Museum von Konstantinopel', *Jahrbuch der asiatischen Kunst* II, 1925, pp. 123–7.

Güreşsever, Gönül: 'Ağustos 1968 Iznik çini fırınları kazısı sırasında çıkarılan stuko buluntular', (Stucco Finds During the Excavation of a Kiln at Iznik in August 1968), *I. Ü. Ed. Fak. Sanat Tarihi Yıllığı* II, 1966–8, pp. 200–8.

Otto-Dorn, Katharina: 'Türkische Grabsteine mit Figurenreliefs aus Kleinasien', *Ars Orientalis* III, 1959, pp. 63–76.

Otto-Dorn, Katharina: 'Türkisch-islamisches Bildgut in den Figurenreliefen von Achtamar', *Anatolia* VI, 1961/2, pp. 1–69.

Otto-Dorn, Katharina: 'Türkisch-islamisches Bildgut in den Figurenreliefs der Klosterkirche von Achtamar', *First International Congress of Turkish Arts: Communications Presented to the Congress,* Ankara, 1961, pp. 279–82.

Ögel, Semra: 'Bir Selçuk portalleri gurubu ve Karaman'daki Hatuniye Medresesi portalı', (A Group of Seljuk Porches and the Porch of the Hatuniye Medrese at Karaman), *Yıllık Araştırmalar Dergisi* II, 1958, pp. 115–19.

Ögel, Semra: 'Selçuk sanatında çift gövdeli aslan', (The Two-Bodied Lion in Seljuk Art), *Belleten* 1962, pp. 529–36.

Ögel, Semra: 'Einige Bemerkungen zum Sternsystem in der Steinornamentik der anatolischen Seldschuken', *Beiträge zur Kunstgeschichte Asiens, In Memoriam Ernst Diez,* Istanbul, 1963.

Ögel, Semra: 'Türk heykelciliğinde insan figürü', (Human Figures in Turkish Sculpture), *Türk Kültürü* No. 4, 1963, pp. 15–20.

Ögel, Semra: *Anadolu Selçukluları'nın taş tezyinatı.* (Carved-Stone Decoration of the Anatolian Seljuks.) Ankara, 1966.

Ögel, S.: 'Der Wandel im Programm der Steinornamentik von den Seldschukischen zu den osmanischen Bauten', *Anatolica* II, 1968, pp. 103–11.

Öney, Gönül: 'Niğde Hüdavent Hatun türbesi figürlü kabartmaları', (The Figural Sculptures from the Tomb of Hudavend Khatun at Niğde), *Belleten* XXXI, 1967, pp. 143–67.

Rice, Tamara Talbot: 'Decorations in the Seljukid Style in the Church of Saint Sophia of Trebizond', *Beiträge zur Kunstgeschichte Asiens, In Memoriam Ernst Diez,* Istanbul, 1963, pp. 87–119.

Rice, Tamara Talbot: 'Some Reflections Aroused by Four Seljukid Stucco Statues', *Anatolica* II, 1968, pp. 112–22.

Turan, Osman: *Oniki hayvanlı Türk takvimi.* (The Turkish Twelve-Animal Calendar.) Istanbul, 1941. (Dil ve Tarih-Coğrafya Fakültesi yayınları, Tarih Serisi, 3.)

Ülgen, A. Saim: 'Divriği Ulu Camii tekstil kapısı ve diğerleri', (The Western Porch of the Great Mosque at Divriği and Others), *Vakıflar Dergisi* V, 1962.

Ünver, A. Süheyl: 'Signatures d'artistes sur quelques pierres tombales et mosquées d'Akchéhir', *Israel Exploration Journal* VII, 1957, pp. 168–77.

Yetkin, Serare: 'Yeni bulunmuş figürlü mezar taşları', (Recently found figural tombstones), *Selçuklu Araştırmaları Dergisi,* I, Ankara 1969, pp. 149–156.

G. *Wood-carving*

Ağaoğlu, Mehmet: 'Unpublished Wooden Doors of the Seljuk Period', *Parnassus* X, 1938.

Berry, Burton Yost: 'Turkish Door Furnishings', *Ars Islamica* I, 1934, pp. 223–9.

Çulpan, Cevdet: *Rahleler.* (Koran Stands.) Istanbul, 1968.

Denike, B.: 'Quelques monuments de bois sculpté au Turkestan occidental', *Ars Islamica* II/1, 1935, pp. 69–83.

Karamağaralı, Halûk: 'Çorum Ulu Camiindeki minber', (The Minbar of the Great Mosque at Çorum), *I. Ü. Ed. Fak. Sanat Tarihi Yıllığı* I, 1964–5, pp. 120–42.

Oral, M. Zeki: 'Anadolu'da sanat değeri olan ahşap minberler, kitabeleri ve tarihçeleri', (Important Wooden Minbars in Anatolia, Their Inscriptions and Historical Data Concerning Them), *Vakıflar Dergisi* V, 1962, pp. 23–77.

Ögel, B.: 'Selçuk devri Anadolu ağaç işçiliği hakkında notlar', (Notes on Anatolian Wood Carving of the Seljuk Period), *Yıllık Araştırmalar Dergisi* I, 1956, pp. 199–220.

Ögel, Semra: 'Anadolu ağaç oymacılığında mail kesim', (Bevelled Cutting in Anatolian Wood Carving), *I. Ü. Ed. Fak. Sanat Tarihi Yıllığı* I, 1964–5, pp. 110–19.

Riefstahl, Rudolf M.: 'A Seljuk Koran Stand with Lacquer-Painted Decoration in the Museum of Konya', *The Art Bulletin* Vol. 15, No. 4, 1933, pp. 361–73.

H. *Metalwork*

Baykal, Ismail: 'Turkish Writing Tools', *Türkiye* 1, 1954, pp. 21–6.

Ettinghausen, Richard: 'The Wade Cup', *Ars Orientalis* II, 1957.

Ettinghausen, Richard: 'Turkish Elements in Silver Objects of the Seljuk Period of Iran', *First International Congress of Turkish Arts: Communications Presented to the Congress,* Ankara, 1961, pp. 128–34.

Kühnel, Ernst: 'The Character of Seljuk Art with Special Reference to Metal-work', *Proceedings of the Second International Congress of Persian Art,* London, 1931, pp. 13–14.

Kühnel, Ernst: 'Der mamlukische Kassettenstil', *Kunst des Orients* 1, 1950, pp. 55–68.

Nandor, F.: 'Der Bronzeguss und Nomaden Kunst', *Eurasia Septentrionalis Antiqua* IX, Prague, 1929.

Ögel, Bahaeddin: 'Türk kılıcının menşe ve tekâmülü hakkında', (The Origin and Evolution of the Turkish Sword), *Ankara Üniversitesi Dil ve Tarih-Coğrafya Fakültesi Dergisi* VI, 1948, pp. 431–60.

Rice, D. S.: 'Studies in Islamic Metalwork', *Bulletin of the School of Oriental and African Studies* XIV, 1952; XV, 1953; XVII, 1955; XXI, 1958.

Sauerlandt, Max: *Edelmetallfassungen in der Keramik.* Berlin, 1929.

Sözer, M. and Orgun, Z.: 'Türk tezyin sanatında kilit süsleri, kapı kuşak ve rozasları ile anahtar ağızları', (Forms of Locks, Corner Decoration, Rosaces and Keys in Turkish Decorative Art), *Arkitekt* 1941, pp. 159–65.

Stone, George Cameron: *A Glossary of the Construction, Decoration, and Use of Arms and Armor.* Portland (Maine), 1934.

Yetkin, Şerare: 'Bir tunç sfenks', (A Bronze Sphinx), *Türk Kültürü* 16, 1964, pp. 48–50.

Zaky, Abd al-Rahman: 'On Islamic Swords', *Studies in Islamic Art and Architecture in Honour of K. A. C. Creswell,* Cairo–London, 1965.

I. *Books and Calligraphy*

Babinger, F.: 'Die grossherrliche Tughra', *Jahrbuch der Asiatischen Kunst* 1925.

Baltacıoğlu, Ismail Hakkı: *Türklerde yazı sanatı.* (Turkish Calligraphy.) Ankara, 1958.

Baykal, Ismail: '*Hat sanatı*', (Calligraphy), *Güzel Sanatlar Mecmuası* II, 1940, pp. 33–48.

Blausteiner, Kurt: 'Beispiele osmanischer Buchkunst aus der Zeit Sultan Selim II. und Sultan Murads III', *Wiener Beiträge zur Kunst und Kulturgeschichte Asiens* X, 1936, pp. 34–55.

Bombaci, A.: 'Les tougras enluminées de la collection de documents turcs des Archives d'Etat de Venise', *II Congresso Int. di Arte Turca, Venezia, 1963,* Napoli, 1964, pp. 41–57.

Cahen, Claude: 'La tuğra seljukide', *Journal Asiatique* CCXXXIV, 1947, pp. 167–72.

Coomaraswamy, Ananda: 'Arabic and Turkish Calligraphy', *Bulletin of the (Boston) Museum of Fine Arts* XXVII, 1929, pp. 50–7.

Çığ, Kemal: *Hattat Hafız Osman efendi.* (The Calligrapher, Hafız Osman Efendi.) Istanbul, 1948.

Çığ, Kemal: *Türk kitap kapları.* (Turkish Book Binding.) Istanbul, 1970.

Inal, Ibnülemin Mahmud Kemal: *Son hattatlar.* (The Last Calligraphers.) Istanbul, 1955.

Ismail Hakkı (Baltacıoğlu): 'Türk yazılarının tetkikine medhal', (An Introduction to the Study of Turkish Scripts), *Ilâhiyat Fakültesi Mecmuası* 1927, pp. 111–36.

Kühnel, Ernst: *Islamische Schriftkunst.* Berlin–Leipzig, 1942; 2nd ed. Braunschweig, 1963.
Kühnel, Ernst: 'Die osmanische Tughra', *Kunst des Orients* II, 1955, pp. 69–82.
Melek, Celâl: *Şeyh Hamdullah.* Istanbul, 1948.
Moritz, B.: Article: 'Arabische Schrift', *Enzyklopedie des Islam,* Leiden, 1913, pp. 399–410.
Uzunçarşılı, I. Hakkı: *Tuğra ve pençeler ile ferman ve buyuruldulara dair.* (*Tuğras, Pences, Firmans* and *Buyuruldus.*) Istanbul, 1941. (Off-print.)
Ünver, A. Süheyl: *Hattat Ahmet Karahisarî.* (The Calligrapher Ahmed Karahisarī.) Istanbul, 1948.
Ünver, A. Süheyl: *Kâtipzade Mehmet Refi'.* Istanbul, 1950.
Ünver, A. Süheyl: *Müzehhip Karamemi.* (The Gilder Karamemī.) Istanbul, 1951.
Ünver, A. Süheyl: *Hattat Şeyh Hamdullah.* (The Calligrapher, Sheykh Hamdullah.) Istanbul, 1953.
Ünver, A. Süheyl: *Türk yazı çeşitleri.* (Forms of Turkish Script.) Istanbul, 1953.

J. *Leather*

Anon.: 'Debağat maddeleri', (Substances Used in Tanning), *I. köy ve ziraat kalkınma kongresi,* Ankara, 1938.
Atasoy, Nurhan: 'Shoes in the Topkapı Palace Museum', *Journal of the Regional Cultural Institute,* Teheran, 1969, Vol. 2, No. 1, pp. 5–32.
Gernross, O. and Öncü, Cahit: 'Old Turkish Leathers', *La Turquie Kémaliste* 48, 1947, pp. 17–22.
Öz, Tahsin: 'Turkish Decorative Arts and Turkish Shoes', *Türkiye* 1, 1954, pp. 47–52.

K. *Glass*

Anon.: *Türk camcılığı sergisi.* (Exhibition of Turkish Glassware.) Ankara, 1947.
Charleston, R. J.: 'The Luck of Edenhall', *The Connoisseur,* Feb. 1959, p. 35.
Eyice, Semavi: 'La verrerie en Turquie de l'époque byzantine à l'époque turque', *Annales du 4e Congrés des Journées Internationales du Verre,* Ravenne–Venise, 1967, pp. 162–82.
Gray, Basil: 'Gold Painted Glass Under the Seljuks', *II Cong. Int. di Arte Turca, Venezia 1963,* Napoli, 1965, pp. 143–9.
Lamm, C. J.: *Mittelälterliche Gläser und Steinschnittarbeiten aus dem nahen Osten.* 2 vols., Berlin, 1930.

INDEX OF NAMES

Persons, Peoples, Dynasties (roman); Places, Monuments, Museums, Book-titles and well-known Objects *(italic)*

NOTE

Titles and nicknames preceding a personal name are transposed to follow it (thus Khwāja Aḥmad appears as 'Aḥmad, Khwāja'). The prefix al- has been omitted only when it occurs at the beginning of a name.

In the case of monuments the principle has been to list a monument located in a town under the name of the town (thus the tomb of Ashık Pasha appears under 'Kırşehir', the Sahib Ata Mosque under 'Konya'), but a monument not in a town is listed under its own current name (e.g. 'Sarı Han'). Some suburbs of well-known cities are listed separately: Çekirge as well as Bursa, Üsküdar as well as Istanbul.

Some entries in this Index refer the reader to the Index of General Subjects which follows.

INDEX OF NAMES

INDEX OF NAMES

INDEX OF NAMES

INDEX OF NAMES

INDEX OF NAMES

INDEX OF GENERAL SUBJECTS

INDEX OF GENERAL SUBJECTS

INDEX OF GENERAL SUBJECTS

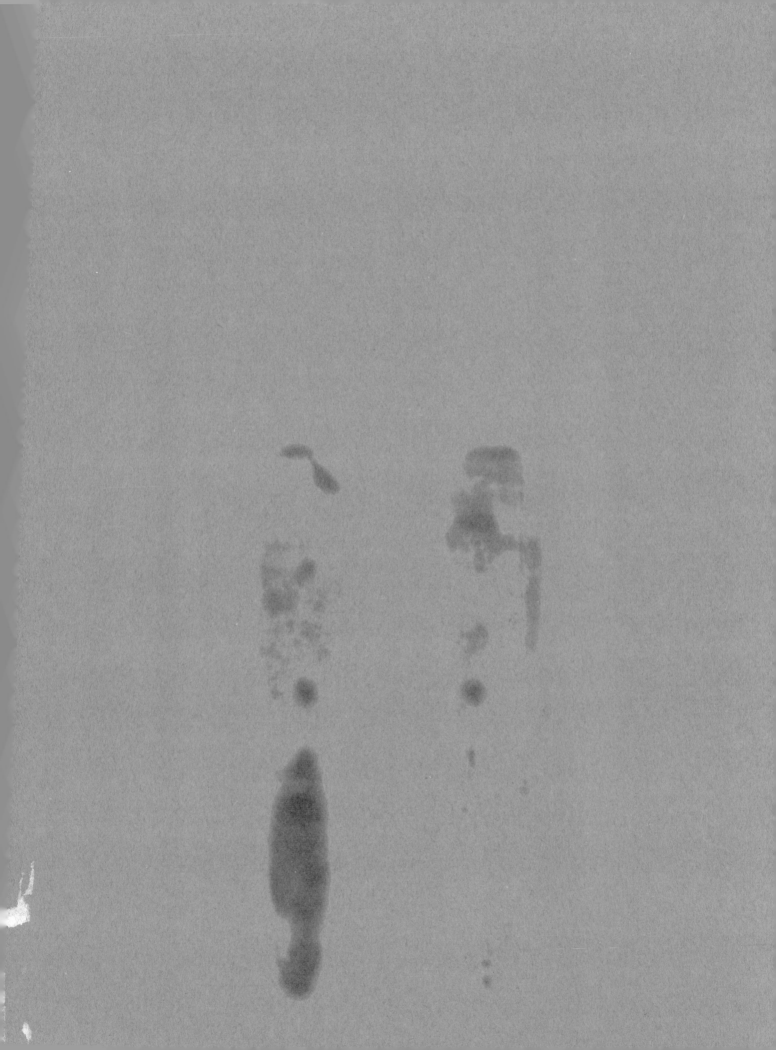